THE LETTERS OF THOMAS MOORE

Oxford University Press, Amen House, London E.C.4

GLASGOW NEW YORK TORONTO MELBOURNE WELLINGTON
BOMBAY CALCUTTA MADRAS KARACHI LAHORE DACCA
CAPE TOWN SALISBURY NAIROBI IBADAN ACCRA
KUALA LUMPUR HONG KONG

THOMAS MOORE by Sir Thomas Lawrence

THE LETTERS OF THOMAS MOORE

EDITED BY

WILFRED S. DOWDEN

VOLUME I

1793–1818

OXFORD
AT THE CLARENDON PRESS
1964

PRINTED IN GREAT BRITAIN

TO

BETTY ROSE

AND

LOREL ANNE

PREFACE

THE main source of information about Thomas Moore and his circle has heretofore been Lord John Russell's edition of the poet's *Memoirs, Journal and Correspondence* (London, 1853–6). Russell's disposition of the letters is ill-adapted for use by either the casual reader or research scholar. The 447 letters by Moore are dispersed over three non-consecutive volumes of an eight-volume work. Thus volume I contains the editor's 'Preface', the 'Memoirs', a few 'notes' (which have more the appearance of an introduction than annotation), and letters dated 1793–1813. Those written between 1814 and 1818 are printed in the first part of the second volume, the remainder of which is devoted to that portion of Moore's diary covering the period 1818–19. All of the 365 letters in the first two volumes were written before 1819, while volume VIII consists of an unwieldy mixture of the journal, Lord John Russell's 'Postscript', and eighty-two of Moore's letters, most of which were written after 1819, although there are a few of earlier date which were not included in the first two volumes. Russell's edition has not been reprinted, and its availability is limited.

The present edition combines the letters printed in Russell's work with more than twice as many collected from published and unpublished sources. The originals of most of the letters published by Russell were destroyed, so that for these texts we are dependent upon his edition. Since he did not use brackets to indicate an editorial interpolation, it is often difficult to determine whether he or Moore dated a letter. In cases where it was possible, Russell's dating has been accepted without indicating whether the date was his or Moore's. A typical date line in Russell's edition gives the place, day of the week, followed by a long dash, and finally the year, as, for example, 'Kegworth, Thursday,——1812'. One must assume that Moore wrote 'Kegworth, Thursday', and that the '1812' was added by the editor. In most of these cases, which are numerous, the month and, in a few letters, the day date has been added and placed in brackets. Thus the letter cited above now appears in this manner: 'Kegworth, Thursday [September] 1812.' It has also been necessary to change the dates given by Russell to a number of letters, but in each case the reason for doing so is explained in a note. Some of the dates may be incorrect, and doubts about others are indicated by question marks. With this exception and one other minor alteration noted below, Russell's text and those of other printed sources have been followed *literatim et punctuatim.*

The extracts of letters in Thomas Crofton Croker's *Notes from the Autograph Letters of Thomas Moore to Mr. Power* (New York, 1854) are not reproduced in this edition since it would be impossible to do so with any degree of accuracy. Croker compiled his book from a sales catalogue, and much of the work is, as the title implies, merely annotation and summary. It is difficult to determine, for example, whether the quoted excerpts are from one or from several letters of different dates. The following item is typical: 'Six letters, 4to., 8vo., 4th, 9th, 13th, 24th, and 30th March, 1818.' This entry is followed by a series of quotations, but with no indication of which quotation belongs to which letter. Under these circumstances it seemed best simply to cite Croker's book as another aid to an understanding of Moore's connexion with his music publisher James Power.

Originals or photographic copies of unpublished letters were followed as closely as was consistent with sound editorial policy. When typescript copies were provided, this fact is noted and the transcript followed *verbatim.* In the interest of a consistent and attractive format, the return address (including that on letters taken from printed sources) is placed above the date, and dates which are supplied from the postmark or from internal or other evidence are placed in brackets. Dates which Moore placed at the close of the letters have been moved to the beginning and marked with an asterisk. Moore's punctuation, spelling, and capitalization have been followed as closely as practicable, although there were instances when it was necessary to make arbitrary decisions. It seemed better, for example, to change his consistent spelling 'oflock' to the standard 'o'clock' than to explain his peculiar orthography in a note each time it occurred. Superior letters which appear in the originals have been retained, but for typographical reasons the period which Moore placed after or under the raised letter in such abbreviations as 'M^{r}' has been omitted. A few significant words and phrases which Moore struck out are included in brackets in the text, but most of his deletions have been ignored since they do not change the meaning of the letters or furnish additional information.

Provenances are given at the beginning of each letter in the left margin. Necessary annotation, almost totally wanting in Russell's edition, has been added. Many people mentioned by Moore or with whom he corresponded are identified in the Glossary of Proper Names; but he had many friends and, in his early years at least, was a name-dropper. Although he has introduced me to many interesting people, living and dead, I cannot claim to have become acquainted with everyone he knew. I have also attempted to identify quotations and allusions, but since Moore's erudition proved greater than mine, some of these have been placed in a file of curiosity-ticklers, which must form part of the residue of every editorial project.

W. S. D.

Rice University,
Houston, Texas.

ACKNOWLEDGEMENTS

THERE have been so many favours granted me that I cannot hope to acknowledge each of them separately; 'I can no other answer make but thanks, and thanks, and ever thanks.' Nevertheless, special acknowledgement is due to those who have aided me most directly. I am more than grateful to Mr. Geoffrey Carnall, Dr. Ian Jack, and Professor Hoover Jordan, who read the manuscript and from their knowledge of nineteenth-century literary history in general and Thomas Moore in particular made many valuable suggestions. I am particularly indebted to Professor Alan D. McKillop, whose knowledge of English literary and social history has prevented me from going astray more often than I have. I am also grateful to Sir John Murray, K.C.V.O., D.S.O., for permitting me to transcribe his large collection of Moore letters and for the hospitality shown me while working in his offices.

Moore's letters are located in public and private collections throughout Great Britain and the United States, and I am deeply indebted to the staffs of the various libraries whose services and resources I have used: the British Museum; the University of Edinburgh; the Firestone Library, Princeton University; the Quaker Collection, Haverford College; the Widener and Houghton Libraries, Harvard University; the Henry E. Huntington Library; Dr. Williams's Library; the National Libraries of Ireland and Scotland; the Clements Library, University of Michigan; the J. Pierpont Morgan Library; the New York Public; the Nottingham Public; the Historical Societies of Maine and Pennsylvania; the John Rylands Library; Trinity College, Dublin; the Victoria and Albert Museum; and the Sterling Memorial Library, Yale University. There are also letters at the University of Lund, Sweden; the University of Bergen, Norway; and the National Library of Copenhagen; and grateful acknowledgement is accorded Professor Nils Erik Enkvist, Åbo Akademi, Åbo, Finland, for providing photostatic copies and typescripts of these letters. Duke University furnished microfilms of Moore's letters to Mary Shelley in Lord Abinger's collection and, acting under his authorization, granted publication privileges, which Lord Abinger has latterly verified. These letters are now in the Carl H. Pforzheimer Library, and Mr. Carl H. Pforzheimer, Jr., has graciously confirmed Lord Abinger's permission. There are also fourteen other letters in the Carl H. Pforzheimer Library, which are published with the permission of the Carl and Lily Pforzheimer Foundation, Incorporated.

More than common thanks are due to Dr. Hardin Craig, Jr., and the staff of the Fondren Library, Rice University, for their unflagging interest in this edition and for their assistance in assembling an excellent collection of originals, photostats, and microfilms of Moore's correspondence.

I wish also to acknowledge by name those who have permitted me to use letters in their possession: Dr. James C. Corson, University of Edinburgh; Mrs. Mercia Dalby, Castle Donington, Derbyshire; His Grace the Duke of Devonshire; Lieutenant-Colonel M. O'Connell Fitz-simon, Dublin; the Earl of Ilchester; Mr. Oscar E. Lancaster, Washington, D.C.; Mr. William Lefanu, Librarian, the Royal College of Surgeons, London; the Earl of Lytton; Dr. Herbert O. Mackey, Dun Laoghaire, Ireland; Mr. B. Y. McPeake, London; Professor Willard B. Pope, University of Vermont; Professor Chester L. Shaver, Oberlin College; and Mr. Robert Taylor, Princeton, New Jersey. Mrs. Doris Langley Moore provided a typescript of an important letter from Moore to Byron and rendered other valuable assistance.

I wish also to thank Earl Bertrand Russell, who, as heir to Lord John Russell, Moore's literary executor, granted his permission for these letters to be published.

At the risk of being accused of Moore's youthful folly of name-dropping, I must recognize others who have assisted in various ways: Professor Carroll Camden, for lightening the load considerably by providing secretarial service when it was most needed; Miss Mildred Christian, for directing my attention to an important letter which might otherwise have been overlooked; Professor Hardin Craig, Sr., for frequent advice and encouragement; Dr. William S. Dix, for providing photostats of letters in the Firestone Library and for interceding on my behalf with the owners of other collections; Professors David Bonnell Green, Thomas O. Mabbott, William H. Marshall, and Louis Peck, for assistance in locating individual letters and larger collections; Professor John E. Jordan, for transcribing letters not available to me and for frequent encouragement and advice; Professor Leslie Marchand, for directing my attention to the letters in Lord Abinger's collection; Professor Thad N. Marsh, for frequent advice in the writing of notes; Professors Leo Hughes, Donald Mackenzie, Robert Myers, and John E. Parish, for assistance in locating elusive quotations; the Right Reverend Monsignor John K. Ryan, for presenting to the Fondren Library a letter from Moore to Mary Shelley; Professors J. D. Thomas and Frank Vandiver, for frequent advice about details of publication; Professor George Williams, for helpful suggestions on the preparation of the introductory material; Mr. Jan B. Gordon and Miss Jeannette Favrot, for assistance in proof-reading and in preparing the index; Mr. Tadhg Gahan, for calling attention to a letter in the *Anthologia Hibernica*; Mr. A. M. Humphries, for furnishing information about one of Moore's neighbours in Wiltshire. Special thanks are due to the typists, particularly Mrs. H. K. Payne, Mrs. R. C. Ragland, and Mrs. I. E. S. Edwards, who also made valuable suggestions concerning textual readings.

I wish to thank the Administration and Board of Governors of Rice University for a leave of absence which enabled me to complete this edition, and the American Philosophical Society for a timely grant which made possible six months of study in England.

The encouragement and assistance of my wife, who has worked side by side with me from the beginning, is at once my principal inspiration and greatest reward.

CONTENTS

VOLUME I

VOLUME II

LIST OF PLATES

LIST OF REFERENCES

THIS list includes the principal works used in the preparation of this edition. Other references are cited in the notes with an abbreviated title or by the name of the author or editor.

Allgemeine Deutsche Biographie, Leipzig, 1875–1912.

Biographie Universelle, Paris, 1854–8.

Burke's Peerage, Baronetage and Knightage, London, 1956.

Cambridge Bibliography of English Literature, Cambridge, 1941.

Coleridge, Ernest Hartley, ed., *The Works of Lord Byron: Poetry*, London, 1898–1904. 7 vols. (Cited in the notes as Byron, *Poetry*.)

Collins's Peerage of England, edited by Sir Egerton Brydges, London, 1812.

Dictionary of American Biography, New York, 1928–58.

Dictionary of National Biography, London, 1917–59.

Halévy, Élie, *A History of the English People in the Nineteenth Century*, London, 1949–52. 6 vols.

Jones, Frederick L., ed., *The Letters of Mary W. Shelley*, Norman, 1946. 2 vols.

Jones, Howard Mumford, *The Harp that Once—: a Chronicle of the Life of Thomas Moore*, New York, 1937.

Lavisse, Ernest, *Histoire de France Contemporaine: depuis la Révolution jusqu'à la Paix de 1919*, Paris, 1921. 10 vols.

Lecky, W. E. H., *A History of England in the Eighteenth Century*, London, 1919–25. 7 vols.

Lippincott's Pronouncing Biographical Dictionary, New York, 1930. 5th edition.

Macmanus, M. J., *A Biographical Hand-List of the First Editions of Thomas Moore*, Dublin, 1934.

Marchand, Leslie, *Byron: a Biography*, New York, 1957. 3 vols.

Moore, Doris Langley, *The Late Lord Byron*, London and New York, 1961.

Moore, Thomas, *Letters and Journals of Lord Byron: with Notices of His Life*, London, 1830. 2 vols.

Moore, Thomas, *The Poetical Works*, edited by A. D. Godley, Oxford, 1924. (Cited in the notes as *Poetry*.)

Moore, Thomas, *The Poetical Works, Collected by Himself*, London, 1841–2. 10 vols.

Moore, Thomas, *The Works of Lord Byron: with His Letters and Journals, and His Life*, London, 1834. 17 vols.

Neue Deutsche Biographie, Leipzig, 1953.

Nouvelle Biographie Generale, Paris, 1860.

Prothero, Rowland E. (Lord Ernle), ed., *The Works of Lord Byron: Letters and Journals*, London, 1898–1901. 6 vols. (Cited in the notes as *LJ*.)

List of References

Russell, Lord John, ed., *The Memoirs, Journal and Correspondence of Thomas Moore*, London, 1853–6. 8 vols.

Strong, L. A. G., *The Minstrel Boy: a Portrait of Tom Moore*, London, 1937.

Webster's Biographical Dictionary, Springfield, Mass., 1943.

INTRODUCTION

WASHINGTON IRVING is reported to have said that one could as easily get a book out of Thomas Moore as a letter, and Moore often remarked that he relegated his correspondence to the tag end of each day when his hand was weary with transcribing and his eyes dim with reading. From these statements one might draw the erroneous conclusion that Moore neither wrote many letters nor had much to say in those he did write. That he was a prodigious correspondent is attested by the number of letters published in this edition, which is only a fraction of those he must have written during the seventy-three years of his life. As for content, no claim can be made for Moore as a great letter writer, in the sense that other English poets have been great. He lacked the eloquence of Byron, the stateliness of Keats, and the ebullience of Shelley. Moore looked upon the letter primarily as a means of communication, not as a medium of artistic expression. Nevertheless he could, when he turned his mind fairly to the task, produce epistles of artistic merit, as is revealed in the letters written from America to his mother in 1803 and 1804. Moore was impressed by both the natural scenery and the socio-political conditions in America, and he described them in a manner which foreshadows the diaries of such English travellers of the mid-century as Captain Marryat, Mrs. Trollope, and Charles Dickens. Furthermore, when he wrote to his friends Lady Donegal and her sisters, and to Samuel Rogers, Lord Byron, Leigh Hunt, the Marquess of Lansdowne, Lord John Russell, or Lord Holland, his style assumed a sparkle akin to that in the best of the *Irish Melodies* and was enlivened by an impressive array of quotations ranging from the Greek and Latin of Homer and Virgil to Shakespeare and the poets of his own age. This excellence was not sustained, however, and if Moore's letters were to be published solely because of their artistic worth, the editor would have to discard many of them.

It is therefore hoped that something other than a demonstration of Moore's talents as a letter writer is achieved by this edition. It brings together for the first time published material with more than twice as many letters which have never before been printed, and it places Moore in a different light from that in which he has heretofore been viewed.

Mention of Moore's name often evokes a tolerant smile indicative of certain popular misconceptions. He is most frequently thought of as a 'minor poet' of the sentimental school—the author of 'The Last Rose of Summer', 'Believe Me if All Those Endearing Young Charms', 'The Harp That Once through Tara's Halls', and other lyrics dealing with Irish history and independence or extolling the charms of an Irish colleen. He was a dilettante, say his detractors, a popular versifier absorbed in the social whirl of London, the centre of attention in the fashionable *salons* where he sang his songs. He is the young man who rose from the lower class (a grocer's son) to become the golden boy of the Whig circle at Holland House.

Some of these opinions are true; others are only half true; and many are completely erroneous. He was often found in the drawing-rooms of the London *élite*, and it is quite apparent that he enjoyed being there, for 'Tommy loved a lord'. But his visits were not purely social. His letters to the music publisher James Power indicate that one purpose in singing at such gatherings was to present his songs to the public, who did, after all, like to hear him and were afterwards eager to purchase. He also enjoyed his associations with the Whigs at Holland House, but it is apparent from the letters to John Easthope, editor of the *Morning Chronicle*; Leigh Hunt, publisher of the *Examiner*; Edward R. Moran, editor of the *Globe*; and from his acquaintance with other newsmen to whom he submitted political squibs and lampoons that he was a respected spokesman for the Whigs.

The letters to James Power point to the manner in which Moore viewed his own work as a lyricist. He insisted that his verses be judged as songs, not as poems; and to study his verses in any way except as songs is both irrelevant and unjust. Their unity is achieved by the blending of the lyric with the music, and he knew that a line which might appear faulty alone could well be exactly right in conjunction with the music for which it was written. For this reason he objected to the publication of the *Irish Melodies* and the *National Airs* apart from the music, and it was not until 1821 that he yielded to pressure and allowed them to be published as poems rather than as songs.

The charge that Moore was a dilettante whose sole interest was in pleasing the socially *élite* of London is best refuted by the entire corpus of his letters, which reveal him as a diligent workman, who spent the bulk of his time at remote places like Mayfield Cottage, Derbyshire, and Sloperton Cottage, Wiltshire, far from the social whirl of London, writing lyrics, political satire, and prose in order to earn enough to feed and clothe his wife and five children. He went up to London at infrequent intervals primarily for business reasons; and social engagements waited upon business. The letters show that he enjoyed warm family ties extending from his immediate hearth to that of his mother and father in Ireland. They reveal him in the midst of a constant battle against poverty, working assiduously in spite of the chronic illness of his wife and the death of all five of his children. But if this diligence was admirable it was also debilitating. It is obvious that Moore could not have been a major poet under the best of circumstances, but it is equally obvious that he could have been a much better one if he had not felt it necessary to spend his time writing, for the sake of expediency, poems which often had only local and occasional interest.

The hitherto unpublished letters show him to be the close friend and confidant of some of the most important literary, political, and social figures of the day, and they evidently regarded him with respect. It is not likely that such men as Scott, Byron, Murray, the Marquess of Lansdowne, Lord John Russell, and Lord Holland were all equally myopic in judging character and competence.

Perhaps the most dramatic letters in this collection are those written to Lord Byron in 1810 and 1811, in which Moore chose the most audacious and elaborate method of becoming acquainted with a well-known figure since Boswell met Rousseau. From the point of view of the literary historian and critic, the most revealing letters are those written to John Murray, Mary Shelley, John Cam Hobhouse, and Douglas Kinnaird about the biography of Byron. It is apparent from the correspondence that his relations with John Murray and Mary Shelley were most cordial and that the latter furnished valuable information for his project. It is also evident that Hobhouse gave him as little assistance as possible and objected to the biography from the beginning, while Kinnaird looked upon Moore's plan for a life of their mutual friend with open hostility. In these relationships are revealed the two paradoxical aspects of Moore's character. When dealing with people like Mary Shelley and John Murray, who respected him as a writer and person, he was forthright and open. But he met coolness and hostility with an obsequious attitude which often goaded his antagonists to further scorn. Thus, when Hobhouse wrote 'You will write . . . a very clever and a very saleable book. But I shall be most agreeably surprised if you accomplish those higher objects which you must propose to yourself . . .' Moore replied, 'However flattering it might be to my vanity to find a person like you entertaining the same partial opinion of my talents that others do, be assured that you cannot think much more humbly of them than I do myself. . . .'

Thomas Moore could not be placed among the 'great guns of our modern Parnassus', as he once called Wordsworth, Coleridge, and Southey; he was not Prince Hamlet, nor was meant to be. Yet his achievements were far from mean. The *Irish Melodies*, of which he published ten numbers in the twenty-seven-year period 1807–34, are justly ranked as of foremost importance in the tradition of national songs. His *National Airs* brought to England and Ireland some of the best central and southern European music, for which he wrote lyrics that enhanced the beauty of the melodies. Although his significance as a political writer is now lost, in his day he was recognized as an important satirist and spokesman for the Whig Opposition. He also produced an impressive amount of prose. He wrote extensively for the important journals of the day, and at various times was offered the editorship of *The Times*, the *Edinburgh Review*, the *Metropolitan*, and the *Keepsake*, all of which offers he declined. He tried his hand at the novel, published a four-volume *History of Ireland*, and wrote the standard biography of Lord Edward Fitzgerald. He was an early chronicler of the life of Richard Brinsley Sheridan, and his *Life of Byron* stands today as the best of the early biographies and a corrective to attacks by Leigh Hunt and others. The letters here published provide a different perspective in which to view Moore as a writer, and they present a body of material which permits an objective evaluation of his character.

LIST OF LETTERS

List of Letters

List of Letters

1815

1. *To his Mother*

Russell, i. 79, no. 1

August 12th, 1793.

We all expected your arrival, at least to night, when your letter of to-day quashed our hopes of a sudden, and informed us you were still in Wexford. For God's sake, will you ever be home? There's nothing here heard but wishes for your return.

'Your absence all but ill endure,
And none so ill as
Thomas Moore.'

N.B. Excuse my scrap of rhyme; for you know poets will out with it.—Poets! very proud, indeed; but don't mention it.

2. *To the Editor of* Anthologia Hibernica

Anthologia Hibernica, ii (1793), 299[1]

Aungier-Street
Sep. 11. 1793.

Sir,

If the following attempts of a youthful muse seem worthy of a place in your magazine, by inserting them you will much oblige,[2]

A constant Reader,
TH.M. S M . . RE.

3. *To his Mother*

Russell, i. 80, no. 2

[March 1799]

I have at length (Heaven be praised!) got something like a home; and any commands for me will be most *thankfully attended to* at No. 44. George Street.[3] I assure you that I felt extremely delighted after my long journey to find myself at length a *fixed star*. The

[1] Transcript provided by Mr. Tadhg Gahan, Dublin.

[2] 'To Zelia, on Her Charging the Author with Writing too Much on Love', Moore's first published poem.

[3] See letter No. 747, to Mary Shelley, 26 Nov. 1827. Moore went to London in order to enter the Middle Temple.

lodging which Mr. Masterson provided for me is a very comfortable little room on the second floor, at six shillings per week; which they tell me is rather cheap, considering the present time of the year, when the world is flocking to London. The woman who keeps the house washes for Mrs. Masterson, and some others: this, you know, is also a convenience to me. My journey up was exceedingly expensive, though Mr. M. tells me it does not exceed the usual calculation. One circumstance, which certainly added to the expense, was my being obliged to take the mail from Chester instead of the coach, which I told you in my letter I expected would set off next morning; but I was mistaken: I should have waited till the morning after that, and two days and three nights passed *alone* in Chester, in the state of mind in which I then was, would have been too much for me to support; so I took to the mail; that was three guineas and a half, which, with 1£. 16*s.* 6*d.* from Holyhead, the guinea for my passage, and the other contingent expenses (in which I was obliged to conform to the other passengers) has made the whole about eight guineas. Mr. M. tells me that the Parkgate way is not by the half so much. So *that* shall be the way by which I shall return, for I will certainly, with God's will, see you in summer.

'The summer will come when the winter's awa,
And I'll be to see thee, in spite of them a'.'

Let me have a letter immediately. Write to me that you are all well; that you expect to see me in summer; and I shall be as happy as absence from all that I hold dear will allow me to be.

Yours ever.

P. S. Mr. and Mrs. M. are uncommonly attentive. I have not given any of my letters yet. Love to my dear father, my dear Catherine, and my dear little Ellen. Never was mortal in such a hurry as I am.

4. *To his Mother*

Russell, i. 82, no. 4

44. George Street, Portman Square
Friday, 5th April, 1799.

I hope Warren was time enough to correct the omission which I made with regard to my residence. You cannot conceive how impatient I am to hear from you, and you ought not to let me remain long ungratified. Tell me whether you think my lodging is very dear; I assure you I find it extremely comfortable; they have my breakfast laid as snug as possible every morning, and I dine at the traiteur's like a prince, for eightpence or ninepence. The other day I had soup, bouilli, rice pudding, and porter, for ninepence halfpenny; if that be not cheap, the deuce is in it. I am sure you will be delighted, too, when I tell you that Mr. Masterson has lent me a piano; that which he had in Ireland; a very good one; for Sally has one of Longman's by hire, and, indeed, she has made a wonderful proficiency. She has a very nice harp also, and is beginning to learn on it. Would you believe it? Mr. M'Mahon is here, and as deep in the gallipots as ever; apothecary and man-midwife! no less. I have dined with him, and find him exceedingly friendly. Nugent, to whom Mr. Dowling introduced me, has been particularly attentive. I scarcely saw any one of the persons to whom my letters were directed, but left the letters with my address. I have had three or four notes from them, regretting their not having been at home, and expressing a wish that I should call on them, but all in *the morning*.

I have been but at one play since I came, for I do not like going alone, and I have not found any one that would accompany me. As I have not, therefore, yet much interesting description to give you, I will tell you one or two anecdotes of my journey, by which you may conjecture how a novice like me was annoyed, and which will account for the gloomy letter which I wrote to you from Chester. We came into Holyhead at night, after a most tedious and sickening passage. The first thing to be done was to get a place in the Chester mail of next morning. The mail was full, but a gentleman told me that he would wish to resign his place, and that if I chose I might personate him, and answer to his name. I accordingly paid him, and when the names of the passengers were called over, answered to his. Before I went to bed, Mr. Patrickson represented to me strongly the danger of such counterfeiting in times like the present, which you may be sure prevented me from much sleep that night, but in the morning I contrived to have my proper name inserted. Well, when I was at Chester, I felt myself particularly unpleasant. Alone, and as sooty as a sweep, I wandered like a culprit through the streets, though conscious that no body knew me. While I was at breakfast in the inn (for you know I stayed there a day) a frantic fellow came in, who had just ridden post from Warrington, and after chasing the maids all about the house, and beating them, came into the room where I was, sat down with me, told me that he had just escaped from a strait-waistcoat, boasted of having killed a woman and child the night before in the theatre of Warrington, and finally, as he had never been in Chester before, he would wait for me, and we should walk through the streets together! Well, well! with some difficulty I got rid of this dangerous gentleman, and met very soon with one still more so, for a sharper is surely more dangerous than a madman. The mail set off from Chester with only two passengers; we took up two more at Northampton, one of whom, though a young man, soon appeared to be, what my father calls, an *old stager*. He had been on the Continent lately, talked of his hunters (though rather shabby in his appearance), and was going to London then only to get rid of a little money. When he knew that I was going to the Temple, and had never been in London before, he thought he had found a *nice subject*, and paid the most servile attentions to me. 'He would shew me the pleasures of the metropolis, we should go to the play together, dine together,' &c. By the bye, it came out in conversation that he had been up all the night previously playing cards. In fact, he forced me to put up at the same inn (when we arrived) at which he did; was so *glaringly civil* as to offer to carry my portmanteau for me; ordered a room for himself and me; and bid the waiter take my coat, and brush it well, while we were at breakfast. When I mentioned my wish to go to a friend's in Manchester Street, who, I expected, had a lodging provided for me, he advised me to devote two or three days *to seeing* London. Observe, he said that he had sent his portmanteau before him, but, strange to tell, *it had not arrived!* He cursed the fellow that he gave it to—and what could he do? He could not go out without a clean cravat and shirt. Hints upon hints demanded the loan of them from me. I, however, did not open my portmanteau. When I was resolved to go to Manchester Street he accompanied me, and extorted a promise that I should meet him in a couple of hours. Well, well, well! now came another embarrassment. The first question almost Mr. M. asked was, 'What have you done with your luggage?' 'Left them at the inn.' 'Did you give them in charge to the master of the house?' 'No.' 'Did you get them booked?' 'No.' 'Have you the key of the room?' 'No.' Off he sent me in a hackney coach; and, to be sure, I was not a little trembling for my portmanteau. Well, well, well, well! I got my luggage, left word for the kind gentleman that it was not in my power to meet him, and I have never seen him since. This one circumstance will make me believe all that I shall ever be told of the schemers of London. There were a thousand other little traits about him, which I have not time to detail, but they confirmed me in his character. Give my love to my father; *mille choses à Catherine et Ellen.* Yours to eternity.

5. *To his Father*

Russell, i. 85, no. 5

April 29. 1799.

I received your letter just when I was hurrying out to dinner, but I must stop to acknowledge its reception, and to assure you that nothing could come more seasonably than its contents; for the expenses of my board had left me penniless, and as there are some fees necessary on the first day of dining, I must have lost my term if the remittance had been two days later, as, after Friday, it would be impossible to serve it. Everything, however, is now as it should be. I sat near an hour with Lord Moira this morning, and am to dine with him on Saturday. He is extremely polite; so indeed are all the people to whom I had letters, and I was mistaken when I told you they took little notice of them. I was on Sunday at a little party at Lady Peshall's, and was introduced very particularly to Col. De Bathe and Capt. Plunket (Lord Dunsany's son). I have returned to my old habits of reading and scribbling again. I stay the forenoon always at home, and generally have a little cold dinner in my room, which never costs me more than a shilling. But I am staying too long; I will write to you immediately again, and will certainly answer my little Catherine's letters. I am uneasy that my mother's cough is not better. Remember me affectionately to her, and believe me ever yours.

How are aunt and uncle (J. and J.)? If you ever see Croker,[1] ask him did he receive my letter.

6. *To his Father*

Russell, i. 86, no. 6

May 11. 1799.

I am distressed to the very heart at having given you all such uneasiness; but indeed the situation was so new to me, that I am sure you are neither surprised nor angry with me for having expressed myself with such querulous irritation. You have, ere this, received another letter, which I doubt not will amuse you; but I hope this one will arrive time enough to efface any uneasy ideas that *either* might have excited in your minds. I must confess that I feel I have acted very ungenerously in not having rather suffered a little inconvenience, than distress for a moment, by any melancholy complainings, the hearts of those so affectionately dear to me. I could

[1] John Wilson Croker. See the Glossary of Proper Names.

cry for what I have done; but *do* forgive me. I feel that you live to make *me* happy, and surely I could not embitter *your* peace, my dear, dear father and mother! Oh, when shall I be able to repay your goodness!

I did not receive your letter with Mozart's introduction till last night; or you might have been saved the pain which my last letter may perhaps have given you; but I am convinced your good sense made you rejoice that I found such an independent method of resource in my difficulties, as only for it I should have forfeited my term.[1] I will now go with my draft to the post office. Everything is as it should be, but I cannot be in spirits till I hear that your uneasiness is dissipated. *Do* write and tell me so. Farewell my dearest, best of fathers. God give you all the happiness which you merit. Yours ever, ever.

7. *To his Mother*

Russell, i. 87, no. 7

May 15. 1799.

My dearest Mother,

My father's letter of the 8th, which I have just received, has affected me extremely: it shows me how ungenerous, how cowardly were my complaints; and convinces me more and more of the affections of my beloved father and mother. However, forget what I have done, and believe that I want nothing to make me perfectly happy but the assurance that those fears which I so thoughtlessly excited are now completely dissipated. But indeed, my dearest mother, I do not remember that, in the midst of all my foolish despondence, I ever harboured the least suspicion of your neglect; and if I expressed anything like it, be assured it was owing to the agitation of my mind, which was disturbed by the *novelty*, still more than by the *perplexity*, of my situation. But reproach me no more with it. I have repented that letter (Heaven knows!) almost enough to atone for all its imprudence.

I thank my father from my heart for his letter to Mrs. M'M., and will fly with it to her immediately. I have found a very pleasant acquaintance in Mr. Hume: he seems already to feel a particular interest in me, and is a man of considerable talent. I dined last week

[1] This letter implies that Moore had encountered some financial difficulty which he was forced to meet by independent means, in order to pay his fees at the Middle Temple. He had evidently written to his father demanding assistance and was chagrined when he received a draft before his letter could have reached Ireland.

with Miss Dodd's friend, Mr. Phibbs; and to-day I dine with our friend Harden. I need never be out of company if I chose it; but I rather avoid it, and am reproached on all sides with my neglect of visiting. Lady Peshall's family have been very attentive to me, and so has Mrs. Latouche; indeed, if I had indulged in going out often (though here I cannot call it an indulgence), there is scarce a night that I should not be at some female gossip party, to drink tea, play a little crambo, and eat a sandwich. I have been dancing after Mr. Atkinson this long time, and cannot meet him. I will write to my father immediately, and give him an account of my expenses, and likewise submit to him a few ideas which have occurred to me with regard to my future pursuits. My darling mother, shall we meet in summer? Oh! how I long for it! Tell me that you wish it,—that you approve of it,—and I will fly to you. Make Catherine write whenever my father writes: give my love to little Ellen and all, not forgetting my uncle Joice, and (when you write to her) to my aunt. Heaven preserve my father to us, my dear mother, and may we all deserve such a protector. God bless you, and make you happy Farewell.

8. *To his Father*

Russell, i. 88, no. 8

May 22. 1799.

Now that I know your uneasiness is done away, I want nothing to make me happy except that re-union with those I love, which I hope is not far distant. Mr. Gibson called on me yesterday, and gave me a letter of Catherine's, and Mrs. Grierson's delightful little present, for which I shall write her a letter to-morrow. I have called two or three times on Mr. Goulding, but have not yet met him: before I seal this letter, I will go to him again. I dined on Sunday with Capt. Otway; he has been extremely attentive to me, and purely from courtesy; for he is one of those men whom I certainly can have no hold upon. Neither music, nor literature, nor any of these things does he seem to have a relish for *himself*, or to know that *I* am any way acquainted with them. My Lord This and my Lady That form the whole subject-matter of his conversation. I am to be at Mrs. Cologan's to-morrow night, where I believe I shall meet Peter Pindar. She is one of the first private performers on the harp. I dined with Mr. —— the Sunday before last. I find him just like other men who are indebted entirely for their education to themselves. Having never had that idea of subordination which the controul of a superior inculcates, and which is so very necessary to chasten self opinion, they gradually imagine themselves into an all-sufficiency of knowledge, and are generally the most egotising pedants in the world. But a truce with characters; and now for cold calculations of another kind,—my expenses I must confess I have not yet made such an estimate as to enable you to judge with any kind of accuracy. My lodging you know is six shillings a-week, and I pay the man two shillings a-month for cleaning my shoes and brushing my coat. Before I did this I was obliged to pay twopence for my boots every day, and a penny for my shoes. By the bye, I let my boots go to the extreme (though I had got them mended), and I have bespoke a new pair, which will cost me twenty-five shillings, which is a low price here. Indeed, I want a total refitment; my best black coat, the only one I have been able to wear, is quite shabby. The usual expense of my dinner I mentioned to you already. Half-a-crown's worth of tea and sugar serves me more than a week. My washing I cannot accurately estimate, but soon will, and shall inform you more precisely in everything.

I have just been with Mr. Goulding and have got two guineas, so that matter is settled.[1] Give my love to my mother and all. Tell my mother that my next letter shall be to her. Farewell, my dearest father. Believe me, yours most affectionately.

9. *To his Father*

Russell, viii. 37

London
June 6. 1799.

Dear Father,

I am very much inclined to think that I shall see and embrace you this summer. The primary motive which induces me is indeed the melancholy idea of being separated so long from those I love, as I must be if I omit this opportunity; but there are other circumstances which incline me to return; and though they be not strong enough to render it *necessary*, they are enough so to obviate any objections to its *propriety*. The summer is not the period of the year for publication, and all therefore I could do during that time would be to prepare something for my *débût* in winter. This I could do as well in Ireland as here; for as to the idea of turning a literary *hack*, I find it to be such a premature grave of talents, that, till absolute exigence demands, I will not have recourse to it. Then for my study

[1] See letters Nos. 18 and 20 to his mother, 9 Nov. and 14 Dec. 1799. Arrangements had evidently been made by Moore's father for Goulding to advance money to Thomas as he needed it.

of the law, I cannot procure books here; to purchase them were expensive, the public libraries are inconvenient and unsatisfactory, and I am not intimate enough with any legal men to apply to them for the loan of those books that I should find necessary: all this would be obviated at home. I have other reasons, important and otherwise, which altogether make me very much disposed to returning. However, I submit it entirely to your wishes; and I pray you, do not think that my heart is *decidedly* set upon it, for I know that with such a persuasion, your indulgence would lead you to consent, in compliance more with my inclinations than your own judgment.

I sat with Lady Flood to-day for near an hour. Miss Flood is going to be married to a man of very large fortune. Sir Fred. has just come from Ireland about it. I was delighted to hear him give such a comfortable account of the returning appearance of tranquillity in Ireland.

You said in your last letter that my mother was *pretty well:* this qualified expression has made me apprehensive that she was not well. *Do* let me know particularly of *her* health and *your own.* Tell her with what delight I shall meet her, if it prove expedient that I shall return this summer, to enjoy that dear little family circle which absence has taught me to know the whole value of.

Give my warmest love to my dear Catherine. Heaven bless my sweet girl, and make her understanding as progressive as her goodness! Tell little Ellen that '*Brother, Sir*' does not forget her, and remember me most affectionately to my uncle Joice. Is my aunt recovering her health? Send her my loving remembrance; and, for you, my best of fathers, need I tell you with what true affection I am your ever grateful and loving son,

T. Moore.

Thursday night.—Write to [*sic*] immediately your determination. Mrs. M'Mahon will, I believe, travel with me.

10. *To his Mother*

Russell, i. 90, no. 9

June 11. 1799.

* * * I received a letter from Croker which pleased me very much. Does he ever call? He is a friend whom I am resolved to cultivate. London is growing insupportably warm, and will be a dreadful place to remain in all the summer. If I return to you, you must none of you be very inquisitive, for I am such an incurious creature

that I have not seen half the *lions* of this place. I have not yet been to this wonderful Pizarro of Sheridan's, which is putting all London into fevers.[1]

My father complained of my neglect of writing. The interval between my letters was perhaps too long, but you will perceive that I have not omitted one week. Give my love to my dearest father, and bid him write his decision immediately. Remember me to Catherine, to Ellen, to my uncle, aunt, &c.

I have paid 18*s*. 6*d*. for my last term, and will have the same to pay for this. Farewell, my sweet mother. Yours, &c.

11. *To his Father*

Russell, i. 91, no. 11

Thursday, June 20. 1799.

I forgot to mention, with regard to my coat and pantaloons, that Mr. Nugent, if you please, will settle for them with Mr. Herbert's money, and you may pay *him*. I am wishing very much to hear from you. In reading Warren's letter over again, I perceive what I did not observe at first; he tells me that my mother is reconciled to my staying during the vacation. Now, as *that* was, I confess, my chief motive for soliciting my return, because I had in a manner promised it to her; if she be *really* reconciled to my absence, and you not very much inclined to my going over, I will endeavour to have the same self-denial, and all my other objections to my remaining will be easily surmounted. I believe I will wait for your answer to this, if something else does not determine me, for I should be sorry to have no arguments for my return, but my own inclinations. If I go, I shall leave a few of my trifling poems with Hume, to get them published: it is more through a wish to get rid of them, than with any hopes of emolument: if the latter *does* result from them, I can rely on Hume for taking advantage of it.[2] Pray let me hear from you immediately on receipt of this. I perhaps may determine, however, before you write. Love to all. Yours, &c.

[1] Sheridan's *Pizzaro* was produced on 24 May 1799.

[2] Moore is referring to his translation of the *Odes of Anacreon*, which was published in July 1800.

12. *To his Father*

Russell, viii. 39

London
June 25. 1799.

Dear Father,

I am now determined upon going, and only wait for the decision of the bookseller, who has the manuscript of my little poems. If he gives me but as much as will bring me to Ireland, it will be pleasant; though I scarcely can expect more than a free publication, as poems are really, in the present taste of the age, a heavy article on the booksellers' hands. I am glad, however, to get rid of them if I can, on any terms. I will write again before I set off, and I hope to meet you all happy and in health. My last letter I suppose surprised, and, I hope, disappointed you; but you must always allow for the fluctuating oddity of my mind, which can never account for those melancholy little whims which it falls into. I have nothing particular to tell you.

My love to my dear mother, and Catherine and Ellen; to my uncle Joice and aunt, &c.—The day after to-morrow I expect to set off.

Yours, &c.
T. Moore.

13. *To his Father*

Russell, i. 92, no. 12

June 27. 1799.

I was not mistaken in thinking that no immediate emolument would result from those poems.[1] The booksellers shrink from risking anything on a person who has not a *name;* so that one must at first, sacrifice a little expense, or be content with eternal obscurity; and indeed I am so vexed that I could almost determine to acquiesce in the latter. I think I will set off to-morrow, but if I do not, I will write. Oh father! I hope I may one day or other repay you; but Heaven knows how! I am now in such a disposition that one word from you would decide me in staying here. Perhaps I may receive your answer to my letter, the last but one, before I go away. I will go now to the coach office, and if there be a place to be got, I *will* set off to-morrow. I shall feel happy, *very* happy in seeing you, but indeed I shall feel disappointed at the idea of not having in some manner lightened the burthen which is on you. If I can add,

[1] See letter No. 11, to his father, 20 June 1799.

however, one moment of happiness to my poor mother's life by returning, I shall hope that we cannot regret it. Give my love to my sisters, my dear good sisters; and believe me, dearest father, to be your most grateful and affectionate son.

14. *To his Mother*

Russell, i. 91, no. 10

Wednesday [June 1799]

My dearest Mother,

I got Kate's letter, and it was very good of you to think I should be anxious at not hearing so long from home, but lazy Kate might have stretched her commission a little and given me a longer epistle. I think the wearisomeness of this place is beginning almost to make me bilious; after all, there are few samenesses more disagreeable than that of seeing faces you dont care two-pence about, returning periodically and domestically, and mixing themselves as if they belonged to you, with every function of life. Oh solitude! solitude! you hold the very next rank to the society of the few we love. I wish prudence did not keep me away from you, dearest mother, and I should exchange all my fineries for Irish stew and salt fish immediately. Your own,

Tom.

15. *To his Father*

Russell, i. 93, no. 13

Parkgate
July 2. 1799.

Dear Father,

The packet will not sail to-day, and here I am imprisoned for one night more: the place is insipid, my companion is insipid, and all these circumstances combining with my impatience to see my beloved home, make this delay most dreadfully irksome to me. However, to-morrow morning, Captain Brown has pledged himself to sail, and you may expect me, with Heaven's permission, the day after to-morrow or the next, for the winds are very uncertain, and we will hardly be over in less than eight-and-forty hours. I hope I shall find you all well and happy. Tell Billy Warren that I am afraid to see him, as I bring him no new music, except that of Pizarro,[1] which is rather uninteresting and common. Yours, &c.

Love to my mother: I am longing to meet her.

[1] See letter No. 10, to his mother, 11 June 1799.

16. *To his Mother*

Russell, i. 93, no. 14

Chester
Oct. 28. 1799.

I have been detained here to-day, by not being able to secure a place last night.[1] However, I have taken my seat for to-night in the mail, and hope to be in London early, Wednesday morning. Poor Hobart[2] was almost shaken to death, during ninety-seven miles, on the outside of the coach. I have been with him to visit some of his Irish friends here; and we expect to be accompanied to the theatre to-night by Miss Beaver, a very pretty little girl. This will diversify the scene to us, and amuse our time till the departure of the mail. I have long wished for an opportunity of seeing the Chester theatre: there are some good actors here. I hope you will contrive to send my books to me very soon: tell Catherine to take Macbean's Ancient Geography out of the bookcase in your room and send it to me.[3] I forgot too to put the *Pastor Fido* among the books:[4] let her look for it in my room. I do not think I have forgot anything else of importance. The volumes of Anacharsis,[5] Hall, I suppose, has sent home. Our journey was extremely pleasant; very little chequered by adventures, and very little disturbed by accident. I am in very good spirits, and feel very differently from what I felt when I first travelled; except in that affection for you, and that longing to return to you, which, in the farthest part of

[1] Moore returned to Dublin in the summer of 1799. This letter was written, therefore, at the beginning of his second visit to London.

[2] In the index to his edition of Moore's *Memoirs, Journal and Correspondence*, Russell listed Moore's travelling companion as 'Rt. Hon. Hobart', thereby identifying him with the 'Rt. Hon. Hobart' whom Moore mentioned in connexion with a duel between Mathew Dowling and Hobart's secretary (Russell, i. 19). This identification is probably incorrect, since Robert Hobart (1760–1816), fourth Earl of Buckinghamshire, was Chief Secretary to the Lord Lieutenant of Ireland (1789–93), Governor of Madras (1794–8), Secretary of War for the Colonies (1801–4), and would undoubtedly be in a different social circle than that to which Moore was accustomed at this time. It is unlikely that Moore would have spoken of him familiarly as 'poor Hobart', or that he would have taken lodgings in the same house as the poet (see letter No. 18, to his mother, 9 Nov. 1799).

[3] Alexander Macbean, *A Dictionary of Ancient Geography, Explaining the Local Appellations in Sacred, Grecian and Roman History* (1773).

[4] Pastor Fido (pseudonym for Allan Blayney), *Festorum Metropolis. The Metropolitan Feast, or the Birth-day of our Saviour Jesus Christ* (1652).

[5] Moore is probably referring to J. J. Barthelemy's *Voyage du Jeune Anacharsis en Grece* (1788).

the world, never could desert me. Send me what I have mentioned, and remember me; for indeed I am,

Your fond and affectionate,

T. M.

17. *To his Mother*

Russell, i. 94, no. 15

Manchester
Thursday night, half-past Ten.
[October 1799]

My dearest Mother,

I have been obliged to come round by Manchester, from being disappointed last night of a seat on to Lichfield. To-day I came twenty-six miles of my journey in a canal boat, at the cheap rate of *three* shillings; and, in about *four* hours hence, I shall be off in the mail for Derby, so as to reach Donington[1] to dinner to-morrow. This is the state of my affairs at present, and but for the uncomfortable hours of darkness I have before me in this night's journey, I am as well and contented as either you or I could wish me to be.

My canal journey to-day was not unpleasant. Contrasted with the rattling of the mail, its movement was as agreeable as it was new, and our way lay through a very pretty country. Love to father and dear girls. Yours, my dearest mother.

18. *To his Mother*

Russell, i. 95, no. 16

Nov. 9. 1799.

Dear Mother,

By some strange error I did not receive Catherine's letter till to-day, when it was given to me with the subsequent one from my father. I was, I confess, extremely anxious, and they relieved me not a little. I should have told you that I took up four guineas from Mr. Goulding, out of which I have bought, in the extra way, a pair of boots (six and twenty shillings) and a little writing portfolio, which I have promised myself this long time. I hope you have got my letter with the inclosure for Cuming; Nugent will write to him immediately. Tell Dr. Stevenson he may expect a letter from me very soon, and that I dine with Incledon to-morrow, when he promises to introduce me to Irish Johnson [*sic*].[2]

[1] Donington Park, the Earl of Moira's estate, near Derby.

[2] Moore consistently spelled Johnstone's name in this way. See the Glossary of Proper Names.

Hobart has taken the first floor under me, but does not intend to continue. I wish he would; for I stay at home very much, and our breakfasting together takes off the *ennui* of *total solitude*. I suppose I shall soon have my books over, and shall pay attention to my father's wishes with regard to Mr. Brownrigg. I am very domestic, and have full leisure to think of all my dear friends at home. Do not forget me, any of you. My love to Billy Warren. Warmest remembrances to father and sisters.

Yours, yours.

19. *To his Mother*

Russell, i. 96, no. 17

Nov. 14. 1799.

Dear Mama,

I have left now so many days of this week without writing, that my letters will come 'not single *spies*, but in *battalions*.'[1]

Beresford Burston and I will dine together to-morrow or the next day, I believe. He appears to me to be drinking deep the intoxications of this place. I was out very late last night at a party at the Honourable Mrs. Gardiner's. She is an *English* woman, but has an *Irish heart*. On Sunday last you know I was to dine at Incledon's. Johnson and I got very great: he is to introduce me to Colman, the manager and author. I met there too Dr. Mosely, the king's physician. He took my address, and seemed to wish the cultivation of an acquaintance: he is in the first circles. Poor Incledon is deplorably hoarse: we might say to him, what he himself said to Peter Duffey (coal factor) the first time he heard him sing, 'By the holy St. Peter, you hav'nt a *note* in your *sack*.' Miss Biggs, the present heroine of Drury Lane, dined there, and gave me her orders for the ensuing evening. Lord Moira is in town. I left my card with him yesterday. I am very much afraid that you did not get my letter with the inclosure for Cuming; let me know immediately. I have not got my breakfast yet, and as Shakespere says, 'with veins unfill'd we're apt to *pout* upon the morning.'[2] Has the music-book been procured from Mrs. Grierson's for Dr. S.? I hope it has. Farewell, my good mother. Believe me, with the tenderest remembrances to my father and my dear little girls, yours ever.

[1] *Hamlet*, III. iv. 78.
[2] *Coriolanus*, v. i. 50.

20. *To his Mother*

Russell, i. 97, no. 18

Dec. 14. 1799.

I had intended to write earlier in the week, but was waiting for the printing of the proposals, the first proof of which I enclose to you. I had yesterday a long visit from a Mr. Biggin—a very famous and very respectable man here. By the bye, it is from *him* the coffee biggins[1] take their name, and from *them* he has taken his money. He has a box at the Opera House, and promises me frequent admission. Johnson [*sic*], of Covent Garden, I hear, sings some of my songs in company. I wish Cuming would be more active in his drawing. Nugent has begun the head of Anacreon. I am to be at a large party on Wednesday at Mrs. Campbell's, and on Friday at Lady Rich's, and am perfectly stout again. I will write very early next week, and tell you more news. I have got ten guineas from Mr. Goulding, and must immediately get a couple more; but I shall not now require such expense, for dining at home, the hiring of a sofa, which I was obliged to do, rather expensively, and coach-hire, were inevitable expenses. I hope, however, I shall clear at least a hundred guineas, by Anacreon. Love to all. Yours ever.

I shall soon get the rest of the printed papers, and will send them to you.

21. *To his Mother*

Russell, i. 98, no. 19

Dec. 19. 1799.

I hope the printed papers, which I enclosed, went safe and undamaged:[2] they are very nicely executed, and that I owe entirely to Hume, who has taken the whole negociation with the bookseller for me on himself: he has procured that I shall be announced in the next Reviews: every thing goes on swimmingly; but why is not Cuming's drawing sent out before this? I will inclose him, perhaps to-morrow, a few of the odes for his designs; and pray entreat of him to lose no time, and spare no trouble, in the execution of them. I am getting a good number of names here, and have received *two hard guineas* already from Mr. Campbell and Mr. Tinker, which I hope will be lucky. They are the only guineas I ever kissed; and

[1] The inventor of a kind of coffee-pot with a strainer. The *OED* gives the date 1803 for the use of the surname applied to the invention.

[2] Moore had probably sent his mother subscription forms for his translation of the *Odes of Anacreon.*

I have locked them up religiously. Mr. Gardiner sent a paper of my proposals, with a very flattering letter, indeed, to the Duchess of Devonshire, and another to Mrs. Fitzherbert. I must immediately send some of them to Captain Atkinson, Grierson, the Provost, &c. &c. I shall be greatly surprised if my friends in Dublin do not make it an ample subscription. Do not be diffident in your applications. I have learned other things here, but shall be long before I conquer my Irish *mauvaise honte*. Hume has given me the name of Lord Cloncurry (of the Tower), whose physician he is. I dined with Mr. Biggin on Sunday. I was mistaken when I told you that his money was made in the coffee pot business; they were only inventions of his.[1] He is a man of very easy fortune, and quite a virtuoso: he is a great chemist, mechanic, musician, and he has undertaken to eradicate my bilious complaint. A charming woman made the third at a very elegant dinner. She is the most exquisite performer I ever heard on the piano; and he has a beautiful organ, which she plays in the grandest cathedral style. They have lately been at Brussels, and collected all the newest music on the Continent. I never had such a banquet. Dearest mother, are you quite well, and in spirits? Give my love to my best of good fathers, to Catherine, Ellen, my uncle, &c. &c., and believe me, yours.

I got the bill on the merchants: in the next letter I hope to send you a new glee of mine, which Longman is printing!

22. *To his Mother*

Russell, i. 101, no. 21

Jan. 6. 1800.

I have just received a very *interesting* letter from my father, in which, though he has not been very eloquent, he has enclosed eight pounds or so. I wrote to you on Saturday a letter which I am sure you did not understand; however, it is now no matter, as the business is settled. I wrote to the Marquis of Lansdowne, to Bath, enclosing my *state* letter of introduction, with some plausible apologies and compliments, and a paper of my proposals. I received a very polite answer from him, requesting that his name should be put down, and that I should call on him any morning about eleven o'clock, when he comes to town, which will be very shortly. Dr. Lawrence has read my Anacreon; paid wonderful attention to it; and has written a Greek ode himself, which he allows me to publish.[2]

[1] See letter No. 20, to his mother, 14 Dec. 1799.

[2] Moore's comment on Dr. Lawrence's criticism of his *Anacreon* is sanguine and probably intentionally ambiguous. Lawrence was careful: the odes 'are,

I have got Mrs. Fitzherbert's name, and Mr. Biggin promises me the Duke of Bedford's. Everything goes on delightfully. Tell Cuming not to let a creature see the odes which I enclosed to him for the designs, but to send them back to me with the drawings; and all as soon as possible. The opening of the opera is deferred every night, on account of some misunderstanding with regard to the license. This annoys me, for I expect I shall be there every night with Mr. Biggin and Mrs. Birom. I am become this lady's pupil in thorough bass.

My next shall positively be to my dear Catherine: she must not, however, be affronted: she ought to consider how much I have on my hands—Anacreon, *thorough bass*, &c. &c.

23. *To his Mother*

Russell, i. 102, no. 22

Feb. 4. 1800.

I received my father's letter yesterday, and I am sorry to find that your enrolment is diminishing so soon; but he said that he enclosed me the list of subscribers, and I found no such thing in the letter. I have got the Duke of Bedford's name, and I believe shall have his interest, for Mr. Biggin is to show him some of the work: in short, my list is about fifty, without including Mr. Solly, who is very attentive to me, or Major Archdall, with whom I have dined two or three times, and who has introduced me to a Mr. Cope, of Manchester Square, with whom I am to dine to-morrow. I have not heard anything from Lord Moira; so I shall write to him very soon. Let Cuming send me the drawings immediately. Nugent is very much advanced in the engraving from the Provost's picture. Whatever damp I might have felt at the idea of the subscription slackening was, I assure you, my dear mother, infinitely compensated by being told that your health was better than it had been: Heaven preserve it long to make us happy! As the time approaches for my return, I begin to be still more impatient for it. I find the retouching and finishing my Anacreon to be an increasing and almost endless labour. I am at it night and day; it will soon be in the press, and shall fly over before me, to harbinger my return. I hope it will succeed. Success makes every one more welcome, but it cannot make me more so to you, can it, my dear mother? Give the warmest remembrances of my soul to my good, good father.

in many parts, very elegant and poetical. . . . To confess the truth, however, they are in not a few places, rather more paraphrastical than suits my notion . . . of translation' (Russell, i. 99).

24. *To his Mother*

Russell, i. 103, no. 23

Thursday, March 20. 1800.

My dearest Mother,

All is well again, and I am again quite stout. Once more laid on my back, under the physicians, I have once more shaken them off, and am drinking bottled porter and old port wine every day. Dearest mother, how anxious I have been at not being able to write to you! and I know now that you are all tremble and anxiety at the long interval there has been between my letters; indeed, the last I wrote was just caught in a lucid interval of ease, when I was allowed to sit up for an hour; and happy enough did it make me to avail myself of it in writing to my own darlings. I have not wanted for care and nursing of the best kind. Dr. Baillie, the first physician here, has attended me every second day, and Woolriche, the surgeon, twice a-day. I shall in my next letter tell you fully what was the matter with me. It began like my old pain, in the side, and they first tried calomel, but that failed, and they were obliged to let it form an abscess, which has now completely discharged itself, and I feel as healthy, as full of appetite and spirits as ever; a little weak, that's all. God bless you. Don't be the least uneasy. I am as one in full health.[1]

25. *To his Mother*

Russell, i. 104, no. 25

Saturday [April or May 1800]

My dear Mother,

I have got the Prince's name, and his permission that I should *dedicate* Anacreon to him.[2] Hurra! hurra! Yours ever.

26. *To his Mother*

Russell, i. 104, no. 24

May 14. 1800.

* * * I am just going out to dinner, and then to two parties in the evening—Mrs. Harwood's and Dr. Grant's. This is the way we live

[1] Moore had in fact been in great danger from a large abscess in his side. He eventually diminishes the illness not to alarm his mother [Russell's note]. See note No. 1 to letter No. 122, to his mother, 30 Apr. 1806, for a suggestion that Russell may have been incorrect in dating this letter 1800 instead of 1806.

[2] *The Odes of Anacreon* was dedicated to the Prince of Wales. See letter No. 32, to his mother, 4 Aug. 1800.

in London, no less than three every evening. *Vive la bagatelle!* 'Away with melancholy.'

27. *To his Mother*

Russell, i. 104, no. 26

June 9. 1800.

* * * How I long to return to you: as soon as the books are published and distributed, you shall see me. I have written a Greek ode, which is now before the tribunal of Dr. Lawrence,[1] and, if he approve of it, I shall have it prefixed to the Anacreon. *This,* I hope, will astonish the scoundrelly monks of Trinity, not one of whom, I perceive, except the Provost and my tutor,[2] have subscribed to the work. Heaven knows they ought to rejoice at anything like an effort of literature coming out of their leaden body! I can do without them; but tell Phipps that I will not put F.T.C.D. after his name, as I should be ashamed of the world's observing that but one of the fellows of the university where I graduated, gave his tribute to a classical undertaking of this kind. They are a cursed corporation of boobies! and if it were not for my friend, their Provost, the public should know my opinion of them. * * * I was last night in company with Godwin.

28. *To his Mother*

Russell, i. 105, no. 27

June 21. 1800.

I am surprised at not having heard from home near this week past. I hope you are all well; and, Heaven knows! I wish I were with you. I have already begun this piece, and only wait for the expression of your wishes to go on with it.[3] It *may* succeed and it *may not;* but still, my dearest mother, you will feel that I have made the effort, and then I shall fly to your arms 'like a young bridegroom, dancing to his love.'[4] I have been obliged to adopt a particular plot prescribed to me, so that I must be considered as connected in the writing as well as the music. This is one reason that I do not wish it to be known that I am engaged in such a thing; but if a hundred

[1] See letter No. 22, to his mother, 6 Jan. 1800.

[2] Dr. Kyle was provost when Moore was at Trinity College, Dublin. Phipps was a fellow of the college and Moore's tutor.

[3] *The Gipsy Prince,* which was produced at the Haymarket Theatre on 24 July 1801. Moore's collaborator on this venture was Michael Kelley, who took the leading role.

[4] The quotation has not been identified.

or two hundred pounds be the result of it, why, we shall have no reason to regret it. At all events, we shall meet, I hope, in the course of a month, and we shall *indeed* be very happy, for *you* deserve to be happy, and I feel that I am, perhaps, not unworthy of it. Farewell, my sweet mother God bless you.

29. *To his Mother*

Russell, i. 106, no. 28

July 5. 1800.

My dearest Mother,

* * * I hope you got my Anacreon, which I enclosed to Cocke. How did you look at it? What did you feel? Oh! I know what you felt, and I know how you looked! My heart is with you, though I am so delayed from meeting you. Good God! when we *do* meet, may it be in happiness! Write to me, my dear father and mother; tell me you are in health and content, and I shall then be as happy as absence from you will allow me. Farewell. 'Forget me not.'

30. *To his Mother*

Russell, i. 106, no. 29

July 12. 1800.

I am trying every day to be off to you, but distributing this book is taking up my time; and waiting to be introduced to the Prince. I met his brother, Prince William, the other night, at a very elegant party at Lady Dering's, and was introduced to him. A young girl told me, that he had been asking her questions about me and my birth, parentage, &c., with all the curiosity of the royal family. I was obliged that night to sing every one of my songs twice. The day before yesterday I was at a splendid dejeuner of Sir John Coghill's: we had charming music. I sang several things with Lord Dudley and Miss Cramer (sister to Sir J. Coghill). These people I was introduced to by Lord Lansdowne. I got your welcome letter; my account from my dear ones at home is heaven to me. I hope the Anacreon will soon be with you, and the *young boy* soon after them. Oh heavens! how happy we shall meet! God send it,—and immediately 'a *speedy* meeting and *soon,*' as an *Irishman* would say. You see how conceited I'm grown. Love to all. My heart is with you.

31. *To his Mother*

Russell, i. 107, no. 30

July 28. 1800.

I hope in a very few days to be able to leave London and see all those I have been so long, so tediously separated from. I am delighted to find by my father's letter, that Hume has made your mind so happy in regard to me. He is certainly an inestimable young man. I never met with any one more capable of friendship, or more adapted to cherish it. He has a peculiar delicacy (which must always make him an amiable companion), never to touch upon any thing grating to one's feelings. I could write a volume about him, and even if he had not *one* estimable quality, still gratitude for his interest in my welfare should tie me to him. I hope he will dine with you some day; and on that day there will not in Europe be three more honest souls together.

32. *To his Mother*

Russell, i. 107, no. 31

August 4. 1800.

I was yesterday introduced to his Royal Highness George, Prince of Wales. He is beyond doubt a man of very fascinating manners. When I was presented to him, he said he was very happy to know a *man of my abilities;* and when I thanked him for the honour he did me in permitting the dedication of Anacreon,[1] he stopped me and said, the honour was *entirely* his, in being *allowed* to put his name to a work of such merit. He then said that he hoped when he returned to town in the winter, we should have many opportunities of *enjoying each other's society;* that he was passionately fond of music, and had long heard of my talents in that way. Is not all this very fine? But, my dearest mother, it has cost me a *new coat;* for the introduction was unfortunately deferred till my former one was grown confoundedly shabby, and I got a coat made up in six hours: however, it cannot be helped; I got it on an economical plan, by giving two guineas and an *old coat,* whereas the usual price of a coat here is near four pounds. By the bye, I am still in my other tailor's debt. To change the topic, I have heard Lord Moira's opinion of my Anacreon (not from himself, for, when I saw him, he very elegantly thanked me for a vast deal of gratification which it had given him); but he had spoken a vast deal of it to a gentleman who told *me:* said there were scarce any of the *best* poets who had been

[1] See letter No. 25, to his mother, April or May 1800.

so strictly grammatical in language as I had been,—that the notes discovered a great extent of reading,—and that, in short, it was a very superior work.

Do not let any one read this letter but yourselves; none but a father and a mother can bear such egotising vanity; but I know who I am writing to—that they are interested in what is said of me, and that they are too partial not to tolerate my speaking of myself. * * *

33. *To his Mother*

Russell, viii. 40

Donnington Park
Dec. 31. 1800 (at night).

My dear Mother,

This is from my bed-chamber at Donnington Park,[1] where I arrived at two o'clock to-day, through snows mountain deep; the cross roads were impassable; so that I was obliged to take a round, which has made it a little expensive: but it can't be helped, it has not made much difference. Nothing can be more princely than the style of this place, nor anything more flatteringly polite than my reception here. Lady Charlotte[2] told me she regretted very much that I was not here during the Prince's stay, and that she had written to her mother to beg of her to hurry me. The Prince, too, she told me, expressed a wish that I had met him. Dearest Mother! there is no fear of my not doing *everything*. Keep up your spirits, my little woman, and you'll find I'll make you as rich as a nabob. But I am now far away from you, and that is the only idea that can hang heavy on my mind; but, dear Mother, be happy and contented, and then you'll be everything to us. Your *excessive* solicitude for us is the *only thing* we can blame you for. I shall not stay here more than a day or two, certainly, for I find my portmanteau tormentingly troublesome. I dread the packing of it again; and I have to *root* into it for everything I want. Lord Moira has but this moment left me, after attending me very politely to show me my bed-room.

Good bye.

Thomas Moore.

I believe I left my little brooch behind me. Take particular care of it, and send it or enclose it by the first opportunity. I may, perhaps, not be able to write again from this, on account of the uncertainty of their sending off a post-boy; but I shall write the moment

[1] The Earl of Moira's estate.

[2] Lady Charlotte Rawdon. See the Glossary of Proper Names.

I arrive in London. Send the enclosed letter under cover to 'Earl Granard, Castle Forbes, Longford.'

34. *To his Mother*

Russell, i. 108, no. 32

Jan. 3. 1801.

My dearest Mother,

Still at Donington; but I am sure I shall leave it tomorrow. Lord Moira wishes me to stay, but I shall promise in a little time to return here, which is the best way to escape pleasantly. There cannot be anything more delightful than this house,—an inimitable library, where I have the honour of being *bound up* myself, a charming piano, and very pleasant society. What can be more delightful however? I am so anxious to get to London that I *must* fly away. * * *

35. *To his Mother*

Russell, i. 109, no. 33

London
Jan. 5. 1801.

* * * I was not allowed to leave Donington Park till I had promised that, as soon as leisure allowed me, I should return. They were, indeed, uncommonly polite. The morning I left it, breakfast was ordered an hour earlier than usual to accommodate me, and Lord Moira requested I should return as soon as I could. * * *

36. *To his Mother*

Russell, i. 109, no. 34

Jan. 27. 1801.

Dearest Mama,

Forgive me for only writing a *billet doux*, but I have written by this post to Capt. Atkinson and Lady Moira, and have not time to say more than that I am very well, and in high spirits. What do you think? Lord Moira, who came to town but yesterday, called on me in person to-day, and left his card: is not this excellent? I got dear Catherine's letter, and shall answer it immediately. Yours totally and eternally.

37. *To his Mother*

Russell, i. 109, no. 35

Monday, Feb. 2. 1801.

* * * I dined on Saturday in company with Suett and Bannister. Read the piece to them.[1] Suett is quite enchanted with his part, particularly the mock bravura.

38. *To his Mother*

Russell, i. 110, no. 36

March 1. 1801.

My dearest Mother,

You may imagine I do not want society here, when I tell you that last night I had *six* invitations. Everything goes on swimmingly with me. I dined with the Bishop of Meath on Friday last, and went to a party at Mrs. Crewe's in the evening. My songs have taken such a rage! even surpassing what they did in Dublin. Let me know if the Steeles are in Dublin, and write to me oftener. Sweetest, dearest mama! keep up your spirits and health till we meet, which shall, please Heaven! be in summer. Yours dearly.

39. *To his Mother*

Russell, i. 110, no. 37

March 6. 1801.

My dearest Mother,

* * * There is not a night that I have not three parties on my string, but I take Hammersley's advice, and send showers of apologies. The night before last, Lady Harrington sent her servant after me to two or three places with a ticket for the 'Ancient Music,' which is the king's concert, and which is so select, that those who go to it ought to have been at Court before. Lady Harrington got the ticket from one of the Princesses, and the servant at last found me where I dined. You may be assured I hurried home and dressed for it immediately. These attentions from such great people are no harm, and they are flattering. * * *

[1] *The Gipsy Prince*, Moore's light opera.

40. *To his Mother*

Russell, i. 111, no. 38

March 18. 1801.

My dearest Mother,

Never was there any wight so idly *busy* as I am—nothing but racketting: it is indeed too much, and I intend stealing at least a fortnight's seclusion, by leaving word at my door that I am gone to the country. I must 'tie up the knocker, say I'm sick—I'm dead!'[1] I last night went to a little supper after the opera, where the Prince and Mrs. Fitzherbert were: I was introduced to her. * * *

I dine with Lord Moira to-morrow, and go in the evening with Lady Charlotte to an assembly at the Countess of Cork's. I assure you I am serious in the idea of being at least for a fortnight incog. * * *

41. *To his Mother*

Russell, i. 111, no. 39

March 24. 1801.

I find Grierson leaves this but to-day: he has been so occupied with business that I have seen very little of him. I never told you that, at the time I came here, I found I was near 70£. in Hume's debt: he is now paid by the sale of the copyright, and has left another debt of strong *obligation* behind, for he is a very honest fellow. You see how I push through these matters. Ah! my dear mother, with the favour of Heaven, there is no fear of me; if you are but happy, I have everything I can wish for. I have not been able to get down so far as Keinvan's yet: it is (as Major Swayne says) eight miles into that cursed city! I shall soon, however, take the walk and get my five guineas. What do you think, young Lord Forbes and another young nobleman dine *with me* to-morrow! This was a thing *put on me*, and I shall do it with a good grace.

I assure you I am six feet high to-day after discharging my debt of 70£. yesterday, and I have still some copies on my hand to dispose of for myself. The new edition will soon be out:[2] it will be got up very handsomely: perhaps if I send you over twenty copies of the last which I have, you may pick up so many guineas there for them; but the manner of sending them is the thing. Love to all.

[1] Pope, *Epistle to Dr. Arbuthnot*, ll. 1–2.

[2] The second edition of *The Odes of Anacreon* appeared in 1802.

42. *To his Mother*

Russell, i. 112, no. 40

Saturday, March 28. 1801.

My dearest Mother,

* * * I was last night at a ball, which (as *we* say) *swept the town*—everybody was there—two or three of the Princes, the Stadtholder, &c. &c. You may imagine the affability of the Prince of Wales, when his address to me was, 'How do you do, Moore? I am glad to see you.' * * * I kept my piece back too long.[1] I am afraid they will not have time to bring it out this season, and it is too expensive for Colman's theatre. He has read it, however; is quite delighted with it; and wishes me to undertake something on a more moderate scale for the little theatre, which perhaps I shall do. But, please God! I must, I think, see my dear ones in summer again. Don't let me be forgot in your lodgings: keep a corner for Tom. Love to you all—to the whole rookery.

43. *To his Mother*

Russell, i. 112, no. 41

Wednesday, April 1. 1801.

How d'ye do, my dearest mother? Did you see my name in the paper among the lists of company at most of the late routs? This is a foolish custom adopted here, of printing the names of the most *distinguished personages* that are at the great parties, and Mr. *Moore*, I assure you, is not forgotten. I have an idea of going down to Donington Park, to seclude myself for about a month in the library there: they are all in town, but Lord Moira tells me I may have an apartment there, whenever I wish. 'Tis a long time since I heard from you. Are you all well and happy? Grierson has not left this yet. I dined yesterday with George Ogle, and he was there. I met the Prince at supper at Lady Harrington's, on Monday night; he is always very polite to me. You cannot think how much my songs are liked here. Monk Lewis was 'in the greatest agonies' the other night at Lady Donegal's, at having come in after my songs: ''Pon his honour, he had come for the express purpose of hearing me.' Write to me soon, dearest little mama, and tell me you are well.

[1] *The Gipsy Prince*. See letter No. 28, to his mother, 21 June 1800.

44. *To his Mother*

Russell, i. 113, no. 42

Saturday, April 18. 1801.

My dearest Mother,

I go on as usual; I am happy, careless, comical, everything I could wish; not very rich, nor yet quite poor. All I desire is that my dear ones at home may be as contented and easy in mind as I am. Tell me are you all happy and comfortable? I do not hear from you half often enough. The other day I dined with the Dowager Lady Donegal: we had music in the evening. Lady Charlotte Rawdon and I were obliged to sing my little glees three times. I go to Donington in about a week, I think: about that time my poems will be all printed. I suppose Captain A. told you they are coming out as 'The poetical works of the late Thos. Little, Esq.'[1] You shall have a copy over immediately. I wrote a long letter to *Miss Catherine Little* this week. Make her answer me soon.

45. *To his Mother*

Russell, i. 114, no. 43

Saturday, April 25. 1801.

My dearest Mother,

I am expecting every day to leave town, and on Tuesday I hope to effect it. I look to a new vein of imagination entirely in the solitude of Donington. I have seldom, never indeed, been two days alone, and I expect that in such a situation, with the advantage of so fine a library, I may produce something far beyond any of my past attempts. I dined *en famille* with Lord Moira on Thursday last, and he told me every thing was prepared at Donington for my reception. * * * I hope the post will be convenient enough to allow my regular correspondence; indeed, I have no doubt of it, and my darling dears shall hear from the Hermit of the Castle all the progress of his fanciful lucubrations. What delays my little Catherine's letter? I am anxious for it. I shall let you know the day before I leave town, in what manner you are to direct your letters to me. I am well, happy in spirits; thinking hourly of the dear ones at home, and anticipating the pleasure I shall have in rejoining them in summer.

[1] *The Poetical Works of Thomas Little* appeared in 1801.

46. *To his Mother*

Russell, i. 115, no. 44

Donington Park
Tuesday, May 5. 1801.

My time here by no means hangs heavily on me, notwithstanding that I am so little accustomed to solitude. I rise rather early, breakfast heartily, employ the day in walking or *hunting*—among old books, dine off two courses, no less; in the evening sing down the sun like a true Pythagorean, and then seasonably take to my pillow, where I sleep sweetly, nor dream of ambition though beneath the roof of an earl. Such is my diary. * * * My love comes more pure to you now from the clear air of Donington; take it, my dear mother, and believe me yours ever.

47. *To his Mother*

Russell, i. 115, no. 45

Wednesday, May 13. 1801.

* * * It is now a fortnight since I came to Donington: it has not by any means seemed tedious to me; and I think another week will be the conclusion of my visit. I shall let you know particularly when I leave it.

48. *To his Mother*

Russell, i. 115, no. 46

Donington Park
May 21. 1801.

I am now more than three weeks at Donington, and in that time have received but one short letter from home,—this is not fair. I am sure *my* regularity ought to be a little better rewarded. My father I excuse. I trust and hope from my soul he has business to keep him from writing; but the little idle gipsy, Catherine, who can have no other employment than to improve herself, ought surely to make correspondence with me one medium of that improvement. I am almost growing anxious from this silence, to *me* so very gloomy; and I sometimes dread that all is not right at home, or the common occupations of the day could never so interrupt your writing to me. Tell me truth, my darling mother, are you all happy and in health? Make Catherine write to me oftener: there are a thousand little nothings of the day's news which I should like to hear, and which it is her province more immediately to communicate. Let her not mind postage either; I throw away many a shilling foolishly, which I should much rather bestow on a little intelligence from dear home.

I never committed a *murder* till I came to Donington, but I've been shooting young rooks every morning for this week past. You cannot imagine how rosy I am grown: these good hours would make an Adonis of me, so that, in pity to the Chloes, I must dissipate when I go to town again. I shall, I believe, make out the month here: next Wednesday I look to leaving Donington, and I think not sooner. Good bye, dear mother. Your own,

Tom.

49. *To his Mother*

Russell, i. 116, no. 47

Saturday, June 6. 1801.

My dearest Mother,

* * * My little poems are very much admired here, and have increased my fame.[1] I hope I shall soon get my shirts and cravats. Atkinson is as cordial and friendly as I could expect almost from my father. We dined together yesterday at Mrs. Fancourt's: we have contrived indeed not to separate in our enjoyments since he came. You cannot imagine how much my name is gone about here: even of those poems my bookseller sells at the rate of twenty copies a-day; and the shabby demand of Ireland for fifty copies (which Grierson has written over) will surely appear very contemptible to this. It is not his fault, however; and, indeed, I am very indifferent about it, for they are not very liberal to the style of my youthful productions. Lord Moira had one of the first copies.

50. *To his Mother*

Russell, i. 117, no. 48

46. Wigmore Street, Cavendish Square.
June 16. 1801.

My dearest Mother,

I know you will forgive my irregularities in writing at present, when you know that I am as well as possible, and as happy as good spirits and a vast deal of pleasant company can make me. The night before last I was at the most splendid ball that has been given this season, at the Duchess of Devonshire's; and I returned

[1] Moore is referring to *The Odes of Anacreon*. See letter No. 50.

at four this morning from another, given by Sir Watkin W. Wynne. This work will soon be over, so you need not dread my having too much of it. Carpenter has thought it most prudent to defer publishing my book till Christmas:[1] the only inconvenience attending this is, that I must be drawing on him in the meantime, without anything going on to liquidate it; but this he has no objection to. I am only afraid it will delay my visit to dear home beyond what I expected, as my only plan now is to go to Donington, to Lord Moira's, where I shall be at less expense than in town. Lord Moira, last night, went a great round out of his way to set me down at Sir Watkin's, from Mrs. Duff's, where we met at a large rout. He is uncommonly kind and attentive. I think the reports about him have again died away. Love to father, dear Kate, and Nell. Yours ever, dearest mother.

51. *To his Mother*

Russell, i. 118, no. 49

Nov. 26. 1801.

My dearest Mother,

* * * I find the papers here have all been quoting passages from my Anacreon for public notice. This your readers of the '*Packet*' in Dublin never could spy out, though they could be lynx-eyed to anything they thought unfavourable. Accordingly, we never heard of this from them. * * *

52. *To his Mother*

Russell, i. 118, no. 50

Monday, Jan. 4. 1802.

My dearest Mother,

This letter I know has been *waited* for, but in leaving Donington I was hurried into the omission of it. I arrived in town yesterday with Curran, who kept me in an uninterrupted fit of laughter all the way. We had a dance at the Park the night before I left it, and I footed it away merrily till four o'clock in the morning. Tell Kate that I, immediately on receiving her letter, copied out the song for Lady Elizabeth, and gave her some lessons in singing it. I shall tell in my next letter what I think about her excursion to Castle Forbes. I was obliged to come to town to try and get this

[1] Moore is referring to the second edition of the *Odes of Anacreon* (1802). *The Poems of Thomas Little* appeared later in the summer of 1801. They were reviewed in the *Monthly Magazine*, xii (Sept. 1801), 106–7.

music into hands. The second edition of Anacreon is published, and it is certainly very beautifully got up. The print is universally thought to be like, and he is selling off hundreds of them singly. There is a copy at the binder's for my dears at home. * * *

53. *To his Mother*

Russell, i. 119, no. 51

Saturday, Jan. 30. 1802.

My dearest Mother,

I am flying off to the Temple this instant to eat my dinner; it's about two miles and a half, so I have little time to write. I don't know which, Kate or I, is generally in the greatest hurry. I go in the evening to a *Blue Stocking* supper at Lady Mount-Edgecumbe's; it is the first this season, and I shall be initiated. The Hon. Mrs. Damer, the Misses Berry, &c. &c., form the *coterie*. I met all my old fashionable friends at a rout last night, the opening of the season,—300 people. I wait my answer from Dalby, Lord Forbes' tutor, to arrange my plans for leaving London; it is necessary to me for some time.

Love to all dears at home. Tell me how Hobart's play comes on.[1] Tell him I have attempted something, but don't like what I have done.[2] I had rather write merely the words, and Stevenson compose the music. * * *

54. *To his Mother*

Russell, i. 119, no. 52

Monday, Feb. 1. 1802.

The idea of Lord Moira's coming into administration begins to be entertained very strongly here. Heaven send it! I have heard from Dalby, and shall about the end of this week go to Donington. The Granards seem to approve very much of my resolution in leaving the seductions of London for a month or two of study. You may have some idea of the increasing popularity that follows my Anacreon, when I assure you that on Saturday last Carpenter sold *ten* copies of the new edition in the course of the day; and so, more or less, every day.

[1] See letter No. 16, to his mother, 28 Oct. 1799. Hobart's play has not been identified.

[2] Moore is referring to *The Gipsy Prince*. See letter No. 28, to his mother, 21 June 1800.

I am going to a rout at Lady Talbot's to-night. There is a volume of designs from the Anacreon, I hear, preparing for publication by some eminent artist. I breakfast with Monk Lewis to-morrow morning in order to go to see them. Tell Stevenson he could not at present choose anything more likely to catch the public than his publication of the glees from Anacreon: it is universally read, and hardly can be said to have been known till now. I do not hear from you half so often as I should wish. Bid Kate never to wait for a frank, and to write very often. Dear, darling mother, your own boy,

Tom.

55. *To his Mother*

Russell, i. 120, no. 53

Monday, March 4. 1802.

My darling Mother,

I don't know how I let Saturday pass without a letter, but I believe I was in a little fuss about a civil kind of scrape that the good nature of some of my fashionable friends brought me into. While I was away, they did me the troublesome honour of electing me into a new club they have formed, and it was on Saturday that I thought I had to pay my subscription. However, I have more time for it than I imagined, and, when the debt is discharged, I must get quietly out of the business, highly sensible of the honour they have done to my pocket. I am deferring too long my letter to my dear uncle, but to-morrow I think it shall be done. The people will not let me stay at home as much as I wish, and I sometimes wish all the duchesses and marchionesses *chez le diable*. * * *

56. *To his Mother*

Russell, i. 121, no. 54

March 6. 1802.

Dearest Mother,

I find, by to-day's paper, that we are all at *loggerheads* again. I believe what my countryman says is true, 'that the French can never be at peace but when they are in some war or other.'[1] Why

[1] On 6 Mar. 1802 an article on the state of affairs in France appeared in *The Times*. The writer observed that many people felt that the incorporation of the Italian Republic with France was a step toward war; that the 'orders for revictualling our Fleets cast a considerable despondency over the public mind'; that the transactions at Lyon (concerning the incorporation of the Italian Republic) caused an interruption in the negotiations at Amiens (where a treaty

is Kate so long silent? She has not acknowledged either of the letters which I wrote to her. I am getting quite rosy with the air of this fine weather. Nothing could take me to town now but *Banti's* benefit. She plays the chief man herself, and Mrs. Billington *la prima donna;* there's a treat! I have some shows myself here; I went last night to look at the satellites of Jupiter, through a telescope, with Dalby; and this morning I was introduced to Dalby's sweetheart! How do you like the way 'Lady Fair' is got up?[1] My best love to dear, good father. I pray for you all every night.

57. *To Joseph Atkinson*

Morgan Library

April 19th 1802*

My dear Sir J.

I feel a very sincere pleasure in dedicating to you the second edition of our friend Little's poems.[2] I am not unconscious that there are many in the collection, which perhaps it would be prudent to have altered or omitted; and, to say the truth, I more than once revised them for that purpose. But, I know not why, I distrusted either my heart or my judgment, and the consequence is that you have them in their original form.

Non possunt nostros multae Faustine liturae
Emendare jocos: una litura potest.[3]

I am convinced however that, though not quite a casuiste relâché, you have charity enough to forgive such inoffensive follies; you know, the pious Beza was not the less revered for those sportive Juvenilia which he published under a fictitious name, nor did the levity of Bembo's poems prevent him from making a very good Cardinal.

Believe me, my dear friend, with the
truest esteem,
Yours

T. M.

with France was finally signed later in 1802); and that a number of political arrests of distinguished people had been made in Paris, a fact which boded ill for freedom of speech and press in France. Moore was probably concerned about the 'revictualling of our Fleets' since an article pointing out the seriousness of this situation appeared in *The Times* on 5 Mar.

[1] 'Oh Lady Fair. A Ballad for Three Voices' (1802).

[2] The second edition of *The Poetical Works of Thomas Little* contained this dedicatory preface.

[3] Martial, *Epigrams*, IV. x. 7–8.

58. *To his Mother*

Russell, i. 121, no. 55

Saturday, May 1. 1802.

My dearest Mother,

It is very, very long since I heard from home: what is my little Kate about? The Granards are still lingering here. * * * Lady Granard is uncommonly kind. I think I should rather wish Kate to go with them to Castle Forbes, if I *can* (as I expect) help her to rig herself out for it. London is most killingly gay, and my spirits keep up to its gaiety. Have you got the heads by Maurice Fitzgerald? I dine to-day with Lady Donegal and her sister; *none* but the trio of us. The day of the great illuminations I breakfasted with the Lord Mayor, dined with Lord Moira, and went in the evening to Mrs. Butler's, the Duchess of Athol's, Lady Mount-Edgecumbe's, and Lady Call's, which was a ball, where I danced till five in the morning.

59. *To his Mother*

Russell, i. 122, no. 56

Thursday, June 3. 1802.

My dearest Mother,

I this morning received Kate's account of your dance, but she did not tell me who were of the party. The Union Masquerade on Monday was rather a Bartholomew Fair business, though tickets sold for *fifteen* guineas each. Mrs. Fancourt, as *Wowski*, was the best dressed and supported character I ever saw. I accompanied her as Trudge. The Morning Post of to-day, I see, speaks of her, though they do not know her name, and says she was attended by '*Anacreon Moore.*' I had a long conversation with Lord Moira yesterday about going to Brunswick with Lord Forbes: it is his wish decidedly, and he begged me to consider, what beyond my expenses would make it unnecessary for me to draw on this country. Do not breathe a word of this. I am still looking out for some one to take charge of the dresses for Kate. I am going to publish Memory.[1] It depends now upon Lord Moira how soon I shall visit my dear, dear home; it may be immediately, it may not be for two months or so. See you all, I must of course, before I arrange any plan whatsoever about Brunswick. Love to my good father, dear Kate, and Ellen. Yours, dearest mother.

[1] Probably 'To . . . 1801', *Poetry*, p. 66.

60. *To Viscount Strangford*

National Library of Ireland

June 20th 1802*

My dear Strangford—

Your letter I believe followed Lewis to Scotland, for he was on his way thither the day you wrote it, & a week's travelling has brought it at last to me—it finds me retired from all the racketting of London, at a little cottage not a hundred yards from Denham's far-famed Hill,[1] up to the chin in folios, and as busy at scribble-scribble as the *damned* goddess of indolence (Vacuna, I believe ?) will let me— I do any thing but what I ought to do, and I nearly shattered my fore-finger into pieces the other day by firing forsooth with a pistol, to show the versatility of my talents— I can with difficulty write yet.

Lewis and I parted in the full blow of friendship—he asked me before he went to make him a present of the books I had published, and I did do so, though I felt very much inclined to answer him out of Martial—

> Exigis, ut donem nostros tibi, Quinete, libellos,
> Non habeo, sed habet bibliopola Tryphon ([*illegible*] Carpenter)[2]

Between ourselves, my dear Percy, and in the beaten way of friendship, I *must* condemn your levity about Mrs Walpole—it was unworthy of you—you made a discovery almost inevitable, and you *must* know too that this is not Diplomatique, for whatever a man may think of a woman, he should *seem* to respect her for indulging him, or he will hardly be indulged by any other—no, no—I agree with my friend Tom Brown that

> Of all the crimes on this side hell,
> The blackest sure's to —— and tell.[3]

And you are right in saying 'le *jeu* ne vaut pas *la chandelle*' *for such games* should be kept quite *in the dark*— I have seldom seen her since, but I have heard from Lewis that she is very miserable about the conversations her conduct gave birth to—

I am delighted to find that your present intentions coincide so much with the advice I have so often given—publish the translations from Camoëns most certainly—[4] I have seen your *gems* upon

[1] Cooper's Hill, near Egham, Surrey.

[2] Martial, *Epigrams*, IV. lxxii.

[3] Thomas Brown, *Amusements Serious and Comical*, ed. Arthur L. Hayward (New York, 1927), p. 292.

[4] Lord Strangford published *Poems from the Portugese of Camoëns* in 1803.

the *dunghill* of the Poetical Register, and I am convinced that a collection of such things would do you infinite credit—besides you are already well known & looked to, and celebrity would tread upon the very heels of Publication—

Bayle has no article upon Camoëns, but though I do not exactly remember, I should think Mickle has made every profitable research upon the subject— Moreri gives a short sketch of his life, and mentions the collection of his poems under the title of Rimas de Luis de Camoens [*sic*] —ses autres ouvrages, (he says) sont perdus— We are referred by Moreri for information about Camoens [*sic*] to Nicolas Antonio, Bibliotheca Hispanica—and particularly to Baillet, Jugement des Savans. Tom 7— I have some volumes of this last work, but not the one he refers to— There is a little volume called the Revolutions of Literature, translated from the Italian of Carlo Denina, in which there are some trifling remarks on the Literature of the Spanish, scarcely however worth your attending to—he applies to their *poetry* the criticism of another upon their *oratory* 'a string of absurdities, of witticisms without judgment, of subtleties without solidity, of words without meaning'—is there any truth in all this? There is certainly but poor antithesis—[1]

Write to me as soon as you receive this, and tell me you forgive my morale de galanterie—

Yours, my dear Strangford
very sincerely
Thomas Moore

Direct to me Post Office Egham Surry [*sic*]

61. *To his Mother*

Russell, i. 123, no. 57

Saturday, July 18. 1802.

* * * I am happy to learn that the Catch Club have done themselves so much justice by their tribute to Stevenson.[2] I wish he were here; he would soon, I think, put down Kelly. Poor *Mick* is rather an

[1] Pierre Bayle, *Dictionnaire Historique et Critique* (1696); William Julius Mickle, *The Lusiad, or the Discovery of India. An Epic Poem,* translated from Camoëns (1776); Louis Moreri, *Dictionnaire Historique* (1674); Nicolas Antonio, *Bibliotheca Hispana Nova* (1672); A. Baillet, *Critique des Savants* (1725); Carlo Giovanni Maria Denina, *An Essay on the Revolutions of Literature,* translated by J. Murdoch (1771).

[2] The Catch Club, a London society, the full title of which was 'The Noblemen and Gentlemen's Catch Club', was formed in 1761 to encourage the composition of canon, catches, and glees. The Club granted occasional prizes for outstanding work in musical composition, but since no prize was given in 1802, the tribute to Stevenson must have been of a different kind.

*im*poser than a composer. He cannot mark the time in writing three bars of music: his understrappers, however, do all that for him, and he has the knack of pleasing the many. He has compiled the Gipsy Prince extremely well, and I have strong hopes of its success.

62. *To his Mother*

Russell, i. 123, no. 58

Monday, Sept. 20. 1802.

My dearest Mother,

I have been kept very busily employed in viewing all the beauties of this country, which are, indeed, extremely interesting; and I hope in a very short time to describe them to you by word of mouth. I had the courage the other day to descend into a coal-pit, 360 feet depth: never was anything so true a picture of the infernal regions; very few, except those condemned to work in them, venture to visit them. I was let down in a bucket, and, indeed, expected to *kick* it before I got up again. The deuce take Mr. Holmes, wherever he is; though I hope by this time, at least, the box has arrived. I received Kate's last letter, enclosed to me, from Egham. As soon as I can get off from this place I shall, please Heaven! lose no time in flying to you. Who could Kate have been with at Seapoint? Love to dearest father, and my little girls. The Atkinsons have quite flattered me by the account they gave of Ellen. Good by, dearest mother.

63. *To his Mother*

Russell, i. 124, no. 59

Nov. 17. 1802.

My dearest Mother,

I have come to town just time enough to see Lord Moira, with whom I dined yesterday at the Cocoa Tree. Lord Hutchinson was of the party. Lord Moira expresses very warm regret at the disappointment I have met with; and I feel not a doubt that, as he has now more *power* than before, he certainly has not less *will* to do me service. Every one has met me with smiles; not a frown, even from my tailor! My chief anxiety now is about the money I owe my dear uncle.[1] *Do* bid him write, and set my mind at ease. Let him not consult his delicacy, but say fairly whether he is pressed for it, as I *can* make an effort to pay him immediately.

[1] Moore had been forced to borrow money from his uncle Joyce Codd.

Dearest mother, is it not a pity, when I am brought so near you, that I must deny myself the gratification of instantly being amongst you; but I *must* work off these scores, and, thank Heaven! I have it abundantly in my power. I think I shall go to Donington: there I shall be still nearer home; and when seeing you all is to be the crown of my task, it cannot fail to sweeten and accelerate my labours. I find they have had frequent reports here that I was *dead.* I hope they did not reach *you.* I never was more *alive* in my life.

I am so anxious to get a lesson from dear Kate upon the pianoforte, and to hear little Ellen warble. Well, well! it must be enough for me to know you are all well, for some time at least. God bless you, and my father, and sweet girls.

64. *To his Mother*

Russell, i. 125, no. 60

Thursday night, March 24. 1803.

My dearest Mother,

* * * I have had a letter from Lord Forbes since he went. From what he says, his uncle's opinion seems to be that war is inevitable! Sad days we are thrown upon: the world will never be in amity, I fear. * * *

65. *To his Mother*

Russell, i. 125, no. 61

Sunday morning, April 17. 1803.

My dearest Mother,

I have been busier than you imagine all this last week, transcribing part of my work for the press. I *do* really think *transcribing* must be the punishment for bad poets in hell; there is nothing so tiresome.[1] It is now a good while since I heard from home, but I know my prattling correspondent is absent, and my father perhaps too much occupied to write: however, I hope to day's post may tell me you are all well, and as I could wish. I would very gladly give up my solitude now, but I have still a vast deal to do, and must stay a little longer. Lord Strangford is publishing his translation of Camoens [*sic*] with Carpenter.[2] I got some proof sheets of it, which Lord S. sent me here, and I think it will do him very great credit. I hope, my dearest mother, you walk out these glorious days: there

[1] Moore was at work on the third edition of the *Poems of Thomas Little,* which appeared in 1803.

[2] See letter No. 60, to Viscount Strangford, 20 June 1802.

never was such fine weather in the memory of any one about me, at the time of the year. Nobody has told me whether the notes to my uncle and Mrs. Mills arrived: pray, bid my father mention. I believe I told you I had a letter from Lewis. There are no less than three families about this country who are teazing me to spend the spring at their houses: so, you see, I am not without my usual resources. Good by, darling mother.

66. *To John Dalby*

Mrs. Mercia Dalby

Thursday—May 12th 1803*

My dear Dalby— I have just missed Lord Forbes to my very great disappointment—it is reported here, through the fashionable circles, that they are all gone to *physic* themselves in the Country—but you will soon find out ('quum sis *nasutus*')[1] whether this be true or not—tell Lord Forbes he will find a dose of *Salts* at a shop near me, which will do him more good than the whole Materia Medica— I have as yet been a very *owl* of *Propriety*, and have not been once into Bond St. but in the *dusk*—my time is coming on however, and I wish you would offer up a few prayers for me, as I shudder at the gripe of Demon Dissipation— Carpenter has offered me £400 for the Volume,[2] which is pretty well—but I think I shall do better by letting it go in the old way—he is very sanguine about the success of it, and from what I can learn, it has excited *some* curiosity certainly— I have not yet been to St. James's Place, but expect I shall reach it to-day— My lodgings are *No. 19 High Street, Marylebone,* where you will have the goodness to direct any letters that may have come for me since—perhaps before I seal this letter, I may hear of some friend who will receive them under cover for me —if not, they can come in a parcel— I shall send Widdowson his money when I receive the stockings, and at the same time shall discharge my debt to *your Holiness*—

Cleanthes and Lamia have gone to sleep, *together*, since I came to town, but as soon as I am settled in my lodgings, I shall waken them *rousingly*—I know you doubt this—but you shall see.[3]

Bowles the Poet, I hear, objects strongly to my Title—but I shall certainly not change it—

[1] *Nasutus* means 'nosey' as well as 'clever'.

[2] Moore was at work on *Odes, Epistles and Other Poems* but had to delay publication until after his return from Bermuda. Carpenter published the work in 1806.

[3] Cleanthes was a Stoic philosopher, and Lamia a gay and witty courtesan; hence Moore indicates that his conduct is characterized by neither extreme.

I hope the *Piano* is safely restored— Remember me to all friends at Donington—tell your sister Mary there is another Glee published here in answer to 'Oh Lady Fair', and dedicated to *me*—it is not worth sending, or she should have it. Best remembrances to Mrs Dalby, and believe me, my dear Dalby,

Yours very sincerely,
Thomas Moore

Present my respects to his highness Count Beaujolois, and tell L^{ds} Forbes & Rancliffe I hope they will not stop long at the Park—

67. *To his Mother*

Russell, i. 126, no. 62

Thursday, May 13. 1803.

Lady Granard left town on Monday. I sent by her a little inclosure of five pounds for Ellen's music. I hope I shall be able to follow it up more *nobly*. There is nothing but masquerades going on here. I was at Mrs. Orby Hunter's, in the character of a little Irish boy just come to London, and had a vast deal of fun. I go to-morrow night to Martindale's; there are twenty guineas offered on every side for a ticket for this, which is a fête given by one of the clubs. I am going as Lingo.[1]

68. *To his Mother*

Russell, i. 126, no. 63

Friday, May 20. 1803.

My dearest Mother,

Yesterday I received my good father's letter: it was quite a cordial to me, and *decided* my conduct instantly. Never could I have had the faintest idea of accepting so paltry and degrading a stipend, if I had not the *urging* apprehension that my dears at home wanted it; but Heaven be praised that you are not in *instant* necessity for an assistance which necessity alone could reconcile.[2] I will do *better* for you, at least *as well*, by means more grateful to my feelings. The manner in which Mr. Wickham communicated the circumstance to me would disgust any man with the least spirit of independence about him. I accordingly, yesterday, after the receipt of my father's letter, enclosed the Ode for the Birthday, at

[1] A character in Samuel Arnold's *Agreeable Surprise* (1783).

[2] In 1803 Lord Moira and Joseph Atkinson persuaded William Wickham, the Chief Secretary of Ireland, to establish an Irish Poet Laureateship, which was to be conferred upon Moore.

the same time resigning the situation, and I slept sounder last night in consequence, than, I assure you, I have done for some time. It would place me on '*a ladder*' indeed, but a ladder which has but the *one rank*, where I should stand stationary for ever. Feeble as my hopes are of advancement under government, I should be silly to resign them, without absolute necessity, for a gift which would authorize them to consider me provided for, and leave me without a chance of any other or further advantage: it would 'write me down an *ass*'[1] and a *poet* for ever! Having considered the matter much since I came to town, and found every instant fresh reason to be disgusted with it, I consulted every one I met with upon the subject, and every one, *except* Croker, advised me peremptorily to reject it. Carpenter's conduct is uncommonly liberal. When I told him that my only motive for retaining it was a very particular use to which I had applied the stipend, he insisted I should not hesitate upon that point, as he was ready, abstracted from our business-account, to pay a hundred a-year for me till I could discharge him and pay it myself. So you see my resources. The only thing I was anxious about was Lord Moira and my dear inestimable friend Atkinson, whose interest had been so actively employed to procure it for me; but Lord Moira has totally relieved my mind upon the subject, by assuring me, that whatever resolution I adopted should meet with *his* concurrence; and I trust that Atkinson's good sense and liberality will in the same way induce him to forgive the necessity which obliges me to decline the favour as totally incompatible with my feelings. I shall write to him to-morrow.

There is a very promising *periodical work* to commence in about a month or two, in which I bear the principal part.[2] We have all advanced fifty *pounds* each, and I expect it will very soon *double* the *income* of the laureateship to me: so why should I burthen my mind with a situation whose emolument is so contemptible, compared to the ridicule which is annexed to it. Love to the dear girls when you write. God bless you, good father and mother, and your own,

Tom Moore.

I send this by post, lest any accident happen. I should be glad, if you have no objection, that you would *send* this letter to Captain Atkinson, as I have not time to write to him till to-morrow; and I wish him to be as soon as possible apprised of my resignation.

[1] *Much Ado about Nothing*, IV. ii. 77–80.

[2] No more is known of the plans for this periodical than is recorded in this letter.

69. *To his Mother*

Russell, i. 128, no. 64

Saturday, July 16. 1803.

My dearest Mother,

I was gratified with a letter from my father, which, I must confess, is rather a *singular* pleasure; but I always console myself with the idea that he is more profitably employed.

I have agreed for the piano for dear Kate: it will be sent off in a few days to Liverpool, and from thence to Ireland. I hope it will arrive safe. It is not by any means as good as I could wish for her, but it is sweet toned, and of course much better than the wretched machine she has at present. I think, as soon as you have received the new one, you had better sell the old trumpery, if any one will give a guinea for it. On Tuesday next I shall be off to Donington. Good by, sweet mother.

70. *To his Mother*

Russell, i. 129, no. 65

Twelve o'clock, Sunday night, Aug. 7. 1803.

My dearest Mother,

I am going to town to-morrow morning on a business which *may* prove as fallacious as all the rest have been, but which I think myself bound to follow up, as it will possibly in the end be productive of something, even if it be not itself a desirable object. Lord Moira told me to-day that he had had a letter from Tierney, offering him the gift of a place which government had left at his (Tierney's) disposal. It must be something far from contemptible, as Lord M. told me, in confidence, Tierney was under obligations to him, and that this was the first opportunity he had of, in any manner, repaying them.[1] I fear, however, it is a situation not in either of these countries; and I fear it *solely* from the violence which a *wider* separation would cause to your feelings, my dearest mother: as for my *own* part, I should not consider any sacrifice of either comforts or society at all to be avoided, if it promised me a permanent subsistence and the means of providing for those I love. I have hopes that even if it *be* necessary to leave this country, the place may be considerable enough to allow you all to accompany

[1] This is the first reference to the post as Registrar of the Naval Prize Court in Bermuda, to which Moore was appointed, through Lord Moira's influence, by George Tierney, Treasurer of the Navy. For the outcome of his Bermuda venture see letters Nos. 81 and 111, to his mother, 19 Jan. 1804 and 22 Aug. 1805. See also other letters written from America in 1804.

me. This would be delightful; but I know nothing certain of it yet. I take a letter to Tierney from Lord Moira, and the circumstances will of course be explained to me. Be assured, however, that I will do nothing without the total concurrence of your *feelings* as well as your *judgment*.

Poor Lord Moira met with a very disagreeable accident the other evening. As he was leaving the judges' dinner at Leicester, he fell in going down stairs and hurt his back, I think, very seriously; for he has been in very great pain ever since, and cannot rise from a sofa without assistance. It is a pity that hearts like his should be perplexed by such common casualties of life, which should be only reserved for the every-day pedlars of this world. He is indeed most amiable. I hope, however, it will not long be troublesome.

This journey is a new expense and perplexity to me, which I, of course, could by no means forsee. However I am very well able for it both in purse and spirits; and God knows but it may be a 'tide in my affairs' which will 'lead to fortune.'[1] Fortune or not, I am still the same, your own devoted Tom.

71. *To John Dalby*

Mrs. Mercia Dalby

Monday Septemb^{r} 5th 1803—*

My dearest Dalby— I believe I am about to bid you a long, very long farewell— You have heard, I dare say, of the situation I have been appointed to in Bermuda,[2] and I think a fortnight more will see me a-float for my destination— I have every reason to expect it will be considerably advantageous to me—the climate is the sweetest in the world, and, during the war, the registrarship is generally lucrative, so that, for a young adventurer like me, it would be silly to neglect such a promising opportunity of advancement— I have been a good deal puzzled about the moveables I left behind me at Donington, but I know your usual goodness will assist me in this predicament, and I could not have entrusted my key to any other person—in the first place, my papers & letters are scattered very carelessly in my Portmanteau, and *you* are one of the few who can feel how much value I attach to them— You will accordingly, I am convinced, take care of and pack them up safe for me— You will also find in the trunk, a little *steel bandage* which I generally wear when I take exercise, from an apprehension I have long had (I believe without any cause), of a *Hernia* in my right groin— I have not had any want of it since I came to town,

[1] *Julius Caesar*, IV. iii. 218.

[2] See letter No. 70, to his mother, 7 Aug. 1803.

but you will have the goodness to cover it up securely at the bottom of the box— You will see, if I mistake not, that old [*Meursius*][1] which I ran away with from our young friends, and you may either restore it to the Library or consign it to 'combustion dire'— You will also find a little blue book, which I stole from F. and which you had better doom to the same 'Index expurgatorius.' You will not be long in discovering that it merits such a fate most seriously— These, my dear Dalby, are all the *delienti* parts of your commission—as to the shirts, coats, and those other *exoterics*, you may stuff them in as well as you can, and pray let me have them in town as soon as possible— You will forgive, I trust, this very inordinate trouble I give you, but after you have arranged the papers &c you can get the chambermaid to do the rest & merely *preside* over the operation— My bottles of perfume & my *exquisite milk* of *Roses* I leave in legacy to either Mrs Dalby or your sister, whichever is most anxious to preserve 'the odour of my memory'— My *Hamper* you will have the goodness to open, & make proper use of every thing *therein contained*, only sometimes remembering to drink the health of him who will be very far absent from you— So much for my last Will and Testament—

My unfortunate work must remain unfinished & of course unpublished—[2] Carpenter bears the disappointment with great philosophy—but *not* 'philosophy of *pleasure*', I perceive—

Lord Moira is very well— I have the honour of breakfasting 'solus cum solo' with him every morning—

I inclose, beside the Key, a letter which was sent to me to take to your sister— Best love & remembrances to all, my dearest Dalby— 'Vive memor nostri' & believe me, in whatever latitude I may be cast, warmly & sincerely yours

Thomas Moore

There is, I believe, in my portmanteau, a collection of Latin poems called 'Hortus Amoris' which you will have the kindness to replace in the Library—

I receive my Letters Patent to day, which stamp me 'Registrar to the Court of Admiralty at Bermuda' ! ! !— 'Euge, Poeta!'[3]

Widdowson, tell him, shall receive the money for my stockings before I go—

[1] This name is partially illegible. The spelling given here seems to be the most likely, in which case Moore is referring to Johannes Meursius (1579–1639), a Dutch classical philologist and historiographer, author of many archaeological monographs and editor of the works of several Greek writers, reprinted in Gronovius's *Thesaurus Antiquitatum Graecarum* (1697–1702).

[2] Moore's *Epistles, Odes, and Other Poems* was not published until 1806.

[3] Persius, *Satires*, i. 75.

72. *To his Mother*

Russell, i. 132, no. 67

Saturday, Sept. 10. 1803.

My dearest Mother,

I have just got my father's letter, which has made me *very happy*. I am quite consoled by the idea of your keeping up your spirits so well, and I entreat of you to let nothing depress them in my absence, for I shall come home, please that Heaven which watches over me, better stocked in constitution as well as pocket than I ever should become by loitering here. I find Bermuda is a place where physicians order their patients when no other air will keep them alive. I am still uncertain about the time of my going, but I pray that Merry may not leave me behind. I could not possibly have such another opportunity. * * * I mentioned to another friend of mine, Woolriche, the surgeon, what I had asked of Atkinson, and he said if it failed, or was not time enough, *he* would contrive to manage it for me. These are Englishmen! without any profession or ostentatious promises, but with a soberly liberal readiness to help the man who is worthy of being helped. Oh! the *gold mines* of sweet Ireland! God Almighty bless you and keep you in health and happiness till I return. I will write again on Monday. Your own,

Tom.

73. *To his Mother*

Russell, i. 133, no. 68

Monday, Sept. 12. 1803.

My dearest Mother,

I enclose you a note I received from Merry yesterday, by which you will perceive that everything is in train for my departure. Nothing could be more lucky. I shall have *just* time to prepare myself; and all difficulties are vanishing very fast before me. Heaven smiles upon my project, and I see nothing in it now but hope and happiness. Tom Hume is arrived, to my very great delight, as his kindness will materially assist in smoothing the path for me. He is a perfect enthusiast in the business, and says that nothing could be presented so totally free from every alloying consideration,—so perfectly adapted to my disposition, constitution, and prospects; and he is right. If I did not make a shilling by it, the new character it gives to my pursuits, the claim it affords me upon government, the absence I shall have from all the frippery follies that would hang upon my career for ever in this country, all these are objects invaluable of themselves, abstracted from the pecuniary.

[The rest of the letter is torn away. *Russell's note.*]

74. *To his Mother*

Russell, i. 134, no. 69

Sept. [20], 1803.

My dearest Mother,

To-morrow morning Merry has fixed on for going to Portsmouth, and to-morrow night I shall follow him. We may be detained there a long time before the ship sails. Tell my dear uncle that I cannot sufficiently thank him for his readiness in supplying my wants: I don't know what I should have done without him, as there is a number of little contigent necessities for which I should otherwise have been obliged to trench on my hundred pounds. * * * I think I shall find Mr. and Mrs. Merry very agreeable companions. They are but lately married, and she has been a fine woman. Our passage they seem to fear will be tedious; but I shall write to you from on board, and take the chance of meeting some ships which may bring letters for us to England. Among the *lighter* sacrifices I make, the poor pianoforte is included. I shall be strangely at a loss without that favourite resource of mine. However, I must carry music in my heart with me; and if that beats livelily in tune, 'twill supply the want of other harmonies. In case of my finding that I shall stay long in the island, an instrument shall be sent after me. I hope to find Kate advanced in all that is elegant and polished on my return; and the little Nell I expect to see—anything but tall and termagant. God bless and preserve our whole circle. * * *

75. *To his Mother*

Russell, i. 135, no. 70

Portsmouth
Thursday, Sept. 22. 1803.

Just arrived at Portsmouth, and the wide sea before my eyes, I write my heart's farewell to the dear darlings at home. Heaven send I may return to English ground with pockets *more heavy*, and spirits *not less light* than I now leave it with. Everything has been arranged to my satisfaction. I am prepared with every comfort for the voyage, and a fair breeze and a loud yo-yo-ee! are all that's now wanting to set me afloat. My dear father should write to Carpenter, and thank him for the very friendly assistance he has given me: without that assistance the breeze would be fair in vain for me, and Bermuda might be sunk in the deep, for any share that *I* could pretend to in it; but now all is smooth for my progress, and Hope sings in the shrouds of the ship that is to carry me. Good by. God bless you all, dears of my heart! I will write again if our departure is delayed by any circumstance. God bless you again, and preserve you happy till the return of your

Tom.

Urge Stevenson to send Carpenter the songs: I shall write to him. Sweet mother, father, Kate, and Nell, good by!

76. *To his Mother*

Russell, i. 135, no. 71

Oct. 10. 1803.

My own dear Mother,

There is a ship in sight which we suppose to be homeward bound, and with that expectation I prepare a few lines, which I trust in Heaven will reach you safe, and find you all well and happy. Our voyage hitherto has been remarkably favourable. In the first week we reached the Azores, or the Western Islands, and though our second week has not advanced us much, from the almost continual calms we have had, yet the weather has been so delicious that there is but little to complain of, and in another fortnight we hope to be landed in America. We are at present in latitude 33° or thereabouts, and in longitude 38°. Though this you cannot well understand yourself, yet you will find many who can explain it, and I know all minutiae about my situation must be interesting to you now. I have had but one day's sickness, which I feel has been of service to me; and though we are now in as warm a climate as I shall have to encounter, I find not the least inconvenience from the heat, but am convinced it will agree most perfectly with me. Nothing could possibly be more pleasant than the accommodations of this ship; and though I shall never feel much passion for voyaging, yet it scarcely could be made less disagreeable than it is to us. The table we sit down to every day is splendid, and we drink Madeira and claret in common: but I am beginning to gossip with you, when I have hardly time to say what is necessary. Make Stevenson give all the songs he can possibly make out to Carpenter. I hope the packet I sent through Erche, from Portsmouth, has arrived safe. Keep up your spirits, my sweet mother; there is every hope, every prospect of happiness for all of us. Love to darling father, to my own Kate and Nell. I am now near two thousand miles from you, but my *heart* is at *home*. God bless you. The ship is brought to, and our lieutenant is just going aboard, so I must stop. Your own,

Tom.

I wrote a line to Carpenter by a ship we met off the Western Islands: I hope he has got it. Here is a *kiss* for you, my darlings, all the way from the Atlantic.

77. *To his Mother*

Russell, i. 137, no. 72

Norfolk, Virginia
Nov. 7. 1803.

Safe across the Atlantic, my darling mother, after a six weeks passage, during which my best consolation was the thought and remembrance of home, and the dear hope that I should soon be assured of what I anxiously persuaded myself, that you were all well and happy. We met a ship off the Western Islands, which was bound for Lisbon, and I took the opportunity of sending a letter by it, with, I fear, but very little chance or expectation of your ever receiving it:[1] if, however, it has been so lucky as to reach you, you have some part of that solicitude removed, which you must, dear mother, most cruelly feel at such a new and painful trial of your fortitude. Heaven send that you have not suffered by it! Keep up your spirits, my own dear mother: I am *safe*, and in health, and have met friendship and attention from every one. Everything promises well for your dear absent boy; and, please God! there will be a thousand things to sweeten our reunion, and atone to us for the sacrifice we are making at present; so let me entreat of you not to yield to those anxieties, which I now guess by myself how strongly you must suffer under. Our passage was rather boisterous upon the whole, and by no means kept the flattering promise the first week of it gave us; but the comfort of our accommodations and the kindness of the captain, which was exhibited towards me particularly, served very much to render it not only supportable, but pleasant. * * * With Cockburn, who is a man of good fashion and rank, I became extremely intimate; and, the day we landed, he took a seal from his watch, which he begged I would wear in remembrance of him. Never was there a better hearted set of fellows than the other officers of the ship: I really felt a strong regret at leaving them,—the more so, as it then, for the first time, appeared to me, that I was going among strangers, who had no common medium of communion with me, and who

[1] See letter No. 76, to his mother, 10 Oct. 1803.

could not feel any of those prepossessing motives for partiality, which those to whom my name is best known have always found strong enough to make them kind and attentive, almost at first sight, to me. This, I assure you, weighed heavy on me the night I quitted the ship, and though I knew I was to be presented to the British consul here, under the auspices of Mr. Merry, and so might be tolerably sure of every attention, yet I dreaded meeting some consequential savage, who would make me regret the necessity of being under an obligation to him. I was, however, most agreeably disappointed. I found the Consul, Colonel Hamilton, a plain and hospitable man, and his wife full of homely, but comfortable and genuine civility. The introduction I brought him from Lord Henry Stuart was of no little weight, as it told him the light I was considered in in England; and on my mentioning Lord Moira by accident, I understood from him that they were old friends in America, and that he should be happy to show his remembrance and love of Lord Moira by attention to any one whom he honoured with his friendship. I shall, of course, mention all this when I write to Lord M. I am now lodged at the Consul's with Mr. and Mrs. Merry, where we have been entertained these two days, in a manner not very elegant, but hospitable and cordial. * * * They will set off in a day or two for Washington, and on Wednesday next (this is Sunday) I think I shall have an opportunity of getting to Bermudas: it is not a week's passage, and I am so great a sailor now, I shall think nothing of that. Colonel Hamilton will give me letters to every one of consequence in the islands. I am much more hardy, dear mother, than I ever imagined; and I begin to think it was your extreme tenderness that made either of us imagine that I was delicate. In the course of our passage towards the southward, it was so hot, that the thermometer was at 90° in the shade; and about five or six days afterwards, when we came along the American coast, a pair of blankets was scarcely enough at night, the weather became so suddenly cold. Yet this violent change has not the least affected me, and I never was better in health, or had a more keen appetite. I often thought of my dear father's 'sea-room' when we were rolling about in the vast Atlantic, with nothing of animated life to be seen around us, except now and then the beautiful little flying fish, fluttering out of the water, or a fine large turtle floating asleep upon the surface. This Norfolk, the capital of Virginia, is a most strange place; nothing to be seen in the streets but dogs and negroes, and the few ladies that *pass for white* are to be sure the most unlovely pieces of crockery I ever set my eyes upon. The first object I saw on entering Colonel Hamilton's drawing-room was a harpsichord, which looked like civilisation, and delighted me extremely; and in the evening we had a Miss Mathews, who played and sung very tolerably indeed; but music here is like whistling to a wilderness. She played some of dear Kate's lessons, which brought the tears into my eyes with recollection. I saw some of my own songs among the music-books, and this morning I met with a periodical publication full of extracts from my Anacreon and Little's poems, and speaking of me in the most flattering terms of eulogium. All this is very gratifying; it would be so naturally at any time, and is now particularly so, from the very few hopes I had of being cheered or welcomed by any of those little pleasures or gratifications I have been accustomed to so long. They tell me that the people of Bermuda are very musical, and I find Admiral Mitchell and his squadron winter there, so that I shall not be very much at a loss for society; and as I intend to devote all my leisure hours to the completion of my work, my time may be filled up not unpleasantly. From what I have heard, however, since I came closer to the channels of correct information, I strongly suspect that we shall not, dearest mother, be long separated. I am delighted that we all had the resolution to enable me to make the effort, but as that is the chief point, and almost the only one I ever expected to attain by the step, I believe I shall not find enough, otherwise advantageous, to induce me to absent myself long from my home-opportunities of advancement. My foot is on the ladder pretty firmly, and that is the great point gained.

When I was leaving Portsmouth, just on the instant of my coming away, I folded up a packet in a hurry, which I enclosed to Jasper Erche,[1] but (I believe) forgot to direct it inside. There were some songs in it for Stevenson to arrange. I anxiously hope it arrived safe. At the same time I had a letter written to Captain Atkinson, but not having time to fold it ashore, I was obliged to send it back by the boat which left us to return to Portsmouth. This too I have hopes arrived safe; but my confusion was so great, that I cannot now remember what I wrote or what I did. Explain all this to my dear good friend Atkinson, and tell him he shall hear from me by the next opportunity. It astonishes me to find that Colonel Hamilton does not recollect him, for he knows Doyle and Marsh, and all Lord Moira's old cronies. If Atkinson could get Lord Moira to write a few words about me to Hamilton, I think it would be of singular service to me while I remain at Bermuda. Show him this letter, and give him with it the warmest remembrances of my heart. I trust Stevenson has not forgotten me, and that he has by this time furnished poor Carpenter with some means of freeing himself from the incumbrances I feel he has submitted to for me.

[1] See letter No. 76.

If any delay has taken place, do, dear mother, conjure him from me to give all the assistance he can in collecting my songs, and forwarding the publication of them. This business I have very much at heart, and shall be extremely grateful to Stevenson if he accomplishes it for me.

I have this instant received an invitation to dinner from one of the Yankees of this place: if the ambassador and his lady go, of course *I* will. Oh! if you saw the vehicles the people drive about in here, white coaches with black servants, and horses of no colour at all; it is really a most comical place. Poor Mrs. Merry has been as ill-treated by the musquitoes [*sic*] as she is by every one else. They have bit her into a fever. I have escaped their notice entirely, and sleep with a fine net over my bed. The weather now is becoming too cold for them, and indeed a little too much so for me. I shall be glad to escape to the mild climate of Bermuda, which I still hear is the sweetest and most healthy spot in the world; but I am sorry to find that meat is rather a scarcity there, and that it is sometimes no fish, no dinner. He that can't feed well, however, upon good poultry, fish, and fruit of all kinds, ought to be condemned to eat roast mutton all the days of his life; and this, my dear mother, in your mind and mine, would be sufficient punishment for him. Tell my beloved, darling father, that if there is anything in the mercantile way which he can learn, that I may assist him or Mr. Gillespie in here, they shall find me a steadier fellow than I am afraid I have hitherto appeared (at least to Mr. G.), and I shall manage for them like a solid man of business. Seriously, though I know nothing at present about the trade here, it is not impossible but something may occur to Mr. Gillespie in which I may be made useful. * * *

78. *To his Mother*

Russell, i. 142, no. 73

Norfolk, Virginia
Nov. 28. 1803.

My darling Mother,

By a ship which sailed last week for England, I wrote you the first account of my arrival at Norfolk, safely and prosperously, as I could wish.[1] Heaven speed the letter to you, my sweet mother! It is very painful to be uncertain upon a point so interesting, as the little communication we are allowed must be to us all; but it is impossible to answer for the arrival of my letters, and I shall be doomed to still more uncertainty at Bermuda. I must, therefore,

[1] See letter No. 77, to his mother, 7 Nov. 1803.

take every opportunity that presents itself, and it will be very unfortunate, indeed, if some of my communications do not reach you. I have now been here three weeks, waiting for a ship, to take me to Bermuda. I could scarcely have hoped, dear mother, to bear the voyage and the climate so well, as (thank Heaven!) I hitherto have done. Since I left England, I have had but one day's illness, which was the mere ordinary sea-sickness, upon coming on board. There are two or three points I am very anxious about: first, whether you got the packet I sent from Portsmouth, folded in a hurry, and, I believe, not properly directed, but which contained an enclosure of songs for Stevenson; secondly, whether Captain Atkinson received a letter I sent ashore by the pilot-boat, to be put in the post-office; and again, whether you, dear mother, got the letter I wrote you on the passage, by a ship bound for some part of the Continent.[1] If these have been fortunate, all is well. Mr. and Mrs. Merry are gone to Washington, after remaining here more than a fortnight. I am lodged at Col. Hamilton's, the British consul, from whom I have experienced all possible kindness and hospitality; and if any of the squadron off this station touch here in their way from Halifax to Bermuda (where they are to winter), I shall be the luckiest fellow in the world, for I am sure of a passage with them, without expense, and most comfortably. Dear darlings at home! how incessantly I think of you: every night I dream that I am amongst you: sometimes I find you happy and smiling as I could wish: sometimes the picture is not so pleasant, and I awake unhappy, but surely Heaven protects you for me, and we shall meet, and long be united and blessed together. In that hope I bear absence with a lighter heart, and I entreat of you, sweet mother! to look on it with the same cheerful confidence—the same consoling dependence on that God of all pure affection, who sees how we love each other, and has, I trust, much prosperity in store for us. I shall lose no opportunity whatever that occurs of writing to you, and saying how affairs go on. My dear father, I am sure, will often give me the consolation of seeing his hand. Good Kate and Nell too must not be idle, but show me that their thoughts are frequently employed upon me.

I write this merely as a *duplicate* of my last letter, to tell you of my arrival, and let you know how I am at present situated: never was my health or spirits better.

Tell Capt. A.[2] everything: show him my letters: he has my heart's warmest remembrances, and I will write to him by this or the next opportunity. I kiss you all. God bless you. Your own, Tom

[1] See letter No. 76, to his mother, 10 Oct. 1803.

[2] Captain Joseph Atkinson. See the Glossary of Proper Names.

79. *To his Mother*

Russell, i. 144, no. 75

Norfolk
Dec. 2. 1803.

Again, my dearest mother, I avail myself of an opportunity which just offers for Ireland, and again I repeat what I have said in my former letters, lest they should be so dreadfully unfortunate as not to reach you. I arrived here this day month in perfect health; am lodged at the British consul's, where I have found the most cordial hospitality, and only wait an opportunity of getting to Bermuda. When I was leaving Portsmouth I sent off a packet for you, with songs enclosed for Stevenson.[1] I trust they have arrived safe, and that Stevenson has lost no time in assisting Carpenter's publication. I left with the latter some words to be written under the title of 'Come, tell me, says Rosa,'[2] acknowledging to whom I am indebted for the air: lest he should forget them, let my father write to remind him. I sent too, from Portsmouth, a letter for Capt. Atkinson, the arrival of which I am very anxious about: mention all these points when you write. When you write! Oh, dear mother! think it is now three months since I had the sweet consolation of seeing any memorial of home. This is a long period, and much may have happened in it; but I hope, I trust, I depend on Heaven that it has preserved you all well and happy for me, and that we shall not long be this dreary distance asunder. My good Father! how often, how dearly, I think of *him*, and *you*, and *all!* I feel how anxious your hearts must be at the long interval you have passed without hearing of me, but the letter I wrote to you in the third week of our passage, and sent by a ship bound for some part of the Continent,[3] if it reached in any reasonable time, must have been a happy relief to your solicitude. I did not regret so much the foul winds we had afterwards, because they were fair for that vessel which bore some tidings of comfort to my dear home. Oh, if the wretches have been neglectful, and not forwarded the letter! But I will hope the best, and think that, long before this, you have seen my handwriting and are comforted, dear mother. The kindness of these good people, the Hamiltons, is fortunate and delightful to me. If I were not so completely thrown upon it though I should be more gratified by, and enjoy it more pleasantly: but is it not a most lucky thing, when I am obliged to remain here, to be

[1] See letter No. 76, to his mother, 10 Oct. 1803.
[2] *Poetry*, p. 72.
[3] See letter No. 76, to his mother, 10 Oct. 1803.

received cordially by a family whose hospitality is of that honest kind which sets one at home and at ease, as much as is possible in such a situation. I have been obliged to get a servant, and am fortunate enough to have one who cannot speak a word of English, which will keep me famously alive in my French. It is extraordinary that I cannot, even here, acquire any accurate information with respect to the profits of my registrarship. One thing is *certain*, that a Spanish war *alone* can make it worth a very long sacrifice of my other opportunities, and our government has so long hesitated upon that point, that it seems now more doubtful than ever. However, I am too far from the source of information to guess how politics stand at present. Perhaps we are at this moment engaged in a Spanish war; if so, *tant mieux pour Jeannette*. I know that my friends in Dublin will all be very angry that I do not write to them by the same opportunities I have found for writing to you, but I can't help that; till I have satisfied myself pretty well with respect to *your* certainty of hearing from me, I confess I cannot think much about any one else. This is, however, the third letter I have written since my arrival, and the winds and waves must be cruel indeed if they do not suffer at least one of them to reach you. The next opportunity I shall make use of to write to my dear friend Atkinson. Tell him so, and give him my warmest remembrances: they are not the less warm for being Transatlantic. Absence is the best touchstone of affection: it either cools it quite, or makes it ten times warmer than ever it was; and I can never judge how I *love* people till I *leave* them. This is a strange climate; yesterday the glass was at 70°, and to-day it is down to 40°. I consider myself very hardy to bear it so well: my stomach has seldom been in such good order, nor my whole frame more braced and healthy. If Bermuda agrees so perfectly with me, I shall return to you the better for my trip. Return to you! how I like to say that, and think it, and pray for it. Dear mother, kiss Kate and Nell for me. I need not bid Kate read, but I bid little Ellen, and they must both apply closely to their music. I expect such a treat from them when I go home; for, indeed, there is a sad dearth of that luxury in these parts. God bless you again and again. The captain waits for the letters; he goes to Cork. Ever your own.

80. *To his Mother*

Russell, i. 147, no. 75

Norfolk, Virginia
Dec. 10. 1803.

My darling Mother,

You will have received, I hope, long before this arrives, two letters which I wrote since the one I now enclose.[1] I am extremely unhappy at the delay, for I know how you must have suffered in the interval; but the ship Ritson, by which I sent the enclosed letter soon after I landed, returned yesterday so much damaged by the bad weather that she could not get on to England, and had been obliged to put back. Can any thing be more unlucky? I so pleased myself with the idea that you were by this time apprised of my safety, for it is now near five weeks since the Ritson sailed, and to have the letter come back to me thus is quite dreadful. God grant, my dearest and beloved mother, that you have had resolution to combat the solicitude you must have endured so long. I was perfectly happy in the hopes that a quick passage would have attended the ship which bore you the intelligence of my arrival, and every thing else has turned out so fortunate with me, that this is the only subject of regret I have met with. If you however, my dear mother, have got well over it, as I trust in Heaven you have, there is nothing else which at present gives my heart one painful thought: is not this delightful for you to hear? The expectation I expressed in all my letters, that some of the ships of war bound for Bermuda would touch here is gratified most fortunately. Captain Compton of the Driver is arrived, and I go with him. Nothing could be more lucky; beside the safety and comfort of such convoy, it saves me between twenty and thirty guineas, which I should have to pay for passage and provision in a merchantman. He gives me a very favourable account of Bermuda, and I have no doubt of passing my time very pleasantly there. Every thing is succeeding to my utmost wishes, and my spirits are as wild as ever you have witnessed them. Till this cursed Ritson returned with my poor dear letter, I had not one uneasy thought, for even my regrets at the distance that separates us was softened by the hope that you would soon hear of my safety, that you would be happy in the promise of good fortune that awaits us, and that no very distant day would see us in the possession of all our hearts wish for.

I have not time, darling mother, to say more, for the ship that takes this goes away in a few hours. In less than a week, I think, Captain Compton sails for Bermuda, and I shall have an opportunity of writing again before we go. God bless you—Father, Kate, Nell, and all dears. * * *

[1] Evidently letter No. 77, 7 Nov. 1803.

81. *To his Mother*

Russell, i. 148, no. 76

Bermuda
Jan. 19. 1804.

My darling Mother,

Here have I been more than a week, without any opportunity of sending a letter even to take its chance at sea in some of the cruisers, since none have arrived or left this during that time; and it gives me so much uneasiness to think you should be long without hearing of me, that I am hardly so selfish as to bestow a thought upon my own privation. Yet indeed, dearest mother, it is a very cruel privation to have been now near five months without a whisper of intelligence from home; and if every thing here was as prosperous as I have been flattered into supposing, this dreadful anxiety would embitter it all; and the brightest advantages of the situation would be very dearly purchased. In coming from Norfolk hither we had most tremendous weather: you may guess what it must have been to an inexperienced sailor, when all the officers of the ship declared they seldom, scarcely ever, had encountered such serious and continual gales of wind. The passage, however, was pretty short for this season of the year; we made it in seven days, though for three days of that time we remained without venturing to set a stitch of sail, and of course lost as much as we gained of our way. Yet I bore it all so stoutly, that, would you believe it, dearest mother! on the day of the worst gale we had, I eat the heartiest dinner of beefsteaks and onions that ever I have made in my life; though, as during the whole time of the passage, we were obliged to be tied to the table at dinner; and at night, when the ship was rolling her sides into the water, and when it was in vain to think of sleeping from the noise and the motion, I amused myself in my cot by writing ridiculous verses and laughing at them. Sailors, to be sure, think nothing of all these storms; but I *do* say, for a novice, it requires a little philosophy to be so cool and careless in such new and uncomfortable situations. Indeed, there has never been a severer winter than this upon the coast of America, and often, very often, darling mother, have I dreaded that you would see some accounts of the storms and the accidents that have happened, and that your heart, already too apt to catch at an intimation of danger, would find in these accounts too much food for its solicitude. I felt some regret, indeed not a little, in leaving the Hamiltons at Norfolk. Mrs. Hamilton cried, and said she never parted with any one so reluctantly. The colonel gave me the warmest letters of introduction to every one that could be serviceable or amusing to me here; and as I know dear mother loves to see anything which flatters her boy, and shows he is not neglected in his absence from her, I enclose one of these letters, which by the merest accident has returned into my possession, and which, being to one of the young sea captains, I have reason to think is not half so strong as some others.

These little islands of Bermuda form certainly one of the prettiest and most romantic spots that I could ever have imagined, and the descriptions which represent it as like a place of fairy enchantment are very little beyond the truth. From my window now as I write, I can see five or six different islands, the *most distant* not a mile from the others, and separated by the clearest, sweetest coloured sea you can conceive; for the water here is so singularly transparent, that, in coming in, we could see the rocks under the ship quite plainly. These little islands are thickly covered with cedar groves, through the vistas of which you catch a few pretty white houses, which my poetical short-sightedness always transforms into temples; and I often expect to see Nymphs and Graces come tripping from them, when, to my great disappointment, I find that a few miserable negroes is all 'the bloomy flush of life' it has to boast of. Indeed, you must not be surprised, dear mother, if I fall in love with the first pretty face I see on my return home, for certainly the 'human face divine'[1] has degenerated wonderfully in these countries; and if I were a painter, and wished to preserve my ideas of beauty immaculate, I would not suffer the brightest belle of Bermuda to be my housemaid. But I shall refer you for a fuller description of this place to a letter I have written to my good friend Atkinson; and to come to the point which is most interesting to us, dear mother, I shall tell you at once that it is *not* worth my while to remain here;[2] that I shall just stop to finish my work for Carpenter,[3] which will occupy me till the spring months come in, when the passages home are always delightfully pleasant, and that then I shall get upon the wing to see my dear friends once more. I perfectly acquit those whose representations have induced me to come out here, because I perceive they were totally ignorant of the

[1] *Paradise Lost*, iii. 32–36. 'The bloomy flush of life' has not been identified. It could be an adaptation of these lines from *Paradise Lost*.

[2] Finding the position in Bermuda unprofitable, Moore appointed a man named Sheddon, the nephew of two London merchants, as his deputy. For further details and the outcome of the Bermuda venture see letter No. 535, to Lady Donegal, 2 Apr. 1818, and No. 610, to Mrs. Belcher, 27 Oct. 1821. See also his diary for 1819–21 (Russell, iii).

[3] *Epistles, Odes, and Other Poems*, which he began before he left England but did not publish until 1806.

nature of the situation. Neither am I sorry for having come; the appointment is respectable, and evidently was considered a matter of great patronage among those who had the disposal of it, which alone is sufficient to make it a valuable step towards preferment. But this is all; so many courts have been established, that this of Bermuda has but few prize causes referred to it, and even a Spanish war would make my income by no means worth staying for. I have entered upon my business, however, and there are two American ships for trial, whose witnesses I have examined, and whose cause will be decided next month: it is well to be acquainted with these things. I have seen too a little more of the world, have got an insight into American character and affairs, have become more used to inconveniences and disappointments, have tried my nerves and resolution a little, and I think very considerably improved my health, for I do not remember ever to have been more perfectly well than I am at present. All these advantages are to be calculated, and as they reconcile me completely to the step I have taken, I have hopes that my darling father and you will consider it in the same favourable light, and not feel much disappointment at the damp our expectations have experienced. Please Heaven! I shall soon embrace you all, and find you in health and happiness once more; and this will amply, dearly repay me for much more exertion than I have yet made towards your welfare. How I shall enjoy dear Kate's playing when I return! The jingle they make here upon things they call pianofortes is, oh! insupportable. I hope Carpenter has not forwarded my books to America, for, if he has, they run a risk of being lost; let dear father inquire about them. In one of the last English newspapers, I was shocked beyond measure at reading of poor Biggin's death: it made me feel the horrors of absence, which keeps one from knowing these calamities till they come by surprise, and without any preparation to soften their impression. It made me resolve almost not to look into another English paper till I return. In closing my letter now, it is a very uncomfortable feeling to think that, perhaps, not a word I have written will reach you; however, Heaven speed it! I will write by as many chances as I can find, let the letters be ever so short, in order to make it more likely that you will receive some of them; and, accordingly, I shall reserve Atkinson's letter for another ship, which sails soon after the one that takes this. Best love to my adored father: I hope Providence favours his exertions for the dear ones about him. Darling Kate and Ellen have my heart with them always. There is a little thing here very like Nell, only much darker, and I go very often to look at her. God bless you, sweet mother, for your own, own affectionate,

T. M.

82. *To his Mother*

Russell, i. 152, no. 77

Bermuda
Jan. 24. 1804.

My dearest Mother,

I have written you a long letter, which I sent by the way of Norfolk from this place; but for fear any unfortunate chance should rob you of it, I take the opportunity of a ship going to the West Indies, which at least doubles the likelihood of your hearing of my arrival in Bermuda in health and in spirits, dear mother, as good as I have had ever to boast of. As I have every hope that you will receive the letter I sent to Norfolk, and as I am given but a moment's time for the dispatch of a few words at present, I shall merely repeat the most important things I have to say, and tell you that in *May or June I expect to sail for England!* yes, darling mother, to see and embrace you once more, since there is nothing here worth staying for, and I have acquired every advantage which I looked to in the excursion.

You cannot conceive how much the change of scene and climate has improved my health; and though the pecuniary value of the situation is not enough to authorise my stay here, yet I have derived quite enough of pleasure and instruction from the step to make me by no means regret having undertaken it. Dear, good darlings at home, how I long to hear of you! Oh! think what a painful interval it is, sweet mother, to have been five months without a word from home. I could hardly have hoped to bear it so well, but we shall all meet soon again, please Heaven! and be happy; and the talking over the past will sweeten the present, and the absence we have endured will endear us more closely to each other. It is now near twelve o'clock. I have just returned from a grand turtle feast, and am full of callipash and Madeira: the ship that takes this is to depart before daybreak, and I shall hardly be time enough to send it to the captain; but in full trust and expectation that you will receive the other letter I have written, in which I have told a few more particulars, I shall kiss you, in fancy, dear mother, and have done, giving a thousand loves to good father, and my own Kate and Nell. God bless you. I shall take every opportunity of writing. Yours, yours, most affectionately, darling mother.

83. *To his Mother*

Russell, i. 154, no. 78

St. George's, Bermudas
Feb. 17. 1804.

My dearest Mother,

Every ship that comes, I look with impatience to, as bringing me some intelligence from some friends at home; but I am still disappointed, and it is now five months since I saw the last dear paper that brought the *odour of home* on it to me. I begin to fear that it is not unlikely I may be on my return to England before any news of you can reach me; for, unfortunately, I did not know myself, nor therefore could I instruct you in, the most frequent and safe method of forwarding letters to me. The address I gave you, however, in everything I wrote from Norfolk (Col. Hamilton, His Britan. Majesty's Consul, Norfolk, Virginia) ought soon to bring me something, and I hope in Heaven it may. From Norfolk I sent you several letters, and this is now the third I have written from Bermudas. In the former one I told you of my resolution to return in the spring, unless some appearances, much more flattering than the present, should make it expedient for me to remain a little longer; though *that* I scarcely look to, as even a war with Spain would render my situation by no means adequate to the sacrifice I make in absence. My health has never been more perfect or regular than at present; indeed, it is almost impossible to be ill in such a delicious climate as this island enjoys in the winter. Roses are in full blow here now, and my favorite *green peas* smoke every day upon the table. I have been extremely fortunate here (as indeed Providence seems to please I should be everywhere) in conciliating friendship, and interesting those around me in my welfare. The admiral, Sir Andrew Mitchell, has insisted upon my making his table my own during my stay here, and has promised to take me in his ship to America, for the purpose of getting a passage home to England, there being no direct conveyance from this little corner thither. They threaten me here with an impeachment, as being in a fair way to make bankrupts of the whole island. There has been nothing but gaiety since I came, and there never was such a *furor* for dissipation known in the town of St. George's before. The music parties did not long keep up, because they found they were obliged to trust to me for their whole orchestra; but the dances have been innumerable, and still continue with very great spirit indeed. The women dance in general extremely well, though, like Dogberry's 'writing and reading,' it 'comes by nature to them,'[1] for

[1] *Much Ado about Nothing*, III. iii. 14.

they never have any instruction, except when some flying dancing-master, by the kindness of fortune, happens to be wrecked and driven ashore on the island. Poor creatures! I feel real pity for them: many of them have hearts for a more favourable sphere; but they are here thrown together in a secluded nook of the world, where they learn all the corruptions of human nature, without any one of its consolations or ornaments. The ship by which I send this letter goes to Providence, in the Bahamas, an express having arrived from that place to the admiral for a reinforcement, as they dread an attack from the remains of the French army of St. Domingo, who are at this moment actually preparing at Cuba for a descent. If this conduct of the Spaniards does not produce a war, we have peaceable ministers indeed. But I must not talk to you of politics, darling mother, for I have only time to bid you kiss all the dears around you for me. Tell my darling father, that I shall be able to talk to him about West India trade on my return. Throw your arms about his neck for me, and bless the dear girls from their own remembering and affectionate brother. God bless you all, for yours truly and ever,

Tom

84. *To his Mother*

Russell, i. 156, no. 79

Bermuda
March 19. 1804.

My dearest Mother,

I take every opportunity of writing that offers, though perfectly uncertain whether my letters will ever reach you. This is now the fifth time I have written since my arrival in Bermuda, besides a letter to Atkinson, one to Carpenter, &c. &c., which I beg you will apprise the latter of, in case any accident should have interrupted my communications. Oh! darling mother, six months now, and I know as little of *home* as of things most remote from my heart and recollection. There is a ship expected here daily from England, and I flatter myself with hopes you may have taken advantage of the opportunity, and that to-morrow, perhaps, may bring me the intelligence I pine for. The signal post, which announces when any vessels are in sight of the island, is directly before my window, and often do I look to it with a heart sick 'from hope deferred.'[1] I am, however, well and in spirits; the flow of health I feel bids defiance to melancholy; and though now and then a sigh for home comes over me, I soften it with sweet hopes, and find in

[1] Proverbs xiii. 12.

the promises of my sanguine heart enough to flatter away such thoughts. There have been as many efforts at gaiety here as I could possibly have expected in so secluded a nook of the world. We have a ball or two every week, and I assure you the weather is by no means too hot for them; for we have had some days so cold, that I almost expected to see a fall of snow, miraculous as that would be in a region so near the sun as this is. A week or two since I rode into (what they call) the country parts of the island: nothing could be more enchanting than the scenery they showed me. The road lay for many miles through a thick shaded alley of orange trees and cedars, which opened now and then upon the loveliest coloured sea you can imagine, studded with little woody islands, and all in animation with sail-boats. Never was anything so beautiful! but, indeed, the mission I went upon was by no means so romantic as my road. I was sent to swear a man to the truth of a *Dutch invoice* he had translated. 'Oh! what a falling off is there.'[1] Indeed I must confess that the occupations of my place are not those of the most elegant nature: I have to examine all the skippers, mates, and seamen, who are produced as witnesses in the causes of captured vessels. I should not, you may be sure, think a moment of the inconveniences of the situation, if the emoluments were anything like a compensation for them; but they are not; and accordingly, dear mother, you will soon have me with you again. About May, I dare say, I shall be able to leave Bermuda; and I shall endeavour, if my purse will compass it, to see a little more of America than before I had an opportunity of doing; so that, about the end of summer, darling mother, you may *look to the signal-post* for your Tom, who will bring you back a sunburnt face, a heart not the worse for the wear, and a purse, like that of most honest fellows, as empty as—richer fellows' heads! Never mind though! I am young and free, and the world is a field for me still. While I have such motives for exertion as *you*, my dear father, and sisters, I may say 'warring angels combat on my side.'[2] I shall leave this letter open, in case I have anything further to add, as the brig which is to take it, I find, does not sail till to-morrow.

I have but just time to close my letter in a hurry, as the vessel is on the point of sailing. God bless you, my sweet mother, my own dear father, and good, *good* little girls. Write to Carpenter to say I sent a letter to him last month, and that I shall be the bearer of my work to him myself.[3] Give my dearly remembered Joice the best

[1] *Hamlet*, I. v. 47.

[2] *Richard III*, v. iii. 176. 'God and good angels fight on Richmond's side.' Moore evidently had this line in mind. The quotation has not otherwise been identified.

[3] *Epistles, Odes, and Other Poems.*

wishes of my heart; and to all those who love or recollect me, say everything kind that you can imagine me to feel. Again Heaven bless you all, for your own,

Tom.

I enclose some letters for people here: the English one you will get franked, and that to Switzerland you must have put into the Foreign Office in London, not in Dublin. I kiss you, darlings.

85. *To his Mother*

Russell, i. 158, no. 80

New York
May 7. 1804.

My dearest Mother,

I have but just time to say, *here I am*, after a passage of nine days from Bermuda;[1] never was better; and the novelty of this strange place keeps me in a bustle of spirits and curiosity. The oddest things I have seen yet, however, are young Buonaparte and his bride.[2]

My plans are not settled yet. Captain Douglas, of the Boston frigate, who brought me here, sails in a few days for Norfolk, whither I shall accompany him; and my intention is, if I can manage it, to come up by land through the States, and rejoin him at Halifax, from whence I believe he will be sent to England,—a fine opportunity for me, and I anxiously hope it may occur so. I go to the theatre this evening, and to a concert to-morrow evening. Such a place! such people! barren and secluded as poor Bermuda is, I think it a paradise to any spot in America that I have seen. If there is less barrenness of *soil* here, there is more than enough of barrenness in intellect, taste, and all in which *heart* is concerned. * * *

I have no more time; my heart is full of the prospect of once more seeing and embracing you, dear mother, good father, and my own Kate and Ellen. God bless you. I wrote to Carpenter and Lord Moira by the same ship. Your own Transatlantic Tom.

[1] The frigate *Boston* sailed from Bermuda on 25 Apr. 1804.

[2] Jerome Bonaparte served as a lieutenant in the navy in the West Indies and on a visit to the United States met Elizabeth Patterson, of Baltimore, whom he married in 1803. In 1805 Napoleon declared the marriage null, ostensibly because it took place without the consent of the Emperor.

86. *To his Mother*

Russell, i. 159, no. 81

Aboard the Boston,
Sandy Hook, thirty miles from New York
Friday, May 11. 1804.

My darling Mother,

I wrote to you on my arrival at New York, where I have been near a week, and am now returned aboard the frigate, which but waits a fair wind to sail for Norfolk. The Halifax packet is lying along side of us, and I shall take the opportunity of sending this letter by her. At New York I was made happy by my father's letter of the 25th January, and dear Kate's of the 30th, which make four in all that I have received from home. I had so very few opportunities at Bermuda, and they were attended with so much uncertainty, that I fear you may have suffered many an anxious moment, darling mother, from the interruption and delay of the few letters I could dispatch to you. But, please Heaven! we shall soon have those barriers of distance removed; my own tongue shall tell you my 'travel's history,'[1] and your heart shall go along with me over every billow and step of the way. When I left Bermuda I could not help regretting that the hopes which took me thither could not be even half realised, for I should love to live there, and you would like it too, dear mother; and I think, if the situation would give me but a fourth of what I was so deludingly taught to expect, you should all have come to me; and though set apart from the rest of the world, we should have found in that quiet spot, and under that sweet sky, quite enough to counterbalance what the rest of the world could give us. But I am still to seek, and can only hope that I may find at last.

The environs of New York are pretty, from the number of little fanciful wooden houses that are scattered, to the distance of six to eight miles round the city; but when one reflects upon the cause of this, and that these houses are the retreats of the terrified, desponding inhabitants from the wilderness of death which every autumn produces in the city, there is very little pleasure in the prospect; and, notwithstanding the rich fields, and the various blossoms of their orchards, I prefer the barren, breezy rock of Bermuda to whole continents of such dearly purchased fertility.

While in New York, I employed my time to advantage in witnessing all the novelties possible. I saw young M. Buonaparte,[2]

[1] *Othello*, I. iii. 139.

[2] See letter No. 85, to his mother, 7 May 1804.

and felt a slight shock of an earthquake, which are two things I could not often meet with upon Usher's Quay. From Norfolk I intend going to Baltimore and Washington; if possible also to Philadelphia and Boston, from thence to Halifax. From Halifax I hope to set sail in the cabin where I now write this letter for the dear old isles of the Old World again; and I think it probable, that twelve months from the time I left England will very nearly see me on its coasts once more.

I thank dear Kate for the poem she has sent me; it is written, I believe, by a Mr. William Smith, some of whose things (extremely pretty) are in the Metrical Miscellany; a collection of poems published by my little friend Mrs. Riddell.[1] But why doesn't Kate say something about Nell?

My first object when I return shall be to discharge my obligations to Carpenter: as I must, for that purpose, seclude myself entirely, the less you say about the time of my return the better. The completion of the work I have in hand will much more than extricate me from all engagements I am under. My dear uncle shall not want his money *one moment* after my arrival: tell him so, with my heart's truest and affectionate remembrances. God bless you, darling mother. Kiss them all round for me, father, Kate, and Nell together. Your own,

T. M.

87. *To his Mother*

Russell, i. 161, no. 82

Baltimore
Wednesday, June 13. 1804.

I am now, dearest mother, more than three hundred miles from Norfolk. I have passed the Potomac, the Rappahannock, the Occoquan, the Potapsio, and many other rivers, with names as barbarous as the inhabitants: every step I take not only *reconciles*, but *endears* to me, not only the excellencies but even the errors of Old England. Such a road as I have come! and in such a conveyance! The mail takes twelve passengers, which generally consist of squalling children, stinking negroes, and republicans smoking cigars! How often it has occurred to me that nothing can be more emblematic of the *government* of this country than its *stages*, filled with a motley mixture, all 'hail fellow well met,'

[1] *The Metrical Miscellany: Consisting Chiefly of Poems hitherto Unpublished*, edited by Maria Riddell (London, 1802). The following poems by 'W. Smyth' are included: 'I checked my sighs, Antonio cried'; 'Stanzas on a Bower Facing the South'; 'The Night Her Empire Had Resigned'; 'The Maid with Bosom Cold'; 'To Laura'; and 'When Brightly Glows the Western Wave'.

driving through mud and filth, which *bespatters* them as they *raise* it, and risking an *upset* at every step. God comfort their capacities! as soon as I am away from them, both the stages and the government may have the same fate for what *I* care. I stopped at Washington with Mr. and Mrs. Merry for near a week: they have been treated with the most pointed incivility by the present democratic president, Mr. Jefferson; and it is only the precarious situation of Great Britain which could possibly induce it to overlook such indecent, though, at the same time, petty hostility.[1] I was presented by Mr. Merry to both the secretary of state and the president. * * *[2]

I hope, my darling mother, that all I write to amuse you may meet your eye, and find your heart in a mood to enjoy it. Oh yes, be happy, my own mother! be *you* but well and happy, and no sorrow can come near any of us. I know, in saying this, I speak for *all*; for my dearest, beloved father, and the sweet, good girls; we all hang on you equally. Never did Heaven form a heart more kind than I have found in Mrs. Hamilton of Norfolk, and she has caught the way to my heart by calling herself my *mother*. She sends a pair of ear-rings by me to Kate with the sincerest affection possible: she loves you all through me. I shall leave this place for Philadelphia on to-morrow, or the day after. I shall see there poor Edward Hudson, who, if I am rightly informed, has married the daughter of a very rich bookseller, and is taken into partnership by the father. Surely, surely, *this country* must have cured him of

[1] Mr. and Mrs. Merry attended dinner at the White House on 2 Dec. 1803, and evidently felt that Jefferson offered an affront to their dignity by saying nothing as a member of the House of Representatives stepped ahead of Merry to sit by the wife of the Spanish minister. There is reason to doubt Merry's statement, however, since there is no indication that he had been invited to sit by the Spanish lady. There is also reason to assume that the Merrys were inclined to put themselves forward more than was fitting. Jefferson once noted in a letter to William Short that Mrs. Merry, not liking a seat assigned to her at a later dinner, was led to the head of the table by her husband, and when a Mrs. Gallatin offered to relinquish her own seat, took it without saying a word (see the *American Historical Review*, xxxiii. 832–5). An account of the social difficulties of Mr. and Mrs. Merry can be found in Henry Adams, *History of the United States during the Administration of Thomas Jefferson*, book ii, chapter xvii.

[2] When Merry presented Moore to the President, Jefferson looked down at the poet in absolute silence, and Moore's dislike of him became so great that in the verse epistle 'To Thomas Hume, Esq., M. D.' (*Poetry*, pp. 116–18) he alluded to the libel that Jefferson kept a black mistress. Moore also added a note to the poem, saying that Jefferson occupied only a small portion of the White House, abandoning 'the rest to a state of uncleanly desolation. . .'. He later regretted these youthful indiscretions and his early condemnation of the United States (see letters Nos. 471 and 554, to John E. Hall, June 1816 and 12 July 1818). For further details concerning Moore's attitude toward Jefferson and the United States see Jones, *The Harp that Once*—, pp. 78–79.

republicanism. Farewell, my sweet mother; Heaven preserve you to me, and to the dear ones about you, who have always my heart and soul with them. Yours and theirs for ever.

I was going to tell you about writing to me, but that is unnecessary, for in less than six weeks I hope to sail from Halifax for England. I am going to the northward just in right time, before the violent heat sets in, and the Halifax summer is delicious.

Philadelphia, June 16.

I have brought this letter on with me from Baltimore, as there was no opportunity likely to occur from thence. I travelled all night in one of the most rumbling, wretched vehicles. O dear! I am almost tired of thus jogging and struggling into experience. I have seen Edward Hudson: the rich bookseller I had heard of is Pat Byrne, whose daughter Hudson has married: they are, I believe, doing well. I dine with them to-day. Oh, if Mrs. Merry were to know that! However, I dined with the Consul-general yesterday, which makes the balance even. I feel awkward with Hudson now; he has perhaps had reason to confirm him in his politics, and God knows I see every reason to change mine. Good by, sweet mother. Your own everywhere.

88. *To his Mother*

Russell, i. 163, no. 83

Passaick Falls
June 26. 1804.

My dearest Mother,

I *must* write to you from this spot, it is so beautiful. Nothing can be more sweetly romantic than the cascade of the Passaick; and yet I could not help wishing, while I looked at it, that some magic could transform it into the waterfall of Wicklow, and then but a few miles should lie between me and those I sigh for. Well, a little lapse of time, and I shall be, please Heaven! in your arms. But there have ships come, darling mother, from Dublin, and I have received no letters; none with a date more recent than January: perhaps they have been sent on to Col. Hamilton, and I shall get them at Halifax. God send I may; but till then I cannot feel at ease. Not a line has reached me from Carpenter since I left England. I sometimes forget the contingencies and accidents which delay and embarrass the forwarding of letters, and almost begin to think myself neglected by those at home; but I ought to recollect how very short a time I have been stationary anywhere, and I shall look with hope to Halifax for the long arrears of comfort which begin to impoverish the treasury of my spirits, rich as it is in stores of consolation and vivacity.

My reception at Philadelphia was extremely flattering: it is the only place in America which can boast any literary society, and my name had prepossessed them more strongly than I deserve. But their affectionate attentions went far beyond this deference to reputation; I was quite caressed while there; and their anxiety to make me known, by introductory letters, to all their friends on my way, and two or three little poems of a very flattering kind, which some of their choicest men addressed to me, all went so warmly to my heart, that I felt quite a regret in leaving them; and the only place I have seen, which I had one wish to pause in, was Philadelphia.[1]

The Boston frigate, in which I expect to return, is now watching the French frigates (off New York), which are come to steal away young Mister Buonaparte: this, perhaps, will a little delay her arrival at Halifax, where I hope to be in less than a fortnight. Never was I in better health; I drink scarcely a drop of wine, which is a plan I am determined to adhere to, as I have always found wine heating and injurious to my stomach. * * *

89. *To John Erskine Douglas*

Rice University

New York
Thursday, June 28th [1804]

My dear friend— After struggling with ye break-neck roads of Virginia and the break-heart girls of Philadelphia, here I am, much, *much* later than I ought to be, and if you scold me for loitering, I am afraid I shall partly deserve it— I had intended to go aboard you to-day, but the Boat leaves this much later than I imagined and I dread the heat and the return to night— I had totally given up the idea of Canada from the delays I was *forced* and *seduced* to make on the road, but since I have heard of your present stationary employ, I begin to think it is not impossible I may yet have time sufficient for the journey— I have found a companion, a young Irishman, whom I shall be glad to take aboard and introduce to you— Notwithstanding the Heat, I should go down to the Hook to-day, if they had not given me to understand that you had some

[1] For an account of Moore's experiences in Philadelphia see Harold M. Ellis, *Joseph Dennie and his Circle* (Austin, Texas, 1915); Albert H. Smyth, *The Philadelphia Magazines and their Contributors* (Philadelphia, 1892); and Ellis P. Oberholtzer, *The Literary History of Philadelphia* (Philadelphia, 1906).

idea of going out on a short cruise immediately— Can *I* be of any service to you, or add any great *weight* of *metal* to you in your engagement with these damned French poltrons [*sic*]?—[1] You *might* make a *Powder-Monkey* of me—but I have got so much inflammable matter in me from my contact with the Philadelphian girls, that I am afraid my interference might endanger the Magazine—however, do with me what you will—and, for Heaven's sake, let me know whether you can give me time for Niagara— I would not risk my going home with *you*, you know very well, for all the Niagaras that I could wish were deluging this Country—but if I can manage it, I should be very happy— Good bye. God give you blessing & victory—

Yours entirely
Thos Moore[2]

90. *To John Erskine Douglas*

Maggs Sales Catalogue # 292, June 1912, p. 54

Sunday Night [June or July 1804]

I have scarcely ever been so annoyed as I was yesterday at not being able to join your party aboard; but, believe me, it was by no means my fault. After dining till two o'clock at the ball on Friday I had myself roused up at *six* yesterday in order to be time enough in St. George's to attend you, and I refused a most pressing invitation to dine at the speaker's, which otherwise I should have accepted, as an opportunity of seeing the *natives*—after these efforts, which I take no merit from, as it was in my old pursuit—fun) [*sic*] when I came to the cursed ferry, they could not pass our horses, we waited and waited till it was quite hopeless and we were forced to cross without them and walk home. . . .

91. *To Joseph Dennie*

New York Public

New York
Monday July 2nd 1804

My dear Denny [*sic*]. I have scarcely found a moments [*sic*] leisure since I left my friends in Philadelphia to tell how warmly I remember them and how much I regret the very hopeless farewell I

[1] Douglas's 'stationary employ' was to watch several French frigates, which had come to spirit away Jerome Bonaparte, who, with his bride, was then visiting New York. (See letter No. 88, to his mother, 26 June 1804.)

[2] This is the letter to which Douglas replied on 29 June 1804 (Russell, i. 165).

have taken—but I trust they will do me the justice to believe that they live in my recollection and this oer [*sic*] the wide waters of the Atlantic shall be no Lethe to the liveliness of my gratitude. The Falls of the Passaic delighted me extremely & I feel quite indebted to Mr Meredith for having urged me to visit them— Niagara (*which I have* resumed my *resolution to see*) must be almost too tremendous to produce sensations of pleasure— I know not whether it is, that I feel the magnificence of Nature to an excess almost painful or that I have some kind of *kindred* affection for her miniature productions but certainly I rather dread such grandeurs as those of Niagara, and turn with more pleasure to the 'minora sidera' [*sic*] of Creation— You remember Akenside— But Waller longs, All on the margin &c &c—[1]

I have mentioned you comme il faut in a letter to Mrs Merry, which (as you will have a formal presentation from Thornton) is, I think the most certain way of making you 'in greges' at once—

Tomorrow I think of setting out for Albany and shall be obliged I suppose to give up all expectation of hearing from you till I reach Halifax where you must direct for me to the care of Sr Andrew Mitchell K B &c &c—

I shall have but time now to transcribe you a little poem which I wrote on my way from Philadelphia and which I beg you will give to Mrs Hopkinson with my best regards at the same time to her and her very admirable husband—[2] I am looking anxiously for Ewing—

Yours my dear Dennie
very sincerely—
Thomas Moore.

92. *To his Mother*

Russell, i. 166, no. 85

Saratoga
July 10. 1804.

My darling mother, I hope, has received the letter I wrote from the Passaick Falls. Since that I have passed a week in New York, but

[1] The reference is to the following passage:

But Waller longs,
All on the margin of some flowery stream
To spread his careless limbs amid the cool
Of plantane shades, and to the listening deer
The tale of slighted vows and love's disdain
Resound soft-warbling, all the live-long day.
Pleasures of Imagination, iii. 558–63.

[2] Probably 'Alone by the Schuylkill a wanderer rov'd', *Poetry*, p. 119.

was afraid to write from thence, through fear you might be uneasy at my being there in so warm a season. Till the day before I left it, there was no appearance of any infection: on that day, some reports of yellow fever *were* made, and indeed I have no doubt the visitation of this calamity will be as dreadful this year, as any that has preceded. I have now come two hundred miles from New York, and if anything can add to the blessing of the health which I feel, it is the idea of having left such pestilence behind me. Oh that you could see the sweet country I have passed through! The passage up the Hudson river gave me the most bewildering succession of romantic objects that I could ever have conceived. When it was calm, we rowed ashore and visited the little villages that are on the river: one of these places they have called *Athens*, and there, you may imagine, I found myself quite at home. I looked in vain though for my dear *gardens;* there were *hogs* enough, but none of *Epicurus's* herd.[1] If you, or sweet Kate, could read *Latin*, I would quote you here what I allude to; but you have not 'been at the great feast of languages, or stolen the scraps,'[2] so I'll not tease you with it. Two or three days ago I was to see the Coho Falls on the Mohawk river, and was truly gratified. The immense fall of the river over a natural dam of thirty or forty feet high, its roar among the rocks, and the illuminated mist of spray which rises from its foam, were to me objects all new, beautiful, and impressive. I never can forget the scenery of this country, and if it had but any endearing associations of the heart (to diffuse that charm over it, without which the fairest features of nature are but faintly interesting), I should regret very keenly that I cannot renew often the enjoyment of its beauties. But it has none such for me, and I defy the barbarous natives to forge one chain of attachment for any heart that has ever felt the sweets of delicacy or refinement. I believe I must except the *women* from this denunciation; they are certainly flowers of every climate, and here 'waste their sweetness'[3] most deplorably. Dear mother, I know you will be pleased with a little poem I wrote on my way from Philadelphia; it was written very much as a return for the kindnesses I met with there, but chiefly in allusion to a very charming little woman, Mrs. Hopkinson, who was extremely interested by my songs, and flattered me with many attentions. You must observe that the Schuylkill is a river which runs by, or (I believe) through, Philadelphia.

[1] An allusion to *Kepoi*, the garden in Athens, in which Epicurus held his school. For 'Epicurus's herd' see Horace, *Epistles*, I. iv. 13 (*Epicuri de grege porcum*).

[2] *Love's Labour's Lost*, v. i. 39.

[3] Gray, *Elegy in a Country Churchyard*, stanza 14.

[Lines
Written on Leaving Philadelphia

—Τηνδε την πολιν φιλως
Ειπων· επαξια γαρ. SOPHOCL. *Oedip. Colon.* v. 758.

Alone by the Schuylkill a wanderer rov'd,
 And bright were its flowery banks to his eye;
But far, very far were the friends that he lov'd,
 And he gaz'd on its flowery banks with a sigh.

Oh Nature, though blessed and bright are thy rays,
 O'er the brow of creation enchantingly thrown,
Yet faint are they all to the lustre that plays
 In a smile from the heart that is fondly our own.

Nor long did the soul of the stranger remain
 Unblest by the smile he had languish'd to meet;
Though scarce did he hope it would soothe him again,
 Till the threshold of home had been prest by his feet.

But the lays of his boyhood had stol'n to their ear,
 And they lov'd what they knew of so humble a name;
And they told him, with flattery welcome and dear,
 That they found in his heart something better than fame.

Nor did woman—oh woman! whose form and whose soul
 Are the spell and the light of each path we pursue;
Whether sunn'd in the tropics or chill'd at the pole,
 If woman be there, there is happiness too:—

Nor did she her enamouring magic deny,—
 That magic his heart had relinquish'd so long,—
Like eyes he had lov'd was *her* eloquent eye,
 Like them did it soften and weep at his song.

Oh, blest be the tear, and in memory oft
 May its sparkle be shed o'er the wand'rer's dream;
Thrice blest be that eye, and may passion as soft,
 As free from a pang, ever mellow its beam!

The stranger is gone—but he will not forget,
 When at home he shall talk of the toils he has known,
To tell, with a sigh, what endearments he met,
 As he stray'd by the wave of the Schuylkill alone.][1]

1 *Poetry*, p. 119. Russell cited the poem but did not include it in his text.

I am now near the spot where the accomplished but ill-fated Burgoyne incurred the first stain which the arms of England received from the rebel Americans.[1] The country around here seems the very home of savages. Nothing but tall forests of pine, through which the narrow, rocky road with difficulty finds its way; and yet in this neighbourhood is the fashionable resort, the watering-place for ladies and gentlemen from all parts of the United States. At Bell Town Springs, eight miles from this, there are about thirty or forty people at present (and, in the season, triple that number), all stowed together in a miserable boarding house, smoking, drinking the waters, and performing every necessary evolution in concert. They were astonished at our asking for basins and towels in our rooms, and thought we might 'condescend, indeed, to come down to the *public wash* with the other gentlemen in the morning!' I saw there a poor affectionate mother who had brought her son for the recovery of his health: she sat beside him all day with a large fan, to cool his 'feverish brow,' and not a moment did she rest from this employment; every time I passed her I saw her at it with the sweetest patience imaginable. Oh! there is no love like mother's love; the sight made me think of home, and recalled many circumstances which brought the tears of recollection and gratitude into my eyes.

I enclose you a scrap from a New York paper of last week, which will show you I do not pass unnoticed over this waste, and it will please our dear Kate's friend, Mrs. Smith, to see her poem selected even in America. God bless you all. Love to my darling father, and the good girls. From your own devoted son,

Tom.

93. *To his Mother*

Russell, i. 168, no. 86

Geneva, Genessee Country
July 17. 1804.

I just pause a moment on my way to give one word to my dearest mother. I hope the letter I wrote, four or five days since, from Seenectady [*sic*], will find its way to you. Since then I have been amongst the Oneida Indians, and have been amused very much by the novelty of their appearance. An old chief, Seenando, received me very courteously, and told us as well as he could by broken English and signs, that his nation consisted of 900, divided into three tribes, entitled the Wolf, the Bear, and the Turtle; poor,

[1] Burgoyne surrendered to Gates at Saratoga on 17 Oct. 1777.

harmless savages! The government of America are continually deceiving them into a surrender of the lands they occupy, and are driving them back into the woods farther and farther, till at length they will have no retreat but the ocean. This old chief's manners were extremely gentle and intelligent, and almost inclined me to be of the Frenchman's opinion, that the savages are the only well-bred gentlemen in America.

Our journey along the banks of the Mohawk was uncommonly interesting: never did I feel my heart in a better tone of sensibility than that which it derived from the scenery on this river. There is a holy magnificence in the immense bank of woods that overhang it, which does not permit the heart to rest merely in the admiration of *Nature*, but carries it to that something less *vague* than *Nature*, that satisfactory source of all these exquisite wonders, a Divinity! I sometimes on the way forget myself and even you so much, as to wish for ever to remain amidst these romantic scenes; but I *did not* forget you; you were *all inseparable* from the plans of happiness which at that moment might have flattered my fancy. I can form none into which you are not woven, closely and essentially.

To-morrow we shall set out for the *Falls of Niagara!* After seeing these (which I shall consider an era in my life), I shall lose no time in reaching Halifax, so as to be ready for the sailing of the frigate. I told you in a former letter, that it is this lucky opportunity of a passage *gratis* to England which has induced me to devote the expenses of my return to the acquisition of some knowledge respecting this very interesting world, which, with all the defects and disgusting peculiarities of its natives, gives every promise of no very distant competition with the first powers of the Eastern hemisphere.

We travel to Niagara in *a waggon:* you may guess at the cheapness of the inns in this part of the country, when I tell you that, the other night, three of us had supper, beds, and breakfast, besides some drink for two or three Indians who danced for us, and the bill came to something less than seven shillings for all. I must own the accommodations are still lower than their price; nothing was ever so dirty or miserable; but powerful curiosity sweetens all difficulties. I shall not have an opportunity to write again for some time, but I shall send you thoughts enough, and you must imagine them the dearest and most comfortable possible. When I say, 'for some time,' I mean a fortnight or three weeks. Good by. God bless you, dears. Oh! that I could know how you are at this moment. Your own,

Tom.

94. *To his Mother*

Russell, i. 170, no. 87

Chippewa, Upper Canada
July 22. 1804.

Dearest Mother,

Just arrived within a mile and half of the falls of Niagara, and their tremendous roar at this moment sounding in my ears. We travelled one whole day through the wilderness, where you would imagine human foot had never ventured to leave its print; and this rough work has given a healthier hue to my cheek than ever it could boast in the Eastern hemisphere of London. If you look at the map of North America, you will be able to trace my situation. I have passed through the Genessee country, and am now between Lake Erie and Lake Ontario. Such scenery as there is around me! it is quite dreadful that any heart, born for sublimities, should be doomed to breathe away its hours amidst the miniature productions of this world, without seeing what shapes Nature *can* assume, what wonders God *can* give birth to.

I have seized this momentary opportunity, dear mother, for writing a line to you, which I will entrust to the waggoner who returns to Geneva, from which place I last wrote to you. Heaven send you may receive all the letters. I feel they would interest even a stranger to me, then what must they be to you! Love to dear father and girls. Your own,

Tom.

I am now on British ground; we arrived yesterday evening to dinner, and drunk the King's health in a bumper. Just going to see the Falls. Good by.

95. *To his Mother*

Russell, i. 171, no. 88

Niagara
July 24. 1804.

My dearest Mother,

I have seen the falls, and am all rapture and amazement. I cannot give you a better idea of what I felt than by transcribing what I wrote off hastily in my journal on returning. 'Arrived at Chippewa, within three miles of the Falls, on Saturday, July 21st, to dinner. That evening walked towards the Falls, but got no farther than the Rapids, which gave us a prelibation of the grandeur we had to expect. Next day, Sunday, July 22d, went to visit the Falls.

Never shall I forget the impression I felt at the first glimpse of them which we got as the carriage passed over the hill that overlooks them. We were not near enough to be agitated by the terrific effects of the scene, but saw through the trees this mighty flow of waters descending with calm magnificence, and received enough of its grandeur to set imagination on the wing; imagination which, even at Niagara, can outrun reality. I felt as if approaching the very residence of the Deity; the tears started into my eyes; and I remained, for moments after we had lost sight of the scene, in that delicious absorption which pious enthusiasm alone can produce. We arrived at the New Ladder and descended to the bottom. Here all its awful sublimities rushed full upon me. But the former exquisite sensation was gone. I now saw all. The string that had been touched by the first impulse, and which *fancy* would have kept for ever in vibration, now rested at *reality*. Yet, though there was no more to imagine, there was much to feel. My whole heart and soul ascended towards the Divinity in a swell of devout admiration, which I never before experienced. Oh! bring the atheist here, and he cannot return an atheist! I pity the man who can coldly sit down to write a description of these ineffable wonders; much more do I pity him who can submit them to the admeasurement of gallons and yards. It is impossible by pen or pencil to convey even a faint idea of their magnificence. Painting is lifeless; and the most burning words of poetry have all been lavished upon inferior and ordinary subjects. We must have new combinations of language to describe the Falls of Niagara.'

* * * * * *

So much for my journal; but if, notwithstanding all this enthusiastic contempt for matter-of-fact description, you still should like to see a particular account of the Falls, Weld, in his Travels,[1] has given the most accurate I have seen. On the Sunday morning before I left Chippewa, I wrote you a letter, darling mother, which I entrusted to the waggoner (who was going back) to have it forwarded.[2] Oh! if the stupid scoundrel should have neglected it. Since the day I left New York (July 4.) this is the fourth letter I have written to you. How dreadfully provoking if they have miscarried. Never was I in better health than I have been during my journey. This exercise is quite new to me, and I find the invigorating effects of it. My heart, too, feels light with the idea that the

[1] Isaac Weld, the Younger, *Travels through the States of America, and the Provinces of Upper and Lower Canada during the Years 1795, 1796, and 1797* (London, 1799).

[2] See letter No. 94, to his mother, 22 July 1804.

moment is approaching when I shall fly on the wings of the wind to the dear embrace of all that is dear to me. God bless you, loves. I pray for you often and fervently; and I feel that Heaven *will* take care of us. A thousand kisses to dear father and the girls, from their own boy on the banks of Lake Ontario. Again God bless you, dearest mother. Ever, ever your

Tom.

96. *To John Erskine Douglas*

Maggs Sales Catalogue # 292, June 1912, p. 54

Niagara
July 29th 1804

Guess the fidget I am in at being detained in this miserable place, already more than a week, and with but little prospect of release from it— Water! Water! I have always hated thee in every shape, medium and mixture! the Grand Toper has not a truer *hydrophobist* under him. Nothing could get on more famously than my journey, till I arrived on the borders of this said Lake Ontario & ever since I came, the wind has been so fair for our passage (if we had a vessel) that it is impossible any vessel can get in to take us. I have fretted myself so much in this time, that as Shakespeare says I have almost 'crept into the jaundice, by being peevish.'[1] To think of my being too late for you at Halifax is quite distracting. . . .

Indeed, indeed, my dearest friend, I never can sufficiently thank you for having persuaded and facilitated my visit to this wonderful place. I pity from my heart all those who are doomed to breathe away their lives among the miniature productions of Nature, without seeing what shapes she can assume, without knowing what wonders God *can* produce.[2] Of those stupendous Falls, it is impossible to attempt any description— 'Go and see them' is all I shall ever say to any one who inquires what they are—and it is well worth a long privation of many of our ordinary pleasures, to taste but a moment's impression which the first glimpse of them makes on the mind. . . .

[1] *Merchant of Venice*, I. i. 85.
[2] See letter No. 94, to his mother, 22 July 1804.

97. *To his Mother*

Russell, i. 173, no. 89

Quebec
August 20. 1804.

My darling Mother,

After seventeen hundred miles of rattling and tossing through woods, lakes, rivers, &c., I am at length upon the ground which made Wolfe immortal, and which looks more like the elysium of heroes than their death-place. If any thing can make the beauty of the country more striking, it is the deformity and oddity of the city which it surrounds, and which lies hemmed in by ramparts, amidst this delicious scenery, like a hog in armour upon a bed of roses.

In my passage across Lake Ontario, I met with the same politeness which has been so gratifying, and indeed convenient, to me all along my route. The captain refused to take what I know is always given, and begged me to consider all my friends as included in the same compliment, which a line from me would at any time entitle them to. Even a poor watchmaker at Niagara, who did a very necessary and difficult job for me, insisted I should not think of paying him, but accept it as the only mark of respect he could pay to one he had heard of so much, but never expected to meet with. This is the very nectar of life, and I hope, I *trust*, it is not vanity to which the cordial owes all its sweetness. No; it gives me a feeling towards all mankind, which I am convinced is not unamiable: the impulse which begins with *self*, spreads a circle instantaneously around it, which includes all the sociabilities and benevolences of the heart. Dearest mother! you will feel this with me. I cannot write more now; the fleet which sails for England is on the point of sailing. To-morrow or next day I am off for Halifax, where I shall bid my last adieu to America, and fly home to my darlings once more. Love to all. Your own boy.

98. *To his Mother*

Russell, i. 175, no. 90

Windsor, Nova Scotia
Sept. 16. 1804.

My darling Mother,

I arrived at Halifax last Tuesday week, after a passage of thirteen days from Quebec. I wrote to you while at Quebec; but from what I have since heard of the time of the fleet's sailing from there, it is likely this letter may reach you first. Well, *dears of my heart!* here am I at length, with the last footsteps upon American ground, and on tiptoe for beloved home once more. Windsor, where I write this, is between forty and fifty miles from Halifax. I have been brought hither by the governor of Nova Scotia, Sir J. Wentworth, to be at the first examination of a new university they have founded.[1] This attention is, as you may suppose, very singular and flattering; indeed, where have I failed to meet cordiality and kindness? They have smoothed every step of my way, and sweetened every novelty that I met. The governor of Lower Canada, when I was on the point of leaving, sent his aide-de-camp to the master of the vessel which was to take me, and begged it as a favour he would defer sailing for *one* day more, that I might join a party at his house the next day. All this cannot but gratify my own sweet mother, and she will not see either frivolity or egotism in detail. All along my route I have seized every opportunity of writing to you, and it will be more than unfortunate if my letters do not reach you. You cannot imagine how anxious I have been lest I should lose the opportunity of the Boston frigate home; for I have been unavoidably detained a month beyond my time, and the orders of service are imperious. I know that with all Douglas's friendship, he could not wait for me, and I almost gave up the hope. But, still lucky, I have found him here refitting, and *in about three weeks we shall sail for England.* How my heart beats with delight to tell you this. I have got Kate's letter of the 29th. God bless her! dear, good girl.

You must not be surprised at such a scatter-brained letter, for I have this instant heard that the packet leaves Halifax before I return thither, and I scribble these dithyrambics (just risen from dinner) to send into town by a gentleman who goes in the morning.

Tell Carpenter I am coming with a volume of poetic travels in my pocket;[2] and tell Kate I have learnt some of the '*Chansons des Voyageurs*' in coming down the St. Lawrence, which I hope before three months, at the utmost, to sing for her. Love to good father and girls, and good by. Sweet mother, your own,

Tom.

There is a nephew of Lord St. Vincent's sent out here on the same wild-goose chase with myself; so it is beyond a doubt they thought them good appointments.[3]

[1] King's College, Windsor, established in 1790.

[2] 'Poems Relating to America', *Poetry*, pp. 93–130.

[3] The nephew was probably Edward-Jervis Ricketts, second Viscount St. Vincent, whose father was a merchant in Jamaica.

99. *To Joseph Dennie*

The Critic (New Series), ix (1888), 270

Halifax, Nova Scotia
Sept. 29th 1804

My dear Denny [*sic*]:

I am very much afraid that you have never received either my letter from New York or that from Niagara. In the former I sent you my Schulkyll verses,[1] which I have not seen in any *Port-Folio* that has reached me, and in the latter I scribbled for you the outline of a Spirit's Song or Hymn which I had just begun and wanted your opinion of.[2] I regret extremely that my long detention at Niagara interfered with the visit I intended to your friends at Boston. If any little airy intelligence could have informed me on my way, that Captain Douglas would not sail so soon as he originally intended, I might have devoted that time to the 'animo candidiores' of Boston, which I have now wasted upon the barren rocks of Halifax. I have seen, however, the chief beauties of upper and lower Canada, and they have left impressions upon my heart and fancy which my memory long shall love to recur to. If the soil be not very ungrateful, the new thoughts it is scattered with, will spring up, I hope, into something for your hand to embellish by *transplanting*. Indeed, my dearest Dennie, I cannot speak half my acknowledgments to you for the very cordial interest you feel in my reputation, and for the truly beautiful *frames* of eloquence in which you take care to *set* all my little miniatures. Nothing can be more flattering than what you have said of me since I left you, and I only wish that I was *deserving* of such Eulogies. I am quite distressed to find that, with my own books, they have sent me on your *Political Register and Huddesford's Miscellany*. I hope it has been no derangement to you, and I return them with this letter. I enclose you, too, a couple of the poems which my lines to the Invisible Girl gave rise to. I wish I had that which produced the visible Lady's reply, but its purport may be gathered from the answer, and it was by no means so good or animated. The printed copy I send is the only one I have. The French poem is written by a son of Lord Trimlestone's, and is a tolerable imitation of the style of Bernard de Bernis. The latter part of it alludes to a conversation I had with him the day before upon the Platonic philosophy.[3] I hope

[1] See letter No. 91, to Joseph Dennie, 2 July 1804.

[2] 'Song of the Evil Spirit of the Woods', *Poetry*, p. 120.

[3] The poems to which Moore refers were published in the *Port Folio*, v (19 Jan. 1805), p. 15. The first, entitled 'La Fille Invisible—a T. M.', is in the style of François Joachim de Pierre de Bernis (1715–94), who wrote short

to sail in about a week hence, and you shall hear from me immediately on my arrival in London. Till then I must remain in your debt for my following year, etc., etc. God bless you, my dear fellow. If you die before me, I shall borrow the epitaph of Martial upon Rufus for you:

> Pectore tu memori nostros evolvere lusus,
> Tu solitus nostros, Rufe, tenere jocos
> Accipe cum fletu moesti breve carmen amici, etc. etc.[1]

My best and warmest remembrances to our friends, the Hopkinsons and Merediths. To Jacques give a *brother-poet's* love, with all the *warmth* of the craft and without one grain of the fiction of it. I have read his tribute to Hamilton. It is

> as sweet a stream of eloquence
> As Athens knew.[2]

Yours, again and again, most truly,
Thomas Moore.

Since I have copied out the French poem for you, I begin to think it is not so *good*, and I am *sure* it is not so *short* as I thought it at *first*. My hand is tired with transcribing it. Do not say *I* sent you these poems: They are too full of flattery, tho' few people *hate* me more cordially than the person who wrote the English one.

100. *To his Mother*

Russell, i. 176, no. 91

Plymouth, Old England once more
Nov. 12. 1804

I almost cry with joy, my darling mother, to be able once more to write to you on English ground. After a passage of eight-and-twenty days, here I am, without a blemish either in heart or body,

poems and '*bouquets poetiques*', as he called them. The second is addressed 'To T. M. Esq., on the Invisible Girl's Letter to Him'. It was submitted 'by a visible girl' and is signed 'Clara'. A headnote to the visible girl's poem reads, 'Soon after Mr. Moore published his verses "To the Invisible Girl", some of the wits addressed to him her *second* reply. This we have never been able to obtain. The following subsequent address, by a *visible* girl was handed about in the polite circles.'

The last twelve lines of the French poem deal with platonic love.

For Moore's 'Invisible Girl' see *Poetry*, p. 60.

[1] Martial, *Epigrams*, VI. lxxxv. The complete passage reads as follows:

> pectore tu memori nostros evolvere lusus,
> tu solitus totos, Rufe, tenere iocos,
> accipe cum fletu maesti breve carmen amici
> atque haec apsentis tura fuisse puta.

[2] Not identified.

and within a few hundred miles (instead of *thousands*) of those that are dearest to me. Oh dear! to think that in ten days hence I may see a letter from home, written but a day or two before, warm from your hands, and with your very breath almost upon it, instead of lingering out months after months, without a gleam of intelligence, without any thing but dreams—[*here the letter is torn*]. If the idleness I have had was voluntary or intentional, I should deserve to pay for it; but without giving me any thing to do, my friends have increased the necessity of my doing something. However, there is one satisfying idea; which is, that I am not at a loss for employment, and that I have it within my own power, in the course of two or three months, to draw the sponge over every pecuniary obligation I have contracted. How few in a similar situation could say this! and how grateful do I feel to Heaven, and my dear father and mother for those means! * * *

101. *To his Mother*

Russell, i. 177, no. 92

Saturday (after my return from Bermuda)
[November 1804]

My darling Mother,

I have only just time to tell you that the Prince was extremely kind to me last night, at a small supper party at which I met him: every one noticed the cordiality with which he spoke to me. His words were these: 'I am very glad to see you here again, Moore. From the reports I heard, I was afraid we had lost you. I assure you (laying his hand on my shoulder at the same time) it was a subject of general concern.' Could anything be more flattering? I must say I felt rather happy at that moment. The idea of such reports having reached him—his remembering them upon seeing me, and expressing them so cordially—was all pleasant, and will, I know, gratify my dear father and mother's hearts. I saw him afterwards go up to Lord Moira, and pointing towards me, express, I suppose, the same thing.

It was at Lord Harrington's. I enclose you the invitation I received from Lord Petersham, because it is friendly, and because nothing else could have induced me to break the studious retire ment I have adopted. I am delighted I went. God bless you all.

102. *To John Dalby*

Mrs. Mercia Dalby

Donington Park
Monday [November 1804]

My dear Dalby

Tho I sincerely rejoice in the cause that has taken you from the old spot, yet I very sensibly feel the effects of it, and have nothing now to talk with but books, which in general are a very bad substitute for *you*—but am I not to see you at all, my dear fellow? Oh! I have seen much, felt much & indeed learned much since I left you— We have a great deal to commune over, and I am anxious for a sight of you— Come then soon, and let us make some arrangements for meeting as often as possible while I am here—give my kindest wishes & remembrances to Mrs Dalby, and believe me, unaltered by Transatlantic [influence,

Your warm friend
Thomas Moore

I have some debts of *money* as well as gratitude to settle with you.][1]

103. *To his Mother*

Russell, i. 178, no. 93

27. Bury Street, St. James's
Wednesday, Jan. 11. 1805.

My darling Mother,

I find that London itself, with all its charms, will be unable to seduce me from my present virtuous resolutions. I work as hard as a Scaliger all the mornings; and a dinner now and then with Lady Donegal or Mrs. Tighe is the utmost excess I allow myself to indulge in. I have often thought, and what I feel now confirms me in it, that I never was in such even spirits, as when employed to some purpose of utility. I don't know though that even the worldly necessity I am under of doing something would be sufficient to urge me so industriously, if I were not impelled by my anxiety to get to Ireland; and, please Heaven! about six weeks hence will, I think, see me on my way thither.

'Tis a long time since I have heard from you. The Moiras are just come to town.

[1] The section in brackets is not in Moore's hand, this portion of the letter having been erased and then supplied by someone else.

God bless my dear father and mother, and spare them to their Tom.

I have just finished the epistle to Kate, and have talked politics to her in it.

104. *To his Mother*

Russell, i. 81, no. 3

Sunday [January 1805][1]

I have only this half sheet of paper to write upon, dearest mother, and it will easily hold all the news I have to tell you. I am at this moment in very ill humour with myself for having been seduced into three days' idleness, which has done my health and spirits no harm I confess, but has robbed me of so much profitable addition to my work, and added a little link to the long chain that is between us. However, I shall make up for it without difficulty. I was presented this morning to Mr. Foster, who recollected having known me before, and was civil. I go to his house this evening. Never was anything half so kind or good-natured as dear Lady Donegal. I must tell you a trait of my landlady in Bury Street. A few days before I came here, I happened to ask her about some tailor she knew, saying, at the same time, that I meant to change mine, on account of his not treating me well, in urging me for the *small balance* of a *very large* bill I had paid him. The good woman took that opportunity of telling me that all her money was at her banker's, and would be much better to be employed by me than to lie idle, and that she requested I would make use of any part of it to any amount I might have occasion for. I could not help crying a little at such kindness from a stranger, told her I did not want it, and went and thanked God upon my knees for the many sweet

[1] Russell was evidently incorrect in placing this letter among those written in 1799. He probably based his decision on the 'trait of my landlady in Bury Street' (see the text of the letter), assuming that this was the same incident as that described in the *Memoirs* (Russell, i. 74). The *Memoirs* were written several years after the events related in them, however, and it is possible that Moore remembered the kindness of the lady but forgot the particulars; but since the incidents do differ in details, it is more likely that he is referring to different occasions.

There is no evidence in other letters that Moore lived at the Bury Street address before he sailed for America in October 1803; he took up residence there after his return in November 1804. Mention in this letter of his desire to visit Ireland and of the kindness of Lady Donegal seems to be in keeping with the sentiments expressed in letters Nos. 103 and 105, to his mother, 11 Jan. and 6 Feb. 1805. Thus there appears to be enough evidence to justify an assumption that the letter was written in January 1805, after his return from America.

things of this kind he so continually throws in my way. It is now terribly long since I heard from home. God bless you all. Your own,

Tom

105. *To his Mother*

Russell, i. 179, no. 94

Wednesday, Feb. 6. 1805.

My dearest Mother,

If I were not so occupied, the time would go very heavily that keeps me from you. It is extremely lucky for me that none of my lounging friends are in town, or I should not have half the leisure I now enjoy, nor look forward to so speedy a release from my business. Though it has been a great sacrifice, I am happy that I resolved not to indulge myself with a sight of home till I completed my task, for it gives me a whet of industry which no other object could inspire: still, where are dear Kate's letters? I have just finished an epistle to Lady Donegal: no one deserves such a compliment better; she is the kindest creature in the world.

Poor Mrs. Tighe has had a most dreadful attack of fever, and a very serious struggle for life: her surmounting it gives me great hopes that she has got stamina enough for recovery.

Are you quite well, darling mother? It is long *indeed* since I heard from you; and perhaps you will complain the same of me; but I am such a stout fellow, there is no need for anxiety about me. God bless you all. Your own,

Tom.

106. *To Mary Godfrey*

Russell, i. 179, no. 95

Tuesday [February] 1805.

I write to-day, merely because I *said* I would—(a reason, by the bye, which I have sometimes been perverse enough to let operate in quite a contrary direction), but it is now half past five o'clock, and I have been all the day beating my brains into gold-beater's leaf, wherewith to adorn and bedaub the Honourable Mr. Spencer,[1] and the last sound of the bell-man is now fading most poetically upon my ears, so God bless you! Heaven reward you both for the pleasant feelings and sweet recollections you have given me to

[1] Probably a reference to William Spencer, to whom Moore addressed a poem in the *Epistles, Odes, and Other Poems*. See the Glossary of Proper Names.

enliven my task and my solitude; they are quite a little *Tunbridge lamp*[1] to me, and will throw the softened light of remembrance over everything I shall do or think of. God bless you both again and again. I shall not attempt to tell you the feelings I have brought away with me, but if I have left *one* sentiment behind, of the same family, of the *remotest kin* to those you have given me, I am but too happy. I have not stirred out these two days. The weather is very dreary and 'suits the *scribbling* habit of my soul;'[2] but my fire burns bright, and, we flatter ourselves, so does our poetry; so that between the two, and the sweet, comfortable recollection of my friends at Ramsgate, I contrive to keep both heart and fingers at a proper degree of temperature, just a little below *salamander heat.* Ever your own, and dear Lady Donegal's,

T. M.

107. *To his Mother*

Russell, i. 180, no. 96

Saturday, March 30. 1805.

My darling Mother,

I gave Mrs. Tighe the little glee[3] yesterday to copy and send to Kate. I am sure it will be popular. I should be glad she would show it to Stevenson, to know if there be anything *glaringly* wrong in the harmony. Perhaps the second voice might be improved at the words 'We'll sing at St. Anne's our parting hymn,' but I rather doubt it. I cannot see the postman pass my door every morning without a little bit of a grudge to Kate, that he brings nothing from her to me. I have now 'sighed away Sundays' more than once since I saw any thing from home but my dear good father's letter.

Every one that I ever knew in this big city seems delighted to see me back in it: this is comfortable, and if the flowers strewed before me had a little *gold leaf* on them, I should be the happiest dog in the world. All in good time; but it is strange that people who value the *silk* so much, should not feed the *poor worm* who wastes himself in spinning it out to them. Lady Donegal is the dearest creature in the world. God bless you all. Your own,

Tom.

[1] Lady Donegal and her sister lived part of the year at Tunbridge Wells, where Moore visited them.

[2] Not identified.

[3] 'The Canadian Boat Song', *Poetry*, p. 124.

108. *To Lady Donegal*

Russell, i. 181, no. 97

Tuesday [March or April] 1805.

Another devilment has just come across me that will prevent my leaving town to-morrow: but on the day after, by all that's least brittle and breakable in the world, by women and wine-glasses, love and tobacco-pipes, I'll be with you by the time the coach arrives, most *punctually:* now pray, believe me this once: besides, I'll tell you what, or (as Lord Grizzle says), 'shall I tell you what I am going to say?'[1] General Phipps has made a dinner for me, to meet George Colman in the beginning of next week: now, by stopping in town to-morrow, I shall open a little loophole of escape for myself, and so get off the necessity of returning to town so soon as I otherwise should do. I own I am a little terrified by Rogers's account of your multitudinous company-keeping at Tunbridge, but I hope you are quieter than he represents you. I like Rogers better every time I see him. Yours on Thursday, and always,

T. Moore.

109. *To George Thomson*

B.M. Add. MS. 35263, f. 265

Donington Park
Tuesday Night* [16 July 1805][2]

Sir.

I feel very much flattered by the application with which you have honored me,[3] and the idea of being associated in any manner with Haydn[4] is too tempting to my vanity to be easily resisted—At

[1] A character in Fielding's *Tom Thumb*. The quotation occurs in Act I. iii. 20. The line does not appear in the early editions of the play (1730, 1731, 1737, 1751, 1776), but it is to be found in some texts based on acting versions. See, for example, *The Modern British Drama: Operas and Farces* (London: printed for William Miller, Albemarle Street, 1811), v. 54.

[2] Hadden gives this as the date, although the original in the British Museum is undated.

[3] Thomson wrote to Moore in May 1805, asking him to supply words for a trio of Welsh airs. Although Moore promised several times to supply the lyrics (see letters Nos. 129 and 131, to Thomson, 11 July and 6 Aug. 1806), they were never produced. Burns wrote for Thomson from 1792 to 1796. For a good account of correspondence with Moore and others see J. Cuthbert Hadden, *George Thomson, the Friend of Burns: His Life and Correspondence* (London, 1898).

[4] Some of the airs were harmonized by Joseph Haydn.

present however I am so strictly pledged not to divert one moment from the poems I am engaged in, that I fear, if you require the songs immediately, I can hardly bestow on them all the attention I should wish—but if your publication is not very urgent, I know of nothing that would give me more sincere[1] pleasure than to contribute the humble efforts of which I am capable to a work so elegant & interesting as that which you are employed in—

Pray, let me know the *longest* time you can afford me, and I shall then be able to answer you more satisfactorily on the subject.

I have tried the airs you were so good as to send, and like the two first extremely—the last, to my taste, is not nearly so pretty; but perhaps it will improve on repetition.

The cordiality with which you praise the young trifles I have published is of course very grateful to me, far as I am from agreeing with you in the opinion you so flatteringly express of them—

I have the honour to be,
Sir
Y[r] very obliged and humble Serv[t]
Thomas Moore

To M[r] G. Thompson [*sic*]

110. *To his Mother*

Russell, i. 183, no. 99

Saturday, Aug. 17. 1805.

My dearest Mother,

Kate's letter has given me a vast deal of pleasure, as it shows me how comfortably you coalesce with my dear uncle's family. Tom Hume goes off at last to-morrow: he has endeavoured to *reason* me into going with him; but when I can resist the *true feelings* that impel me to it, the *false reasons* he brings for such a step have been easily resisted; and *false* they are, for I am bound, not only by *agreement* but by *honour* to Carpenter, to finish this work[2] without any unnecessary delay, and as long as he has the slightest objection, I should consider myself trifling with *both* if I interrupted it. I am getting on very nicely, and I know my darling mother sacrifices with willingness a little present gratification to the pleasure of seeing me with a mind unburdened by any sense of duty unperformed—don't you, dearest mother? Pray let me know in some of your letters what yourself, Kate, and Ellen, are chiefly

[1] Hadden (p. 194) inserts '[genuine]' here and notes, 'Word torn away here by the seal'. The present editor had no difficulty in reading the text as given.

[2] *Epistles, Odes, and Other Poems,* which Carpenter published in 1806.

in want of in the useful way: I should not like to take you any unnecessary baubles, but wish to turn my *galanteries* to account: you must not be delicate in telling me, for I shall not be so in saying whether I can compass what you want. God bless you. Ever your own,

Tom.

111. *To his Mother*

Russell, i. 184, no. 100

Thursday, Aug. 22. 1805.

My dearest Mother,

I think I shall on Monday go for a couple of days to Tunbridge again: these little trips are of service to me, though, indeed, I am now quite stout and well. I am quite happy at having corresponded with my darling father's wishes in retaining my situation at Bermuda. I have no doubt that it will turn out something to me: the men I have appointed are of the most respectable in the island;[1] and I shall get a friend of mine to write to the new governor, and beg him to have an eye to my little interests in that part of the world. Heaven bless all. Poor Mrs. T.[2] is ordered to the Madeiras, which makes me despair of her; for she *will not* go, and another *winter* will inevitably be her death. Your own,

Tom.

112. *To Viscount Percy Strangford*

De Fonblanque, *Lives of the Lords Strangford* (London, 1877), p. 111

[September 1805]

I am sorry to find that you are not employed in anything better than cyphers and dispatches; though why should I say sorry when there is nothing in the world I pant for so much as release from all drudgery of fancy—this slavery of imagination I am bound to?[3] My dear fellow, you are happy! If it was even Father Barbosa's works you were obliged to translate from morning till night, I would do it with delight for such a respectable exemption from literature as you enjoy. I am so weary, so subdued, with my 'primrose path' of nonsense, that I would rather scribble anything now than poetry, and I look at a desk in Threadneedle Street with a more wistful eye than I would at Ariosto's inkstand.

[1] The reference to 'the men I have appointed' is not clear. Moore appointed as his deputy in Bermuda a nephew of the Sheddons, merchants in Bedford Square. (See letter No. 81, to his mother, 19 Jan. 1804.)

[2] Mrs. Tighe.

[3] Moore was at work on *Epistles, Odes, and Other Poems* (1806).

113. *To his Mother*

Russell, i. 185, no. 102

Nov. 2. 1805.

My dearest Mother,

It is now near six o'clock, and I have hardly time to say How d'ye do? I have been sitting this hour past with Lady Harrington: she is very kind to me, and says the more and oftener she sees me in Ireland, the better.

The whole town mourns with justice the death of Nelson:[1] those two men (Buonaparte and he) divided the world between them—the land and the water. We have lost ours.

I got my dear father's letter, and forgive Tom Hume for the many kind affectionate things my charge has produced from you [*sic*]. Your own,

Tom.

114. *To his Mother*

Russell, i. 186, no. 103

Nov. 8. 1805.

My dearest Mother,

This weather is only fit for poets, lovers, and murderers: there is hardly light enough to pursue any other calling. It is now but four o'clock, and I can scarcely see to write a line. I am just going to dine third to Rogers and Cumberland: a good poetical step-ladder we make—the former is past forty and the latter past seventy.

I wish I could hope to dance at Eliza A.'s ball. I have not capered much since I left Bermuda; though I forget myself—at Tunbridge, my toe had a few fantastic sallies. God bless you all, dears, and good friends. Your own,

Tom.

They say now Lord Powis is going as lord lieutenant.[2] I don't know him at all.

115. *To his Mother*

Russell, i. 187, no. 104

Donington
Monday [November, 1805?]

My dearest Mother,

* * * I was at a beautiful little fête champêtre at Mrs. Siddons's cottage on Saturday evening: it was the most fairy scene I ever

[1] Nelson was killed at the Battle of Trafalgar on 21 Oct. 1805.

[2] Moore evidently meant that Lord Powis was to be made Lord Lieutenant of Ireland. He did not receive the appointment.

witnessed; and even the duchesses and countesses looked romantic in the illuminated walks. Bless you, darling mother. Ever your own,

Tom.

116. *To J. McMahon*

Rice University

Aungier Street*
Monday* [*c.* 1805][1]

My dear Sir— I feel quite unhappy at not having had an opportunity of paying my respects to you in the country, and I trust you have not so far lost your former good-opinion of me as to think that I am ungrateful or forgetful of your Kindnesses to me— Mrs McMahon too I have never ceased to remember with the warmest gratitude— If I could know where your head-quarters are when you come into town, I should contrive to meet you some day—pray, let me know—

Carpenter charged me with many good-wishes for you & the promptitude of your offer to stand bail for him gave him the most sincere pleasure & gratitude— Believe me with best regards to Mrs Mac.

Your very attached friend
Thomas Moore.

117. *To Matthew Gregory Lewis*

Harvard College Library

[*c.* 1805]

My dear Lewis— I hope the Postman knows some better way of getting into your house than I could find out, for I have been twice in Gerrard St, and given each time as many knocks as there are Muses without [*sic*] about as many curses as there are Graces—but they would not let me in— By the same token, your door is a green one & has a Lion's head upon it & is nearly opposite Nassau St—all which I tell to remove the suspicion from your mind of my being a Diplomatist—

Ever yours
T. Moore

Where is Psyche? I begin to tremble about her.[2]

[1] Watermark 1805.

[2] Mrs. Tighe.

118. *To his Mother*

Russell, i. 187, no. 105

Wednesday, Jan. 22. 1806.

Dearest Mother,

The town has been a good deal agitated to-day by various reports about Mr. Pitt's death.[1] It still seems uncertain; but every one appears to agree that he cannot live. What a strange concurrence of circumstances we have witnessed within this short period. Something bright, I hope, will rise out of the chaos; and if a gleam or two of the brightness should fall upon me, why, Heaven be praised for it!

I am quite stout again, but have not yet ventured upon wine. Nothing ever was like the ferment of hope, anxiety, and speculation that agitates the political world at this moment. They say the King will certainly offer the premiership to Addington, but it is strongly expected that Addington will refuse it.

Good by. God bless you all. Your own,

Tom.

119. *To his Mother*

Russell, i. 188, no. 106

Tuesday, Feb. 6. 1806.

My darling Mother,

I am quite in a bewilderment of hope, fear, and anxiety: the very crisis of my fortune is arrived. Lord Moira has everything in his power, and my fate now depends upon his sincerity, which I think it profanation to doubt, and Heaven grant he may justify my confidence.[2] Tierney goes to Ireland,[3] so *there* a hope opens for dear father's advancement. In short, everything promises brilliantly; light breaks in on all sides, and Fortune looks most smilingly on me. 'If that I prove her haggard,'[4] no hermit or misanthrope has ever fled further or more heartily from the commerce of mankind than I shall from the patronage of grandees. But this sounds like doubt of Lord Moira, which I hate myself for feeling. I have not seen him yet, nor do I expect it for some days; but the instant anything turns out one way or other, you shall know it.

[1] William Pitt died on 23 Jan. 1806.

[2] In 1805 Lord Moira was made Master General of Ordnance. Moore's hopes for a government appointment were not fulfilled at this time, however. Lord Moira was at first vague and later offered him a small position, which Moore declined. (See letter No. 124, to his mother, 8 May 1806.)

[3] Tierney was appointed President of the Board of Control in 1806.

[4] *Othello*, III. iii. 260.

God bless us all, and turn this dawn of our hopes into full daylight, I pray of him. Your own,

Tom.

120. *To his Mother*

Russell, i. 188, no. 107

Thursday, Feb. 8. 1806.

My darling Mother,

I this morning breakfasted with Lord Moira, and have had all my doubts about his remembrance of me most satisfactorily removed: he assured me in the kindest manner that he had not for an instant lost sight of me; that he had been a good deal burdened by the friends of others (alluding to the Prince); but that he still had a very extensive patronage, and would certainly not forget me. What gave me most pleasure of all, and what I am sure will gratify *you*, dearest mother, is his saying that he could *now* give me a situation immediately, but that it would require residence abroad, and he added, 'We must not banish you to a foreign garrison.' I answered, 'that, as to occupations, I was ready to undertake any kind of business whatever.'— 'Yes,' says he; 'but we must find that business *at home* for you.' I deferred writing till to-day that I might have this interview to communicate to you, and I know you will share my satisfaction at it. God bless you, dears. Your own,

Tom.

I have hopes that Tierney will go chancellor of the exchequer to Ireland,[1] which will give me an opportunity of putting in a word for father.

121. *To his Mother*

Russell, i. 189, no. 108

Wednesday, Feb. 14. 1806.

My dearest Mother,

I can hardly trust or listen to the hopes which every one is forcing upon me now from the change that is taking place in administration. Certainly, if Lord Moira comes in, I may look with confidence to something good.[2] He has so often assured me (and particularly once, when he believed he was just about to join the government, and when I could not doubt of his sincerity), that I

[1] See letter No. 119, to his mother, 6 Feb. 1806.
[2] *Ibid.*

cannot let my heart mistrust his interest in my advancement for an instant. Darling mother! think how delightful if I shall be enabled to elevate you all above the struggling exigencies of your present situation, and see you sharing prosperity with me while you are yet young enough to enjoy it. God bless you, dears. A little time will determine the success of my friends, and their goodwill towards me. I am quite stout again. Your own,

Tom.

My best congratulations to dear uncle and aunt on their new relation.

122. *To his Mother*

Russell, i. 190, no. 109

April 30. 1806.

My dearest Mother,

I cannot help now thinking of the poor Negro, who said, when he was going to be hanged, what a hard thing it was for a poor man 'to die and he no sick.' With all the feelings of health about me, and such roses and *even* lilies in my face as there never were there before, I am obliged to lie up again for a week or so, in order to give the *coup de grace* to my maladies; in short, the abscess, though quite well, would not close, and I have within these two hours undergone a little operation for the purpose of closing it, which has given me more pain than I have felt yet, and will confine me for about eight days.[1] It is a good thing to know, however, that, at the end of those eight days, I shall be turned out sound and perfect as I ever have been in my life.

I have received a letter from Mrs. Tighe, and shall answer it when I get off my back.

Now that I have written this letter, I feel almost afraid that you will be fool enough to be alarmed at it; but if you saw my cheeks at this moment, almost bursting with health and cheerfulness, you would even *laugh* at the little pain that I feel. Your own,

Tom.

[1] See letter No. 24, to his mother, 20 Mar. 1800. Moore either had a recurrence of the trouble in his side at this time or the first letter in which he mentions the illness was incorrectly dated 1800 instead of 1806 in Russell's edition. There is not sufficient evidence, however, to justify changing the date in the present edition.

123. *To his Mother*

Russell, i. 191, no. 110

Monday, May 5. 1806.

My dearest Mother,

Here I lie, fat and saucy, eating and drinking most valorously, reading and writing most wisely, but not stirring an inch.[1] On Monday or Tuesday I am to be relieved from this impalement, and after two or three days, which it will take me to heal, I shall be quite well again. Lord Moira sent Lord Rancliffe to me this morning, to ask me to dinner; but of course I can't go.

I am glad to see that the elements are taking the opportunity of my illness (or rather confinement), and are amusing themselves with all sorts of rain, hail, and inclemency; for that makes me hope that they will be able to afford me a little sunshine, when it will please my surgeon to rid me of this *stitch in my side*. In order that you may understand this joke, I must inform you that I have at this moment a large skein of cotton passed through my side in the most seampstress-like manner possible. God bless you all. Best love to dear uncle and aunt. Your own,

Tom.

124. *To his Mother*

Russell, i. 191, no. 111

Thursday, May 8. 1806.

My dearest Mother,

Lord Moira sent Lord Rancliffe to me the other day, to say that he had a small appointment to give away, which I might have till something better offered.[2] I weighed the circumstances well, and considered both the nature of the gift and the advantages it would bring to me: the result of which deliberation was, that I determined to decline the offer. I wrote, however, a very long letter to Lord Moira upon the subject, explaining the reasons of my refusal, and stating the circumstances of my present situation; from all which it appeared to me better to wait till something worthier both of *his* generosity and *my* ambition should occur: at the same time I suggested how much less difficulty there would be in finding some appointment for my dear father, which, while it relieved my mind from one of its greatest causes of anxiety, would make me even much more devoted and grateful to him than any favour conferred

[1] See letter No. 122, to his mother, 30 Apr. 1806.
[2] See letter No. 119, to his mother, 6 Feb. 1806.

on myself. The enclosed note is in answer to my letter; and it gives me much pleasure, as showing me both his approbation of my bold and manly language about myself, and his attention to the solicitude which I expressed about my father. Good by. God bless you all. I believe I shall be let out to-morrow. Your own,

Tom.

125. *To Joyce Codd*

Russell, viii. 39

Wednesday [May 1806][1]

My darling Brother,[2]

This has been a most delicious day, and I have been basking about the streets in great happiness; everything looked so new and so bright to me—the coaches all made of gold and the women of silver; besides, every one was so glad to see me, and I saw one poor man who had been as ill as myself, and we met like two newly-raised bodies on the day of resurrection,—so glad to see each other's bones with a little flesh on them again. I met Mr. Thompson, and he looked at me, but not taking me for myself, he passed on; indeed, he never saw me before without a flannel gown and a sofa. Well, it is a most sweet thing to feel health returning, and if my side but keeps well, and the sun keeps shining, I have some very, very happy weeks before me. I am now in the 8th week of my illness, and this is the first day I have *walked* out, though I have been *twice* with Lady D.[3] in the carriage. I hated coming back to my room and my sofa to-day, but as it was the first time, I could not venture to stay out.

God bless all ours. Tell my dear *uncle* how stout I am getting, and give her dutiful nephew's love to my aunt.

Your own
Tom.

[1] Evidently basing his decision on Moore's first account of his illness in letter No. 24, 20 Mar. 1800, Russell dated this letter simply 'Wednesday, 1800'. Moore's remarks about taking his first walk after the long illness, however, indicate that it was probably written in May 1806. See letters Nos. 122, 123, and 124, to his mother, 30 Apr., 5 May, and 8 May 1806.

[2] His uncle by the mother's side, whom he called by the name of brother [Russell's note].

[3] Lady Donegal.

126. *To his Mother*

Russell, i. 192, no. 112

Monday, May, 1806.

My dearest Mother,

I missed one letter this last week, for which I cry '*peccavi;*' but I enclose something now to you, which will, I think, make you feel very happy; and I hope that, by the time this reaches you, Atkinson will be returned and at hand to arrange every thing about my father's appointment.[1] You must not say a word to any one about this promise of Fox's, as it would be wrong on many accounts.

I believe I told you the kind things the Prince said to me about my book.[2]

I feel uncommon spirits, which I hope every thing will justify me in. All around me looks bright and promising, and the respectability of the situation they intend for me flatters my hopes most delightfully.

God bless you all. Best love to dear uncle and aunt. You may tell *them* of Fox's promise. Your own,

Tom.

Why does not saucy Kate write to me about my book?

127. *To J. Taylor*

Morgan Library

Scotland Yard, Whitehall
June 4. 1806.

Dear Sir,

I thank you for the present of the Parody, which appears to me to have much merit, & if you think the time & circumstances are not too materially changed, might be printed in your proposed miscellany. But you are the best judge.— Perhaps any composition which holds up Jacobins to contempt & ridicule, if it is good, should be preserved. I hope such times will not recur; but it is best to be prepared against them.— I am, &c. &c.

Y^rs most
faithfully
T. M.

[1] Lord Moira secured John Moore's appointment as Barrack-master of Island Bridge in Dublin. See the letter from Lord Moira to Moore, Russell, i. 193.

[2] *Epistles, Odes, and Other Poems.*

128. *To his Mother*

Russell, i. 193, no. 114

Wednesday [June] 1806.

My dearest Mother,

I have seen Lord Moira, and presented him my father's thanks.[1] He told me, that it is one of the *Irish* commissionerships I am to have, and that these will not be arranged till those in England are settled. He spoke with the utmost kindness to me; and I am sure, when he has it in his power, I need not doubt his good-will to serve me. He said, at the same time, that there was nothing to prevent my visiting Ireland, as he should not forget me; so that, I think, in about a fortnight I shall take flight for the bogs. Darling mother! how happy I shall be to see you!—it will put a new spur on the heel of my heart, which will make life trot, for the time at least, sixteen miles an hour. I trust in Heaven that you are recovering, and that I shall find you as you ought to be. Ever your own,

Tom.

Love to uncle and aunt.

129. *To George Thomson*

B.M. Add. MS. 35263, f. 270

Bury St., St. James
Wednesday 11th July*[2] [postmark 1806]

My dear Sir— I feel quite ashamed at my not having, long before this, acknowledged the kindness of your very elegant present— I was already well acquainted with the work, but did not possess it among my collection—

I have been so unfortunate as to lose the airs which you sent me to Donington Park, and I need not tell you how very imperfectly one could expect to write words upon the mere skeleton of metre which you have given me, without knowing & feeling the spirit of the music to which they are to be wedded—it would be like those distant, diplomatic courtships to which poor Princes and Princesses are doomed—[3] Have the goodness to let me see copies of the airs again, & I shall endeavour to put the best of my humble powers in requisition for them—

[1] See letter No. 126, to his mother, May 1806.

[2] Hadden (p. 196) dates this letter 16 July. 11 July appears to be the correct date.

[3] See letter No. 109, to George Thomson, 16 July 1805.

You may send them under cover to *Mr Stokes* (without directing them to me) and let that be again in another envelope directed to *William Fawkener Esqr &c. &c. Whitehall*— And now, I shall beg of you to do me a favour through the same channel— The Edinburgh Review will be published by the time you receive this, and if you will immediately forward me a Copy of it under the covers I have mentioned, you will do me a kindness which I shall feel very grateful for— I am obliged to leave London for Ireland about the latter end of next week, and wish to see what your secret Tribunal says of me before I go—

I have not time to read what I have written, but hope you will be able to make it out & that you will do me the honour to believe me

Very truly yours
Thomas Moore

130. *To Mary Godfrey*

Russell, i. 194, no. 115

Wednesday, July, 1806.

I certainly may say to *you* as Cowper says to one of his correspondents, that 'you understand trap,' for nothing was ever more skilfully anticipated than the scolding which you know you deserved from me, and which you were resolved to be beforehand with. Sheridan himself could not manage an impeachment against money-defaulters with a more unblushing brow of innocence, than you have assumed in charging me with neglect; after your having remained a fortnight at Worthing, with nothing on your hands but your gloves, and nothing to distract you but Chichester, and yet, during that whole time, not feeling *one twitch* of the pen (a disorder too that I know you to be at other times so subject to), nor thinking it necessary to bestow one moment of your idleness upon the 'poor forsaken *gander*' whom you left *hissing hot* upon the pavement of London, with a pain in his side and the wind-colic in his heart, with the dust in his eyes and the devil in his purse, and in short with every malady, physical, pthisical, and quizzical, that could shake the nerves of a gentleman, or excite the compassion of a lady; and there are you, between *sunbeams* and *mists*, between *Ossians* and *Chichesters*, taking a whole fortnight to consider of it, before you would even say, 'How are you now, sir?' Well—I forgive you, though I cannot help thinking it the very refinement of Irish modesty, the very quintessence of the bogs, to follow up such delinquency with an attack instead of an apology; it is like Voltaire's Huron, who, when they send him to confession, seizes the unfortunate priest, whirls him out of his sentry-box, and forcing him down upon his knees, says, 'Now, you must confess to me!'[1] * * *

Now as to *Worthing*, when *am* I to visit you? I *solemnly and assuredly* hope to leave London for Ireland *about the latter end of next week, or the beginning of the following one*. Lord Moira has told me that my absence will not interfere with anything that he has in prospect for me; that the commissionership intended for me is to be in Ireland; and that, *if there are any such appointments*, I am to have one of them.[2] Such are my plans, and such my hopes. I wait but for the arrival of the Edinburgh Review, and then 'a long farewell to all my greatness.'[3] London shall never see me act the farce of gentlemanship in it any more, and, 'like a bright exhalation in the evening,'[4] I shall vanish and be forgotten. Say how and when I am to go to you. Ever yours,

T. M.

On Saturday, if you have got to Worthing, I think I shall be able to go down to you: this at least imposes upon you the task of writing to me to-morrow to let me know.

131. *To George Thomson*

B.M. ADD. MS. 35263, f. 274

27 Bury St., St. James's
Wednesday* [6 August 1806]

Dear Sir— I received the airs which you sent me & shall have much pleasure in writing words to them, though I confess I could have wished you had selected some prettier[5] melodies for me—the last air of the three appears to me particularly flippant and uninteresting—[6] I must say however that as yet I have played them but *once*, so that perhaps I may like them better when I have become more intimate with them— I have received the Review and cannot tell at present whether I am indebted to *you* for sending it, as it was

[1] Voltaire, *L'Ingénu, Histoire véritable* in *Œuvres Complètes* (Paris, 1826), lx. 21.

[2] See letter No. 128, to his mother, June 1806.

[3] *King Henry VIII*, III. ii. 351. Moore was anxiously awaiting the review of his *Epistles, Odes, and Other Poems* (see letter No. 131, to George Thomson, 6 Aug. 1806).

[4] *King Henry VIII*, III. ii. 226.

[5] Hadden inserts '[—more attractive]' and notes, 'Part of the letter torn away by the seal'. The present editor had no difficulty in reading the text as given.

[6] See letter No. 129, to George Thomson, 11 July 1806.

forwarded to me to the country & I have not asked my bookseller whether it was a copy inclosed by you or the one which he serves me regularly— If I am in your debt however, I have some hopes of being able to repay you *in person*, as I think it likely I shall soon visit Edinburgh— I was agreeably disappointed by the article on my Volume of Poems—there is all the *malignity* which I expected, but not half the *sting*, and I hope I shall always be lucky enough to have such dull, prosing antagonists—[1] Will it be too much trouble for you to answer me a question by return of Post?—does Mr *Jeffrey* (one of the persons concerned in the Review) reside in Edinburgh, and is he there at present?—you see I make you pay very dear for the nonsense which I intend to write to your music, but I trust you will excuse the liberty which I take & believe me

Yours &c
Thomas Moore

132. *To Viscount Percy Strangford*

De Fonblanque, *Lives of the Lords Strangford* (London, 1877), p. 112

[August 1806]

My dear Strangford,

I have owed you a letter for a long time, and now that I do write, it will perhaps be for the last time. I have thought it proper to call out Mr. Jeffrey, who has been so long abusing you and me, and we are to fight to-morrow morning at Chalk Farm. . . .[2] The cloth has been but just taken from the table, and though to-morrow may be my last view of the bright sun, I shall (as soon as I have finished this letter), drink to the health of my Strangford with as unaffected a warmth as ever I felt in the wildest days of our fellowship. My dear friend, if they want a biographer when I am gone, I think in your hands I should meet with most kind enbalmment, so pray say something for me, and remember me as one who has felt your good and social qualities, who at this moment recalls with pleasure the days he has passed with you, and who hopes that

[1] Moore's *Epistles, Odes, and Other Poems* was reviewed in the *Edinburgh Review*, viii (July 1806), 456–65. The tone of the article may be discerned from the following quotation: '[Moore] is indebted, we fear, for the celebrity he enjoys to accomplishments of a different description [than "singular sweetness and melody of versification"]; and may boast, if the boast can please him, of being the most licentious of modern versifiers, and the most poetical of those who, in our times, have devoted their talents to the propagation of immorality. We regard his book indeed, as a public nuisance' (p. 456).

[2] See letters Nos. 133 and 134, to Mary Godfrey and Lady Donegal, August 1806.

his good genius to-morrow will allow him to renew them hereafter. So good-bye, and God bless you.

Yours while I live,
T. Moore.

133. *To Mary Godfrey*

Russell, i. 207, no. 116

Monday [August 1806]

I have just time to tell you that this morning I was fool enough (as I know you will call it) to meet Mr. Jeffrey by my own invitation, at Chalk Farm, and that just as we were ready to fire, those official and officious gentlemen, the Bow Street runners appeared from behind a hedge, and frustrated our valorous intentions, so that we are bound over to keep the peace for God knows how long. William Spencer is the cause of this very ill-judged interruption, though he had pledged his honour to keep the matter as secret as the grave.[1] I never can forgive him; for at this moment I would rather have lost a limb than that such a circumstance had happened. And so there is all my fine sentimental letters which I wrote yesterday for posthumous delivery to your sister, you, &c. &c., all gone for nothing, and I made to feel very like a ninny indeed. Good by. I have not yet had time to read your letter. Best love to Lady Donegal and your sister. Ever your

Tom Fool till death.

134. *To Lady Donegal*

Russell, i. 209, no. 117

Tuesday [16 August 1806]

You will see that I am doomed inevitably to one day's ridicule, by the unfortunate falsehood which they have inserted in all the morning papers, about the loading of our pistols; but, of course, a contradiction will appear to-morrow, signed by our seconds, and authorised by the magistrate. This is the only mortifying *suite* that this affair could have, and Heaven knows it has given me

[1] Francis Jeffrey's review of Moore's *Epistles, Odes, and Other Poems* appeared in the *Edinburgh Review* for July 1806. (See letter No. 131 to George Thomson, 6 Aug. 1806.) Moore challenged Jeffrey to a duel, and they met at Chalk Farm early in August. William Spencer, one of the seconds, had either purposely or accidently told of the meeting, which was interrupted by the police. The duelists were taken to the Bow Street prison, where they remained until bail could be arranged by Samuel Rogers. For complete details see Russell, i. 199–207, which is Moore's own account of the affair.

unhappiness enough. Do not scold me, dearest Lady Donegal; if the business was to be again gone through I should feel it my duty to do it; and all the awkwardness that results from it must be attributed to the ill-judged officiousness of the persons who were sent to interrupt us. To be sure, there cannot be a fairer subject for quizzing, than an author and a critic fighting with pellets of paper.[1] God bless you. Tell every one as industriously as you can the falsehood of to-day's statement, and stem, if possible, the tide of ridicule till our contradiction appears. Love to your dear sisters. Ever your attached,

T. M.

135. *To Lady Donegal*

Russell, i. 212, no. 119

Monday, August [17], 1806.

I have the pleasure to tell you that this morning I had a pacific meeting with Mr. Jeffrey at Rogers's, and received from him the most satisfactory apologies for the intemperance of his attack upon me. He acknowledged that it is the opinion, not only of himself but his friends, that the Review contained too much that was exceptionable, and that he is sincerely sorry for having written it. He has given me a statement to this purpose in his own autograph, which concludes thus: 'I shall always hold myself bound to bear testimony to the fairness and spirit with which you have conducted yourself throughout the whole transaction.' Is not this all pleasant? I know you will be glad to hear it. The letter which you will see in to-morrow's Post was a very necessary step, and will put an end

[1] When Moore asked for the pistols after his duel with Jeffrey (see letter No. 133, to Mary Godfrey, August 1806), he was informed by the officer who returned them that no bullet had been found in Jeffrey's weapon. Moore hurried to Horner, Jeffrey's second, who went with him to the Bow Street station, and explained that he had supervised the loading of the pistols and that they were both charged at the time of the meeting. The police were satisfied with this explanation. A statement, signed by the seconds, was to have appeared in the press the following day; but Hume, Moore's second, became frightened of having his name connected with the duel and refused to sign. Moore's own statement denying that any foul play had been intended appeared in the *Morning Post* for 18 Aug. 1806.

When the statement about the duel was sent by the police to the press, one of the editors, whom Moore designated as 'a countryman of my own (named Q——),' changed the word 'bullets' to 'pellets', in which form it was copied by all the other papers.

For Moore's controversy with Byron over the outcome of the duel see letters Nos. 168 and 197, to Lord Byron, 1 Jan. 1810 and 22 Oct. 1811.

to every misconstruction of the affair;[1] so that (for the first time since I took the business into contemplation) I feel 'my bosom's lord sit lightly on his throne,'[2] and the sooner I receive your congratulations upon the subject the better. Ever yours,

T. M.

I have now done with these *bulletins*, and shall write you *letters* hereafter.

136. *To Lady Donegal*

Russell, i. 210, no. 118

Aug. 29. 1806.

I have been looking for a frank (like that best of all thrifty good girls, Miss J* * *), in order to send you back Hayley's letter, which is as pretty a specimen of the old gentleman's twaddling as I could wish to see. But the last person I asked for a frank was Humphrey Butler; and he told me if I had applied before the Union he could have given me one,—which, however satisfactory it was, made me resolve to keep Hayley's letter from you a little longer, and I shall return it the instant I get a cover, and not a soul shall see it, I assure you. Lord Moira has written to me a very kind note, in consequence of my communicating to him the explanations which I had from Jeffrey, and he assures me 'he feels uncommon satisfaction that it has terminated so pleasantly.' If I were just now seated upon the couch, with my legs turned up, I could show you this letter; but, as I am not, I must only give you an extract from it, thus:—'I feel perfectly for you how disagreeable it is to be obliged to start one's self as the butt for all the wild constructions of the public; misrepresentation, in some way or the other, is the inevitable lot of every one who stands in such a predicament; but the squibs against you were only momentary, and a *fair tribute to the spirit with which you vindicated your character will remain*.'[3]

This high Spanish approbation of my conduct has given me much pleasure, as I know it will to you; indeed, nothing can be more gratifying than the generous justice which every friend whose opinion I value has done to my feelings upon this occasion. I was particularly happy to hear that Horner, the other day, at Holland

[1] Moore is referring to the duel with Jeffrey and the public statement published in the *Morning Post* on 18 Aug. See letters Nos. 133 and 134, to Mary Godfrey and Lady Donegal, August 1806.

[2] *Romeo and Juliet*, v. i. 3.

[3] See letter No. 133, to Mary Godfrey, August 1806. See also letter No. 137, to Joseph Atkinson, August or September 1806, where this passage is quoted in a slightly different form.

House, spoke warmly in praise of what he called 'the mixture of feeling and fortitude which my conduct exhibited.'

I met your friend the Duke of York, and the Duke of Cambridge, in a dinner party of eight only the other day at Harry Greville's. In short, I do nothing but *dine;* yesterday at Ward's, to-day at Lord Cowper's, &c. Somebody told me, and made my heart flutter not a little, that you are coming to town before your Tunbridge trip. I believe it was Chichester that '*whispered* the flattering tale,'[1] but I am almost afraid to believe it. I should in that case see you once before I go to bury myself among my St Chrysostoms and Origens,[2] and to shake hands with a dearer father than whole centuries of such fathers. Carpenter is to give me forty pounds for the Sallust,[3] and I wait but for this forty-pounder to discharge me at one single shot to Dublin.

Best love to dear Mary (why shouldn't I call her Mary, as well as that old ridiculous Hermit?), and to sister Philippa, too, a thousand remembrances. Ever yours, most truly,

T. M.

I suppose you have heard of this officious clerk of the Bank's accusation of Lord Moira. I know no more than you have read in the papers.

137. *To Joseph Atkinson*

William Lefanu

Saturday [August or September 1806]

My dearest friend. I am sure you were happy to hear that my affair with Jeffrey has terminated so satisfactorily—[4]his concessions were of the most generous & even friendly kind—he assured me that if he had known the least of the character which I hold among those I live with, he never should have written such an article—confessed that it was exceptionable in many respects, and in short was very sorry it had ever appeared—all this he said to me, and allowed me to mention it to my friends—at the same time he gave me a written declaration, disclaiming all intentions of personality and concluding thus. 'I shall always hold myself bound to

[1] A parody of 'Hope Told the Flattering Tale', a popular song of the early nineteenth century.

[2] By referring to St. Chrysostom (345–407) and Origen (185–254), two Greek fathers of the Church and early Christian theologians, Moore indicates that he is going to visit predominantly Catholic Ireland.

[3] Moore wrote a prefatory life of Sallust for Arthur Murphy's translation of Sallust's works, which Carpenter published in 1807.

[4] See letter No. 133, to Mary Godfrey, August 1806.

bear testimony to the fairness & spirit with which you have conducted yourself throughout the whole transaction'— This tribute of praise with which he has honoured *my* conduct, I can pay back with interest to *his own*—he is a most excellent, gentlemanlike fellow—pray, mention all this to everyone—particularly to Forbes & Tom Sheridan, both of whom, I think, know Jeffrey—Lord Moira has been kind enough to write me a letter on the subject, and concludes it thus— 'The squibs against you were only momentary, while a fair tribute to the spirit with which you vindicated your character will remain'— In short, whatever service or injury the affair may do me in the gross world's eyes, the *âmes choisies* among whom I live do me the most flattering justice throughout it all— I dare say there is misrepresentation enough in Ireland—but I beg you will disseminate as much as possible the explanation which Jeffrey has made me & the high opinion of his manliness with which he has sincerely inspired me.

[I dare say you have heard these stinging stories about one noble & admirable friend but the whole world does me the justice to reject all belief of it for an instant— In his letter to me I believe he spoke *feelingly* when he said 'I feel for you how disagreeable it is to start oneself as the [*illegible*] for the wild constrictions of the Public misrepresentation in some way or other is the inevitable lot of every one that stands on such a predicament'— This is all of course private.][1] I hope to be free from my *jobs* in about *ten days* at the farthest, and happy shall I be, Heaven knows! to find myself once more among a few who love me— Few, very few I know they are in Ireland— I dine with Ward to-day for the second time this week— He & I were on a visit for a few days to Putney, and I slept in the room where Pitt died—

Next week I go for two or three days to Brocket-Hall, Lord Melbourne's, the most récherché house in all the fashionable world, & the most difficult of access.

Love to all—what a
hasty, gossiping scribble!
Every your own
T. M.

[1] The section in brackets is an interlineation by another hand. Moore's script was almost totally erased and is illegible. For a reference to the attack on Lord Moira see letter No. 136, to Lady Donegal, 29 Aug. 1806, where the passage from Moira's letter is quoted in a slightly different form.

138. *To Mary Godfrey*

Russell, viii. 59

Remston, Leicestershire
Sept. 20. 1806.

'Thus far into the bowels of the land have I marched on without impediment.'[1] I know you will say I am an odd fellow, and as long as you say no worse of me, I shall be contented. Why didn't I write all the last fortnight that I have been *Septembrisé* in town? Why didn't I apprise you that I was about to transport my illustrious carcase hither? And why didn't I—but the only answer I can make to Why didn't I? is Why—I didn't. The fact is, I was neither happy nor comfortable, and I did not like to throw the shade of my mind upon paper for you, though little bodies do not in general cast great shadows; yet you cannot imagine what an eclipse I spread around me whenever my orb becomes opaque with sorrow, or that the light of the heart does not shine pleasantly through me; and this has been the case all this fortnight past. I have had every possible *colour* of annoyance,—*brown* study, *blue* devils, not forgetting '*green* and *yellow* melancholy'[2]—in short, I have been a 'rainbow ruffian' (as some sentimental poet styles a well-dressed soldier), and my *reflections* on paper would have been all of the prismatic kind. 'Oh, this learning! what a thing it is!'[3] But to come to the plain matter-of-fact (which, you know, I love as well as I do roast mutton), I was fidgetted and teased by my impatience to get away from London, and by the impossibility from day to day of accomplishing it for want of those *paper-wings* which are so necessary to the *flights* of even poets themselves. I have, however, contrived to fly thus far; and oh! that I had the wings of a *Lottery Pigeon*, that I might flee away and be in Dublin. I hope in two or three days to manage this. I came down here in a new carriage of Rancliffe's, with his German servant to frank me along ('base is the slave who pays'),[4] and the title of 'My Lord' lavished on me all the way; not without some little surprise that his Lordship had *grown* So much of late. I was unfortunate enough to be just in time for the Leicester Races, where I went with '*burning* eyes of love'[5] after my long night's travel, and figured away at the ball in the evening to the

[1] *King Richard III*, v. ii. 3.
[2] *Twelfth Night*, II. iv. 114.
[3] *The Taming of the Shrew*, I. ii. 163.
[4] *King Henry V*, II, Chorus, 100.
[5] A figure of speech used several times in his poetry. See, for example, *Poetry*, p. 59 ('The Ring') and p. 83 ('Hymn to Love').

tune of Paddy O'Rafferty[1] till three or four o'clock. The Duchess of Rutland was there. Think of her dining *in ordinary* with about two hundred Leicestershire *racers* and *graziers*, in their boots just fresh off the race-ground, staring at her with all their eyes and mouths. She did the honours in a most *queenish* style; and I asked one of these turf gentlemen whether he did not think she was a fine '*Monarch Mare*.' Now this is a joke even still more distant from your comprehension than jokes in general, because it is a familiar designation among sportsmen for the female descendants of a certain famous gentleman whom they call *Monarch*; and I assure you that it had all the 'jest's prosperity' among the black-legs.

Best love to Lady Donegal: direct your next letters under cover to Edward Connor, Esq., War Office, Dublin Castle. Yours,

T. M.

139. *To Lady Donegal*

Russell, viii. 62

Dec. 4. 1806.

I have often said that correspondence between friends should be like the flow of notes in music,—if too long an interval is allowed to take place between the tones, one loses the *chain* of song, the idea of melody is interrupted, and we listen to the sounding note (when it comes) with faint, or at least diminished, gratification. Is it not exactly so with letters? But all I can say is, that it was *you* who taught me this bad practice; and that if I had not found you so slow to *answer*, I never could have become so slow to *write*. *Action* and *reaction* is as much a law of friendship as it is of nature; and it is but too natural for my writing to cease in proportion as it finds your *answering* so tardy. This causation, I know, includes us both: but I call all the gods to witness that yours is the greatest share of the guilt; and if you will but show promptitude in answering this letter, you will find me as true a hero as ever *exchanged paper* with an antagonist. Dublin has at length become gay; but it is a kind of *conscript* gaiety, in which the people assemble with all the ill-grace of French *volontaires forcés*. There is nothing, however, but dinners,—daily, dull, d—n—ble dinners; and I have time to do little more than 'faire le saut de l'Allemand, du lit à la table et de la table au lit.' The Bedfords have been very civil to me, and have had me to dinner and at private parties with them. The Harringtons, too, are gracious, but it is 'leather and prunella.'[2] My heart

[1] Moore's 'Drink of This Cup' (*Poetry*, p. 218) was written for the Irish air 'Paddy O'Rafferty'.

[2] *Essay on Man*, iv. 203.

is sick of them all, and I see nothing for me but to become either one of Bonaparte's King-lets, or enlist among Sir Francis Burdett's bludgeon-men. Any little hopes I have had of advancement are gone. Among the great, both in England and Ireland, there is nothing now left but pride, self-interest, and, I think, a fatal insufficiency, whose day of trial seems to be near, and whose fate may be too much what it deserves. The country parts of Ireland are in a most disturbed state. Under the name of *Threshers*, the United Irishmen are again organising; and the prophecy-mongers tell us that Bonaparte is the Grand Thresher, who is described as coming to 'thresh the nations.' Certainly no one ever performed a mission more completely. Our Judges are going down, under strong escorts, to these disturbed parts of the country; but Judges are not the people to send against *Threshers*. In short, the lightning is flashing in our eyes, and some people will not see it; the thunder is rolling in our ears, and some people will not hear it. But the bolt will fall, and then (as young Rousseau said, going to bed without his supper) 'Good bye, roast beef!'[1]

I was delighted to see that our friend General Spencer has got a regiment. But where is he? I have seen no account of that expedition since I left London.

It goes to my heart to think that it will be so long before I meet you again, and that you will be caring less and less for me every day of that time. I know your opinion about absence, and I dread so much that you speak from feeling and from practice! I have sometimes indeed, in my own case, found my stock of recollections nearly exhausted, and then I confess that the eyes of the object were the only warehouse where I could lay in a new store, genuine and fresh; but these were recollections meant merely for light 'summer wear,' and not even expected to last. I shall hope, however, that ours is of a different texture, and that even if it does diminish, the wear of it, like that of gold, will be so slow and insensible, as not to make us feel any loss in its value. I shall go to Donnington village when I leave this, and there bury myself, as I have no idea any longer of letting my light shine, like the sun in the Zodiac, for the *illumination* of *monsters*.

Pray give my best remembrances to your sisters. Tell Miss Godfrey that if she would not stand upon the ceremony of hearing

[1] When ordered to bed without his supper as a punishment for mischief-making, the young Rousseau bade each member of the company good night and then bowed politely to a roast turning on the spit, saying, 'Good night, roast beef'. As a reward for his sally he was allowed to stay and eat with the others. See *The Confessions of Jean Jacques Rousseau* (New York: Random House, n.d.), p. 31.

from me by this post, and write immediately, it would give me a very high opinion of her benevolence. I shall fire a letter at her to-morrow or next day. But this day I happened to dine at home, and, behold, you have the fruits of it.

'Tis now ten at night, and my brains give no light,
And the Postman rings ding-dong.[1]

So good bye. Believe me,
Yours very cordially,
Thomas Moore.

Atkinson, to whom I have sent this to be franked (too late) begs his most cordial remembrances, and hopes that he is not forgotten by your Ladyship.

140. *To Mary Godfrey*

Russell, viii. 61

Dublin
[December] 1806.

I hope Lady Donegal received the letter which I wrote to her on my arrival here,[2] though I think if she had, she would have been honest enough to have repaid it before now; and *I* should not have delayed so long answering your *very dear* letter, if I had not been for these five or six days laid up in my old way on the sofa, not so much with illness as with the dread of illness. I had two or three broad hints from my side that it intended to recommence operations; so, without waiting for the attack, I adopted that 'stirring little man, Bonaparte's' system, and marched an army of leeches over it immediately; a little hostile blood has been spilt, and everything, I am happy to say, seems restored to its former tranquility. You cannot imagine how desperately vulgar and dreary this place is! I have not even Mrs. Tighe to comfort me, but I expect she will be in town in a week or two. I regret very much to find that she is becoming so 'furieusement littéraire:' one used hardly to get a peep at her blue stockings, but now I am afraid she shows them up to the knee: however, I shall decide for myself when I see her, as certainly this city, among the other features of a country town which it has acquired, has not forgotten that unfailing characteristic, *scandal*. If it were not for my own dears immediately about me, and the old books of Tanaquil Faber in St. Patrick's Library, I should die the death of the desperate here. I have been received

[1] Not identified.

[2] See letter No. 139, to Lady Donegal, 4 Dec. 1806.

certainly with every possible mark of attention: most of the men of situation have left their cards with me, and, amongst the rest, the new Provost of the University, who as being the depositary of the morals of the country, and personally a very High Priest into the bargain, gave me more pleasure by his visit than any of them. The Harringtons have asked me two or three times to dinner; and this very day I was to have been presented at a private audience to the Duke of Bedford, but he has not come to town on account of illness I believe, and it will not take place till to-morrow. All these things, to be sure, are merely *feathers in the cap*, but they are feathers I like to shake in the eyes of some envious people here amazingly. I entreat of you to write often to me. Your last letter was like summer sunshine to me—not only bright but warm, not only luminous but comfortable. That blessed ingredient, *affection*, which would sweeten the homeliest draught, comes doubly sweet in the Falernian you sent me, and I beg of you to repeat the dose as often as possible.

Best love to Lady Donegal and your sister Philippa.

Ever yours,

T. M.

141. *To the Earl of Moira*

Huntington Library

52 Aungier St.*

Friday* [January 1807]

My Lord— I should suppose that it is as *pleasant* to your Lordship to be asked for what you *can* give as I know it is *painful* to you to be solicited for what you can*not*, and the request which I now take the liberty of making, I should hope comes under the former description— The situation which your Lordship's goodness has procured for my dear Father is now his only means of subsistence, as the attention which it requires renders it utterly impossible for him to undertake any other pursuit, and if there were some little accommodations allowed him, which I believe are generally attached to his situation, he could support his family on it and supply their humble wants very comfortably—[1] *A House* is the great object to which he looks, and a few words from your Lordship would be so effectual in procuring him that convenience, that I have no hesitation in begging you to interpose them for him—if this were once done, I should consider my dear family so safely

[1] Lord Moira, who was at this time Master General of Ordnance, had arranged for John Moore to be appointed Barrack-Master of Island Bridge, Dublin.

provided for (at least while my father lives) that my heart should feel no further wish nor my tongue breathe one further prayer—

And now, my Lord, for the last time to mention myself to your Lordship—I have begged of Dalby to procure me a little lodging in the village of Donnington,[1] to which I shall retire as soon as my visit in Ireland is over, and what I have to entreat is that your Lordship will allow me (in case Dalby should feel any difficulty in procuring me a lodging) to go to the Park till I can settle myself in the Village— It would be worse than imprudent, it would be *dishonest* of me to return to the same mode of life which I have hitherto pursued in London, & my literary exertions will be completely adequate not only to my support in the country but to my releasement (I should hope) from all the difficulties I have involved myself in— Do not, my Lord, suppose that this is the language of despondency— Your Lordship has already by what you have done for my father, lightened my heart of its only burthen, and if you can but facilitate for him what I now request, you will leave me *nothing* to feel towards you but the very fullness of gratitude & satisfaction, nor shall I ever again from this moment obtrude one word about myself upon your attention.

I have the honour to be your Lordship's very obliged & devoted Servant

Thomas Moore.

Mr Tierney has answered my letter of congratulation civilly—

To

the Earl of Moira

142. *To John Dalby*

Mrs. Mercia Dalby

Monday Febr 2nd 1807*

My dear Dalby—Though you would not answer my letter about the portmanteaus, yet I flatter myself you will feel some pleasure in satisfying me upon the subject I now trouble you with— In about a fortnight I [*MS. cut*] be able to leave Dublin, and Donington is

[1] See letter No. 142, to John Dalby, 2 Feb. 1807. Moore made the same request of Dalby five years later (see letter No. 220, to John Dalby, 10 Mar. 1812). Since this letter and No. 220 are undated, there is a possibility that an error has been made in assigning dates and that Moore asked the favour only once. This letter bears an 1805 watermark, however, and reference to the 'situation' which Moira procured for Moore's father and the fact that the letter was written from Dublin indicate that the date was early in 1807. The letter to Dalby (No. 220) has a Bury Street return address, and other letters written at that time refer to Moore's request. One can only conclude that he asked his friend on two occasions for assistance in finding a house.

once more [*MS. cut*] my 'verum secretumque μȣσειον'— Lord Moira has given me permission to make it my abode as long as I like, and that will now be for a considerable time, I assure you—[1] What I wish of you, is to apprize the servants of my intention and to find out for me what is the present state of the establishment— I believe my old friend Mrs Briers is gone, which I shall be very sorry for, but I dare say there are still quite enough to make a Poet comfortable, & I shall be most happy once more to bury myself up to the chin in folios, and to *be lost* to the *world* in order to find *myself*— There has been nothing here but stupid racketting ever since I came— The Duke & Duchess of Bedford have been very civil to me, and have had me at all their dinners and private parties—but, my dear Dalby, I have learned how to value this glittering, unprofitable kind of life—it is all *winter sunshine, dazzling*, but *cold*; and even its *brightness* ceases to amuse me.

Pray, write to me, as soon as you have informed yourself of the *status quo* for me, and direct under cover to Edward Connor Esqr War Office, Dublin Castle—

I beg my best remembrances to Mrs Dalby and your sister, and am, my dear fellow,

Yours most sincerely

[*Signature cut out*]

I have written the latter part of this letter in my friend Joe Atkinson's office, who sends you his cordial recollections & will be much obliged by your enquiring of Mr Dawson how his *Mules* are— He wrote to Mr D. about them, but received no answer—

143. *To Mary Godfrey*

Russell, i. 217, no. 121

Dublin

Monday, Feb. 23. 1807.

I am quite ashamed of myself—at which you ought to be very much delighted, because it humiliates me most profoundly before you, and gives you ten times more merit in my eyes than I would condescend to allow you if I felt that I had exactly done what I *ought* to do; but, indeed, if you knew the efforts I am obliged to make to throw some sort of *ballast* into the little pleasure-boat of my existence—if you knew how difficult I find it to *square* the gains and losses of *time*, and set off the savings of the morning

[1] See letter No. 141, to the Earl of Moira, January 1807.

against the expenditures of the night, you would not be very hard upon me, but would be very glad to hear that I have contrived to study about three hours and a half every day since I came here. And though I have said every morning, in going to old Patrick's Library, 'Well, I shall return time enough to-day for the post,' yet once I get into that bewildering *seraglio*, what with making real love to one, flirting with some, and merely throwing my eye upon others, the whole day has passed in dalliance, and I have hardly had time enough afterwards to make myself decent for company. I have now, however, bid adieu to this harem, and have made up my mind for a week's idleness before I leave Ireland, which will be, I hope, on Friday or Saturday next, and then once more for Donington, for the Muses, and for *you!*—dear Donington! dear Muses! and dear *you!* Sorry am I to think, however, that both *you* and the *Muses*, however you may visit my thoughts, must be equally *invisible* to me; and I would willingly give up the society of my whole *Nine* just to be, as I could wish, with my *Two* in Davies Street. By my Two here I mean you and your sister Philly, for Lady Donegal has long forgotten me.

I suppose you have been amused a good deal by the reports of my marriage to Miss * * *, the apothecary's daughter. Odds pills and boluses! mix *my* poor Falernian with the sediment of phials and drainings of gallipots! Thirty thousand pounds might, to be sure, *gild* the *pill* a little; but it's no such thing. I have nothing to do with either Sal. Volatile, or Sall * * *; and I don't know *which* would put me into the greatest *purgatory*, *matrimony* or *physic*. The Novice of St. Dominick is bringing out an opera here, for which I am most wickedly pressed to write a prologue; but I shall run from it, and leave Joe to do it.[1]

What you communicated to me about Jeffrey pleases me extremely, because it justifies my conduct most amply, and does honour to both of us.[2] I have written nothing since I came here, except *one song*, which every body says is the best I have ever composed, and I rather prefer it myself to most of them. When am I to sing it to you? Oh! *when, when?* I am an unfortunate rascal, that's certain.

You may direct your answer to this to Donington, and I have

[1] Lady Morgan published the four-volume *Novice of St. Dominick* in 1805. She was encouraged, under Whig patronage, to bring out *The First Attempt*, the opera to which Moore refers. It was produced on 4 Mar. 1807, and ran for several nights. Moore probably meant that he was leaving the task of writing the prologue to Joseph Atkinson.

[2] For an account of the duel with Jeffrey and its settlement see letter No. 133, to Mary Godfrey, August 1806.

full reliance on your being my *sick heart's nurse* while I am there. God bless you. Very much yours,

Thomas Moore.

I would have sailed with *Miss Linwood* the other night, only I was afraid she would give me a *stitch* in my *side!!*

144. *To Sir John Stevenson*[1]

Moore, *Works* (Philadelphia, 1831), p. 316

Leicestershire*
Feb. 1807*[2]

I feel very anxious that a Work of this kind should be undertaken. We have too long neglected the only talent for which our English neighbours ever deigned to allow us any credit. Our National Music has never been properly collected;[3] and while the composers of the Continent have enriched their operas and sonatas with melodies borrowed from Ireland—very often without even the honesty of acknowledgment—we have left these treasures in a great degree unclaimed and fugitive. Thus our airs, like too many of our countrymen, for want of protection at home, have passed into the service of foreigners. But we are come, I hope, to a better period both of politics and music; and how much they are connected, in Ireland at least, appears too plainly in the tone of sorrow and depression which characterises most of our early songs. —The task which you propose to me, of adapting words to these airs, is by no means easy. The poet, who would follow the various sentiments which they express, must feel and understand that rapid fluctuation of spirits, that unaccountable mixture of gloom and levity, which composes the character of my countrymen, and has deeply tinged their music. Even in their liveliest strains we find some melancholy note intrude—some minor third or flat seventh—which throws its shade as it passes, and makes even mirth interesting. If Burns had been an Irishman (and I would willingly give up all our claims upon Ossian for him,) his heart

[1] This extract from Moore's letter to Sir John Stevenson was quoted as part of the 'advertisement' to the first number of the *Irish Melodies*.

[2] The dating of this letter as 'Feb. 1807' caused some difficulty in determining the correct date of the first number of the *Irish Melodies*. Percy H. Muir, 'Thomas Moore's Irish Melodies 1808–1834', *The Colophon*, part xv (September 1933), discusses this question and proves that they were actually published in April 1808.

[3] Moore later added the following note to this comment: 'The writer forgot, when he made this assertion, that the Public are indebted to Mr. Bunting for a valuable collection of Irish Music; and that the patriotic genius of Miss Owenson has been employed upon some of our finest Airs.'

would have been proud of such music, and his genius would have made it immortal.

Another difficulty (which is, however, purely mechanical) arises from the irregular structure of many of those airs, and the lawless kind of metre which it will in consequence be necessary to adapt to them. In these instances the poet must write not to the eye but to the ear; and must be content to have his verses of that description which Cicero mentions, '*Quos si cantu spoliaveris, nuda remanebit oratio.*'[1] That beautiful air, 'The Twisting of the Rope,' which has all the romantic character of the Swiss *Ranz des Vaches*, is one of those wild and sentimental rakes which it will not be very easy to tie down in sober wedlock with poetry. However, notwithstanding all these difficulties, and the very little talent which I can bring to surmount them, the design appears to me so truly national, that I shall feel much pleasure in giving it all the assistance in my power.

145. *To his Mother*

Russell, i. 219, no. 122

Donington Park
Monday night, March, 1807.

My dearest Mother,

I arrived here on Sunday to dinner, after a very pleasant journey, during which Crampton recovered from his trance, and gave us the plots of all the new pantomimes, &c. I parted with him at Birmingham, and gave a sigh towards London as I turned out of the road; but it is all for the better. I am here re-established in *all* my former comforts, and though most of my old friends are gone, yet the two or three that remain know me well enough to be attentive. I was a little dismayed at entering, as the place never before in my time looked half so deserted; but I am quite comfortable now, and shall not stir from this except for Ireland, unless some good star should shine out upon the London road to justify, by golden reasons, my resignation of solitude.

I forgot to bring Bunting's Irish Airs with me;[2] get them from Power; and if any one that you know is coming, they can bring them for me as far as Lichfield, and send them from thence by the coach to Derby. Get Miss Owenson's too;[3] the Atkinsons will give them to Kate for me. Love to all dears. God bless you.

Tom.

[1] Cicero, *Orator*, 183.
[2] Edward Bunting, *General Collection of Ancient Irish Music* (1796).
[3] Sydney Owenson (Lady Morgan), *The Lay of an Irish Harp* (1807).

146. *To his Mother*

Russell, i. 220, no. 123

Donington Park
Thursday, March, 1807.

My darling Mother,

It maketh me marvel much that I do not hear from home; but I suppose Kate is writing such long letters to Anne Scully, that she has not a scrap of paper left to say, 'How d'ye do' on to *me*. I have not heard yet from Mrs. Tighe, but of course you have sent to inquire, and will let me know how she is. The day before yesterday (St. Patrick's) was kept here with great festivity: of course I *bled* freely for the saint; a kind of blood that works more miracles than even St. Januarius's.[1] I am, indeed, quite tranquil and happy here, and shall not feel the least wish to leave it till summer, if I find that I can with any decency remain.

I danced away among the servants on Tuesday night with a pretty lacemaker from the village, most merrily.

Old Cumberland has devoted a page of his Memoirs in the second edition to *me*, which pleases me more than I can tell you.[2] What he says is so cordial, considerate, and respectful, and he holds such a high and veteran rank in literature. God bless you. Yours,

Tom.

147. *To Mary Godfrey*

Russell, i. 220, no. 124

Donington Park, Loughborough
Friday morning, March, 1807.

Though I think you do not care much to know 'my whereabout,' or I should have had a letter here as I petitioned, yet I cannot help telling you that here I am, and here shall be, for God knows how long. I am made very comfortable, and it certainly is friendly of Lord Moira to do me these little kindnesses; but the main point is still wanting: '*Il me donne des manchettes, et je n'ai point de chemise.*'[3] I read much more than I write, and think much more than either; but what does it all signify? The people of Dublin, some of them, seemed very sorry to lose me; but I dare say by this time they

[1] Januarius, Bishop of Benevento, was beheaded about A.D. 305. A cathedral was erected over his grave at Naples, where it is believed that his blood exerts great power in checking the eruptions of Vesuvius.

[2] Richard Cumberland, *Memoirs of Richard Cumberland Written by Himself* (1806–7).

[3] Not identified.

treat me as the *air* treats the *arrow*, fill up the gap and forget that it ever passed that way. It is a dreadful thing not to be necessary to one's friends, and there is but *one* in the world now to whom I am anything like a *sine quâ non.* While that one remains, *il faut bien que je vive;* when that one goes, *il n'y a plus de necessité.* You see I have brought no wife with me from Ireland, notwithstanding all that the kind match-makers of this world did for me. I was very near being married the other night here at a dance the servants had to commemorate St. Patrick's Day. I opened the ball for them with a pretty lacemaker from the village, who was really *quite beautiful*, and seemed to break hearts around her as fast as an Irishman would have broken heads. So you see I *can* be gay.

Have you met with old Cumberland's second edition? He has spoken of me in a way that I feel very grateful for, and if you ever see him, I wish you would tell him so.[1] How go on Spenser[2] and Rogers, and the *rest* of those agreeable rattles, who seem to think life such a treat that they never can get enough of it?

Write to me immediately upon receiving this; and to bribe you, after such a stupid letter, I will write you an epitaph that will make you laugh, if you never heard it before:

'Here lies John Shaw
  Attorney at law;
And when he died,
  The devil cried,
"Give us your paw,
  John Shaw,
Attorney at law!"'

Yours,
T. M.

148. *To his Mother*

Russell, i. 222, no. 125

Wednesday, March, 1807.

My dearest Mother,

We know nothing decisive yet about the ministry. The last accounts gave me rather a hope that Lord Moira would stay in, though I don't know whether one would wish him for his own sake to continue, after his public vow not to serve with the Duke of Portland: if however, as it is said, the Prince takes the part of the

[1] See letter No. 146, to his mother, March 1807.

[2] Moore spells the name here with an *s*, but his remark aptly describes William Robert Spencer. See the Glossary of Proper Names.

new arrangement, he will most certainly stay in.[1] It is all a bad business for the country. Fine times, to be sure, for changing ministry, and changing to such fools too! It is like a sailor stopping to change his shirt in a storm, and after all putting on a very ragged one. I see Lord Hardwicke is very active in the business, so I suppose he will return to Ireland. I got Kate's *one* letter in the course of three weeks, and congratulate her much on her activity. Love to all. Your own,

Tom.

149. *To Lady Donegal*

Russell, i. 224, no. 128

Donington Park
Monday, April 27. 1807.

'We are commanded (says Cosmo de Medici) to forgive our *enemies*, but I cannot find that we are any where ordered to forgive our *friends*.'[2] Now, though this is a very deep and good saying of Cosmo's, yet it is not at all applicable to you; for, notwithstanding that I *did* suspect you of a sort of *leze amitié*, a kind of compassing and imagining the death of our friendship, yet I now entirely acquit you, and hope every thing from your loyalty in future. As to absence, I have said very often, and I believe to you among others, that recollections are too like the other perishables of this world, and that it is hard even for those who take the best care of them, to keep up a stock without a supply now and then; so that, though I feel I am strong in that article at present, yet I trust for all our sakes I shall be able to open shop in Tunbridge this year, and shall come back 'laden with *notions*,' as the Americans call their fancy goods. I suppose you will only allow *love* to come under the head of *fancy* goods, but I am afraid all the feelings of our heart have but too much of *her* manufacture in them. I am here very busy, and yet if I were to try and tell you about *what*, it would puzzle me a little: only this I must inform you 'to God's pleasure and both our comforts,' that I am not writing *love-verses*.

[1] Lord Moira did not serve under Lord Portland because the latter supported the Union Act, which carried during Portland's term as Home Secretary. Lord Moira opposed the measure in a speech delivered in March 1799. Both Portland and Hardwicke supported Catholic emancipation in Ireland, however, a cause dear to the heart of Moira.

[2] Quoted by Sir Francis Bacon in *Apothegms*, 143: 'Cosmus duke of Florence was wont to say of perfidious friends, "that we read, that we ought to forgive our enemies; but we do not read that we ought our friends."'

I begin at last to find out that *politics* is the only thing minded in this country, and that it is better even to *rebel* against government, than have nothing at all to do with it; so I am writing politics: but all I fear is, that my former ill-luck will rise up against me in a new shape, and that as I could not write *love* without getting into—, so I shall not be able to write *politics* without getting into *treason*. As to my gaiety and dissipation, I *am* to be sure *very* dissipated, for I pass my whole time among *knowing-ones* and *black-legs*, the former in the *library*, the latter in the *rookery:* it is true, I see some *white* legs now and then upon the lawn, but I have nothing at all to do with them, I assure you.

I had a long letter from America the other day; and what do you think? My Epistles were, in January last, going through their *third* edition there! and Carpenter is only just now getting out his *second*, of which I have seen some proof-sheets, and they are very beautiful. My correspondent tells me that, to the last edition that had come out in America, there was prefixed 'some account of the author,' but he had not yet seen it. A pretty account, I dare say, it is; but there is some glory in being even abused so generally; and I have that at least in common with most of the great men who have lived, just as I am little like Horace, and love dozing in the morning like Montaigne: it is comfortable to resemble great men in anything. Tell Miss Godfrey that I cry '*peccavi*,' and beg pardon for what I said in my last billet, but that I said it merely for the pleasure of transcribing that epigram, which I knew she would like, and which is written by her friend, the man that wrote '*Mille fois*,' &c. I shall send her a palinode in a day or two, that is (for fear she should expect any thing great from this hard Greek word) my recantation, justification, and renunciation of the *aforesaid* and all other errors thereunto belonging and appertaining, and what not. You must know I have been reading law very hard, and you must not wonder at its breaking in in my style. *I am determined on being called to the Irish bar next year*. Best remembrances to your dear sisters, and believe me, yours most truly,

Thomas Moore.

150. *To his Mother*

Russell, i. 223, no. 127

Sunday, April, 1807.

My dearest Mother,

The time flies over me here as swift as if I was in the midst of dissipation, which is a tolerable proof that I am 'arm'd for either field,' for folly or for thought, for fiddlers or philosophers. The family do not talk of coming till June, and, if that be the case, I shall not budge. From this to Ireland shall be my only move. Tell the Atkinsons that, to show them I have not forgot their choice scraps, I send them one which I found in a paper of last year, and which I think too good to be lost. I am anxious to hear whether my packet of letters, which I entrusted to Jane, arrived safe.

Good by. I have been writing letters since eight o'clock, and my breakfast is coming up. Ever your own,

Tom.

151. *To his Mother*

Russell, i. 226, no. 129

Wednesday, April, 1807.

My dearest Mother,

I take both exercise and your Spa in plenty. What put it into Kate's head, or rather into her *hand*, to write me such a *beautiful* letter last time? I never saw anything like it; it was quite a picture. Seriously, it was very nice writing, and if she keeps to that the girl may do.

Sweet weather this. The May thorns are beginning to open their eyes. The new ministers are in full blossom of folly and prosperity, and the *snows* and the *Parliament* have dissolved away. I wish I were in Dublin now, and I would make speeches on the hustings for Grattan. Good by. God bless you all. Ever your own,

Tom.

152. *To his Mother*

Russell, i. 227, no. 130

April, 1807.

My dearest Mother,

I don't know what your Irish skies have been doing all this month (I suppose *raining*, as usual), but *here* we have had the severest frost and snow till yesterday, when I think a change in the administration of the weather took place: before then it was what Dr. Duigenan would call a *white-boy* administration, for we had nothing but snow. My 'Pastor Fido,' Dalby, has been prevented from coming to see me as he used to do, by his wife's illness, which is a great loss to me; but the time never hangs heavy, and reading, writing, walking, playing the pianoforte, occupy my day sufficiently and delightfully, without either 'the tinkling cymbal' of talk, or 'a gallery of moving pictures' about me.

You need not mind Miss Owenson's airs;[1] for I can do without them till I go to Ireland.

God bless you, dearest mother. I got Kate's letter on Monday. Ever your own,

Tom.

Best love to the barrack-master.

153. *To his Mother*

Russell, i. 227, no. 131

Saturday, April, 1807.

I send an inclosure for Power, which you will forward to him immediately. Carpenter is preparing a second edition of the Poems,[2] to be printed splendidly by Ballantyne, of Edinburgh. I hope these *fellows* will get in again; but if the King dissolves Parliament, their chance, I fear, is but indifferent. However, my resolution is taken, and I care no longer about them. If I am to be poor, I had rather be a poor counsellor than a poor poet; for there is ridicule attached to the latter, which the former may escape: so make up your minds to having me amongst you. I shall exchange all my books for a law library, and knock down my music with the first volume of Coke upon Lyttleton.[3] Why does not Nell write to me? She promised when I came away. God bless you all. Your own,

Tom.

154. *To his Mother*

Russell, viii. 65

Thursday, April, 1807.

My dearest Mother,

I got letters from all the little circle the other day except yourself. Tell dear Ellen I was very happy to welcome her preface to our correspondence, and that I hope she will not lag like other people; though indeed I retract all my blame of Kate, for she has been very good to me. I am going to-day to the first gay thing I have had since I came—indeed, I have not seen a face but Mary Dalby's, and that but once a week, since I came; but to-day I gig it to Ashby, nine miles off, where I dine with Parson M'Doual, Lady Loudoun's cousin, and then proceed in the evening to a concert

[1] See letter No. 145, to his mother, March 1807.

[2] *Epistles, Odes, and Other Poems.*

[3] Sir Edward Coke, *The First Part of the Institutes of the Laws of England, or a Commentarie upon Littleton* (1628).

and ball, consisting of Ashby amateurs and amateuresses; and I expect to find my corked-up spirits flying like spruce-beer or soda-water. I assure you, whenever I meet any one to talk to now, they suffer for my long silence by myself, and my fits of oratory are prodigious. God bless you, dearest mother! My father's letter gave me most sweet comfort. Ever your own

Tom.

155. *To Mary Godfrey*

Russell, i. 228, no. 132

Tuesday night, May 26. 1807.

These good people are come down upon me at last; so there is an end at once to all my musings and meditations. They have brought so many *Misses* with them too, that my muse, I think, must shut up her *paper*-mills and go into the *linen*-trade. But there is *one* thing, I assure you, I write to you with some pleasure now, because I *want* you more. Except when I *actually* HAVE the society of those I love, I am never so much *with* them as when I am alone; and though this may sound very Irish, I flatter myself it is Irish in much more than sound. All my pursuits, all my thoughts in solitude have a reference to my dear and distant friends. I enjoy my own feelings *best*, when I think *they* would sympathise in them, and am never proud of what I do, except when I can hope *they* will approve of it; but in the bustle of such society as I have now, neither my feelings or my business are worthy of being associated with such friends as you are, so that I begin to miss you exceedingly, and am glad to fly to a quiet moment like this, when I can call you back and tell you that my heart is fit to receive you. There is another circumstance by which you are a gainer in my present situation, and that is *comparison*. Oh the sweet happy days of friendship and boiled mutton! how unlike were you to the disguised hearts and dishes, the iced wines and looks, of my present dignified society. But I am beginning to talk too sentimentally for your wag-ship. You must know I shall soon leave this; but I wish to Heaven either I or you could know that I shall leave it for Tunbridge. I am afraid, alas! that Ireland must be my destination again, and that I must leave our friendship to take care of itself, without any looking after, for six or seven months longer: this is a hard case, but the *softest* hearts meet with the *hardest* cases in this world. I wish such precious souls as yours and mine could be *forwarded* through life with 'This is glass' written on them, as a warning to Fortune not to jolt them too rudely; but if she was not blind, she would see that we deserve more care than she takes of us.

She would see that *I* ought to be allowed to go to Tunbridge, and that *you* ought to be without ache or ailment to receive me there. You always speak so *waggishly* about your own grievances (and, indeed, other people's) that I cannot collect from what you say of your illness, whether you are really very bad or not; but I sincerely hope it was more fatigue than ill-health that you complained of. Ever yours,

T. M.

On Thursday I shall be *seven and twenty* round years:[1] drink my health, and more sense to me.

156. *To his Mother*

Russell, i. 230, no. 133

May, 1807.

My dearest Mother,

There is a fishpond here, which Lord Moira has always been trying to fill; but he couldn't; and it has long furnished me with a very neat resemblance to *my own pocket*, which I dare say he would like to do the same with, but couldn't. This pond however, in the late rain, has got the start of my pocket, and is brimful at this present writing, which will delight his lordship so much that I am afraid he will come down in a hurry to look at it. Believe me, your own,

Tom.

157. *To his Mother*

Russell, i. 230, no. 134

Donington Park
Thursday night, June, 1807.

My dearest Mother,

I beg, when you write to Kate, you will scold her, for making Melfield a pretext to avoid writing to me. I get on here very well. The ice begins to thaw on all sides, according as we know each other better; and if idleness were not the root of all evil to me at present, I could lounge away my time here very agreeably. We still have no other man amongst us but Lord Moira and the old Duke de l'Orge.

[1] According to a medal made from a Spanish dollar, which was prepared at Moore's birth, he would have been twenty-eight at this time (see Russell, i. 2). The medal, which gives the date 28 May 1799, is now in the British Museum.

I wait but for some supplies I expect to decide upon my movements from home. London I certainly shall avoid, though Carpenter presses me very hard to go there; and the only excursion I can possibly be tempted to, before I set out for Ireland, is to Tunbridge, to see Lady Donegal. However, even this is by no means probable at present, and I think, in about a fortnight, you may count upon seeing me. I wish, dearest mother, you would have a look-out in the neighbourhood, for either two tolerable rooms or one very excellent, large bed-room for me, where there would be some one merely to bring me up breakfast. I shall work very hard all the summer. Love to all dears. From your own,

Tom.

158. *To his Mother*

Russell, i. 231, no. 135

Donington Park
Saturday [June] 1807.

Not one letter this long time, my darling mother. I should think Kate sleeps even longer than she used to do and doesn't get up till post-time is over. (Here I was thinking of London post-time, which I wish to Heaven you were as well acquainted with as I am.) Dublin is again, I find, or rather *still*, the seat of wrangle and illiberal contention. The Roman Catholics deserve very little, and even if they merited all that they ask, I cannot see how it is in the nature of things they should get it. They have done much towards the ruin of Ireland, and have been so well assisted by the Protestants throughout, that, between them, Ireland is at this instant as *ruined* as it need be.

Lord Moira is again called to town; I suppose upon some errand quite as useless as the rest. He takes Buxton in his way; and I suppose will return here from London to escort his lady to Edinburgh.

I should be glad they were all there now, for I thrive in my solitude amazingly. God bless you, dearest mother. I hope your health is better than I think it. Love to my good father, and the girls. Your own,

Tom.

159. *To Mary Godfrey*

Russell, i. 232, no. 136

Saturday [June ?] 1807.

That racketting old Harridan, Mother *Town*, is at last *dead:* she expired after a gentle glare of rouge and gaiety at Lady L. Manners' masquerade, on Friday morning, at eight o'clock; and her ghost is expected to haunt all the watering-places immediately. I hope I shan't meet the perturbed spirit at Tunbridge, for this is to notify that, in *the course of to-morrow,* you will see your humble servant on the ——; what's the name of the place? No matter, but *there* I shall be to-morrow, if Fortune have but one smile left, or if Joddrel's barouche can hold me. Yours most faithfully,

T. Moore.

160. *To Lady Donegal*

Russell, i. 235, no. 138

Saturday, April 29. 1808.

Though I don't much care how light and inconsiderate I may seem to the world in general, yet with regard to the opinion of *friends* I am not altogether so indifferent; and therefore, though I allow the good people of Dublin to think (as indeed I have told them) that it was the toss-up of a tenpenny token which decided me against going to London, yet to *you* I must give some better signs and *tokens* of rationality, and account for my change of mind in somewhat a more serious manner. As this task, however, is very little to my taste, seeing that I would rather vindicate any one else than myself, the present *exposé* must serve for 'all whom it may concern;' and I therefore enjoin you to make the said document known unto our friend and *cozen*, Miss Mary, not forgetting our trusty and well-beloved Rogers, to the end that we may be no farther troubled therewith. In the first place, then, my motives for going to London may be comprised under the heads of *pleasure* and *ambition*, and the purest part of the former object you must take solely to yourselves, for (though, I confess, the taste of pleasure has not *quite* yet left my lips) the strongest attraction that my Epicureanism would have in London at present is the pleasure of being near you, with you, and about you,—'About you, goddess, and about you.'[1] Well, then, there's the *pleasure* of the thing settled. Now, with respect to the *ambitious* part, I don't know that

[1] *The Dunciad*, iv. 249–52.

I can be quite so explicit upon that head, for the objects of all *ambition* are generally as vague as they are distant; and luckily for the humble people of this world, those joys that give most pleasure to the heart are easiest defined and easiest attainable. I thought, however, that by republishing those last poems with my name, together with one or two more of the same nature which I have written, I *might* catch the eye of some of our patriotic politicians, and thus be enabled to serve both *myself* and the *principles* which I cherish;[1] for to serve one at the expense of the other would be foolish in one way and dishonourable in the other. Though, however rash it would be to sacrifice myself to my cause, I would rather do it a thousand times than sacrifice my cause to myself. How happy when the two objects are reconciled! Well, against these motives of pleasure and ambition, I had a sad array of most cooling considerations; indeed, many of the reasons why Austria should not go to war were the very reasons why I should not go to London—an *exhausted treasury, dilapidated resources*, the necessity of seeking subsidies from those who would fleece me well for it in turn, the unprepared state of my *capital*, &c. &c. 'I have here a home, where I can live at but little expense, and I have a summer's leisure before me to prepare something for the next campaign, which may enable me to look *down upon* my enemies, without *entirely looking* up to my friends; for, let one say what one will, *looking up* too long is tiresome, let the object be ever so grand or lovely, whether the statue of Venus or the cupola of St. Paul's.' Such were my reflections, while I waited for the answer to a letter which I had written to Carpenter, sounding him upon the kind of assistance which he would be willing to give me, and suggesting that, as it was entirely *for his interest* that I should go over (to get the work through the press which I left in his hands), I thought he ought at least to defray my expenses. His answer was so niggardly and so chilling, that it instantly awaked me to the folly of trusting myself again in London without some means of *commanding* a supply, and I resolved to employ this summer in making wings for myself against winter to carry me completely out of the mud. I have not time to add any more to this, which I have written in a great hurry, and have not now time to read over again; but I trust you will be able to make out from it very good and sufficient reasons for the sacrifice which I have doomed myself to make in not going to London this year. With respect to sister Mary's intelligence of my being in love, I shall answer that charge to

[1] Moore is probably referring to *Corruption and Intolerance, Two Poems Addressed to an Englishman by an Irishman* and *The Sceptic, a Philosophical Satire*, both of which appeared in 1809 (*Poetry*, pp. 131–45).

herself, and shall only say that I wonder *she* is not sick of imputing to me a sensation of which, I am sorry to say, I have not felt one flutter these three years. Do not forget me; above all things do not forget me.

T. M.

161. *To Joyce Codd*

Russell, i. 239, no. 140

Donington Park
Monday [June 1808]

My dearest Uncle,

Though my pen has been slow to congratulate you, my heart, I assure you, has not been behind-hand in the interest we must all feel in whatever regards your happiness; but I have been obliged to keep my wits in such a hot-house for this work, that plain prose is a thing I have hardly time to condescend to, and I could have written you a dozen of epithalamiums at shorter notice than one letter. While *you* are so well occupied with one fair one, no less than *nine* are tormenting *me*,—the nine Miss Muses, from the cold country of Parnassus, with nothing but their wits to keep them in pin-money! Seriously, my dear uncle, nothing has ever come nearer to my heart than the joy I have felt at your progress to happiness in every way. In taking to yourself what you love, you have secured the only sweet consolation in this world for those rude shocks which the hard corners of life must give now and then even to him who most cautiously turns them. *Few* may those corners be to *you*, dear uncle, and that love may *cover* them with *velvet* for you is my prayer and my confidence. I am quite anxious to see and know your chosen one. I dare not yet say when that can be, but I look to a happy summer amongst you with delight, and I trust to your goodness for conciliating her kind opinion of me. My dear mother and Kate, I know, love her, and I am sure will come as close as she can draw them to her, and altogether I think there will not be *one inequality* on the *perfect little circle* of affection we shall form.

God bless you. Best and dutiful love to my dear aunt, and believe me, my good uncle, yours most truly,

Thomas Moore.

162. *To his Mother*

Russell, i. 238, no. 139

Wednesday, August, 1808.

Dearest Mother,

For fear you should think I love to tantalize, I shall say no more about my departure till I am quite fixed upon the time; but one thing, I hope, will give you pleasure, and that is, that I have a task before me, which will keep me pretty long amongst you; but I must contrive to have lodgings in town, as my chief business will be with the libraries: so pray have your eye about for something comfortable.

This next year, with a little industry and economy, will, I expect, make me quite independent even of friends (I mean of my debts to them); for I have been offered *a thousand pounds* for a work which I think I can finish within the year, and which I intend to dedicate to Rogers.[1] God bless you, dearest mother. Ever your own,

Tom.

I quite threw away the Melodies; they will make that little smooth fellow's fortune.[2]

O Kate! the laziest Kate in Christendom!

163. *To John Dalby*

Mrs. Mercia Dalby

Dublin
October 17th [1808]

My dear Dalby— I left here in a most deplorable way for want of my portmanteaus, which Lord Rancliffe could not venture to inflict the weight of upon his fine jim-crack post chaise. You will oblige me more particularly than I can tell you till we meet, if you will either go yourself or send to Remstone & ask the servants on what day my portmanteaus were booked at Loughborough—it is not impossible that they may still lie slumbering in the warehouse, as contented as if they were doing the thing I liked best in the world—do, my dear fellow, make every enquiry possible about them, and you will oblige me infinitely— I have done little more

[1] This is the only mention in Moore's letters of such an offer, and *Lalla Rookh* (1817) is the only poem in his *Complete Works* which is dedicated to Rogers.

[2] Moore is probably referring to William Power, who first proposed that the poet write words to a set of Irish airs, for which Sir John Stevenson would arrange the music. See letter No. 144, to Sir John Stevenson, February 1807.

yet than hug & embrace my friends after so long an absence—indeed I have scarcely recovered my breath from all the kissings and smotherings which I found ready for me—God bless you, my dear Dalby, best remembrances to Mrs D. to the little rosy cherub & to your sister Mary.

Ever yours
Thomas Moore

Write to me under cover to Edward Connor Esqr War Office Dublin Castle.

164. *To John Erskine Douglas*

William L. Clements Library, University of Michigan

January 14th 1809*

Welcome home, my dear Douglas— I have but this instant read of your arrival in the last Packet that reached me, and I seize the moment to tell you how delighted I feel at your return & how I regret not being in London to meet you— I wrote two or three letters to you while you were away, and until you let me know whether you received them, I shall not repeat any thing they contained— I hope to be in London in a little more than *two months* hence, when I trust you will not have left it— You will find me as high in spirits and as low in every thing else as usual— But I shall be able to take over with me a *few hundreds* this time (*honestly come by*, I assure you, however that may make you stare) and then your agent & I shall have our settling day— It went to my heart to find that you were not making any captures while you were away to atone for the *ruin* which I & others of your needy friends must bring upon you— I rather think you *did not* receive my letters, as I mentioned something upon this subject with respect to my Bermuda Treasury,[1] which would have been doing *justice* to yourself & *kindness* to me, but it has not been done—

There is some little gaiety going on here, of which of course I am not without my share— The gallant Sir Arthur (our Secretary) took his leave of us a night or two ago with a Ball at which I danced till five o'clock— He has been making a great fool of himself here with Lady Argile, to the no small misery of his interesting little wife— Our Duke too is playing the same game with Lady Edward Somerset— 'To it, luxury! pell-mell'—[2] I met them all last night at Lady Harrington's, and there was really more of the *Vice* than the *Royalty* in their conduct—

[1] Moore is referring to his position as Registrar of a Naval Prize Court in Bermuda, which he had deputized.

[2] *King Lear*, IV. vi. 119.

God bless you, my dearest Douglas. Let me hear from you soon & direct to me under cover to *Edward Connor, Esqr War Office, Dublin Castle*—

Ever yours
Thomas Moore.

165. *To his Mother*

Russell, i. 240, no. 141

Friday morning [December] 1809.

My dearest Mother,

From what I have heard of our poor Richard, I fear you must prepare your heart for *the worst;* and I am happy to think that you have not been very sanguine in your hopes for his recovery, as this will soften your feeling of a calamity, which, I own, requires *all* the softening that philosophy and preparation can give it.[1] As for myself, he is the first dear friend it has ever been my fate to lose; and though he did not bring me close enough into intimacy to leave any very sensible void in my life, yet I am too well convinced of his worth and his warmth, and the zeal with which he would have stood by us in every extremity, not to feel his loss most deeply and sorrowfully. It is for *you* however, dearest mother, that I most particularly feel it. Those who die as he did, are not to be pitied; but I know how much and how justly you will lament him. You must not, however, let it sink too deep, darling mother; but while you mourn for the dead as he deserved, remember what you owe to the living. Indeed I dread less from your *grief* than I did from your *anxiety:* the latter had *hope* to keep it alive, while the former will naturally yield to time and good sense and consolation. It is for *us* who are still left to you to do all in our power to make you forget the melancholy loss which you have suffered, and as those who are deprived of *one sense* have generally the *remaining ones* more lively and exquisite, so I trust you will find in the love of those who still live for you, but an increased sensibility to everything in which your happiness is concerned.

I mean to go out on Sunday to you, and shall stay till your mind has recovered a little from the first feelings of this event. Dearest mother, your own,

Tom.

[1] Moore's uncle Richard Joyce Codd died in 1809.

166. *To Joseph Atkinson* (?)

William Lefanu

Worthing
Wednesday* [December 1809][1]

My dearest friend—

I have come here for a day or two, partly to visit our dear friends, the Donegalls, previous to my flight for Ireland, and partly to elude the invitation to dinner which the Pss of Wales honoured me with, and which I thought it expedient, in the present times, to avoid, though it is the third time she has flattered me with the proof of condescension—say nothing of this *to any person whatever*— I consulted Lord M. on the subject & was happy to find my conduct sanctified by his approbation. I shall not now think of any thing but my visit to Ireland, and I hope, though you *have* played the *censor* with me lately, I shall find that the 'rumores senum severiorum' float only about your lips, without influencing farther, & that there is not one wrinkle more upon your heart than there used to be— I should be sorry to see that *Hebe*,[2] which has played so long about you, and retained her smile in spite of sixty years' services—I should be sorry to see her turned into an old *Hanah More* at last, and become a Piety in Pattens just as her illumination was most necessary—[3]

With respect to your advice about my recantation, I see in it the same solicitude for my reputation & advancement, which has made you all along worth a legion of guardian-angels to me—but I own I think it would be an unnecessary exposure of what very few *know* & that very few care little about— The Strumpet of Babylon gives me but little trouble, and I do not think I need *afficher* my connection with her, or wish for a divorce either *a mensâ* or *a thoro* as long as no one sees me eating the transubstantiated bread of the *former*, or bending my knee to the scarlet whoredoms of the *latter*.

The post goes out sooner than I expected—so I must let this nonsense go *without ballast*—except you will admit as a *makeweight* (what I assure you, is *sterling*) the best good wishes of my heart for you & yours eternally.

Ever your attached
T. M.

[1] Moore was in Ireland in January 1810, and the tone of this letter indicates that it was written just before his departure from England.

[2] Daughter of Zeus and Hera. She was associated with perpetual youth.

[3] Hanah More published such pamphlets as 'Village Politics' and 'Repository Tracts', which proved very successful and led to the foundation of the Religious Tract Society. She devoted the latter part of her life to philanthropic activities and her name became a byword for rigorous, conservative piety. *Piety in Pattens*, the title of a play by Samuel Foote, produced in 1773.

167. *To his Mother*

Russell, viii. 74

Donnington Park, 1809.

My dearest Mother,

I think I have got into some mistakes in my reckoning, and whether I have given you a letter too little or too much I cannot at this moment determine. A squire in the neighbourhood here came and forced me over to dine with him and Lord Robert Manners, and I *dawdled* away two days with them, which has deranged all my calculations. The letter that Kate asks about was written for publication, but not in the manner that Sir John's luminous biographer has introduced it: it makes part of a prospectus which I wrote for Power, and which I dare say you have seen by this time printed on a single sheet. The letter was never written to the Knight, or you may be sure I should not have been so ill-bred as to quote Latin in it.[1] I have lost all my comforts here already. The house is arrayed in all its company-dress, and waits in prim expectation of their arrival, like the poor maids of honour in George II.'s time, who used to sit up all night in arm-chairs with their heads drest, in order to be ready for court next morning. I can't stir an inch without meeting some crimson carpets, &c., that must be spotless for my lady's eye when she comes. God bless you. Ever your own

Tom.

By the bye, there is the best Irishism in that said 'Dublin Magazine' that ever I met with. The editor in a note upon the last cover very gravely entreats the reader to 'keep in mind' that Miss Owenson's portrait *is not* Sir John Stevenson's.

168. *To Lord Byron*

Moore, *Byron*, ii. 81

22, Molesworth Street,* Dublin
January 1. 1810.

My Lord,

Having just seen the name of 'Lord Byron' prefixed to a work entitled 'English Bards and Scotch Reviewers,' in which, as it appears to me, *the lie is given* to a public statement of mine,

[1] Moore is referring to the letter prefixed to Part I of the *Irish Melodies* (see letter No. 144, to Sir John Stevenson, February 1807), in which he expresses his interest in a collection of melodies, since Ireland's 'National Music has never been properly collected'. Jones, *The Harp that Once*—, p. 104, says that the letter was addressed to Stevenson, which Moore here denies.

respecting an affair with Mr. Jeffrey some years since,[1] I beg you will have the goodness to inform me whether I may consider your Lordship as the author of this publication.

I shall not, I fear, be able to return to London for a week or two; but, in the mean time, I trust your Lordship will not deny me the satisfaction of knowing whether you avow the insult contained in the passages alluded to.

It is needless to suggest to your Lordship the propriety of keeping our correspondence secret.

I have the honour to be
Your Lordship's very humble servant,
Thomas Moore.

169. *To Lady Donegal*

Russell, i. 241, no. 142

Jan. 3. 1810.

I was quite sorry to hear from Rogers that you have had another attack of those sad fainting fits which used to annoy you so last year, and think you are very right in trying Baillie, instead of your old *state* physician Sir Francis. I shall be more anxious than, I fear, you will give me credit for, till I hear that you are recovered; and if you do not let me know immediately, even by a short bulletin, how you are getting on, I will never play Paddy O'Rafferty for you again. You will perceive by my seal that death has been a visitor in my family; and indeed it is the first time that I have had to lament the loss of any one very dear to me. My poor uncle, who went to Madeira, with but faint hopes of recovery from a decline,

[1] Moore is referring to the following passage in the *English Bards*:

> Can none remember that eventful day,
> That ever glorious, almost fatal fray,
> When Little's leadless pistol met his eye,
> And Bow-street Myrmidons stood laughing by. (ll. 458–61)

In a note explaining the passage Byron remarked that 'the balls of the pistols, like the courage of the combatants, were found to have evaporated'.

The lines allude to the famous near-duel between Moore (the 'Little' of line 3) and Jeffrey (see letter No. 133, to Mary Godfrey, August 1806). Byron has it that Moore's pistol was empty, whereas the original rumour was that Jeffrey's was not loaded. Marchand (*Byron*, p. 300 n.) suggests that Byron had either heard this version of the story or deliberately changed it to make Jeffrey appear to be lacking in courage. Nevertheless, this passage still contradicted Moore's public statement that both pistols were loaded. See letters Nos. 197 and 200, to Lord Byron, 22 and 29 Oct. 1811.

died there in four days after his arrival.[1] I am so hourly prepared for these inroads on our social happiness, that the death of even the healthiest friend about me could scarcely, I think, take my heart by surprise; and the effect which such calamities are likely to have upon me will be seen more in the whole tenor of my life afterwards, than in any violent or deep-felt grief of the moment: every succeeding loss will insensibly sink the level of my spirits, and give a darker and darker tinge to all my future hopes and feelings. This perhaps is the natural process which many a heart goes through that has to survive its dearest connections, though I rather think it is not the commonest way of feeling those events, but that, in general, the impression which they make is as *short* as it is keen and violent; and surely it is better to have one moment *darkly blotted*, with the chance of the next moment's washing it all out, than to possess that kind of sensibility which puts one's whole life into mourning. I am not doing much; indeed, the downright necessity which I feel of doing something is one of the great reasons why I do almost nothing. These things should come of their own accord, and I hate to make a *conscript* of my Muse; but I cannot carry on the war without her, so to it she must go. London is out of the question for me, till I have got ammunition in my pocket, and I hope by April to have some combustibles ready. How a poor author is puzzled now-a-days between quantity and quality! The booksellers won't buy him if the former be not great, and the critics won't let him be read if the latter be not good. Now, there are no two perfections more difficult to attain together, for they are generally (as we little men should wish to establish) in inverse proportion to each other. However, I must do my best.

Take care of yourself for *my* sake, best and dearest friend; and with warm remembrances to our well-beloved Mary, believe me, most faithfully yours,

Thomas Moore.

Many a year of happiness and good health to you both.

170. *To James Power*

Russell, i. 243, no. 143

Dublin
[January or February] 1810.

My dear Sir,

If you have no objection, I rather think I shall take the liberty of drawing upon you very soon for whatever sum you may find it convenient to accommodate me with, and I shall discharge the

[1] See letter No. 165, to his mother, December 1809.

obligation, *partly* in songs, or *entirely*, as you may think fit. I shall wait your answer, and propose, with your consent, to draw upon you either at *two* months for thirty pounds, or at *three* for fifty: in the latter case I shall take up *twenty* of the same myself, as I should not have songs enough for the whole; and in return for the kindness of the accommodation, I shall not avail myself of your offer of twelve guineas, but content myself with *ten*. I have some idea of writing a song for Braham, and *that*, if it succeeds, shall be among the number.

I have no objection to your brother knowing this negotiation between us, but I would rather have the telling of it to him myself, as, without some explanation, he would have a right to think me very extravagent of late, knowing how much he has accommodated me in; but the truth is, a very expensive honour has been conferred upon me, in the shape of admission to our leading club house here, which urges me more than I expected at this moment. Your answer as soon as possible will oblige.

Yours very truly,
Thomas Moore.

You will of course consider these particulars between us as sacred from every body except your brother: he already is aware that it is my intention to give you songs occasionally, according to the promise I made you. Direct to me, 22. Molesworth Street, Dublin.

171. *To James Carpenter*

Morgan Library

Monday Feb^r^ 13* [*c.* 1810]

My dear Carpenter— When people say you are *dis*obliging, they ought only to say you are *forgetful*— Where are the copies of Corruption, of Sallust, the numbers of the *Cabinet*[1] & other things which I expected in my bundle?— Ah! you are a sad fellow— I have very nearly completed my materials for the two volumes, and I rather think I may take a trip over to you myself to get them through the Press for you, as it would be endless to have the Proofs sent over here—what do you think?—I shall hide myself in some corner or other in your neighbourhood, and just stay till the book is printed— I think it would be worth your while to pay my

[1] *Corruption and Intolerance, Poetry*, p. 131. Moore wrote a prefatory life of Sallust for Arthur Murphy's translation of that historian in 1807. *The Cabinet; or Monthly Report of Polite Literature*, vols. i–iv (1807–8).

expenses for the convenience & expedition of the thing, not to mention the pleasure of my company to eat some stewed beefsteaks with you— Let me hear from you about this— The new manager here *had* some idea of bringing out an old business of mine, the Troubadours, transmogrified into a Melo-Drama, and the Third Night would have been very convenient to me, as I should have touched at least *five hundred* by it—but alas! *Mother Goose* has cast me out completely— Remember me to those about you & believe me, my dear Carpenter

Most truly yours
T. Moore

172. *To James Carpenter*

Rice University

Monday* [February or March 1810]

My dear Carpenter—I find I am in a little hobble about the Bill my Aunt's attornies have of mine, as the source to which I looked for taking it up has disappointed me—so that I fear I must make use of your name (*merely* your name) to help me through it— The sum is a hundred, but I am trying to make the part I shall draw upon *you* for as small as possible—[1]

Ever yours
T. Moore

[1] Moore was in need of money during the early months of 1810. He mentioned the fact to Lady Donegal (to whom he seldom wrote about money matters) in letter No. 169, 3 Jan. 1810, and he requested a loan from Power in letter No. 170, Jan. or Feb. 1810. His need is further attested in letter No. 171, to James Carpenter, where he asked that the publisher pay the expenses of a trip to London, so that Moore could see a volume (probably *A Letter to the Roman Catholics of Dublin*, April 1810) through the press. In letter No. 173, July 1810, he made another rare, but nonetheless pointed remark about his financial difficulties to Lady Donegal, indicating that his hopes for emolument from the *Letter to the Roman Catholics* had been in vain.

Moore's relations with Carpenter at this time were such that he called on the publisher frequently for financial assistance. After 1810, however, his affiliations with James Power, Thomas Longman, and John Murray were more cordial, and he turned less frequently to Carpenter for aid.

173. *To Lady Donegal*

Russell, viii. 83

July, 1810.

I shall not attempt to defend myself; for it would really require more sophistry and more impudence than (bad as I am) I possess, to think of proving that I am not *quite wrong* in having so long deferred writing to you. But is there not *some* little grace in this avowal? and would it not require the hardest heart in the world to be angry with me after such an humble confession of my errors? I *know* you will forgive me; because, after all, you understand very well yourself the sort of unwillingness one has to take up a stitch that has long dropped in a correspondence; and though I think I am as sure of your heart as of any heart in this world, yet I do firmly believe that '*yours sincerely*' is the only part of a letter that you take any real pleasure in writing to me—isn't it so? As for myself, there are a *few* in the world for whom I would *willingly* shed my last *blood*, and yet I *cannot help* being sparing of my *ink* to them. I know sister Mary thinks this very odd, for she would sooner draw a pen than a sword at any time; but it is my *weakness*, and a very lazy weakness it is, I confess,—one great inconvenience of which is that my letters, when they *do* come, are only apologies for those that did *not* come, and my not having written is almost the only thing I have to write about. Pope says that 'Heaven first *sent letters;*'[1] but if it required *answers* to the letters it sent, I am afraid that Heaven would have found me an unpunctual correspondent.—So much for the main subject of my epistle; and now, having made such a bad hand of what I have *not* done, I wish I could give you even a tolerable account of what I *have* done; but, I don't know how it is, both my mind and heart appear to have lain for some time completely *fallow*, and even the usual crop of *wild oats* has not been forthcoming. What is the reason of this? I believe there is in every man's life (at least in every man who has lived as if he knew how to live) one blank interval, which takes place at that period when the gay desires of youth are just gone off, and he has not yet made up his mind as to the feelings or pursuits that succeed them—when the last blossom has fallen away, and yet the fruit continues to look harsh and unpromising—a kind of *interregnum* which takes place upon the demise of *love*, before ambition and worldliness have seated themselves on the vacant throne.

[1] *Eloisa to Abelard*, l. 51.

* * * I am now on a visit with a man who has ten thousand a year, and who keeps the best table within the bills of mortality; but the house, notwithstanding, is most preciously dull; the cook and I are the only *savans* on the establishment, and the *sauce* is the only thing *piquante* I have to deal with in it. I intend however, if I can, to turn my seclusion to account, and to write something *marketable* for this next year; for money I *must* have, if the Muses were to die for it; and of all the birds of the air, the *gold*finch's notes [*sic*] for me. By-the-bye, talking of money, you insult me in a most pointed manner by never once touching upon the subject in any of your letters. You seem to think it quite as ridiculous to mention money-matters to *me*, as it would be to write to Hammersley about the Loves of the Plants;[1] but I'd have you to know—seriously, I take it rather unkind of you you [*sic*] that do not tell me how you are getting on with those sad samples of nobility you have to deal with, for though my hard fate prevents me from being any thing but a burthen to you, yet you ought to do me the justice to feel that I am anxious about all that concerns you, and that to know the *worst* from yourself is better than being made to fear everything bad by others. Mrs. Crookshank, about a month ago, told me some circumstances which gave me much and real pain. Ah! nothing goes *right* in this world, *except* for *those* with whom everything (*please God*) will go *wrong* in the other. Really, one is obliged to feel either very profanely or very piously, when one sees the kind of persons that are put upon the black list in this life. Do, pray, let me know something about your affairs, and do not for an instant suppose that I am not as warmly and anxiously alive to everything connected with you and your happiness, as I was when near you, and as I ever, while I live, shall continue to be.

I hope you did not dislike my dedicatory letter to you.[2] It was sent to the press before I recollected that I ought to have asked your permission for the step, and it was this afterthought that made me resort to the awkward expedient of putting only the initials of your name. Most people here think it is Lady Downshire, which is very stupid of them, though perhaps *you* will not be sorry for the transfer. As to politics, I begin rather to hope that the kind of change most for *my advantage* (and perhaps most for the advantage of the country) will take place next sessions, and that the Whigs

[1] A joke at the expense of Byron's London banker Hammersley, who, according to Moore, would not appreciate or understand Erasmus Darwin's *Loves of the Plants* (1789).

[2] The *Irish Melodies* were dedicated to 'the Marchioness Dowager of Donegal'.

will come in, in spite of my other friends the Reformists, who seem to be dropping off the perch very fast indeed; and certainly never did *dirtier sticks* ascend in the *bright shape* of rockets than some of these said Reformists have proved themselves to be. Cobbett is contemptible; Wardle is in the mud; and Burdett himself is, I believe, beginning to think that politics, like 'poverty, brings a man acquainted with strange bedfellows.'[1] When I mention my hopes from the Whigs, I found them chiefly upon the impression which my last pamphlet has made among them.[2] I have had letters of the most flattering kind possible from Grattan, Lord Lansdowne, Lord Moira, the Duke of Bedford, &c., and the language which they use, particularly Lord Lansdowne and the Duke of Bedford, looks very like a persuasion in their minds that I might be somewhat useful to them. But I was almost forgetting to tell you of the strange honour that came by surprise upon me the other day. I received a letter from Stockholm, through Hammersley's house (where it had been detained *about a year*), informing me that I had been elected a Knight of the illustrious, secular, equestrian, and chapteral Order of St. Joachim,[3] on account of my reputation for literature on the Continent. This, you know, is one of the orders made hereditary in the family of Nelson. I thought for a moment that it was a *hoax*, and the name of the saint appeared to me very well chosen, being easily convertible into St. *Joke-him;* but upon applying to Naylor, the Windsor genealogist, and others, to whom this letter from the Vice-Chancellor of the order referred me, I found it to be all a most illustrious and chapteral matter-of-fact; so I am now Sir Thomas Moore, K. J., elect. I have not yet answered the letter, but it is my intention respectfully to decline the honour, as literary knights (even if the knighthood were acknowledged) are anything but reputable personages in the eyes of John Bull, to whom the respect for authorship that exists on the Continent is as unintelligible as their cookery, and goes against his stomach quite as much.

[1] An old proverb. It was used by Bulwer-Lytton in *The Caxtons*, part iv, chapter 4, l. 849, and Thackeray refers to 'that dismal proverb which tells us how poverty makes us acquainted with strange bedfellows' in *Roundabout Papers: on Some Carp*, part 2, l. 863.

[2] Probably *A Letter to the Roman Catholics of Dublin*, which appeared in Dublin in 1810.

[3] See Moore's *Poetical Works* (London, 1841), vol. ii, pp. xxv–xxvi, where Moore recorded the invitation to become a member of the order of St. Joachim. He noted that Lord Nelson, the Duke of Bouillon, and Colonel Imhoff were members. He wrote to Monsieur Hansson, Vice-Chancellor of the order, declining the honour.

And now, good bye. Give dear sister Mary my best and warmest regards; tell her I shall write just as long a letter to her very soon, and that *that* letter and another will be about long enough to cover the space between this and our meeting, which I trust will be a happy one; and to which I shall carry just as warm a heart and as constant a spirit (I mean in friendship) as ever.

Yours,
T. M.

174. *To James Power*

Morgan Library

Monday [*c.* July 1810]

My dear Sir—

Notwithstanding my '*positively*', I now send only the Song, and shall keep the Duett, till I have something *very good* to send with it— I was a little uneasy at not hearing from you yesterday, as I fear you are teazed about your boy & other matters— I hope you think the Preface in its present state worth making the alteration for & recollect the expense is to be set down to me— When you are next making a parcel, I wish you to send me the last Quarterly Review—I intend after this time to order it from Murray regularly—

Did you see the mention of my name the other day in the Morning Chronicle, in an Essay on the Drama, calling upon me, Byron, Scott, Campbell &c to turn our talents *fairly* to the stage; & so, with the blessing of God, I will, as soon as my present stumbling-block is removed—

I have not forgot my promise about the Melologue,[1] but my first attempt at it has been a failure—

Best regards to Mrs Power from hers &

Yours most faithfully
Thomas Moore

I wish you would enquire at Butler & Whitaker for the remaining numbers of Handel for me— I have to as far as *37*— Mrs Ready is gone to Ireland, I suppose, to lay *violent* hands on the Knight

[1] The *Melologue on National Music* was recited at Kilkenny on 2 Oct. 1810, and published in 1811.

175. *To Lady Donegal and Mary Godfrey*

Russell, viii. 82

Birmingham
Monday [December] 1810.

I am so far on my way to you, and just wait to take breath before I encounter the various kinds of feelings that I shall have upon my arrival. It is a sad thing to be ashamed to meet one's friends, and I should be sorry to think that I have any such feeling about me; yet, when I know that I have so long disappointed the wishes and hopes of those who are interested about me, it is impossible not to dread such reproachful salutations as 'I am sorry you did so,' and 'I wonder you didn't do so,' and a thousand other anxious comments, which one must only feel without answering. But the good nature and the true cordiality with which I *know* I shall be received in Davies Street, give me courage to meet even the reproaches which perhaps may be mingled with them; and all I intreat of you is that, for a little while at least, you will neither ask me what I *have* done, or even what I *mean* to do, but draw upon your *first* good opinion of me (if that fund be not entirely exhausted) to enable you *still* to look forward with a hope of something good and respectable from me. To tell you that I mean to give up society would be only to make you smile and remember how often that wise resolution has been *paraded* by me: but *years* make some difference even in fools, and though they may not give us *wisdom*, they do a good deal in changing the *objects* of our folly. After this preparatory letter, which, I am afraid, has always the clumsiness of a pioneer without his strength, I shall bid you good bye till Wednesday or Thursday, when I mean to have a hearty shake of the hand with you in Davies Street. This letter is to *both*, as my friendship is.

Ever faithfully yours,
Thomas Moore.

176. *To his Mother*

Russell, i. 244, no. 144

Bury Street
Saturday, Dec. 1810.

My dearest Mother,

I arrived here on Wednesday; but was so hurried at first that I had scarcely time to send for pen, ink, and paper to write. I bid Power, however, to whom I wrote about business, let you know of my arrival; and you may be assured of my continuing frequent and punctual as usual. I have written a most pathetic little letter to Connor, which I would hope will make my dispatches pass glibly through his hands. Lord Moira is out of town, and so is Rogers. Lady Donegal, however, is at her post, and as steady as ever. It is strange that two years should have made so very little difference. I came into my rooms, as if I had left them but last week; my flannel-gown airing at the fire; my books lying about the tables; and the very same little girl staring in at me from the opposite windows. I found Miss Godfrey asleep in the evening, as usual; and, as usual she wakened with a joke. I found my landlady as fond of me; and Carpenter as fond of himself as ever. In short, nothing seems altered but myself.

The King has got bad again within these two days past. God bless you, my dearest mother. Ever your own,

Tom.

I hope you got my letters from Holyhead and Birmingham.

177. *To his Mother*

Russell, i. 244, no. 145

Monday, Dec. 1810.

My dearest Mother,

I am told that the report of the physicians is very unfavourable, and that a regency will be proceeded on immediately,[1] with no other change for some time, however, than the introduction of Lord Moira into the cabinet. I left my name this morning at Carlton House.[2]

You would be amused if you knew all the letters and visits I am receiving from booksellers, music-sellers, managers, &c., with offers for books, songs, plays, &c. I rather think I may give something to Covent Garden; but I know you will be happy to hear that I am able to *keep* myself *up*, without any precipitate engagement or involvment of any kind, and that I am not hurried or urged from *any quarter*. Best love to father and the dear girls. From ever your own,

Tom.

I have seen the Sheddons about my Bermuda treasury, and they say I may expect to receive something very shortly.[3]

[1] The Regency Bill was passed in January 1811.

[2] The residence of the Prince of Wales.

[3] The Sheddons were the London merchants whose nephew was Moore's deputy in Bermuda.

178. *To his Mother*

Russell, i. 245, no. 146

Wednesday, Dec. 1810.

My dearest Mother,

I am going on very quietly here, and have, as yet, seen nobody but the Donegals.

My cough is a good deal better; and I begin to think that the little waterfalls in Mrs. Booth's room tended considerably to keep me coughing.

They say now there will be measures taken for a regency; but, for some time, I do not think there will be any material change in the Ministry. Lord Moira is still out of town.

I am happy to find, dearest mother, by Kate's letter, that you have got better of the illness you had after I left you. If my letters are any medicine to you, you shall have the dose regularly, 'as before;' and I hope, in the course of some time, I may have something *cordial* to mix up with them. Ever yours,

Tom.

179. *To his Mother*

Russell, i. 246, no. 147

Friday, Dec. 1810.

My dearest Mother,

The plot begins to thicken here very fast, and yesterday was expected to be a hard-fought day. I have not heard yet what was the result, but I think some time must yet elapse before there will be such a change of administration as I can take advantage of.

I have often *said* I was careless about the attractions of gay society, but I think, for the first time, I begin to *feel really* so. I pass through the rows of fine carriages in Bond Street, without the slightest impatience to renew my acquaintance with those inside of them.

Best love to all dears about you. Ever affectionately your own,

Tom.

180. *To Lady Donegal*

Russell, i. 246, no. 148

Jan. 3. 1811.

I wonder whether you have as beautiful a day before your eyes this moment as I have. 'The green blood dances in the veins'[1] of

[1] Not identified.

the young rose trees under my window, and the little impudent birds are peeping out as boldly as if it were May-day. I am afraid, however, it is rather a rash speculation of theirs: like Spanish patriots, they are bursting out too soon, and General *Frost* will some night or other steal a *march* upon them. You may conclude from all this that I write to you from a garden; and so I do, from a garden most romantically situated at the end of Dirty Lane, which leads out of Thomas Street, well known in the annals of insurrection for

'The feast of treason and the flow of punch.'[1]

On my right is the 'hanging wood' of Kilmainham, and from my left I catch the odoriferous breezes of a tanyard; so that you must not be surprised if such a sweet and picturesque situation should inspire me with more than usual romanticity. I am certainly, somehow or other, in most sunshiny spirits to-day; and I believe the principal reason of it is, that I have resolved this morning to be in Davies Street in the course of a fortnight. *Don't tell any one*, but I think my having *resolved* it is the *only thing* likely to prevent its taking place. I cannot find in my heart to let you have a revolution, without being up in town to attend it. You know most Irishmen are amateurs in that line, and I have not a doubt but John Bull soon means to give us a specimen of his talents for it. What will your friend the Duke[2] turn to? He may become a schoolmaster, like Dionysius, and instruct young gentlemen in the 'art of polite letter writing;' and if he will condescend to join the *Quakers*, we shall have another union of the houses of York and Lancaster. I am afraid you will be angry with me for laughing in this manner at such serious events and such illustrious people, but I cannot help it; at least *to-day* I cannot help it; and if I do not send off this letter till to-morrow, you shall have a most loyal and dismal postscript to make up for my profane and 'unparliamentary' levity. It is some comfort to you to think that *all* your countrymen are not such refractory reprobates as I am, and that there is but little fear of our incurring much suspicion for honesty or independence, while Messrs. B. and C.[3] are alive to vindicate our characters. But why do I talk politics to you (in which we don't agree) when there are so many pleasanter things in which we *do?* One of them, I flatter myself, is the wish to see each other, and in that I seriously

[1] A parody of Pope, 'The feast of reason and the flow of soul', *Satires, Epistles, and Odes of Horace*, Satire I, book ii, l. 127.

[2] The Duke of York [Russell's note].

[3] Probably Bryan, an Irish politician, and Canning, who was at that time Foreign Secretary.

think we shall soon be gratified. Now be sure you meet me with all your heart and soul, for my stay will be but short. I stay a good deal at home with my father and mother here, eating boiled veal and Irish stew, and feeling very comfortable; in short, very much the same diet and feelings which I was used to in Davies Street; only that those about me *know* how much I love them, which you and *Mary* sometimes *pretended not* to know.

Rogers has not answered my letter, but I shall fire another at him soon.

This little note is a specimen of the sort which I intend to write to you *often* now; for, indeed, it is a sad thing to be long without knowing how this hard world deals with those who are away from us; and though I would willingly dispense with telling you about myself, yet it is a cheap price after all to pay for the delight of hearing from you.

Tell me something, when you write, about the political *secrets* of London, and particularly say whether you have heard any thing about the *Plenipo's* difference with the Prince Regent.[1] Ever yours,

T. M.

Best love to sister. Many happy returns of this year.

I have been waiting in awful suspense for a letter about the tickets, but I fear that Fortune's usual *blindness* to *merit* will leave *us* in the lurch as well as many other excellent people. 'Call me not fool till Heaven shall send me fortune,'[2] is as much as to say that we wise personages need never expect a 20,000£. prize in the lottery. But how *very* convenient it would be! How much it would brighten up all my views of politics, law, divinity, &c. For what *I* cared, they might send Mr. Percival[3] to be second in command to St. Narcissus, or employ Sheridan's nose in bringing about a *thaw* for the armies in Finland; but there's nae sic luck for us, I fear. You are very right in saying that every pursuit is a lottery, and *my* ticket-wheel is my *head*, from which I draw ideas sometimes *blank* enough, God knows; but the fact is, I have kept Cupid too long for my drawing-boy, and as he is quite as blind as Fortune, it is no

[1] Moore is referring to the Prince's differences with Perceval, the Prime Minister. When it became apparent, late in 1810, that a regency would be established, Perceval notified the Prince of the restrictions to be imposed upon the Regent: restrictions from making peers, from granting offices in reversion or pensions, from dealing with the King's property, and from having custody of the King's person. The Prince prevailed upon his brothers to sign a protest against these restrictions, and the Duke of Sussex spoke against them in the House of Lords.

[2] *As You Like It*, II. vii. 19.

[3] Obviously Spencer Perceval, the Prime Minister, whose name Moore often misspelled.

wonder that nothing *capital* has come forth, but I have dismissed him this good while. * * *

181. *To his Mother*

Russell, i. 249, no. 149

Saturday, Feb. 1811.

My dearest Mother,

I forgot whether I told you that my excellent friend Douglas was among the many persons enriched by the old Duke of Queensbury's will.[1] He has been left 10,000£. I saw him this morning for the first time these six years; I believe, *five* at least: he has never written a line to me during that time, and after an hour's conversation to-day he said, 'Now, my dear little fellow, you know I'm grown rich: there is at present seven hundred pounds of mine in Coutts's bank; here is a blank check, which you may fill up while I am away, for as much of that as you may want.' I did not of course accept this offer, but you may imagine what my feeling was at this unexampled instance of a man bringing back the warmth of friendship so unchilled, after an absence of five years. I never heard anything like it.

I got dear Ellen's letter, which is beautifully written, and I hope she will often let me have such. Ever your own,

Tom.

182. *To his Mother*

Russell, i. 250, no. 150

Saturday, March, 1811.

My dearest Mother,

I dined with Lord Holland on Wednesday, and yesterday with old Sheridan, who has been putting us off from day to day as if we were his creditors. We had yesterday Lord Lauderdale, Lord Erskine, Lord Besborough, Lord Kinnaird, &c. &c. My old friend, Lady A——, still faithful in her faithless way, took me to dinner in her carriage. I have at last got a little bedroom about two miles from town, where I shall fly now and then for a morning's work. It was quite necessary for me, if I did not mean to starve gaily and fashionably in London, though, indeed, the starvation part is not very likely.

[1] It was William Douglas, fourth Duke of Queensbury, who died in 1810, not Charles, as Russell's note states.

I have found a method of getting a second-hand paper, or rather a second-*day* paper, at rather a cheap rate, and I have long been wishing for it, in order to indulge you, my darling mother, with a sight of London paper and type once more. I send the first to-day, and direct it to my father at Island Bridge. It is the Morning Post, a terrible hack in politics: however, I have some hopes of getting it exchanged soon for a more liberal paper. Best love to all dears about you. From your own affectionate,

Tom.

183. *To his Mother*

Russell, i. 251, no. 151

Saturday, April, 1811.

My dearest Mother,

I have been so busy preparing the enclosed packet for Power, that I have hardly left myself time to say more than I am very impatient to hear from you; as I long to know whether you have taken my prescription of airing and jolting, and whether it has made you stout again.

I am just now in a quandary of doubt about the levee. To dress or not to dress, that is the question: whether 'tis nobler keeping in my pocket seven guineas, which 'twill cost me for a waistcoat, or &c. &c. If Lord Moira was in town I would consult him and ask him to take me, which is another weighty point to be looked to. I rather believe, I shall wait till there is another levee. Ever yours, darling mother,

Tom.

184. *To Lord Holland*

The Earl of Ilchester[1]

27 Bury St.*
Tuesday* [*c.* April 1811]

I am afraid your Lordship does not care about *Music*, and there is nothing else worthy of your notice in the *Melologue* which I have the honour of sending to you—except perhaps two or three common-places about Liberty, which, as applied to Spain, I rather think you will not disapprove of—[2]

[1] Transcript provided by the Earl of Ilchester. This letter was printed in Princess Marie of Liechtenstein's *Holland House* (London, 1874), ii. 84. She added a note saying that 'some of' in the phrase 'some of the sentiments against Whiggism' (paragraph # 2) is an interlineation, 'as if, looking through what he had written, Moore wanted to retract part of his recantation.'

[2] The *Melologue upon National Music* was published early in 1811. For the two songs concerned with Spanish liberty and patriotism see *Poetry*, p. 305.

I also venture to send for your perusal a Pamphlet,[1] which, from the narrow range of its circulation, has never, I dare say, reached your Lordship's eye—the only claim it has upon your attention, & the only reason I have for troubling you with it, is the manner in which *one name*, every way dear to you, is introduced in it—For the rest, I only tried it as an exercise in a style of writing very new to me, and I regret & recant most heartily some of the sentiments against Whiggism, which it contains—but I went to it hot from reading Bolingbroke, the Craftsman, &c. &c.

If your Lordship will but accept it as a mark of my respect, and not think me presumptuous in the manner of offering it, you will make me very happy.

I have the honour to be,

Very much your obliged Serv[t]
Thomas Moore

185. *To his Mother*

Russell, i. 252, no. 152

Saturday, May, 1811.

My dearest Mother,

I have been these two or three days past receiving most flattering letters from the persons to whom I sent my Melologue.[2] I was, however, much better pleased to get dear Kate's letter with news from home, as the long silence you all kept was beginning to make me a little uneasy.

Jeffrey, my Edinburgh friend, is in town: we have called upon each other, and I am to meet him to-morrow morning at breakfast with Rogers: to-day, I shall touch the two extremes of anarchy and law, for I dine with Sir F. Burdett, and go in the evening to Lord Ellenborough's.

Tell Kate I cannot give any opinion of Miss Owenson's novel;[3] for *one* reason, i.e. because I have not read a line of it. Ever yours, my dearest mother,

Tom.

[1] Probably his *Letter to the Roman Catholics of Dublin* (April 1810), which was occasioned by the reaffirmation of the Irish clergy in March of their stand on the veto question. In it Moore attacked the demogoguery of Irish politics, stated his belief in the freedom of the mind, and advocated tolerance, good sense, and expediency in dealing with the Catholic question.

[2] See letter No. 174, to James Power, *c.* July 1810.

[3] Lady Morgan's *Woman; or, Ida of Athens* appeared in 1809, and *The Missionary: an Indian Tale* in 1811. Moore could be referring to either.

186. *To James Corry*[1]

Russell, viii. 90

June 4. 1811.

My dear Corry,

You have every reason to be very angry with me—but I really have such an unconquerable aversion to writing letters, that I have often thought that Captain Brady's resolution not to answer anything but a *challenge* was the most peaceable way of getting through life.[2] But I feel myself particularly reprehensible in not attending to *your* letter; not only because it was the most agreeable I have received since I left Dublin, but because it was so good-natured of you to write to me *at all*, after my 'angel visits, few and far between,'[3] to Lurgan Street. However *you* may forgive me, I can by no means be so lenient to myself for having *seemed* (for it was only seeming) so insensible to the many repeated kindnesses I have experienced from you and Mrs. Corry; but distractions of various kinds beset me in cities, and it somehow happens that those I love best come off worst with me. I rather think you will understand what I mean; and indeed both you and Mrs. Corry show that you *feel* what I mean, by continuing your kindnesses to me through all chances and changes, through all my neglects and abberations. I have not yet had a *business* day with Power, which means that we have not yet *got drunk* together; but he is good enough to be one of my allies next Monday, when I take the chair at a dinner of the gentlemen educated at Dublin College. I wish, with all my heart, that *you* could pop your *nose* in amongst us. Beecher has the misfortune to be *English*-bred, and so cannot be with us.

With respect to the opening lines of the Prologue for Kilkenny,[4] I am afraid you must fill up the *hiatus* with stars, for, poor as they were, I have robbed them of their only trinkets for a song in the next number of the Melodies; therefore you must give it only as a fragment, and say '*Caetera desunt*,' the rest is *not decent*, or some such cause.

Pray do not translate any of my Latin for Mrs. Corry, but give her, in plain English, my warmest remembrances, and tell her it

[1] Strong, *The Minstrel Boy*, p. 141, mistakenly identifies James Corry with the Irish politician Isaac Corry, whom Moore also knew. The error is understandable, since Moore often referred to the two men in the same entry in his diary. Almost invariably, however, when he mentioned the elder Corry, he used the full name. See the Glossary of Proper Names.

[2] The allusion is not clear.

[3] Blair, *The Grave*, l. 588; Campbell, *The Pleasures of Hope*, ii. 378.

[4] The prologue written and spoken by Moore at the opening of the Kilkenny Theatre, October 1809.

gave me sincere pain to hear of her illness; but that I strongly hope I shall see her here with all her good looks and (may I say?) kind smiles in summer.

Ever yours, my dearest Corry,
Thomas Moore.

You see I have presumed upon your privilege to enclose a letter, which you will oblige me by sending as soon as possible.

187. *To Thomas Longman*

Russell, i. 263, no. 161

Bury Street, St. James's
Wednesday [19 June] 1811.

My dear Sir,

I am at last come to a determination to bind myself to your service, if you hold the same favorable dispositions toward me as at our last conversation upon business. To-morrow I should be very glad to be allowed half an hour's conversation with you, and, as I dare say, I shall be up all night at Carlton House,[1] I do not think I could reach your house before four o'clock.

I told you before that I never could work without a retainer. It will not, however, be of that exorbitant nature which your liberality placed at my disposal the first time I had the honour of applying to you; and I still beg, as before, that our negotiations may be as much as possible between ourselves. Whatever may be the result of them, I shall always acknowledge myself indebted for the attention I have already experienced from you, and beg you to believe me, dear sir, faithfully yours,

Thomas Moore.

188. *To his Mother*

Russell, i. 254, no. 155

Friday, June 21. 1811.

My dearest Mother,

I ought to have written yesterday, but I was in bed all day after the fête,[2] which I did not leave till past six in the morning. Nothing was ever half so magnificent; it was in *reality* all that they try to imitate in the gorgeous scenery of the theatre; and I really sat for

[1] See letter No. 188, to his mother, 21 June 1811.

[2] Moore is referring to a fête held at Carlton House on 19 June 1811, to celebrate the establishment of the Regency. See letter No. 187, to Thomas Longman, 19 June 1811.

three quarters of an hour in the Prince's room after supper, silently looking at the spectacle, and feeding my eyes with the assemblage of beauty, splendour, and profuse magnificence which it presented. It was quite worthy of a Prince, and I would not have lost it for any consideration. There were many reports previous to it (set about, I suppose, by disappointed *aspirants*), that the company would be mixed, &c. &c.; but it was infinitely less so than could possibly be expected from the strange hangers-on that all the Royal Brothers have about them, and of course every thing high and noble in society was collected there. I saw but two unfortunate ladies in the group (mother and daughter) who seemed to 'wonder how the devil they got there,'[1] and everybody else agreed with them. While all the rest of the women were outblazing each other in the richness of their dress, this simple couple, with the most philosophic contempt of ornament, walked about in the unambitious costume of the breakfast-table, and I dare say congratulated each other, when they went home, upon the great difference between their becoming simplicity and the gaudy nonsense that surrounded them. It was said that Mr. Waithman, the patriotic linendraper, had got a card; and every odd-looking fellow that appeared, people said immediately, 'That's Mr. Waithman.' The Prince spoke to me, as he always does, with the cordial familiarity of an old acquaintance.

This is a little *gossiping* for you, dearest mother, and I expect some in return from Kate very soon. God bless you. Ever your own,

Tom.

189. *To his Mother*

Russell, i. 256, no. 156

Monday [June or July] 1811.

My dearest Mother,

I did not write on Saturday, as I was a little nervous about my reading to the manager; but I came off with him ten times better than I expected, as I have indeed very little confidence in my dramatic powers.[2] He was however very much pleased, and said its only fault was, that it would be too good for the audience, that it was in the best style of good comedy, and many more things, which, allowing all that is necessary for *politeness*, are very encouraging, and I begin to have some little hopes that it may succeed. I was very much amused by Kate's astonishment at my full-dated and

[1] Pope, *Epistle to Dr. Arbuthnot*, l. 169.

[2] Moore is referring to his musical *M. P., or the Blue Stocking*, which he read to Arnold, the manager of the Lyceum Theatre.

full-signed letter. I suppose I had been writing a few *formal* epistles before it. Kate says that Boroughes is very curious about *franking;* but he has rather a curious mode of doing it, as the letter of my father's (which she says he franked the week before) I *never got*, and this last one of hers (which she says he *also* franked) I paid postage for. By the bye, I had begun to feel a little uneasy at not having heard from my dear father so long, and the only consolation I had was seeing some of his directions of the newspapers at Power's.

I am right glad to hear that little Dolly's lover, after holding out as long as Saragossa,[1] has surrendered to her at last. Ever your own, my dearest mother,

Tom.

Do not mention my opera to any one, and bid Kate muzzle old Joe upon the subject.

190. *To Mrs. Mills*

Harvard College Library

Jenkinstown
July 24th* [1811][2]

I am afraid you will think that I played you false—but to you, who know how little I do things by *premeditation*, I need hardly say that I did not *intend* to stay so long in this place—[3] The fact is, my Muse has been for some time *in the family way*, and she has such a fair prospect of a happy delivery here, that I cannot find it in my heart to disturb her by changing—I shall therefore just wait to see what God sends, and as my Muse is generally *confined* in the *open air* (being an Irish Muse) I shall expect the child's features to be full of sun-shine, and in that case I shall take it to Cradockstown to shew it to you.

I was quite unhappy to hear from Kate that your health & spirits are still far from good—do, pray, take care of yourself, and *get fat* in some other way than you generally are— Mills has eleven children (counting *you*) and that is quite enough— Best regards to him—& believe me most sincerely yours,

Thomas Moore

[1] A town in Spain which was besieged by the French in 1808–9. The bravery of Augustina, 'the Maid of Saragoza', was celebrated by Byron in *Childe Harold*, I. liv–lvi.

[2] This is evidently the letter which Moore enclosed in that to his mother dated Friday, July 1811 (letter No. 191).

[3] Moore was then living at Donington Park, and probably refers to that rather than to 'Jenkinstown'.

191. *To his Mother*

Russell, i. 257, no. 157

Donington Park
Friday [July] 1811.

My dearest Mother,

I got Kate's last letter here from town, and am delighted to think that you are all well and happy. Nothing can equal the luxury of this house, especially since *Monsieur's* arrival.[1] I can imagine that it may be surpassed, but I am sure it *seldom* is: the Prince of Condé and the Duke of Bourbon have come with him.

How does Herbert's play go on?[2] Tell him I wish to have a particular description of the situation in which he desires to have the *song* introduced, and I shall endeavour to make out something suitable to it.

If I could, I should like very much to return to Ireland with Lord and Lady Granard; but it is not very probable. Send the enclosed letter to Mrs. Mills: it will save her so much postage, and I ought to have written to her.

Love to Kate, dear father, and yourself,

Tom Moore.

192. *To Lady Donegal*

Russell, i. 257, no. 158

Saturday, August 17. 1811.

* * * * * *

The season is now, indeed, so far gone, that I should not wonder if I were yet to have you witnesses of my first plunge;[3] and oh! if I could pack a whole audience like you, with such taste for what is good, and such indulgence for what is bad; but I think there is not in the world so stupid or boorish a congregation as the audience of an English playhouse. I have latterly attended a good deal, and I really think that when an author makes them laugh, he ought to feel like Phocion[4] when the Athenians applauded him, and ask what

[1] Lord Moira.

[2] James D. Herbert, a friend of Moore's family in Dublin, was best known for his *Irish Varieties* (1836). The play to which Moore refers has not been identified.

[3] Moore is referring to his forthcoming musical *M. P., or the Blue Stocking.* See letter No. 193, to Leigh Hunt, 6 Sept. 1811.

[4] In his 'Life of Phocion' Plutarch notes that when in difficulty the Athenians turned to the wisest and most astute man among them as their leader, regardless of how often he opposed their sentiments. Thus, when Phocion, who often disagreed with them, was applauded by the Athenians, he asked his friends, 'Have I inadvertently said something foolish?' See *Plutarch's Lives* (Modern Library Edition), p. 900.

wretched *bêtise* had produced the tribute. I have been a good deal and most *loyally* alarmed, lest a certain catastrophe should interrupt the performances at the playhouses; but I believe there is no fear whatever, and that I may be very well satisfied if my piece is not dead and d—d before he is—(N.B. before he is *dead*, I mean—don't mistake me). His conversation latterly has been all addressed to George the First.[1]

Your sister bids me give an account of my mode of living, and I promise to do so in my next letter, which now that I am released from my joke-manufactory, shall follow up this in closer order than I have hitherto preserved; but, in the meantime, I know I cannot tell you too often, that I am more rationally happy than ever I was; that, to compensate the want of worldly advantages, I have found good sense, simplicity, kind-heartedness, the most unaffected purity, and *rightness* of *thinking* upon every subject connected with my welfare or comfort.[2]

I have no news for you. Rogers is still at his brother's in Shropshire. I suppose you saw the account in the paper of the apartments at Windsor into which the poor King was turned loose, and suffered to rage blindly and frantic about, like Polyphemus in his cave.[3] I never read anything more melancholy; the mockery of *splendour* which, they said, was preserved in these preparations (that he might knock his head royally against velvet and satin), made the misery of his situation so much more glaring and frightful, that I am quite happy to find it was all a fabrication.

I shall write to *dear Mary* next week. I have *told my Bessy* that you know it, therefore you may write without restraint. Ever most truly yours,

T.M.

I would enclose this through the War Office, but the paper is too *thin* for stranger eyes.

[1] The reference is to the illness of George III, the state of whose health was reported by *The Times* on 3 Aug. 1811, as follows: 'We regret to state that His Majesty has experienced another severe relapse, and that great apprehensions were entertained of a repetition of those violent paroxysms by which he has been recently so much reduced, and from which he had enjoyed some remission for a short interval.' Bulletins on the King's health were issued daily throughout August.

[2] This paragraph and the last in the letter indicate that Moore had informed Lady Donegal and her sister of his marriage to Bessy Dyke, which took place on 25 Mar. 1811, even though he had not yet told his parents. See letters Nos. 207 and 208, to his mother, November or December 1811. See also letter No. 198, to James Corry, 24 Oct. 1811.

[3] One of the Cyclopes, into whose cave Odysseus wanders and is imprisoned. He and his men escape by blinding Polyphemus.

193. *To Leigh Hunt*

B.M. Add. MS. 37210, ff. 153 and 154

Bury St.
Saturday* [September 6, postmark 1811]

My dear Sir—

It was my intention upon receiving the last letter with which you favoured me, to answer it by a visit and that immediately—but I was hurried off to the country by the sickness of a friend, and since my return I have been occupied in a way that makes me very unfit society for *you*—namely in writing bad jokes for the galleries of the Lyceum—[1] To make the galleries *laugh* is in itself sufficiently degrading, but to *try* to make them laugh & *fail* (which I fear will be my destiny) is deplorable indeed— The secret of it however is that, upon my last return from Ireland, in one of those moments of weakness to which poets & their purses are but too liable, I agreed to give Arnold a piece for the Summer, and you may perceive —by the lateness of my appearance, with what reluctance I have performed my engagement—

It will no doubt occur to you, upon reading the first page of this note, that the whole purport of it is *to ask for mercy*—but the kind terms in which you have spoken of some things I have written makes me too much interested in your *sincerity* to ask for, or *wish* the slightest breach of it— I have no doubt that, in this instance you will treat me with severity, and I am just as sure that, if you do, I shall have *deserved* it—only say that you *expected something better* from me, and I shall be satisfied—[2]

I must now (tho late) thank you for your last Reflector—the poem, to which you were good enough to direct my attention, interested me extremely—there is nothing so delightful as those alternate sinkings & risings, both of feeling & style, which you have exhibited in those verses, and you cannot think how gracefully it becomes the high Philosophy of your mind to saunter now & then among the flowers of Poetry— Do indulge her with a few more walks, I beseech you.[3]

[1] Moore's opera *M. P., or the Blue Stocking* was produced at the Lyceum on 9 Sept. 1811.

[2] Moore was so apprehensive about the venture that he wrote a letter to the London papers calling the piece a bagatelle and denying that it had political implications. Arnold, the manager of the Lyceum, issued a counter statement, declaring the 'brilliant and unqualified success' of the musical. It had an initial run of eleven days and several revivals. With the exception of that in *The Times*, the reviews were favourable. See letter No. 194, to Leigh Hunt, 11 Sept. 1811.

[3] Moore is probably referring to 'Atys the Enthusiast; A Dithyrambic Poem Translated from Catullus, with Prefatory Remarks', *The Reflector*, (1811), 165–74.

I am afraid you look upon me as a bad politician, or you would likewise have bid me read the fine article, entitled (if I recollect right) 'A Retrospect of Public Affairs'— It is most ably done— but you write too well for a politician—and it is really a pity to go to the expence of *fulminating gold* when *common gun-powder* serves the purpose just as well—[1]

I shall not call upon you now till I have passed the ordeal—but till then & ever believe me, my dear Sir,

Yours with much esteem
Thomas Moore

The fragment which Carpenter told you I had for the Reflector was *wickedly* political— Some of the allusions have now lost their hold, but you shall see it & perhaps something may, with your assistance, be yet made of it.

194. *To Leigh Hunt*

B.M. Add. MS. 37210, f. 158

27 Bury St.
Wednesday* [11 September 1811]

My dear Sir.

I have not the least fear that *you* will make any ungenerous use of the anxiety which I express with respect to your good opinion of me— I dare say you have read in the Times of yesterday the very well-written & (I confess) but too just account which they give of the *shooting* of my *fool's* bolt on Monday—the only misrepresentation I can accuse them of (& *that* I feel very sensibly) is the charge of Royalism and Courtier-ship which they have founded upon my foolish clap-trap with respect to the Regent—this has astonished me the more as the opera underwent a very severe cutting from the Licensor for the very opposite quality to Courtiership, & it is merely lest *you* should be led into a similar mistake (from the little consideration you can afford to give to such nonsense) that I trouble you with this note.[2]

If the child's plea 'I'll never do so again' could soften criticism,

[1] 'Retrospect of Public Affairs' was a periodical essay which appeared in each number of *The Reflector*.

[2] *The Times* reviewed Moore's *M. P., or the Blue Stocking* on 10 Sept. 1811. After noting that the light opera was produced before one of the 'fullest and most fashionable audiences ever seen in the Lyceum', the reviewer wrote, 'We cannot attempt to give *the plot*, which has literally nothing of the firmness or frame of a plot,—nothing to make a substratum for the pun, and the jest, and the gibe, and *proh nefas*, the clap-trap into which Mr. Moore's sudden affection for Royalty and Regency suffered him occasionally to descend.'

LORD BYRON by Thomas Phillips

I may be depended upon, from this moment, for a most hearty abjuration of the Stage & all its heresies of Pun, equivoque & claptrap— however *humble* I may be in *other* departments of literature, I am quite conscious of being contemptible in this—

Yours, my dear Sir, very truly
Thomas Moore

Did you receive a note I sent you about a week ago?[1]

195. *To Mary Godfrey*

Russell, viii. 91

Sept. 11. 1811.[2]

My unfortunate opera was at last launched the night before last;[3] and though the actors expected so much from it, I doubt whether it will turn out at all so attractive as they supposed. I have not seen it myself yet; but last night I am told it went off without the slightest opposition, and to-night I dare say I may venture, without danger to my nerves, to go and see it. I knew all along that I was writing down to the mob, but that was what they told me I must do. I however mingled here and there a few touches of less earthy mould, which I thought would in some degree atone for my abasement. I am afraid, however, I have failed in both: what I have written up to myself is, they say, over-refined and unintelligible; what I have written *down* to *them* is called vulgar. I have therefore made a final resolution never to let another line of mine be spoken upon the stage, as neither my talents nor my nerves are at all suited to it. I must tell you, at the same time, that the piece has (what the actors call) *succeeded*, the second night having been fully attended and unanimous in applause. Most of the paper critics too have been friendly; the 'Times' making a most formidable exception.[4] The article in that paper yesterday was really a brain-blow, from the style in which it was written and the candour with which it affected to praise me in other departments of literature: they however made a most ridiculous and unaccountable mistake in accusing me of royalism and courtiership, when the fact is, the piece was dreaded by us all as dangerous from the opposite quality, and I had a long struggle with licenser [*sic*] for the retention of several most ticklish passages about bribery. The worst of it is,

[1] See letter No. 193, to Leigh Hunt, 6 Sept. 1811.

[2] Russell erroneously dated this letter 'Dublin, Sept. 11. 1811'. Moore was in London when his opera was produced.

[3] See letter No. 193, to Leigh Hunt, 6 Sept. 1811.

[4] See letter No. 194, to Leigh Hunt, 11 Sept. 1811.

that I fear Arnold means to trick me out of all but the first advance that he made me in the spring; this is too bad. However, you shall know more when I have ascertained his intentions.

I shall now take to my poem, and do something, I hope, that will place me above the vulgar herd both of worldlings and of critics; but you shall hear from me again, when I get among the maids of Cashmere, the sparkling springs of Rochabad, and the fragrant banquets [*sic*][1] of the Peris. How much sweeter employments these than the vile joke-making I have been at these two months past!

Best love to dear Lady Donegal from hers and yours ever,

Thomas Moore.

196. *To Edward S. Foss*

Rice University

Wednesday Morning*
[Postmark 18 September 1811]

Sir—

I have had the honor of receiving your letter and am extremely flattered by the kind terms in which you speak of my Opera—Your suggestion about the Glee is perfectly judicious & I shall try whether the imperfection can be remedied—the over-sight with respect to Sir C's carriage is quite glaring, and I shall have it corrected—[2]

I am, with many thanks,
Your very humble servt
Thomas Moore.

[1] Evidently a misreading of 'bouquets'. Moore is referring here to *Lalla Rookh*, which was not completed and published until 1817.

[2] Moore's note is a reply to a letter from Foss, dated 16 Sept. 1811, the original of which is now in the Fondren Library of Rice University. Foss praised Moore's opera but felt it his duty to tell the author of two 'imperfections' which marred it. In the scene in Leatherhead's shop when Miss Harlington and her attendant Susan meet Du Ranier, Foss found it 'out of all probability' that the two girls would sing a glee before one whom they knew only slightly. He suggested that the number be introduced to the audience by Du Ranier, who would comment on his fondness for music, particularly glees, and illustrate his appreciation by quoting the first line of Moore's song. The girls, with providential coincidence, would remember and sing it.

The second flaw concerned the overturning of Sir Charles Canvass's carriage. At the time the accident occurs, Sir Charles speaks of his 'leaders', indicating that he was driving four-in-hand to a barouche. Later he refers to the accident as happening to his 'curricle'. Foss suggested that the actor be instructed to substitute the word 'barouche'.

197. *To Lord Byron*

Sir John Murray

27 Bury Street, St. James's
Tuesday October 22nd [1811]

My Lord—

As I understood, soon after your Lordship's return to England, that a melancholy event had occurred in your family, which must have very painfully occupied all your thoughts,[1] I forbore from troubling you with the subject upon which I now have the honour of addressing you; and, indeed, if in what I have to say at present there were any thing of hostility or unkindness towards you, I should think it too soon even *now* to disturb you unpleasantly from your retirement. But I trust you will find that, notwithstanding the injury of which I complain, the spirit in which I address you is neither revengeful nor ungenerous.

It is now about three years since I wrote a letter to your Lordship, upon seeing your name advertised before the second edition of 'English Bards & Scotch Reviewers.'[2] I was in Ireland at the time, and not having seen more than the *advertisement* of *this* Edition, I was ignorant of your Lordship's intention to leave England so soon— Accordingly, you had sailed before my letter arrived in London, and it is very possible it may never have reached you— The purport of it was to ask some explanation with respect to a certain note upon your Lordship's poem, in which, professing to relate the circumstances of my meeting with Mr Jeffrey in 1806, you appear to me to *give the lie direct* to a public statement of mine, which appeared in most of the newspapers with my name affixed to it, about a week after the meeting with Mr Jeffrey took place.

It is useless now to speak of the step, with which I intended to follow up that letter. The time, that has elapsed since then, though it has done away neither the injury nor the feeling of it, has so very materially altered my relative situation in life—has laid me under so many obligations to friends, and fettered me with so many serious responsibilities, that I should consider myself, at present, not only selfish but unprincipled, were I to consult any punctilious feeling of my own, at the risk of leaving undischarged the many duties which I owe to others. The only object, therefore, which I now have in writing to your Lordship is merely to preserve some consistency with the letter which you may have formerly received from me, & to prove to you that the injured feeling still remains,

[1] Byron's mother died on 1 Aug. 1811.

[2] See letter No. 168, to Lord Byron, 1 Jan. 1810.

however circumstances, at present, may compel me to be deaf to its dictates.

When I say '*injured feeling*', I must again assure your Lordship that there is not one vindictive sentiment in my heart towards you— I mean merely to express that *uncomfortableness* under a charge of falsehood, which must haunt a man of any feeling to his grave, unless the insult be retracted or atoned for, and which if I were not sensibly alive to, I should indeed deserve much worse than ever your Lordship's satire could inflict upon me. So *very* far am I, however, from treasuring any ungenerous revenge, that it would give me this moment the most heart-felt pleasure, if, by any kind, candid & satisfactory explanation, you would enable me to ask for the honour of your intimacy, and let me try to convince you that I am *not exactly* the kind of person, who would set his name to a mean and cowardly falsehood.

I have never mentioned *to any one* my former letter to your Lordship, nor ever hinted at the feeling which your work excited in me, except to one person, who is, I believe, an intimate friend of your Lordship's. If, however, you should feel inclined to meet my sincere wishes for reconcilement, I shall mention the subject to my best & most valued friend, *Mr Rogers* (whose worth & talents your Lordship seems justly to appreciate) and I have no doubt that he will be most happy to become a mediator between us.[1]

I have the honour to be, my Lord, Your Lordship's very humble Servant

Thomas Moore

To
the Rt. Honble
Lord Byron

198. *To James Corry*

Russell, viii. 96

Thursday, Oct. 24. 1811.

My dear Corry,

Now for it—I am quite ready for you—proof sheets—play bills —I'll dash through all with you. Seriously, my dear fellow, though

[1] On 27 Oct. Byron replied to Moore's letter in the following manner: 'The advertisement you mention, I know nothing of. . . . With regard to the passage in question, *you* were certainly *not* the person towards whom I felt personally hostile. On the contrary, my whole thoughts were engrossed by one, whom I had reason to consider as my worst literary enemy. . . . I can neither retract nor apologize for a falsehood which I never advanced' (*LJ*, ii. 60–63).

not altogether *désauvré*,[1] yet I am just now in want of an interposing relief to more serious studies, and I know of nothing better for the purpose than our Kilkenny undertaking; so don't spare me, but as many tons burden as your franks are allowed to carry, freight away without any remorse,—the linen trade will be all the better for it.[2]

You perceive I have been qualifying myself still further for the task by putting on the sock in *writing* as well as *acting*, but I am sorry to say I feel it rather *slipshod* on me. You will see a resurrection (when you read me) of many jokes that were tolerable in *their lifetime*, but which wear rather 'a *ghastly smile*' in their present cold-blooded reappearance. *One* of those *revenans* you will recognise as having once given some signs of life in a letter to *you;* but there are many of them which not all the efforts of the Humane Society (and the audiences are very much of this description) could warm back into any respectable state of animation.[3]

I wish you would tell Dalton that, tolerant as I am (from sympathy) of those who will not write letters to their friends, yet (like Mr. Perceval, &c.) there is a certain point at which my toleration stops; and Dalton is degenerating into such very licentious silence, that, with all my liberality upon the subject, I must say that he abuses his privilege.

There is no news that you'd care to hear of, except that the Prince is to have a villa upon Primrose Hill, connected by a fine street with Carlton House, and is so pleased with this magnificant plan, that he has been heard to say 'it will quite eclipse Napoleon.' It is feared too that Mr. Perceval, by *this* and *other* '*primrose paths* of dalliance,' is finding his way very fast to the Regent's heart.

[1] The word is probably *désœuvré*, meaning unoccupied, idle, or unemployed.

[2] Moore and Corry had evidently projected a written account of the Kilkenny amateur theatrical group. See letter No. 237, to James Corry, 29 June 1812. For a good summary discussion of the Kilkenny Theatricals see Jones, *The Harp that Once*—, chapter vi. The main source of information about the venture is *The Private Theatre of Kilkenny, with Introductory Observations on Other Private Theatres in Ireland before it was opened* (1825). The group was started in a theatre built in 1794 by Robert Owenson. The theatre was a financial failure and was taken over in 1802 by several amateurs who organized the 'Kilkenny Theatricals'. Moore became associated with the company in 1808 at the instigation of his friend Joseph Atkinson. He appeared as David in *The Rivals*, as Mungo in *The Padlock*, as Spado in *The Castle of Andalusia*, and as Trudge in *Inkle and Yarico*. He returned in 1809 to repeat some of his roles and to speak his prologue, lamenting the death of Mr. Lyster, one of the founders. While associated with this group, he met Bessy Dyke, whom he married on 25 Mar. 1811.

[3] Moore is referring here to his opera *M. P., or the Blue Stocking*. See letter No. 193, to Leigh Hunt, 6 Sept. 1811.

When you write, or rather when you *research*, do not forget that some little *biographical traits* of our *brotherhood* would form a very useful feature of your investigation.

Ever most truly yours,
Thomas Moore.

199. *To Lady Donegal*

Russell, i. 262, no. 160

Monday, Oct. 28. 1811.

My opera has succeeded much better than I expected, and I am glad to find that Braham is going to play it at Bath; but I have been sadly cheated. What a pity that we 'swans of Helicon' should be such geese! Rogers is indignant, and so am I; and we ring the changes upon * * * and * * often enough, God knows, singing of them like Cadet Roussel's children, '*L'un est voleur, l'autre est fripon—ah! ah!*' &c. &c., but it all won't do.[1]

I suppose you have heard that I have had the magnificent offer of Lucien Bonaparte's poem to translate, and that I have declined it.[2] I wrote to ask Lord Moira's advice about the matter, and his answer contained one thing most comfortably important in my opinion, as showing his thoughtfulness about my future interests; he bid me, in case I should find the poem unobjectionable in its political doctrines, to mention the circumstances to McMahon, and get the Prince's assent to my translating it, adding, that if I could wait till he arrived in town, he would mention it to the Prince himself.

The Prince, it is said, is to have a villa on Primrose Hill, and a fine street, leading direct from it to Carlton House. This is one of the 'primrose paths of dalliance' by which Mr. Percival is, I fear, finding his way to the Prince's heart.

I have nothing more to say now, but that I am as tranquil and happy as my heart could wish, and that I most anxiously long for the opportunity of presenting *somebody* to you. If you do not make haste, I shall have *two* somebodies to present to you.[3] Ever yours,

T. Moore.

[1] Guillaume Joseph Roussel, 'Cadet Roussel' (1743–1807), was the subject of a series of popular songs. Although the exact lines which Moore quotes have not been located, they were probably taken from one of the numerous verses of the song beginning '*Cadet Roussel a trois maisons*'.

[2] Lucien Bonaparte's two-volume poem *Charlemagne*, translated by S. Butler and Francis Hodgson, was published by Longman in 1815.

[3] See letter No. 208, to his mother, November or December 1811.

200. *To Lord Byron*

Sir John Murray

27 Bury Street, St. James's
Tuesday Oct[br] 29. 1811

My Lord—

Your Lordship's letter is, upon the whole, as satisfactory as I could expect—[1] It contains all that, in the strict *diplomatique* of explanation I could require, namely—that you had never seen the statement which I supposed you to have wilfully contradicted—that you had no intention of charging me with falsehood—and that the objectionable passage of your work was not levelled personally against *me*— This is all the explanation that I have a right to demand, and, of course, I am satisfied with it.

There is one little point, in which your Lordship has mistaken me, and in which I must beg leave to set you right. I have *not said* that I commissioned any friend to wait upon you, at the time when I first took notice of your publication. The fact is (as I have stated) that I merely wrote a letter to you from Ireland, which, as I was ignorant of your Lordship's address, I inclosed to a man who transacts business for me in London (*Power* in the Strand) and desired that he would find out where you lived— He went accordingly to your Publisher who told him you were not in town, but that he would take charge of the letter & give it to M[r] Hodson[2] (I think) who would forward it to your Lordship— Had I been on the spot myself and known the distant ramble upon which your Lordship had gone, I should, of course, have withheld this letter till your return—as it was, when I heard the journey you had undertaken, I had very little hopes of the letter's ever reaching you, and I find, by what your Lordship says, that it *never did*—

The gentleman, whom I mentioned as the *only* person to whom I ever *hinted* the sort of feeling your words had excited in my mind was Captain Ross (*Archibald*—I forget his regiment) and to him I only spoke of it slightly and passingly in conversation, upon his saying that he had the honour of being intimate with your Lordship— I was wrong however in stating that he was the *only* person to whom I ever communicated any part of my feelings upon the subject; I ought to have mentioned that there is a friend of mine in Dublin, whom I consulted upon the terms of my first letter, before I sent it—allow me also to add that I have the *copy* of that letter by me, if your Lordship should feel the least inclination to see it—

[1] See letter No. 197, to Lord Byron, 22 Oct. 1811.
[2] Francis Hodgson. See the Glossary of Proper Names.

I have descended, my Lord, into these minute particulars, because I confess I do not feel *quite* easy under the *manner* in which you have dwelt upon the miscarriage of that first application to you.

As your Lordship does not shew any great wish to proceed beyond the rigid *formula* of explanation, it is not for me to make any further advances— *We Irishmen*, in businesses of this kind, seldom know any medium between decided hostility and decided friendship; but, as any approaches towards the *latter* alternative must now rest with your Lordship, I have only to repeat that I am satisfied with your letter and that I have the honour to be, in perfect good-will and with sincere respect for your talents[1]

Your Lordship's very humble Servant
Thomas Moore

To the Right Hon[bl]
Lord Byron, &c. &c.

201. *To Lord Byron*

Sir John Murray

Bury Street
Wednesday Evening [30 October 1811]

My Lord—

You have made me feel the imprudence I was guilty of in wandering from the point immediately in discussion between us—[2] I shall now, therefore, only say that, if, in my last letter,[3] I have correctly stated the substance of your Lordship's explanation, our correspondence may, from this moment, cease forever; as with that explanation I declare myself satisfied.

I have the honour to be,
my Lord, your Lordship's
very humble Servant
Thomas Moore

If the letter in M[r] Hodgson's care should prove to be mine, your Lordship will oblige me by destroying it.[4]

To the Rt Hon[bl]
Lord Byron

[1] On 29 Oct. Byron replied to this letter, saying in part, 'Was I to anticipate friendship from one, who conceived me to have charged him with falsehood? . . . I should have felt proud of your acquaintance, had it commenced under other circumstances; but it must rest with you to determine how far it may proceed after so auspicious a beginning' (*LJ*, ii. 64). See letter No. 202, to Lord Byron, 31 Oct. 1811.

[2] Moore had wandered from the point in making overtures of friendship, which Byron was unwilling to accept until the main issue was settled. See Byron's letter to Moore, *LJ*, ii. 64.

[3] Letter No. 200, to Lord Byron, 29 Oct. 1811.

[4] Byron had suggested to Hodgson that Moore's letter of 1 Jan. 1810 (letter

202. *To Lord Byron*

Sir John Murray

Thursday [31 October 1811]

My Lord

I answer your last note with great pleasure—[1] I was afraid your Lordship had totally mistaken me, and began most heartily to repent of the openness by which I had exposed myself to misconstruction & repulse— I find however that my reliance upon your generosity was not misplaced— I shall now mention the subject, for the first time, to my friend Rogers, and, as I know he has long wished for the pleasure of your Lordship's acquaintance, we cannot have a better person or a better mode of bringing us together—

I expect him in town tomorrow morning.

I have the honour to be, my Lord

Your Lordship's very humble Servt

Thomas Moore

(turn over)

I open my note again to say that I thank you for your delivery with respect to the letter in Mr Hodgson's hands, and shall, according to your Lordship's desire, receive it.[2]

203. *To Lord Byron*

Sir John Murray

Chelsea

Friday Three o'clock [1 November 1811]

My Lord—

I have the honour of inclosing a note which I have just received from my friend Mr Rogers— I perceive that he makes a reservation of *tomorrow*, and together with his note I have received one from

No. 168), which Hodgson had held back pending Byron's return to England, be opened in Moore's presence. In reply to this note from Moore, however, he said that if the letter in Hodgson's possession should prove to be the one in question, it 'should be returned *in statu quo* to the writer; particularly as you expressed yourself "not quite easy under the manner in which I had dwelt on its miscarriage"'. (See letter No. 200, to Lord Byron, 29 Oct. 1811.) Byron concluded his letter by saying, 'You have now declared yourself *satisfied* and on that point we are no longer at issue. If, therefore, you still retain any wish to do me the honour you hinted at, I shall be most happy to meet you, when, where, and how you please, and I presume you will not attribute my saying thus much to any unworthy motive' (*LJ*, ii. 65). See letter No. 202, to Lord Byron, 31 Oct. 1811.

[1] Byron's letter of 30 Oct. (*LJ*, ii. 65).

[2] See letter No. 201, to Lord Byron, 30 Oct. 1811. See also Byron's letter to Hodgson, *LJ*, ii. 71.

Lord Holland, asking me to meet him there on Sunday; but if that day should be more convenient to your Lordship than any of the succeeding ones, I can answer for it that no engagement will prevent Mr Rogers from receiving us at his house, and *I* think the sooner we shake hands in amity the better—

I have not been at my lodgings since yesterday morning, when I answered your Lordship's note of the preceding evening—[1] in sending you the inclosed therefore I take for granted that no other communication has arrived from you in Bury St. since then.

I have the honour to be,
my Lord, your very obliged
& humble Servant
Thomas Moore

To the Rt. Hon.
Lord Byron

Your Lordship will oblige me (if not at home when this note arrives) by sending your answer to Bury St. as soon this evening as meets with your convenience.[2]

204. *To Lord Byron*

Sir John Murray

Friday Evening [2 November 1811]

My Lord—

I shall take the liberty of letting Mr Rogers know that *on Monday* you will dine with him—[3] I am sure he will feel much flattered by the terms in which your Lordship has spoken of him— You cannot think more highly of him than he deserves, I assure you—[4]

His hour of dining is *six*

I have the honour to be very
truly your Lordship's
obliged Servant
Thomas Moore

To the Rt Hon
Lord Byron

[1] Letter No. 202, to Lord Byron, 31 Oct. 1811.

[2] Byron replied on 1 Nov., saying that he would not want to interfere with Moore's Sunday engagement and that if 'Monday or any other day of the ensuing week' would be convenient to Moore and Rogers he would be glad to accept the invitation (*LJ*, ii. 66).

[3] See letter No. 203, to Lord Byron, 1 Nov. 1811. Byron and Moore met at the home of Samuel Rogers, at a dinner which was also attended by Thomas Campbell. Rogers left an account of the dinner in *Table Talk of Samuel Rogers*, pp. 231–2 (reprinted in *LJ*, ii. 66–67 n.).

[4] See Byron's letter to Moore, 1 Nov. 1811 (*LJ*, ii. 66).

205. *To James Corry*

Russell, viii. 98

Wednesday, Nov. 4. 1811.

My dear Corry,

I have only time at this moment to thank you for all your communications, great and small, and to tell you that I have sent the *covers* of your *packets* to Sir Francis Burdett, that he may make a speech about them at the opening of Parliament. I suppose you have heard that during the Talents' administration Windham received an express from Lord Grey, which made a great sensation in every town it passed through, but which turned out (upon opening the gilt despatch-box) to be the *annonce* of a battle between Gulley and Gregson, sent by the Foreign Secretary to the War Secretary 'upon public service.'[1] I thought of this when I received your Linen Board enclosures. What an enormous book you mean to make of it! *μεγα βιβλιον μεγα κακον.* A great book is a great evil.[2] (N. B. writing Greek when a man is in a hurry!) Seriously, I fear we must either reject much of the printed materials, or considerably diminish the scale upon which it is executed. Such a heavy book upon such a light subject would be quite an anomaly. Think what can be done to reduce its corpulence; for really it rather terrifies my little muse to be wedded to such a Mr. Lambert[3] of a book as it must necessarily be when preface, plates, &c. are added to its present bulk. I find I have only time now to throw out these few hints; but I shall write more fully in a day or two.

Your kindness in thinking of my interests gives me the sincerest pleasure and gratitude. What you and Dalton were talking of (an author's night) would be not only serviceable, but flattering to me; and I should like to be *surprised* with such a favour exceedingly. As you have been good enough to ask how you can serve me, the following quere will show that I take you at your word: What are the *longest dates* at which you could get *two bills* upon *Power* in *Dublin* cashed for me, being for the sum of one hundred pounds

[1] Gulley and Gregson were two boxers of the age. Moore mentioned them in his diary (Russell, v. 301), referring to a remark made by Lord Lyttleton to Lord Plunket after Lord Eldon had shaken Plunket's hand: 'That reminds me of Gregson and Gully shaking hands together before they *set to*.'

[2] Moore is referring to the history of the Kilkenny Theatricals, which he and Corry had projected. (See letter No. 198, to James Corry, 24 Oct. 1811.)

[3] Daniel Lambert (1770–1809) was reputed to be the most corpulent man of whom there is authentic record. At one time his weight was 739 pounds. His name became synonymous with hugeness. George Meredith, in *One of Our Conquerors*, mentions 'the Daniel Lambert of cities', and Herbert Spencer refers to 'a Daniel Lambert of learning' in his *Study of Sociology*.

each? I wish to know this immediately (though I ought to have prefaced it with another question, which is, whether you would get them cashed for me at *any* date). I want the money for the approaching Christmas, and he has this sum at my disposal, but wants as long a shot for paying his bills as Acres did for killing his man.[1] So pray, without mentioning the circumstance to any one, let me know what you can do without inconveniencing yourself, and believe me to be,

Most hastily, but as *sure* as if I were *slow*,

Yours,
T. Moore.

206. *To Lord Byron*

Sir John Murray

Monday Evening [November 1811][2]

My dear Lord Byron—

I have just received my letter and thank you for taking so much trouble about it—[3] I am ashamed to find that my memory has deceived me in more than one circumstance attending it— Instead of having been written 'near three years' ago, I find it is dated January 1st 1810—and instead of having inclosed it to Power, as I told you, I now recollect that I only desired him to enquire at Cawthorne's whether it had arrived, and whether it had been received by you; to which application Cawthorne returned the answer I have already stated—

I have been in the country almost ever since I had the pleasure of seeing you—and lately, indeed, have not been very well; but I shall call at your door some morning this week, and shall be very happy if I find you at home disengaged—

I have very often wished to belong to the Alfred,[4] since you told me that you were so constant a visitor there—

Ever very sincerely your Lordship's
faithful Servt
Thomas Moore

To the Lord Byron

[1] Bob Acres, a character in *The Rivals*, finds his courage 'oozing out at the palms of his hands', declines to fight a duel with Ensign Beverly (Anthony Absolute), and resigns his claim to Lydia Languish.

[2] This letter was written after 17 Nov., since Byron wrote to Hodgson on that date, requesting him to return Moore's letter of 1 Jan. 1810 to its author (*LJ*, ii. 70).

[3] Letter No. 168, to Lord Byron, 1 Jan. 1810.

[4] Byron's club at 23 Albemarle Street. It was established in 1808 and was active until 1855. Among its members were William Gifford and Sir James Mackintosh.

207. *To his Mother*

Russell, i. 252, no. 153

[November or December] 1811.[1]

My dearest Mother,

I have just seen Lady Donegal, as kind and delightful as ever. Her praises of *you*, too, were not the *worst* recommendations she returned with. She came last night. I breakfast with her on Monday, and dine to meet her at Rogers's on Tuesday; and there is a person to be of both parties whom you little dream of, but whom I shall introduce to your notice next week. God bless you, my own darling mother. Ever your own,

Tom.

208. *To his Mother*

Russell, i. 253, no. 154

Tuesday [November or December] 1811.

My dearest Mother,

You will be sorry to see this letter unfranked; but Connor has written to me to say, that he did not authorise any one to tell us that the channel of the War Office was again opened: he has added, civilly, that he regrets it very much, &c. &c: however, do not fear, darling mother; I shall find some ways of letting you have your two letters a-week notwithstanding. It was but two days ago I got my dear father's letter about the letting of the house. If I thought, for an instant, that this resolution arose in any degree from any feeling of *hopelessness* or disappointment at my marriage,[2] it would make me truly miserable; but I hope, and, indeed, am confident, dearest mother, that you do me the justice to be *quite* sure that this event has only drawn closer every dear tie by which I was bound to you; and that, while my readiness to do every thing towards your comfort remains the same, my power of doing so will

[1] The date of this letter (May 1811) as given in the Russell edition is evidently incorrect. Even though Moore had told Lady Donegal and Mary Godfrey of his marriage (see the letter from Mary Godfrey, Russell, i. 259, no. 159), he did not introduce his bride to either sister until after he had written to Lady Donegal on 28 Oct. 1811 (letter No. 199), when he said '. . . I most anxiously long for the opportunity of presenting *somebody* to you. If you do not make haste, I shall have *two* somebodies to present to you.' It is quite apparent from this letter that they had already met Bessy. He must have informed his parents of his marriage after October, therefore, instead of in May, as is commonly supposed. See also letter No. 208, to his mother, November or December 1811.

[2] See letter No. 207, to his mother, November or December 1811.

be, please God! much increased by the regularity and economy of the life I am entering upon. Indeed, I *may* be a little too alive to apprehension; but it struck me that there was rather a degree of coldness in the manner in which my dearest father's last letter mentioned my marriage; and if you knew how the cordiality and interest of all my friends has been tenfold increased since this event, you would not wonder, my darling mother, at the anxiety which I feel lest those, whom in this world I am chiefly anxious to please, should in the least degree withhold that full tribute to my conduct which my own conscience tells me I deserve, and which the warm sympathy of all my other friends has given such a happy and flattering sanction to; but I know I am (like *yourself*) too tremulously alive upon every subject connected with the affection of those I love, and I am sure my father by no means *meant* to speak coldly.

With respect to letting the house, I do believe (if you really *like* to leave it) that it would be the best thing you could do. I know you want a little society, and in lodgings more convenient to those you are acquainted with you could have it. Besides, I should think my father might get something handsome by letting it, as that neighbourhood has become so much more promising since he took the place. All I want is, that you should not leave it from any fear that I shall be unable to do anything in future towards helping you through any occasional difficulties you may encounter; for, on the contrary (even if the present change in politics does not do all it ought to do for me), I have every prospect of having it more in my power to assist you, in my little way, than ever; and, if my father wants some money now, let him only apprise me, and draw on Power for it without hesitation.

I have not a minute to write more: my next letter shall go through Lord Byron.[1] Ever yours, dearest mother,

Tom.

209. *To James Corry*

Russell, viii. 100

Friday, Dec. 13. 1811.

My dear Corry,

Many thanks for your kindness in offering so promptly to *translate* my English into *Spanish*, 'cum *notis*,' &c. &c. The sooner the *version* is done, the better; I enclose the *original*.

[1] Although Russell dated this letter May 1811, it was evidently written after October, since Moore did not meet Byron until that month and hence would not have asked him to frank letters. See letters Nos. 197 and 200, to Lord Byron, 22 and 29 Oct. 1811.

Though Power is of such *longue haleine* in the bill way, I think the number of resting-places you offer him cannot but satisfy him.

Give my very best remembrances to Mrs. Corry; and tell her, though given in a letter upon money-matters, they have not a tinge of *the dross* about them.

I shall keep my dramatics for another letter.

Ever yours, in haste,
Thomas Moore.

Send the enclosed letter to Power. By-the-bye, I forgot to ask whether your powers of *import* (in the *franking* way) are as unlimited as your *export* privileges; because a friend of mine has a *young child* he wants to *frank over*.

210. *To his Mother*

Russell, i. 264, no. 162

[December] 1811.

My dearest Mother,

I find the Master of the Rolls is in town, and, if possible, I shall go in to meet him.[1] There is so much call for the opera, that I have *made* a *present* of it to little Power to publish;[2] that is, *nominally* I have *made* a *present* of it to him, but I am to have the greater part of the profits notwithstanding. I do it in this way, however, for two reasons—*one*, that it looks more dignified, particularly after having made so light of the piece myself; and the *second*, that I do not mean to give anything more to Carpenter, yet do not think it worth breaking with him till I have something of consequence to give Longman. Little Power is of wonderful use to me, and, indeed, I may say, is the first *liberal* man I have ever had to deal with. I hope both for his own sake and mine, that his business will prosper with him. Ever your own,

Tom.

211. *To Lord Byron*

Sir John Murray

Saturday [December 1811]

Dear Byron—

It was quite refreshing to see your autograph once more, for you have of late *reduced* your letters (I suppose upon the Peace

[1] Until 1852 the Master of the Rolls was chief of the twelve assistants to the Lord Chancellor.

[2] *M. P., or the Blue Stocking* was published in 1811.

Establishment)[1] most parsimoniously— I know of old your 'grand talent pour le silence', when once you set fairly in, & I am delighted that your billet of yesterday has broke the spell— I am indeed *very* busy—but I don't think I could bear our not meeting as philosophically as you profess to do— In the course of to-day or tomorrow I shall take a chance of finding you at home.

Ever yours
T. Moore

212. *To Thomas Longman* (?)

Rice University

Bury St.*
Sunday 1811*

I send you a Manuscript which was left with me some time since, that I might use my interest with your house to publish it— I cannot take upon myself to recommend the work, as, to say the truth, I have not read three pages of it— But, if you will favour me with some civil apology for not publishing it (in case it should not meet your approbation) you will much oblige

Yours very truly
Thomas Moore

213. *To Leigh Hunt*

B.M. Add. MS. 37210, f. 156

Bury St.
Monday Evening [*c.* 1811]

My dear Sir—

I am just about to step into the Mail for a week's absence from town, & have only time to say that I have received your letter, which I have read with gratitude & admiration— How you, who write so much in public, can *afford* to write so well in private, is miraculous— I shall take your books with me, and hope to tell you all I think & feel about them at Buckinham [*sic*].

[*Signature erased*]

[1] By 'Peace Establishment' Moore means the amicable settlement of the difficulties occasioned by Byron's allusion to Moore in *English Bards.* See letters Nos. 197 and 204, to Lord Byron, 22 Oct. and 2 Nov. 1811.

214. *To Lady Donegal*

Russell, i. 265, no. 163

Saturday, Jan. 4. 1812.

I did not like to write to you during the first moments of your unhappiness, because indeed there is nothing harder than to know what to say to friends who are in sorrow, and the best way is to feel with them and be silent. Even now, I am afraid if I speak honestly, I shall confess that a selfish feeling is predominant with me, and that I am much more grieved by your absence, which is *my* distress, than the cause of it, which is *yours*. This after all, however, is very natural, and I am sure you will give me more credit for sincerity in *missing* you whom I know and love, than in mourning over your brother whom I scarcely was lucky enough to be even acquainted with. Most happy shall I be to see you back once more from a country which could have but little charms for you at any time, but which the sadness and perplexity you have met there now must render particularly gloomy and disagreeable. I shall be the more happy at your taking your leave of it for ever, as I have every hope and thought of being able to live in England myself; and the more I narrow my circle of life, the more seriously I should want such friends as you in it. The smaller the ring, the sooner a gem is missed out of it: so that I own I shall not be *quite* easy till you are once more upon English ground.

I have been living very quiet and very happy, with the exception of those little apprehensions which I must naturally feel at the approaching trial of poor Bessy's strength. She is very delicate indeed, but her spirits and resolution are much better than they were at first.

I was going to talk to you about being god-mother, but as you will not be here at the time, we shall wait till the *next*, though I sincerely hope they will come 'like angel visits, *few* and *far between*.'[1]

Rogers has been at Lord Robert Spencer's this fortnight past, but I have this instant got a note from him asking me to a tête-à-tête dinner.

On Sunday last I dined at Holland House. Lord Moira took me there and brought me back. There is no guessing what the Prince means to do: one can as little anticipate his measures as those of Buonaparte, but for a *very different reason*. I am sure the powder in his Royal Highness's hair is much more settled than any thing

[1] A common poetic figure. See, for example, Blair, *The Grave*, ll. 586–589, and Campbell, *The Pleasures of Hope*, ii. 378.

in his head, or indeed heart, and would stand a puff of Mr. Percival's much more stoutly. At the same time I must say, that there are not the same signs of his jilting Lord Moira, as there are of his deserting the rest of the party. Lord M. is continually at Carlton House, and there was a reserve among the other statesmen at Holland House on Sunday in talking before him, as if they considered him more in the *penetralia* of the sanctuary than themselves: it was only in groups after dinner that they let out their suspicions upon the subject. Lord Moira has not, for a long time, been so attentive to me as since his last return to London.

I never am let to write half so much as I wish; but now that I have broken the chilling ice which the last sad misfortune cast between our communications, you shall hear from me constantly. Ever your attached friend,

Thomas Moore.

215. *To Lord Byron*

Sir John Murray

Sunday Night* [January or February 1812]

My dear Byron—

I have been writing so many letters to-night that I am quite sleepy, and have only wakefulness enough to trouble you with the two inclosed notes, which you will dispatch by the Twopenny for me—but I shall write tomorrow or the day after— I have a most immortalizing scheme to propose to you—or rather, what is better, a most amusing one—in the literary way— You & I shall write Epistles to each other—in all measures and all styles upon all possible subjects—laugh at the world—weep for ourselves—quiz the humbugs—scarify the scoundrels—in short do every thing that the mixture of fun & philosophy there is in both of us can inspire. What say you? but I am too dozy to talk more about it now—it would bring out every thing we might publish or not, comme vous voudrez—

Good night, my dear Byron,

Ever yours affectionately

Thomas Moore

216. *To his Mother*

Russell, i. 267, no. 164

Saturday [February] 1812.

My dearest Mother.

I never had such a *flattering*, but embarrassing scene as yesterday. I dined at Lord Holland's, and there were the Duke of Bedford, Lord Grey, Lord Morpeth, &c. Their whole talk was about my poem, without having the least idea that I had written it: their praises, their curiosity about the author, their guesses, &c., would have been exceedingly amusing to me, if there had been *no one* by in the secret; but Lord Holland knew it, which made me a good deal puzzled how to act. Nothing for a long time has made such a noise. The copy I had for you has been forcibly taken away from me by Lord Holland this morning; but I dare say it will be in the papers to-day or to-morrow, and at all events I will not close this letter till I try whether I can get Rogers's copy, or Lord Byron's, for you.[1]

Rogers has this instant sent me a present of a most beautiful reading-desk, which puts the rest of my room's furniture to the blush. God bless my darling mother. Ever your own,

Tom.

I am going to dine with Croker on Monday.

217. *To Lady Donegal*

Russell, i. 268, no. 165

Saturday [February] 1812.

I take advantage of a frank, and have but one moment to say that I am a papa! and, contrary to my express intentions, it is a little girl.[2] It is well for you that I have not time now to tell all I feel about your neglect of my last letter. *You* I forgive a little, because you don't like writing; but it is so unlike dear Mary, that I am afraid I am beginning to be forgotten. The Berrys and C. Moore

[1] On 13 February 1812, after he had been made Regent, the Prince wrote to the Duke of York explaining that his sense of duty to 'our Royal father' had prompted him to retain the Tories in power. As a consequence the Whigs felt that they had been betrayed. Moore composed his 'Parody of a Celebrated Letter' (*Poetry*, p. 164), which was privately printed and circulated among the Whigs of Lord Holland's circle. It was a direct attack on the Prince's shallowness, faithlessness, and heartlessness; and many people read in it a threefold indictment of his desertion of the Whigs, the Catholic cause, and Mrs. Fitzherbert.

[2] Anne Jane Barbara, Moore's first child, was born on 4 Feb. 1812.

hear continually, and Rogers, indeed, very often taunts me with the preference shown to them; but I tell him I have no doubt they deserve it, however I may lament that I have *lost* such *valued ground* to them. *Will* you be god-mother to my little girl? I would not add to your responsibilities in the child line, if the god-father, who is rich and generous, did not *ask* to stand for the very purpose of taking care of the little one, if any thing should happen to us. Therefore it is the high, precious, *heart-felt sanction* (the *honour* I would say, if it were not too cold a word), the *sanctification* which your name would give to my present happy tie. This is what I want, and what I am sure you will grant me.

I hardly know what I write, but I shall be more collected next time. We are all doing well. Ever your attached friend,

Thomas Moore.

218. *To Lady Donegal*

Russell, i. 269, no. 166

[February] 1812.

I wrote to you last week; at least I sent a letter directed to you, which, I dare say, like the poor poet's 'Ode to Posterity,' will never be delivered according to its address. Instead of directing to Leinster Street, as you bid me, I have dispatched it to *Killarney*, with the same idea of shortness that the Irishman had when he said, 'my name is Tim, but they call me O'Brallaghan *for shortness*,' I dare say it will be some weeks before it reaches you, which, however, I hope it *will* do at last, as there were some little family details in it not quite fit for the eyes of the uninitiated: for instance, there is an account of a *birth*, and rumours of a *christening*, and a modest request that you would take the poet's first production under your patronage; seriously, I have been unreasonable enough to ask that you would allow me to give your name to my little daughter; and I have at the same time told you, that I would not have added to your responsibilities in this way, only that the god-father, who is rich enough to buy all Parnassus, has taken the worldly risk entirely upon himself, and left only the spiritual and godly responsibilities to your ladyship, who will, I am sure, be as *willing* as you are *able* to undertake it.[1]

I also threatened you with a little overflowing of my heart on the subject of your silence to me; but this I feel too deeply to venture upon in a letter. Charles Moore tells me that you are certainly coming in April, and Charles Moore has been indebted to my

[1] See letter No. 217, to Lady Donegal, February 1812.

anxiety to know something about you, for two or three visits, which otherwise I might not perhaps have paid him; for, after all, though I can bear *participation* in what I value, I am very impatient of *monopoly*, and nothing but my real wish to know that you are well and happy could make me submit to inquire news of you from a person who so *totally* engrosses your attention. You never before left a letter of mine so long unanswered as the one I last sent to Leinster Street.

One thing is pretty certain, that you will soon be rid of me. In Lord Moira's exclusion from all chances of power, I see an end to the long hope of my life; and my intention is to go far away into the country, there to devote the remainder of my life to the dear circle I am forming around me, to the quiet pursuit of literature, and, I hope, of goodness. It will make me very unhappy to be forgotten by you, but not half so much so as I should be if I thought I *deserved* it. I [have] not time for more. Ever your sincere friend,

Thos. Moore.

I have not time to look over this, but I fear there is a little *spleen* in it; and the truth is, that the political events of these few days, so suddenly breaking up all the prospects of my life, have sunk my spirits a little, so forgive me if I am either unjust or ill-natured.

219. *To Mary Godfrey*

Russell, i. 270, no. 167

Friday, March 6. 1812.

Your letters have made ample amends for your silence, and I am always ready to believe, at a minute's notice, the kindest assurances of recollection which you can make me; indeed, I cannot hear them renewed too often, and I should not wonder if there were at the bottom of all my *complainings* a little lurking wish to draw these kind professions from you rather than any serious supposition that I am *really* either forgotten or supplanted. No, I believe I have a ninety-nine years lease of your hearts, which is *pretty nearly* as long a term as I shall want them for; and you may set up the sign of the *Angel* over them afterwards. I suppose I can tell you nothing in politics that you have not heard already; but I dare say I should give a very different colouring to my intelligence. Your correspondent is one of the *livery-servants* in politics, and his sentiments of course take the colour of his facings; but *I*, thank Heaven! (and it consoles me for my poverty) am free to call a rascal a rascal wherever I find him, and never was I better disposed to make use of my privilege. You seem to think, both Lady Donegal and you, that the late events are likely to depress my spirits; and I am not sorry that you *did* think so, because the affectionate things it has made you say to me are too sweet to be lost; but I rather believe, if you were here to see with what a careless spirit I bear it all, you would be of opinion that consolations and condolences are thrown away upon me. The truth is, I feel as if a load were taken off me by this final termination to all the hope and suspense which the prospect of Lord Moira's advancement has kept me in for so many years. It has been a sort of *Will-o'-the-Wisp* to me all my life, and the only thing I regret is that it was not extinguished earlier, for it has led me a sad dance.[1] My intention now is, as I have told you already, to live in the country upon the earnings of my brains, and to be as happy as love, literature, and liberty can make me. I think of going somewhere near Lord Moira's for the sake of the library; and though I shall have but few to talk *to* me, I will try to make many talk *of* me. This now shall be my only ambition, and I mean to lay the whole *lever* of my mind to it. Lord Moira has behaved with all that delicate high-mindedness, which those who know him well expected from him. When he told the P. that in a very short time he should make his bow and quit the country, this precious gentleman began to blubber (as he did once when he was told that Brummel did not like the cut of his coat), and said, 'You'll desert me then, Moira?' 'No, sir,' says he; 'when the friends and counsels you have chosen shall have brought your throne to totter beneath you, you will then see me by your side to sink, if it should so please God, under its ruins with you!' He is certainly going to Vienna.

(To Lady D.)

Your answer about my little girl was so long coming, and mamma was so impatient to have her made a Christian (seeing, as she said, that 'children always *thrive better* after it'), that I was obliged to take my chance for your consent; but not wishing to presume too much, we have not placed you in the *van* of responsibility, but merely made you bring up the rear in the following long army of names, 'Anne Jane Barbara Moore.'[2]

We are all well, at least *pretty* well, for poor Bessy is sadly altered in looks; indeed, so totally, that, though she says nothing ails her, I cannot think how health can be compatible with such pale emaciation, and am therefore not a little anxious about her. I hope you will come before we leave London. Ever most sincerely yours,

Thomas Moore.

[1] Moore is referring to the Prince Regent's decision to retain the Tories in power. Lord Moira and other Whigs were in consequence out of office, and Moore's hopes for patronage from Moira vanished. See letter No. 216, to his mother, February 1812.

[2] See letter No. 217, to Lady Donegal, February 1812.

220. *To John Dalby*

Mrs. Mercia Dalby

27 Bury St., St. James*
Tuesday, March 10th* [1812]

My dear [Dalby][1]

When friends have no chance of ever seeing each other again (which I have long feared was *our* case) there is nothing so tantalizing & indeed melancholy as their corresponding together— If it be any thing like a true sentiment that 'Death & absence differ but in name' I think a letter from those we never hope to meet again is as gloomy a visitor as the ghost of those who are departed— Accordingly I dare say I never should have written another line to you, if I had not to communicate the agreeable news (to *me* at least highly agreeable) that we are not only, I hope, soon to meet, but most probably *long* to be near each other— The late events in politics, (which I dare say have surprized *you* as much as they have done others) have completely extinguished the hopes I have looked to now for so many years, of having something done for me whenever [Lord Moira] should have it in his power—[2] The game is now completely up, and [Lord Moira] himself so entirely despairs of any brighter prospects that it is confidently said to be his intention *soon to quit England altogether*—and before I proceed farther, my dearest [Dalby], let me beg of you to keep all the circumstances of this letter a secret from *every one* for some time— With respect to myself, as I am now thrown totally upon my own exertions, and as my own exertions are quite incompatible with the idleness of London life, I have adopted the resolution of retiring to the country, and, of course, [Donington], from the convenience of [Lord Moira]'s Library and from the advantage of having a friend like you so near me, is the place of all others in which I wish to fix my retreat— You may recollect how often I have projected this at times when I had little thought of ever being drawn to it. However when I say 'drawn to it', do not suppose that it is a step which I take unwillingly—far from it— I have, thank heaven! every certainty of making an ample livelihood by literature, and I am convinced that I shall feel more true tranquility, and certainly a more independent spirit in a life of such pursuits than I should ever have enjoyed in the vulgar walks of office—at least it is the best philosophy to *persuade* myself that such will be the advantages I shall gain by exchange— Now, my dear friend, what I want of you is to look out *industriously* for

[1] Brackets in the text of this letter indicate that the names of persons and places, which were erased, have been supplied from the context by the editor.

[2] See letter No. 219, to Mary Godfrey, 6 Mar. 1812.

a *neat house* for me in the neighbourhood of [Donington], not too small nor yet too large, and if it has a good garden so much the better— It must be unfurnished, but, of course, may have as many conveniences in the way of fixtures &c, as it chuses, and I need not say that *cheapness* is one of the objects to be attended to in your choice— I found lodging so inconvenient in [Donington] that I *must* have a *house*, particularly as my prospect is to stay many years among you, and I cannot say how grateful I shall feel to you, if you will lose no time in executing my behest for me—[1] It may be either in the Village or any where around within two or three miles walk of the [Park], and I must intreat you also to *keep* the *matter* a *secret* till I have consulted freely with [Lord Moira] upon my intentions, and informed him of all my plans, views &c. &c.

I know you will forgive all the trouble I impose upon you, & I beg you to believe me, my dearest [Dalby.]

Yours ever most truly
Thomas Moore

221. *To James Perry*

National Library of Ireland

Friday Evening [26 March 1812, *not in Moore's hand*]

My dear Sir— I sent you some more doggerel— I heard the thing of to-day *abused* pretty well for its stupidity—but I rather think that was owing to your having puffed it off too much to Tierney yesterday—however don't betray me *ever*—as for *one hit* I may have a *dozen failures*.[2]

I should like very well to go on buffooning this way, but it takes up as much time as more important things, and this is what I cannot afford at present—however, if you think it worth your while, there is *one way*, in which you can not only oblige me very much, but secure a quicker and brisker fire from me than I have maintained as yet, and that is by *lending* me for six months one hundred

[1] Moore made the same request of Dalby in 1807. See letter No. 141 to Lord Moira, January 1807.

[2] See letter No. 222, to James Perry, 27 Mar. 1812, which was printed in the *Morning Chronicle* as a preface to one of the satires. Moore is perhaps referring here to the poem which accompanies that letter.

Moore began writing squibs for the *Morning Chronicle* early in 1812 and continued to contribute through 1842. It is impossible to identify all of the satires written by him, since many of them are signed merely with a letter— 'O' or 'R', for example. For a good discussion of Moore's contributions to newspapers see Jones, *The Harp that Once*—, pp. 341–2. A number of squibs and lampoons are identified in letters addressed to Perry and Easthope, which are included in this edition.

pounds— I say 'lending' and for 'six months,' because it does not *fetter* either of us, and at the end of that time, if you should think the labourer has not been worth his hire, I shall repay you—indeed I should hope (as I shall take more pains with what I do) that a collection of the best of them in a volume would very amply *overflow* my debt at the end of that time— Pray, have not the least delicacy in refusing my proposal, if you dislike it— I cannot deny that I want the money, but (thank the Muses!) I have at least *nine* different ways of getting it.

(Turn over)

Ever sincerely y[rs]
T. Moore

[*On reverse side*]

If you have any better or more extensive plans to propose to me, I am quite ready for them—

222. *To James Perry*

National Library of Ireland

Morning Chronicle
Friday, 27 March 1812.

To the Editor of the Morning Chronicle
Sir

I was conversing with a friend of mine yesterday, on the alarming appearances of the times, and the very little prospect of any alteration for the better, when after some deliberation, he proposed the following remedy as the only means of arriving at the bottom of the evil and producing a fundamental change in the Councils of the Empire—He proposes to engage some personable elderly lady, who will suffer herself to be cooped and fattened, till she *outweighs* every other lady by a stone or two— 'We must then' says he 'give her full power and proper instructions, and this is the only chance we have of saving the Country—' Philosophers state it to be one of the great laws of gravitation, 'that the attraction of bodies is in the proportion of the quantity of matter they contain'—and as the attraction of *female* bodies, seems very much regulated by the same law at present, my friend's reliance upon the effects of an increase of matter, does not appear to be at all chimerical, or ill founded— I therefore submit his proposal through the medium of your patriotic paper, and requesting a few hints, with respect to the shortest fattening process, from any of the Noble feeders, of (what is called) *new light* mutton, I am, Sir

Yours &c
Q

P. S. It ought to be mentioned, that one lady has been tried in the balances against the favourite, and has been found wanting—the following is a pretty accurate account of the experiment.[1]

223. *To John Dalby*

Mrs. Mercia Dalby

Saturday [March 1812]

My dear Dalby—

I wrote to you near a fortnight since upon a subject about which I am not only very much interested but about which I am in a *very great hurry*, and you have gone on quietly *never minding* me all the time—[2] Now, this is to notify to you [*sic*] that if you do not answer me by return of Post, and tell me something (satisfactory or *not* satisfactory) upon the subject I wrote to you about, you shall 'never more be officer of mine.'—[3] If I do not soon get a house at

[1] This letter and the three poems accompanying it are not in Moore's hand. Two of the poems are to be found in the *Poetical Works*: 'Extracts from the Diary of a Fashionable Politician' (*Morning Chronicle*, 30 Mar. 1812) and 'News from Country Cousins' (*Poetry*, pp. 168 and 579). To the former Moore added the following lines in the 1841 edition of his works: 'While gentle H—rtf—d begg'd and pray'd / For "*Young I am, and sore afraid.*" '

The following squib, with which the letter is concerned, was not included in the 1841 edition:

'Let us see, said the R—t, *which* heaviest weighs,
Britannia, or——, and lo! he displays
The balance to try them, high hanging in air
With the Goddess placed *here* and her Ladyship *there.*
They were both of them, ladies of pretty good weight
But Britannia had been rather sickly of late,—
For she'd got in the hands of a d—mnable Quack
Who had very near laid the poor Dame on her back,—
And in spite of her vigour and proud resolution,
Had almost destroyed her good old Constitution,—
Besides too 'twas rumoured, to add to her fright,
That the *Doctor* was coming to finish her quite,—
Then, no wonder, alas! the poor lady was thin
And unable to weigh down the scale she was in,
For the Dame on the other side, sitting, G— bless us,
Was equal, at least, to three whole Marchionesses
Accordingly, scarce had her most noble r—p
Been placed in the balance, when down it came plump,
And the R—t exclaimed, while he viewed them together,
'Poh! weighed against——, Britannia's a feather!—'

See also letter No. 221, to James Perry, 26 Mar. 1812.

[2] See letter No. 220, to John Dalby, 10 Mar. 1812.

[3] *Othello*, II. iii. 249.

Donington I shall go somewhere else—therefore in the direct ratio of your anxiety to have me near you must be your alacrity in executing my commission. [*The remainder of the letter is missing.*]

224. *To his Mother*

Russell, i. 273, no. 168

Friday night [March] 1812.

My dearest Mother,

After long wishing and waiting, I got a letter from my dear father to-day, and I quite jumped at it with impatience, after the long silence you have all kept. I hope *now* however, since I have told you of the convenience of inclosing to Lord Byron, that you will let me hear a *little* oftener about you; for, indeed, all this time that Kate has been with you, you have been three writers in family, and I am but one; besides *I* write for the public, and Kate and Nell have little other authorship than gossiping now and then to me, which I hope they will afford me oftener.

I think of taking a little tour the beginning of next week, to look for some rural retreat somewhere, as I am quite weary of London, and I find my friend Dalby is confined with an illness which may prevent him for some time investigating the neighbourhood of Donington for me.[1]

I wish, whenever you have a good opportunity, dear mother, you would send me the remainder of my books, as I am collecting a library, and am resolved to get all together that I can. Tell Kate she must leave her Boileau to me in her will. I owe her many books still, and, as soon as I can get an opportunity, I will send her Lord Byron's book (which is *every thing* now),[2] and one or two more new publications.

My Lord Byron liked so well the way I conducted my *own* affair with him, that he chose me as his friend the other day in a similar business, and I had the happiness of bringing him through it without going to extremities. When I say that 'he liked so well,' &c., I don't mean that he gave that as a reason for employing me, but I think it was a tribute that amounted to pretty much the same thing, and I was flattered by it accordingly.[3]

[1] See letter No. 220, to John Dalby, 10 Mar. 1812.

[2] *Childe Harold*, Cantos I and II, which appeared in 1812.

[3] Byron chose Moore as his representative in an affair with Harry Greville. A settlement was made peacefully when Leckie (Greville's second) asked Moore to mark out of an offensive letter from Greville to Byron all the objectionable sentences. Moore complied, Greville wrote the letter again (not knowing who had acted as censor), and all ended amicably. (See Russell, ii. 229.)

I am quite sorry, my darling mother, to find that you have had your winter cold; but the sweet season that we feel now will, I trust, quite restore you.

I shall take care and not write anything in the papers. Poor Hunt is *up* for his last article but one against the Prince.[1] God bless you, darling mother. Ever your own,

Tom.

225. *To his Mother*

Russell, i. 274, no. 169

[March or April] 1812.

My dearest Mother,

I have not had an answer from Dalby yet, but am in the same mind about retiring *somewhere*, and I should prefer Donington both from the society and the library.[2] Lord Moira told me himself that he meant to withdraw entirely from politics, so that I look upon all hope from him in this way as completely extinguished, and must only look to myself for my future happiness and independence; indeed, I rather think, from the appearance of the times, that the best of the great ones hold their places and possessions by a very precarious tenure, and he that has nothing to *fall from* is the only one that has nothing to fear. I don't know whether I told you before, (and if I did not, it was my uncertainty about it for some time which prevented me,) that the Powers give me between them *five hundred* a-year for my music; the agreement is for seven years, and as much longer as I choose to say. This you will own (however precarious, as depending on their success in business) is very comfortable as long as it lasts, and shows what may be done with my talents, if exerted. You will not mention this much. As soon as I have leisure to finish a long poem I have in hand,[3] I shall get a good sum for it, which will, I hope, enable me not only to pay my debts, but to assist my dearest father with something towards *his*

[1] On 9 Dec. 1812 John and Leigh Hunt were prosecuted and imprisoned for publishing an attack on the Prince Regent in the *Examiner* for 12 Mar. 1812. The article was a reply to a poem in the *Morning Post*, which lauded the Prince as the 'Maecenas of the Age', the 'Glory of the People', and an 'Adonis of Loveliness'. In answer the *Examiner* said, in part, 'this *delightful, blissful, wise, pleasureable, honourable, virtuous, true*, and *immortal* prince was a violator of his word, a libertine over head and ears in disgrace, a despiser of domestic ties, the companion of gamblers and demireps, a man who has just closed half a century without one single claim on the gratitude of his country or the respect of posterity.' (Quoted in *LJ*, ii. 205 n.)

[2] See letter No. 220, to John Dalby, 10 Mar. 1812.

[3] Moore was at work on *Lalla Rookh*, which was not published until 1817.

establishment. So you see, darling mother, my prospect is by no means an unpromising one, and the only sacrifice I must make is the giving up London society, which involves me in great expenses, and leaves me no time for the industry that alone would enable me to support them: this I shall do without the least regret.

My friend Lord Byron's poem is doing wonders,[1] and there is nothing talked of but him every where; he certainly is * * *

[*The rest of the letter has been lost.*][2]

226. *To James Carpenter*

Rice University

Donington
Monday [postmark April 14, 1812]

My dear Carpenter—

I meant to have answered your last note in person, but having told my friends that I was leaving town several days before I actually did, I was afraid to venture into Bond St— We should have had you with us, but poor B. was very ill indeed— I was obliged to get medical advice, and it appeared she had every symptom of approaching decline, and requires to be taken very great care of—this makes me more anxious to get her into the country & accordingly I am come down here upon a reconnoitring trip— I have forgot this some time to tell you that I keep my lodgings in Bury St. for the season & that you may fearlessly direct every one for me thither— We shall have dinner at '*both our houses*' when I return—

Pray, send me Copies of *Corrupt. & Intol.*—my *Letter to the Catholics* and one of the Parody,[3] *by tomorrows* [*sic*] *mail*—for my friend Dalby— Keep the latter in *hands* till I return.

Ever sincerely yours
Thomas Moore

Direct 'Castle Donington, Loughborough'[4]

[1] *Childe Harold*, Cantos I and II.

[2] Russell's note.

[3] For 'Corruption and Intolerance' and the 'Parody of a Celebrated Letter' see *Poetry*, pp. 131 and 164. The *Letter to the Roman Catholics of Dublin* appeared in 1810.

[4] The end quotation mark has been supplied by the editor.

227. *To James Corry*

Russell, viii. 108

Kegworth, Leicestershire
Friday, May 19. 1812.

My dear Corry,

We have at last got down to our country retreat, where I have no doubt of surmounting all my difficulties. If we had staid much longer in town, the curiosity to see 'Moore's wife,' combining with the kindness of my friends, would have ruined us. She was asked to the three most splended assemblies in London, and Lady Lansdowne's disappointment at her not going to hers was quite diverting. I know all this will give you pleasure, my dearest Corry. What are we to expect next after the late horrors in London? Some change may take place in politics now, but I build no longer upon such phantasies.[1] Ever yours, with best regards,

T. Moore.

Mr. Corry.

228. *To John Wilson Croker*

John Wilson Croker, *Correspondence and Diaries*, i. 52

Keyworth, Lancashire [*sic*]
May 22nd [1812].

I dare say you have heard of my having appeared suddenly to my friends in the new characters of a husband and a father. If I were quite sure that you feel interested enough about an old friend to wish to know the particulars of my marriage, you should know them. At all events, I hope it will give you pleasure to learn that, though I thought it necessary to conceal the business so long (from everyone but my friends Rogers and the Dowager Lady Donegal) yet the moment the revelation took place, all my friends took the excellent creature I have married most cordially by the hand, and Lady Loudoun and Lady Charlotte Rawdon were among the first to visit her. They knew the story, and could not but respect her. I should have been most happy to have made her known to you, but I found it impossible to stand the expenses of town, and therefore made a hasty retreat into Lord Moira's neighbourhood, where, with his fair library and a happy home, I hope to live a life of peace and goodness, and to become at last, perhaps, respectable.

[1] See letter No. 219, to Mary Godfrey, 6 Mar. 1812.

I am glad to take the opportunity of troubling you with the inclosed letter to show you that I am not unmindful of your good opinion nor indifferent to your remembrance of me.

Ever yours,
Thomas Moore.

229. *To James Power*

Russell, i. 277, no. 171

Wednesday, May 23, 1812.

My dear Sir,

I send you the commencement of our fifth number,[1] and I am glad we have begun so auspiciously, as I think it will make a very pretty and popular duet.

Many thanks for your inquiry at the inn, but we have got our things. They were carried by mistake to Derby.

I have written two more verses to the inclosed air, as I mean now to finish as I go on.

You cannot imagine what a *combustible* state this country is in—all the common people's heads are full of revolution. Yesterday the bells of this and the neighbouring villages were ringing all day for the change of Ministry.[2] Pray, let me know everything curious that comes to your knowledge in music, literature, and politics. Bessy sends best regards. Ever yours,

Thomas Moore.

230. *To Thomas Longman*

Harvard College Library

Private Bury St.

Thursday Morning [May 1812]

My dear Sir—

Before I say a word about *business*, allow me to entrust to you a little secret of mine, with the custody of which you will not be long burdened, as once I am quietly in the country, I do not care how much it is proclaimed—the secret is that I am *married*, and have been so near fourteen months past—the circumstances that attended it you shall know when we talk together, but the only persons privy to it at the time were my friends Mr Rogers, the Dowr

[1] The fifth number of the *Irish Melodies*, 1813.

[2] See letter No. 219, to Mary Godfrey, 6 Mar. 1812. The ringing of bells came as an aftermath to the change of ministry occasioned by the assassination of Perceval by John Bellingham, a bankrupt broker.

Lady Donegall & her sisters, and Power in the Strand— I have, within this fortnight past, made it known to a few more friends, Lord Moira's family &c.—but I wish it not to circulate much farther till after my departure— I have had a house all this time at Brompton and have this morning packed off all my furniture to the little Cottage I have taken in Leicestershire—[1] Now, (to slide by a delicate transition into *business*) I find that the very exhausting process of moving a family has drawn so much upon my last supply from Power that I shall be completely in the *shallows* for the remainder of the quarter, unless *you* can muster up confidence enough in me to make another advance of the same amount as the former—in order to lighten the risk a little, I will deposit immediately in your hands some manuscript things of mine, which I fear nothing but my death would give any value to, but which might be some sort of security in your hands against any event of that kind. They consist of a tolerably large fragment of a kind of Novel which I began, (about perhaps a hundred pages) and some light political things, many of which have appeared and made some noise, tho I have not *acknowledged* more than one or two—with these I will likewise deposit a poem with notes (which I must however send you from the country, as it is packed up) called 'an Ode upon Nothing', which got a medal from the Historical Society in Dublin College, and was the subject of much contention afterwards in College, till I removed it from the Books of the Society myself, and I believe Croker of the Admiralty is the only person who now has a copy of it— It occupies a good deal of space, and is a whimsical thing enough, but as it was written during the boyish times of my Little's Poems, I doubt whether any friend of mine would wish to see it published— You shall have it however to lie by you— Another condition I would wish to make is that (after you have seen *cursorily* the things I give you) you would allow me to seal them up till I shall feel myself entitled to ask them back from you, or till any accident befalling me shall put it in your power to make use of them—[2]

In offering you these trifling securities, I am well aware how insufficient they are, and that I have chiefly to depend upon your trust & good-will towards me for the favour which I take the liberty of asking; and if you are disposed to feel sufficient of both towards me to contribute so considerably to my comfort at present, I shall consider it an additional tie between us in the long literary connection which I trust we shall maintain— I had hoped to be near

[1] The Moores moved to Kegworth, in Leicestershire, in the spring of 1812.

[2] The unfinished novel is probably 'The Chapter of the Blanket. A Fragment.' The 'Ode upon Nothing' was evidently never published.

giving you my Poem now, but I am sorry to say that the disturbed life I have led between the *pretence* of living in town & the reality of living out of it has not been at all favorable to its progress—[1] I shall have full time however now to attend to its completion.

I must tell you (and pray do not mistake my motive in telling you) that Carpenter is unceasing in his offers of kindness & assistance, and that, of course, I have declined them all since the period of my agreement with you— I mention this in order to have the opportunity of assuring you that even a refusal of assistance from *you* would not excite a regret in me for the discontinuance of my connection with *him*— To do him justice, he is very anxious that I should consider all his offers as made upon the score of *friendship* not of *business*; but, tho I shall always like him, & be happy to keep upon good terms with him, I am too well aware how hard it is to draw the line between friendship & business in pecuniary matters ever to be indebted to him another shilling— I enter into this explanation lest you should suspect me of the mean little management of playing him off against you by mentioning his offers to me.

If you are inclined to oblige me, pray write a line as soon as you can to say 'Yes',—or if it be '*No*', still let me have it written, for I had rather have this ugly monosyllable in my eyes than my ears, and as soon as I know your determination, I will call upon you— I am completely dependent upon your decision for my ability to follow my furniture— Very truly yours

Thomas Moore.

It would do in *fifty pounds* now, and the rest in the course of a month or so.

231. *To J. Taylor, Sun Office*

Rice University

Wednesday* [May 1812]

My dear Sir—

You have given me a most lucky opportunity of telling the Public *my own* opinion of Mr. P.—[2] Pray, if possible, let the inclosed be in this evening correctly—

A thousand, thousand thanks for your good-nature—

Yours ever

T. Moore.

[1] Moore is referring to *Lalla Rookh,* which was published in 1817.

[2] Moore could be referring to his 'Lines on the Death of Mr. P—rc—v—l', *Poetry*, p. 452. Spencer Perceval, First Lord of the Treasury and Chancellor of the Exchequer, was shot and killed at the House of Commons on 12 May 1812 by one Bellingham, a timber merchant who felt he had been wronged by the Russian government and the British ambassador to Russia.

232. *To Lady Donegal*

Russell, i. 286, no. 180

Kegworth
[May] 1812.

This is merely an experiment to try how I can get at you through the Woods and Forests,[1] and as soon as I have cleared the vista, we shall have many a peep at each other. We arrived here safe and tired, though, I must say, I never made a journey with less fatigue, for we had the inside of the stage to ourselves, and it was like traveling in the family coach. Bessy is quite pleased with our new house, and runs wild about the large garden, which is certainly a delightful emancipation for her after our very limited domain at Brompton. But we are still in all the horrors of settling, and if a life could be found worse than that of 'buttoning and unbuttoning,' it would be packing and unpacking. We talk often over your kindness to us the morning we came away, and *I* think often of your kindness to me every morning I have ever seen you. God bless you for it all; and, as I intend now to go to church every Sunday, you shall have many a prayer offered up for you; none of your worn-out devotions, that have been hacked till they are good for nothing, but bran-new prayers, that (at least *in church*) are very little the worse for the wear. Love to dear Mary and your sister, from theirs and yours ever,

T. M.

233. *To his Mother*

Russell, viii. 103

Tuesday [May] 1812.

My dearest Mother,

I went and dined at the Park yesterday. Lord Moira seems to think that this late victory, instead of confirming the Ministers in their seats, will rather undermine them by tending to *increase* the power of Lord Wellesley, who goes hand in hand with *him*; but I fear he is too sanguine.[2] He has set about *retrenching* at last most manfully, and has dismissed no less than *twenty servants*. There is no doubt but in a few years this system will set him on his legs again.

[1] Lord Glenbervie, Commissioner of the United Lands and Forests, was franking some of Moore's letters. See letter No. 239, to Mary Godfrey, June 1812.

[2] See letter No. 237, to James Corry, 29 June 1812.

I am going to dine with the Stories of Lockington. They offered to send their carriage for Bessy if she would come; but her back gets so weak and painful after dinner, that it is uncomfortable to her to go into society.

I am beginning to be anxious about a letter from home, and hope, my darling Mother, that you have no returns of your summer illness. Yesterday and to-day are, at last, *true warm* summer with us.

Ever your own,
Tom.

234. *To James Power*

Russell, i. 284, no. 178

Thursday, June 12. 1812.

My dear Sir,

I hope you got my little parcel last week with the Tyrolese air,[1] and that I soon shall hear from you about Stevenson. I got the proofs you sent through Lord Glenbervie; but unfortunately it was most deceitful intelligence that Joe Atkinson gave me about the War Office being again opened to me, for it is as shut as ever; and all I can do is to send my packet back to Lord Glenbervie, and get him to frank it to Ireland. You shall have the proofs at the same time. I wish we could get the Irish airs your brother has. Pray write to him about them.

What an unexpected turn these long delayed arrangements have taken! I cannot suppose, however, that the House of Commons will allow these *invalided* gentlemen to go on with the Ministry. The tone in which you write about *my* political expectations is as liberal as usual, and very cheering to me. I do not think I ever met any one who feels so rightly about me as you do.

Do you think do the Americans mean *seriously* to put a few hundreds a year in my pocket?

Within this week past I feel something like settlement to business; *and ten days shall seldom pass over my head* without your seeing some proofs of my industry.

Mrs. Power is very good-natured to think of little Nanny, and Bessy means very soon to write her a long account of all our domestic felicities. You certainly *must* come down to us: we have already a room which is called Mr. Power's room.

Believe me, with the best regards of Bessy and myself to Mrs. Power and you, ever sincerely yours,

Thomas Moore.

[1] 'Merrily Every Bosom Boundeth: the Tyrolese Song of Liberty', *Poetry*, p. 314.

235. *To Mary Godfrey*

Russell, i. 290, no. 182

Monday, June 22. 1812.

You must take every line I write to you now as pure matter of friendship, without one grain of self-interestedness in it, for my Lord Glenbervie has given me free leave to make use of him *on my own account*, and so I am now independent of you, and might crack my fingers at you, if it were not for a little sneaking kindness that makes me think of you even when you are *not* doing me services; a sort of repose, in which you so seldom indulge yourself, that I ought to avail myself of every such short opportunity as you allow me for the display of my disinterestedness.

I thank you very much for the pamphlet, and if you think the Quarterly Review will come within the limits of Lord G.'s privilege and good-nature, Power shall now and then trouble you with one for me. I would not ask you to send me the Edinburgh, because that is growing too heavy to be franked.

They are preparing at Donington for Lord Moira, but I should suppose he is tied too fast by the ribbon to come away; and, in the mean time, I meet very good company at the Park, both ancients and moderns, Greeks and Persians; and the best of it is, I have the privilege of bringing home as many of them as I please to a visit with *me*.

I have heard nothing whatever of Lord Byron, and I dare say he will return to London without my seeing him. Lord Tamworth called upon me yesterday, but I was at church!

From what I see of this place,[1] I have the pleasure to tell you that I think we shall be able to live very cheaply in it. There is no fear of my getting too fat with eating; the market is as bad nearly as that of Bermuda, where they ring a bell to announce the *event* of their going to kill a *creatur*.

Bessy is plagued with headaches. *You* never say anything about your health, but I think often of those vile attacks you have, and wish you would tell me whether they are less frequent. Ever yours,

Thomas Moore.

I shall write to Rogers this week, but I am ill myself to-day with a pain, something like rheumatism, in my shoulder: it may, however, be a strain which I have got in *hoisting* little Barbara. How is *your* little Barbara?

[1] Kegworth, Leicestershire, near Donington Park, Lord Moira's estate.

236. *To William Gardiner*

Russell, viii. 109

Kegworth
June 24. 1812.

Dear Sir,

The more you do me the honour of *valuing* the assistance you expect from me, the more I lament my thoughtlessness in offering it; for I ought to have recollected (when Miss Dalby told me that you wished some verses of mine) that I am no longer a free agent in the disposal of my writings,—at least of those *connected with music*,—having given, by a regular deed, the *monopoly* of all such productions of mine to the Messrs. *Powers* of London and Dublin. These legal trammels were so new to my muse, that she has more than once forgotten herself, and been near wandering into infidelity, very much, I assure you, from the habit of setting no price upon her favours; but I think you will agree with me that it is worth while keeping her within bounds, when I tell you that the reward of her constancy is no less than *five hundred* a year during the time stipulated in the deed. For not complying with your request I need offer no better apology; but for inconsiderately promising what I could not perform I know not what I can say to excuse myself, except that (and believe me I speak sincerely) the strong wish I felt to show my sense of your merits made me consult my *inclination* rather than my *power;* and it was not till I had actually begun words to one of your airs that I recollected the *faux pas* I was about to commit.

I thank you very much for the sermons,[1] which I am reading with great pleasure, and I beg you to believe me, very sincerely yours,

Thomas Moore.

237. *To James Corry*

Russell, viii. 110

Monday, June 29. 1812.

My dear Corry,

I have waited for your *post-liminious* letter till I am out of patience, and though I doubt whether this will catch you in Dublin, yet it shall take its chance; and the first thing I feel impatient to express is my very sincere sorrow at the account which you give me of Mrs. Corry's health. I was not a little glad to hear, however, that

[1] Sermons by Robert Hall. [*Russell's note.*]

Cheltenham was recommended to her, as it gives us some faint chance of seeing you both in our humble mansion at Kegworth. Pray bring her. I think it would do her good to see us so happy; and Bessy shall be her handmaid and nurse, and smile her into health again.

I am afraid your plan of a short season at Kilkenny will not do. So few of your *staunch sitters-out* will think it worth while to go for that short period; and, then, it is too narrow a mark also for your *chance* visitors to hit: when they had the space of three weeks they were sure to make some part of it convenient to them, the least intervention of business now will make them give it up as hopeless; however, you may try, it will add a few pages more to my book,[1] and if I have to record a failure (*quod Deus avertet!*) it will produce a *variety* which I did not expect.

Politics are, as you say, going to the Devil. I don't know what to make of my friend Lord Moira's conduct.[2] A sword when put into the water will look crooked, and the weak medium of Carlton House may produce an *appearance* of *obliquity* even in Lord M—. But both the sword and he, I trust, are as bright and straight as ever. God bless you.

Ever yours,
T. Moore.

[1] This statement furnishes evidence that Moore was either writing the book on the Kilkenny Theatricals from materials furnished him by Corry or that he was collaborating with Corry on it. Moore published his article on 'Private Theatricals' in the *Edinburgh Review* for October 1827, and it is quite possible that he had a hand in *The Private Theatre of Kilkenny* (1825). For further evidence of their collaboration see letter No. 198, to James Corry, 24 Oct. 1811.

[2] After the death of Perceval, the task of forming a new ministry was given to Lord Wellesley, who failed in the attempt. In June 1812 Lord Moira was authorized to consult with Lords Grey and Grenville on the formation of a new cabinet. Disagreements arose, negotiations were broken off, and Lord Liverpool was made Prime Minister. Throughout the proceedings, Lord Moira, from necessity, supported the Prince Regent, for which he was criticized by his Whig colleagues. In June of that year he was invested with the Order of the Garter, and in November appointed Governor-General of Bengal and Commander-in-Chief of the forces in India.

Realizing that Moira would not have a worth-while post for him in India and being unwilling to accept anything in England by 'exchange of patronage,' Moore gave up all hope of receiving anything from the man to whom he had looked for aid in securing a government position. See letter No. 281, to Lady Donegal, December 1812.

238. *To Edward T. Dalton*

Russell, i. 292, no. 184

Kegworth
Monday, June 29. 1812.

My dear Dalton,

Do not think that I did not deeply *feel* your letter because I have been slow in acknowledging it. I am one of the ruminating animals, you know, and chew the cud of a letter long after others would have swallowed and forgotten it. Really and sincerely the most solid benefit you could do me (and I know no one who would be more ready to do me one) could not affect me more strongly than the kind, prompt, and cordial feeling with which you received the intelligence of my marriage. It has been a happy marriage indeed, my dear Dalton, and I doubt whether I could have arrived at a wife by any other process that would have made me equally sure of her attachment, purity, and disinterestedness. You know we found, with some degree of pleasure upon both sides, that Mrs. Dalton and she had taken a strong fancy to each other, even at the distance by which they were then separated; and it will give me the most heartfelt pleasure to see them side by side, a sort of *companion pictures* in friendship to *you* and *me*. I don't know when this time will arrive, but, whenever it does, it will be sure to make me happy.

I am ashamed to say a word about the '*olim promissum carmen*' for the club, except that I own it cooled my zeal a little to find that Power and Corry have never heard a syllable about it;[1] and as I know, of course, that they would be among the first of the *élite*, I thought that nothing but your abandonment of the idea could have kept them from knowing something about it. I have written a song very lately, which I think would suit Mrs. Dalton, and I intended it should accompany this letter, but I find I *must* write again to you in a day or two about some business with Stevenson, and the song shall go then.

What a mess you must have made of poor M.P., in Dublin! They are playing it, I see, at the Lyceum again.[2]

I wish (as you have so often thought of retirement in England) that you would come and live near us here, and let us be happy and

[1] Moore is probably referring to Richard Power and James Corry, two friends of his acting days with the 'Kilkenny Theatricals', 1808–9.

[2] Moore's opera *M. P., or the Blue Stocking* was revived at the Lyceum in October, 1811; January and February 1812; August 1815; and October 1816; but there is no indication that it was produced in June 1812. It was staged in Dublin, as Moore says.

musical together. Lord Moira's library, which I will insure you the use of, and the use of *my* voice as a third, now and then, in our old favourites, Haydn and Mozart, would make a country life pass, not only pleasantly but profitably. Living here is as cheap as any poet or musician could wish; and, for myself, I see every prospect of being able, in a few years, to be *just* to my friends as well as grateful, and gradually to emancipate myself from debts of all kinds. But I am forgetting all this time your plaguy plan, which of course will keep you in Ireland, and puts an end to the vision of having you here completely.

Our little child, which is quite a *fairy*, and was very puny at first, is getting as fat and merry as a young sucking cherub.

You shall hear from me again very soon, and in the meantime believe me ever, your sincere friend,

Thomas Moore.

I did intend to send this to Corry for you, but as it is doubtful whether he is in Dublin, you shall pay postage for it.

239. *To Mary Godfrey*

Russell, i. 280, no. 173

Kegworth
Wednesday [June] 1812.

This is *not* 'the long letter next week,' so don't mistake it for it. Campbell, you know, says that 'coming events cast their shadow before;'[1] so this is only the *shadow* of the coming letter, which you shall have, please pen and ink, before next Tuesday. The first glass of wine of *my own* that I've drunk since I came here was the day before yesterday to the late Ministry, and (as we say in Ireland) 'sweet bad luck to them.'[2] I feel more indifferent about chances and changes than ever I did in my life, which makes it more likely, perhaps, that I shall get something good out of them, for Fortune is one of those ladies who are piqued by indifference, and generally makes her advances to those who could contrive to do very well without her.

I took Bessy yesterday to Lord Moira's, and she was not half so much struck with its grandeur as I expected. She said, in coming out, 'I like Mr. Rogers's house ten times better;' but she loves everything by association, and she was very happy in Rogers's house. By the same rule, I think 56. Davies Street would excel, in her eyes, every mansion in the Lady's Almanack.

[1] Campbell, 'Lochiel's Warning'.
[2] See letter No. 237, to James Corry, 29 June 1812.

Good by. I was very near forgetting though, that you have kept me in sad suspense about a packet (one of those that were sent to you) which comes from Bermuda, and which, I shrewdly suspect, contains *money;* if you had had a suspicion of this, I know you would have contrived, somehow or other, to put wings to it for me; but I dare say you sent it flying yesterday. Good by again. Ever yours,

Thomas Moore.

I am sorry the old *Woodman*[1] is going out; but we shall get somebody else perhaps.

Since I wrote the above, I have received the packet from you, and it is *money* indeed! Bessy imputes this luck entirely to a little robin redbrest that has haunted us these two days.

240. *To his Mother*

Russell, i. 281, no. 174

Kegworth
Wednesday [June] 1812.

My dearest Mother,

You missed one letter from me last week on account of my bustle in town, but now that I am returned (and right happy to get back), you shall have your weekly dues as regular as ever. I came yesterday morning, very much fatigued indeed with sitting up all night, and I found Bessy and the little one pretty well. Bab *had* been very ill during my absence, on account of something wrong they gave her to eat at Dalby's, but she is now getting round again.

I dined with Lord Moira again a day or two before I left town, and from what I could collect from him and others, I do not think there is much probability of his going over to Ireland. He will not go without full powers of emancipation, and those they will not give him. The Chancellor is the dire stumbling-block in the way both of him and the Catholics.[2]

This little trial of London has only made me love my quiet home and books better. Indeed, I want but *you*, darling mother, and my good father and Ellen with me to confine all my desires within this dear circle. My friends in London were astonished at my *fat.* Ever your own,

Tom.

[1] Lord Glenbervie, who was first Chief Commissioner of the United Land and Forest Department.

[2] John Scott, first Earl of Eldon, was Lord Chancellor of England, 1801–6 and 1807–27. He opposed Catholic Emancipation.

241. *To his Mother*

Russell, i. 282, no. 175

Tuesday [June] 1812.

My dearest Mother,

I dined with Lord Moira yesterday, and I fear I shall be obliged to go there again to-morrow. I say 'I *fear*,' because I do not like to leave Bessy alone; and, besides, she is always so anxious about my returning at nights, which are now growing dark: however, to-morrow is Lady L.'s birthday, and as they will most probably be off in a day or two more, I think I shall go. I believe I told you about her kindness in undertaking to consult her own physician in London about Bessy's health. She is to call upon us the day after to-morrow, for the purpose of hearing accurately from Bessy herself the state of her health, and getting Dr. Clarke's opinion upon it when she arrives in town. I got the paper my dear father sent me with Curran's speech. I am delighted to find that Lord Moira is regaining so fast the popularity which he lost for a moment with the Catholics; and, indeed, from the general aspect of affairs, I don't think it at all improbable that we shall see him lord lieutenant of Ireland this next year.

I have had a very kind letter from my friend Colonel Hamilton. Bessy was to have written to-day, but she has Mary Dalby with her, and therefore only sends her love. Ever your own,

Tom.

Let me know whether my letters go regularly now.

242. *To James Power*

Russell, i. 282, no. 176

Friday [June] 1812.

My dear Sir,

I got the parcel yesterday, which I find you had sent off before you received my letter through Lord Glenbervie. I shall therefore dispatch this by post, lest there should occur any delay in its reaching you; and I have to ask pardon for having omitted answering two or three questions in your former letters. In the first place, with respect to a subject for the engraving to this number, I agree with you that the Minstrel Boy would be a very good subject, and more simple than Love, Wit, and Valour, which occurred to me as offering a tolerable field for the fancy of a good artist; but the other is, as you say, very national, and I should suppose you mean the boy to be taken when fallen on the ground and tearing away the strings of his harp. The title of 'Merrily oh!' I would have as follows: 'The Tyrolese Song of Liberty; a national air, arranged with English words, and dedicated to Miss Rawdon:'[1] but I should like to see it as arranged for a single song before you print it, if that be not already done, or at least a proof of it.

With respect to which of the songs I mean for the *Book*, that is entirely as you may think proper yourself; you are the best judge of the mode in which they will tell to most advantage. The order of the Melodies I shall think over against Tuesday, when I will send you those back you may wish for, through Lord Glenbervie. Let me know by letter to-morrow, which of the manuscripts you sent you wish returned.

If you have a verse of 'Oh! see those Cherries,' beginning 'Old Time thus fleetly,' it is all I have written or intend to write to it.[2]

I shall finish the number of the Melodies this month. I am sorry to find that there is no air in it at all likely to suit my own singing, which does not tell well for the number. When I write to your brother, I will bid him send me some more: there is one lately published by him with words of Curran's, but it is no great things.

I looked over Gardiner's preface as you desired me, and if the subject you were thinking of be a New Version of the Psalms, I am afraid that is a task that would be sure to bring disgrace upon me, for I agree with Dr. Johnson, that such a work must 'necessarily be bad.' But I'll tell you what I should be very glad to undertake with Stevenson, and that is, a series of Sacred Songs, Duets, &c.; the words by me, and some of the airs.[3] If you think this would do, I shall very readily join him in it.

I am still without any further intelligence about Lord Moira's plans. Ever yours, my dear sir,

Thomas Moore.

243. *To James Power*

Russell, i. 284, no. 177

Thursday, June, 1812.

I send you the Tyrolese air, which I have just written words to, and I think it goes beautifully.[4] Pray let me know whether anything more is done with Stevenson; if not, I shall send you up

[1] *Poetry*, p. 314.
[2] See letter No. 268, to James Power, November 1812.
[3] Moore's *Sacred Songs* appeared in 1816.
[4] 'Merrily Every Bosom Boundeth', *Poetry*, p. 314.

a letter, which you must forward to him with my songs to be arranged. The second verse of 'Cease, oh! cease,' is to be thus:

> 'Say, oh! say no more that lover's pains are sweet,
> I never, never can believe the fond deceit.
> *Thou* lov'st the wounded heart,
> *I* love to wander free;
> So, keep thou Cupid's dart,
> And leave his wings to me.'[1]

This will sparkle better in the page. Ever yours,

T. M.

244. *To James Power*

Russell, i. 285, no. 179

Thursday night [June ?] 1812.

My dear Sir,

I am sincerely sorry to put any *drag* upon the *wheel* of a business, which seemed to run so glibly and prosperously to-day; but, upon mentioning the kind of *forms* which we had used in our agreement to the friend with whom I consult about everything of this kind, he made me feel the very great irregularity I had been guilty of, in putting myself totally in the power of your brother and you, while I had not a *line* in return to give me the least claim or binding upon *you.* I need not tell you how much I wish our compact to depend solely upon the good-will and convenience of all those concerned in it; but still it is rather sinking *me* into a comparative nothingness in the arrangement to make me write a formal agreement to *your* terms, without letting me have one line in writing from *you* to guarantee an equal observance of the stipulations on your side. Indeed, I am well convinced that it is only from oversight that you or your brother could have proposed such a very unequal arrangement, and I therefore feel less hesitation in begging that you will both return me the letter I have written you, and let us strike out some mode of giving a form to our agreement, in which the securities may be somewhat more regular and reciprocal. I am, my dear Sir, most sincerely yours,

Thomas Moore.

[1] 'Cease, oh Cease' was not included in the 1841 edition of Moore's works and hence not in the Oxford edition, edited by A. D. Godley; but it is to be found in the Albion edition, published by Frederick Warne (1891), p. 620.

245. *To William Gardiner*

Russell, i. 296, no. 186

Tuesday, July, 1812.

My dear Sir,

I have but just time to thank you for your beautiful book, which I am playing through with the greatest delight.[1] The subjects are most tastefully selected, and admirably arranged. Your copy for Lord Moira I will willingly take charge of, and you had better lose no time in sending it, as it is doubtful how long they will stay at Donington Park.

I find I shall have an opportunity of forwarding your Sermons to you in the course of the week.[2] Yours very truly,

Thomas Moore.

246. *To Lady Donegal*

Russell, viii. 113

Kegworth
[13 August] 1812.

I went over and dined with the Moiras yesterday, and saw poor Lord M. in his Star and Garter, which he sat down to dinner in, with a couple of parsons and myself, to celebrate the Prince's birth-day![3] They leave this, I believe, next week, and it is a fine thing to see at last the manly resignation with which he is disbanding whole regiments of servants and horses, and reducing his expenditure to a scale which can hardly exceed two or three thousand a year. I feel most deeply interested about him; and both he and she have given me new cause for the warmest gratitude by their kind attentions to Bessy. Rogers and I had a very pleasant tour of it, though I felt throughout it all, as I always feel with him, that the fear of *losing* his good opinion almost embitters the *possession* of it, and that though, in his society, one *walks upon roses*, it is with constant apprehension of the *thorns* that are among them.

* * * * * *

He left me rather out of conceit with my poem, 'Lalla Rookh' (as his fastidious criticism generally does), and I have returned to it with rather an humbled spirit; but I have already once altered my

[1] Gardiner had probably sent Moore a copy of his *Sacred Melodies from Haydn, Mozart, and Beethoven*, which was first published in 1812.

[2] See letter No. 236, to William Gardiner, 24 June 1812.

[3] The Prince Regent was born on 12 Aug. 1762.

whole plan to please him, and I will do so no more, for I should make as long a voyage of it as his own 'Columbus'[1] if I attended to all his objections. His *general* opinion, however, of what I have done is very flattering; he only finds fault with *every part* of it in detail; and this you know is the style of his criticism of characters —'an *excellent* person, *but*—'

I find my hour draws near, and I have talked so much of Rogers that I have only time to say I hope Tunbridge has made you both as stout as in our best days of Tunbridge happiness.

Best love to dear Mary, and believe me,

Ever yours,
T. Moore.

247. *To James Power*

Russell, i. 297, no. 187

Wednesday, Aug. 13. 1812.

My dear Sir,

I was in hopes I should be able to send to you the ballad for Mr. Ashe to-day, in order that Stevenson might have it to take with him to Cheltenham to-morrow. I have not, however, been able to please myself in it; but by to-morrow's post I think I shall at least succeed so far as to send you *one verse*, which you can forward after him, if he is gone, and I can write the remainder afterwards, one verse being quite enough for him to set to. In the meantime I shall write at the other side some words, which I think, with a gay and elegant air, might be made popular. I could add a third verse if it was thought absolutely necessary; but the idea is so completely put into the *two*, that I had much rather leave it as it is, and I think there is enough of it. Bid Stevenson take pains with it, and not repeat *too often* the last line. Am I to see him here? If he does not think it worth while to take Kegworth in his wanderings, I shall never have a good opinion either of his *taste* or his *friendship*.

Best regards to Mrs. Power from us both. Bessy has just had visits from Lady Tamworth and Lady Rumbold. We are unluckily in the *thick* of fine people here. Ever sincerely yours,

Thomas Moore.

1.

'She has beauty—but still you must keep your heart cool;
She has wit—but you must not be caught so:
Thus *Reason* advises—but Reason's a fool,
And 'tis not the first time I have thought so,

[1] Rogers published *The Voyage of Columbus* in 1812.

Dear Fanny!
'Tis not the first time I have thought so.

2.

'She is lovely—then love her, not let the bliss fly,
'Tis the charm of youth's vanishing season:
Thus *Love* has advis'd me, and who will deny
That Love reasons much better than Reason,
Dear Fanny!
Love reasons much better than Reason.'[1]

My name may be put to these words. I intend to alter the second line of the second verse.

248. *To James Power*

Russell, i. 350, no. 240

Monday [14 August 1812]

My dear Sir,

I write to you with 'Going, going,' in my ears, and it has occurred to me, as the product of the sale is very uncertain, and it is a great object for us to be off on Thursday, it is just *possible* that, after paying our bills, we may not have money enough to carry us on, for we have been obliged to get clothes, &c., and even I (from being disappointed by Campbell) have been compelled to employ a Donington tailor. All these things must of course be discharged before we go, and as it is of some moment to us (from what I told you about the income tax) to get away immediately, I should be glad, for certainty's sake, that you could contrive to send me a few pounds by to-morrow's post. I have great hopes we shall not want it, and in that case I will send it back to you.

I am sorry you have altered your own arrangement about the music, as I dare say it is better than mine.

I was going to say I would send 'The Valley lay smiling'[2] to-morrow, but I have great fears that Bessy has put it up; therefore, to make sure, inclose a proof to-morrow, and you shall have it back, with the words on Thursday. I expect 'Savourna Deilish'[3] back from your brother every day, and then we shall be quite done. The Lord send us safe out of Kegworth. Ever yours,

T. M.

[1] *Poetry*, p. 312.
[2] *Poetry*, p. 203.
[3] ''Tis Gone, and Forever, the Light We Saw Breaking', *Poetry*, p. 209.

I'll Think of You Waking and Sleeping

'You love me, you say, for the light of my eyes,
And if eyes would for ever shine clearly,
You need not, perhaps, give a reason more wise,
For loving me ever so dearly.
But beauty is fleeting, and eyes, I'm afraid,
Are jewels that spoil in the keeping,
So love me for something less likely to fade,
And I'll think of you waking and sleeping:
Dear youth!
I'll think of you waking and sleeping.'[1]

Here is a verse, my dear sir, which I hope Stevenson will be able to make something of; it will require that mixture of lightness and feeling which no one knows better than his knightship. You ought to have had it by yesterday's post, but I got a sudden summons the day before to dine at the Park and celebrate the Prince's birthday,[2] which, you may suppose, I did with all due solemnity and sincerity; the wine was good, and my host was good, so I would have swallowed the toast if it had been the devil! The second verse of the above song ends, 'I'll think of you sleeping and waking, dear youth,' which I think makes a good burden and title. I expect my *Quarterly* from you; send it by the coach immediately. Ever yours,

T. M.

249. *To James Power*

Huntington Library

[Augst 19th 1812, *not in Moore's hand*]

My dear Sir—

I return the Songs— I like the way the Warrior[3] is done very much, and it may now, I think be put in—

I have marked the changes that may be made in 'Dear Fanny'—[4] and as I intend to make two or three alterations in the second verse, you may take some opportunity of sending it back to me corrected, & I'll add the second verse.

[1] This stanza was not included in the 1841 edition of Moore's works.

[2] See letter No. 246, to Lady Donegal, 13 Aug. 1812, where Moore mentions the celebration of the Prince's birthday. This letter was probably written on 14 Aug. 1812, rather than in 1813, as given in Russell's edition.

[3] 'The Dying Warrior', *Poetry*, p. 299.

[4] *Poetry*, p. 312.

I have not the Haydn Song ready for to-day, but you shall have it by my next dispatch—[1]

Ever yours
T. Moore.

250. *To Leigh Hunt*

B.M. Add. MS. 37210, f. 160

Wednesday [postmark August 20, 1812]

My dear Sir—

I am very sorry to find by your Examiner of Last Sunday that you are ill, and I sincerely hope, both for the sake of yourself and the world, that it is not an indisposition of any serious nature— I have very often, since I left town, had thoughts of writing to you —not that I had any thing to say, but merely to keep myself alive in your recollection till some lucky jostle in our life's journey throws us closer together than we have hitherto been— It is *not* true, however, that I have had nothing to say to you—for I have to thank you for your Poem in the Reflector, which I would praise for its beauty, if my praises could be thought *disinterested* enough to please you—but it has won my heart rather too much to leave my judgment fair play, and the pleasure of being praised by *you* makes me incapable of returning the compliment—[2] All I can tell you is that your good opinion of me in general is paid back with interest tenfold, and that my thoughts about you are so well-known to those I live with, that I have the pleasure of finding you acknowledged among them by no other title than 'Moore's friend'— I suppose you have heard that I suddenly burst upon my acquaintances last spring, in the [two] characters of husband & father,[3] and I hope you will believe me [*MS. damaged*] (though my little intercourse with you might have made such a confidence impertinent on my side) I often wished to make you one of the very few friends, who know the secret of my happiness & witnessed my enjoyment of it— I rather think too that if you were acquainted with the story

[1] Moore made use of several of Haydn's airs. See, for example, the *Sacred Songs*, *Poetry*, pp. 254 ff.

[2] Moore is referring to the following passage in *The Feast of the Poets*, which first appeared in *The Reflector*, No. IV, article x:

> There are very few poets, whose caps or whose curls
> Have obtain'd such a laurel by hunting the girls.
> So it gives me, dear Tom, a delight beyond measure
> To find how you've mended your notions of pleasure.

[3] Moore married Bessy Dyke on 25 Mar. 1811, and his first child, Anne Jane Barbara, was born on 4 Feb. 1812. He did not publicly announce his marriage until the spring of 1812. See letter No. 230 to Thomas Longman, May 1812.

of my marriage, it would not tend to *lower* me from that place, which I am proud to believe I hold in your esteem—I have got a small house & large garden here in the neighbourhood of Lord Moira's fine library, and feel happy in the consciousness that I have *indeed* 'mended my notions of pleasure', and that I am likely, after all, to be what men like you approve— Mrs Moore & I have been for these ten days past on a visit to our noble neighbour, who is, at length, preparing for an old age of *independence* by a manly & summary system of retrenchment— He has dismissed nearly all his servants, and is retiring to a small house in Sussex, leaving his fine Park & Library here to *Solitude & me*— How I have mourned over his late negotiation! A sword looks crooked in water, and the weak medium of Carleton House has given an appearance of obliquity even to Lord Moira, but both the Sword & he may be depended upon still—at least I think so.[1]

I was very much flattered by your taking some doggerel of mine out of the Morning Chronicle some months since, called 'The Insurrection of the Papers'.— I don't know whether you saw 'The Plumassier' about the same time—[2] It was mine also, but not so good— I hope next year, when I have got over a work I am about, to help you with a few shafts of ridicule in the noble warfare you are engaged in, since I find that you have thought some of them not unworthy your notice.

With best regards to Mrs Hunt, and your *little child*, for whom I could supply a *companion-picture*, I am, my dear Sir,

Most truly yours
[*Signature effaced*]

251. *To James Power*

Russell, i. 298, no. 188

[August] 1812.

My dear Sir,

I send you the song for Braham in this parcel. I feel almost sure he will like it. You had better take my copy to him, and tell him that what I have put as bass now must be turned into accompaniment. He may alter as he likes, and, as soon as I know he approves of it, you shall have the second verse, which I will make applicable to any purpose he may wish it for. I am just going into Ashbourne

[1] Lord Moira's political downfall was brought about partly by his support of the Prince Regent, which was not approved by his Whig friends. See letter No. 237, to James Corry, 29 June 1812.

[2] *Poetry*, pp. 164 and 167.

with this parcel, and to get my bill changed: if I succeed, I will send it by the morning's post. Yours ever,

T. M.

First Verse.

'Has sorrow thy young days shaded,
As clouds o'er the morning fleet?
Too fast have those young days faded,
That even in sorrow were sweet.
Does Time with his cold wind wither
Each feeling that once was dear?
Come, child of misfortune! hither,
I'll weep with thee, tear for tear.'[1]

252. *To Mary Godfrey*

Russell, i. 299, no. 189

Kegworth
[August?] 1812.

I have only time to say two words, and that is to beg you will send me a kiss a-piece by Rogers, who, you know, is coming down to me on Sunday next. I forget who the man was that set fire to his house after the Constable Bourbon had been in it;[2] but I believe I shall do the same by mine (though from a different reason) after this memorable visit. I shall be so happy to have had a right good, excellent friend under my *own* roof!

The Moiras are come, and I am just going to do the honours of the country to them. Millions of thanks for your last letter. I knew your head was bad, though you would not tell me of it. Ever yours,

T. M.

N.B. This is *really* only a note; but such a letter as will follow it!

253. *To his Mother*

Russell, i. 299, no. 190

Kegworth
[August or September] 1812.

My dearest Mother,

I know you must be anxious about your little grandaughter's (only think—your grand-daughter!!) getting over her weaning, and I have great delight in telling you that she hardly seems to have

[1] *Poetry*, p. 206.

[2] Probably a reference to a legend connected with Charles de Bourbon, who quarrelled with Francis I and was a French expatriate in Italy. See the Glossary of Proper Names.

missed the nurse at all, but has taken to the bread and milk as naturally as if she and it were old acquaintances.

I believe I shall have to fly up to London in a day or two about some business with Power and Stevenson, and I shall avail myself of the opportunity of calling upon the Sheddons about my deputy at Bermuda,[1] though I rather think now there will be no American war.

A draft which I sent out to Colonel Hamilton some time ago (in payment of money which he quite *forced* upon me when I was going upon my tour in America) shared the fate of my other arrears from my old deputy, and was never paid; so that I have been obliged, since his arrival, to produce *forty pounds!* Nothing could be more kind about it than my old friend the colonel, for he never mentioned the circumstance, and it was only by a round-about way I found out that he had not been paid.

God bless my darling mother. Lady Loudoun and Lord M. called upon us on their way to town, and brought us pine-apples, &c. How shockingly Lord M. has been treated in the Edinburgh Review.[2] It quite goes to my heart to think of his having exposed himself to such profanation of abuse. Ever your own,

Tom.

254. *To William Gardiner*

Russell, ii. 101, no. 351

Tuesday evening
[August or September 1812][3]

My dear Sir,

One would think by our anxiety to detain you that we had a *presentiment* of something worth your staying for; and, strange

[1] The Sheddons, merchants in London, were uncles of Moore's deputy in Bermuda. See letter No. 81 to his mother, 19 Jan. 1804.

[2] 'Authentic Correspondence . . . Relating to the Proceedings of the Marquis of Wellesley, and of the Earl of Moira, . . .', *Edinburgh Review*, xx, no. xxxix (July 1812), pp. 29–38. The article is a criticism of the 'All the Talents Administration', which was formed in 1812. It is extremely critical of Lord Moira's support of the Prince and notes that 'whatever doubts we may form of the conduct of the opposition, we have none whatever of the conduct of Lord Moira,—of the very objectionable part which he has acted, and the very serious abasement of his political character, in the opinions of all men'. Lord Moira saw, says the writer, an opportunity of doing something 'suprafine' for display, i.e. of interposing between the Prince and the barons. The result was that he hurt the opportunities of the opposition by preventing the Prince from granting what the party deserved. He also hurt himself with the Catholics in his attitude toward their cause.

[3] This letter is dated 1816 in Russell's edition, which is an obvious error

to say, an attraction has but this moment occurred, which, I am sure, to *you* is irresistible. My friend Rogers (who, I told you, left me a month or two since), returning by Kegworth, and not finding me there, has come by the evening coach, and is now sitting by the pianoforte at Mr. Peach's, waiting the effect of this note in bringing you back to us.[1] He is a warm admirer of your music, and is anxious to see the author before he leaves Leicester, which must be early in the morning; therefore pray come immediately. Ever yours,

T. Moore.

255. *To his Mother*

Russell, i. 300, no. 191

Donington Park
Thursday night [September] 1812.

My dearest Mother,

To-day I drove Bessy over to our own house to see dear little Barbara, whom we found quite well and in high spirits. I think it would have pleased you to see *my wife* in one of Lord Moira's carriages, with his servant riding after her, and Lady Loudoun's crimson travelling cloak round her to keep her comfortable. It is a glorious triumph of good conduct on both sides, and makes my heart happier and prouder than all the best worldly connections could possibly have done. The dear girl and I sometimes look at each other with astonishment in our splendid room here, and she says she is quite sure it must be all a dream. Indeed, Lady Loudoun's attentions are most kind and delicate. We think of going on with Rogers the day after to-morrow to see Matlock, which is a most beautiful place, within four-and-twenty miles of this.

God bless you, my darling mother. Ever your own,

Tom.

since the Moores were living at Kegworth in 1812 and left it in April 1813. Clayden, *Rogers and His Contemporaries*, i. 234, makes a similar mistake, claiming that Russell dated the letter too early.

[1] Moore is probably referring to the visit from Rogers in September, at which time the two friends made a trip together to Matlock, near Ashbourne. See letter No. 252, to Mary Godfrey, August 1812. See also letter No. 255, to his mother, September 1812.

256. *To his Mother*

Russell, i. 301, no. 192

Kegworth
Thursday [September] 1812.

My dearest Mother,

I am just returned from a most delightful little tour with Rogers. We left Donington on Sunday (poor Bessy being too ill and too fatigued with the ceremonies of the week to accompany us), and went on to Matlock, where I was much charmed with the scenery, and from thence proceeded to Dove Dale, which delighted me still more. It is the very abode of Genii. I parted with Rogers at Ashbourne, and came home yesterday evening. I found Bessy by no means well, but the little thing in high spirits. We are both right glad to be quietly at home again. Nothing could equal the kind attentions of Lord M. and Lady Loudoun; the latter gave Bessy the most cordial advice about her health. The day we were coming away Lord M. took me aside, and asked me in his own delicate manner about the state of my pecuniary affairs; and when I told him that I had every prospect of being comfortable, he said, 'I merely inquired with respect to any *present* exigence, as I have no doubt there will soon be a change in politics, which will set us all on our legs.' This was very pleasant, as being a renewal of his pledge to me, though I fear the change he looks to is farther off than he thinks. Ever your own,

Tom.

I am afraid, on account of my tour, you will be stinted to *one letter* this week.

257. *To Edward T. Dalton*

Russell, i. 304, no. 195

Thursday [September] 1812.

My dear Dalton,

Just when I received your letter, and almost ever since, I have been occupied by a *job* which has taken up all my thoughts and time; but now I am free to think of goblets and flowers again, without the *amari aliquid* of business to embitter them; and the first thing I shall do will be your Charter Glee, if I can get time enough to anticipate that *consummation* of all Baviuses and Moeviuses—Mason.[1] At all events, I will write the words; and even though they

[1] Bavius and Maevius were poetasters satirized by Virgil and Horace. Moore is probably referring to the printer W. Mason.

should not be time enough to get the dip in the baptismal font of your club, they will do for the ceremony of *confirmation*. I have not a moment now to say more. I am off to-morrow night to Donington, where I shall not, however, make any long stay.

The beginning of next week you shall have a *Plenipo* letter from me. Best remembrances to Mrs. D. from hers and yours ever and ever,

T. Moore.

258. *To James Power*[1]

Huntington Library

Wednesday* [October 1st 1812, *not in Moore's hand*]

My dear Sir—I have only time to tell you I arrived safe & sleepy yesterday morning—and to ask a thousand pardons for having left you so much in the style of a *schemer*, for I find I did not even pay for my *washing*, and the salt-fish gave likewise *leg-bail* for itself—but I don't know which it was my shortness of *time* or of *money* that occasioned these over-sights—whichever it was, I am sure you will forgive me—

I have found here a letter from your brother announcing to me the intelligence that he has had his little child christened *Thomas Moore*—what do you think of that? *Yours*, if a little girl, will of course be Miss *Melody Power* to keep him in countenance—

I have found Bessy & the little thing *only* pretty well—but (notwithstanding you made me so comfortable) I am right glad to get back.

You shall soon have more Melodies—

Ever yours
T. Moore

259. *To Edward T. Dalton*

Russell, i. 305, no. 197

Wednesday, Oct. 7. 1812.

My dear Dalton,

I was in London when your letter arrived here, or it should have been answered sooner, and now and then I have been *dreaming* of answering it *in person* at Kilkenny; but it has been *only* dreaming, for the thing would be quite impracticable. I would not give a rush to go without taking Bessy with me, and that would be 'double,

[1] This letter was included in Russell's edition (i. 304, no. 196).

double toil, and trouble,' which I never could attempt; besides, she is not in a portable state at present; but how I should have delighted to exchange places with the dear girl, and see her in the boxes and myself on the stage.

I, of course, saw a good deal of Stevenson in London, and, if he 'in aught may be believed,' we may expect him down here to pass some days with us: he is as boyish and paradoxical as ever, and makes the grave matter-of-fact Englishmen stare wherever he goes. I have one or two *inert* subjects to play him off upon here, and expect a good deal of amusement from it. I see the run of Code's piece is already interrupted after only six or seven nights in sequence; indeed, but for the base abuse of Buonaparte, and the clap-trap allusions to the Spaniards, it could not have stood at all, for it is *pestilently bad*, and Stevenson's music is seldom at all worthy of him.[1]

I had heard of your fame with the commissioners before you mentioned it, and heartily congratulate you not only upon your enjoyment of the *sweets* of place, but (much more) upon your keeping yourself free from its *corruptions*. Every day more and more convinces me that there is but *one* RIGHT way of thinking upon political subjects, and that few take the wrong one who have not some flaw in their *hearts* as well as their *heads*. There was some faint negotiation, I believe, lately with Lord Moira, about the lord lieutenancy of Ireland; but he will not *always* be their dupe, and I only hope he may live long enough to prove, that, though he forgot himself, he has never forgot his country. I don't know whether I have written to you since Bessy and I were on a visit at Donington Park, but it would give you, I am sure, heartfelt pleasure to see the kind, the familiar, and cordial attentions with which both Lord Moira and Lady Loudon [*sic.*] treated her. Lady L. has written to her since she went to town, and there is a degree of good feeling and good taste in the unformal and hearty manner she writes, that will always make me both respect and love her; for she has with others the character of being cold and high, which makes her relaxation in this instance more amiable and well-intentioned.

I am flattered more than I can tell you, by Mrs. Dalton's anxiety to get the song I promised, and must tell you how truly flattered I felt at Stevenson's saying (when I sung him another I have done since), 'How finely Olivia would sing that!' but, I fear, you must

[1] Henry Brereton Code and Sir John Stevenson collaborated on *Spanish Patriots a Thousand Years Ago, an Historical Drama*, which was produced in Dublin in 1812. For further information about Code see the Glossary of Proper Names.

wait till you either see *them* in print, or *me* in Dublin; for I thought it but right to sound little Power with regard to the propriety of giving copies, and he did not seem to wish it. This must also be an answer to your request of a song for Kilkenny, though I doubt whether I have one that would suit your purpose.

Tell Power that I called on my *fellow-labourer* Cardon[1] when I was in town, and was sorry to find that he had been very ill, and obliged to go to the country. If I have a right to make any request of the manager, it is that he will not too hastily determine this to be the last season: tell him this, and with my hearty good wishes to him and all his merry men, and a hope that I may be sometimes remembered over their claret, believe me, my dearest Dalton, ever your attached friend,

Thomas Moore.

My Bessy's best regards to you and Mrs. Dalton.

260. *To his Mother*

Russell, i. 307, no. 198

Kegworth
Thursday [October?] 1812.

My dearest Mother,

Bessy has received your letter, and if you could witness the pleasure it gave both her and me, you would think it was the only one thing in this world which we wanted to make us *quite* happy; but there is still more wanting, and that is the delight of our being all together in love and quiet; and, please God! I trust that happiness is not very far distant; though on every account it would be imprudent of me to break in upon the leisure and profitable retirement I am enjoying at present. I shall let you pay the postage of this letter, as I shall not trouble Corry till my next. I feel a little compunction about him, as his letters do not go free; but their postage is all paid by the board. However, once or twice a week will not break the Great Linen Board of Ireland. You shall have a letter from Bessy herself with my next, but to-day she is very busy preparing for a tea and supper party which she gives to-morrow evening to some of the *Natives* here. I am much afraid that Lord Moira has ruined his reputation as a statesman. The only thing that can save him is (what I suppose he reckons upon) the present Ministry giving up the Catholic question; in which case he will, of course, go to Ireland. But if they deceive his hopes in this respect, I look upon

[1] Probably Anthony Cardon, an engraver. See the Glossary of Proper Names.

him as a gone man with the Catholics, the country, and, what is worse, *himself.* I shall send a letter for Kate with my next packet. God bless my dearest mother and father. With the best love and duty of our hearts, believe me, ever your own,

Tom.

Love to dear Nell.

261. *To the Earl of Moira*

Russell, viii. 124

Kegworth
Nov. 4. 1812.

(Extract.)
My Lord,

I had the pleasure of hearing of your lordship's appointment near a week ago from those friends in this neighbourhood to whom it was communicated; but I did not feel myself authorised to address you upon the subject till I had received the intelligence from those public sources through which it is now known to every one.[1]

Though I read the fate of Ireland in your government being withheld from her, and though I think her last, last hope is now leaving her, yet I cannot but congratulate your lordship on being removed to so honourable an appointment, far away from the contemplation of evils which you are not suffered to remedy or even alleviate.

Thomas Moore.

To the Earl of Moira.

262. *To Mary Godfrey*

Russell, i. 311, no. 201

Friday, Nov. 6. 1812.

I take the opportunity of an inclosure to Lord Glenbervie to say a word or two in answer to my dear Mary's letter which I received yesterday. I have, as yet, had no communication whatever from Lord Moira on the subject of his appointment, which proves at least that he has no idea of taking me with him, because little men require some time for preparation as well as great men, and he is

[1] Lord Moira was appointed Governor-General of Bengal and Commander-in-Chief of the forces in India. See letter No. 237, to James Corry, 29 June 1812.

to sail the beginning of January.[1] Neither do I think it very probable (eaten up as his patronage will be by the hungry pack of followers who surround him) that he will be able to procure me anything at home worth my acceptance: what's more, if he *were* able, I doubt whether I would accept it. My reasons for this another time. But, notwithstanding my expectations are so far from sanguine, I cannot help feeling a good deal of anxiety till the thing is determined one way or other.

Poor Lord Moira! his good qualities have been the ruin of him.

'Que les vertus sont dangereuses
Dans un homme *sans jugement*.'

They must keep him out of the reach of all Indian *princes*, or the Company's rights will be in a bad way. A shake by the hand from a *tawny* prince-regent, and a plume of *heron's feathers* to wear upon birthdays, would go near to endanger our empire in India. This is too severe, but it is *wrung* from me by his criminal gullibility to such a —— as the Prince.

I have not a moment more to lay about me at my friends, or *you* should come in for a lash or two. Do you think you ever do? No, by the pure and holy flame of friendship, *never*! And so good-by to both of you. Ever your attached,

T. M.

263. *To James Power*[2]

Pforzheimer Misc. MS. 309

[Postmark November 12, 1812]

My dear Sir—

I have but just got your letter, and have only time to say that if you can let me have but three or four pounds by return of Post, you will oblige me— I would not have made this hasty & importunate demand on you, but I have foolishly let myself run dry without trying my other resources & I have been this week past literally without one sixpence.

Ever with most sincere good-will,
the pennyless

T. M.

[1] See letter No. 261, to Lord Moira, 4 Nov. 1812, and No. 237, to James Corry, 29 June 1812.

[2] This letter was included in Russell's edition (i. 314, no. 204).

264. *To James Power*

Russell, i. 316, no. 206

Langley Priory
Thursday, Nov. [13] 1812.

My dear Sir,

It was most ungracious of me to send you such a hurried and begging scrawl as I did yesterday,[1] after receiving such letters from you as never had their equal for kindness and solidity of friendship; but the truth is we have been kept on a visit at a house where we have been much longer than I wished or intended,[2] and simply from not having a shilling in our pockets to give the servants in going away. So I know you will forgive my teazing you—and now to return to your letters with respect to my India hopes. I cannot at all express to you how deeply, and *thoroughly*, I feel in the prompt and liberal kindness which you have shown on this occasion: I shall *never* forget it. I do not think it at all probable, however, that I shall have to draw upon the rich *Bank of Friendship* I possess in you; for Lord Moira's not having sent me any communication as yet shows, that at all events he does not look to taking me out with him in any situation, for such an intention would require my being apprised of it in time to prepare. However, he is expected here on Monday, and I shall then know all.

My being here at a distance from my manuscripts makes it impossible for me to send you any inclosure, but as soon as I return, I shall attack business industriously again.

You may laugh at my ridiculous distress in being kept to turtle-eating and claret—drinking longer than I wish, and merely *because* I have not a shilling in my pocket—but however paradoxical it sounds, it is true. Best regards to Mrs. Power. Ever yours, my dear sir,

Thomas Moore.

You will not get this till Saturday, but I dare say between this and then I shall hear from you.

[1] This sentence, which probably refers to letter No. 263, to James Power, 12 Nov. 1812, makes it clear that Russell's date of 18 Nov. 1812 for this letter is incorrect.

[2] Moore was visiting his friend Richard Cheslyn, owner of Langley Priory.

265. *To James Carpenter*

Victoria and Albert Museum, Forster Collection, MS. XXIX, No. 409

Friday* [20 November 1812]

My dear Carpenter— Tho I am appointed Private Secretary to the Gov. General of India with a salary of four thousand a year (vide *Observer* of last Sunday)[1] I do not forget my old friends, and send you this hasty line to show you my remembrance— I had a long letter from Lord Moira last week, but there was not a word in it of Secretaryships, Salaries, or Thousands, and till he comes down here (which we expect every day) I do not know whether he means to do *any* thing or *nothing* for me—in the mean time I am employed for this fortnight past in a way very unlike a person expecting *Princely* Patronage; for I have been writing down (as I told you I would) all my Regency Squibs, and shall have them published for me by some of those respectable booksellers in New-gate Street or thereabouts— I am writing a good many more & in order to give a bond of union to them, I have taken up Hook's idea of the Two-Penny Post-Bag, which tells in Rhyme amusingly—[2] I am glad you liked the Hare &c.— I hope soon to have an opportunity of sending you more—

If you did not make such poor mouths, I would ask you to *lend* me twenty pounds till Christmas—for my payings-away in town left me but small stock to go on with here & I must not draw again till the middle of December— If you *can* spare so much till then you will oblige me, and I shall repay you punctually—

Bessy is much better than she was, and the little thing is so much improved you would not know her— She breasts this frosty weather as hardy and rosy as a young Winter-Cherub, if there *be* such an animal.

Ever yours, with best regards to Mrs C.

Thomas Moore

Not a word about the Twopenny Post-Bag—in about six weeks I will give it to you.

[1] 'Mr. Thomas Moore, celebrated for his translation of Anacreon, is mentioned as being likely to accompany the Earl of Moira to Bengal, in the capacity of Private Secretary, which office is supposed to be worth between 4 and 5,000 £. a year.' The *Observer*, Sunday, 15 Nov. 1812.

[2] Moore's *Twopenny Post Bag* was published in 1813.

266. *To James Power*

Harvard College Library

Tuesday* [postmark Kegworth, November 23, 1812]

My dear Sir—

I sat down to write you a long letter this morning according to my *threat* of Friday; but I was not in the humour for it—indeed I never *can* be in the humour for doing any thing that is at all likely to run counter to your feelings—but the delicate situation in which I am placed between you, and the danger I fear there is lest the world should suspect I stood quietly by, *taking advantage of the dissention of two brothers*, and *leaving* to the side that *it is* most for my *interest*, this fear it is that haunts me & makes me anxious to tell you what I have *all along* felt & thought upon the subject—in a few words, I do not think we shall appear to have done fairly in taking advantage of your brother's surrender of my letter to substitute another kind of compact for *that* which he prefers and to which, when he was in town, we *virtually* pledged ourselves—he has done nothing since to forfeit his right to that kind of agreement, and whatever his former conduct may deserve, or however good *our* intentions may be, the simple transaction will never, I fear, appear otherwise to the world than a wish on *your part* to have your brother in your power, and a no very delicate subserviency to my own interest on *my* part—putting this matter of character out of the question too, I think every one will be of opinion that your brother, contributing such a proportion to the annuity settled on me has a full right to pay his share in any manner he thinks proper, and however our bond may secure us in the eye of the law, I would sooner throw it into the fire & myself after it than produce it *against* that *letter* which your brother returned to me—if he had been contented with the present arrangement (as you always assured me he would be at last) I would, in deference to your wishes, have forborne from any interference; but as he is not, I certainly feel it due to candour to declare that I think he has every right to the sort of arrangement he demands, and that however we may be borne out by the *bond* in resisting him, we shall never stand clear in the code of honour & fairness for it— To shew you how *entirely* I consulted *your* wishes in agreeing to the Bond (supposing too at the same time that your Brother would at last agree to it) I need only mention that when I asked my friend Rogers's advice about it, he declared *against it*—not on account of any unfairness there appeared to him in it (for he did not know all the circumstances) but from the idea of a man of business that two names to a deed were better than one— This I never mentioned to you before, because I was in hopes every thing would be arranged at last according to your wishes— Now, however, that your brother seems to *demand* the arrangement we at first agreed to, I feel myself called upon to declare that, in my opinion, *he has a right to it.*[1]

Trusting that I shall be *any thing* but *lowered* in your esteem by this open avowal of my sentiments, and hoping that it is quite unnecessary to repeat all the friendship my heart feels towards you, and all the sincere wish I feel to go hand in hand with you thro life in every thing that is conducive to our mutual happiness, I am, my dear Sir,

Most faithfully your
T. Moore

I have hardly made this *legible*, as I have been running after every Coach in expectation of Stevenson—at last I saw his *name* in the Guard's list, with 'Failed' opposite it— *Failed* indeed!—tell him he may stay where he is— we had a blazing fire in his bed-room, & our *best breakfast* on the table for him—but he shall meet a *cold reception* whenever he chuses to come after this.

I did not mean to make this a long letter!!

267. *To James Carpenter*

Pforzheimer Misc. MS. 304

Monday* [postmark November 24, 1812]

My dear Carpenter— I wrote to you on Friday under cover to Lord Glenbervie,[2] and asked, in a *careless side-long* way, for the loan of

[1] The idea for the *Irish Melodies* actually originated with William Power in Dublin, but James Power seemed to consider them his exclusive property, so that relations between the two brothers became strained. William retained the original deed of sale, and the result of their argument was that James filed a bill in the Irish court of chancery on 16 July 1816, seeking to compel William to give him sole rights to sell the *Melodies* in Great Britain. In July 1817 William sued James for £5,000 damages, but a compromise was reached out of court. James finally received exclusive publishing rights for the last four numbers of the *Melodies*, although he was supposed to send copy to William. He complied by sending copy for the seventh number (1818), but not for the eighth (1821). When William hired Stevenson to write music for the words to the eighth number, James, who had already engaged Henry R. Bishop for the eighth, ninth, and tenth, got out an injunction against his brother. This letter indicates that Moore attempted this early to bring about a fair settlement, even though he probably sided with James in the question of publication rights. For a more detailed account of the negotiations see Jones, *The Harp that Once—*, pp. 158–9.

[2] See letter No. 265, to James Carpenter, 20 Nov. 1812.

twenty pounds till Christmas—but I now find I must repeat the request with more *serious sadness*, for I cannot do without the money, and you will find me punctual—you know you magnificently offered to let me draw for twenty pounds a month upon you!—but far was it from me to take advantage of such princeliness—all I want now is a *loan* for *this month*, and if you *really* are too poor to oblige me I will send you up a draft upon Power at 31 days for the sum—tho I would rather, *much* rather you could afford to do it in the other way— Lord Moira comes down to-day and my fate will be decided whether I am to be an Indian nabob, or a thorough working-day poet for the rest of my natural life— Sir John Stevenson meditates a visit to me, and actually went so far towards it as to pay for his place in Saturday's mail, which however brought down only his name with the word 'Failed' opposite it—[1] It is not impossible however that he may come to-day or tomorrow, and if he does I shall ask you for the dish of fish you promised me— When you are sending down the fish, could you contrive to put up the Rejected addresses with it? I mean the *Genuine* ones—[2]

Let me hear from you by return of Post & believe me

Yours ever
Thomas Moore.

268. *To James Power*

Russell, i. 317, no. 207

Tuesday [November] 1812.

Your contribution of ten pounds came very seasonably, and was just sufficient to release me from my turtle-eating confinement and pay about a month's house expenses at home.[3] I gained one point beside the turtle at the High Sheriff's; for upon my singing one song that pleased him very much, he said, 'By God! I'll exempt you from the militia to-morrow;' and he did accordingly, on the next day (which was the meeting for the purpose), with '*military commission*,' under my statement with respect to Bermuda, and I am exempt. I had a long letter from Lord Moira on Friday last, and (what you will think very extraordinary) there was not a single word in it about me, or any *expectations* I might have from him. It was merely and solely to explain to me *why* he had taken the

[1] See letter No. 266, to James Power, 23 Nov. 1812.

[2] Moore is probably referring to *Rejected Addresses, or the New Theatrum Poetarum*, published by James and Horace Smith in 1812.

[3] See letter No. 264, to James Power, 13 Nov. 1812.

appointment,[1] the little negotiation he had with Ministers upon the subject (it being the act entirely of the Prince), *the utter hopelessness of justice being done to Ireland*, and his own determination, expressed to Ministers, to give the Catholic cause his most energetic support if it should be brought on before his departure. All this elaborate explanation shows not only his own sensibility upon the subject, but certainly proved very flatteringly the anxiety he felt with respect to my good opinion of his conduct. I cannot, however, but think it very singular that, after the renewed pledges and promises he made me so late as the last time he was here, he should not give the remotest hint of either an intention or even a wish, to do anything for me. I shall be exceedingly mortified, indeed, if he should go away without giving me an opportunity of at least *refusing* something, which is most probably the way I would treat any offer he could make me; but I should like to have at least this gratification. However, as he tells me at the end of his letter that he will be here the beginning of this week, I must suspend all further opinion till he comes. For one reason, however, I shall most heartily rejoice at his appointment, and that is, for its having brought forth your friendship, my dear sir, and exhibited it to me in such fulness of heart, as was never before surpassed. I return you your letters. With respect to 'Fortune may frown,' I shall like to talk to Stevenson about it: but if he is determined not to come down, we must only let it take its chance. By-the-bye, you mentioned his saying 'that it could not be better.' Had you it to show him, or have *I* it? I shall make a search to-day, and shall let you know more about it in my next. I like the way he has done the songs you sent very much. You may place them just as you please, putting the grave and gay alternately, and I think you had better begin with 'Oh the Shamrock!' or, if you like better, 'The Minstrel Boy.' I should like to reserve for the last places (in the hope that we may get something better), 'The Valley lay smiling,' 'One Bumper at Parting,' and 'Oh! had I a bright little Isle.' I object to the latter for its music only, as the words are among my happiest, but the air is not elegant. The deficient line in 'If e'er I forget Thee' is 'That e'en the past errors of boyhood may be.'

The following is the second verse of 'Oh! see those Cherries:'—

'Old Time thus fleetly his course is running,
(If bards were not moral, how maids would go wrong),
And thus thy beauties, now sunn'd and sunning,
Would wither if left on their rose-tree too long.

[1] See letter No. 261, to Lord Moira, 4 Nov. 1812.

Then love while thou'rt lovely, e'en I should be glad
So sweetly to save thee from ruin so sad:
But, oh! delay not, we bards are too cunning
To sigh for *old* beauties, when young may be had.'[1]

Yours ever, my dear sir, most faithfully,

Thomas Moore.

All I say to you about Lord M. is, of course, in confidence.

269. *To his Mother*

Russell, viii. 105

Kegworth [November] 1812.

My dearest Mother,

Lord Moira is appointed Governor-General of India, and he and Lady Loudoun, with the three eldest children, are to sail in January next.[2] I cannot possibly tell at present what effect this very important event will have on my destinies, but it appears to me the worst way in the world that he could be provided for for my interests, though the only way by which *his own* could be served in the present state of politics, and the ruined condition of his finances. What he will propose to me I cannot imagine, but they are coming down here in a fortnight, and then I shall know all. I wrote a letter from Cheslyn's to you by Friday's post, and I hope you received it; it was to say that my dearest Father might depend upon my assisting him through his December difficulties. I only want to know the sum he will require, and the time.

We passed five days at the High Sheriff's very gaily, eating turtle, playing, singing, and dancing.

I am quite in a fidget about Lord Moira's intentions, and shall be till I see him.

Ever my darling Mother,
Your own
Tom.

[1] For 'Oh the Shamrock', 'The Minstrel Boy', 'The Valley Lay Smiling', 'One Bumper at Parting', and 'Oh Had We Some Bright Little Isle' see *Poetry*, pp. 201–3. 'Fortune May Frown' and 'If e'er I Forget Thee' were not included in the 1827 edition of Moore's works or in that collected by himself in 1841, which was reproduced by Godley. 'Oh, See Those Cherries' (the last stanza of which is that quoted here) is not in Godley's edition but can be found in Moore's *Melodies, Songs, Sacred Songs, and National Airs* (New York: W. B. Gilley, 1825).

[2] See letter No. 237, to James Corry, 29 June 1812, and No. 261, to Lord Moira, 4 Nov. 1812.

270. *To James Power*[1]

National Library of Ireland

Tuesday* [November 1812]

My dear Sir—

I suppose you have heard this (to *me*) very important news of Lord Moira's being appointed Governor General of India— Himself, Lady Loudoun & the three eldest children are to sail in January next— What effect this will have upon my destinies I cannot at present conjecture, but it must be something very tempting indeed, which would take me so far from all I have hitherto loved & cultivated— He could, of course, get me something at home by exchange of patronage, but I cannot brook the idea of taking any thing under the present men, & therefore it will be either *India* or *nothing* with me— If he goes off without me, which is most probable, all I have left for it is, hand in hand with you, to make my own independence & I trust contribute to yours— There will be an end then to all expectation from patronage, and *our Plan* will be the only object to attract all my attention and energy— I am at present, as you may suppose, in rather a fidgetting suspense & shall be till my fate is decided one way or the other, which cannot be till I see Lord Moira himself & he intends, I find, coming down here in a fortnight—

I inclose you the last letter I had from your brother— You perceive he still clings to the idea of separate deeds—[2] Did you tell him I had written a poem to prefix to my Picture? I am glad he is thinking of an engraving from it—and think it was not a bad plan to induce him to let us have it—

Bessy & I have been passing these five last days very merrily at the High Sheriff's—eating Turtle & Turbot, singing, dancing &c. &c.

I am going to attack 'Savourna Deilish'—[3] it is a hazardous effort after Campbell, but I will put my shoulder to it—

Best regards to Mrs Power from hers & yours

ever

T. Moore.

Stevenson is a shabby fellow & I quite give him up—

Of course you will not mention to your brother that I have sent you his letter, but it was the shortest way of letting you know its contents.

[1] This letter is included in Russell's edition (i. 308, no. 199).

[2] Moore is referring to the deeds to the *Irish Melodies*. For details see letter No. 266, to James Power, 23 Nov. 1812.

[3] ''Tis Gone and Forever, the Light We Saw Breaking', *Poetry*, p. 209.

271. *To his Mother*

Russell, i. 312, no. 202

Friday [November] 1812.

My dearest Mother,

I have heard nothing more about Lord Moira's plans yet; his stay in India is to be but three years, and I should hope that that time will be sufficient to bring his finances round again. I have had a letter from the Donegals, full of anxiety about *my* hopes and views upon the subject.[1] I do not think myself that Lord Moira (eaten up as his patronage must be by the hungry pack of followers he has about him) will be able to offer me anything of that importance that would tempt me to go so far from home; but, certainly, if he offered me any place of great emolument, I do not think I should be just either to myself or any of those who depend upon me to refuse it. In this, however, my darling mother, I shall consult *your* wishes first and chiefly. You will never find me otherwise than your obedient and affectionate Tom; and though I took *one* important step of my life without consulting you,[2] it was one which I knew you would approve when it could be explained to you; and you shall always guide me as you did when I was a baby at your apron-string.

My good Bessy is quite at my disposal in everything, though naturally not without her fears of the unknown seas and distant regions. I shall let you know the moment I hear anything.

We are quite anxious about poor Kate. Ever yours,

T. Moore.

272. *To his Mother*

Russell, i. 315, no. 205

[November] 1812.

My dearest Mother,

I have heard nothing more since I wrote last. The newspapers have all had it that I am going to India, and some of them have been kind enough to give me a salary of four thousand a-year.[3] I believe, however, the fact is, what was in the Morning Chronicle of yesterday, that Lord Moira has not yet made any appointments. We expect him down here every day, and then all uncertainty will be cleared up. In the meantime, my darling mother, I think you need not have the slightest dread of my being tempted out to India, as I am quite sure Lord M. will not be able (even if he be willing) to offer me anything important enough to justify me in submitting

[1] See the letter from Mary Godfrey, Russell, i. 309, no. 200.
[2] Moore is referring to his marriage.
[3] See letter No. 265, to James Carpenter, 20 Nov. 1812.

to such banishment. I wish he would only let me live at the Park while he is away, and I should be satisfied. However, there is no speculating upon what he will do till I see him, and it is as likely as anything that he will *do nothing*.

We are still very anxious about Kate. My Bessy is much better, and the little thing breasts this frosty weather as hardy and rosy as a young winter-cherub, if there *be* such an animal. Love to all. Ever your own,

Tom.

273. *To James Power*

Pennsylvania Historical Society

[Dec 4 1812, *not in Moore's hand*]

My dear Sir—

I was from home yesterday leaving Bessy on a visit with some friends at Leicester, while *I* go to Lord Moira's for a day or two— I shall then have an opportunity of speaking with him— My absence from home since Tuesday prevented my receiving your letter till this moment, but I hope you have not hesitated to put my name on the Bill—you have my full leave of course—

I have walked from Loughbro [*sic*] and have but an instant to write—you shall hear from me from Lord Moira's, whither I am just setting out to walk, making in all near twelve miles.

Best regards to Mrs Power—
Ever Yours—
T. Moore

274. *To James Power*

Russell, i. 322, no. 211

Dec. 4. 1812.

My dear Sir,

Stevenson left us this morning, and we had great difficulty indeed in getting all his distracted commodities together for him. He copied out, 'Oh, fair! oh, purest!'[1] yesterday, and wrote rather a pretty glee to some words I selected for him. He also tried a song to Rogers's 'Once more, enchanting Girl;' but he failed in it completely. I had not the least idea that the Spanish things had not been done by him in town, and therefore was careless about looking over them with him, knowing how little they required; but upon examining them since he went away, I find they are just in the same state as when I wrote them. I must, therefore, send him the only two of them that will want correction.[2] We dined at my friend

[1] *Poetry*, p. 260.

[2] There are two Spanish airs in the *Melologue on National Music* (*Poetry*, p. 305) and one ('The Castillian Maid') in *Ballads, Songs, and Miscellaneous Poems* (*Poetry*, p. 314).

the rector's yesterday, which took up almost all of the little time we had after your departure.

On Saturday I was equally unlucky at Lord Moira's, as on the former day.[1] Lord M. was out shooting, and Lady Loudon [*sic*] ill; but this morning he has *at last* written me a note, expressing his expectation that I would have stayed and dined last week; and sending us a large basket of hares, venison, pea-fowl, &c. We regretted it did not come while you were here to share it with us; the more so, as this basket of game is all, I am sure, I shall ever get from his lordship. I hope you found Mrs. Power well. Ever yours,

T. M.

275. *To James Power*

Russell, i. 324, no. 213

Sunday, Dec. 21. 1812.

My dear Sir,

The above is the air from Crotch,[2] and it has puzzled me more than any air we have had since the commencement of the Melodies, except perhaps the 'Fairy Queen.'[3] It is to be sure a most irregular strain. The only way I could get over the difficulty was by those convenient triple rhymes, 'Wearily,' &c.;[4] but I find it very hard to find ones equally tripping and graceful for the second verse. The above has taken me four days in twisting and altering, and I am yet far from satisfied. I mean it as the song of a *Leprechaun;* little Irish fairies, you know, that will stay as long as one looks at them, but the moment you look aside they are off. My next shall certainly be 'Savourna Deilish,' and then *Lochaber*,[5] which Crotch gives as an Irish air. If the Tyrolese air be not in hand, pray let Mr. Bennison alter the melody to the way I had it originally (see at the bottom of the music lines on the other side); as, though I took Stevenson's advice in changing it for the glee, I feel it is much more characteristic for the song as I had it at first.

I had a very pleasant and good-natured letter from Stevenson in answer to mine. He says he hopes to meet me in London in March.

[1] See letter No. 281, to Lady Donegal, December 1812.

[2] Moore drew upon Crotch's *Specimens of Various Styles of Music* (*c.* 1807) for some of the airs in his *Irish Melodies*.

[3] 'By the Hope within Us Springing', *Poetry*, p. 192.

[4] There is no Irish melody in the collection which has the 'convenient triple rhymes "Wearily," &c.' in the first stanza. The Tyrolese air ('Merrily Every Bosom Boundeth', *Poetry*, p. 314) does have rhymes in the second stanza ending 'wearily, oh'.

[5] For 'Savourna Deilish' see letter No. 270, to James Power, November 1812. 'Lochaber' is not included in the *Irish Melodies* or in the *Ballads and Songs*.

I mean to send him the two Spanish airs to Ireland,[1] if you have no objection, as he has promised to send them back by *return of post.* I did not like venturing them to Sandbach till I knew he was there, and then it was too late.

I shall be much obliged by your sending the Quarterly Review with the parcel you are making up, and pray send to Carpenter for my Edinburgh one, and let it come too. You will find I shall be very busy in my vocation from this on't, and few weeks, if *any*, shall pass, without your seeing some proofs of my activity. I do not forget the four original songs I have to do yet, but I suppose you will not be very angry if you do not get them till January: *you* are always in *advance*, and *I*, alas! in *arrears;* but time will make all even. Yours ever, with best regards to Mrs. P.,

Thos. Moore.

276. *To James Power*

Rice University

Tuesday* [postmark December 30, 1812]

My dear Sir—

I received the proofs &c.—and shall make a parcell of them tomorrow for you—with Merrily oh![2]—the alteration I wished in the latter is not of much consequence—indeed tho the other is the real & most characteristic melody, I rather think the way it *is* will be most easy & popular— I shall also send you tomorrow a very pretty Sicilian air,[3] which I met with this last week & which turned me aside from my Melodies— The words are at the other side, and I hope you will like them—

Bessy is in expectation of a letter to-day, announcing the happy result of Mrs Power's Christmas Box— She thanks you very much for the Music—

You will be glad to hear that Bessy has consented to my passing next May in town alone— To take her would be too expensive, and indeed it was only in my representing to her that my Songs would all remain a *dead letter* with you, if I did not go up in the gay time of the year and give them life by singing them about, that she agreed to my leaving her— This is quite my object— I shall make it a whole month of company and *exhibition*, which will do more service to the sale of the Songs than a whole year's advertizing—[4]

[1] See letter No. 274, to James Power, 4 Dec. 1812.

[2] *Poetry*, p. 314.

[3] There are several Sicilian airs in the collection of *National Melodies.* See *Poetry*, pp. 237, 242 (2), 244, and 246.

[4] The fifth number of the *Irish Melodies* (1813).

I have a plan, when I return to London *for good* (that is, for our grand project) which I hinted once to you, and which cannot fail to make money—both by *itself* & the publications that will result from it—which is a Series of Lectures upon Poetry & Music, with specimens given at the Piano-Forte by myself—very *select* you know; by subscription among the highest persons of Fashion—it would do wonders—

Ever yours.
T. Moore—

I have made many mistakes in copying out the words, but Williams, the mad parson, is playing on his walking-stick at the other side of the table.

277. *To James Corry*

Russell, viii. 129

Monday, Dec. 30. 1812.

My dear Corry,

A right merry Christmas to you and yours! You have contributed not a little to enliven mine by the inclosure which accompanied your last letter, amounting to 181 £. 14 *s.* 2 *d.*, as well as I can recollect, for the sum is wonderfully '*mutatus ab illo*'[1] since the day before yesterday.

And now to return to our editorial labours,[2]—first premising to you that you are the treasure of treasures in this line of industry, and that you would be worth any money to an *omne-editing* man like Walter Scott. Indeed, if the linen trade could spare you to literature (where you certainly would be much more at *home*), I think you and I together might set up such a book manufactory as would leave the Stephenses and Gronoviuses quite behind us.[3] Never was anything so clear and convenient as the arrangement you have made of the papers for me. There are, however, two, I think, wanting (beside those which you marked down as deficient),

[1] *Aeneid*, ii. 274.

[2] This is the task mentioned in letter No. 237, to James Corry, 29 June 1812. See also letter No. 198, to Corry, 24 Oct. 1811.

[3] Two families famous for their printing: the Estienne (Latin Stephanus) family of France and the Gronov (Latin Gronovius) family of Holland. Henri I (d. 1520) founded the Estienne business and was succeeded by his sons François (1502–50), and Robert I (1503–59). They established the house in Geneva and printed classical works, the Bible, and a French-Latin dictionary. Johann Friederich Gronov (1611–71) and his descendants were noted scholars, who produced a number of scientific and classical works, including *Thesaurus Antiquitatum Graecarum*.

and I have the memorandum of them among my papers, but not just at hand now, to tell them to you. I wish we could get rid of the prologues and epilogues altogether. I dare say there are not six lines 'nantes in *gurgite vasto*'[1] which are worth saving. I include my own in this denunciation, for they are both *very bad*,[2] and I think it is much better to let our posterity *imagine* what sallies of wit and fancy must have been struck out during the Institution, than to embody such a mass of evidence against ourselves *to the contrary*. In my opinion a slight sketch of the progress of private theatricals in Ireland, a list of the company of Kilkenny for each season, with the plays acted, and the casts of the principal characters; a series of portraits of those chiefly concerned, with brief notices of their talents, &c., would comprise all that could be in the least degree interesting, and would be a much more tasteful monument of our establishment than this ponderous load of play-bills, and this swarm of 'wounded snakes,' that 'drag their slow lengths along'[3] in the form of prologues and epilogues. This, however, is merely my opinion; it makes not the least difference in *my* part of the business, only that I feel I should be deficient in proper zeal for this undertaking if I did not both *think* of what would be *best*, and *tell* what I think fairly. At the same time I by no means expect that any one of you will agree with me; and indeed, as perhaps the feelings of some of our oldest members might be hurt by the sacrifice of so large a portion of the materials, I by no means press it. All, therefore, I shall suggest is, that as there *must* be a *canister* at the *tail* of the book, it ought to be of as *light construction*, and as little of a *trumpery canister* as possible. Selections, perhaps, might be made, and you would find me a true *Brutus* in this task, for my own children should be the first to go to the block. Talking of my own children, there is a very awkward error of the press in the answer to the Charitable Institutions which I wrote. I do not quite remember the words of the sentence, but it is something like 'whatever difficulties, &c. &c., by your co-operation we were enabled to surmount *them*,' where the word 'them' is omitted, to the no small mutilation of the grammar and construction. I suppose the same error was in the Kilkenny paper.

When you first mentioned the idea of an 'author's night,' I thought it was merely one of those momentary speculations which

[1] *Aeneid*, i. 118.

[2] The epilogues and prologue written by Moore and included in the 1841 edition of his works are 'Occasional Epilogue, Spoken by Mr. Corry, in the Character of Vapid', 'Prologue Written and Spoken by the Author', and 'Epilogue Written for Lady Dacre's Tragedy of Ina', *Poetry*, pp. 527, 528, and 717. Moore is referring here to the first two of these.

[3] *Essay on Criticism*, ll. 352–3.

flash before one's eyes and vanish; but as you seem to be, with true friendly feeling, following up the intention, I think it but fair to tell you that I would by no means accept of it. If Dublin had many such ingredients in its mixture as you, Power, Dalton, and a *very* few more, I would look upon a tribute of this kind as not only advantageous, but honourable, and should reckon up the '*golden* opinions' of *such* 'sorts of men' with great pleasure;[1] but alas, alas! to lay myself under an obligation to —— and ——, and to have tickets, ostensibly for my benefit, circulating among the low, illiberal, puddle-headed, and gross-hearted herd of Dublin (that 'palavering, slanderous set,' as Curran once so well described them to me),— this, my dear Corry, would never do. No, no! a man must indeed think with the often-quoted *night-man* of antiquity, 'bonus odor nummi ex *re quâlibet*.'[2] Who would receive it reeking from such uncleanly sources? I love Ireland, but I despise Dublin; nor has it one claim on my gratitude (speaking of it as a public) to prevent my doing so. I have never been valued by them as I am here, and I question whether, even in a *lucrative* point of view, you would not be grievously disappointed in your hopes of making a house for me. My 'Melologue' (which is good writing compared to such a thing as 'M. P.')[3] never, that I know of, drew a soul to the theatre in Dublin. Therefore, pray put it out of your head, my dear friend, and tell Dalton and Power my reasons, at the same time assuring them that I feel as I ought all their goodness in proposing it.

I am truly happy to hear that Dalton has got such a comfortable addition to his income. If anything could spoil such a good fellow as Dalton, I think accepting a place from the hands of Wellesley Pole would go near to effect it; but I am convinced his *heart* is place-proof, which, in these times, is saying a good deal for it. Your description of the *Pole's* turning towards the *milky way* is highly amusing.

Well, I have written enough, God knows! so good bye, my dearest Corry, and believe me,

Ever sincerely yours,
Thomas Moore.

I dined with a party of statesmen yesterday,—Tierney,

[1] *Macbeth*, I. vii. 32.

[2] Juvenal, xiv. 204. The quotation should read: 'Lucri bonus est odor ex re/Qualibet.' Emperor Vespasian placed a tax on public toilets, and when asked about this means of raising money replied in this manner.

[3] *Melologue upon National Music* (*Poetry*, p. 303), and *M. P., or the Blue Stocking*, which was produced at the Lyceum on 9 Sept. 1811.

Ponsonby,[1] Erskine, &c. They all look very *blue*, and not the *Prince's blue*, I assure you.

I wish you would frank the enclosed letter to Joe Atkinson, *Atanna, Ballynakill*. He wouldn't thank the angel Gabriel for a letter, if it was not franked.

278. *To his Mother*

Russell, viii. 103

Friday [December?] 1812.

My dearest Mother,

I am very anxious indeed at not hearing from home. *You* were ill when Ellen wrote last, and our dear Kate was on the eve of her trouble;[2] on both of which accounts I am very solicitous about hearing from you. Bessy is getting, I think, a good deal better, and very much, I believe, by the means of milk and chocolate. I know milk does not agree with you, darling Mother; but I should suppose *chocolate* would, and it is very strengthening.

Did you see the account of the 'Religious Liberty' Dinner at Kilkenny, where they gave, 'Thomas Moore, and the Union of Patriotism and Poetry?' They so seldom do me justice in Ireland, that I rather suspect I was indebted to a man from London, who was there, for this compliment.

Make Ellen write immediately, with full particulars both about yourself and Kate; and believe me, my dearest Mother,

Ever your own,
Tom.

279. *To his Mother*

Russell, i. 319, no. 208

Tuesday [December] 1812.

My dearest Mother,

Lord Moira arrived at the Park yesterday evening, and I am just now preparing to call upon him, so that we soon shall be put out of suspense, though I have made up my mind pretty well to expecting *very little*.[3] Captain Thomson, an old American comrade of his, has been appointed private secretary; and that, you know,

[1] Moore is referring either to George Ponsonby, leader of the Whig opposition, or to John Wilson Ponsonby, fourth Earl of Bessborough, a Whig leader. See the Glossary of Proper Names.

[2] Moore's sister Catherine was expecting her first child. The baby died soon after birth (see letter No. 279, to his mother, December 1812).

[3] See letter No. 281, to Lady Donegal, December 1812.

was the place which all my friends would have it, right or wrong, was to be mine. Indeed, when I say, I expect *very little*, I mean that I expect *nothing:* for, as he disclaims all connection with Ministers, there is nothing to be looked for to his interest with them, even if I were inclined to wish that he should exert it for me; and, as to India, he will offer me no situation important enough to tempt me to emigrate to such a distance; so that I am most likely to remain as I am; and, please God! there is no fear of me.

We are so anxious about Kate. Bessy *is* even more than I, for she has a deep horror of what Kate has to go through. Ever your own,

Tom.

280. *To his Mother*

Russell, i. 320, no. 209

Thursday [December] 1812.

My dearest Mother,

I have as yet only seen Lord Moira for a moment; he was shooting in his fields, and merely said, 'You see a school-boy taking his holiday;' and he must be most happy to get a little repose and relaxation after London.[1]

We were so delighted to hear of darling Kate's happy delivery. God send they may both continue well!

I am just now setting off with Sir John Stevenson (who came down to me, accompanied by Power, on Tuesday) for a concert and ball at Leicester.

I am quite sure Lord Moira will do nothing whatever for me. Your own, *own*,

Tom.

281. *To Lady Donegal*

Russell, i. 320, no. 210

Tuesday [December] 1812.

I have but just time to tell you that I have at last had an interview with Lord Moira. He has fought very shy of me ever since he came here. I had heard that he had nothing left to give, the Royal Family having *put upon him* three clerks, the only remaining places of his household that he had to dispose of; so that I was well prepared for what occurred between us. He began by telling me that he 'had not been *oblivious* of me—had not been *oblivious* of

[1] See letter No. 281, to Lady Donegal, December 1812.

me!' After this devil of a word there was but little heart or soul to be expected from him. He was sorry, however, to add that all the Indian patronage he was allowed to exercise *here* was already exhausted; if, however, on his going to India, he should find anything worth my going out for, he would let me know. In the meantime, he had a right to expect that Ministers would serve his friends here, in exchange for what he could do to serve their friends in India, and that he would try to get something for me through this channel. To this I replied, that, 'from *his hands* I should always be most willing to accept anything, and that perhaps it might yet be in his power to serve me; but that I begged he would not take the trouble of applying for me to the patronage of Ministers, as I would rather struggle on as I was than take anything that would have the effect of tying up my tongue under such a system as the present.'

Thus the matter rests, and such is the end of my long-cherished hopes from the Earl of Moira, K. G. &c. He has certainly not done his duty by me: his *manner*, since his appointment, has been even worse than his deficiencies of *matter;* but (except to such friends as you) I shall never complain of him. He served my father when my father much wanted it,[1] and he and his sister took my dear Bessy by the hand most cordially and seasonably; for all this I give him complete absolution; and, as to disappointment, I feel but little of it, as his late conduct had taught me not to rely much upon him.

If you can read this, you will be very ingenious: I shall write more legibly very soon; and, with best love to my dearest Mary, I am ever yours,

T. Moore.

282. *To James Power*

Russell, i. 323, no. 212

Kegworth
[December] 1812.

My dear Sir,

Many thanks for your truly *eloquent letter*. I have since written to Lord Moira (in order to put the matter upon record) the substance of what I said to him,[2] and have added that, with respect to his promise of letting me know if anything good should occur in India, I must beg he would dismiss *that too* entirely from his

[1] Lord Moira had arranged for Moore's father to be appointed Barrack Master of Island Bridge, Dublin. See letter No. 126, to his mother, May 1806.

[2] See letter No. 281, to Lady Donegal, December 1812.

thoughts, as it was too late in the day for me to *go on expecting*, and that I must now think of working out my own independence by industry. Between ourselves, my dear friend, I have not so much merit in these refusals as I appear to have, for I could see very plainly, through Lord Moira's manner, that there was very little chance of his making any proper exertion for me whatever, and, putting conscience out of the question, policy itself suggested to me that I might as well have the merit of declining what it was quite improbable would ever have been done for me. After this, what do you think of his lordship? I cannot trust myself with speaking of the way he has treated me. Gratitude for the past ties up my tongue.

I certainly never wrote a second verse to Mrs. Ashe's song; but here is one fresh from the mint, and not bad either:

'If haply these eyes have a soul underneath,
By whose flame their expression is lighted;
A mind that will long like an evergreen breathe,
When the flower of the features is blighted.
And if soul be the tie of those fetters of bliss,
Which last when all others are breaking;
Oh! talk not of beauty—but love me for this,
And I'll think of you sleeping and waking;
Dear youth!
I will think of you sleeping and waking.'[1]

If I had had the air I might perhaps have suited the words to it better. Let these words be copied correctly, and call the song 'I'll think of you sleeping and waking.'

'Savourna Deilish' is on the anvil.[2] You shall have it this week.

I have had another letter with another proposal from your brother, but there is no time now to enter upon it.[3] When I write next, you shall know it. Ever yours, with best regards and anxious wishes for Mrs. P.,

Thomas Moore.

I have got a tolerably pretty air out of Crotch's book for the Melodies, which I have *half written* words to.

[1] This song is not in the 1841 edition of Moore's works and has not been otherwise identified.

[2] See letter No. 270, to James Power, November 1812.

[3] See letter No. 266, to James Power, 23 Nov. 1812.

283. *To Edward T. Dalton*

Russell, i. 325, no. 214

Friday [December] 1812.

My dear Dalton,

I am quite distressed at the serious tone in which you speak of my silence. I flattered myself that you were so sure of your place in my heart and mind, that however you might be angry with me (and I own deservedly so) for not writing to you on this occasion, you would impute it to anything but the *least little* shade of change in my most fixed and never-altering regard for you. A cloud or two should not make the barometer sink, and it will not be *my* fault if it does not remain up to *clear*, *settled*, *sunshiny* weather between you and me for ever. I have written to two persons on the subject of my interview with Lord Moira[1] (Bryan and P. Crampton), and I should not have *repeated* the detail to the *latter*, if I did not know that the two channels had no sort of communication with each other, and that they would each serve as a conduit for the statement in very opposite directions. I most heartily hate a dry repetition of 'says he' and 'says I,' and it is entirely my wish that all my friends should know the particulars. Even now, my dearest Dalton, all I shall do is to refer *you* to one of the above channels or conduits; Bryan's pipe, I believe, being nearest to you. My writing so soon to Bryan upon the subject arose from his having launched a most wrongful sarcasm at me for a flourishing little tirade which I gave him in one of my letters about the unambitious happiness of my present life, and the independence I felt of all places, princes, and patrons. To this he answered by asking me, 'whether the grapes were not rather sour?' This was before Lord Moira had the least prospect of coming into power; and though I had perfectly made up my mind as to what should be my conduct on such an event, I did not like to boast any further of a virtue which was so little likely to be put to the test. As soon, however, as I had done what I thought right, I felt, I own, a little impatient to give my very best *practical* refutation of Bryan's sarcasm, and hence arose my speedy communication to him. You need not mention to him my telling you this. I have no doubt he meant it sincerely, and even kindly, though certainly his letter in approbation of what I *have done* is much slower in coming than his suspicion of what I *would* do. As to Crampton, my letter to him was in answer to a very anxious and urgent inquiry which he wrote to me on the subject. So now, my dear Dalton, I hope I have explained enough to convince you, that it is not from any *preference* of others

[1] See letter No. 281, to Lady Donegal, December 1812.

for my confidential communications, that the circumstances should have reached you from anybody but myself.

I am happy to tell you that Lord Moira has shown no disapprobation whatever of the tone in which I have thought it right to decline his interest for me with Ministers; so far from it, I have within these few days received a present from him of fifteen dozen of excellent wine. Tell Stevenson this. I know he will be glad to hear that my threatened abandonment of the black-strap is deferred a little longer.

I mean to be in town about April or May to pass a month. If you will let me know your movements in time, I shall shape mine to meet them. Bessy expects to be confined in February, and as soon as she is well enough to be left alone, it is my intention to go to town.

I most anxiously wish to hear (and so does Bessy) that your dear Olivia is well over her crisis. Stevenson *did* seem to like my wife, and it shows his taste, for she is a girl '*comme il y en a peu.*'

I don't see why you should not come and take me up here in your way to London. Ever yours,

T. Moore.

284. *To his Mother*

Russell, i. 328, no. 215

Kegworth
Tuesday, Dec. 1812.

My dearest Mother,

We have been very much affected, indeed, by poor Kate's loss; and the only consolation we can either feel or suggest, is its having occurred before the poor child could have taken any more than its natural hold upon her affections. A little time hence it would have been a sad loss indeed, as we can well feel when we look at little Barbara, whose rosy cheeks, however, and dancing eyes forbid us, thank Heaven! to have any such apprehensions.[1]

The Moiras set off for town yesterday; they called here in passing, and Lady Loudon [*sic*] was very kind, indeed, to Bessy. Lord M. told me he had given orders for game, &c. to be brought to me; and Lady L. made me a present of a book, which she recollected me expressing a wish for about five or six months ago, with her own name in it. I was glad of all this for one reason, because I had written Lord Moira a letter since I saw him last, repeating the substance of what I had said in our interview; and,

[1] Moore's sister Catherine was married to a Mr. Scully. Her first child died soon after birth. There is bitter irony in the reference to Barbara, who died on 18 Sept. 1817, from injuries received in a fall.

also, begging him to dismiss from *his* mind, as I should from *mine*, his promise with respect to considering of a place for me in India, as it was *too late* in the day for me to *go on expecting*, and I must now think of working out my own independence by industry. The letter, though written respectfully and gratefully, was in a tone which he must have felt a good deal, and which, therefore, I thought might possibly displease him; but, if it did, he concealed it, and was full of kindness.[1]

My chief uneasiness at the misfortune that has happened at home, dearest mother, is the shock that it has given you, and my fears that it may hurt you; but, for God's sake, let no such circumstance rob us of one moment of your dear health or happiness.

I hope my father got my letter desiring him to draw upon Power in the Strand (Mr. James Power, 34. Strand), for twenty-five or thirty pounds, whichever he chooses, or indeed, for the whole fifty, if necessary; but I rather think I shall be able to send him the remainder in cash about the beginning of January. Ever your own,

Tom.

285. *To his Mother*

Russell, i. 329, no. 216

Kegworth
Tuesday [December] 1812.

My dearest Mother,

I had a very kind letter from Rogers on Sunday, inclosed in one from Lord Byron. Rogers has seen a good deal of Lord Moira, and gives a lamentable account of his low spirits, and the sort of self-consciousness of failure there hangs about him. I pity him most sincerely. Rogers tells me that he hears nothing but praises of my conduct; which is very pleasant to be told, though I want nothing but my own heart and conscience to tell me I have acted rightly.

Dalby went up to London yesterday to take leave of the Moiras: I believe, only for Bessy's state, I should have paid them the same mark of respect myself. Good by, my own darling mother. Ever your own,

Tom.

Our little Barbara is growing very amusing. She (what they call) *started* yesterday in walking; that is, got up off the ground by herself, and walked alone to a great distance, without any one near her. Bessy's heart was almost flying out of her mouth all the while with fright, but I held her away, and would not let her assist the young adventurer.

[1] See letter No. 281, to Lady Donegal, December 1812.

286. *To James Power*

Boston Public Library

[January 1813]

My dear Sir— I do not like to defer answering your letter till Tuesday, as I am impatient to say that I shall plague you no longer with your brother's proposals— They are made so plausibly, that I am always puzzled what to say to them— I shall now do as you have advised— I will this next week write to him for his account, and tell him that I must adopt measures for paying it myself, without any reference to his portion of the annuity, which must be remitted regularly to you—

I had got into my head very foolishly that my year ended with 1812, and tho I am glad to find that I have so much 'time to the good' for finishing my Number of Melodies to my satisfaction, yet I feel somewhat alarmed about the enormity of my Saturday's draft on you, as it makes, I fear, a most tremendous anticipation of my next year's resources, and must inconvenience you in proportion— What led me into my confusion about the *time* was my having, I believe, *anticipated* in the same manner at the beginning of 1812— But I never kept any thing like an *account* of my receipts before I came here—therefore of any sums received at the beginning of the year I have not the slightest recollection—but since *May* I have drawn upon you, I believe, for fifty pounds some time after my arrival—for £100 in September—and for £100 more on Saturday last—this, with a ten pound note in November and four or five pounds when you were here is all I have down in my book as having *received* from you—(what you have *paid* for me is another account)— Now, if I have put down *all* my drafts upon you since May correctly, these sums, together with what I *anticipated* of the present year before I came down here, must leave me very little even of your brother's portion untouched for the remainder of the time, and therefore a great part of my draft of Saturday will fall unseasonably & prematurely upon you— When I speak this way of your 'brother's portion', I am considering it as we did last year (improperly I know) to be left to be paid at the end of the year— but I ought rather, *in the spirit of our bond*, talk of the five hundred pounds at once, without separating your portions— In this way then, what I fear is that there remains so little of my five hundred pounds to me now, as to throw a great part of my last draft upon the resources of next year, & that I am, like Bonaparte, drawing out the conscription of 1813 before its time—Pray, set me right upon all these points, when you have a leisure moment, and never conceal from me any inconvenience you may feel in meeting my drafts, as I have always resources to which I can apply on an emergency—

We are naturally still more anxious about Mrs Power from your last accounts than ever—pray, give us a line *instantly* when she is out of suspense—

Ever yours
T. Moore.

I have made a glee of the Finland Air, and I mean to send it to Stevenson this next week, with the two Spanish Airs—the mode I shall adopt is to inclose them to my *Father* for him, and make him stick close to Stevenson, and not let them out of his own hands to the Knight, but see them done by him & send them back—

287. *To James Power*

Russell, i. 331, no. 218

Friday [January] 1813.

My dear Sir,

I dare say you will be surprised at not hearing from me so long, but the truth is I have been *stealing* a week or ten days from you to do a little job, which I think will get me out of Carpenter's debt, and, if I can make a good bargain with him, put money in my pocket. I have collected all the little squibs in the political way which I have written for two or three years past, and am adding a few *new ones* to them for publication. I publish them, of course, anonymously, and you must keep my secret.[1] Carpenter being the Prince's bookseller, is afraid to publish them himself, but gets some one else. I am much mistaken if they do not make a little noise. What a pity it is that such things do not come from *our book-shop* in the *Strand*, but *these* would not *keep*, and there is no fear but I shall find *more* against that is opened [*sic*]. I consider every little reputation I can make, my dear sir, as going towards the fund I am to throw into our establishment, and though I shall, of course, *deny* the trifles I am now doing, yet, if they are liked, I shall be sure to get the credit of them.

In the mean time I have not been idle in the musical way, but have an original song nearly ready for you, and after I have dispatched my politics, you shall see what a fertile month I shall make February. I would not have turned aside for my present job, only that I found I have a little time over, and that, indeed (as I have already said), everything that I can get fame by tells towards our future prospects; it is like establishing a credit.

[1] *The Intercepted Letters, or the Twopenny Post-Bag* appeared in March 1813.

We were of course delighted to hear of Mrs. Power's safe arrival of a boy; we had been indeed sincerely and unaffectedly anxious about her.

I shall send your copy of Walker's answer when I have something to send with it; or do you want it immediately?

What I inclose for Carpenter is the beginning of my squibs. It is to be called 'Intercepted Letters, or the Twopenny Post Bag.'

Will you find out for me how many ponies Lady B. Ashley gave the Princess Charlotte; or, at least, how many the latter drives.[1] Ever yours,

Thomas Moore.

288. *To James Carpenter*

Rice University

[January 1813]

My dear Carpenter—

I return the Proof—and by my next communication you shall have the remainder of the *new* part—we shall get on expeditiously when we get to the old ones—I think I shall take the Epistle of Pope Joan[2] out of the Pious Women[3] for this, as it is *misplaced* there, and it has long been my intention not to publish it with them—

As to the number to be done, you are the best judge of what effect you think it will have, but I think a *few* is far the best—say 250 or 300— Tell me in your next who you have got to publish it—and tell me too what you think of my putting in the Parody on the P.'s Letter among the old ones— I shall insert 'the Insurrection of the Papers' certainly, and *that* is at least as much known to be mine as the Letter— all we can do is to say that some of them may be mine, but I know nothing of the rest, nor of the Collector of them, and, in this way, I think I may put in the letter— The Advertisement shall run thus 'Intercepted Letters or the Two-penny Post-Bag—to which are added a few trifles that have already appeared in the Morning Chronicle, Examiner &c among which are The Insurrection of the Papers, the Plumassier, the New Costume of the Ministers, the Sale of the Tools &c. &c. by a member of the Poco-curante Society.'—[4]

The Sale of the Tools appeared in the M. Cronicle [*sic*] a month ago,[5] and it was but on Sunday last put into the Examiner— As

[1] The first squib in the *Intercepted Letters* is 'From the Pr—nc—ss Ch—rl—e . . . to the Lady B—rb—a Ashl—y'. It is a parody of a note thanking Lady Barbara for a gift of ponies.

[2] *Poetry*, p. 159.

[3] The *Pious Women* was a satirical work planned by Moore but never completed or published.

[4] *Poetry*, pp. 164 ff.

[5] *Morning Chronicle*, 21 Dec. 1812.

these things have made some noise, it will be a good puff to put them in the Advertisement—

I can trust this Proof, I think, to the care of the Printer, tho if it be not very inconvenient, I should like to see the revise.

Poor Bessy is very near calling out, and I am of course all anxiety about her— The little thing is getting as rosy and healthy as I could wish her—

You will see me in town towards the latter end of April for a month or six weeks, and indeed I think, if I could manage it, I would go & live near London altogether— I hope then Mrs C. & my dear Bessy will be close friends—

Ever yours
T. Moore

When you are sending a Parcell [*sic*] next pray get me the two new Plays, Coleridge's and Jameson's— Mr Smith's Epilogue is no great things—[1]

289. *To his Mother*

Russell, i. 332, no. 219

Friday [January] 1813.

My dearest Mother,

I am sending a good many letters off to-day, and have only time to say God bless you. I got my darling father's letter yesterday, and am delighted to find that you are recovering your fatigue and anxiety. My poor uncle Garret! I had a letter from him about six weeks ago, asking me to get his two sons out in Lord Moira's suite.

My cold is quite well, and poor Bessy, though she gets but little sleep at night, is keeping up pretty well. Ever your own,

Tom.

290. *To his Mother*

Russell, i. 333, no. 220

Friday [January] 1813.

My dearest Mother,

I had a long letter yesterday from Rogers, who is returned from his northern tour. He says, with reference to my interview with

[1] Coleridge published *Remorse* (a revision of *Osorio*) in 1813. Robert Francis Jameson's play *A Touch at the Times* was produced at Covent Garden on 6 July 1812. Other plays by him were *The Students of Salamanca* and *The Invisible Bridegroom*, both of which appeared in 1813, the former at Covent Garden on 23 Jan. The epilogue could refer to *Rejected Addresses*, by Horatio and James Smith, published in 1812.

Lord Moira, 'You have acted, my dear Moore, quite nobly and like yourself.' He assigns a number of excuses for Lord Moira's conduct, which indeed are all very just; and even what I most complained of (the shyness and distance he kept with me) appears to Rogers, and even now to myself, as the very natural result of his inability. Rogers has told Lord Holland the circumstances, who thinks of it all as we do.

Bessy is doing I think very well now: much better.

291. *To his Mother*

Russell, i. 333, no. 221

Friday [February] 1813.

My dearest Mother,

We got my darling father's letter a day or two ago, and Bessy was delighted at its being such a long one. I am almost sorry that you are letting poor Kilmainham Lodge, and I would enter my protest against it, only that I think, by getting into town, your spirits, my dearest mother, will have a much better chance of being kept alive. As to paying me back any of what you have had, don't think about it; when I want it *very badly*, I will tell you. I forgot, in my two or three last letters, to ask of my father what was the date of the bill he drew upon Carpenter. Let him write to tell me on receipt of this, and not mind paying postage at any time.

You shall have immediate intelligence when poor Bessy is over her confinement. We have had repeated letters from Stevenson's friend, Mrs. Ready, of the most *cordial* description. She is within forty or fifty miles of us, and is very earnest indeed in her invitations to us to go there. Nothing could be more seasonable than her invitation for I wanted exactly such a quiet place to leave Bessy at when I go to town. There are people enough immediately near us that would be too glad to have her, but there is not one of them without some objections, except the Peach's, at Leicester, and they, I believe, will be away from home. Ever your own,

Tom.

292. *To James Power*

Russell, i. 334, no. 222

Tuesday [February] 1813.

My dear Sir,

Having *broke* the *neck* of my job for Carpenter,[1] I am returning to my other pursuits, and yesterday wrote a little song, which I

[1] Moore was at work on *The Twopenny Post-Bag.*

hope you will think pretty. I shall give you the words at the other side, and you shall have the air on Friday.

Walter Scott's Rokeby[1] has given me a renewal of courage for my poem, and once I get it brilliantly off my hands, we may do what we please in literature afterwards. Rogers's criticisms have twice upset all I have done, but I have fairly told him he shall see it no more till it is finished. Did you ever see much worse songs than those in Rokeby? Ever yours, my dear sir, most truly,

Thomas Moore.

1.

'The brilliant black eye
May, in triumph, let fly
Its darts without caring who feels 'em;
But the soft eye of blue,
Tho' it scatter wounds too,
Is much better pleas'd when it heals 'em,
Dear Jessy.

2.

'The black eye may say,
"Come and worship my ray;
By adoring, perhaps, you may move me!"
But the blue eye, half hid,
Says from under its lid,
"I love, and am yours if you love me!"
Dear Jessy.

3.

'Oh! tell me, then, why,
In that lovely blue eye,
No soft trace of its tint I discover?
Oh! why should you wear
The only blue pair
That ever said "No" to a lover?
Dear Jessy.'[2]

293. *To James Power*

Russell, i. 335, no. 223

Monday [February] 1813.

My dear Sir,

As I shall have a pretty large packet to send to-morrow for Lady Donegal through my old Woodman,[3] I write *now* in answer to

[1] Scott's *Rokeby* was published in Edinburgh in 1813.

[2] *Poetry*, p. 311.

[3] Lord Glenbervie.

yours of yesterday. I should have sent you the music of 'The brilliant black eye' on Friday, but I found I had put it in the wrong time, and have been obliged to copy it over again.[1] You shall have it next Friday, with another I am about.

From the state of my poem, and the industry I mean to carry it on with this year, I think we need not look to a more distant period than next year (1814) for the commencement of our book-concern;[2] as the poem (if it succeeds well enough to encourage you to the undertaking) will be the last thing I shall put out of my own hands. I should like therefore, with your permission, to make the *Dictionary of Music* my object this year, for two reasons, first, because, being prose, it will enable me to give my fancy more undistractedly to my poem; and secondly, because, being a kind of mixed work between literature and music, it would be a good thing to begin with, and would slide us quietly from your present business into the other.[3] All this, however, we shall discuss more fully together in April, and in the mean time I shall continue to make my notes and preparations for the Dictionary.

Bessy still up. Ever yours,

T. Moore.

294. *To James Power*

Russell, i. 336, no. 224

[February 1813]

My dear Sir,

I send you the 'Rose Tree,'[4] which are the prettiest words I've written for some time; also the Finland air.[5]

Ever yours,
T. Moore.

295. *To James Power*

Russell, i. 339, no. 229

March [2] 1813.

My dear Sir,

I received the proofs yesterday, and shall send them back under cover to Lord Glenbervie to-morrow. You will hardly believe that

[1] See letter No. 294, to James Power, February 1813.

[2] *Lalla Rookh* appeared in 1817.

[3] Moore never published the dictionary of music, and there is no evidence that the project ever went beyond the planning stage.

[4] *Poetry*, p. 310.

[5] 'I Saw the Moon Rise Clear', *Poetry*, p. 312.

the two lines which I had (with many hours of thought and *glove tearing*) purposed to insert in the vacant place, displeased me when I wrote them down yesterday, and I am still at work for better. Such is the easy pastime of poetry! You shall have four more Melodies ready this week, so that you will not be delayed for me. I agree with Stevenson in not very much liking the air from Crotch, but I cannot at all understand why your brother, when he communicated this piece of intelligence, did not send a better air in its stead from his boasted Connemara stock. Perhaps some will come with the proofs: if so, for God's sake! lose no time in sending them, as I again say I am far from satisfied with the number as it is.

You are very good to think so much about poor Bessy.

It was my intention to ask of you and Mrs. Power to do us the favour of standing sponsors for the little girl, as it would create a *kind* of relationship between us, and draw closer (if they require it) those ties which, I trust, will long keep us together. But I am obliged to confine the request to *Mrs.* Power, and leave *you* for some future and (I hope) very-far-off little child; for our rector, Doctor Parkinson, very kindly *offered*, of himself, to be godfather, and it is such a very flattering tribute of his good opinion to us, that I could not hesitate in accepting it. I have a long letter to write to you about my schemes for going to town: my heart almost failed me about it; but it appears to me so very *useful* a *measure* for the *concern*, that, after much fidgetting consideration of the subject, I have devised a plan, which I think will enable me to do it without much distressing any of us.

I am afraid the Post Bag will not do. It is impossible to make things *good* in the very little time I took about that, and Carpenter, with his usual greediness, has put a price on it far beyond what it is worth; so that, I suppose, it will go to sleep.[1] I have, however, taken pretty good care, in the preface, to throw it off my shoulders, and the only piece of waggery I shall ever be guilty of again is a Collection of Political Songs to Irish airs, which, you know, I mentioned once to you, and which I should like very much to do. Your brother would be afraid to display them in Dublin, I think; but what say you? More to-morrow. Ever yours,

T. Moore.[2]

[1] See letter No. 300, to his mother, March 1813.

[2] There is a fragment of this letter in the Harvard College Library. It is dated 'March 2nd 1813' rather than 23 Mar., as given in the Russell edition.

296. *To Mary Dalby*

Russell, i. 337, no. 226

Tuesday, March 16. 1813.

My dear *Mary*,

About six o'clock this morning my Bessy produced a little girl about the size of a twopenny wax doll.[1] Nothing could be more favourable than the whole proceeding, and the mamma is now eating buttered toast and drinking tea, as if nothing had happened. Ever yours,

T. Moore.

I have been up all night, and am too fagged to write more.

297. *To his Mother*

Russell, i. 342, no. 231

Tuesday, March [23] 1813.

My dearest Mother,

* * * * * *

You know it was this day week she lay in.[2] Well, on Sunday morning last, as I was at breakfast in my study, there came a tap at the room-door and in entered Bessy, with her hair in curl, and smiling as gaily as possible. It quite frightened me, for I never heard of any one coming downstairs so soon, but she was so cheerful about it, that I could hardly scold her, and I do not think she has in the least suffered for it. She said she could not resist the desire she had to come down and see how her crocuses and primroses before the window were getting on.

My father's letter yesterday gave us great pleasure.

I am sending notice of quitting, to my landlord, this month. Ever your own,

Tom.

298. *To his Mother*

Russell, i. 338, no. 227

Tuesday [March] 1813.

My dearest Mother,

I have written to Corry to send me a piece of Irish linen, and, by whatever opportunity he sends it, you can let me have my

[1] Moore's second child, Anastasia Mary.

[2] See letter No. 296, to Mary Dalby, 16 Mar. 1813.

Boileau that Kate left, and some of my other books, particularly the three volumes of Heyne's Virgil:[1] he will let you know, I dare say, when he finds the opportunity.

I inclosed a dispatch for my Bermuda deputy to Croker yesterday, to send out for me. I was glad to see a pretty good list of ships taken the other day, but I find the admiral and squadron have gone there later this year than ever they did before, which was very uncivil of them.

Little Bab is somewhat restless with her eye-teeth, but is otherwise quite well. Poor Bessy is very weak, but is altogether much better than she was with Barbara. Ever your own,

Tom.

Do you get my two letters a-week regularly?

299. *To his Mother*

Russell, i. 338, no. 228

Tuesday [March] 1813.

My dearest Mother,

As I gave you a long letter last time, I may the better put you off with a short one now, particularly as I have so many to write this morning.

Bessy is getting on amazingly, and already looks better than she has done for a long time; indeed, she says she has not felt so well since her marriage.

I do not know whether I told you that our worthy friend the rector has offered to be godfather to the little girl: it was his own free offer, and is a very flattering testimony of his opinion of us. Ever your own,

Tom.

I suppose Lord Moira is off. Carlo Doyle has sent me, as a keepsake, four very pretty volumes of French music.

300. *To his Mother*

Russell, i, 342, no. 232

Kegworth
Thursday night [March] 1813.

My dearest Mother,

I write this over night, because I am obliged to go early in the morning to Donington Park, as I want to consult the library for

[1] Christian Gottlob Heyne edited the works of Virgil (Leipzig, 1767–1775), 4 vols.

many things before we set off. Only think of my anonymous book: it goes into the *fifth* edition on Saturday or Monday.[1] This puts me quite at ease about the money my father has had, and I *insist* that he will dismiss it entirely from his mind. Little *Statia* went through her christening very well, and we had the rector, curate, and Mary Dalby to dinner afterwards. You have, of course, long perceived that they are both, Barbara and she, *little Protestants*.

I have great hopes that this will be a prosperous year with me, and that I shall gradually be able to get rid of all my debts. Mrs. Ready (who seems to be a most warm-hearted person), upon my writing to her that we were quitting our house, and meant to look out for a pleasanter one and a cheaper, wrote back that she was most happy to hear it, and that we need not look further than Oakhanger Hall (her place) for a residence, that she was fitting up half of the house to receive us, and that we *must* make it our home as long as we lived in the country. Was not this unexampled kindness? She also offered herself as sponsor to the little child, and begged we would defer the christening till we came to her, when their son-in-law, the new dean of Exeter (who, with his wife, is to meet us there) would perform it; but this was impossible, as we had already godfathers, godmothers, and parson provided.

There never was anything like the rapid sale of my Post Bag. There was great praise of it in a very clever paper of Sunday last, which, if it is not gone astray, I will send you in the morning. Ever your own,

Tom.

301. *To James Power*

Russell, i. 343, no. 233

Tuesday [March] 1813.

My dear Sir,

I send the proofs; and, by the next time of my inclosing, I shall have four Melodies more for you. In order to give you a little idea of the difficulty I have in pleasing myself, I have written down at the top of the proof as many of the *rejected* couplets as I could remember; they are *not one third* of those I have manufactured for the purpose; so that you see I do not *write* songs quite as easily as our friend the Knight composes them. Tear off these lines before you send them to the printer.

With respect now to my going to town, I must first premise, that it is chiefly from my persuasion of your wishing it very much that I

[1] At least eleven editions of the *Twopenny Post-Bag* appeared in 1813. The sixteenth edition was published in 1818.

am so anxious to effect it; because, though of course there is nothing I should like myself much better, yet, in the present state of my resources, I should consider it proper (if only my own *gratification* were concerned) to sacrifice my wishes to prudence; and, understand me, my dear sir, I say this, not from any vulgar idea of enhancing, or making a compliment of my going; I hope you think me too sensible to have any such silly notion; but it is for the purpose of impressing on your mind how much I *begin* to set *business*, and the interests of *our concern*, above every other consideration, either of pleasure or convenience. In this respect I hope and feel that you will find me improve every year.

Now you know it has always been my intention to give notice to my landlord this month, and Mrs. Ready (Stevenson's friend) has given us so many and such pressing invitations to pass the summer with her, that I mean to take her at her word;[1] and indeed am quite happy to have such a place to leave Bessy in while I am in town, for she would not like staying at home (besides the saving of house expense while she is out), and there are objections to every one of the places to which she has been invited in this neighbourhood. So that the offer of such a quiet, goody retreat as Ready's is every way convenient. What do you think of this? Having arranged all this, you will observe there will be left scarcely two months of my remaining six, to occupy this house;[2] and my idea is, before we start, to sell off whatever furniture we do not mean to move, to employ the intervening time in looking out for a house both cheaper and pleasanter elsewhere; and so to have done with this entirely. I have sucked pretty well out of the library,[3] and shall be able, I think, to wean myself of it without injury; indeed, I have got quite sufficient materials out of it for my poem;[4] and as to my musical works, it has nothing to assist me there, so that I now consider myself free to choose where I can live cheapest and most retired during the remainder of my rural exile. We are too much in the midst of my fine acquaintances here, and are obliged to keep up an appearance which might be dispensed with in a more retired situation. Now turn these things over in your mind for me. I am at my wits' ends for *the supplies*, and would give a good deal to have a little conversation with you about the best means of getting through the difficulties which this next month, April, has in store for me. This is what I hinted I should like to run up for a day or two soon to talk with you about, and I think it not unlikely

[1] The Moore's were invited to visit Oakhanger Hall. See letter No. 306, to Mary Dalby, 8 Apr. 1813.

[2] The cottage at Kegworth.

[3] Lord Moira's library at Donington Park.

[4] *Lalla Rookh.*

I shall; but, observe me, I do not intend to let you suffer one minute's inconvenience by my *derangement.* The sale of my *immoveables* here will pay all bills, and get me up to town; but your brother's bill, my aunt's, my father's!! do not be alarmed; I am safe from all these but your brother's; but I want (if I can) to take them from the shoulders they are on to my own. There is my rent too, which, I believe, I ought to pay immediately. Ever yours,

T. Moore.

302. *To his Mother*

Russell, i. 346, no. 234

Kegworth
Wednesday [March] 1813.

My dearest Mother,

We are just returned, and I have missed my regular day of writing; but Sir Charles Hastings (Lord Moira's cousin) came over for us to Donington on Monday, and made us go to Wellesley Park, his place, and dine and sleep there: indeed, he wanted us to stay a month, and it was only by promising we should go again that he let us away at all. Lady Hastings was very kind to Bessy.

We brought Mary Dalby with us to stay a week. I shall write again on Friday. Love to dearest father and Nell. Ever your own,

Tom.

303. *To James Power*

Rice University

Thursday Night* [March 1813][1]

My dear Sir—

What I send now is *not* the one I promised, but you shall have that, with the words & setting of Jessica[2] (if we are not to send it to Ireland) next week—

I shall be glad to hear from you whether there is any chance of getting Bunting's Collection—[3]

Mrs Ready left us yesterday, and almost cried & tore her hair to make us go with her to Buxton—but we were hard-hearted— She is a good-natured woman, with all her nonsense, for she has taken great offence with me because I will not let her lend me two or

[1] Part of the watermark is torn away by the seal, but that which is visible reads '18–0', probably '1810'. The letter was dated March 1813, by comparison of its content to that of letter No. 301, to James Power, March 1813.

[2] *Poetry*, p. 317.

[3] Bunting's *General Collection of Ancient Irish Music* (1796).

three hundred pounds— I am sure I do not know where it is to come from, if I accepted it—

Ever yours, my dear Sir, most truly
Thomas Moore.

304. *To Leigh Hunt*

B.M. Add. MS. 37210, f. 162

Kegworth Leicestershire
Thursday [postmark April 2, 1813]

My dear Sir—

I was well aware that, on the first *novelty* of your imprisonment you would be over-whelmed with all sorts of congratulations & condolences, and therefore resolved to reserve *my* tribute both of approbation & sympathy till the gloss of your chains was a little gone off, and both friends & *starers* had got somewhat accustomed to them—[1] If I were now to tell you half of what I have thought and felt in your favour during this period, I fear it would be more than you know enough of me to give me credit for; and I shall therefore only say (in true Irish phrase and spirit) that my *heart* takes you by the *hand* most cordially, and that I only wish heaven had given me a brother, whom I could think so well of & feel so warmly about— I hope to be in London in about four or five weeks, when one of my first visits shall be to Horse-monger Lane, and I trust I shall find your restrictions so far released as to allow of my not merely *looking* at *you* thro the bars, but passing an hour or two with you in your room—

I have long observed and (I must confess) wondered at your *retenue* about Lord Moira—and have sometimes flattered myself (forgive me for being so vain, and so little just, perhaps, to your sense of duty) that a little regard for *me* was at the bottom of your forbearance—for you have always struck me as one, whom nature never destined 'accusatoriam vitam vivere', and who, if you were to live much among us Lilliputians of this world, would soon find your giant limbs [*MS. damaged*]d with a multitude of almost invisible *heart*-strings—but be this as it may, I must acknowledge (with a candour, which is *wrung* from me) that Lord Moira's conduct no longer deserves your approbation—and when I say this, I trust I need not add, that it *no longer has mine*— His kindnesses to me, of course, I can never forget—but they are remembered, as

[1] In December 1812 John and Leigh Hunt were convicted, sentenced to two years in prison, and fined £500 for publishing an attack on the Prince Regent in the *Examiner* for 12 Mar. 1812. (See letter No. 224, to his mother, March 1812.) Leigh Hunt's room in Surrey Jail became a meeting-place for friends who shared his liberal views.

one remembers the kindnesses of a faithless mistress, and that esteem, that reverence, which was the soul of all, is fled—his thoughtfulness about me indeed remained to the last, and, in the interview which I had with him, immediately on his coming down here after his appointment, he said, that, tho he had nothing sufficiently good in his *Indian* patronage to warrant my taking such an expensive voyage, yet it was in his power, by *exchange* of patronage with ministers to serve me *at home*, and that he meant to provide for me in this way—to which I answered, with many acknowledgements for his friendship, that 'I begged he would not take the trouble of making any such application, as I would infinitely rather struggle on as I am than accept of any thing under such a system'—I must add (because it is creditable to him) that this refusal, tho so significantly conveyed and still more strongly afterwards by letter, did not offend him, and that he continued the most cordial attentions to us during the remainder of his stay—[1] I know you will forgive this egotism, and would perhaps trouble you with a little more of it, if the unrelenting Post-time were not very near at hand.

My Bessy has given me another little *girl*, which was one of the very few wrong things she does, for I meant it to be a boy—[2] If the lively anxiety and interest of a very pure & natural heart be gratifying to you, you have had it from her throughout— Do you recollect meeting me and her one day?

Best regards to Mrs Hunt from
Yours
[*Signature effaced*]

305. *To William Gardiner*

Russell, i. 302, no. 193

Wednesday night, twelve o'clock
[April 1813][3]

My dear Sir,

I send you my last parting words. To-morrow morning we are off, and be assured that we leave some of our best recollections

[1] For details of Lord Moira's appointment to the position as Governor General of Bengal and of Moore's refusal to accept anything from him by exchange of patronage see letter No. 237, to James Corry, 29 June 1812, and No. 281, to Lady Donegal, December 1812.

[2] Moore's second daughter, Anastasia Mary, was born on 16 Mar. 1813.

[3] Although Russell placed this undated letter with those written in 1812, the date given above is more nearly correct, since the text seems to allude to Moore's move from Kegworth in April 1813.

with *you*. Hall the carrier will take you your books on Saturday, and I hope they may arrive safe.

I am in your debt for my comforts the last winter, but I hope to pass through Leicester at no very distant period, when this and *higher matters* shall be settled between us.

I can scarcely see to write, so weary with the fatigues of packing, bill-paying, &c. &c. Bessy joins in best remembrances to you, with yours very truly,

Thomas Moore.

306. *To Mary Dalby*

Russell, viii. 141

Oakhanger Hall
April 8. 1813.

My dear Mary,

Bessy is so occupied with Mrs. ——,[1] that she has not a moment to spare for writing to you, and therefore has deputed the very agreeable but hasty task to me. What do you think? On our arrival within four miles of this place, we heard (what I had often strongly anticipated) that poor old ——[2] was dead! He died the day but one before we came. You may imagine the perplexity this threw us into, for I regarded our visit as completely frustrated, and I passed a miserable night at the miserable inn of Sandbach, turning over in my mind, with an anxiety I have seldom felt, the extreme awkwardness of our situation, and the difficulty I should find in disposing of myself and the dear little group along with me, after our abandonment of house, furniture, and everything like a home. The morning, however, soon dissipated all this gloom; for, in answer to a note which I sent Mrs. ——, there arrived a gay barouche, and two smiling servants, who conveyed us and our baggage hither, and, if there was not such a thing as a *corpse* still in the house, you would scarcely suppose that Death had ever showed his ugly face within the walls. The son-in-law and daughter are expected every hour, and after the will-reading and funeral are over, I think we shall all be as if nothing had happened. Mrs. —— takes most violently to Bessy, and as dispossession from Oakhanger (if at all) will not be enforced for at least a year, we shall get on for three or four months quite as pleasantly as we expected. The place is beautiful. We have a suite of delightful rooms that open into each other — a bedroom, my study, and a room for the maid and

[1] **Mrs. Ready, who had invited them to spend the summer at Oakhanger Hall. See letter No. 301, to James Power, March 1813.**

[2] **Mr. Ready.**

Barbara; and I write to you now at a window that looks over a sweet little lake and a glorious country. Your little daughter was very ill indeed on our arrival, but we have got a wet-nurse for her, and she already begins to recover and revive.

Bessy sends her best love,—she is always talking to them about you. Ever, my dear Mary, your sincere friend,

Thomas Moore.

307. *To James Power*

Russell, i. 347, no. 236

[April?] 1813.

My dear Sir,

I send you the four more Melodies. You see I have changed my mind about 'Oh! had I a bright little Isle;' the fact is, I thought the words too pretty for the air, and have been at the *bother* of writing two convivial verses for it, which now go for nothing, as I hit upon a second verse to the former words, which makes it altogether (*I will* say) so *pretty* a *poem*, that I think it will grace our pages more than the convivial one. Mind, when I praise my own things in this way, it is only by comparison *with* my own; and in this way I have seldom done anything I like better than the words of 'Oh! had I,' &c.

I am very glad you sent me 'You remember Ellen;' as I have been in great perplexity between 'One Bumper' and 'The Valley lay smiling;' but what you now have are certain, and arranged as I wish.

Did I send you the names of 'Ellen' and 'The Minstrel Boy?'[1] I must look for them. Ever yours,

T. Moore.

308. *To James Power*

Russell, i. 347, no. 237

Thursday [April] 1813.

My dear Sir,

I have been thinking ever since I got your last very kind letter, what plan I could hit upon for something popular for you; and I think I have it. There is one Mr. Tom Brown, whose name now would bring him (I well know) any sum of money, and you shall skim the cream of his celebrity; these shall be ready for publication soon after my book (not before for the world). 'The First Number of

[1] For the poems mentioned in this letter see *Poetry*, pp. 202–5.

Convivial and Political Songs, to Airs original and selected, by Thos. Brown the Younger, Author of the 'Twopenny Post Bag.!' Ever yours

T. Moore.

309. *To his Mother*

Russell, i. 351, no. 241

[May] 1813.

My dearest Mother,

I am going to send this through my old channel, Lord Glenbervie, because there is some music in it which I wish to arrive at its destination as soon as possible. I had a letter yesterday from Bessy;[1] they are all well, except that the parrot has bit one of little Bab's fingers.

I must contrive some way of sending you my Post Bag: it is now in the seventh edition; but I am sorry to find that Carpenter has not kept the secret of its being mine as faithfully as he ought.

I have been busy ever since I came to town about the Melodies, and have not appeared or visited any one yet.

I hope, my own dear mother, that you are all as well and happy at home as my heart wishes you to be, though this you can hardly be. However, take care of yourself and keep up your spirits, my darling mother: I hope we may yet all live together. I was sorry to find my father saying that his hand begins to shake. God send him long health to bless us all. Ever your own,

Tom.

310. *To Mary Dalby*

Russell, viii. 104

Oakhanger
Wednesday [June 1813]

My dear Mary,

I arrived here the latter end of last week, and immediately set out upon a *cottage hunt* to Wales, 'the cheapest country in England!' How much people are deceived at a distance!—its cheapness is all a flim-flam, and nothing remains as it used to be, but its glorious scenery.

We are now packing up to retrace our old steps home towards Derbyshire, &c. &c., and if we are not stopped short by some pretty resting-place near Ashbourn [*sic*], you may perhaps see us

[1] Bessy stayed at Oakhanger Hall during May while Moore was in London.

back among the Kegworthies once more. At all events, I think, we shall be very near you.

* * * * * *

I write this, by command of Bessy, who is buried in trunks, packing-cases, &c. I fear she has been a sad truant in the way of letter-writing since I left her.

Ever yours,
T. Moore.

311. *To James Corry*

Russell, viii. 143

Abergeley
Sunday, June, 1813.

My dear Corry,

I seize the very first quiet moment I have had for two months to give you some little account of myself, and ask pardons innumerable for my long and most criminal silence; but, if you know the way (or rather the million ways) I was pulled about in Town, and the difficulty I found in snatching a minute for my *daily* letters to Bessy, you would forgive me without hesitation, and only think of congratulating me on being released from a bustle and dissolution, always so bewildering, and now become so very uninteresting to me. I went through it, indeed, quite as a task, for I thought it a good thing to see and be seen a little, and to put the springs of my town friendships in play again, lest they should grow rusty from disuse. You will be glad, I am sure, to hear that, in this point of view, I have every reason to be delighted with my visit; I never met with more kindness, and certainly never with half so much deference, or half so many flattering tributes to me both as a man and an author. My conduct with Lord Moira is known to all those whom one is anxious to please, and I find it has got me indeed much more credit than I deserve for it. You will be surprised, too, to hear that the *Post-bag* has done me infinite service,—so differently do things sometimes turn out from what their tendency, at the first cursory glance, appears to be! Whether it be from any talent shown in it, or its courage, or the general dislike towards the Prince, nothing I ever wrote has gained me so much *pleasant* fame.

I am here *cottage-hunting*, but with so little success that I believe I shall try back towards my old ground in Derbyshire, or thereabouts. Wales is certainly so far from everything civilised, that nothing but its scenery and its cheapness could recommend it to one. The former, of course, remains always beautiful; but as to *cheapness*, it is become quite a humbug: if I may parody a line of my friend Byron's,—

'Beef, mutton, poultry fails, but Nature still is fair.'[1]

Your letter, inclosing the draft, travelled to Kegworth, Cheshire; and at length, after these easy stages, reached me in town, from whence it returned, both letter and draft, unanswered, unaccepted, unannealed, to Cheshire again, where it now lies; but the moment I get back again you shall have the valuable instrument you enclosed, with all the validity that a poet's name can give it. A bill like this resembles those animals that lie in a torpid state for months together, and I shall be but too happy if I am able to *waken* it into *cash* in November.

Give my best regards to Mrs. Corry, and believe me, my dear Corry, ever your very attached friend,

Thomas Moore.

312. *To his Mother*

Russell, i. 352, no. 242

Ashbourne
Saturday night [June] 1813.

My dearest Mother,

Within these few hours I have succeeded in taking a cottage; just the sort of thing I am likely to like,—secluded, and among the fields, about a mile and a half from the pretty town of Ashbourne, in Derbyshire.[2] We are to pay twenty pounds a-year rent, and the taxes about three or four more.

Mrs. Ready has brought us on here in her barouche, and we have had a very pleasant journey of it.

Bessy bids me make a thousand apologies to dear Nell for not writing, but she has been so bustled about she has not had a moment.

You must direct to me now, Mayfield, Ashbourne, Derbyshire.

Best love to all from your own,

Tom.

[1] 'Art, Glory, Freedom fail, but Nature still is fair.' *Childe Harold*, II, lxxxvii.

[2] The Moores moved to Mayfield Cottage, near Ashbourne, Derbyshire, in June 1813.

313. *To his Mother*

Russell, i. 358, no. 247

Mayfield
Thursday night [June] 1813.

My dearest Mother,

Dear Bessy and I are quite busy in preparing our little cottage, which was in a most ruinous state, but which is already beginning to assume looks of comfort. The expense of remaining at the inn, while it is preparing, is the worst part of the business. My darling mother, how you would delight, I know, to see us when we are settled! I have taken such a fancy to the little place, and the rent is so low, that I really think I shall keep it on as a scribbling retreat, even should my prospects in a year or two induce me to live in London. I wish I had a good round sum of money to lay out on it, and I should make it one of the prettiest little things in England. Bessy still begs a thousand pardons of Ellen, but her bustle increases upon her, and she must only atone by long, long letters when she gets into the cottage. Mind, you must direct, 'Mayfield Cottage, Ashbourne, Derbyshire.' Every your own,

Tom.

314. *To his Mother*

Russell, i. 358, no. 248

Mayfield Cottage
Monday night [June] 1813.

My dearest Mother,

I got my dear father's letter yesterday, and I assure you we both heartily sympathise in the impatience which you feel for our meeting: but, darling mother, it would be (I am sure you are convinced) the height of imprudence for me to go to such expense, and indulge in so much idleness as a trip to Ireland would now entail on me. Next spring it is almost certain that I shall be able to see you all embracing one another. To-morrow we shall remove from the inn to the house of the farmer from whom we have the cottage, and in a few days more I expect we shall sleep under our own roof. To-day, while my dear Bessy was presiding over the workmen, little Barbara and I rolled about in the hay-field before our door, till I was much more hot and tired than my little playfellow. The farmer is doing a vast deal more for us in the way of repairs, but still it will take a good sum from myself to make the place worthy of its situation; and, luckly, the Post Bag has furnished me with tolerable supplies for the purpose. God bless my own dear ones at home. Ever your

Tom.

315. *To Mary Godfrey*

Russell, viii. 132

Mayfield Cottage
Thursday night [June] 1813

We slept in our cottage, for the first time, last night, after having served an ejectment on the *ghosts*, who have been its only occupants for some time past. We have the luck of getting into haunted houses; for our Kegworth mansion, though as matter-of-fact a *barn* as ever existed, must needs affect the *spirituel*, and had actually the reputation of being *troubled*. There is certainly every conveniency *here* that a ghost could require, and we see nothing like a habitation from our windows, except just the upper part of an old church, which stands at half-a-mile distance among the trees; so that we really are (as our landlord pronounces it) as *lural* as possible, and I feel quite happy at my emancipation from the methodists and manufacturers that swarmed about us at Kegworth. We are, however, as yet, but very imperfectly settled, and, till I can get my little library up comfortably, the fields are my study; my 'books in the running brooks, sermons in stones,' &c. &c.[1] We have had an exceeding good riddance of our widow, who is about the most trumpery person I ever met with, and the more tiresome and oppressive to us, as we were obliged to seem grateful to her for a vast deal of really very good-natured but, at the same time, very disagreeable civilities. She is romancing about coming to live near us! but I sincerely hope some captain or other may lay hold of her and her jointure, and spare us the pain of *cutting* so very dear a friend.[2]

We walked this evening into Ashbourne, and brought back some peas for our supper, which Bessy carried in a little basket upon her arm, as happily and prettily as any market-girl in Derbyshire.

One of the very few pleasures I look forward to, that do not depend upon *myself*, is that of hearing frequently from you and dear Mary; so mind you do not disappoint me, and let me hear all the gossip you can collect for me.

Ever yours.

Best remembrances to sister Philly.

T. M.

Do not tell Rogers you have heard from me till I have time to write to him, which will be in a day or two.

[1] *As You Like It*, II. i. 12–14.

[2] Probably Mrs. Ready, whom they visited at Oakhanger Hall in April and May. She brought them to Mayfield Cottage (see letter No. 312, to his mother, June 1813).

316. *To Mary Dalby*

Russell, i. 360, no. 250

Mayfield Cottage, Ashbourne,
Thursday evening [June] 1813.

My dear Mary,

We had the courage to take possession on Tuesday week last, after having served an ejectment on *the ghosts*, who have been the only tenants here for sometime past. Isn't it odd that we should have the luck always to get into haunted houses? This lonely, secluded little spot is not at all a bad residence for ghosts; but for our old matter-of-fact barn at Kegworth to pretend to be haunted was too much affectation. Within these few days the place begins to look habitable about us; my poets and sages have raised their heads from the packing-cases, and very *creditable* chairs, tables, &c., are beginning to take their places round the walls.

Bessy is highly delighted with her little cottage, and whenever any new improvement is made, she says, 'How Mary Dalby will like this when she comes!' We have not yet found out the Matchetts, but there were two or three stray ladies the other evening reconnoitring the cottage when we were out, and making a sort of offer at a visit, who, we believe, are friends of the Matchetts' [*sic*]: They were of the Cooper family.

Bessy and I had a day at Dovedale together, before we left Ashbourne, and it was a very happy day indeed. She shall write to you very soon, but (whether it is an invention of her laziness or not, I don't know) she says the agreement was that *I* should write the first letter: so now you have it, and now let us hear from *you*. I have near a dozen epistles to scribble this evening. Ever yours faithfully,

Thomas Moore.

317. *To Lady Donegal*

Russell, i. 362, no. 252

Ashbourne, Derbyshire
Saturday night [June] 1813.

I am settled at last, and I would not write till I could tell you so. I have got a small rural cottage among the fields, near the pretty town of Ashbourne; rent twenty pounds a-year, and taxes about three more. I have not time at this moment to say anything else, but that I have every prospect of quiet and happiness. I have received a very flattering letter from Whitbread, apologising for not cultivating or courting my acquaintance while I was in town, and requesting me to undertake something for Drury Lane.

Your little god-daughter is growing the sweetest and most interesting little thing in the world. Bessy sends best remembrances. More in a day or two. Ever cordially yours,

T. M.

318. *To his Mother*

Russell, i. 363, no. 254

Mayfield
Thursday evening [June] 1813.

My dearest Mother,

We are to dine out (for the first time) to-morrow: indeed the natives here are beginning to visit us much faster than I wish. Mrs. Rain called upon Bessy yesterday: they have a fine place here called Wooten Hall.

Our cottage is upon a kind of elevated terrace above the field, which has no fence around it, and keeps us in constant alarm about Bab's falling over, so that I shall be obliged to go to the expense of *paling:* it will cost me, I dare say, ten pounds, for the extent in front is near sixty yards.

I find I am a great favourite with this celebrated Madame de Stael [*sic*], that has lately arrived, and is making such a noise in London: she says she has a *passion* for my poetry.[1] Ever your own,

Tom.

319. *To his Mother*

Russell, ii. 28, no. 286

Mayfield Cottage, Ashbourne,
Thursday night [June 1813][2]

My dearest Mother,

We last night went into Ashbourne to see a phantasmagoria and automatons, and supped afterwards with our neighbours the Coopers. We found several cards of visitors on our return home; amongst others the Arkwrights, who live in Sir B. Boothby's fine place, Ashbourne Hall. I am glad he has called on me, for he was the person opposed to Lord Rancliffe in the Nottingham election,

[1] Madame de Staël was in London in June 1813.

[2] Mention in the second paragraph that the paling had been placed around the lawn at Mayfield indicates that Russell's dating of this letter in 1814 was incorrect. It must have been written soon after the family moved to the Cottage. See letter No. 318 and No. 320, to his mother, both dated June 1813.

and it shows he bears me no grudge for my zeal in his antagonist's cause.

We are very glad to get back to our quiet little cottage, which has been a good deal improved since we left it, by the addition of the paling, and little Barbara runs about now without any fear. She is again very well, though I think still cutting more teeth. God bless my darling mother. Ever your own,

Tom.

320. *To his Mother*

Russell, i. 346, no. 235

Thursday night [June] 1813.

My dearest Mother,

We have had a very kind invitation from Honeybourne (Joe Atkinson's brother-in-law, who lives within twelve or thirteen miles of us) to go and pass some days with him. On Monday we are asked to dine at Rain's, and though we sent an apology, saying we expected some visitors, they wrote back again to request we would bring the visitors; so that I don't know how we are to get off: but, without a carriage, these distant trips to dinner are very bad proceedings.

Mary Dalby has left us, and Barbara says, '*Koopsch gone.*' Our green paling is up—our gravel walks are nearly made, and we begin to look very neat and snug.

Poor Bessy is not very well these two or three days past, but Barbara is quite stout.

Good night, my darling mother. Ever your own,

Tom.

321. *To Mary Godfrey*

Russell, ii. 23, no. 281

Mayfield
[June, 1813]

I ought to have thanked you both much sooner for your very enlivening pair of letters. In my absence from all your fine London *fêtes*, I ask no better festival than one of these letters of an evening, and they have as *illuminating* an effect (upon our faces at least) as a despatch from Lord Wellington has among *you.* I assure you Bessy rubs her hands with as much glee as I do when she sees your seal, and says, 'Now for a nice letter from Lady D. and Miss Godfrey,' so that you are very much mistaken when you think that Friendship does not thrive in a cottage as well as Love; and I only wish you were near me, that you might see how pleasantly they would go together, and be, 'like Juno's swans, coupled and inseparable.'[1] I have had a great number of letters lately from Lord Byron.

By the bye, how is the Giaour liked? and how does Rogers seem to bear the review of Columbus?[2] It is in many parts most insidiously done, and the accusing him of *haste* is really too impudent a humbug, when they and all the world know so entirely to the contrary. I am very glad to hear that I am in such high favour with that *Begum* of *literature*, Madame de Staël.[3] Rogers has told me much more to the same purpose: that she says 'she has a *passion* for my poetry,' &c. &c. I should like very much to see her, though you know how shy I am of this kind of animal, and that Goldsmith's young Marlow is not more afraid of a *modest* woman than I am of a learned one.[4] However, as I am told she is good-natured, and too much of the true lioness to hurt a little terrier like me, I think I would venture within the reach of her claws. We have been visited by some of the *respectables* in this neighbourhood, as, luckily, there is no fashion; though I have already met with a blooming old lady of sixty, who writes poems in *imitation of me*, about 'Coming to bowers,' &c. &c.: altogether, though, we are very well off for quiet, and I hope will continue so.

I send you herewith a little job to do for me. Will you take the trouble of sending John to Perry's for me with the inclosed draft? It will be paid perhaps immediately, perhaps not till next day; but, as soon as you get it, inclose it in a frank to me. It is not in payment for Chronicle squibs, for I have not once taken to my *Brown* studies since I left town; but Perry discounted a bill on Power for me two or three weeks ago, and this is part of the amount.

Ever, with best love to Lady D. (to whom I shall write soon about her kindest of all kind offers of a lodging in Davies Street) and remembrances to sister Philly, yours, most truly,

Thomas Moore.

[1] *As You Like It*, I. iii. 75.

[2] *The Giaour* was published by John Murray in June 1813. *The Voyage of Columbus*, a fragmentary epic, was written in 1810 and published in 1812. William Ward, third Viscount Dudley, gave an unfavourable review of it in the *Quarterly Review*, vol. ix, no. xvii (March 1813), 207–18, in which he accused the author of undue haste in composing it.

[3] See letter No. 318, to his mother, June 1813.

[4] Young Marlow is a character in *She Stoops to Conquer*. He is bashful and reserved, except with barmaids and servants.

322. *To his Mother*

Russell, i. 361, no. 251

Thursday evening [June or July] 1813.

My dearest Mother,

We have this day got our curtains up and our carpets down, and begin to look a little civilised. It is a very sweet spot indeed, and I do not recollect whether I told you that I only pay twenty pounds a-year for it; and the taxes will be about three or four more. This is not extravagant, and, though it be a little nutshell of a thing, we have a room to spare for a friend, or for you, darling mother, if you could come and visit us. How proud Bessy would be to have you, and make much of you!

We heard, a day or two ago, of our little Statia, that she is thriving finely. The only drawback on my dear Bessy's happiness is the being removed from her little child so far. She has hardly had time to get acquainted with it yet; but it would have been a great pity to take her away from a nurse that seemed to be doing her so much justice.

Best love to father and Nell from us both. Bessy says she *will not* write till the house is settled. Ever your own,

Tom.

323. *To James Corry*

Russell, viii. 144

Ashbourne
July 1. 1813.

My dear Corry,

At last I have found a resting place, and you may now direct to me, in the true poetic style, to 'Mayfield Cottage, Ashbourne, Derbyshire.' I have got a pretty little stone-built cottage, in the fields by itself, about a mile and a half from the very sweetly situated town of Ashbourne, for which I am to pay twenty pounds a-year rent, and the taxes come to three or four pounds more; but though this sounds so cheap, yet the expenses of furnishing, and the beautiful capabilities of the place, which tempt one into improvement so irresistibly, will make it, I fear, rather a dear little spot to me. Once done, however, to my mind (if the supplies will enable me to do it so), I think I shall not be easily induced to quit it, but shall keep it on still as a *scribbling retreat*, even though I should, in a year or two, find it more to my purpose to live in London; but certainly until my *Grande Opus* is finished,[1] I could not possibly have a more rural or secluded corner to court the Muses in. We are fitting up a little room for a friend; and though

[1] *Lalla Rookh.*

it has but a low ceiling and cottage windows to it, yet I flatter myself we could make you and Mrs. Corry comfortable in it, if you would take us in your way to Matlock, Buxton, or any other given gay place you may be bound to. We are within four miles of that most poetical of all spots, Dovedale.

At length, my dear good fellow, after my long, long incubation, I have hatched your draft into something like an acceptance; and all I ask is, if it passes out of your own hands, that you will give me timely notice, that I may be fully prepared to ward off the '*irrevocabile* telum.'[1]

I do not remember whether I told you that I was solicited very flatteringly, while I was in town, to lecture at the Royal Institution next year. Campbell has just concluded his lectures. I should not have disliked it, but by Rogers's advice and that of some other friends (who thought it *infra dig.*) I declined it. A day or two since I received a very cordial letter from Whitbread, containing a most urgent entreaty that I should undertake something for Drury Lane.[2] This, however, I shall not think of till after my poem.

Write soon, my dear Corry, and tell me all about the health and happiness of yourself and your dear Maria.

Ever yours, faithfully,
Thomas Moore.

My Bessy and babes are quite well, and would *all* jump with joy to see you.

324. *To James Power*

Russell, i. 353, no. 243

Mayfield, Ashbourne, Derbyshire
Tuesday, July 1. 1813.

My dear Sir,

I have great pleasure in telling you that I have got a cottage very much to my liking, near the pretty town of Ashbourne. I am now, as you wished, within twenty-four hours' drive of town, and I hope, before the summer is over, we shall see you at Mayfield. I have much to do, and many efforts to make, before I can put the cottage in a state to receive us. More in a day or two. Ever yours,

T. Moore.

I have had a most flattering letter from Whitbread, entreating me earnestly to write something for Drury Lane.[3]

[1] See letter No. 311, to James Corry, June 1813.
[2] See letter No. 317, to Lady Donegal, June 1813.
[3] See letter No. 317, to Lady Donegal, June 1813, and No. 323, to James Corry, 1 July 1813.

325. *To James Power*

Pforzheimer Misc. MS. 305

[Postmark July 14, 1813]

My dear Sir— At the other side I send you the words to the Finland Song with the second verse I have just finished;[1] and before the end of the week you shall have something else of my promised performances— What you offer about the Opera is very tempting indeed; particularly, as I have (since I wrote to you last) plucked up courage enough to look into the dreadful little book you gave me at parting, and find to my infinite horror that I have no more to draw this year, but that at the end of it I shall be ten pounds in your debt!—Tho I felt that this must be the case, yet the actual proofs of it staring before my face, in black and white, quite staggered me for a day or two— I am now however a little recovered from the shock, and though this state of our accounts makes your proposal doubly tempting, yet I fear I could not possibly undertake both my Poem & an Opera this year & do all that justice to both which it is your interest as well as mine that I should—for, believe me, that I consider *your* interest very much in the anxiety I feel about my Poem,[2] so much indeed do I consider my duty towards you to be paramount to all others in the way of business, that if I did not think the success of the Poem a very material circumstance in your favour as well as my own, I should not feel justified in giving a moment to it away from any task it is your wish I should undertake; and it is principally from my desire to get the Poem forward that I have chosen a number of the melodies as my musical work for this year; because I shall naturally feel less solicitude about such an old established job than I should about any thing new we should embark in—and you may depend upon it that, after this year, whether I am lucky enough to finish the Poem or not, you shall hear no more about it as standing in the way of any thing you wish me to undertake—

With respect to your brother, I fear he will make me suffer for the pains I took to get him connected with us—but I shall be very grateful indeed for your keeping off as much of his annoyance from me as possible— If *you* are displeased with my Advertisement or the intention expressed in it, you have but to say so, & it shall be altered—but I dare say I shall have your sanction in not troubling my head about any criticism or objection of his— So that I may

[1] *Poetry*, p. 312. [2] *Lalla Rookh.*

leave entirely to yourself the explanation you think proper to make, both with respect to this year's works, and the announcement we agree to put forth in the Advertisement— Pray, tell me how soon you think the numerous delays he is throwing in your way will enable you to bring out this Number—[1]

I have never yet been in any situation so retired & suited to business as our present little Cottage, and I think I shall live in it for ever, if something better than ordinary does not turn up for me.

Best remembrances to M[rs] Power from Bessy. Your poor dear little girl!

from Ever yours
T. Moore

I saw the moon rise clear
On hills and vales of snow,
Nor told my fleet rein-deer
The track I wish'd to go.
But quick he bounded forth,
For well my rein-deer knew
I've but one path on earth
That path which leads to you!

The gloom that winter cast
How soon the heart forgets,
When summer brings, at last,
Her sun that never sets.
So dawn'd my love for you,
And, chacing every pain,
Than summer sun more true,
Twill never set again!

326. *To James Power*

Russell, i. 353, no. 244

Mayfield Cottage
Thursday evening, July 17. 1813.

My dear Sir,

I thought to have sent you a song by this post, but I cannot finish it without a pianoforte. I am, however, to get one upon *hire* next week, and in the mean time I am touching up the preface. It will not be *quite* as long as Twiss's.[2]

[1] For details of the difficulties between the Power brothers see letter, No. 266 to James Power, 23 Nov. 1812.

[2] Horace Twiss wrote the preface to *A Selection of Scottish Melodies*, music

I think it is better for me to pay half-a-guinea a month for a pianoforte, than venture upon a new one. Recollect I am in your debt eight or nine pounds upon the last one.

This is the first day I have been able to establish a sitting-room for myself, so you may suppose I have not been able to do much.

I hope you liked the second verse of the Finland song. I have one or two old things of mine to send you, when I get the pianoforte. Poor *M. P.*,[1] I see, is on again. Ever yours,

T. Moore.

327. *To his Mother*

Russell, i. 363, no. 255

Thursday [July] 1813.

My dearest Mother,

We are going to-morrow to return the visit of the Rains: our neighbours, the Coopers, lend us their carriage. You see we fall on our legs wherever we are thrown.

I had a long letter from Lord Byron yesterday: his last thing, the Giaour, is very much praised, and deservedly so; indeed, I think he will dethrone Walter Scott. Ever, my darling mother, your own,

Tom

328. *To James Power*

Russell, i. 348, no. 238

Wednesday [July] 1813.

My dear Sir,

With respect to the Spanish airs, I like the title you propose for the Song of War very well, but not the other. I think it would be better, perhaps, to put 'Vivir en Cadenas, a celebrated Spanish air,' &c. As to the words, I certainly did not intend to put any more verses, but if they are too short as they are, or, if you wish it, of course I shall lose no time in writing more, and, while I wait your answer, I shall be trying what I can do. Ever yours,

Thomas Moore.

by Henry R. Bishop and words by Twiss (London, 1814). The collection was reviewed in the *Monthly Review*, lxxiv (June 1814), 187–91. The writer remarked that 'Mr. T's preface, which (to use a Trans-atlantic phrase) is *lengthy*, consists principally of a dissertation on inversion in poetic language' (p. 188). Since Power was the publisher, Moore probably saw the collection before it appeared in print.

[1] *M. P., or the Blue Stocking*, Moore's musical comedy.

Did I tell you that Murray has been offering me, through Lord Byron, some hundreds (number not specified) a year to become editor of a Review like the Edinburgh and Quarterly?[1] Jeffrey has fifteen! I have, of course, not attended to it.

329. *To James Power*

Russell, i. 349, no. 239

[July] 1813.

My dear Sir,

I send you a second verse to 'Vivir en Cadenas,'[2] and I am glad that I have written it, for I think it is *not bad*. I have written it under the notes, as I suppose it will be engraved with the music. Here follows the second verse to 'Oh! remember the Time:'

'They tell me, you lovers from Erin's green isle
  Every hour a new passion can feel;
And that soon, in the light of some lovelier smile,
  You'll forget the poor Maid of Castile.
But they know not how brave in the battle you are,
  Or they never could think you would rove;
For 'tis always the spirit most gallant in war,
  That is fondest and truest in love.'[3]

With respect to Murray's proposal,[4] I feel (as I do every instance of your generosity) the kindness and readiness with which you offer to yield up our scheme to what you think my superior interest; but, in the first place, I do not agree with you, that this plan with Murray would be more for my ultimate advantage than that extensive one which I look forward to with you; and, in the next place, I do not think I would accept now *ten thousand* pounds for anything that would interfere with the finishing of my poem, upon which my whole heart and industry are at last fairly set, and for this reason, because, *anticipated* as I have already been in my Eastern subject by Lord Byron in his late poem,[5] the success he has met with will produce a whole swarm of imitators in the same

[1] See Byron's letter to Moore, dated 22 July 1813 (*LJ*, ii. 223), in which Byron conveys Murray's proposal to Moore.

[2] 'From Life without Freedom', *Poetry*, p. 312.

[3] 'Remember the Time', *Poetry*, p. 314.

[4] See letter No. 328, to James Power, July 1813.

[5] *The Giaour* appeared in June 1813, thereby anticipating Moore's *Lalla Rookh*, which was not published until 1817. For an account of this popular interest in Eastern subjects see W. C. Brown, 'Thomas Moore and English Interest in the Middle East', *SP*, xxxiv (1937), 576. See also Hoover H. Jordan, 'Byron and Moore', *MLQ*, ix (1948), 429.

Eastern style, who will completely *fly-blow* all the novelty of my subject. On this account I am more anxious than I can tell you to get on with it, and it quite goes between me and my sleep.

I have not time now to write more; but good night, and God bless you! Ever yours most sincerely,

Thomas Moore.

330. *To James Power*

Russell, i. 354, no. 245

[July] 1813.

My dear Sir,

I have drawn upon you again, as I dare say before this you know. I am also, with your permission, going to take another liberty with your name, and that is (do not be frightened) to draw upon you at *six* months for fifty pounds. It is merely as a *matter of form*, for the upholsterer at Derby, to whom I am to give it, means to let it lie in his desk, and I am to pay it off by instalments; he did not demand this of me, and therefore, if you dislike it, there is no necessity; but I should feel more comfortable, and less under obligation to him, if he had this in his hands till I can gradually get out of his debt. We are resolved to take our furniture with us, whenever we go to London, as this buying and re-buying is a very losing concern. You shall next week have the first symptoms of my returning industry for the shop, and I must do something every week now, to make out my task for the year, which is nearly at an end. Indeed, if I had no one but yourself to deal with, I should not scruple now to ask for three or four months total liberty from you; as I am convinced, with your spirit and our united views, you would see how amply such time lost in one way would be made up to us in another; but I dread your brother, and while I should not like to ask the favour of him, I feel that he would not have the same prospective interest in granting it, so that my best way is to do as much as I can, and then, after the Book,[1] I am 'yours till death.' Indeed I am not quite sure that this Book (at least a great part of it) must not be yours also. I am still writing away *songs* in it, and how the property of them is to be managed, God and you only know. But no matter; you cannot have too much for what you *merit* of me; and if you can but get me through my debts to friends gradually, and keep this cottage over my head, you may dispose of me and mine as you please. An operatic drama will be the first thing the moment the Book goes to

[1] *Lalla Rookh.*

press, and I will set my shoulders to it, you may be sure. I have had a letter from Lord Meath, who was chairman of the first meeting of Dalton's Amateur Glee Club, expressing the delight which the members all felt at 'my composition,' and communicating to me my unanimous election as honorary member. I had a letter from Corry, dated the morning of the meeting, saying that great things were expected from the glee, as Stevenson said he had never been so lucky in anything: so I wish you joy of the firstfruits of our co-operation.

Did you see the quotation of 'Oh! had I a bright little Isle,'[1] in the Chronicle, with the praise of 'exquisitely beautiful,' before it. Best regards to Mrs. Power. I fear very much, from what you hint about her, that Bessy and she are keeping each other in countenance; but Providence, I hope, will look after us. A good peace with France and a good piece at Drury Lane will do wonders for us. Ever yours,

T. Moore.

I dare say, from the explanation you give me, that the arrangement of 'Oh, doubt me not!'[2] is quite correct; but it is the most *discordant correct* thing I ever heard in my life.

331. *To Leigh Hunt*

B.M. Add. MS. 37210, ff. 164, 165

Mayfield Cottage
Ashbourne Derbyshire
Thursday evening* [July 1813]

My dear Hunt—

I take advantage of an envelope to send you greeting from my new habitation, where, I am sure you will be glad to hear, I am much more *poetically* situated than I was at Kegworth, which, to say no worse of it, is a very unlovely village, and where (as the Kegworthies chiefly consist of manufacturers and methodists) I heard nothing but hymns and stocking-frames all day long—*here*, however, I have no such *muse-less* people near me, but have got into a solitary little Cottage in the fields, where the only thing *like* a habitation I see from my windows is an old romantic church half a mile off among the trees—and really, without affectation, I think I begin to feel that the 'genius loci' has no inconsiderable influence on my mind, and that I am writing better for the select company of trees, cows and birds I have got into— I have started afresh with my Poem—[3] (as the Sailors term it) 'taken a new departure' and I

[1] *Poetry*, p. 203. [2] *Poetry*, p. 204. [3] *Lalla Rookh.*

like myself much better this time of setting out than I did before. How are *you* getting on? singing away, I hope, 'like *committed Linnets*'[1]—(by the bye, what a good parable you might draw between the feelings described in the pretty prison-poem of Lovelace's, and your own about the 'sweetness, mercy, majesty &c.') I wish very much you would copy out for me what you have done of your Poem[2] since I left town—and I wish this, more from my anxiety about your success, than from any idea that my criticisms could be of use to you—but I will tell you honestly all I feel & think about it, and there is *just a chance* that my remarks may be of some service—tho my *chief* motive for asking it is to gratify *myself*—I think what I am most likely to differ with you about is the use of some unusual words in which you appear inclined to indulge, and some of which struck me as ungraceful—above all things too, I deprecate such rhymes as that you have made to Aha!—the gratuitous R of the cocknies after words ending in A is inadmissible, I think, *even* in doggerel rhymes, tho poor Harry Greville [*MS. damaged*]—lonel) thought them fr [*MS. damaged*] rhymed verses, not on [*MS. damaged*] language.

> 'This heart is glowing with desire
> For thee, my lovely, sweet Maria!'

Mind, whenever I presume to speak to you ex cathedra of Poetry, you must be generous enough not to throw his *practice* in the face of the Preacher, but listen to me as gravely as you would to a sermon of the Rev. Sir H. B. Dudley's against adultery, or a charge from Lord Ellenborough about indecorous expressions—[3] or if you *will* institute odious comparisons, in my present self-satisfied state (for 'omnia nostra dum nascuntur placent') I would say 'compare with my *present* practice not with my *past*'—

If you consent to send me your verses as you write, and feel any compunction about making me pay postage for them, you may send your packet under cover to the Marchioness Dow^r of Donegall, 56 Davies St. Berkeley Square, and she will get it franked to me—

In the hope of soon hearing from you
I am, my dear Hunt
[*Signature effaced*]

[1] Lovelace, 'To Lucasta, Going beyond the Seas'.

[2] Moore could be referring to either *The Feast of the Poets* (1814) or *The Descent of Liberty, a Mask* (1815).

[3] Although Sir Henry Bate Dudley took orders and after his father's death succeeded to the rectory of North Fambridge, most of his time was spent in London, where he became well known as a man of pleasure. As Lord Chief Justice of England, Lord Ellenborough was a forceful speaker but was noted for using intemperate language.

I have just been reading a very amusing book of Gretry's upon Music, and he says, speaking of a *tristesse* he imagines there is in the sound of a *clarionet*, that if a man in prison should *dance*, it ought to be to the Clarionet—[1] so you may know your instrument whenever you feel inclined to this exercise—

332. *To Mary Godfrey*

Russell, viii. 134

Mayfield
[July or August] 1813.

I was a good deal relieved from my apprehensions about Lady Donegal by your letter, for though you mention colds, &c., I was afraid, from what Rogers said in his letter, that her old complaint had returned with more violence than usual, as he mentioned that she was obliged to consult Baillie, and I always couple his name with something serious and *clinical*. But indeed, Rogers himself, in the next line to this intelligence, mentioned having met her at Gloucester House the Saturday preceding; which (unless *aqua regalis* or *royal wish-wash* was among the doses prescribed by Baillie), I did not think looked like very serious indisposition. If *wishing* you both well and happy, and free from all the ills of this life, could in any way bring it about, I should be as good a physician for both your bodies and souls as you could find anywhere. So you insist upon my taking my poem to Town with me?[2] I will, if I can, you may be sure; but I confess I feel rather down-hearted about it. Never was anything more unlucky for me than Byron's invasion of this region,[3] which when I entered it, was as yet untrodden, and whose chief charm consisted in the gloss and novelty of its features; but it will now be over-run with clumsy adventurers, and when I make my appearance, instead of being a leader as I looked to be, I must dwindle into an humble follower—a Byronian. This is disheartening, and I sometimes doubt whether I shall publish it at all; though at the same time, if I may trust my own judgment, I think I never wrote so well before. But (as King Arthur, in 'Tom Thumb,' says) 'Time will tell;'[4] and in the mean time, I am leading a life which but for these anxieties of fame, and a few ghosts of debt that sometimes haunt me, is as rationally happy as any man

[1] Moore is probably referring to a three-volume work entitled *De la Vérité* (1802), which dealt with how best to express the composer's political and social philosophies in music.

[2] *Lalla Rookh.*

[3] Moore is referring to Byron's *Giaour*. See letter No. 329, to James Power, July 1813.

[4] Fielding, *Tom Thumb*, I. iii. 51.

can ask for. You want to know something of our little girls. Barbara is stout and healthy, not at all pretty, but very sensible-looking, and is, of course, to be everything that's clever. The other little thing was very ill-treated by the nurse we left her with in that abominable Cheshire, but she is getting much better, and promises to be the prettier of the two. Bessy's heart is wrapped up in them, and the only pain they ever give me is the thought of the precariousness of such treasures, and the way I see that *her* life depends upon *theirs*. She is the same affectionate, sensible, and unaffected creature as a mother that she is as a wife, and devotes every thought and moment to them and me. I pass the day in my study or in the fields; after dinner I read to Bessy for a couple of hours, and we are in this way, at present, going through Miss Edgeworth's works, and then after tea I go to my study again. We are not without the distractions of society, for this is a very gay place, and *some* of the distractions I could dispense with; but being far out of the regular road, I am as little interrupted as I could possibly expect in so very thick a neighbourhood. Thus you have a little panorama of me and mine, and I hope you will like it.

Good-bye. Ever yours,
T. Moore.

333. *To his Mother*

Russell, ii. 27, no. 285

Mayfield Cottage
Monday night [July or August, 1813]

My dearest Mother,

As Bessy is by my side, this letter must all be about Barbara; she bids me tell you she has got her a nice little stuff gown for the winter, in which she looks prettier than in anything she ever wore, and Bessy means to send you a pattern of the gown in my next letter, or rather in her own, for she means to write next time. Barbara now has got her mamma's phrase 'Bird,' and looks at me very significantly, as if she had discovered something wrong I had done, and says 'Oh, Bird!' We have at last heard about Statia, she had been a little ill with her teeth, but was getting quite well again. Bessy looks forward to having her home with great impatience.

We are going to a ball this evening, given by the son of a poet in this neighbourhood. I wish there was always such a vein of gold running beside the vein of poetry, for his father (Gisborne) will leave him fifteen thousand a year. Ever, my dearest mother, your own,
Tom.

334. *To his Mother*

Russell, i. 365, no. 257

Mayfield Cottage
Monday night [July or August] 1813.

My dearest Mother,

It is very late, and I have been obliged to leave you last of half a dozen letters, so that you will come off very badly. We dined out to-day at the Ackroyds, neighbours of ours. You would have laughed to see Bessy and me in going to dinner. We found, in the middle of our walk, that we were near half an hour too early for dinner, so we set to *practising country dances*, in the middle of a retired green lane, till the time was expired. Ever your own,

Tom.

335. *To Leigh Hunt*

B.M. Add. MS. 37210, f. 166

Mayfield Cottage
Monday Evening [postmark August 19, 1813]

My dear Hunt—

Since I wrote to you I received the Examiner, in which you impute two things from the Chronicle to my friend Mr Brown— *For once* you are wrong— The 'Little Man & little Soul' *is* his, but the other is *not*—[1] It is not worth making a paragraph about, but if you can find an opportunity of setting your *squib-readers* right upon this important matter, I should be glad you would, and you may cite Mr Brown's authority both for the avowal & *dis*avowal— This ballad about Abbot is the only flight of nonsense I have taken since I left town— I hope you see my friend Lord Byron often— one of the very few London pleasures I envy him is the visit to Horsemonger Lane now & then.

Faithfully yours
Thos Moore

[1] 'Little Man and Little Soul, a Ballad. Dedicated to the Rt. Hon. Ch—rl—s Abb—t' was reprinted in the *Examiner* for Sunday, 18 Aug. 1813. The squib purports to be an argument between Abbot, Speaker of the House of Commons, and his 'Little Soul' about what he will choose as a suitable subject for a speech to the House. He finally decides that

I will tell the Prince and People
What I think of Church and Steeple
And our patent little plan to prop them up, up, up;
And our patent little plan to prop them up.

336. *To his Mother*

Russell, i. 362, no. 253

[August] 1813.

My dearest Mother,

I sent you the Examiner the other day, with two things in it which, you will see, he imputes to me: he is only right in *one* of them, the only thing I have given to the Morning Chronicle since I left town.[1]

You cannot think how our cottage is admired; and, if ever I am able to *purchase* it, I shall make a beautiful thing of it. Ever your own,

Tom.

Barbara is at this moment most busily engaged about a pair of new top-boots, which I have on for the first time since I came from London, and which she is handling and viewing with great admiration.

337. *To James Power*

Russell, i. 337, no. 225

Thursday [August] 1813.

My dear Sir,

I have only time to inclose a little duet, and to say that I have been disappointed in not hearing from you for so long a time. I told you a little *fib* about the Examiner, and the reason was (as I had not seen the paper) I had no idea he would have taken notice of what I thought a very foolish thing, and was ashamed to acknowledge even to *you;* that is, 'Little Man and little Soul,' the *only squib* I have sent Perry since I left town. The other thing about Sir J. Murray is *not mine*; and, bad as the former one is, I am sorry still more he could impute such a dull thing to me as this parody on Sir J. Murray's letter; there is hardly one bit of fun throughout it.[2] Ever yours,

T. Moore.

'A Close Versification of a Memorable Dispatch,' attributed to 'the author of the *Twopenny Post Bag*,' was also reproduced in the same issue. It is a verse satire of a letter from Sir John Murray to the Duke of Wellington, explaining why the former ordered 20,000 troops under his command to embark at Tarronga on 12 June 1813 leaving all their cannon and ammunition ashore. It is this squib which Moore denies writing.

[1] See letter No. 335, to Leigh Hunt, 19 Aug. 1813.

[2] *Ibid.*

338. *To James Power*

Rice University

Sunday Night Septr 13th 1813

My dear Sir—

I leave some parcels behind for you to dispose of for me— The paper bundle, you will perceive, is directed for Mr Lawrence & to be forwarded to Ipswich by the Coach— The books are to go to Longmans (more carefully folded up) and the little parcel containing some ladies' articles are to go to whatever *dyer* Mrs Power thinks proper—as I do not remember they mentioned any particular one— I know you will excuse all this trouble— We have walked all the way to-day, Hornsey, Highgate & home—& I am a little tired. Good bye.

Ever yours faithfully
Thomas Moore

339. *To James Power*

Russell, i. 364, no. 256

Castle Donington
Friday [September or October] 1813.

My dear Sir,

I took the opportunity of a lift to come on here for a last *rummage* of the library before the bad weather sets in, and I have got more for my purpose out of it, by making it a *business* in this way, than I should, in an idle, sauntering way, if I were in its neighbourhood for twelve months. I only write now to acknowledge your last letter, which was forwarded to me hither. I shall give up the correction in the letter-press, as it is so inconvenient, but I think I shall avail myself of the new plate and the erratum: more of this, however, next week. I shall also have a consultation with you about a point which I perceive your mind is a good deal set upon, and that is, my living in or near London. I certainly fear that embarrassments would soon gather round me there, and my own wish is to stay here at least till you and I fix upon some plan of cooperation; but in this, as on every other point, I am very much inclined to listen to your counsel; and therefore we shall have some talk about it. At all events, I shall stay here till I finish my poem; but my reason for agitating the question now is, that I had some idea of agreeing with the landlord for a short term of years of this place; so think over the matter now, and let me know your whole mind and wishes. Next week you shall have another song. Ever yours,

T. Moore.

340. *To James Power*

Russell, i. 365, no. 258

Oct. 23. 1813.

My dear Sir,

Bessy and I have been on a visit to Derby for a week. I was indeed glad to have an opportunity of taking her for change of air, as she was very ill before we went. We were on a visit at Mr. Joseph Strutt's, who sent his carriage and four *for* us and back again *with* us. There are three brothers of them, and they are supposed to have a million of money pretty equally divided between them. They have fine families of daughters, and are fond of literature, music, and all those elegancies which their riches enable them so amply to indulge themselves with. Bessy came back full of presents, rings, fans, &c. &c. My singing produced some little sensation at Derby, and every one to whom I told your intention of publishing my songs collectively seemed delighted.

I have had another application about Drury Lane in consequence of a conversation at Holland House, and am beginning already (without, however, stopping the progress of my poem) to turn over a subject in my mind.[1] You must be very indulgent to me for a few months, and I promise to make up abundantly for it afterwards. This poem has hitherto paralysed all my efforts for you, but it shall do so no longer than this year, I promise you. You are right in referring your brother to the advertisement of the fifth number for this year's work, and I'll make it a good one too, depend upon it. I suppose you have seen the Monthly Review of June on the Melodies. I am promised a sight of it.[2]

It gave me much pain to hear of your vexations and your illness. I feel *more* than a *partner* to you, and nothing can affect either your health or welfare without touching me most deeply. As yet I have only added to your incumbrances, but I trust *my* time for lightening the load is not far distant. I only hope that this new engagement with Stevenson may not involve you in too much difficulty or uneasiness; but (however you may smile at the oft-repeated and still-distant speculation) I am quite sure it will be in my power, after the sale of my Book, to withhold long enough from

[1] See letter No. 323, to James Corry, 1 July 1813. Moore is referring to *Lalla Rookh*.

[2] The fifth number of the *Irish Melodies* was reviewed in the *Monthly Review*, lxxi (June, 1813), 113–26. The article was favourable and praised the 'pathetic and melancholy' songs, which were better than those of livelier description. The reviewer noted the mixture of politics and poetry and discussed the music as well as the verse.

my share of the annuity to let your resources take breath and refreshment, and by writing the words of an oratorio for Stevenson I may perhaps do something towards rendering *him* more valuable, or a set of songs for him to compose. I shall be most happy to write, leaving it to the merit they may possess and your discretion in the use of my name, whether I shall acknowledge them or not: *indeed, this latter task I should rather like than not, so command me;* only I wish he and I could be together when he is setting them.

I think the title of the Finland air had better be, 'A Finland Love Song, arranged for Three Voices, by Thomas Moore, Esq.'[1] Ever yours,

T. Moore.

341. *To his Mother*

Russell, i. 370, no. 261

Mayfield Cottage
Saturday night [24 October 1813]

My dearest Mother,

We returned from Derby the evening before yesterday,[2] just in time for me to appear in my dignified office of steward at the Ashbourne Ball. It was a tolerably gay ball, and they said I acquitted myself *very properly*. It was, however, a very disagreeable office, as I was obliged to consult *rank* more than beauty, and dance off the first two sets with the two ugliest women in the room. Mr. Strutt, while we were with him, made *me* a present of a beautiful box for my letters, and gave Bessy a very fine ring, a nice ivory fan, and a very pretty antique bronze candlestick, so that we lost nothing by our visit.

We shall now shut up for the winter: this place is much too gay to give ourselves up to. Bessy is quite well, and little Barbara in great spirits. We are very uneasy at not hearing of Anastasia.

Barbara calls me *Tom*, and I try in vain to break her of it, because she hears her mother call me so. Ever your own,

Tom.

342. *To James Corry*

Russell, viii. 158

Ashbourne
Oct. 25. 1813.

My dear Corry,

I did not like to risk writing to you while you were away, as I was afraid my letters might have to follow you from place to place,

[1] *Poetry*, p. 312.

[2] See letter No. 340, to James Power, 23 Oct. 1813.

as Lord Moira's venison followed Joe Atkinson; and whereas the latter was quite *alive*, when it caught Joe, my letters, I fear, would have lost even the little life they had at setting out, in the chace: but now that the cold winds of the North have, I presume, sent you home again, I feel most happy in returning to fresh communion with you, and in asking how the journey has agreed with you, as well *spiritually* as *corporeally*. Mrs. Corry too,—I hope most sincerely she is all the better for it, and I again renew my claims upon a little postscript from her own hand, when next you write to me: now, mind, she must not forget this.

We have got into rather a gayer neighbourhood here than I bargained for, but I am determined to go into a torpid state for the winter, and suck my paws, like the bears; as indeed, if I do not work hard, I shall have little else to live upon;—after all, however, it is better than turning Poet Laureat. What do you think of Southey? Is it not *quite* a pity that such a Pegasus as his should be turned into a royal 'cream-coloured horse' for state occasions?[1] I heartily mourn over him.—You will be sorry, I am sure, to hear, that my Island of Bermuda is far from being a *Cucagna* to me, no island of dainties, but barren of money, as its rocks are of vegetables. I am sure I am cheated, and yet I do not know how to help myself. Bessy and I have been lately on a visit to Derby, and found a nest of young poetesses in a family there that amused and interested me a good deal, particularly as some of them were pretty and natural.

* * * * * *

They are daughters of the *Strutts* (with one of whom we were for a week), three brothers in the cotton trade, who have more than forty thousand a year between them, and, what is much better, love literature, music, and everything else that cotton manufacturers are not likely to love. The Edgworths were our predecessors at their house.

I wish, my dear Corry, you would write to me often: your letters are always the pleasantest I receive, and Bessy quite claps her hands with joy at the sight of a letter from 'dear Mr. Corry:' so, do gratify us with long, very long ones. The only very faithful and voluminous correspondent I have is Lord Byron, which is exceedingly delightful to me, as he is just as gay a companion and correspondent as he is a sombre and horrific poet.

Best regards to Mrs. Corry, and believe me most truly your very attached friend,

Thomas Moore.

I inclose a postscript, or rather inscript.

[1] Southey was made Poet Laureate in 1813.

343. *To James Power*

Russell, i. 369, no. 260

[October] 1813.

My dear Sir,

I luckily received your last parcel yesterday morning, time enough to inclose you back your letters with the proofs. I hope you did not answer Dalton's letter yesterday, for you have quite mistaken one part of it; that which relates to the arranging of my compositions. He by no means intends to exclude the arranging of them; but taking that task as a matter of course, says that, in addition to those, he will arrange whatever of any kind or of anybody else's you may publish, and adds that this he thinks must be an object to you. If you have written, pray write again immediately to do away your misapprehension, as whether you decline the proposal or not, I know you would wish to do it on true grounds, and in this I have no doubt you are quite mistaken. I will venture no opinion upon Stevenson's proposal; at least I *ought not*, perhaps, as I have so much myself, to object to his having a good deal too; but I must own, I think, two hundred a-year, *exclusive* of his great works, is a very fair offer, and as much, perhaps, as you ought to give, though I should regret exceedingly the dissolution of my alliance with him. The following is the corrected passage which I wish you to have engraved in the first verse of 'Thro' Erin's Isle:'

'Where'er they pass,[1]
A Triple grass
Shoots up, with dewdrops streaming,
As softly green
As emerald, seen
Through purest crystal gleaming.'*[1]

*This passage has been altered thus, since the letterpress was printed off, in order to get rid of an awkward double rhyme, which savours a little of doggrel.

I wish the note engraved underneath, if it can be done conveniently.

The preface, song, and duet you shall have in the course of this week. Ever yours,

T. Moore.

[1] *Poetry*, p. 201.

344. *To Edward T. Dalton*

Russell, ii. 87, no. 340

[October 1813]

My dear Dalton,

I think it is a *toss-up* which of us has treated the other the worst, and Mrs. Dalton is the only one of the trio that has done her duty. Give her my best thanks for reminding you of me so often, and tell her that, whenever she finds you *will not* recollect me (let her do all she can), she has nothing for it but to sit down and write me a long letter herself, and she may depend upon a *speedy* answer and *soon*, like Sir William Curtis's peace.[1] In one of Lord Byron's letters to me after I left London, he mentioned having met you, and that Mrs. Dalton sung 'one of my best songs so well that, only for the appearance of affectation, he could have cried.' Was it 'Could'st thou look?' I received the songs you left with Power for me, but have not yet been able, in my own poor performance, to extract much delight from them. I begin to fear, do you know, that both Mrs. Dalton and you are refining yourselves too far into the *super-exquisite* of music, and one reason of my fearing so is that you did not seem to care about *my* humble ballads this last time of our meeting, half so much as formerly. But indeed there was no judging, and still less any enjoying of each other in that vortex of London, in which it is as impossible to find out real opinions and feelings as it is to tell the colours of a top that is spinning. I was more disappointed than my proud stomach would let me tell you at your not making a little effort to come and visit us at our cottage. God knows when I shall have another opportunity of making Bessy known to Mrs. Dalton, for, unless my *paper* wings grow much faster and stronger than they have done of late, they will never be able to sustain the flight of my whole family to Dublin, and Bessy will not be easily persuaded to leave the children behind her. That land of promise, Bermuda, turns out a devilish bad land of performance: I get as near nothing from it as possible.

I am delighted to find that Stevenson and I are in harness together. I only hope the *whip-cord* will hold out with little Power. Tell Sir John that he *must positively* pass the next summer at this cottage with us. If he loves a beautiful country, where every step opens valleys, woods, parks, and all kinds of rural glories upon the eye, this is the Paradise for him, and (to descend lower in the scale) he shall have as good *brown soup* as we gave him in Kegworth. He

[1] Sir William Curtis was a supporter of Pitt and the war; hence Moore's ironic allusion.

and I *must* do something in the dramatic way. I believe I told you I had a long pressing letter from Whitbread to do something for Drury Lane, and I had another communication upon the same subject the other day from Holland House.[1]

I am getting on prosperously with my poem, and hope to be ready, though rather *late*, for this next campaign. I wish you had been a little more communicative about yourself, but it is sufficiently gratifying to me to hear that you are not worse, because it leads me to hope that the complaint has reached that point when it will be no longer troublesome, and perhaps even show symptoms of retiring altogether.

We have got into *much* too gay a neighbourhood, and I enjoyed the high dignity, the other night, of being sole steward to the county ball in honour of Lord Wellington.[2] 'Cock up, Spotty!' as the poet says.

Best regards to my dear Mrs. D. from Bessy and myself, and ditto to yourself from, ever yours affectionately,

Thos. Moore.

345. *To Mary Dalby*

Russell, ii. 30, no. 289

Mayfield
Monday morning [October 1813]

My dear Mary,

We have both been sad truants to you, but Bessy bids me say that as soon as Miss Lawrence leaves her, she will write to you with a punctuality that will astonish you. I suppose you have heard that we have been to Derby; and a very pleasant visit we had of it. I like the Strutts exceedingly; and it was not the least part of my gratification to find a very pretty natural girl of sixteen reading the sixth book of Virgil, and not at all spoiled by it. This is Joseph Strutt's eldest girl, a very nice dancer as well as a classic, and a poetess into the bargain. Indeed, they have quite a nest of young poets in that family; they meet every Sunday night, and each brings a poem upon some subject; and I never was much more surprised than in looking over their collection. I do not think I wrote half so well when I was their age. Then they have fine pianofortes, magnificent organs, splendid houses, most excellent white soup,

[1] See letter No. 340, to James Power, 23 Oct. 1813.

[2] See letter No. 341, to his mother, 24 Oct. 1813. Mention of the application for Moore to write something for Drury Lane and of his serving as steward at the county ball indicates that the letter was written in October 1813, rather than in 1815, as given in Russell's edition.

and are, to crown all, right true Jacobins after my own heart; so that I passed my time very agreeably amongst them, and Bessy came away loaded with presents of rings, fans, and bronze candlesticks. I have wound up my gaieties for the season by being steward to the Wellington ball at Ashbourne, where I danced with your friend Annette, and had another opportunity of seeing the pretty tremble of her eyelids in a poussette.[1]

We have had invitations without end to the Gells of Hopton, the Arkwrights, &c. &c.; but I intend to go into a torpid state for the winter, and give no signs of life to any one of them.

Miss Lawrence has gone about with us everywhere, and is liked very much; she is, indeed, a very sensible, pleasing girl.

We have not heard anything of your little Statia, which makes us very uneasy; but Barbara is in high bloom, and has not forgot Coopsh.[2] Ever yours, my dear Mary,

Thomas Moore.

346. *To his Mother*

Russell, i. 371, no. 262

Monday night [October] 1813.

My dearest Mother,

You cannot imagine what a sensation Bessy excited at the Ball the other night; she was very prettily dressed, and certainly looked very beautiful. I never saw so much admiration excited: she was very much frightened, but she got through it very well. She wore a turban that night to please me, and she looks better in it than anything else; for it strikes everybody almost that sees her, how like the form and expression of her face are to Catalani's, and a turban is the thing for that kind of character. She is, however, not very well; and unfortunately she is again in that condition in which her mind always suffers even more than her body. I must try, however, and keep up her spirits.

Little Baboo is quite well, and is, I think, improving in her looks.

The fifth number of the Irish Melodies is out. We were so hard run for airs, that I fear it will not be so popular as the others. Ever your own,

Tom.

[1] See letter No. 341, to his mother, 24 Oct. 1813. The allusion to the visit to Joseph Strutt in Derby and to Moore's serving as steward at the Ashbourne ball indicates that Russell's date of 1814 was incorrect.

[2] A nickname for Mary Dalby.

347. *To his Mother*

Russell, i. 372, no. 263

Thursday night [October or November] 1813.

My dearest Mother,

I am just returned from the great and grand Public Dinner at Ashbourne, where I assure you they did me high honour, drank my health with three times three, and, after the speech I made in acknowledgement, shouted most vociferously. It is really very flattering to meet with such respect in one's neighbourhood: a place was reserved for me next to the president, the chief magistrate of the place.

Barbara has been to all the festivities, and enjoyed them very much. We have slept the two nights past at Mr. Belcher's, the clergyman's, there.

There was a general dinner this evening of all the young girls and lads of Ashbourne, in the principal street: it was a very gay scene; but I am quite tired: so good night, dearest Mother. Ever your own,

Tom.

348. *To James Power*

Harvard College Library

Thursday* [Decr 4th 1813, *not in Moore's hand*]

My dear Sir—

I could not inclose you the advertisement last Tuesday, as I had to send some other packets thro Lord Glenbervie, but I hope it is time enough now— You perceive it is your own, with a very few alterations—I could not improve upon it, and I think, as Bonaparte has *beaten* his antagonists into *heroes*, I shall *write* you into an *author*— I do not understand what you mean by a flourish to Carpenter, nor by what you say about something I have written 'which will do, with the alteration of Publisher*s* to Publisher'—What document do you allude to here?

The Melo-drama is not Lord Byron's, but you see he has another Poem in the Turkish Style coming out—[1] I wish I could write so fast, but this campaign (the Spring one, I mean) I am *determined* to be ready, and you must only let me be *upon tick* a little in the way of labour, that I may get rid of it quick & *be yours thenceforward and entirely*—

I *must* make use of your name this month, but it shall be the *last* time, till the hundreds I shall *then* have *over*-drawn be repaid you—

[1] *The Bride of Abydos* was published in December 1813.

My Bill to Mrs Pencard comes due some time this month, but if it should be presented to you before I draw, do not mind it— When this is discharged, I shall have paid, within this short time, Col. Hamilton, my Aunt Mrs Pencard, besides that cursed £100 to your brother—and the Poem will pay off all my other old debts;[1] so that I shall start free & unencumbered, when our partnership begins— A long Peace (which I think [we long *deleted*] may expect) will make sunshine weather, I hope, for our undertaking.

Ever yours, with best regards to Mrs
Power,
Thomas Moore

349. *To James Power*[2]

Harvard College Library

Sunday* [postmark December 7, 1813]

My dear Sir.

I received the melodies yesterday evening and am very well satisfied with the whole number, *except* (and it is a dreadful exception) the Air of 'Oh! doubt me not,'[3] which is played the very deuce with by the omission of Stevenson's flat B.— As it stands now, it is quite disgraceful to him & all of us—and it is by no means my fault— I asked Mr Benison indeed, *whether* it would do with the omission of the Flat, but I left the decision entirely to him, without examining the music myself, and he ought to have known enough to see that the Air & Harmony agree together like Cat & Dog, as they are at present— One ought to leave nothing to another's eye, but I am always too diffident of my own opinion in the Musical part— Now we are in the scrape, however, you must be industrious in getting out of it & the Flat must be put in with a pen in every copy you send out, and if you could recall those that are gone for the purpose of correction, it would be advisable— The flat must be marked at the words 'season' and 'reason', and in the accompaniment of the 4th bar, where it occurs with C— This latter correction must be made too in the *Second Voice* of the Duett— There is an F to be made *Sharp* too in the Single Voice setting, at the words 'only shook'— It was Stevenson's devilish whim of putting in the Flat, that originally made all this bungling, and it departs so much from the true setting of the Air, that I really think it would be right to have a little slip printed with an explanation of the whole

[1] *Lalla Rookh.*

[2] This letter was included in Russell's edition (i. 340, no. 230) and dated simply 'Sunday —— 1813'.

[3] *Poetry*, p. 204.

mistake, which you can insert in binding or let lie between the leaves of those that are bound— Write me word immediately whether you think it worth while, & I will send it off to you by the next morning's Post—

We got the Parcell too late last night, for me to look over the airs till this morning, or I should not have let a Post pass without apprizing you of this mistake.

God bless you, my dear friend,
Ever yours
T. Moore

Bessy is very anxious to know more about Mrs Power & the Children—so be explicit, when you have time for it.

350. *To Mary Dalby*

Russell, viii. 152

Mayfield
[December] 1813.

My dear Mary,

Bessy leaves the *literary* part of your letter for me to answer. Lord Byron's last poem *did give* me (I am sorry to tell you) a deep wound in a very vital part—my story; and it is singular enough, for he could not know anything about it. Your brother and Mary Matchett are both in extremes on the subject of his bride [*sic*].[1] He *could not* write anything bad, but it would have been much finer if he had taken more time about it. He is half-way or more through *another* poem, 'The Corsair.'[2]

Bessy would have written more if she had not been so ill, and so would I if I were not so busy.

What does Sir C. Hastings mean by saying Bonaparte is not a great man? I almost agree with him about the Ministers; though, if they have not come round to the good cause, the good cause has certainly come round to them.

Ever yours,
T. M.

[1] Byron published *The Giaour* in June and *The Bride of Abydos* in December 1813. Moore is probably referring to the latter, although the oriental theme of each anticipated his *Lalla Rookh*.

[2] *The Corsair* was published in January 1814.

351. *To Lady Donegal*

Russell, viii. 135

Mayfield
[December] 1813.

You may be assured that I was anything but angry on reading your kind lecture: the only thing is that I think you *quite* mistook me, for, as far as I can recollect, my feelings were by no means those of *levity* when I wrote that letter, and if they wore that air, it was only from the habit one has got of giving a light turn to everything, the present age being so very anti-sentimental that every one is obliged to go in gay masquerade, and 'no black dominos are admitted' on any account. As for the rest, I believe you and I differ a little in our opinion of virtue—at least if you think, as you seem to do, that there would be more merit in having *lost* one's former propensities than in *conquering* them: in *my* mind the struggle makes all the virtue.

'When the sea is calm
All boats alike show mastership in floating'.[1]

It is he that steers steadily onward, in spite of the surge of passion beneath, and the songs of Sirens around, who deserves the praise of resolution and virtue; and I cannot help thinking that I, poor Scaramouche,[2] here, with all my love of pleasure and of folly as fresh on me as ever, yet leading a life of patriarchal purity, and *happy* in it, am a much greater hero in virtue than if all my said propensities were gone to sleep, and I had nothing to do but put on my night-cap and snooze quietly by their side. I know you will say that this is a very ticklish situation for poor virtue to be placed in;—but no matter, the more danger the more honour; and bad as it is to go wrong from *too much* feeling, it is, at least, a duller thing to go right only from the *want* of it. I have a lovely, pure, and attached wife, and a smiling, rosy, pug-nosed child, one look from whom, if I were in the very claws of Old Nick, would loosen his grasp and restore me to heaven again. And now, having given you one of those open confessions that are as good for the soul, they say, as other aperients are for the body, I must tell you that my book, such as it will be (for various calamities of criticism, anticipation, forestalment, &c., have made it very unlike what it was intended), shall most certainly come out in the course of this spring.[3] What

[1] *Coriolanus*, IV. i. 7.

[2] Scaramouche, an adaptation of the Italian *scaramuccia,* meaning 'skirmish', was a stock character in Italian farce. He was a cowardly, foolish boaster, who was constantly beaten by Harlequin.

[3] *Lalla Rookh.*

a nice opportunity it would be now, while Jeffrey's in America![1] When some savage French reviewer died, Bensarade wrote an epigram, which ended,

'Dieu merci!—Je vais faire imprimer mon livre'.[2]

What you tell me about Mackintosh is very delightful, if the compliment does not die, under the editor's bow-string, before it meets the light. So many pretty things have been lately *going* to happen to me! I was *going* to be very rich from the American war, and Lord Byron tells me he was *going* to dedicate the 'Bride of Abydos' to me.[3] If you come to that, 'how do *you* like the "Bride of Abydos?"' In the country we never know *how* we like things till we hear how you like them in London.

I have not time for more now. Best love to Mary.

Ever yours,

T. M.

We had a grand ball here the other night, and you cannot imagine the sensation that Bessy excited; her dress was very pretty, and 'beautiful,' 'beautiful,' was echoed on all sides. I was (as the poet says) as pleased as Punch!

The note to Longmans is of some consequence, so pray let it go soon: the twopenny-post will do.

352. *To John Murray*

Sir John Murray

Mayfield Cottage, Ashbourne, Derbyshire
Sunday Evening* [1813, *not in Moore's hand*]

Dear Sir—

You were once good enough to cash a Bill at Lord Byron's request, for me, and I now take the liberty of asking you to do me a similar favour—the inclosed is the last fruits of a certain uncourtly production of mine;[4] but this is a secret which I trust you will keep for me better than I have been able to keep it for myself—

It is only very lately that I have applied with any degree of earnestness to the poetical Work I am employed upon,[5] and I hope to be ready for *the hammer* before the end of Spring—

[1] Jeffrey sailed for New York on 29 Aug. 1813, landing on 7 Oct. He left the United States on 22 Jan. 1814 and landed at Liverpool on 10 Feb.

[2] Not identified.

[3] Byron's *Bride of Abydos* was dedicated to Lord Holland. Byron dedicated *The Corsair* to Moore.

[4] Probably the 'Parody of a Celebrated Letter' (1812), *Poetry*, p. 164.

[5] *Lalla Rookh.*

I shall be much obliged by your sending me the Quarterly Review as it comes out, beginning with the number just now published— As it is not worth making a coach parcell [*sic*] of itself alone, have the goodness to direct it to Power's 34, Strand for me.

Very much Yours
Thomas Moore

The sooner you can make it convenient to send me cash for the inclosed, the better—that is, if it be not inconvenient to you to do it *at all*.

353. *To John Cooper*

Yale

Monday* [*c*. 1813]

My dear Sir—

Will you have the goodness to send the inclosed Letters to Ashbourne for me this evening? and I shall be much obliged, if you will let your man bring me from Wheatley's two quires of the paper I usually get from him.

Truly yours
Thomas Moore

354. *To Lady Donegal*

Russell, ii. 3, no. 264

Monday, Jan. 10. 1814.

Why don't you write to me? Why don't you write to me? Why don't you write to me? Two-pence to be paid upon the inclosed, and forwarded directly. Lord Byron dedicates his Corsair to me,[1] and from this on't lords are to dedicate to poor poets, instead of poor poets dedicating to lords. Mrs. Wilmot has written to me to furnish her with an epilogue for her tragedy, with fine flourishes about its being the wish of Messrs. Sheridan, Whitbread, &c. &c.[2] I have taken time to consider. Last packet brought me proposals of being elected librarian to the Dublin Society, 200£ per annum, coals, candles, and to be qualified in *German* for it, at half an hour's notice, by Mr. Professor Feinagle. Every body thinks me a person of some consequence except you two sisters there, in Davies Street; and unless you give some *signs of life* in the course

[1] *The Corsair* appeared in January 1814.

[2] Moore wrote the epilogue beginning 'Last night, as lonely o'er my fire I sat' (*Poetry*, p. 717) for Mrs. Wilmot's tragedy *Ina* (1815).

of this week, I shall hand you over to the Humane Society for resuscitating persons in said condition. Ever yours notwithstanding,

T. Moore.

355. *To Samuel Rogers*

Russell, viii. 168

Jan. 13. 1814.

My dear Rogers,

Living in the fields, as we do, we cannot stir a step without pioneers and shovels, and I cannot find it in my heart to send a servant into Ashbourne through the waste, so that I am obliged to lay hold on any unfortunate person who brings me a message, and make him useful to me by taking ten times as many messages back again. Just such a *return*-courier is now in the house, and I take the opportunity of writing by him a very few lines, lest you should leave Lord Spencer's before you receive at least an acknowledgment of your very, very kind letter from Althorpe. I can hardly wish you where *I* am in this very *anti*-cottage weather, but I wish heartily we were together somewhere, for I want you, *selfishly* want you, often; and the glimpses I get at you through letters, is something like what we have of the sun at this season,—very bright, but distant and cheerless: yet not cheerless, either, except in comparison with the same kind things, said *à quattr'occhi* over a good fire, with one of your best smiles illustrating every word. That's what I want, and that is what, for some months to come, I fear I shall not have. Lord Byron dedicates his 'Corsair' to me, which I look upon as a very high niche in the Temple indeed,—to be placed so near *you*, too! Between you and Lord Holland I fear I shall have applied to me the *reverse* of the famous epigram,—

'Wisdom and Wit full-sized were seen,
And Folly, at *small length*, between.'[1]

I think there are few more *generous* spirits than Lord Byron's, and the overflowing praise he has lavished on me in his dedication (if he preserves that of which he has sent me a copy) is just such as might be expected from a profuse, magnificent-minded fellow,

[1] *The Giaour* was dedicated to Samuel Rogers, *The Bride of Abydos* to Lord Holland, and *The Corsair* to Thomas Moore. These lines were first attributed to Jane Brereton, 'On Mr. Nash's Picture at Full Length between Busts of Sir Isaac Newton and Mr. Pope'. They can also be found in Lord Chesterfield's 'On the Picture of Richard Nash . . . between Busts . . . of Newton and . . . Pope at Bath'.

who does not wait for the scales to weigh what he says, but gives praise, as sailors lend money, by 'handfuls.' Let others think what they will of it, he has made *me* very proud and happy; and the more he commits his judgment for my sake, the more grateful, of course, I must feel for his goodnature.

My *return* post-boy is clamouring below stairs, so I must have done, and shall write to you a longer letter next week, directed to St. James's Place.

Ever yours affectionately,
Thomas Moore.

356. *To his Mother*

Russell, ii. 8, no. 269

Thursday, Jan. [13] 1814.

My dearest Mother,

Lord Byron has sent me a proof sheet of his Dedication, and I hope he will keep it as it is, for nothing was ever so flattering or gratifying: as I have just said in a letter to Rogers, 'the overflowing praise he lavishes on me is exactly what might be expected from a profuse, magnificent-minded fellow, who does not wait for scales to weigh what he says, but gives praise, as sailors lend money, *by handfuls*.'[1] I shall keep the proof till I see whether he makes any alteration, and shall then send it you with any difference there may be.

We are almost completely blocked up by snow, and cannot stir without pioneers and shovels in our van. I have had a proposal from Dublin to stand for the librarian of the Dublin Society, with a promised prospect of success; but 200£ a year and residence on the spot are but poor temptations, and I have declined it. Ever, my darling mother, your own,

Tom.

357. *To James Power*[2]

Pennsylvania Historical Society

Wednesday

This letter was written to go off on Tuesday, but the young Ladies had not their packet ready—so that they must take the place of my own inclosures on Friday, and I shall send my two Songs by the way of *Davies* St. the beginning of next week—in the mean-time,

[1] See letter No. 355, to Samuel Rogers, 13 Jan. 1814.

[2] This letter was included in Russell's edition (ii. 4, no. 265).

as I trust you will think this letter worth ten-pence, it shall go by itself—

Monday Jan^{r} 17 [1814]

My dear Sir—

I did not intend to have any communication with you till Friday; but as I have been requested by the Coopers to send the inclosed, I must give you the trouble of forwarding them—and I think I shall not inflict another packet on my friend Lord Glenbervie, till this day week, when you shall have the two jobs of the present week— I was very much delighted to receive your two last letters, tho I did not answer the one about your excursion to France so soon as you seemed to wish, concluding that there is *as yet* no hurry, tho certainly I have no doubt of a Peace taking place very soon—and then, my dear Sir, after I have seen my poor Bessy safe over her *July production*, I shall be at your command for a short Musical Trip at a day's notice—beside the pleasure of our being together, I think it is quite necessary for you to have some one with you that speaks French, and I have but little doubt that we shall make the excursion tell—

I have had a letter from old Sheddon, in which there is no money but some sort of promise, which I can hardly understand, of remittances I may expect, he says, on account of last year— Heaven grant it! They can never come amiss.[1]

Lord Byron's new Poem is dedicated to me, and as it will be a fortnight yet before it appears, I will give you a taste of what he says, which I flatter myself, will be a cordial to you— 'I take this opportunity of adorning my pages with a name consecrated by unshaken public principle & the most undoubted & various talent. While Ireland ranks you among the firmest of her patriots—while you stand alone the first of her Bards in her estimation, and Britain repeats & ratifies the decree—permit one, whose only regret since the commencement of our acquaintance has been the years he had lost before it began, to add his humble suffrage of friendship to the voice of more than one nation'— Then at the end he says 'it may be of some service to me that the man who is the delight both of his readers and his friends—the poet of all circles and the idol of his own—permits me here & elsewhere to subscribe myself &c. &c.'—[2] Is not *this* very fine? They may [say] the praise is *laid on with a trowel*, but at least it is a *golden* trowel that lays it on—

[1] See letter No. 81, to his mother, 19 Jan. 1804.

[2] See the dedication to *The Corsair*, Byron, *Poetry*, iii. 223–6.

Best regards to Mrs Power from Bessy & myself & believe me, my dear Sir,

Ever cordially yours
Thomas Moore

Monday——

I suppose you saw that the Tyrolese Glee was sung at the great dinner given to Mr Canning in Liverpool.—[1] When you have any parcell [*sic*] to send us, I wish you would put up some *dried sprats* from your neighbour Hicksons, 170.—

358. *To William Gardiner*

Russell, ii. 5, no. 266

Mayfield Cottage
Wednesday, Jan. 19. 1814.

My dear Sir,

I have a thousand apologies to make for not answering your letter sooner, but I rather think I must have *dreamed* that I had done so, for though I have thought of you often since, it was without the least symptoms of remorse, till this morning I was awakened to a full sense of my wrong towards you by discovering your letter in the *un*answered side of my letter-box. I hope by this time you have recovered from the effects of Mr. Cheslyn's method of 'teaching your young idea how to shoot,' and that you will in future keep out of the way of such *unpoetical* things as guns, squires, rabbits, &c.* The Prince was very gracious to you, and no one can be more so when he chooses. To give the devil his due, he is very fond of music, and that is one great step towards redemption, at least where you and I are the judges.

We are here, in a very delightful situation, where we should be most happy if you would pay us a visit. You must not come, however, till we have better *cottage*-weather, as, in these snows, we cannot stir a step without pioneers and shovels in the van.

When are we to have your second volume? Pray give our kindest regards to our *well-remembered* friends in High Street, and say that we have often meditated a visit to them, and shall hardly let another summer pass without putting it into execution.

Will you take the trouble of telling Clarke to send me a bill of the things he made for me, and believe me, very truly yours,

Thomas Moore.

What do you think of my friend Buonaparte? like most of our modern dramatists, he *falls off in the last act* deplorably.[2]

[1] 'The Tyrolese Song of Liberty', *Poetry*, p. 314.

[2] Napoleon had suffered a defeat and retreated to France after the three-

**Note by Mr. Gardiner:*— 'This alludes to my having been persuaded, much against my will, to join a shooting party, at which some stray shots from my friend's gun, firing at a rabbit, wounded me in the knee, and I returned to the hall bleeding.' [*Russell's note.*]

359. *To Edward T. Dalton*

Russell, ii. 7, no. 267

Thursday, Jan. 25. 1814.

My dearest Dalton,

I have just heard that you are at Lord Bective's, and very ill there: for goodness' sake, my dear fellow, *do* let me hear from you, or, if you dislike writing yourself, I am sure Mrs. Dalton will let me have a line of intelligence about you. If the letter I wrote to you some time since did but *half* justice to the anxiety I felt to hear from you, I am certain you would not have left me so unaccountably long without that gratification. My appearance as a 'sweet singer of Israel'[1] is near at hand, and I want to know whether you will let me dedicate the first number to *you*, and whether I may call you, 'My dear Dalton,' *in print?*[2] Answer these two questions immediately, as the printer's devil's claws are extended over me, and there is no time to lose. Yours ever affectionately,

T. Moore.

360. *To James Power*

Russell, ii. 9, no. 271

Thursday, Jan. 29. 1814.

My dear Sir,

You did not, of course, receive my letters of last week till late in this. We have been so blocked up here that I have not been able to take my exercise, and from this cause, and a very bad cold, I have been upon the whole rather unfitted for my studies. I send you, however, a Song, and an Irish Melody, which I have altered from one in Crotch's collection;[3] it is the second verse I have sent with it, as I am not yet satisfied with the first, and indeed shall

day 'Battle of the Nations' at Leipzig, and his victory over Blücher and Schwarzenberg (January–February 1814) had not yet occurred. Hence it looked as if this were his 'last act'.

[1] 2 Samuel xxiii. 1.

[2] The first number of the *Sacred Songs* (1816) was dedicated to Edward Tuite Dalton.

[3] William Crotch, *Specimens of Various Styles of Music* (*c.* 1807).

have some alterations to make in this second one. I am resolved to make this number, at least in *words*, better, if possible, than any one of them; there are some old airs for it that will admit of a fine measure for poetry. From what I hear of the fifth number, I begin (though you know how dissatisfied I was with it) to think it will not let down the character of the work: it is, at all events, much better than the third. One good sign is, that I find different people choosing different favourites from it. Lord Tamworth said to me at the Derby ball, 'Moore, you never wrote anything so good as "The Young May Moon;"'[1] but our sixth shall be a *smasher*. I mean to write the regular number through before my year is out, to leave nothing for your brother to complain of; but I will positively protest against its publication till I think it all excellent; and what are over may be laid by, till we recommence the work.

I am determined, as soon as my poem is published,[2] to give all my soul and body to the stage and music. I shall not be deterred even by a *failure*, for I mean to throw so much of the best writing I can muster up into what I do, that even should the galleries damn it, I may have the critics on my side.

I don't know whether I told you that I have had a request from the party lately at Whitbread's to write an epilogue for Mrs. Wilmot's forthcoming tragedy.[3] I have said that I will try, and the manuscript is on its way to me; it ought to have come last week, and I hope no accident has happened to it. There is no time to lose, as she comes out in February. I shall take pains with it. I think the oftener I rub my skirts to the Dramatic Muse the better, and who knows but (if I receive something from Bermuda) I may take a trip myself to town to school Miss Smith in her recitation of it. Ever yours,

Thomas Moore.

361. *To his Mother*

Russell, ii. 7, no. 268

Tuesday, Jan. 1814.

My dearest Mother,

I am sorry to find you are as wretchedly off with snow in Dublin as we are here; it made me quite sad to read of the miseries they are suffering in the Liberty, &c. Our roads have been completely blocked up, and we had four mails due yesterday. I expect by the

[1] *Poetry*, p. 202.

[2] *Lalla Rookh.*

[3] See letter No. 354, to Lady Donegal, 10 Jan. 1814. Mrs. Wilmot's tragedy *Ina* was produced in 1815.

post Mrs. Wilmot's tragedy,[1] for which I have half promised to write an epilogue; but, unless it is pathetic enough to *melt* its way to me, I fear I shan't get it in time. We struggled through the snow to see Statia yesterday, and were delighted to find her improving very fast: she has cut two teeth.

Lord Byron's poem comes out on Tuesday next: I shall contrive to send you over a copy. Ever your own,

Tom.

362. *To his Mother*

Russell, ii. 9, no. 270

Mayfield Cottage
Thursday [January] 1814.

My dearest Mother,

I forgot to mention in my last, that my *bile* was quite gone again, and I am this moment returned from a long walk with as good a colour on my cheeks as even you, my darling mother, could wish to see.

Barbara has this moment interrupted me with her often-repeated demand for 'pretty mookis,' which means 'pretty music,' and I have accordingly set her up on a chair at the pianoforte, where she is inflicting all sorts of tones on my ears. I hope she will continue as fond of it as she is now.

Best love to dear father, Nell, and Kate, from your own,

Tom.

363. *To James Power*

Trinity College, Dublin

Thursday* [January 1814]

My dear Sir—

The threatened Packet has made its appearance, and I find it is not so enormous as to have prevented my sending the manuscripts with it—however, as they are not ready, you shall have them the beginning of next week.

I have nothing to add to my letter of yesterday, except I believe I forgot to tell you that I have been applied to (with every promise of success) to stand for the Librarianship of the Dublin Society,[2] 200 a year, coals, candles, &c. &c.—but, as residence in Dublin

[1] See letter No. 354, to Lady Donegal, 10 Jan., and No. 360, to James Power, 29 Jan. 1814.

[2] See letter No. 356, to his mother, 13 Jan. 1814.

would be necessary, and that would not suit *our* plans, I have declined it—what a pretty little addition, taking in the full use of Library &c. &c. such a thing would be in London!—

Ever yours
Thomas Moore

You will take care & send the inclosed, as soon as possible.

364. *To Miss Smith*[1]

Rice University

Mayfield Cottage, Ashbourne
Monday Febr 21, 1814

My dear Miss Smith—

Will you have the goodness to let me know, as soon as you conveniently can, *when* Mrs Wilmot's Tragedy is expected to appear?—I wrote more than a week ago to ask herself, but I dare say she has not got my letter— I have finished an Epilogue for you, and am much tempted to take it up myself to give you *the Author's* notions of it—but I must first know what time you come out—so, pray, write immediately & tell me.

Very much yours
Thomas Moore]

365. *To Lord Byron*[2]

Lovelace Papers

Monday, Febr 28 [1814]

My dear Byron—

If I were to guess my *dislikes*, as your other friends have done, I should certainly say that *Croker* was the man for tho he & I have made up our quarrel, it is something like the reconciliation of Asmodeus with his brother-devil— 'We embraced and have hated each other ever since'—[3] but notwithstanding this, and that I

[1] Miss Smith was the actress who recited Moore's epilogue. See letter No. 360, to James Power, 29 Jan. 1814.

[2] Transcript provided by Mrs. Doris Langley Moore. Used by permission of the Earl of Lytton and Mr. Gladstone Moore.

[3] Asmodeus is the evil spirit in *The Book of Tobit*, iii. 8, who loved Sarah, daughter of Raguel, and slew the seven husbands given to her in succession. The spirit was then driven into Egypt by the burning of the heart and liver of a fish caught by Tobias and the angel Raphael. Asmodeus is also the principle character in Le Sage's *Le Diable Boiteux* (1707) and *The Devil upon Two Sticks* (1790), by William Combe, a continuation in English of Le Sage's romance. In 1768 Samuel Foote produced a farce with the same English title. It satirized quack doctors and the College of Physicians.

think him quite enough of a *maligno animaletto* to do such a thing, I *do not* believe it was he—it is not his style—there would have been more of a brisk flippancy in the attack, and besides, to give my brother-devil his due, I have heard him speak of you in terms of admiration rather inconsistent (if any thing be inconsistent in such a *lickspittle*) with the language of these Ana— I quite agree with Hotham, that you are not called upon to seek the toad in his lurking-hole, but if he should come across your path, put your foot upon him most certainly— You mistake me in supposing that I had any idea of *avowing* the *Bag*—my only thoughts were about *disavowing* it for Rogers, without in any way saddling it upon my own shoulders more than it is at present. As to Dallas's letter, the statement with respect to the appropriation of the profits of your writings was absolutely called for and could not be withheld in justice both to himself and you—and indeed this explanation gave *me* particular pleasure, for I may *now* tell you that one of the stories which, I was told circulated with most credit in town was that you had given the *proceeds* of the Corsair to *me!* Yet all thro I bore 'well—very well'—rather than break the sacred silence of contempt with which such things should be heard by both of us—[1]indeed, I would not even to *you*, my dear Byron, dignify this wretched nonsense with one more mention, if it had not struck me, from your two last letters,[2] that either this or something else is making you uncomfortable and out of spirits—to tell you it *ought not* will do you, I know, but little good, if it *does*, and therefore all I shall say is that if by my coming to town to you or by doing any thing else in the world that is in my power I can either amuse, serve or in the slightest degree minister to your comfort, I am heartily ready at a minute's notice—too happy if you can discover

[1] On Thursday, 17 Feb. 1814, an article entitled 'Byroniana' appeared in the *Courier*. In it Byron was accused of pocketing money gained from the sale of his poems. R. C. Dallas answered the statement in a letter to the *Morning Post*, Monday, 21 Feb. 1814, saying that Byron had never received money for his poems, that Dallas had been given the copyrights of *Childe Harold* and *The Corsair*, and that Murray could attest to the fact that Byron had not received money for *The Giaour* and *The Bride of Abydos* (see *LJ*, iii. 41–43). The article in the *Courier* also stated that 'Mr. Sam Rogers is reported to have clubb'd with the Irish Anacreon in that scurrilous collection of verses which we have before mentioned, and which were published under the title of the "Twopenny Post-Bag," and the assumed name of "Thomas Brown"'. The writer says that this rumour may be unfounded but that he much prefers it to the fact that the author or authors lurk behind fictitious names. See letter No. 369, to Lord Byron, February 1814. For further details of the attacks on Byron by the *Courier*, *Morning Post*, and *Sun* see *LJ*, ii, appendix vii.

[2] The letters dated 10 and 16 Feb. 1814 (*LJ*, iii. 32 and 38). Byron replied to this letter on 3 Mar. (see *LJ*, iii. 54).

(what I cannot flatter myself enough to find out) any one way in which I can be made useful to you— If I am, after all, mistaken, and you are *not* suffering any unusual uneasiness of mind, pray lose no time in telling me so, for I feel very anxious about you.

Every yours
T. Moore

366. *To James Corry*

Russell, viii. 170

Tuesday, Feb. 28. 1814.

My dear Corry,

I have been very slow in thanking you for your kind panegyric, which had all the features of the warm heart and sound head it came from. I suppose you have before this seen Lord Byron's overflowing eulogium.[1] He has got into a tremendous scrape with the Carlton House faction by the avowal of his 'Lines to the Young Princess.'[2] 'The Courier,' 'Morning Post,' &c. &c. have been all, as he says himself, 'in hysterics' since their appearance; and I have come in for my full share of the bespatterment. When scavengers

[1] The dedication of *The Corsair*.

[2] Moore is referring to 'Lines to a Lady Weeping', Byron, *Poetry*, iii. 45. The lines were occasioned by an incident which occurred at a banquet at Carlton House on 22 Feb. 1812. The Prince Regent expressed 'surprise and mortification' that Lords Grey and Grenville had replied unfavourably to his letter to the Duke of York, in which he explained that his 'sense of duty to our Royal father' had caused him to keep the Tories in power (see Moore's 'Parody of a Celebrated Letter', *Poetry*, p. 164). Lord Lauderdale retorted that the reply did not express the opinions of Lords Grey and Grenville alone, but of 'every political friend of that way of thinking', and that he had assisted in drawing it up. The Prince was so 'suddenly and deeply affected' that Princess Charlotte burst into tears, whereupon the Prince asked the women present to withdraw. (See the *Courier*, 10 Mar. 1812. See also Byron, *Poetry*, iii. 45 n.)

Byron's poem was first published anonymously in the *Morning Chronicle* for 7 Mar. 1812. He later inserted the eight lines in *The Corsair*, and they were published in the first edition of that poem. The *Courier* published an article on 1 Feb. 1814, taking Byron to task for attempting to cause Princess Charlotte to view her father as a disgrace to the realm. Other articles on the subject appeared in the *Courier* on 2 and 3 Feb. and on 5 Feb. the *Morning Post* launched a similar attack. The practical result was that Murray withdrew the offending lines from the second edition, but Byron insisted on their being replaced in the third (see *LJ*, iii. 27).

Moore was 'bespattered' in the *Courier* for 5 Feb. where he was mentioned as the dedicatee of *The Corsair*. He was accused by the same paper on 12 Feb. of 'substituting . . . a party spirit for the spirit of poetry', and his 'Let Erin Remember the Days of Old' was cited as an example of his Irish nationalism.

For details of the attack of the Tory press on Byron see *LJ*, ii. appendix vii. See also Marchand, *Byron*, pp. 434–5.

become assailants, there is no coming very clean out of their hands. Indeed, 'The Courier' has taken the only method such dull dogs could hit upon for annoying Byron, by raking up all his past and *suppressed* abuse of those he is now friends with; and they have quoted the very passage upon which I called him to account (and from which sprung our intimacy), to contrast it with his present praise of me. Byron tells me that till his avowal of those formidable lines to the young Royalty, the Regent always thought they were *mine*.

What has *Bryan* been doing? I have seen some severe strictures upon his conduct; and as I am a good deal interested about him, you will oblige me very much by telling me frankly, and, of course, in perfect confidence, what is the general impression his conduct has made, as I have only seen 'The Dublin Evening Post,' and that paper is naturally under much irritation against him.

The spring is beginning to shine out upon our cottage very deliciously, and my only alloy is that Bessy is not as well and strong for the enjoyment of her garden and flowers as I could wish.

I believe I told you that I had been requested to write an Epilogue for Mrs. Wilmot's forthcoming tragedy.[1] Were *you* of the party with Power to hear her read when you were in London?—if not, ask Power whether the play she read was 'Ina of Sigiswold,' for that is the name of the tragedy to which I have written the Epilogue. I hope it may be done but half the justice to in the speaking that my Kilkenny one was.

I am getting on with my poem,[2] though I begin to tremble about its appearance this season; this, however, shall not interfere with my Grand Memoir—[3] as once over the fit period for publication, I have a long summer for all my jobs before me.

Still in debt to Mrs. Corry! If warm and frequent remembrances are a satisfactory *interest* upon the *debt*, I pay them faithfully; and am, dear Corry,

Hers and yours, very truly,
Thomas Moore.

I have a copy of 'The Corsair' lying by me for you ever since it was published; but I have been startled by the idea that it would be too heavy for your franking privilege. I feel your pulse in that way with an inclosure now, which I must beg you to forward for me immediately.

[1] See letter No. 354, to Lady Donegal, 10 Jan. 1814, and No. 360, to James Power, 29 Jan. 1814.

[2] *Lalla Rookh*.

[3] The projected work on the Kilkenny Theatricals. See letter No. 277, to James Corry, 30 Dec. 1812.

367. *To James Power*

Pennsylvania Historical Society

Thursday* [February 1814]

My dear Sir—

I have just got your parcell [*sic*], but too late to correct & send back the Proof of the Preface by this Post—[1] Thanks for the Sprats—

I wish you would call upon Mr Murray, the Bookseller, and tell him I have received 'The Corsairs' [*sic*] but that I wish he would send me the Poem I wrote for (Sofie) and 'The Missionary'[2] by the Coach—if you have any thing to send me within the next week, you can keep them for me till then—if not bid him send them off immediately—

Braham once told me the same, and I always looked forward to at least having him in my Piece. I should not have the least objection to joining him in doing the music, and as the Piece I meditate will be rather a *Drama* with Songs than an *Opera*, we can easily manage it between us.[3]

I send you a Paragraph out of a Dublin Paper— Will you have the goodness to put the inclosed Petition in a cover directed to 'Mr William Addison, Newington Grein [*sic*], near Stoke Newington', and write in the Cover '*Mr Moore has left Kegworth*'—

I have got Mrs Wilmot's Tragedy at last & must ask you to forgive me this week's work, as I have but a very short time to write the Epilogue in—[4]

[1] Probably the preface to the Sixth Number of the *Irish Melodies* (1815).

[2] Probably *The Missionary*, by Lady Morgan, which appeared in 1811.

[3] Moore did not complete his plans for this 'Drama with Songs'.

[4] See letter No. 354, to Lady Donegal, 10 Jan., No. 360, to James Power, 29 Jan., and No. 366, to James Corry, 28 Feb. 1814. There is some confusion about the date of this letter. A note (not in Moore's hand) at the top of the manuscript gives the date 'Jan or Feb 1815', but mention of Byron's *Corsair* as if Moore had just received it immediately after its publication indicates that the letter was written early in 1814. If Russell's dating of the letters to Lady Donegal, Power, and Corry is correct (and internal evidence proves that it is), then this letter must have been written about the same time, since Moore mentions in almost identical language the fact that he had been requested to write an epilogue for the play. Nevertheless the question of the date on which Moore was asked to write the epilogue is also confusing. The play was produced at Drury Lane on 22 Apr. 1815, over a year after he started work on the epilogue. The issue is further clouded by the fact that Prothero (*LJ*, iii. 195 n.) cites Moore's letter to Power (No. 360, 29 Jan. 1814), but dates it *1815*.

One can only assume that Moore wrote the epilogue early in 1814 and that he expected to see the play performed much earlier than it was. Evidence that he was expecting an earlier performance is found in the last paragraph of this letter.

Am I necessary to you on your Trial?[1] I did not well-understand that part of your letter, but am, of course, at your command in that as well as every thing else, and it will be about the time I should like to go for Mrs W^s^ Tragedy—

Best regards to M^rs^ P.
Ever yours
T. Moore

368. *To Lord Byron*

Sir John Murray

Sunday Evening [February 1814]

My dear Byron—

I have been expecting some announcement of your return to town, and asked Mr Murray about your *whereabouts* in a note I wrote to him, but his answer has not given me the best information —further than that the Corsair is 'liked beyond measure,' which was what I could easily take for granted without his having the kindness to inform me— 'liked'—Werter [*sic*] was angry at this cold word being applied to Ossian,[2] and what would he say to its being used of 'the Corsair'? I may perhaps, as God-father,[3] be suspected of undue partiality for this child, but certainly any thing more fearfully interesting, more wild, touching and 'negligently grand,' I never read even from *your* pen—you are careless, but you can afford to be so, and, whenever you slumber, it is like the albatross, *high in the air* and *on the wing*—the blood upon Gulnare's cheek is terrifically fine—[4] as to *my* part of the Work, I will not render my thanks to you in words, tho I do in *feeling* twenty times a day—but I must tell you what an honest neighbour of mine says of it— 'This makes me like him better than all the rest of his works put together, for it shows he's a *warm-hearted* fellow, which is better than all the genius in the world'—

I write this to catch a flying opportunity for the Post, so must conclude—

Ever yours most faithfully
Thomas Moore

I shall make my old mother so happy by the Copy I have sent her! She will worship you—

[1] A publisher named Walker brought out a pirated edition of the *Irish Melodies*, and James Power sued him before Lord Ellenborough on 28 May 1814. Power had evidently written to Moore about this suit, to which the latter is referring here. See letter No. 377, to James Power, May 1814.

[2] *Die Leiden des jungen Werthers, Erstes Buch* (*am 10 Julius 1771*). See letter No. 555, to James Corry, 13 July 1818.

[3] *The Corsair* was dedicated to Moore.

[4] *The Corsair*, ll. 1582–5.

369. *To Lord Byron*

Sir John Murray

Thursday* [February 1814]

My dear Byron—

You really, as I have often told you before, ought to give me at least two letters for every one of mine— Full of incidents as your own days are, and busy and various as the scene is about you, I should not think myself at all too *exigeant*, if I were to require you to sit down every day for half an hour before dressing-time, and give me an account of all the *hes, shes* and *its* you have had to do with since morning—particularly, as you recollect you have appointed me your Editor & Historiographer, (in case any enraged husband should be the death of you) and a journal of this kind would soon make very respectable material— Do you know that I was all agog about a week ago with the hope of being *forced* to go to town upon business very soon?—but I am disappointed and left without a single pretext for the trip but pleasure, which, tho as good a pretext as a man can well have in this life for any thing, would be a little too *selfish* upon the present occasion for me to be quite satisfied with it—

Now, do, pray write me very long letters, my dear Byron—there is but one great man in this world, besides yourself, that I feel interested about—and that is Bonaparte— We owe great gratitude to this *thunder-storm* of a fellow, for clearing the air of all the old legitimate fogs that settled upon us, and I seriously hope his task is not yet quite over— When he is once off the stage, the Play is over for me—the rest of the Kings may strut over their hour & be d—d!— I inclose you a letter, which you will have put in the Twopenny for me—by the bye, is Rogers annoyed at being suddenly with the Bag?— I had half an intention of clearing him from the imputation, but I did not like to distract that profound contemptuous silence with which (till your friend Dallas's letter) the Courier was so properly treated.[1]

Ever, my dear Byron, yours most truly
Thomas Moore

[1] See letter No. 365, to Lord Byron, 28 Feb. 1814.

370. *To his Mother*

Russell, ii. 12, no. 273

Monday [February] 1814.

My dearest Mother,

I have just been copying out some music to send to Power by this opportunity, so that I have not left myself a moment to say more than that I have got the two newspapers you sent me. I fear my friend Bryan has not done quite right, though I perceive he has not lost ground with the Catholic Board, and I should suppose that illustrious body would have shown their sense of his misconduct if he had been wrong. What a set they are! they make me blush for poor Ireland.

Bessy is not at all well to-day, and it is unlucky, as we have the Coopers to dine with us. Ever your own,

Tom.

371. *To James Power*

Russell, ii. 11, no. 272

[February or March] 1814.

My dear Sir,

I have been disappointed in not hearing from you this week past. I send you words of a song for Stevenson to set: there is a third verse, but the two will do to send him. He may introduce much variety in it. Let the verses be copied out correctly from my manner of writing them. I told your brother in my letter, thanking him for the Irish airs, that you would not bring out the sixth number till it was as perfect as possible, and he has written in reply that he would not, on any consideration, have me hurried in this or any other work till I was completely satisfied with it myself.

Mrs. Wilmot's play does not come out for a month yet, and this extraordinary phenomenon, Kean, is her hero.[1]

You have seen, I suppose, the lashing I have got in Drakard:[2]

[1] See letter No. 367, to James Power, February 1814.

[2] Moore was the subject of the fourth in a series of 'Portraits of Authors', *The Champion*, Sunday, 27 Feb. 1814, pp. 70–71. (*The Champion* was published by John Drakard and edited by John Scott.) The criticism was chiefly of the erotic elements in the *Thomas Little Poems*, 'the naked and deformed sensuality' of which was 'tricked out with such spruceness of dress . . . that poor credulous girls, who know nothing of the matter . . . mistook the disguised demon for a smiling angel, and feared no harm from one who looked so gentle and kind'. The only favourable sentiment expressed in the review concerned the *Irish Melodies*, the reviewer claiming to be aware of the 'very beautiful songs which he has written to old Irish music'. But this faint praise was nullified by the remark that Moore consciously avoided erotic motifs in those poems because

it is an unfair renewal of all the old charges against my early poems; but you perceive the Irish songs are sacred even in this fellow's hands; indeed, these songs are, at present, the main bulwark of my reputation, and I am rejoiced at it for your sake; but I hope to show these gentlemen they are mistaken, when they say there is nothing better in me than I have yet exhibited.

You shall have another melody next week. Ever yours,

T. Moore.

Poor Mr. Kean is now in the honeymoon of criticism. Next to the pleasure of crying a man down, your critics enjoy the vanity of crying him up; but, when *once up* and fixed there, he is a mark for their arrows ever after.

'When first the Fount of life was flowing,
  Heavy and dark and cold it ran,
Every gloomy instant growing
  Bitterer to the lips of Man;
Till Love came by, one lucky minute,
  Light of heart and fair of brow,
And flung his sweetening cordial in it,
  Proudly saying, "Taste it now."

'Then bring the Lyre, to rapture wake it,
  Who one drop of Life would waste,
When the balm of Love can make it
  Fit for Gods themselves to taste?

'Still, though now no longer bitter,
  Still, the Fount in darkness strayed,
Ne'er had morn or noontide glitter
  O'er its cloudy surface played;
Till Wit, the Spirit of the Mountain,
  Stooping from his airy heights,
Came and scattered o'er the fountain,
  All his richest rainbow lights!

'Then bring the Lyre, to rapture wake it,
  Who one drop of Life would waste,
When the beams of Wit can make it
  Fit for Gods themselves to taste?'[1]

The first four lines of each verse ought to be slow and melancholy. I should think the varieties of the expression particularly suited to a three part glee.

he knew into whose hands the music would fall. The writer concluded by noting that political satire was Moore's *forte*.

[1] This poem was not included in the 1841 edition of Moore's works.

372. *To his Mother*

Russell, ii. 59, no. 313

Thursday [3 March] 1814.

My dearest Mother,

We were delighted beyond anything last night to hear of dear Kate's safe recovery. Long life and happiness to both mother and child! Give my best love and congratulations to the whole establishment.

So the wise persons in Dublin believe, upon the credit of the Morning Post, that there is to be an impeachment of Lord Byron! —that would be too ridiculous.[1]

My Drakard's paper of last Sunday has been mislaid by Mr. Cooper, but you have no loss. There was a sort of criticism upon my early poems in it, trying to be very severe, but calling my fancy delightful, my Irish songs very beautiful, &c. Nothing shows me where I stand more than the quantity of shots there are aimed at me.[2]

I wish I could send you Hunt's Feast of the Poets, just republished, where I am one of *the four* admitted to *dine* with Apollo; the other three, Scott, Campbell, and Southey. Rogers, very unfairly, is only 'asked to tea.'[3] I am particularly flattered by praise from Hunt, because he is one of the most honest and candid men I know. Ever yours, my darling mother,

Tom.

373. *To Samuel Rogers*

Russell, viii. 174

Mayfield
April 10. 1814.

My dear Rogers,

Though I owe many letters to many people, and don't owe *you* one at all, yet you see, like Charles Surface,[4] I let my generosity outstrip my justice, and write to you. The last time I heard of you, you were at Hope's with the Donegals; but I dare say, long before

[1] Moore is referring to the attacks on Byron in the *Morning Post* for 8 and 18 Feb. 1814. See letter No. 366, to James Corry, 28 Feb. 1814; *LJ*, ii, appendix vii; and Marchand, *Byron*, pp. 434–5.

[2] See letter No. 371, to James Power, February or March 1814.

[3] Leigh Hunt, *The Feast of the Poets*, in *The Poetical Works* (London, 1860), pp. 197 and 199.

[4] A character in Sheridan's *School for Scandal*, noted for his reckless good nature as opposed to his brother Joseph's shameless hypocrisy.

now, you have bid him and his magnificence farewell (*Spes et Fortuna, valete!*) and are now preparing to take flight somewhere for the Easter. I wish I had Cornelius Agrippa's glass to trace you through your rambles;[1] though it would not do if I could not *hear* as well as *see* you in it; and when *shall* I either see or hear you? I suppose the Donegals have told you that I think of making my next move near to London, and then, what delight I have in anticipating, my dear Rogers, that we shall go on seeing each other every day, perhaps, till the end of our lives. This is a pleasant prospect, and what chiefly determines me to the step, for there are many considerations against it, of sober and shadowy hue, economy, prudence, &c. &c., all which are best consulted in the country; but then I flatter myself I am become steady enough (with Bessy's aid, who is a very Minerva of economy) to resist all the Town's temptations to expense; and then the times are getting cheaper, and I shall, I hope, be getting richer, and to crown all, I shall see you and the Donegals—shall hear music—go laugh at Liston—go walk in Hyde Park, and a thousand other intellectual amusements. Here, I really am in a desert; if I go to a dinner, the dulness of the good people is like suffocation,—I can hardly draw my breath under it. I have hopes, too, that the change of scene may do poor Bessy service, who has fallen off in everything but her sweetness of heart, most sadly; but *you'll* take her by the hand kindly, and *that*, too, will do her good. *Au reste*, I am going on as usual, at the easy rate of ten lines a day, with but little interruption. I made a figure at Derby the other day, at a Lancasterian dinner,[2] where I spoke about fifteen speeches, which astonished not only the company but myself. I have got half entangled with my Derby friend Strutt (you know my unlucky facilities in this way) to accompany him for a fortnight to Paris, in a month or two hence. I am certainly most anxious to take a peep at it before another Revolution, perhaps, lays it in ashes; and as Strutt, I believe, gives me a seat in his carriage, I may not find the opportunity amiss. My ambition has long been to see it with a very different sort of companion, namely, yourself; and who knows but even this may happen some fine spring or other? but the Louvre!—the pictures!—'and echo answers, where are they?'[3] Oh, what a pity I wasn't with you last summer!

[1] An allusion to Cornelius Agrippa's interest in astronomy.

[2] Cf. letter No. 465, to Lady Donegal, 4 Apr. 1816, where Moore mentions a similar dinner of the Lancasterian Society, an organization formed to support the monitorial system of education devised by Joseph Lancaster (1778–1838).

[3] Proverbial. 'I came to the place of my birth, and cried "The friends of my youth, where are they?" and echo answered "Where are they?"' Arab saying.

Give my best regards to your sister, who I hope does not forget Bessy, but will let her come to Highbury with us sometimes.

Ever, my dear Rogers, most truly yours,

Thomas Moore.

374. *To his Mother*

Russell, ii. 17, no. 276

Monday, April 25. 1814.

My dearest Mother,

I will now give you an extract or two from Jeffrey's letter to Rogers. * * * * * Is not this very flattering?[1] There is nothing half so gratifying as winning round such antagonists to praise and friendship.

I shall be off for London on Friday: poor Bessy does not at all like my going, but she would be very sorry I did not. Barbara is in high health and spirits, and little Statia getting on very well. Ever your own,

Tom.

375. *To his Mother*

Russell, ii. 37, no. 296

Ashbourne
Monday [April] 1814.

My dearest Mother,

I congratulate you upon the certainty of peace, though I own I think the French shabby dogs for taking back the Bourbons, and *returning* to *their vomit* so quietly.[2]

I find Lord Byron's being out of town was the reason of my father's last letter coming to me unfranked. We had yesterday a poor French prisoner of Ashbourne to dine with us, who was an officer of Buonaparte's guards. He damns the 'ingratitude' of his countrymen to Buonaparte, and says if he was in his army now he would stick by him to the last. It has been from first to last a strange melodrame, and if it had not been so very bloody, would

[1] Jeffrey wrote to Rogers on 30 Mar. 1814 asking him to request that Moore contribute an article to the *Edinburgh Review*. Jeffrey had in mind an essay on a classical author with translated excerpts from his works. He was prepared to pay thirty guineas for such an article. His praise of Moore was high, and his belief that Moore could assist in raising the quality of the writing in the *Review* seemed genuine (see Russell, ii. 13, no. 274).

[2] Moore is referring to Napoleon's defeat, abdication, and exile on Elba in April 1814. Louis XVIII was placed on the throne.

be very ridiculous. It is that mixture of the tragical and the farcical, which poor wretched human nature exhibits so often.

We are very anxious to hear from you, and hope you still think of the delightful plan of coming to us. Ever your own,

Tom.

376. *To his Mother*

Russell, ii. 17, no. 277

[May] 1814.

My dearest Mother,

I am again in quiet, and again able to renew my regular correspondence, which I know you will forgive the interruption of during my very bustling visit to town. I certainly never was in half such request before, and feel great spirits from finding my character in every way standing so high. I had not time to tell you of my appearance at Power's trial;[1] but Lord Ellenborough's manner to me was of the most marked respect and politeness; and was so far *politic* as well as polite, for he has secured my silence in his favour for ever. I would not from this on't touch one hair of his wig. I send you a report of the trial, in which his compliments to me are noticed.

Did I tell you that I was offered two thousand guineas for my poem while I was in town?[2] My friends thought I might command three thousand; but I should not like to ask more than I could be sure of getting.

Poor Bessy was, as you may suppose, delighted to have me back again. I found Barbara visibly improved in the five weeks I had been away, and little Statia much better.

Bessy sends a collar for Ellen, which she bids me say is only worth acceptance as being worked by herself, and the first she ever worked. God bless you, dearest mother. Ever your own,

Tom.

377. *To James Power*

Russell, i. 367, no. 259

Monday night [May 1814]

My dear Sir,

I received your letter, and yesterday, in the box from Miss Lawrence, got the books and music, for which I thank you very much: the Melodies are bound very neatly.

[1] Power *v.* Walker. See letter No. 367, to James Power, February 1814.

[2] See letter No. 385, to John Murray, 28 July 1814.

What you tell me about the depredations committed on you is most mortifying indeed; I only hope that the loss being spread over so many years will be felt less by you than if it came all at once together. We must be more careful in our book concern.

I have this last week written a charter glee for Stevenson to set for a new musical society that is about to open, with great *éclat*, in Dublin. Dalton is the great promoter of it, and the Duke of Leinster gives his patronage. I send you the words on the other side, and a question has occurred to me which puzzles me not a little. If I have understood you right, your brother is not to have, or at least has not yet, any share in your agreement with Stevenson. Now, what is to be done about the words I write for Stevenson? as your brother certainly has a claim upon all such words, and I do not well see how you are to settle the matter with him. I wish you would, when you write, give me some explanation upon this subject, before I employ myself in any more words for Sir John.

'Who says the Age of Song is o'er,
  Or that the mantle, finely wrought,
Which hung around the Bard of yore,
  Has fall'n to earth, and fall'n uncaught?
It *is* not so: the harp, the strain,
  And souls to feel them, *still* remain.

'Muse of our Isle descend to-night,
  With all thy spells of other years,—
The lay of tender, calm delight;
  The song of sorrow, steep'd in tears;
The war-hymn of the brave and free,
  Whose every note is victory!
And oh! that airy Harp of mirth,
  Whose tales of love, and wine, and bliss,
Make us forget the grovelling earth,
  And all its care on nights like this!'[1]

I am very anxious Stevenson should set this well, for his own sake as well as the sake of the words; particularly as I am told there is an Opposition Club forming against this, under the auspices of Warren, and professedly to the exclusion of Stevenson. I was very sorry to see by the newspaper (the Morning Chronicle), that you have lost your point against Walker in Chancery.[2] Do you care

[1] This poem was not included in the 1841 edition of Moore's works.

[2] See letter No. 367, to James Power, February 1814. Since William Power held the deed to the *Irish Melodies*, James could not prove his claim and lost the suit against Walker.

much about it? I hope not most sincerely, as you have so many other things to plague you.

I have got rather a pretty Irish air, which, with a little of my manufacturing, will do for our next number, and you shall have it, with some other things, soon.

Best regards to Mrs. Power from Bessy, and yours most affectionately,

Thomas Moore.

I wish you would take the trouble of calling upon Sheddon before eleven some morning with this letter, as I have inclosed him Croker's letter (principally to show I have such a friend at the Admiralty) and not wishing to leave it in his hands have begged him to return it to you, when he has read it; so just deliver the packet to him, and wait till he has done with it.

I have written to ask Croker's advice about my Bermuda place, and he has, in a long letter, repeated and enforced what he said before, that my going out myself is the only way of seeing myself done justice to there; but the remedy is worse than the disease. Unfortunately, I entered into a negotiation with my deputy (through the Sheddons) to sell him, for an immediate sum, the whole profits of the office during the war, and I very much fear he is keeping back my share, in order to diminish my opinion of the emoluments, and prevent me from setting too high a price on the situation. Even his uncles, the Sheddons, are displeased with him.[1]

378. *To his Mother*

Russell, ii. 18, no. 278

Mayfield Cottage
Thursday night, June 1. 1814.

My dearest Mother,

Bessy received Ellen's letter this evening, and it rejoiced us exceedingly to hear you were so merry on my birthday: long, long may you be merry on that day, my own dear mother, and may we soon be able to celebrate it all together. This last time even Bessy and I were separated.

Did I tell you that Mrs. Dalton was asked to be godmother to our forthcoming little thing. She has made Bessy very happy by a present of a most splendid cap and frock for it; they are quite the admiration of all our female neighbours.

[1] See letter No. 81, to his mother, 19 Jan. 1804.

I assure you I have the credit here of being a pattern for husbands, on account of my goodness in coming back to Bessy just as all the gaieties were beginning in London; but in this they allow me more credit than I deserve, for I have no great curiosity after emperors (except *ex*-ones), and of the gaieties I had quite enough.[1] Ever, my dearest mother, your

Tom.

379. *To James Power*

Pforzheimer Misc. MS. 303

[Postmark June 9, 1814]

My dear Sir—

I arrived very tired on Saturday evening—not the less so for meeting with very unexpected honours from the fools of Derby, who came out to meet us about a mile from the town (on account of the confirmation of Peace) with ribbons, oak-leaves &c, took the horses from the mail and pulled us thro the town—after we had dined, the same wise animals pulled us out again— We were received at Ashbourne (both places being long remarkable for these fits of frenzy) with the same cavalcade & triumph, and the only thing that amused me in the whole business was an idea that struck me of buying a *whiskered mask*, before we came to Derby, which I made a man in the mail (who had an odd sort of black tufted travelling cap) put on, and he hurraed [*sic*] like a Don Cossack out of the windows—

I have lost no time in doing some of the jobs you wished me to dispatch, and at the other side send you the second verses of two of Stevenson's Songs—the third Song does not please me so much, but I shall complete the Verse that's wanting for it as soon as possible—

Do not omit taking Dalton to the Piano-Forte Place— I find Bessy very symptomatic of an approaching cry-out, but better than she used to be on those occasions. In the first verse of 'When Twilight dews &c' alter the 5th line thus And thou too on that orb so dear,[2]

[1] This is an allusion to the visit of the King of Prussia, the Emperor of Russia, Marshal Blücher, and other continental dignitaries to London in June 1814. Edward Dalton described some of the festivities in a letter to Moore on June 27 (Russell, ii. 19, no. 279), noting particularly the incident at the opera when Princess Charlotte timed her entrance into her box so that it occurred just as the ovation for the Prince Regent and his royal guests was subsiding. See also letter No. 381, to Lady Donegal, 28 June 1814.

[2] *Poetry*, p. 317. The line was altered as Moore suggested.

Second verse of 'When Twilight dews &c'

There's not a garden-walk I tread,
  There's not a flower I see, love,
But brings to mind some hope that's fled,
  Some joy I've lost with thee, love!
And still I wish that hour was near,
  When, friends and foes forgiven,
The pains, the ills we've wept thro here
  May turn to smiles in heaven!

Second verse of 'When I am dead'[1]

  But oh! were mine
  One sigh of thine,
One pitying word [of thine *deleted*] from thee,
  Like Heaven's spheres
  To angel ears
Would be that word to me.
  Howe'er unblest,
  My shade would rest,
While listening to that tone—
  [And oft[2] would die *deleted*]
  Who would not die
  To hear thee cry
'Peace, peace to him that's gone!'

In the first verse of this last song, I wish the second line instead of '*Oh!* lay my head' to be '*Then* lay my head'—[3]

The following alterations too must be made in the music of the 2nd verse—

While list'ning to

Who would not die

[1] 'Peace, Peace to Him That's Gone', *Poetry*, p. 319.
[2] Over *still*, deleted.
[3] The alteration was made.

Let Mr Benison too remove the cadences at the end, as I wished—but perhaps you had better first consult Dalton—

Ever yours most cordially
Thomas Moore

Bessy sends her kindest remembrances to Mrs Power

380. *To James Power*

Pennsylvania Historical Society

Thursday Evening* [June 25th 1814, *not in Moore's hand*]

My dear Sir— I send you a very short, but very pretty Melody—you should have had another, but yesterday we were invaded by a most multitudinous visit from Joe Atkinson and almost all his family, who are come upon a visit to Mr Honeybourne's within 9 or 10 miles of us, and this entirely occupied the time I had set apart for my other Melody— The one I send has a good many verses to it, and is a subject I have long meditated—it is on the *Prince's desertion of Ireland*, and done so as to appear like a Love-Song, in the manner of some other political ones in the Collection—I am sure you will like it, when you see the rest—[1]

I now absolve you from the *locking-up* of the Sacred Song you have of mine— You may send it to Stevenson to set and he shall have more of the same kind, as soon as I can manage them—

Bessy still keeps up, and I think I may venture even to leave her a day to pay a visit to the Atkinsons. I was very sorry and not a little ashamed of myself for not sending you the idea of a transparency—but the truth is the designs I thought of were all too far-fetched, and would have been not only difficult to an artist to execute, but difficult for the mob to understand— *Had* you any thing of the kind?

Best regards to Mrs Power
Ever yours
T. Moore.

381. *To Lady Donegal*

Russell, ii. 21, no. 280

Tuesday, June 28. 1814.

Ladies, who could forget a friend for such poor creatures as the Bourbons,[2] can hardly be expected to have remembered him

[1] 'When First I Met Thee, Warm and Young', *Poetry*, p. 206. Later Moore could not suppress the popular opinion that the poem referred, not to the Prince's desertion of Ireland, but of Mrs. Fitzherbert.

[2] See letter No. 378, to his mother, 1 June 1814.

during the late Imperial proceedings, and therefore I have very quietly made up my mind to your being (as Lord Moira says) '*oblivious*'[1] of me for the last three weeks; but now that these royal persons are gone, and it is the opinion of the Morning Chronicle that we should all 'return to reason and reflection,' I beg leave to call your attention to a certain *un*-royal person in Derbyshire, who is exceedingly anxious to hear all you can tell him about every single soul that has figured away since he left you, from the Emperor of Russia down to Paul Methuen and the Prince Regent. Seriously, I know that you are the very centre of chit-chat; that you have the first bloom and blossom of every good story that's going; and I shall take it very unkind of you, if you do not share some of your treasures with me. Even an old cast-off report, or a thread-bare letter from Elba, is as pretty a present as you can make to a country acquaintance. Talking of presents, my dear Bessy was quite delighted with the very beautiful things you all sent her; and I brought down at the same time a cap and frock for the forthcoming babe from Mrs. Dalton, which quite crowned the offerings. I never came back to her so richly laden before. The Atkinsons are come on a visit to their brother-in-law in this neighbourhood, and invaded our territories in full force the other day. I had long ago rather imprudently told Bessy what old Joe had said to dissuade me from marrying her, and it had dwelt so upon her mind, that she burst into tears upon meeting him. However, she soon recovered, and got on, I think, very well with them. I am sorry not to be able to go to them for a day or two, but I cannot think of leaving her just now. * * * Such family minutiae as I bore you with! but it is what is uppermost just now, for I feel deeply anxious about her, and I know *you* will not laugh at it. These fine days are very favourable to poetry. I have my chair and my manuscript book in the garden, and stay out whole hours. I am quite sure, from the more 'genial current' of thought I feel in summer, that the warm sun of Southern France would suit me exactly.

I send you back the document you were so good as to take so much trouble about; and as there seems to be but one step more to the eleven pounds for the poor sailor, I know you will take it cheerfully for him.

A kiss to bold Barbara. Ever yours affectionately,

T. Moore.

[1] See letter No. 281, to Lady Donegal, December 1812.

382. *To Lord Byron*

Sir John Murray

Wednesday 6 o'clock [June 1814]

My dear Byron—

It is so uncertain at what hour I can get to Lady Jersey's that I shall not ask you to take me there—but I shall meet you *sans faute*—poor Lady Adelaide![1] What a fit you took about her— Fit the second, isn't it?

You kept me awake till daylight this morning, first reading your journal, and then thinking of the *απορργτα* of your story.[2]

Malgré tout ever your
T. M.

383. *To Samuel Rogers*

Russell, viii. 179

Mayfield
Sunday night [June] 1814

My dear Rogers,

I have taken it for granted that you have all been too occupied with your sovereigns, &c.,[3] to give one thought to an humble cottager like myself, and have accordingly refrained from interrupting your 'emperatorial' (as the Myronian Gallery has it) delirium, till the fever had been well sweated off in balls and processions. From what I read in the papers, I conclude that, mad as London has often been, it never was so gloriously mad before; and if I could have known with certainty that another week would have brought on the fit, I should have been very glad to have waited to witness it, though, as it is, I feel so happy and quiet once more with my cottage, and my Bessy, and my books, and my Barbara, that I cannot say I much regret the loss; and I shall the less care about it, if you will write me a long account of all that has been *ridiculous* (for *that* is the best part, after all) in these shows and ceremonies. How does 'our fat friend' go on?[4] among all these

[1] Lady Adelaide Forbes, the daughter of Lord Granard, with whom Byron became acquainted in 1813. Their acquaintance evidently did not develop into a serious romance (see Marchand, *Byron*, pp. 399, 450, and 452).

[2] Byron gave Moore a journal he had kept between November 1813 and April 1814. Marchand (*Byron*, p. 455 n.) suggests that this early Byron intended Moore to be the 'custodian of the relics of his life, if not his biographer'. Corroborative evidence for this conclusion is found in letter No. 369, to Lord Byron, February 1814.

[3] See letter No. 378, to his mother, 1 June 1814.

[4] The Prince Regent. Beau Brummell is reported to have asked Lord Alvanley, 'Who 's your fat friend?'

fighting chieftains, he seems particularly to distinguish himself in what is called *fighting shy*. *Is* he or is he *not* hissed wherever he goes? and is the Princess of W.[1] likely to survive Paul Methuen's speeches in her favour? Tell me all these important points, and likewise, whether you faced the sovereigns in full dress anywhere, and whether they expressed curiosity to see any of *us Authors*, or were merely contented with the Prince Regent, and such food as their worthy chamberlain catered for them? Were they civil to the Opposition, and did Lady Jersey tell them, as she told Prince Paul and many others, that the Regent was a '*bête?*' I *hope* she did.—You see I leave you no excuse for withholding news from me, for I put all the questions that I wish to have answered, and as the Sovereigns leave town on Tuesday, you will have time to attend a little to *me*.

Poor Bessy is beginning to cry out a little, and I should hope in my next letter I shall have to announce the dear girl's safe recovery; her delight at my return, and her gratitude for my hastening it, more than repaid me for a hundred such sacrifices. I have written but sixty lines of my work since I came down; it really required some time to recall my emigrant thoughts, and establish order in the capital again; but I shall now go on vigorously.

Where is Jacqueline?[2] *she* too, I fear, has suffered in this bustle of royalty. Do send her down here as soon as possible out of such company. Ever yours,

T. Moore.

Pray remember me to your sister. One of the things I have thought of since I came away is, how *very* little I saw of your brother Henry while I was in town.

384. *To James Power*

Rice University

Saturday Night* [July 4th 1814, *not in Moore's hand*]

My dear Sir—

Your letter, received this minute, has taken me quite by surprize, but a *word* from you is worth (I was going to say) ten *commandments* from any other quarter—I shall therefore set off on Monday—*my* chief object (and I take for granted it is also *yours*) in my going to town, is for the purpose of seeing Stevenson thro the arrangements of the Sixth Number—for, as to the *Trial*,[3] I am

[1] Charlotte, Princess of Wales.
[2] Rogers's *Jacqueline* was published with Byron's *Lara* in 1814.
[3] See letter No. 367, to James Power, May 1814.

not *necessary* there, and, unless you *particularly* wish my attendance, I had much rather be spared both the vulgar laugh at my unfortunate verses, and the *Old Bailey* sort of language I may expect from the Attorney General—indeed I felt as if I were *gibbetted* the last time; but then it was necessary, and, as it turned out, very important—but now that my being a Plaintiff gives the matter all the consequence it can derive from me, I would rather (unless it appears my presence can be in any way useful) keep out of the way— But, I consider it of the highest consequence that I should be near Stevenson, while he is arranging the Melodies, and for that reason (though you may suppose poor Bessy is just now sadly in want of me) I shall set off to you on Monday—pray try, if there is a bed for me at 33. in Bury S^{t}.

Many thanks for your kindness about the Filtering Stone— The Stone is dear, but the *Gravel* would be a devilish deal dearer, and we should all have it, if we went on drinking our present water.

Ev yours
T Moore.

385. *To John Murray*

Sir John Murray

Mayfield, Ashbourne
July 28th 1814

My dear Sir—

When I was in town some weeks ago Lord Byron communicated to me a proposal which you were kind enough to honour me with on the subject of my Poem—[1] As the Work was not ready, I did not think it necessary to notice this communication, further than by expressing, through Lord Byron, how much I was flattered by your good opinion—as I have since however heard that I am represented by some persons as *asking inordinately* for my Poem, and as this is a charge I feel very uncomfortable under, I think it right to explain to you, that so far from asking inordinately, I

[1] When news of *Lalla Rookh* reached Murray, he offered Moore 2,000 guineas for the work. The Longmans countered with an offer of 3,000 guineas, with the proviso that they be allowed to read it before actually contracting to publish it. Since the poem had been heralded far and wide and was eagerly awaited, Moore probably feared a repetition of the piracy difficulty he had experienced with *The Irish Melodies* and was reluctant to let the work out of his hands. He refused the offer, and the Longmans dropped the stipulation, offering him £3,000 'for a poem the length of Rokeby', which brought from Jeffrey the caustic comment that he hoped this was the only similarity between the two poems. Moore accepted this offer, and *Lalla Rookh* appeared on 27 May 1817. See letter No. 407, to Longman & Company, 17 Dec. 1814.

have never yet had the presumption to fix any price whatever upon it, and that if the appreciation of its value was left to myself, my conscience would direct me to the *lowest* bidder that offered—at the same time I confess my vanity is not a little gratified by the very liberal offers that have *voluntarily* been made to me, and to you, in particular, I feel highly grateful for being the first to pay so solid a tribute to my literary character—

I am still quite free & shall remain so till the Work is ready to go to Press—

Yours very truly
Thomas Moore

386. *To Mary Dalby*

Russell, ii. 30, no. 288

Tuesday [July] 1814.

My dear Mary,

Bessy insists upon my writing you a line, and I'll be generous enough to write you two; indeed I have, at this moment, time for very little more. We were truly sorry at the cause of your not coming to us, and Bessy, who wants the smile of a friend about her just at this moment particularly, is grievously disappointed. However, come to us as soon as you can, and I'll treasure up all my London recollections for you—'my prancings with Mary Ann Skiddy,' &c. &c. If I could have foreseen that this show of emperors, &c. would have taken place so soon, I should certainly have waited for it;[1] but the quiet of my cottage and my books, and my Bessy and my Barbara are so delightful to me after the racketting wits, dukes, and countesses I have been living with, that I but little regret the loss I have had, and can even read of the meeting between those two old profligates, the Regent and Blucher (which affected some of our honest neighbours here even to tears), without one sentimental wish to witness the interview. Barbara is improving beyond my expectations, and little Statia is tolerably well. Ever yours, with both our loves,

T. Moore.

Bessy seals this letter with the tassie she has got for you.

[1] See letter No. 378, to his mother, 1 June 1814.

387. *To James Power*

Russell, ii. 33, no. 292

Aug. 1. 1814.

My dear Sir,

I have received both your letters, and am much delighted by your kind assurances of unaltered, and I trust *unalterable*, friendship. There are, however, one or two things you have said, which I either do not understand quite right, or (if I *do* understand them right) am not *quite* satisfied with, and I am more and more convinced that the only way for me to get spotless out of the scrape is, by adhering to the resolution I made in town, and *totally breaking* the *engagement*. I shall finish the set of twelve sacred songs, as I have begun them, but shall not take anything for them: they shall be a saintly work of supererogation, and a peace-offering to the bond in parting.[1] All *other* matters you and I can talk over when you come here in your way to Ireland, which you *must* do, set out when you will, for let Bessy be up or down (and she is, I am sorry to say, still up) there can always be a *shake down* for *you*. Longman has communicated to me through Perry his readiness to treat on the basis of the three thousand guineas, but requests a perusal beforehand: this I have refused. I shall have no *ifs*. Murray's two thousand *without* this distrustful stipulation is better than the three with it.[2] I mean, in a day or two, to *turn* Carpenter's *stomach* by a communication of these proposals.[3]

I send you the first verse of the glee (which I have succeeded in beyond my hopes) and the duet: the following is the second verse of the duet. I have a third and fourth for it, which are *under consideration*.

'When every tongue thy follies nam'd,
  I fled th' unwelcome story;
Or found in e'en the faults they blam'd,
  Some gleam of future glory.
In e'en thy last, thy fatal fall,
  These arms would still have caught thee;
I could have died, to prove thee all
  My fancy first had thought thee.
    But go, deceiver! go;

[1] Moore is probably referring to his break with Carpenter, which he had contemplated as early as 1811 but could not bring off because he was in debt to the publisher. The success of the *Twopenny Post-Bag* enabled him to pay the debt.

[2] See letter No. 385, to John Murray, 28 July 1814.

[3] See letters No. 395 and No. 397, to James Carpenter, 5 and 14 Sept. 1814.

Some day, perhaps, thou'lt waken
From pleasure's dream, to know
The curse of hearts forsaken!'[1]

I begin to be in high good-humour with this number, but I find I have a devilish deal to do to it yet to satisfy me in the words. Ever, my dear sir, yours most truly and cordially,

Thomas Moore.

What do you think my landlord has had the conscience to ask for this little cabin? a thousand guineas;—to the no small amusement of the country gentlemen.

388. *To James Power*

Huntington Library

Tuesday Evening [Aug. 18th 1814, *not in Moore's hand*]

My dear sir— I write now merely to say that I have done 'Cuislih ma Chree'[2] after many trials, but that I mean to keep it back till I have something more ready, and that I think I shall enable you to give six or seven to the engraver on Monday—you never print more than two verses with the music & therefore where there are third verses, they may lie till the letter-press is begun—this will expedite it as you wish—the Duett of 'When first I met thee' might have been long since with the engraver, as you have the two verses—and I shall be glad if you will tell me *which* of them you mean should have *two verses* printed under the music, that I may dispatch them first—

The title to 'the young Rose' I am almost sure I answered you about long ago—and if I remember it aright it runs thus 'a Duett dedicated (and the words addressed to) Mrs E. T. Dalton by &c.'—this is right—you must mention however somewhere that the subject is from Mozart—

I am very much out of spirits upon various accounts. My perplexity between you & your brother is not one of the least of my anxieties— If I knew *your* wishes exactly as to what I was to do, I should be more at ease—but you do not write your mind openly to me on the subject, and tho I dare say this reserve is right, I am sorry it should be necessary.

Bessy is still up, & suffers much from tooth-ache in addition to her other uneasinesses.

Ever yours very truly
Thomas Moore

[1] The second stanza of 'When First I Met Thee, Warm and Young', *Poetry*, p. 206. [2] Come o'er the Sea', *Poetry*, p. 205.

389. *To Mary Dalby*

Russell, ii. 34, no. 293

Thursday, Aug. 18. 1814.

My dear Mary,

Another girl! but no matter: Bessy is safe over it, and that's all I care for at present. This morning, at ten minutes after ten, Miss Olivia Byron Moore (that is to be) opened her eyes on 'this working-day world,'[1] and one of the first things Bessy thought of was a despatch to you upon the happy event. It is really such a weight off my mind, that I feel as if I had been delivered myself.

Now, in a very few weeks, two or three, we shall be ready for you, and you positively *must* come and help me to get poor Bessy well and fat again. In about one week, I hope to see you at Donington. Ever yours, very sincerely,

Thomas Moore.

Write to Bessy immediately.

390. *To his Mother*

Russell, ii. 35, no. 294

Mayfield
Sunday evening [21 August] 1814.

My dearest Mother,

Bessy is getting on as well as can be expected, and the little thing is as strong as a young lioness. I am taking advantage of this moment to go and read a little at the library at Donington, for an article I have promised Jeffrey to write for the next number of the Edinburgh Review. You'll see me very flatteringly mentioned in the Drakard I send you to-day.

The Atkinsons are come back from Matlock, whither they went last week, and dined and slept at our friends the Coopers on their way: this was on Tuesday last, and, next morning, Bessy made a great effort and walked over to breakfast there: the next morning she produced Miss Olivia Byron Moore.[2] I believe I told you Lord Byron is the godfather.

I send this letter through young Joe, and will continue to do so till old Joe returns; you shall then have them through him. God bless my own darling mother. Ever your own,

Tom.

[1] *As You Like It*, I. iii. 12.

[2] See letter No. 389, to Mary Dalby, 18 Aug. 1814.

391. *To Samuel Rogers*

Russell, viii. 182

Donington
Monday, Aug. 29. 1814

My dear Rogers,

This is by way of answer to a letter of yours which I have *not* received; for I left home on Tuesday last, and Bessy tells me there is a letter from you waiting me there. I am come for a few days' rummage of the Library, on the subject of the *Fathers*, which is to form one of my articles for Jeffrey.[1] People will be a little surprised, I think, at my leaving the mothers and daughters, to take to the *Fathers;* but, heaven knows! it is time for me—a third child![2] only think. My dear Bessy got over it very safely and stoutly, and I left her coming on as well as possible. I took the Derby Races and Ball in my way hither, and met a very tolerable cluster of London stars there: your old friend Miss Fawkener in the character of Mrs. Henry Cavendish; which connection I was so totally ignorant of, that I told her I was quite surprised to meet her in Derbyshire! The Duke of Devonshire has given me a very kind invitation to Chatsworth for next Thursday, to meet the Harringtons, and stay a week; but I do not think I shall go. I have no servant to take with me, and my hat is shabby, and the seams of my best coat are beginning to look white, and—in short, if a man cannot step upon equal ground with these people, he had much better keep out of their way. I can meet them on pretty fair terms at a dinner or a ball; but a whole week in the same house with them detects the poverty of a man's ammunition deplorably; to which, if we add that *I* should detect the poverty of *theirs* in *another way*, I think the obvious conclusion is, that we ought to have nothing to do with each other. At the same time, I think the Duke one of the civilest persons in the whole Peerage; and he took every opportunity of speaking kindly and familiarly to me at Derby.

Are you thinking of France? I have put it out of my head for some time upon many accounts. This reviewing, and my Sixth Number of 'Melodies,' has thrown me back considerably in my work;[3] and if I let pass this next season without producing it, I fear it will turn out a *fausse couche* entirely. I am more anxious than ever that you should keep my secret about the *plan* and the *title*, as I really am so nervous upon the matter, that I have serious thoughts of passing off a pious fraud upon the public, and saying,

[1] See letter No. 395, to James Carpenter, 5 Sept. 1814.

[2] See letter No. 389, to Mary Dalby, 18 Aug. 1814.

[3] Moore was still at work on *Lalla Rookh*.

when I publish these Tales, that they have merely sprung out of the poem I have been employed upon, and that I reserve *that* for publication at some future period. This will not only take away all air of pretension from the Tales, but it will keep indulgence alive by giving a hope of something better unproduced. Don't betray me; —no one but yourself and Bessy knows the truth; and I will not venture to ask your opinion upon the *morality* of the step, lest you should say something to scare me out of it. For my own part, I think every possible trick fair with that animal *ferae naturae*, the Public.

How do 'Lara' and 'Jacqueline' get on?[1] I see them on every table; so I suppose they prosper. There are some of our fair neighbours who read 'Jacqueline' much oftener than their prayer-books.

Ever, my dear Rogers, yours most truly,

Thomas Moore.

I shall not get your letter (to which this is an answer) before Wednesday evening.

392. *To his Mother*

Russell, ii. 32, no. 290

Donington
Friday, Aug. 1814.

My dearest Mother,

I have been to the Derby ball and races on my way hither, and met shoals of my fine friends. The Duke of Devonshire has asked me to pass some time with him next week at Chatsworth, to meet the Harringtons, &c. &c. I don't know whether I shall go. I have been lucky enough to be brought on hither by an old acquaintance of mine in his curricle, and, instead of going to the Turk's Head Inn at Donington, I am very comfortably situated at his house, within a mile and a half of the Park. I left Bessy getting on very well.

I got my father's letter. Best love to him, from his and yours ever,

Tom.

I have heard from Lady Charlotte Fitzgerald. She wishes to tempt me into Devonshire; tells me of a cottage near her, with two acres, and only twenty pounds a-year. But it is much too far off.

[1] Byron's *Lara* and Rogers's *Jacqueline* were published together in 1814.

393. *To his Mother*

Russell, ii. 32, no. 291

Mayfield
Thursday night [August] 1814.

My dearest Mother,

I fear I have been very remiss this week, but my trip to Donington put me out of all my regular ways.[1] I found Bessy, on my return yesterday, doing as well as I could expect, but her appetite is not come yet. She has been in the garden these two days.

I believe I told you the Duke of Devonshire has asked me to pass a week at Chatsworth, to meet the Harrington's [*sic*]. I do not think I shall go, one requiring a man servant at these great houses; and, besides, I have some business which demands my presence at home.

I am grieved to find, my own darling mother, that your health is not so good as it ought to be. For God's sake keep up your spirits, and be well and cheerful to receive all the dear strangers that I mean to introduce to you in spring. You may depend on us, please Heaven! Rogers is gone to France. Good bye. Ever your own,

Tom.

394. *To Edward T. Dalton*

Russell, ii. 36, no. 295

Sunday night [August] 1814.

My dear Dalton,

I could not have two things to tell you more delightful in the telling than first, that Bessy is safe and well; and second, that you and I shall meet in May. I only wish I could make the *partie quarrée* by taking her with me; and indeed the first time she has expressed any regret at not accompanying me, was upon hearing that Mrs. Dalton was to be in London, for she is quite constant to the impression that *Olivia's*[2] face and manner made upon her. I have had a letter from poor Tom Sheridan within these few days, and I told him in my answer, that he was one of the very few fellows in this world who, I thought, might compare with me in the article of *wives*, and *you*, my dear Dalton, are another of this very few; for to have a wife *pretty* as well as *everything* else she *ought to be* is a thing us men ought, morn and night, to bless God for.

I am sorry I cannot put on a long face and be grieved at what you tell me about the tumour; but, besides that I am very sure it

[1] See letter No. 392, to his mother, August 1814.

[2] Dalton's wife Olivia, for whom Moore's third child was named.

is like mine, and of no consequence, I look upon it to be the cause of your coming to London, and therefore cannot (as yet at least) feel very sorry about it.

Tell Mrs. Dalton I think Adelaide a very pretty name, but that as I always value names according to what I feel for those who wear them, I have a strong suspicion that Olivia is, *next* to Bessy, the prettiest name in the whole circle of nomenclature, that therefore I think she was very wrong in not bestowing it upon the little child. Our last God-send is the *weeest* little thing that ever was produced; something like the Countess of Hainault's children at the wax-work, which came 360 at a time;[1] but she is thriving, I believe, and the mother is doing wonderfully.

I shall reserve all the multifarious things I have to communicate till we meet; more particularly as, having to go out early in the morning, I write this letter over night after a dish of spinach and eggs, and a pint of ale; all (except the *eggs* and *ale*) out of our own garden. So you must excuse the *muzziness* you may have detected throughout this epistle, and believe me, in happy anticipation of our coming days together in London, ever sincerely and truly yours,

T. Moore.

I hope to be in town about the first week in May, and if you could but contrive to blindfold Mrs. Dalton, and stop her ears till I arrive, I shall be very much obliged to you.

395. *To James Carpenter*

Morgan Library

Saturday Evening [Sept. 5, 1814, *not in Moore's hand*]

My dear Carpenter— I suppose by my formal announcement of a letter on business, you expect something very formidable—but it all may be dispatched in a few lines, and as I am just now in a hurry, the fewer the better as I think it but fair to tell you that from my friends having circulated the impression that I was open to all bidders for my forth-coming Poem, I have had two or three proposals on the subject—one was an unqualified offer of two thousand guineas—the other an intimation of the probability of my receiving *three* thousand, if I would allow a previous perusal— My answer to all has been that I will make no determination till the Poem is ready for the Press—and to the last in particular, that I will on no account submit to the condition of a previous perusal—[2]

[1] The allusion is not clear.

[2] See letter No. 385, to John Murray, 28 July 1814. See also letter No. 387, to James Power, 1 Aug. 1814, and No. 407, to Longman & Company, 17 Dec. 1814.

This is all, and I thought it but right that you should know it—but I tell it in confidence, and have no doubt that you will keep it faithfully—

And now I have a favour to beg— I am reviewing Boyd's Translation from the Fathers for Jeffrey (which is also a secret) and I want to rob my pious Women of one or two notes for the purpose—[1] Will you entrust it to me once more, and you may be assured of my making good whatever pilferings it may suffer.

Bessy is getting on very well & so is the little thing— She thanks you for the Newspaper. Best regards to Mrs C. & believe me

Yours very sincerely
Thomas Moore

396. *To James Power*

New York Public, Berg Collection

Sunday Night Septr 13th 1814

My dear Sir—

From the letter I received from you, and the answer I wrote in consequence to Stevenson, I was in full expectation of seeing both him & you here in the course of tomorrow—but I have just received a scatterbrained letter from him to say that he means to start on Tuesday morning for Gloucester, which is in an entirely opposite direction to us— Now, what I entreat of you is that the moment you get my letter you will proceed to seize this wild, frolicksome youth—put him into one of the Coaches that leave London for Manchester at two o'clock, and, if possible, put yourself in with him— We really count most sanguinely upon your coming, and have planned a sofa bed for you in my little study—Above all things do not let that reprobate Stevenson escape to Gloucester— If he is resolved upon a Music-Meeting, the finest one in England will be at Birmingham the beginning of October, *and I will go with him to it*—so tell him, we shall expect him here on Wednesday, & you with him— Pray, send by him the last number of the North British Review published by Colbourn, I think—it contains a Review of Bishop Tomline's Refutation of Calvinism—[2] I mention this, that you may know the right one to send me.

[1] In September 1814 Moore contributed an article on Lord Thurlow's poetry to the *Edinburgh Review* and followed this in November with a review of Hugh Stuart Boyd's translation of *Select Passages of the Writings of St. Chrysostom, St. Gregory Nazianzen, and St. Basil.* See the *Edinburgh Review*, xxiii (September 1814), 411–24, and xxiv (November 1814), 58–72. For the 'Pious Women' see letter No. 288, to James Carpenter, January 1813.

[2] Bishop George Pretyman Tomline, *A Refutation of Calvinism* (1811).

I shall have Paddy P. Raferty[1] ready for Stevenson to arrange & shall make him do the Sacred Songs.

Ever yours faithfully
Thomas Moore

I depend upon your sending Stevenson to me—

397. *To James Carpenter*

Harvard College Library

Wednesday Septr 14, 1814

My dear Carpenter—

I have received the manuscript & thank you very much— I find there is but very little in it to suit my present purpose, and shall send it back carefully in a few days—[2]

You had *another* very good reason for not feeling *surprized* at my communication—(besides any talk you may have heard lately)—which is that I myself told you long ago, of the experiment I had consented to try with this Poem, by setting it up to the highest bidder—so that unless you imagined no one would bid, there was nothing whatever 'to surprize' in the present intelligence—[3] It was solely on account of those friends, who were my advisers, that I wished any secrecy to be kept, on the subject, and I am glad to find, by your account, that they themselves have absolved me from this necessity— There is nothing in the competition for my Poem which is not highly honourable & flattering to me, and *you* are the last person that ought to feel hurt at such tributes to my reputation— As to the *liberality* of the offers made me, I have too much reliance on your own generous intentions towards me, to suppose for an instant that *that* can make you uncomfortable— If you feel at all angry with my friends for their interference you have it fully in your power to convince them there was no necessity for it, and I have not the least doubt you will avail yourself of the opportunity— Once over this ordeal, and there is nothing, I trust, can disunite us after—but as I said many months ago, you must come forward liberally, or it will not do—

I am truly sorry to hear of Mrs Carpenter's illness— Bessy & *all* the little things are quite well—

Ever truly yours—I will not say 'with respect' but with cordiality—

Thomas Moore

[1] 'Drink of This Cup', *Poetry*, p. 218.

[2] The manuscript of the 'Pious Women'. See letters Nos. 288 and 395, to James Carpenter, January 1813, and 5 Sept. 1814.

[3] See letters No. 385, to John Murray, 28 July 1814; No. 387, to James Power, 1 Aug. 1814; and No. 395, to James Carpenter, 5 Sept. 1814.

398. *To Lady Donegal*

Russell, ii. 44, no. 302

Mayfield Cottage
Monday, Oct. 25. 1814.

When people go 'upon a tour' (as I saw by the papers *you* did), I make it a rule never to write after them, for it is ten to one that I don't hit them, and then there is so much ammunition lost. But now that I find you are settled in the old *form*, Tunbridge Wells, *have at you*, my lady! I am afraid you will think my phraseology not much improved by my retirement, but as this is the sporting season, I naturally fall into some of the technicals of the art, and I know you will forgive me for making *game* of you, for once in my life. I must certainly, *some time* before I die, have a season with you at Tunbridge Wells, and conjure up a phantasmagoria of vanished hours; indeed, if ever you have seen a phantasmagoria, it is no bad emblem of one's pleasant recollections, for the objects brighten considerably as they get farther off, and so it is with past joys; and those of Tunbridge (though I dare say I thought but middlingly of them while they existed) have acquired a brilliancy in receding back into time, which flashed upon me with full force when I read the other day of the 'Marchioness Dowager of Donegal going to Tunbridge Wells.' I most earnestly implore you both, that however you may take the liberty of forgetting me in other places, you will make it a point to remember me with all your hearts and souls at Tunbridge,—that you will think of our serenade at Miss Berry's,—our dear quiet dinners *at home*,—our hearty laughs at the expense of some of the wise-ones of the party,—and (if your *saint-like* heart does not feel remorse at the recollection) your own innocent and unconscious courtship of the widow for me. This last remembrance is a melancholy one. 'When I consider (says Sir W. Temple) how many noble and *esteemable* men, how many lovely and agreeable women, I have outlived among my acquaintance and friends, methinks it looks impertinent to be still alive.'[1] There are already *three* whom I (at least fancied I) loved, now cold in the earth!

'Then warm in love, now withering in the grave.'[2]

But this is too sad, and perhaps part of it too foolish, to dwell upon; and it was only this plaguy Tunbridge phantasmagoria that put it into my head, assisted, no doubt, by a little melancholy music I

[1] 'Heads Designed for an Essay on Conversation', *The Works of Sir William Temple* (London, 1757), iii. 528.

[2] Pope, *Eloisa to Abelard*, l. 37.

have been playing this evening. But to turn from the foolishly-loved that are *dead*, to the rationally and fondly-loved that are *living*. My Bessy and my little ones, you will be glad to hear, are quite well; and your little god-daughter (though far from pretty) is filling so fast with intelligences, archnesses, and endearments, that she *already* begins to be 'the light of her father's house.' The other (Anastasia) is still at nurse, and getting on very well. I have filled this letter so completely with *sentiment* (after a fashion) that I have no room left for news; but as soon as you answer this, I will write a little more soberly and communicatively, and in the meantime tell you that, whenever I think of *you* and one or two others, I bless my stars that *love* has not been the only article I dealt in in my youth; but that I have still on hand so much of that far less perishable commodity, friendship: and so with this tradesman's metaphor I shall conclude. Ever yours,

T. M.

399. *To Mary Godfrey*

Russell, viii. 188

Oct. 29. 1814.

I ought to have written much oftener lately (I mean much oftener than—not at all), but that I have been most overwhelmingly busy, making up for a whole month's idleness, which was inflicted on me by a visit from my musical friend, Sir John Stevenson. We did something, however, in Power's way, with whom I am again to start, as before, next March. This was my own wish, as I am anxious to keep the rest of this year unencumbered by any more jobs for him, and free for the final completion of my never-long-enough-to-be-expected poem.[1] I suppose you have, before this, seen my *débût* as a reviewer.[2] I have heard nothing of it but from Jeffrey and Byron; the former of whom says 'nothing can be more entertaining or more cleverly written;'[3] and the latter, 'There is wit, taste, and learning in every line of that critique, and by G— I think you can do anything.'[4] My article upon Mr. Boyd's Translations from the Fathers is to be in the next number;[5] and then, I think, I have done.

I am sorry, very sorry, to hear that dear Lady Donegal still suffers from those attacks, and I really think the sooner she tries

[1] *Lalla Rookh.*

[2] For Moore's two articles in the *Edinburgh Review* see letter No. 395, to James Carpenter, 5 Sept. 1814.

[3] See the letter from Jeffrey, 14 Sept. 1814 (Russell, ii. 40, no. 299).

[4] See the letter from Byron, 7 Oct. 1814 (*LJ*, iii. 149).

[5] See letter No. 395, to James Carpenter, 5 Sept. 1814.

other air and other scenes, the better. It is a sad thing to think that there is such sweet sunshine going on in France and Italy, which we might all be enjoying instead of coughing and shivering through the fogs of this most unamiable climate. How *nice* it would be (you recollect my old word) if you should be starting next year at the same time that I set out on my experimental or pioneer visit to prepare the way there for the transportation of my whole family. This is a wicked trick of Mr. Vansittart's, if true, to send the income-tax riding double after all travellers.[1] He sticks to one like the little old man in the 'Arabian Nights.'

My good Bessy is very well, and getting up her looks again; but I am sorry to see this last little one has increased her figure a good deal; and I very much fear she will grow large. She does not like the idea of going to France, and has hopes that I shall be disappointed and give up my resolution, when I have seen it myself; but she makes no difficulties about anything I wish, and I know she would soon get reconciled to the change; but still it is very possible that what she looks to may happen, and that I shall not like the country well enough, upon trial, to make it my residence. The moment I mention its cheapness all her objections vanish. Tell me a little of what you hear about it in this respect when you write.

I agree with you that a great part of 'Lara' is very prosy and somnific; but it has many striking parts, and the death is very fine. 'Lara's' waiting-maid, poor 'Jacqueline,' is in general, I find, thought rather *niaise* than otherwise; which I am sorry for, as Rogers sets his heart upon fame, and his heart is a good one, that deserves what it wishes.

You must not mind the blunders and blots in this letter, as I write it after dinner, with Barbara on my back.

Ever affectionately, with love to Lady D., and kindest remembrances to *Philly*,

Yours,
T. M.

[1] The main feature of Vansittart's budget of 1813 was a general 25 per cent. increase of the customs to raise an extra £1,000,000. The taxpayers were not relieved by the 1814 budget when the Chancellor of the Exchequer found it necessary to maintain the war taxes and raise immense loans from a sinking fund, which he insisted on maintaining.

400. *To James Power*

Russell, ii. 46, no. 303

Oct. 31. 1814.

' 'Tis gone—and for ever—the light we saw breaking,
Like Heaven's first dawn o'er the sleep of the dead,
When Man, from the slumber of ages awaking,
Look'd upward and bless'd the pure light, ere it fled!
'Tis gone—and the gleams it has left of its burning
But deepen the long night of bondage and mourning,
That dark o'er the kingdom of earth is returning,
And darkest of all, hapless Erin! o'er thee.

'For high was thy hope, when that glory was darting
Around thee through all the gross clouds of the world;
When Truth, from her fetters indignantly starting,
At once, like a sun-burst her banner unfurl'd.
Oh, never shall earth see a moment so splendid!
Then, then, had one Hymn of Deliverance blended
The tongues of all nations, how sweet had ascended
The first note of Liberty, Erin! from thee.

'But shame on those tyrants who envied the blessing,
And shame on the light race, unworthy its good,
Who, at Death's reeking altar, like furies caressing
The young hope of Freedom, baptiz'd it in blood!
Then vanish'd for ever that fair, sunny vision,
Which spite of the slavish, the cold heart's derision,
Shall long be remember'd, pure, bright, and Elysian,
As first it arose, my lost Erin! on thee!'[1]

At last, my dear sir, after several days twisting and turning, I have licked this young bear into shape, and a promising cub I am sure you will think it. It is bold enough; but the strong blow I have aimed at the French in the last stanza makes up for everything. I am delighted to have written something to 'Savourna Deilish,' which, though it may not supplant Campbell's words in *singing*, has stuff enough in it to bear some comparison in reading. I am not afraid now of the poetry of this number, though I fear, with all your mildness and toleration, I shall not escape without a few curses on my delays and changes. Talking of changes, the burthen to the first verse of 'When first I met Thee' must, after all, be thus:

[1] The stanzas written to 'Savourna Deilish', *Poetry*, p. 209.

'Find one whose love can glow
Like hers, now lost for ever!'[1]

I have another *botherer* now in 'Sweet Harp,'[2] but it is in fair train. I am impatient to see the design from the Wellington song, and wish you would likewise let me have the list of the songs as Bennison has placed them. I wish those three, the Wellington,[3] Savourna, and Sweet Harp, to come at a tolerable distance from each other.

Upon looking over Stevenson's manuscripts, I find he has left only two Sacred Melodies done, viz. 'Mary Magdalene' (a new setting), and 'This World is all,'[4] which he has done very successfully. He was four or five days hammering away at 'When faint beneath the folding Wings,'[5] and at last took it away unfinished. I am afraid I am too fastidious with him; but certainly he neither did much himself (though working quite enough), nor suffered me to do *anything*. The rest of the things he left are merely airs for the Sacred Melodies, not one of which, I fear, I shall be able to make use of; indeed, without some striking melodies, I shall have but little hope of the success of that work. I have now only two selected ones, that are good. Ever yours,

Thomas Moore.

401. *To Lady Donegal*

Russell, ii. 47, no. 304

Mayfield
Oct. 31. 1814.

I have been lately very much teased, and have had my time much interrupted by a constant succession of visitors. First, I had Sir John Stevenson for near a fortnight. He came upon business that might have been done in three days, and took the whole of that time in *not* doing it. He then wrote to his son to come to him here from London, and the next night changed his mind, and set off for London himself, crossing the son, in a very national and characteristic manner, on the road; and this son has ever since remained

[1] *Poetry*, p. 206. These lines are not in the poem.

[2] Probably 'Dear Harp of My Country', *Poetry*, p. 210.

[3] Although Moore wrote a satirical poem entitled 'Lord Wellington and the Ministers' (*Poetry*, p. 179), he is probably referring here to the *Irish Melody* 'While History's Muse' (*Poetry*, p. 207), which is a plea for the Duke to champion the cause of Ireland, his own country.

[4] 'This World Is All a Fleeting Show' and 'Were Not the Sinful Mary's Tears', *Poetry*, pp. 256 and 258.

[5] This poem was not included in the 1841 edition of Moore's works.

with us here, waiting filially for the father to come back again. By way of episode, Lambart and his wife (Stevenson's daughter), who were at Lord Talbot's in this neighbourhood, must needs come over to see the young gentleman (who is just returned from America), and we have had *them* too to entertain: in short, amongst them all, I have not had a minute of this whole month to myself, and the loss of so much time just now is really a most grievous calamity to me. Nor is the grievance over yet, for the son is still here, inflicting all his mess-room intelligence upon me. But I trust in providence and the mail-coach for bringing Sir John down from London tomorrow, and then the day after, if there is one principle of shame in an Irish bosom, they shall both pack out of my house for Ireland. All this makes me feel the horror of the incursions I should be exposed to (from my countrymen in particular) if I lived what they call *convaniant* to London; and though I shall certainly go near town when I am publishing, I shall as certainly, after that, keep at a respectful distance from it,—at least till I see some chance of being made secretary of state in the new order of things that is approaching. By the bye, have you heard how *soon* the revolution is to take place? You remember the story of a lady who told the King she had seen every fine sight except a coronation, which she wished to see exceedingly. The Lord keep us from a similar curiosity about revolutions; but, for myself, I shall only say, I never saw one, and ——that's all. You must not take this hum-ing and ha-ing too seriously though, for I really believe, after all, that a revolution is a bad sort of thing, and that the only part of the community which deserves to suffer its horrors, are those stupid rulers who might avert it but will not. Such profane talk as this under a secretary's cover is, to be sure, something like smuggling French wares under a bishop's petticoat (if any such smuggling ever took place). But I think the inclosed head will be quite sufficient to frighten away any prying eyes that might peep into the contents of my packet. Ah this head! how cruel it is of you to take it away from me. I may almost apply, in my grief, Voltaire's lines upon sending back Frederic's portrait.

'Je le reçus avec tendresse,
Je le renvoye avec douleur;
Comme un amant, dans sa fureur,
Rend le portrait de sa maîtresse.'[1]

[1] Moore was mistaken about the occasion for the lines and did not quote them quite accurately. The quatrain which Voltaire wrote when he returned the Chamberlain's Key and Cross to Frederick reads as follows:

Je les reçu avec tendresse,
Je vous les rend avec douleur,

But mind, though I give it into your keeping, it is *still mine*, and I know nothing in the world that would induce me to part with it, even in this way, but your command. For I think it a most admirable portrait of a most excellent and highly gifted person; therefore posterity must not lose it.

Will you take the trouble of sending the packet I inclose; and believe me, with my dearest Bessy's best regards, yours and my *very* dear Mary's attached and affectionate friend.

Thomas Moore.

I have not said a word of your kindness in asking us to be your guests; but what *can* one say to such kindness? I shall write again soon.

402. *To his Mother*

Russell, ii. 50, no. 305

Mayfield
Saturday, Nov. 12. 1814.

My dearest Mother,

These 'stormy winds that blow-ow-ow' have very nearly frightened out of my head the thoughts of taking little Baboo over to you, and I dare say I shall put up with their noises till spring, when certainly you shall have the advantage of at least one of the little vociferators. The young Olivia is getting on wonderfully, and is a very lively, pretty baby.

I am going to give a dinner on Monday to some of the gentlemen in the neighbourhood that have been civil to me, and then we mean to shut up and go into a torpid state, like the bears, for the winter. Bessy is all bustle about this dinner, which is to be superfine. Sir Henry Fitzherbert dines with me; he is a very good sort of man, who will be Lord St. Helen's. Bessy shall write to you next week the bill of fare, company, &c.

My dearest father's last letter was written in such good spirits it quite delighted us: make him fat again. Ever your own,

Tom.

Tel qu'un amant dans sa jalouse ardeur,
Rend le portrait de sa maîtresse.

See Theodore Besterman (ed.), *Voltaire's Correspondence* (Genève, 1953–9), xxii. 2.

403. *To James Power*

Russell, ii. 51, no. 307

Saturday, Nov. 12. 1814.

My dear Sir,

I send you on the other side the two verses to 'Forlorn'[1] as (I trust in Providence and the Muse) they will be allowed to stand. 'When first I met Thee'[2] is altered; but as you have by this time engraved it off, it is unnecessary to send you the alterations till I get the proofs. I fear very much there must be a new plate for it, but I request most earnestly that every extra expense I may be the cause of in this way, by either my fastidiousness or caprice (call it which you will), shall be set down to my account.

I have had a letter from your brother, which I shall not know how to answer till I hear from you. He says you have written to him, that you have every reason to think *I* shall act upon the deed this year, and that therefore you request he will send over his last quarter.[3] I have been some time threatening to ask you when the last bill I drew becomes due, as if I can take it up no other way, I must only draw upon you again to gain time, for certainly my decided wish is to be let off all tasks but the Sacred Melodies, and any little occasional things, for the remainder of the year, and that these shall be accepted (as I have already explained) in lieu of the accommodation. Your name shall not be compromised by my renewal of the bill, as I will either get it cashed by a different hand, or if you could pay the other first, I will draw immediately after and give you the money, by which means you will be but a short time out of it. I could, of course, raise this sum with ease in other ways, but I wish not to be dependent upon any one but *you*, and upon you, I hope, I shall long have dependence of every kind. I think whenever we move from this it will be to the neighbourhood of town, for I feel in many ways the inconvenience of being away from you, and I am growing steady enough now, I think, to resist the temptations of London, when it is necessary.

I hope the sketch arrived safe; there was another delay in my letter of next morning; indeed we are obliged very often to trust to any chance messenger we can lay hold of. I fear the engraving will take a long time. I shall send you the second verse of 'Sweet Harp'[4] next time: it is done, and there will *only* be two verses out of four

[1] Evidently the two stanzas which follow the signature, although they do not bear the title 'Forlorn'. [2] *Poetry*, p. 206.

[3] See letter No. 266, to James Power, 23 Nov. 1812.

[4] Either 'Dear Harp of My Country' or 'My Gentle Harp' (*Poetry*, pp. 210 and 211); probably the former, since it has only two stanzas.

or five I wrote for it; you had better print both. Stevenson, I suppose you know, has been appointed to the new Castle chapel, and is continually busy with the Viceroy making arrangements about it. Ever yours,

T. Moore.

1.

'Oh! where's the slave so lowly,
Condemn'd to chains unholy,
 Who, could he burst
 His bonds at first,
Would pine beneath them slowly?
What soul, whose wrongs degrade it,
Would wait till time decay'd it,
 When thus its wing
 At once may spring
To the throne of Him who made it?
 Farewell, Erin! farewell all
 Who live to weep our fall!

2.

'Less dear the laurel growing,
Alive untouch'd and blowing,
 Than that whose braid
 Is pluck'd to shade
The brows with victory glowing!
We tread the land that bore us,
Her green flag glitters o'er us,
 The friends we've tried
 Are by our side,
And the foes we hate before us!
 Farewell, Erin! farewell all
 Who live to weep our fall!'[1]

404. *To Edward T. Dalton*

Russell, ii. 55, no. 309

Saturday, Nov. 23. 1814.

My dear Dalton,

Your letter gave me great pleasure in many ways; but in none so much as in the tone of kindness and cordiality there is throughout

[1] *Poetry*, p. 208.

it, which I assure you was quite *comfortable* to me, and I have great delight in thinking that, whenever we meet, it will be

'With heart as warm, and brow as gay,
As if we parted yesterday.'[1]

When that will be, however, I have as little idea as yourself, for I am more and more convinced every day that this is the only place for *me*,—or, indeed, for *any one;* and therefore, unless you will show that you agree with me in opinion, and transplant yourself and your fair rose and rose-*bud* hither, I am afraid our meeting is rather distant. I am glad to hear that you are writing for the horses; they are the only decent actors going, and nothing *pays* here like your *hippo*-drames. Do you recollect the use I made of Mathilda in the melodrame I began in Dublin, and do you think the plot would be of any use to you? If you do, I will send it over. I shall be most ready and happy to give you all the advice and criticism I can muster up, though I have never, I must say, thought myself any great hand as a critic, and least of all as a critic in the *drama*, for which, I strongly suspect, I have very little aptitude or ability. Not that any one can form any just opinion upon this subject from the M. P.,[2] which was written quite as a hasty job, and therefore gave me nothing but sickness in my stomach from beginning to end; but the point I think I should always fail in is a knowledge of stage effect. Lewis will be of great use to you in this way; there is no man who (as they say) 'knows the *inside* of a theatre' better than Lewis.

I was very much flattered by Stevenson's favourable anticipation of my music; but I *know* he has been disappointed. It was the first time I ever composed airs premeditatedly (for I need not tell *you* that they have always come by chance); and the idea of a task disgusted and disabled me. Again I made an effort to compose for dramatic effect, which took me out of *my own* element, without naturalising me in any *other*. And, lastly, the harmonist and the actors inflicted such improvements on all the airs, that they have lost even the few features of the parent which they brought into the world with them: an instance of this you will see in the way the simple ballad of 'Oh Woman!' is set,—the barbarous pause upon the word 'what' in the second line, &c.[3] Some of these things I have altered for the detached edition of the songs, and Rhodes' fine air[4]

[1] Not identified.

[2] *M. P., or the Blue Stocking*, which was produced at the Lyceum on 9 Sept. 1811.

[3] Evidently one of the songs written for the unfinished 'melodrame'. The only poem in Moore's published works which begins 'Oh woman!' is a piece of juvenilia (*Poetry*, p. 73), and the word 'what' does not occur in the second line.

[4] Probably another air in the unfinished musical.

(which I am sure you delight in, and which I fancy I hear you singing with Mrs. Dalton) will be arranged for four voices, which is the way I always intended it, as much more rich and perfect, but the scene where it was introduced would not allow of it.

Pray tell Mrs. Dalton that she is not to lose her duet by the theft I have made of it for the finale: it was little noticed on the stage, and as the finale will not be printed singly, it has not lost much of its gloss by the exposure; besides, if it even *had* been faded a little, the other words and *her name* would bring it back to life and freshness again.

You will be glad, I know, to hear that I am employed most resolutely and devotedly upon a long poem,[1] which must decide for me whether my name is to be on any of those medallions which the the swans of the temple of fame (as Ariosto tells us) pick up with their bills from the stream of oblivion. The subject is one of Rogers's suggesting, and so far I am *lucky*, for it quite enchants me; and if what old Dionysius the critic[2] says be true, that it is impossible to write disagreeably upon agreeable subjects, I am not without hopes that I shall do something which will not disgrace me.

I think, early in this next year, I shall have a little money, and if you will send me over an account of some of your *minor* debts, I will try and extinguish them: this sounds very magnificent, but it is only *very slow justice*.

Best regards to Mrs. Dalton, and a kiss to the dear little child (which I appoint *her* as my proxy to give), and believe me, dearest Dalton, sincerely your attached friend,

Thomas Moore.

405. *To his Mother*

Russell, ii. 50, no. 306

Mayfield Cottage
[November] 1814.

My dearest Mother,

I have but one moment for one word. I told you, I believe, that I was to give a dinner on Wednesday.[3] It went off illustriously. Power sent me down a fine turbot and lobsters, one of which was really nearly as large as myself. All Ashbourne rings with the fame of this monster.

I am writing so many letters by this inclosure, that I have not time for a word more; but God bless my darling mother. Ever your own,

Tom.

[1] *Lalla Rookh.*

[2] Dionysius or Longinus, *On the Nature of the Sublime.*

[3] See letter No. 402, to his mother, 12 Nov. 1814.

406. *To Lord Byron*

Sir John Murray

Tuesday
½ past five [12 December 1814]

My dearest Byron—

I have not been able to call upon you to-day, and, what is worse, I fear, from an engagement that has been made for me, I shall not be able to meet you at that Deipnosophist Kinnaird's to-night—

I feel Bessy was right in her jealousy of you—if I were to see so much of you as lately, you would be a dangerous rival to her—'how pleasant!'—

I wish you would send me the pattern of the olive Coat you have ordered, as I am about to get one, and, for the fun of the thing, should like to wear your Benedictine livery—[1]

Ever yours
Thomas Moore

Tomorrow we must do something at the Play or elsewhere—

407. *To Messrs. Longman & Company*

Russell, ii. 57, no. 310

London
Dec. 17. 1814.

Dear Sirs,

I have taken our conversation of yesterday into consideration, and the following are the terms which I propose: 'Upon my giving into your hands a poem of the length of Rokeby, I am to receive from you the sum of 3000 £.'[2] If you agree to this proposal, I am perfectly ready to close with you definitively, and have the honour to be, gentlemen, your very obliged and humble servant,

Thomas Moore.

I beg to stipulate that the few songs which I may introduce in this work shall be considered as reserved for my own setting.

[1] Byron sent the pattern for the coat. See the letter to Moore, 14 Dec. 1814 (*LJ*, iii. 163).

[2] Terms of the contract for *Lalla Rookh*:

That upon your giving into our hands a poem of yours of the length of Rokeby, you shall receive from us the sum of 3000£. We also agree to the stipulation, that the few songs which you may introduce into the work shall be considered as reserved for your own setting (Russell, ii. 58, no. 311).

408. *To James Carpenter*

Pennsylvania Historical Society

Saturday—Decr 1814*

My dear Carpenter— It is with very sincere regret I find that we are driven so near a separation in business; but I am no longer my own master in this affair, and I must say your backwardness in it is quite unaccountable—[1] I now find that you would have given me two thousand, and a few days ago I could have accepted it, and with pleasure—but it was indeed very mortifying to me that when the subject of the offers made to me was mentioned, and I was asked 'what Carpenter offered', my answer was necessarily 'nothing'— You of course have reasons to satisfy yourself for this backwardness, but to me it is strange & astonishing, and, tho I am likely to profit by it in a pecuniary way, I regret it most deeply— The proposal Woolriche witnessed was quite casual & unexpected, and I am glad to find you yourself are so just & liberal as to rejoice at such a tribute to my reputation—it is indeed much more than I expected, or (in my own opinion) have a right to; and affords a *practical* answer to those who may doubt of the place I hold in public favour— It will give me but little pleasure, however, if I find that it produces any change whatever in that social & friendly intercourse, which subsists between you and me—this would, I assure you, give me real pain—therefore, whatever you may feel just now, pray, neither write nor speak any thing harsh to me, and let us go on entirely as usual— The matter is not yet conclusively settled, and if there should occur any *hitch* in the proceedings, you may depend upon my readiness to take advantage of it, and return to the old shop with alacrity & pleasure— This is all I can say just now & I hope it is sufficient to show you what I feel toward you & that you will still consider me, as ever,

Your well-wisher & friend
Thomas Moore.

I think of leaving town to-night, and am all in a bustle; but If [*sic*] I can, I shall call upon you—

[1] See letters Nos. 395 and 397, to James Carpenter, 5 and 14 Sept. 1814. Moore is referring here to the fact that he has just completed contract negotiations with the Longmans. See letter No. 407, to Longman & Company, 17 Dec. 1814.

409. *To his Mother*

Russell, ii. 58, no. 312

Mayfield Cottage
Wednesday [December] 1814.

My dearest Mother,

Here I am, returned in safety, after a most lucky visit to town. I received a sum from Bermuda,[1] quite unexpectedly, which my friend Woolriche (who is returned and was with me) insisted upon my instantly delivering up into his hands, and he purchased for me five hundred pounds stock; so that I am now a stockholder, and, as this next year I shall be enabled to increase the deposit considerably, I look forward most sanguinely to being a *rich* old fellow. My other piece of good-luck was concluding *definitively* a bargain with the *Longmans*, whereby, upon my delivering into their hands a poem of the length of Rokeby, I am to receive from them *three thousand* pounds![2] What do you think of that, my darling mother? The poem is not, however, to be out till this time twelvemonth. I have only time to give you a skeleton of my transactions, but my next letter this week shall be fuller. Love to my dearest father and Nell. Ever your own,

Tom.

410. *To Lord Byron*

Sir John Murray

If your servant should be travelling near 34 Strand, pray, send me, a frank for Bessy

33 Duke Street, St. James's
Monday Morning [December 1814]

My dear Byron—

As you would not come *down* to me, *me voici* come up to you—I saw you on Saturday evening, but as I was a Pittite, could not come near you—you did not look worried, and I begin to quake about you—'Speak, brother, speak—is the deed done?'—or when will it be?[3]

[1] From his deputy in Bermuda. See letter No. 81, to his mother, 19 Jan. 1804.

[2] See letter No. 407, to Longman & Company, 17 Dec. 1814.

[3] Moore is referring to Byron's approaching marriage. The latter had informed Moore of his proposal and Miss Milbanke's acceptance in a letter dated 20 Sept. 1814 (*LJ*, iii. 138–40).

I am busy all this day and must in the evening see Miss O'Neil—[1] I shall again venture on the Pit, if I can get nothing better— & to-morrow I shall try & catch you about boxing time—

Ever yours affectionately
T. Moore

If you have any thing to say to me to-day send it to 34 Strand—

411. *To Lord Byron*

Sir John Murray

Monday Morning [*c.* 1814]

My dear Byron— In charity to a poor hired (and tired) hack, who does not belong to himself just now, pray, contrive to be at home to-day about four, as I shall at that hour have a chance of emancipating myself & tomorrow I am off—

Ev^r yours
T. Moore

412. *To his Mother*

Russell, ii. 60, no. 314

Mayfield Cottage
Tuesday [January] 1815.

My dearest Mother,

I have just received my father's letter, and cannot tell you how it grieves me to hear so bad an account of your health. If you think, my darling mother, it would be any comfort for me to run over and nurse you for awhile myself, say but the word, and nothing shall prevent me. But I trust it is only the fatigue of your attendance on my dearest father, and that, with Ellen's care of you, you will soon come about again. We have a contrivance for keeping the feet warm at night—a tin bottle, pretty large, with a screw at one end to keep in the hot water, which we often wish we could send over to you. But I think by describing it to a brazier, he could make it, and there is nothing, I am sure, would be of more service to you; have it made larger in circumference than a bottle, and about a foot and a half long, and you must cover it with flannel, or put it into a woollen stocking; otherwise it is too hot for the feet, the water of course to be put in boiling. Do take care of yourself, my own dearest mother, and, above all, keep up your spirits.

[1] Since Eliza O'Neill's first appearance in London was as Juliet at Covent Garden on 6 Oct. 1814, this letter was probably written after that month. 'Is the deed done' probably refers to Byron's forthcoming marriage (see the letter from Byron, 7 Oct. 1814, *LJ*, iii. 146–50).

The Duke of Devonshire has just passed through here, and has invited us to Chatsworth; I shall go for a day or two, certainly. Poor Anastasia has been very ill, but she is now getting much better. Ever your own,

Tom.

413. *To his Mother*

Russell, ii. 61, no. 315

Mayfield
Monday morning [January 1815]

My dearest Mother,

I am just setting off for the Duke of Devonshire's, from which I shall write to you more fully.[1] I have had some little trouble to rig myself out, as the coat my London tailor sent me down did not fit me, and I have been obliged to have an Ashbourne bungler at me.

There are assembled there the Morpeths, the Boringdons, the Jerseys, the Harrowbys, all lords and ladies, and I shall be, I dare say, the only common rascal amongst them.

Anastasia is quite well, and Bessy is pretty well. The Coopers, two of them, stay with her while I am away. Ever darling mother's own,

Tom.

414. *To James Power*

Pennsylvania Historical Society

Monday 1 o'clock [January 1815]

My dear Sir— Your parcel has just arrived by the Chaise that is to take me off to Chatsworth, so that I have not a moment to look at it or write about the Sketch, which, however, I return, as any thing is better than delay—if the story of the Leprechaun be authentic, keep it so—but let me know whether you do by return of Post, directed to me at Chatsworth, Derbyshire—as I must mention it in the note on the Song—[2] I send you a Sacred Thing to keep the Leprechaun in countenance—you shall have the Second Verse from Chatsworth, with the Proofs—

Ever yours
T. M.

[1] See letter No. 412, to his mother, January 1815.

[2] Moore is probably referring to the following lines in 'The Time I've Lost in Wooing' (*Poetry*, p. 208):

Like him, the sprite,
Whom maids by night
Oft meet in glen that 's haunted.

He describes the Leprechaun in a note to the passage but remarks that Lady Morgan has given a different account in her novel *O'Donnel.*

I rather fear the Cobler is too vulgar for the Style of my Song— I wish now we had chosen another subject.

415. *To his Mother*

Russell, ii. 61, no. 316

Chatsworth
Jan. 25. 1815.

My dearest Mother,

I snatch a moment from the whirl of lords and ladies I am in here, to write a scrambling line or two to you: they are all chattering at this moment about me, dukes, countesses, &c. &c. It is to be sure a most princely establishment, and the following are the company that sat down the first day I came: Lord and Lady Harrowby and their daughter (he is a Minister, you know); Lord and Lady Jersey, Lord and Lady Boringdon, Lord and Lady Leveson Gower, Lord and Lady Morpeth, Lord and Lady Cowper, Lord Kinnaird, the Duke himself,[1] and the Poet *my*self, with one or two more *inferior* personages. I could have wished Bessy were here, but that I know she would not have been comfortable in it. She does not like *any* strangers, and least of all would she like such grand and mighty strangers as are assembled here.

I hope, my own dear mother, I shall find a letter at home from you with better accounts than my father gave us in his last. Ever your own,

Tom.

416. *To James Power*

Russell, ii. 63, no. 318

Sunday night, Jan. 31. 1815.

My dear Sir,

I am just returned from Chatsworth,[2] where I have passed a very delightful time, with many stings of conscience, however, at my being obliged to leave the proofs and sketch unnoticed. With respect to the *latter*, however, I was in hopes I should be able to prevail upon either Lady Cowper or Lady Boringdon (two very tasteful artists) to give me a design for it; but they promised from day to day, and were either unwilling or unable to perform it at last. Lady Cowper, indeed, promised to send me a sketch of it, but we must not wait for her. What do you mean to do about it? I think the best way is to let the man sketch the Leprechaun somewhat like what it was in the last you sent me, but without the cobbler's

[1] The Duke of Devonshire, whom Moore was visiting.

[2] See letter No. 415, to his mother, 25 Jan. 1815.

implements; and as there is so little time to spare, you need not send it me again.

You cannot imagine what a sensation the Prince's song[1] excited at Chatsworth. It was in vain to guard your property; they had it sung and repeated over so often that they all took copies of it, and I dare say, in the course of next week, there will not be a Whig lord or lady in England who will not be in possession of it. Ever, my dear sir, yours most truly and penitently,

Thomas Moore.

417. *To Mary Dalby*

Russell, viii. 192

[January] 1815.

My dear Mary,

You will, I am sure, be sorry at the news Bessy has given you; and I assure you, *you* and the sweet fields about us are the *only* regrets we have in the place ourselves; but what can we do? *Shaw* will not let me have *this* house, and you will not make Mr. Milward let me have his, and with those children in this nutshell I should get crazy (or rather *cracked*, as it's a nutshell);[2] but come see us you *must* as soon as the weather grows fine, and we will then arrange about 'annihilating both space and time'[3] for our meetings hereafter.

I am writing away hard and fast, both at my Poem[4] and the 'Sacred Melodies.' My week at Chatsworth was very delightful.[5] You cannot imagine what a sensation my 'Song to the Prince' produced (which is now four verses): copies were sent off in all directions to all possible Whig lords and ladies.

Bessy is very indignant at Lady Loudon's [*sic*] calling her 'little.' She says it is all owing to *me* that she is supposed to be little.

Yours ever,

T. Moore.

[1] 'When First I Met Thee', *Poetry*, p. 206.

[2] Moore was contemplating a move from Mayfield Cottage.

[3] Pope, *The Art of Sinking in Poetry*, ch. 11.

[4] *Lalla Rookh*.

[5] See letter No. 415, to his mother, 25 Jan. 1815.

418. *To Leigh Hunt*

B.M. Add. MS. 37210, f. 169

Sunday Night [January 1815]

My dear Hunt— It is with sincere regret that I find myself compelled to leave town this time without seeing you— I have been but a week here in a whirl of business—and had set apart Thursday last for a visit to you with Lord Byron, who expressed strong & I am sure *sincere* eagerness upon the subject; but he failed me, and I have not had another moment since— Disappointed as I am myself however, I have the happiness of thinking that *you* are become more independent of the attentions & visits of your friends from the spirits which the near approach of liberty must give you—that you may long enjoy that liberty in health & happiness & at all events never lose it in a worse cause than that you now suffer for is the very warm wish of your friend[1]

[*Signature effaced*]

I have just concluded with the Longmans for my Poem—three thousand pounds!—but I do not come out till this time twelvemonths—[2]

419. *To James Power*

Russell, ii. 64, no. 319

[January] 1815.

My dear Sir,

I did not get your parcel till too late last night to return the proofs by this morning's mail, and now I believe tonight's Pickford will take them as soon to you as the mid-day coach. On Tuesday morning I intend to try my new franker in Lord Bathurst's office, and send you another Sacred Melody. I think I *can promise* to make up *twelve* for you before the end of March, but I am decidedly of opinion we ought to go on till we have twenty-four, or at least eighteen good ones for the first number: you may depend upon my despatching them as quick as possible. I do not expect to get much in Gretry, and that is not at all the sort of music I want to rummage in. I want *lessons* of all kinds, old and new,—Bach, Schubert, Kozeluch, &c. &c., mere rubbish as to *price* (but valuable for our purpose), which, with a little industry, might be collected for a trifle. I know I could do a great deal with such materials, but French

[1] A note (not in Moore's hand) at the top of the manuscript gives the date 'Post, July, 1816', which is evidently a mistake since Hunt left prison on 3 Feb. 1815.

[2] *Lalla Rookh* appeared on 27 May 1817.

operas are the last things I should think of searching in for what I want.[1] Whenever I go to town again, I certainly will go about with a few pounds in my pocket, and do the job myself.

We were in much anxiety at not hearing from you for so long a time after the announcement of your little girl's escape of the crisis. I trust a little time will restore her perfectly; youth soon picks up again.

Pray look after the corrections of the second sheet yourself, and it need not be sent again to me. Have the goodness to spell Leprechaun as Dr. Kelly spells it; there ought, at all events, to be a *c* in it.

I do not like to smuggle anything in without your perfect concurrence, but you will see I have put the date of 1789 as a note upon the Prince's song.[2] This I think quite harmless, and it will prevent (if the idea of an equivoque should occur to any one) the confusion of supposing it to be Mrs. Fitzherbert, or some deserted mistress, instead of Ireland. Leave it or not, however, just as you please.

From your last letter I fear your spirits are not so good as I could wish them to be. If the expediting our Sacred Melodies can cheer you a little, you may depend on my setting my shoulders to it. Best regards from Bessy. Ever yours,

T. M.

420. *To his Mother*

Russell, ii. 66, no. 320

Wednesday night, Feb. 1. 1815.

My dearest Mother,

I meant to have written again from Chatsworth, but we got up so late, and the day was so soon over in various little occupations, that I could not find a minute except for a letter or two I had to write upon business, and I knew you would forgive me. My time was very pleasantly passed there indeed, and it required some resolution to break away from the pressings and remonstrances employed to keep me there longer. Upon my return, I found my dearest father's letter, and it delighted us both to hear that you were even a little better. But indeed, my darling mother, you have no right whatever to yield to low spirits: your children all well and happy, and loving you with all their hearts and souls; and though for a time absent from you, looking forward to being very speedily about you, and

[1] Gretry was a composer of French operas. See the Glossary of Proper Names.

[2] 'When First I Met Thee', *Poetry*, p. 206, was written in June 1814. See letter No. 380, to James Power, 25 June 1814.

showing you how fondly and perfectly they love you. All this ought to give sunshine to your heart, my dearest mother, and keep away everything like depression or despondency. I think it is very likely when we *do* go over to you, that we shall make a long visit of it, and, as Bessy is very cheerful, I think she and the little ones will be new life to you. Anastasia you shall certainly have early in the spring. Love to all. From your own

Tom.

Bessy is still very thin and weakly.

421. *To James Power*

Pennsylvania Historical Society

Thursday Night [Feb^r^ 4th 1815, *not in Moore's hand*]

My dear Sir— I have this minute got your letter of yesterday, and stop the Messenger, while I send in a hurried line for the morning's post, to say how truly we sympathize in your affliction for the state of your dear little girl— Heaven send the change you wait for may be favourable— I had no idea from your first letter about her that her illness was so alarming—pray, do not fail to let us know by Saturday's Post how she is—

Your letter, directed to Chatsworth I did not get till after I had sent off my parcel— As to the Doctor's request, I have, of course, not the least objection—but I do not like the style of his wording— Suppose we say— 'To the gentleman, who favoured me with this Air, I am indebted for many other old & beautiful Melodies, from which &c. &c.'— Nothing better occurs to me at present— 'Scientific' is not one of *my* words—

With anxious expectation of your next letter

I am, Dear Sir, Affectionately yours

Thomas Moore

I have got Isis & Osiris myself & you shall have it with words very soon—[1] it is a magnificent thing.

422. *To James Power*

Huntington Library

Saturday Feb^r^ 18 1815

My dear Sir—

I am exceedingly sorry there should have occurred any delay from your supposing I meant to give more than two verses to 'Dear

[1] See letter No. 423, to James Power, February 1815.

Harp of my Country'—[1] you have all the poetry of the Work this long time.

What you tell me about your difficulties annoys me considerably & I must insist upon your making use of my debenture also— The money will be quite as well with you as in the Funds & I am but too happy at having it at your service— I will inclose it in my packet next week to Greville, and shall enquire of somebody here whether it is necessary to send a power of attorney with it to enable the Broker to sell out—

Bessy is much disappointed at Jane's not coming, and if your want of some person to take care of her down hither, be the only obstacle, say so honestly & I shall have great pleasure in coming up for her— change of air & variety of scene would I am sure be of such service to her, that it is quite a pity she should not have the advantage of them—now, pray, be as generous in accepting kindnesses as you are in doing them, and *let* me have *my* turn sometimes—

Ever yours
T. Moore

423. *To James Power*

Russell, ii. 86, no. 339

Monday night [February] 1815.

My dear Sir,

I send you 'Isis and Osiris,' which I think very beautiful.[2] Tell Stevenson that the alterations I have made in the original are all in submission to his opinion and correction; and I think Bennison had better write out the original opposite my copy, or Stevenson will never take the trouble of comparing them.

On the other side you will find the second verse of the last Sacred Melody I sent you. We shall get on *flamingly*, you'll see.

I hope we shall soon hear of your little girl being in a state to accept our invitation. Ever yours,

Thomas Moore.

'So grant me, God, from every care,
And stain of passion free,
Aloft, through Virtue's purer air,
To hold my course to thee!

[1] *Poetry*, p. 210.

[2] Isis was an Egyptian deity, sister and wife of Osiris and mother of Horus. She was worshipped as a nature-goddess and worship of her spread to western Asia and southern Europe, where she was identified with various local deities. The song which Moore mentions was not included in the 1841 edition of his works.

'No sin to cloud—no lure to stay
My soul, as home she springs;
Thy sunshine on her joyful way,
Thy freedom in her wings!'[1]

424. *To James Power*

Rice University

Wednesday Evening March 3rd 1815

My dear Sir—

By this Post I send you, through Lord Bathurst's office, the Proofs (of which I shall want a revise) & the Advertisement— I write, at the same time, because I have some fears about the safety or punctuality of my new franker, from your saying nothing of the arrival of a packet I sent you off last Friday, with a Sacred Melody— I wish you would make up some parcel (the Revise will do) & send it to the office to be franked to me—directed under cover to Mr Greville, War Department, Downing St.— I am anxious to know whether he may be depended upon—

We are delighted to hear your little Jane is better, & anxiously expect her— The latter end of next week you shall have another Sacred Melody from me.

Ever yours
T. Moore

The new setting of 'Fill the bumper'[2] will do—but Stevenson seems to have resolved upon doing it tastelessly.

425. *To his Mother*

Russell, ii. 69, no. 323

Mayfield
Saturday [26 March] 1815.

My dearest Mother,

You are prepared by my letter of yesterday for the sad news I have to tell you now. The poor baby is dead;[3] she died yesterday morning at five o'clock. Poor Bessy is very wretched, and I fear it

[1] The second stanza of 'The Bird Let Loose in Eastern Skies', *Poetry*, p. 255. The division into two stanzas must have been made by Russell, since Moore states that he is sending the 'second verse' and the lines are printed without separation in the text.

[2] *Poetry*, p. 210.

[3] Olivia Byron Moore was born on 18 Aug. 1814 and lived only a few months. Although Moore did not record the exact date of her death, it must have been in March 1815.

will sink very deep into her mind; but she makes efforts to overcome the feeling, and goes on with all her duties and attentions to us all as usual. It was with difficulty I could get her away from her little dead baby, and then only under a promise she should see it again last night. You know, of course, we had it nursed at a cottage near us. As soon as it was dark she and I walked there; it affected her very much of course, but she seemed a good deal soothed by finding it still so sweet, and looking so pretty and unaltered: she wants to see it again to-night, but this I have forbidden, as it will necessarily be a good deal changed, and I should like her impression of last night to remain. I rather think, my darling mother, this event will bring us all together sooner than I first intended, as the change and your kindness will enliven poor Bessy's mind. Ever your own,

Tom.

426. *To Lady Donegal*

Russell, ii. 70, no. 324

Mayfield
Monday, March 27, 1815.

You have seen by the newspapers that we have lost our poor little Olivia.[1] There could not be a healthier or livelier child than she was, but the attack was sudden, and, after a whole day of convulsions, the poor thing died. My chief feeling has, of course, been for Bessy, who always suffers much more than she shows; and whose health, I fear, is paying for the effort she made to bear the loss tranquilly. I mean, however, as soon as the fine weather comes, to take her over to my mother, who is also in a bad state of health, and pining to see us all: a few months together will do them both good: and I *will* say for them, they are as dear a mother and wife as any man could wish to see together.

What do you think now of my supernatural friend, the emperor? If ever tyrant deserved to be worshipped, it is he: Milton's Satan is nothing to him for portentous magnificence—for sublimity of mischief![2] If that account in the papers be true, of his driving down in his carriage like lightning towards the royal army embattled against him, bare-headed, unguarded, in all the confidence of irresistibility—it is a fact far sublimer than any that fiction has ever invented, and I am not at all surprised at the dumb-founded

[1] See letter No. 425, to his mother, 26 Mar. 1815.

[2] Napoleon left Elba and landed at Cannes on 1 Mar. 1815. He entered Paris on 20 Mar.

fascination that seizes people at such daring. For my part, I could have fancied that *Fate herself* was in that carriage.

Good by: write soon: by your not mentioning my 'Fathers' in the Edinburgh,[1] I take for granted you cannot read it, and 'no blame to you,' as we say in Ireland. Ever yours,

T. M.

What desperate weather! all owing to Buonaparte.

427. *To Leigh Hunt*

B.M. Add. MS. 37210, ff. 170, 171

Mayfield Cottage
Thursday March 30th 1815

My dear Hunt— Many thanks for the Mask—you already know my opinion of it—it will live in spite of the Congress & Bonaparte—and tho the principal maskers have shifted dresses a good deal since, your poetry is independent of the Politics—it has that kind of general & fanciful character of Sir Joshua Reynolds' portraits, which will make it long outlive the frail & foolish heads that sat for it—[2]I see you have been done justice to by a very interesting writer in the Champion— His description of you in your prison-garden is done well & feelingly— I was a good deal surprized, during a visit some time ago to Chatsworth,[3] to find how very little more than the *reputation* of the Champion had reached any of the various Whig Lords there assembled—they had all *heard* it was extremely clever, but I do not think one of them had ever met with it—which I could not help considering a little stupid in their Lordships— Your friend Scott[4] is a fine fellow, and I heartily hope he may have perfect success— I see your imagination was affected as mine was by the description of Bonaparte's meeting with the Royal Army—[5] If that account be true, it is a fact as sublime as any thing that Fiction ever thought of—and I am not at all surprized at the overwhelming effects of such daring—such apparent consciousness of irresistibility—for my own part, I should have thought that *Fate herself* was coming in that carriage— I perfectly agree with *you* on the subject of his restoration—or rather I go beyond you for I am

[1] See letter No. 395, to James Carpenter, 5 Sept. 1814.

[2] Hunt's *Descent of Liberty, A Mask* was published in 1815 and was given a three-column review in the *Champion* on Sunday, 26 Mar.

[3] See letter No. 415, to his mother, 25 Jan. 1815.

[4] Probably John Scott. See the Glossary of Proper Names.

[5] See letter No. 426, to Lady Donegal, 27 Mar. 1815.

decidedly *glad of it*—but—then—*I* am an Irishman—feræ-naturæ—beyond the pale—and my opinions, I believe, are more the result of passion than of reason— If however there is a single Norwegian, Genoese, Saxon or Pole that doesn't agree with me, why—he is a very worthy, loyal sort of gentleman, and I wish his masters joy of him, that 's all—

I suppose you recognized me (by my old pickled & preserved joke about Southey) in the Edinburgh article on Lord Thurlow—but I doubt whether I was equally well known to you as the orthodox critic of the Fathers in the last number—[1] Scott, I saw, gave an extract from me, which was the only sign of life this last article has exhibited since its appearance—

Mrs Moore is much gratified by your remembrance of her— I have had some difficulty in bringing her to bear her late loss with resignation—[2] and I fear her health is paying for the efforts her mind has made—if I had let her grieve more at first, I am sure she would have been better now—which hurts women more, *having* children or *losing* them? I sincerely hope Mrs Hunt may always be unable to answer as to the latter part of this question, & with best remembrances to her, I am,

My dear Hunt, very truly yours
[*Signature effaced*]

Lord Byron is just gone to town— He has got, he tells me the *Dutchess* [*sic*] of Devonshire's House in Piccadilly—

428. *To Mary Godfrey*

Russell, ii. 67, no. 322

Wednesday evening, March, 1815.

Oh for some of those ways of coming together that they have in the fairy tales,—wishing-caps, mirrors, flying dragons, anything but this vile intercommunication of pen and ink. I am afraid we shall never get *properly* into it; and, whenever I get a letter from either of you, it makes me regret my own laziness in this way most bitterly, as I feel you only want '*stirring up*' now and then, like those other noble females, the lionesses at the Tower (no disparagement) to make

[1] See letter No. 395, to James Carpenter, 5 Sept. 1814. The 'old and pickled joke' about Southey appeared on p. 424 of vol. xxiii of the *Edinburgh Review*: 'And now we . . . take our leave of Lord Thurlow;—heartily wishing that, as he styles himself "the Priest" of the Prince Regent, and seems to threaten many more such oblations at his shrine, he would, at once, assume the laurel in form, and emancipate the brows of the present wearer, whose pegasus is much too noble an animal to be doomed to act the part of a cream-coloured horse upon birth-days.'

[2] The death of Olivia Byron Moore.

you (as Bottom says) 'roar an 'twere a nightingale.'[1] Whether you like this simile or not, you really *are* worth twenty nightingales to me in my solitude, and a letter from you makes me eat, drink, and sleep as comfortably again; not that I do any one of those things *over* it, but, without any flattery, It sweetens them all to me. I am as busy as a bee, and I hope too, like him, among flowers. I feel that I improve as I go on, and I hope to come out in full blow with the Michaelmas daisy,—not to publish, you know, but to be finished.[2] I was a good deal surprised at *you*, who are so very hard to please, speaking so leniently of Scott's Lord of the Isles:[3] it is wretched stuff, the bellman all over. I'll tell you what happened to me about it, to give you an idea of what it is to correspond *confidentially* with a *firm*. In writing to *Longman* the other day, I said, 'Between *you* and *me*, I don't much like Scott's poem,' and I had an answer back, '*We* are very sorry you do not like Mr. Scott's book. Longman, Hurst, Orme, Rees, Brown,' &c. What do you think of this for a 'between you and *me*?'

I think there are strong symptoms of the world's being about to get just as mad as ever,—the riots, Lord Castlereagh, Sir Frederick Flood, and Buonaparte![4] What the latter has done will be thought madness if it fails; but it is just the same sort of thing that has made heroes from the beginning of the world; success makes *all* the difference between a madman and a hero.

Bessy is, I hope, getting a little stouter. The little things eat like cormorants, and I am afraid so do *I*. There are two things I envy you in London,—Miss O'Neil and your newspaper at breakfast;

[1] *A Midsummer Night's Dream*, I. ii. 84.

[2] An allusion to *Lalla Rookh*, on which he was still at work.

[3] Scott's *Lord of the Isles* was published early in 1815.

[4] Rioting was common in England from 1810 to 1815, and there were a number of riots in late 1814 and early 1815, to which Moore is probably referring. It is worth noting that a grave outbreak occurred in February 1815, directed against the Act of Agrarian Protection, which was being debated in Parliament.

Castlereagh returned to England on 3 Mar. 1815, after negotiating a treaty with France and Austria. He was hailed as the statesman who brought about a European peace. At the same time Napoleon was marching toward Paris for the '100 days'.

Sir Frederick Flood steadily opposed the Act of Union in Ireland and did not retire from politics after its passage. He continued to sit in the House from 1812 until 1818. This and other blundering moves made him appear ridiculous to many of his countrymen.

Moore is probably referring specifically to Sir Frederick's speeches during the debate on the Corn Laws, in which Flood failed to distinguish himself by making such remarks as the following: he wished 'the House had been in possession of the sentiments delivered at a great public meeting of the county . . . at which were present great numbers of the lay, spiritual, and other agricultural classes'. See Hansard, *Parliamentary Debates*, xxix (22 Feb. 1815), p. 981.

all the rest I can do without manfully. Rogers has written me a long letter from Venice, all about gondolas. Best love to my dear Lady Donegal. Ever yours,

Thomas Moore.

429. *To Lady Donegal*

Russell, ii. 73, no. 326

Monday, April 10. 1815.

Your letter deserved a much speedier answer, both to thank you for the very kind anxiety you have expressed about me, and to set your heart at rest upon the subject of them. If there is anything in the world that I have been detesting and despising more than another for this long time past, it has been those very Dublin politicians whom you so fear I should associate with.[1] I do not think a good cause was ever ruined by a more bigoted, brawling, and disgusting set of demagogues; and, though it be the religion of my fathers, I *must* say that much of this vile, vulgar spirit is to be traced to that wretched faith, which is again polluting Europe with Jesuitism and inquisitions, and which of all the humbugs that have stultified mankind is the most narrow-minded and mischievous; so much for the danger of my joining Messrs. O'Connel, O'Donnel, &c.

Now as to poor Bryan, whom I know you particularly allude to, I believe I need not tell *you* who know me *a little*, that not all his wrong-headedness, nor all the clamours of the world against him, could make me guilty of one minute's coldness towards a man who has shown such genuine, hearty, and affectionate interest about me and mine. He is, I own, a blunder-headed politician; but, luckily both for himself and me, he is no longer a politician, for he has split with the Catholic board for ever. I had almost forgot the 'giving security.' I *do* promise you; and if any needy gentleman, presuming upon my funded property, should venture to hint such a thing, I will tell him I have been sworn upon a hundred pound debenture, never to risk so dangerous a proceeding. Seriously, though it is not very likely any one should ask me, I am aware of the danger there is in so committing one's self; and I only hope, most anxiously hope, that your warning does not proceed from any sad experience of your own.

It is a hard thing that you, who like London, should find it

[1] Lady Donegal wrote to Moore on 30 Mar. warning him not to associate with dangerous 'Irish Democrats' while in Dublin. She mentioned Sir Francis Burdett and 'Mr. B.' specifically and suggested that, even though such people were '*too wrong*' to have any influence on Moore, he should avoid them since the 'association of their names with yours would grieve me most sincerely'. (See Russell, ii. 71, no. 325.)

necessary, or at least prudent, to quit it just now; for I fear *that* is the case. For myself, I know I ought to *pay* before I talk of *lending;* however, I shall only say that my debentures, such as they are, are now and evermore most heartily at your service.

T. M.

430. *Addressee unknown*

Morgan Library

Saturday night [22 April, 1815]

My dear Sir—

The Epilogue looks much less alarming now— It is quite correct —but I have made two trifling alterations, which you will have the goodness to see carefully attended to, and then you need not, I think, take the trouble of sending it me again—

While I write, Ina is in the crisis of her fate—but I can know nothing till Tuesday—[1]

Yours very truly
Thomas Moore.

431. *To Thomas Longman*

Russell, ii. 75, no. 327

Mayfield Cottage
April 25. 1815.

My dear Sir,

I hope to see you in town the beginning of next week. I had copied out fairly about 4000 lines of my work,[2] for the purpose of submitting them to your perusal, as I promised; but, upon further consideration, I have changed my intention: for it has occurred to me that if you should happen not to be quite as much pleased with what I have done as I could wish, it might have the effect of disheartening me for the execution of the remaining and most interesting part, so I shall take the liberty of withholding it from your perusal till it is finished; and *then*, I repeat, It shall be perfectly in your power to cancel our agreement, if the merits of the work should not meet your expectation. It will consist altogether of at least 6000 lines, and as into *every one* of these I am throwing as much mind and polish as I am master of, the task is no trifling one. I mean, with your permission, to say in town that *the work is finished;* and merely withheld from publication on account of the lateness

[1] Mrs. Wilmot's *Ina*, for which Moore wrote the epilogue, was produced at Drury Lane on 22 Apr. 1815. See letter No. 432, to Edward Dalton, 4 May 1815.

[2] *Lalla Rookh.*

of the season: this I wish to do, in order to get rid of all the teazing wonderment of the literary quidnuncs at my being so long about it, &c.; and as the fiction is merely a *poetic* license, you will perhaps let it pass current for me; indeed, in one sense, it is nearly true, as I have written almost the full *quantity* of verses I originally intended.

I shall call upon you on Monday or Tuesday, and hope to find you and your friends in perfect health. Ever yours, my dear sir, very truly,

Thomas Moore.

432. *To Edward T. Dalton*

Russell, ii. 76, no. 328

Mayfield Cottage
May 4. 1815.

My dear Dalton,

I think I might complain a little in my turn now of not having received any answer to my letter; but I will be magnanimous (to say nothing of conscience), and forgive you for once. There were two or three things I omitted telling you in my last, which you had expressed a wish to be informed about. My poem, *imprimis*, I *am* to get *three* thousand for it, *not* four, as that exaggerative father-in-law of yours proclaims.[1] It is to be the length of Rokeby, measured out upon the counter in Paternoster Row; and as to its merits, why, they are to be 'of what colour it pleases God.'[2] Jeffrey says, in a letter I had from him lately, 'I hope it will resemble Rokeby in nothing but length.' As to your kind advice of putting the produce in some funds, I mean to do so with whatever remains over and above the discharge of debts; and as to the time of the poem's appearance, and the money's payment, I think, between ourselves, it can hardly be till near this spring twelvemonth; for, as the article is to consist, per agreement, of at least five thousand lines, and there are but three thousand written, it can hardly be finished off, fit for delivery, before that time, unless I am much more industrious than I have any prospect of being in that idlest of all *poco-curante* places, Dublin. Here I get on most flourishingly; it is, at this moment, while I write to you, but half-past nine, A.M., and we had done breakfast near an hour ago. This, I know, will appear to you about as true as the Courier, or a French bulletin, but you may depend upon the fact, however marvellous.

[1] See letter No. 407, to Longman & Company, 17 Dec. 1814.
[2] *Much Ado about Nothing*, II. iii. 37.

Mrs. Wilmot's play got a most complete damning: the unfortunate epilogue was hardly spoken, and not at all heard: indeed, when the play is in the flames, the epilogue can scarcely escape *singeing* —*tel maitre, tel valet;* and it was a most unlucky tail-piece to a damned drama. 'No, no; your gentle Inas will not do,' was quite an echo to those cursed executioners in the pit; they must have taken it so.[1]

I want you *most* particularly to urge Stevenson in the various jobs he is *not* doing for Power; particularly the Sacred Melodies, and the air to 'The World has not a Joy to give.'[2] I have pledged myself to Power that your influence will procure their speedy completion, and I am sure you will not falsify my assurance. I hope you have seen my first verse to your favourite 'Ho sparso tante lagrime:' it goes beautifully to English words.

Poor Bessy is still very weak, and my chief hope for the recovery of her strength now is sea-bathing, when we get to Ireland. Best regards to Mrs. D. Ever yours,

T. Moore.

433. *To Douglas Kinnaird*

Sir John Murray

Mayfield
Sunday May 21st 1815

My dear Sir— I am not at all surprized at your so easily finding a more worthy colleague than myself— I only wonder a little that this possibility did not occur to you, before you favoured me with an application— Your fear of having too much poetry on the Committee is highly laudable, and I think, what with Lord Byron, Lord Essex and Bradshaw, you have managed your lights and shadows very skilfully—[3]

[1] Moore wrote the epilogue to Mrs. Wilmot's tragedy *Ina* (see *Poetry*, p. 717). He is referring here to the following lines, spoken by the 'blue-legg'd sprite', the daemon who inspires ladies to write tragedies:

> No, no—your gentle Inas will not do—
> To-morrow evening, when the lights are blue,
> I'll come—(pointing downwards)—you understand—till then adieu.

[2] Byron gave the lines 'There's Not a Joy the World Can Give' to Moore, who was to submit them to Power. They were published with music by Sir John Stevenson. On 8 Mar. Byron wrote to Moore: 'An event—the death of poor Dorset—and the recollection of what I once felt, and ought to have felt now, but could not—set me pondering, and finally into the train of thought which you have in your hands.' A year later he noted that these were 'the *truest*, though most melancholy,' lines he had ever written (*LJ*, iii. 183, 274).

[3] On 12 June 1815 Byron wrote to Moore: 'Kinnaird, I hope, has appeased your magnanimous indignation at his blunders. I wished and wish you were on

Tell Byron I shall remember his wishes on my journey, and shall keep a sharp look-out from the Coach-window for 'talent in obscurity'—[1] Shall I try and pick up a few more loose 'strings for the bow' too?

Yours very truly
Thomas Moore

434. *To Samuel Rogers*

Russell, viii. 193

Mayfield Cottage
Monday, May 22. 1815.

Welcome, my dear Rogers, most welcome back again. I was beginning to feel seriously anxious about you, and feared very much I should not hear any tidings of you before my departure—yes, my departure. You have caught me upon the wing for Ireland: this very evening we set off. I have long, you know, been promising my dear mother a sight of her new relations; and, anxious as I was myself to see them altogether, I would willingly have still deferred it a little longer; but the declining health of my mother, and poor Bessy's very delicate state, both in spirits and health, since the loss of our last little child (Olivia Byron),[2] have altogether determined me to sacrifice my own convenience to their gratification. The sight of her little grandchildren will be new life to my mother, and the change of scene and air will be sure to do Bessy service. You will hear from our friends in town that I had determined upon a trip thither, and I now more than ever regret my inability to achieve it, as I should have had at least one shake of the hand from you; but the exchequer was not adequate to the two journeys, and I was obliged to sacrifice London to Dublin. I shall return myself in August; but if the sea-bathing agrees with Bessy, I shall prevail upon her to stay behind me as long as she can take advantage of it.

the Committee, with all my heart.' Kinnaird had written to Byron, enclosing this letter, and saying, 'A pretty scrape I am in with *Moore*. Read my answer and frank it, prythee. I hope you will think it will appease him' (*LJ*, iii. 201 n.). Members of the Sub-Committee for Management of Drury Lane Theatre were Byron, Lord Essex, George Lamb, Douglas Kinnaird, and Peter Moore. (See *LJ*, iii. 191 n. Bradshaw is not listed by Prothero as a member, although both Byron and Moore indicate that he was.) Kinnaird had blundered in withdrawing the invitation for Moore to become a member of the Committee.

[1] Byron had suggested, by way of a joke, that Moore secure Mrs. d'Esterre as an attraction at Drury Lane. She was the widow of J. N. d'Esterre, who was killed in a duel with Dan O'Connell on 3 Feb. 1815. (See *LJ*, iii. 202.)

[2] See letter No. 426, to Lady Donegal, 27 Mar. 1815.

I *have* sold my *Poem* (for so it must be called still) for three thousand pounds![1] There will of course be a revision of the contract, and perhaps a retraction, when I disclose the real nature of the work; but I have gained at least the tribute to my reputation, and I do not much fear any *considerable* diminution of the sum, when they find the same quantum of poetry they have bargained for (5000 lines!), but divided into tales instead of one continued poem. Pray keep my secret about it with your accustomed fidelity. Your calling it 'my tales' in your letter quite startled me—I felt as if the whole thing were known,—for I never call it anything but my poem.

I cannot write any more now, for we are in the very agonies of packing; but you shall hear from me from Dublin.

Your letter from Venice I received, but not till the end of March, when I knew it would be useless to answer it. It made me unhappy for days. How I envy you!

Best regards to your sister. The next time we meet, my dear Rogers, it will be, I hope, for a *long spell*.

Ever, ever yours most affectionately,
Thomas Moore.

435. *To James Power*

Quaker Collection, Haverford College

Tuesday May 30* [postmark June 5, 1815]

My dear Sir—

I have made twenty attempts to write to you, since we arrived (which was on last Friday night), and this is the third or fourth letter I have begun—but you can have no idea of the whirl we are in—all very flattering—every body in hysterics of joy to see us—

What I write now chiefly for is to supply an omission in my last dispatch before leaving the Cottage— I wish a Design to be made of a *Mary Magdalen*—as beautiful as possible—from the words

Like Mary kneel, like Mary weep
'Love much' & be forgiven—[2]

This I should like to be the chief & leading Frontispiece of the Work —it is such a mixture of the Sacred & Profane as will be most characteristic of *me*, and may be made most tasteful & interesting— The other subject & a very fine one will be from the last Melody I sent you 'Sound the loud timbrels'—[3] You may let the Artist form

[1] See letter No. 407, to Longman & Company, 17 Dec. 1814.

[2] 'Were Not the Sinful Mary's Tears', *Poetry*, p. 258. The lines quoted are the last two of the poem.

[3] *Poetry*, p. 257.

his idea upon a comparison of my words with the text in Exodus, Chap. 15. v. 20. 'And Miriam, the prophetess &c. &c.'[1]

I write this actually on a dinner-table among chatterers, drinkers, & all sorts of noise-makers—but I thought it wrong to defer any longer—

Best & warmest regards to Mrs Power & our little friend Jane—Stevenson is almost free of his operatic labours, and means speedily to attack the Sacred Melodies— We have seen your brother, who again offered us his lodgings—but Richard Power has left us his house in Kildare Street, where we are in great comfort and where you will direct to us—No. 7—

Yours ever most cordially
Thomas Moore

436. *To Samuel Rogers*

Russell, viii. 195

June 7. 1815.

My dear Rogers,

I snatch one moment from the bustle of greetings and visitings that assail us here, to tell you of our safe arrival and the thousand hearty welcomes we have met with. If we had as many hands as Briareus,[2] they would be all nearly shaken off. My friend Richard Power, who is now in England, has lent us his house (one of the best in Dublin, with an excellent library,) during our stay, and all Dublin is at our doors, in carriages, cars, tilburies, and jingles, from morning till night, to the no small astonishment of a Derbyshire maid we have brought with us to take care of the little ones. The sight of us has been quite a renewal of the lease of life to my dear good mother and father, and I had the happiest dinner among them all on my birthday,—*far* the happiest I have enjoyed for a long time. They loved Bessy *upon trust*, before they saw her, and the little children are never out of their arms. We are going to pay some visits at country-houses next week, amongst others to Lord Granard's, and altogether I shall have but little breathing-time till my return to the dear cottage, which I hope to achieve before the end of August, and to which (in spite of all the cordial chaos about me) I look forward with a feeling most ungratefully impatient.

I have seen Curran once; he talked of the 'intensity' of your attachment to me, and, for once, I hoped his style was not exaggerative. Of Lord Moira, too, he spoke much, but in a far different

[1] 'And Miriam the prophetess, the sister of Aaron, took a timbrel in her hand; and all the women went out after her with timbrels and with dances.' Exodus xv. 20.

[2] In Greek mythology a giant with one hundred hands and fifty heads.

strain:—'I have mourned over him; I have held an inquest upon the carcase of his dead fame, &c. &c.;' and then finished by a climax quite characteristic of his eloquence,—'that, in short, it was but too true he (Lord M——) had a great dash of the Piper about him!' Notwithstanding all this bad taste, there is nothing like him for fancy.

Do, my dear Rogers, let me hear from you as soon as possible, and direct, 7. Kildare Street, Dublin. Bessy, I hope, is somewhat better, though she hardly knows how she is in this eternal bustle. She has this instant looked over me [*sic*], and bid me not forget 'her love.'

Best remembrances to your sister, from,

Ever faithfully yours,
Thomas Moore.

437. *To Lady Donegal*

Russell, viii. 196

Kilfane
July 3. 1815.

Your letter, which Arthur gave me in Dublin, found me so whirled about in visitings, dinnerings, hand-shakings, &c., that I had not a moment to myself, and I knew you would forgive my deferring my answer till I got a little out of the bustle. Our reception, indeed, has been highly flattering and gratifying, and the attention every one has paid to Bessy is as creditable to themselves as it is pleasant to her and me. We are now with Richard Power's brother, who has a most beautiful place here, and gives us a very hospitable welcome. We have been with the Bryans for a week or ten days, and a few days with Joe Atkinson's daughter, Mrs. T. Kearney. Next week we return to Dublin, that Bessy may get a little sea-bathing, which has been ordered as quite necessary for her; and thence we have two more visits to make, to the Duke of Leinster and Lord Granard, if the latter family shall have sufficiently recovered their grief for poor Hastings* to admit us. What fearful and wonderful things are happening! Tragedy and farce come so mixed up together, that to do justice to the world, we ought to be like the grimacier at Astley's,[1] and cry at one side of the face while we laugh with the other. I

* Honourable Hastings Forbes, killed at Waterloo. [*Russell's note*]

[1] One of several theatres established by Philip Astley (1742–1814), the famous equestrian performer. He founded nineteen equestrian theatres, including Astley's Royal Amphitheatre in London.

suppose it is all over with the Great Nation, and with the Napoleons, both great and small.[1] His Imperial Majesty, I perceive, is coming quietly to England, and you will perhaps have an opportunity of letting your house in Davies Street to him; though I rather think you would burn it to the ground after such profanement, as the gentleman did with his mansion after the Constable Bourbon had slept in it. I am afraid you and I would have some little squabbles about the poor Bourbons if we were together just now; and I hope, for the sake of your repose in this very hot weather, that all the persons around you are thorough coinciding, sympathising, and never-ceasing Tories. Reprobate as I am, I am sure you will give credit to my prudence and good-taste in declining the grand public dinner that was about to be given me upon my arrival in Dublin. I found there were too many of your favourites, the Catholic orators, at the bottom of the design,—that the fountain of honour was too much of a *holy-water* fount for me to dabble in it with either safety or pleasure; and, though I should have liked mightily the opportunity of making a treasonable speech or two after dinner, I thought the wisest thing I could do was to decline the honour. Being thus disappointed in *me*, they have given a grand public dinner to an eminent toll-gatherer, whose patriotic and *elegant* method of collecting the tolls entitles him, I have no doubt, to the glory of such a celebration. Alas! alas! it must be confessed that our poor country, altogether, is a most wretched concern; and as for the Catholics (as I have just said in a letter written within these five minutes) one would heartily wish them all in their own Purgatory, if it were not for their adversaries, whom one wishes *still further*.

I have written to Lord Byron about your Tunbridge friend, though I fear the application will have but little success. Did you hear that *I* was applied to to join the Committee?[2]

Bessy, as you may collect from what I have already said, is not very strong; but the little ones are quite well, and go about with us everywhere.

Best love to dear Mary, and believe me, ever

Most affectionately yours,

T. Moore.

[1] Napoleon's defeat at Waterloo was on 18 June 1815, and his second abdication occurred on 22 June. The 'small Napoleon' refers to Napoleon II, who was named as successor upon his father's defeat.

[2] See letter No. 433, to Douglas Kinnaird, 21 May 1815.

438. *To Samuel Rogers*

Russell, viii. 198

Dublin
Aug. 9. 1815.

My dear Rogers,

I am most anxious to hear something about you. I'm sure you do not like me *in Ireland*, for you never write to me here. There are now two able and full-grown epistles of mine unanswered near three months. However, on [*sic*] matter for that, I do seriously believe that they who *bottle up* their remembrance of each other have it in much higher order and effervescence when they meet, than they who let it out, drop by drop, through the post-office; and I can answer at least for my own being at this moment as strong, cordial, and *racy* as ever, my dear Rogers.

We have made two country tours since I wrote to you, and are now just returned from a three weeks' visit to my married sister in Tipperary. Alas! it would be but a poor return for your delicious pictures of Italy—your 'thoughts that breathed'[1] of the sweet air in which they were born, and your 'words that burned' with the pure sunshine which they described, to give you any account of what I either felt or saw in the foggy, boggy regions of Tipperary. The only thing I could match you in is *banditti;* and if you can imagine groups of ragged Shanavests (as they are called) going about in noonday, armed and painted over like Catabaw Indians, to murder tithe-proctors, land-valuers, &c., you have the most stimulant specimen of the sublime that Tipperary affords.[2] The country, indeed, is in a frightful state; and rational remedies have been delayed so long, that nothing but the sword will answer now. We lost a visit to the Grattans by this barbarous trip—a sort of sacrifice which I am often obliged to make, but which *your sçavoir-faire* [*sic*] so happily always extricates you from. On our return to town last week, in high spirits at the prospect of sailing immediately for England, and getting back to our dear, *doubly* dear cabin once more, poor Bessy had to encounter the shock of finding our darling Barbara (whom we left at my father's) dangerously ill of a bilious fever. Nothing could be more unseasonably distressing. She is now, however, recovering rapidly; and if in a week after the receipt of this you will sit down, like a good fellow, and answer it, your letter may find me, I trust, at Mayfield Cottage.

[1] Gray, *Progress of Poesy*, III. 3. 1. 2.

[2] The 'Shanavests' were Irish Rebels, followers of the 'Rockites', who, in the eighteenth century, fought for Catholic emancipation.

Persia, of course, has suffered by Tipperary; but I shall work double tides to make it up again.[1]

Best regards to your sister from hers and yours, faithfully,

Thomas Moore.

439. *To Edward T. Dalton*

Russell, ii. 79, no. 331

Athassel Abbey, Cashel
Friday, Aug. 22. 1815.

My dear Dalton,

Bryan, as I suspected, will not stir, and Killarney is given up. If it were possible for me to wait *your* time, we could manage, I think, to achieve the business without him; but that's out of the question, and sincerely do I regret that it is so; for I flatter myself Killarney has seldom had, within its enchanted precincts, two souls that would agree better in enjoyment of all its beauties. My sister has been alarmingly ill since we came, from a miscarriage; she is now much better; but a sick house, and a dull, ugly country, render our visit here rather a melancholy proceeding, and I look with some impatience to next week for a release from it. The only *stimulants* we have are the Shanavests, who enter the houses here at noonday for arms, and start out, by twenties and thirties, upon the tithe-proctors in the fields, stark naked, and smeared over with paint like Catabaros [*sic*].[2] The good people of Tipperary will have a bloody winter of it.

Lord Llandaff's is the only fine house in this neighbourhood; but it is one of those unfinished and never-to-be-finished places, which, as far as I can perceive, abound throughout Ireland.

Bessy is all anxiety to hear about Mrs. Dalton; therefore pray let us have a bulletin of her progress immediately.

The rector of this place has just passed the windows on a tithe-hunting expedition, with a large gun in his gig. This is one of the ministers of peace on earth! Ever, my dearest Dalton, your faithful friend,

Thomas Moore.

[1] An allusion to his slow progress with *Lalla Rookh*.

[2] Evidently Russell's misspelling of 'Catabaws'. See letter No. 438, to Samuel Rogers, 9 Aug. 1815.

440. *To Edward T. Dalton*

Russell, ii. 80, no. 332

[Dublin]
Wednesday, Sept. 13. 1815.

My dear Dalton,

Here I am still, kept on from day to day, watching alternately the weathercock and poor Barbara's pulse, and still undecided whether I shall sail alone or wait for her. She recovers strength so rapidly, that I dare say it will end in my staying the few days that Duggan prescribes as necessary for her restoration; but in such a state of doubt and fidgettiness it would be impossible for me to enjoy *any thing*, even you and *Beau-parc;* yet how lovely it must be now!

In last Friday's Morning Chronicle there was the following paragraph, 'We have had so many and such incessant applications for the paper which contains the exquisite *jeu-d'esprit*, entitled "Epistle from Tom Crib," &c., that we shall reprint it to-morrow.'[1] I knew that flash fun would tell in England, though it was all flash in the pan here: *you* were the only one of all I read it to, in the least up to its humour.

That pathetic warrior, Mr. George Lidwill, sailed the day before yesterday for the Pistol Congress, to be holden at Calais on the 20th. I hear that there is a vast assemblage of *amateurs* from Kerry, Galway, and other warlike places expected on the ground.

Stevenson has found out how economical it is to live alone; he says he can now breakfast for a penny per morning. I have no other important news for you; but do write, my dear fellow, do write to me, and let me know how you get on, whether the boil on your neck is troublesome, and whether you are better of those uneasy heats at night. I sat with P. Crampton near an hour and half on Sunday, and again on Monday; he is just now the most spiritied skeleton that can be imagined. Best regards to all around you. Bessy will answer Mrs. Lambert's very kind note before we go. Ever faithfully yours,

T. Moore.

[1] The 'Epistle from Tom Crib to Big Ben' (*Poetry*, p. 455) was first published in the *Morning Chronicle* on 31 Aug. 1815.

441. *To Edward T. Dalton*

Russell, i. 302, no. 194

Tuesday, Sept. 19 [1815][1]

My dear Dalton,

This evening we are off; and if you knew the demands I have had upon every thought and moment during the last week, you would not have written me so cross a letter. I did not *enumerate* to you the various obstacles there were to my going to Beau-Parc, because I thought you would give him credit for *wishing* it *heartily*, and for not allowing mere 'laziness' or 'want of stimulus,' to prevent me. In the first place there was my sister, who came up, at very great risk, to have a few days of us, before our departure. In the next place there was little Power from London, full of fuss and fury, about Cymon, Sacred Melodies, his brother, &c. &c.;[2] and in the last and chief place there was my daily and hourly anxiety about our little girl, lest the efforts making to prepare her for the journey, by air and exercise, might expose her to cold and bring on a relapse of the complaint. Notwithstanding all this, and the offence I knew it would give my sister, to leave her after the effort she had made to come out of a sick bed to take leave of us, your letter was in such a tone of accusation, that I had made up my mind to set off on Sunday for Beau-Parc (of which Corry and Joe Atkinson will be my witnesses), when the arrival of little Power from London on Saturday totally put it out of my power, and has made my last moments here one uninterrupted paroxysm of bustle, wrangling, and anxiety. Now that I have explained everything, I must say you owe me a kind and prompt atonement for the unreasonably angry tone of your last letter; and let me have it by return of post, directed to Mayfield Cottage, Ashbourne, Derbyshire. Be particular in telling me all about your health, and believe me, with best regards to Mrs. D., ever yours,

T. Moore.

[1] Russell dated this letter 19 Sept. 1812. Mention of Mayfield Cottage as a return address, however, proves that it was written later, probably while the Moores were on a visit to Dublin in the summer of 1815. See letter No. 442, to his mother, 29 Sept. 1815, written after his return. See also letters Nos. 439 and 440, to Edward Dalton, 22 Aug. and 13 Sept. 1815.

[2] Probably a reference to 'Cymon and Iphigenia,' one of Dryden's *Fables*, which was based on the *Decameron*, v. i. Moore mentions Dryden's poem in his diary (Russell, ii. 254). The *Sacred Songs* appeared in 1816. For details of the controversy between the Power brothers see letter No. 266, to James Power, 23 Nov. 1812.

442. *To his Mother*

Russell, i. 359, no. 249

Mayfield
Friday night, Sept. 29 [1815][1]

My dearest Mother,

We arrived, as I anticipated in my last, between five and six on Monday evening. It was a most lovely evening, and the cottage and garden in their best smiles to receive us. The very sight of them seemed new life to Bessy, and, as her appetite is becoming somewhat better, I hope quiet and care will bring her round again. I paid the *forty-second* pound to the post-boy that left us at home! This is terrible phlebotomising. However, quiet and economy will bring these matters round again also. If any of you had come with us (and I wish to God you had) you would have been amused to see how company and racket meet me everywhere. A neighbour of ours (Ackroyd) came breathless after our chaise, to say that he had a musical party that night, Sir W. Bagshaw, the Fitzherberts, &c. &c., and we must positively come in our travelling dresses. Bessy's going was out of the question, and I assured him I feared it was equally so with me. Notwithstanding this, Mr. Cooper was dispatched from the party in Lady Fitzherbert's carriage, between eight and nine o'clock, to bring me by persuasion or force, or anyhow.[2] It would not do, however; I sent him back alone, and got quietly to my bed. The children are doing very well, and I am, as usual, stout and hearty. God bless my dearest mother. Ever your own,

Tom.

443. *To Joseph Strutt*

The Living Age, 7th Series, xxiii (1904), 438

Mayfield
Monday [September 1815]

My dear Sir,— It gave me very great pleasure to hear so soon from you after our arrival. I do not indeed think I would have waited much longer without finding some excuse for resuming the

[1] This letter is incorrectly dated 29 Sept. 1813 in Russell's edition. The subject matter indicates that it was written after Moore's visit to Dublin in the summer of 1815. See letters Nos. 439 and 440, to Edward Dalton, 22 Aug. and 13 Sept. 1815. See also letter No. 441, to Edward Dalton, 19 Sept. 1815, for a similar correction of date.

[2] Although Moore mentions the Ackroyds, Sir William Bagshaw, and the Coopers several times in his letters, little is known of them except that they were his neighbours while he lived at Mayfield Cottage. For Lady Fitzherbert see the Glossary of Proper Names. Russell confused her with Mrs. Fitzherbert, wife of the Prince Regent.

correspondence myself. I am sorry to say none of my little group is the better for our Irish excursion—poor Bessy was taken very ill on the road, and it was with some difficulty and much anxiety I got them all home again. After a week more of rest I trust she will be able to enjoy with me the very great happiness which a visit to Derby is always sure to give us, and I shall apprise you as soon as she considers herself well enough. I regret to find that you do not speak of Caroline so sanguinely as the accounts we have had of her recovery would lead us to expect—but perhaps you only mean to surprise us with the favourable alteration, which I hear, and will still hope, has taken place.

We were three weeks in the County Tipperary during our absence, and *mirabile dictu!* were not shot, nor even kilt, which you know ranks lowest on the scale of personal injuries in Ireland. The state of my poor Country is indeed frightful. All rational remedies have been delayed so long, that there is now none left but the sword, and the speedier it is used the more merciful.

France deserves all she suffers. Why did she leave Bonaparte to fight the last battle of her independence—of her very existence—with little more than a hundred thousand men? But, as you say, it is a dreadful precedent, and makes one shudder for the destiny of the rest of the world—though I believe after all laughing is a better thing than shuddering, and if priests, old women and fat Regents are to have everything their own way to laugh at them will soon be the only consolation left us—*à propos* of this, did you read my Irish epistle to my friend Ben ('Ben mio' as the Italians say) in the *M. Chronicle?*[1]

Best regards to my two dear poetesses, and to Miss L. from

Yours very faithfully,
Thomas Moore.

444. *To his Mother*

Russell, ii. 82, no. 333

Derby
Tuesday, Oct. 17. 1815.

My own dear Mother,

I have run over here on a short visit to our friends the Strutts, and to buy a sofa for Bessy, who cannot do without lying down a good deal. Mr. Strutt, who never sees me without *giving* me something, has just made me a present of a very snug and handsome easy chair for my study. They are most friendly and excellent people.

[1] See letter No. 440, to Edward Dalton, 13 Sept. 1815.

I fear I have been a little irregular, my darling mother, this last week, in my correspondence, but I shall make up in the present one. Ever your own affectionate,

Tom.

445. *To Mary Godfrey*

Russell, viii. 200

Mayfield Cottage
Thursday night, Oct. 19. 1815.

There is nothing like demanding an answer by return of post. It is the only way with such correspondents as I am, and I wish you always had some baron or other to put me in requisition, for many is the self-reproach it would save me; but I know no more of said baron than of the man in the moon, nor has William Spencer (who will be 'responsible,' poor fellow! for any thing but his debts) ever written me a single line on the subject; you know, however, I cannot give words for music to any one but Power. I am bound hand and foot,—at least my lyrical *feet*,—and you may tell the Baron it would cost me five hundred a year to give him even so much as a 'Down derry down' of my own composition. Strange that such penalty should be on Tweedle-dum and Tweedle-dee, but so it is, and you can swear to it, for you read the deed. We arrived here two or three weeks since, after the most anxious journey I ever had to encounter. Poor Bessy (who was by no means well when we embarked) suffered so much on a long and sickening passage, from her own illness and attention to the children, that on our arrival at Holyhead, she was most alarmingly indisposed, and it was with great delay and many difficulties that I was able to get her along the road at all. The sight of her own little home, however, and the comfort of being there after the very bothering bustle of our Irish visit, was like magic in restoring her, and though she is still very weak, I have great hopes that rest and care will bring her about again.—Among other welcome things that greeted me at home, was your *thrice*-welcome letter from Tunbridge, and if yours were but 'generous letters that no answer wait,' or if there were any way in which you could know how thoroughly they delight me, and how warmly I remember you both every hour of my existence, without my taking a dirty pen in my hand to tell you so, the whole pleasure of the thing would be as unalloyed as it is delightful; but since it is impossible, I suppose, for me to enjoy that perfection of friendly correspondence, where (as Sir Boyle Roche says) 'the reciprocity would be all on one side,' and where you alone should write and I should read, I must only endeavour to muster up as *much* reciprocity as possible, and if you will even give me two letters for one, I shall be satisfied.

I am returning to work again, but the idleness of our Irish trip, and the necessity of completing my year's job for Power, make sad havoc in my time and thoughts. How unlucky I have been in not seeing Paris before it was 'shorn of its beams!'[1] Often do I think with regret of the opportunity, the golden one, you gave me and I missed. It is a proof perhaps that my life has not been *very* miserable, when I say that the loss of that opportunity is one of the things I *most* regret in the course of it. How do you like the way your friends, the legitimates, are disposing of the world? At all events, the ball is completely at their feet, and we shall see whether old women priests and fat regents, assisted by French renegades and drunken corporals, are, after all, the best agents of Providence for the welfare of mankind.[2] I suppose they are, at least it is but loyal to think so. The boxing epistle *is* mine,[3] the only thing of the kind I have done for a long time.

I have written often to Byron about your Tunbridge friend; but he seems to say, like King Arthur, 'petition me no petitions,'[4] and will not mind me; I will try Kinnaird next.

Love and regards from both to both.

Ever yours,
T. M.

446. *To his Mother*

Russell, ii. 82, no. 334

Oct. 21. 1815.

My dearest Mother,

I returned from Derby on Thursday, and the chair Mr. Strutt gave me was not the only present I received.[5] I owe the man there who furnished our cottage, a balance of about thirty pounds on his bill, and as I could not pay him, I was doubtful whether I should call upon him: however, I plucked up courage and went, and asked to look at a stand to hold my music, which we very much want. He showed me one, price two pounds, very handsome. I asked whether he made any cheaper: 'some,' he said, 'at from thirty-two

[1] *Paradise Lost*, i. 596.

[2] An allusion to the Holy Alliance and other events which took place in Europe after the defeat of Napoleon.

[3] 'Epistle from Tom Crib to Big Ben', *Poetry*, p. 455. (*Morning Chronicle*, 13 Aug. 1815.)

[4] Fielding, *Tom Thumb*, I. ii.

[5] See letter No. 444, to his mother, 17 Oct. 1815.

to thirty-six shillings; but, Mr. Moore, if you will do me the honour to accept that one, as a proof of the high respect I entertain for you, you will flatter me exceedingly.' I, of course, accepted it without hesitation: what do you think of that for an English upholsterer?

Bessy, while I was away, has got the rooms and hall stained, and we look much neater now: often, often, my darling mother, do we wish for you; and Bessy says she never will be quite happy till *you* see how comfortable we are.

Take the earliest opportunity of telling Power[1] that I should have written to him long before this, but I have been waiting for his announcement of the departure of my books. Ever your own,

Tom.

447. *To his Mother*

Russell, ii. 83, no. 335

Wednesday night, Nov. 8. 1815.

My dearest Mother,

Since I last wrote, or rather since Bessy's letter, we got my father's of the 26th, which was so far a comfort to us, but we are still astonished at receiving no later intelligence from you, and I only wait to know that it is not illness which has caused your silence, to give you all a *very good* scolding. Nell promised that now she knew Bessy well, she would write to her continually, and I believe she has sent her but *one* letter since we left you. There never was a creature more anxious about any thing than Bessy is to have your loves and good opinions; and, in addition to Nell's silence, she took it into her head that my father expressed himself coldly and drily towards her in saying, 'Your mother desires me to thank Bessy for the papers.' I tell her this is all nonsense; but *do* make my father say something kind about her in his next.

I hope, my own dearest mother, that to-day's post will put me out of the painful anxiety I feel about you all. God bless my darling mother. Ever her own,

Tom.

[1] **Probably Richard Power in whose home Moore lived while in Dublin. See letter No. 436, to Samuel Rogers, 7 June 1815.**

448. *To his Mother*

Russell, ii. 84, no. 336

Saturday, Nov. 18. 1815.

My dearest Mother,

We are here in the midst of such gaieties as Derby and a large party of lively girls can muster up. Bessy is in high spirits, and looking better than I have seen her for a long time. The Longmans have just sent her down a present of Messrs. [*sic*] Inchbald's Theatres.[1] They are, indeed, very liberal, and have been particularly kind in their offers of money to me, to prevent the sale of my little stock, which I commissioned them to effect for me. I have, however, refused their offer, thinking it more independent not to borrow while I can help it.

If my dear father should be in want of money towards Christmas, he may draw upon me, at sixty-one days, for twenty or thirty pounds. Love to all. Ever my dearest mother's own,

Tom.

449. *To James Power (?)*

New York Public

[*c.* November 1815]

My dear Sir—

I troubled you with a packet of letters to-day through Lord Bathurst's office,[2] in order to try if that channel is still open to us, which will be a great convenience—but, since dispatching that packet, in consequence of being disappointed in some money arrangements I had made, and having a sudden call upon me for my rent, I have been obliged to draw upon you through the banker here for fifty pounds at two months sight, and though this premature draft may, I fear, inconvenience you a little, it will be somewhat counter-balanced by my not having (as I trust will be the case) to draw upon you again for the next quarter— I am at present living at but little expense, being on a visit to some friends, with whom I dare say we shall stay for two months longer.[3]

[1] See letter No. 450, to Mary Godfrey, 6 Dec. 1815.

[2] See letter No. 424, to James Power, 3 Mar. 1815, for his arrangement with Lord Bathurst.

[3] Moore visited the Strutts in Derby in October and November. See letters Nos. 444 and 448, to his mother, 17 Oct. and 18 Nov. 1815.

450. *To Mary Godfrey*

Russell, ii. 84, no. 337

Tuesday, Dec. 6. 1815.

Where is my two for one? Ever since the magnanimous promise in your last, that you would really and truly let me have two of your letters for every one of mine, I have been waiting for the shot from the other barrel like a hero, but none has come, and, therefore, I fire off this little squib at you, just to try your courage, which, I hope, will show itself, by return of post, oozing out (like Acres's) from your fingers' ends.[1] I have no news for you; except that the other day, being inclined to treat Bessy to Mrs. Inchbald's Modern Theatre, in ten volumes, I wrote to Longman's for them; and lo! with a generosity unexampled among bibliopolists, they sent her a present of *all* the plays Mrs. Inchbald has edited, consisting of forty-two volumes splendidly bound, with proof impressions of the plates.[2] I have read *Walter*-loo, since I heard from you. The battle murdered many, and *he* has murdered the battle*: 'tis sad stuff; Hougom*ont* rhyming to 'long,' 'strong,' &c.[3] He must have learned his pronunciation of French from Solomon Grundy in the play—'Commong dong, as they say in Dunkirk.'[4] *Where* is Rogers? I have not heard from him for ages. Four goodly letters has he had from me since I left this for Ireland, and never answered one of them. This is even worse than you, Miss Two-for-one! Best, kindest love to Lady Donegal, from hers and yours faithfully,

Thomas Moore.

* In similar phrase Lord Erskine wrote:

'Of all who fell, by sabre or by shot,
Not one fell half so flat as Walter Scott.'

But Sir Walter only fell as a poet, to rise again as a novelist. [*Russell's note.*]

[1] Bob Acres, in Sheridan's *Rivals*. His courage oozes 'out at the palms of his hands', and he refuses to fight a duel with Ensign Beverly.

[2] The edition Moore requested was *The Modern Theatre* (1809), 10 volumes. He may have received the twenty-five volume *British Theatre, or a Collection of Plays with Biographical and Critical Remarks* (1808). There is no record of a forty-two volume edition. Moore may have been referring to separate editions of plays rather than to a collection such as that of 1808.

[3] Scott's *Field of Waterloo* appeared in 1815. Moore is referring to the following lines:

With every mark of martial wrong
That scathe thy towers fair Hougoumont. (ll. 482–3)
For many an age remembered long
Shall live the towers of Hougoumont. (ll. 496–7)

[4] Solomon Grundy, a character in the younger George Coleman's *Who Wants a Guinea?* (1804), Act III, sc. ii.

451. *To James Power*

Russell, ii. 85, no. 338

Sunday, Dec. 19. 1815.

My dear Sir,

I have only time to send you, according to my promise, the first verses of 'When Day,' &c. which you will, of course, lose no time in engraving.

'Thou art, O God! the life and light
Of all this beauteous world we see:
Its glow by day, its smile by night,
Are but reflections caught from thee;
Where'er we turn, thy glories shine,
And all things fair and bright are thine.

'When Day, with farewell beam, delays
Among the opening clouds of Even;
And we can almost think we gaze
Through golden vistas into Heaven!
Those hues, that wake e'en Light's decline,
So bright, so soft, oh God! are thine.

'When Night, with wings of starry gloom,
O'ershadows all the earth and skies,
Like some celestial bird, whose plume
Is sparkling with unnumber'd eyes:
That sacred gloom, those fires divine,
So grand, so countless, Lord! are thine.'[1]

I have sent off the copy from memory of 'There's nothing bright'[2] to Stevenson, and have entreated him to lose no time in returning it. Ever yours,

T. Moore.

452. *To Samuel Rogers*

Russell, viii. 204

Mayfield Cottage
Dec. 26. 1815.

My dear Rogers,

As this is about the time you said you should be on your return to London, from your bright course through that noble Zodiac you've been moving in, I hasten to welcome you thither, not alas!

[1] *Poetry*, p. 254.

[2] 'This World Is All a Fleeting Show', *Poetry*, p. 256. Each stanza ends with the refrain 'There 's nothing true (bright, calm), but Heaven'.

with my hand, as I could wish,—*that* joy must not be for a few months longer,—but with my warmest congratulations on your safe and sound return from the Continent, and hearty thanks for your kind recollections of me—recollections, which I never want the outward and visible sign of letter-writing to assure me of, however delightful and welcome it may be, in addition to *knowing* that there's sweet music in the instrument, to *hear* a little of its melody now and then. This image will not stand your criticism, but you know its *meaning*, and that's enough—much more indeed than we Irish image-makers can in general achieve. My desire to see you for *yourself alone*, is still more whetted by all I hear of the exquisite gleanings you have made on your tour. The Donegals say you have seen so much, seen everything so well, and describe it all so picturesquely, that there is nothing like the treat of hearing you talk of your travels—how I long for that treat! You are a happy fellow, my dear Rogers; I know no one more *nourri des fleurs* of life, no one who lives so much 'apis matinæ more' as yourself. The great regret of my future days (and I hope the *greatest*) will be my loss of the opportunity of seeing that glorious gallery, which, like those 'domes of Shadukiam and Amberabad,' that Nourmahal saw in the 'gorgeous clouds of the west,'[1] is now dispersed and gone for ever. It is a loss that never can be remedied; but still perhaps our sacrifices are among our pleasantest recollections, and I ought not to feel sorry that the time and money, which would have procured for myself this great gratification, have been employed in making other hearts happy,—better hearts than mine, and better happiness than *that* would have been. With respect to my *Peris*,[2] thus stands the case, and remember that they are still to remain (where Peris best like to be) *under the rose*. I have nearly finished three tales, making, in all, about three thousand five hundred lines, but my plan is to have *five tales*, the stories of all which are arranged, and which I am *determined* to finish before I publish—no urgings nor wonderings nor tauntings shall induce me to lift the curtain till I have grouped these five subjects in the way I think best for variety and effect.[3] I have already suffered enough by premature publication. I have formidable favourites to contend with,[4] and

[1] The wife of the emperor Selim in Moore's *Light of the Haram*, one of the tales in *Lalla Rookh*. She is also the empress in Dryden's *Aureng-Zebe* (1676). Shadukiam and Amberadab are two cities in 'the country of delight—the name of a Province in the kingdom of Jannistan, or Fairy Land . . .'. *Poetry*, p. 401 n.

[2] *Paradise and the Peri*, one of the tales in *Lalla Rookh*.

[3] There are actually four tales: *The Veiled Prophet of Khorassen*, *Paradise and the Peri*, *The Fire-Worshippers*, and *The Story of the Sultana Nourmahal* (*The Light of the Haram*).

[4] Byron's *Giaour*, *Bride of Abydos*, and *Corsair*.

must try to make up my deficiencies in *dash* and vigour by a greater degree, if possible, of versatility and polish. Now it will take, at the least, six thousand lines to complete this plan, *i.e.* between two and three thousand more than I have yet done. By May next I expect to have five thousand finished. This is the number for which the Longmans stipulated, and accordingly in May I mean to appear in London, and *nominally* deliver the work into their hands. It would be then too late (even if all were finished) to think of going to press; so that I shall thus enjoy the credit with the Literary Quidnuncs of having completed my task, together with the advantage of the whole summer before me to extend it to the length I purpose. Such is the statement of my thousands, &c., which I am afraid you will find as puzzling as a speech of Mr. Vansittart's; but it is now near twelve o'clock at night, which being an hour later than our cottage rules allow, I feel it impossible to be luminous any longer—in which tendency to eclipse, my candle sympathises most gloomily.

Your poor friend Psyche is by no means well. I was in hopes that our Irish trip would have benefited her; but her weakness and want of appetite continue most distressingly, and our cold habitation in the fields has now given her a violent cough, which if it does not soon get better, will alarm me exceedingly. I never love her so well as when she is ill, which is perhaps the best proof how *really* I love her. How do Byron and my Lady go on? there are strange rumours in the country about them.[1]

Ever yours, my dear Rogers,
Thomas Moore.

453. *To his Mother*

Russell, ii. 29, no. 287

Mayfield Cottage
[December, 1815]

My dearest Mother,

I know it delights you to hear of instances of friendship towards your own Tom, and I have one now to tell you that gave myself very great pleasure. My friend Douglas (whom I have not, you know, seen more than twice in eight or nine years) has just been appointed admiral on the Jamaica station, and the first thing he did was to offer me the secretaryship.[2] The salary is something

[1] The Byrons agreed on the legal terms of their separation on 17 Mar. 1816. (See Marchand, *Byron*, p. 590.)

[2] According to the *Royal Naval Biography* (London: Longman, 1823), vol. i, John Erskine Douglas was made a Rear-admiral on 4 June 1814, and was

under five hundred a-year, but the perquisites, even in peace, are considerable, and in case of war it is a sure fortune. He also tells me he has a fine house and near one hundred acres of land allowed him, which are all at my disposal. I, of course, have declined it, as the emoluments in peace are not sufficient to counteract the risk of sea, health, and other objections; but the friendliness and *courage* of the offer (considering the interest by which Douglas must have got the appointment) can never be forgotten by me.

We shall be all anxiety now, my dearest mother, to have accounts of your health, and your letters may be inclosed under cover to the person who franks this, 'Richard Arkwright, Esq., Ashbourne Hall, Derbyshire.' Bessy will write to Ellen the next time.

Have all sorts of comforts for yourself, my darling mother, and make my father draw upon me to furnish them: mind this. If we had you here we would nurse and make you well again; and perhaps at the first appearance of spring you will let me run over for you; the change of air and scene would do you good, and we should all return to Ireland with you. Ever your own,

Tom.

454. *To his Mother*

Russell, ii. 89, no. 341

Jan. 1. 1816.

My dearest Mother,

We were most happy to find, from dear Nell's letter, that your cough was gone, and I trust the pain in the side will soon go after it. Bessy has had a most severe bout of it, and is much weakened indeed; but I have just had her out in this sweet spring sunshine, that opens the new year so smilingly, and I think she is much better: her cough though, at night, is still very distressing.

The poor girl, of whose death I told you in my last, we now find died of an attack on the brain, and, during her delirium, she frequently sang parts of 'There's nothing bright but Heaven,'[1] and other Sacred Melodies of mine, which the poor young creature was a great admirer of. Ever my darling mother's own,

Tom.

nominated Commander-in-chief at Jamaica late in 1815. This letter must have been written, therefore, in December 1815, rather than in 1814, as given in Russell's edition.

[1] 'This World is All a Fleeting Show', *Poetry*, p. 256.

455. *To John Erskine Douglas*

Rice University

Mayfield
Saturday Jan[r] 13th 1816

My dear Douglas— We must be shabby enough to put you off from your engagement to us on Tuesday—but our House and ourselves are in such a state, that it would be any thing but kindness to admit you to such a concern— Smoky, wet rooms with a chorus of coughers & sneezers for inhabitants—our Cook at the point of death, and ourselves almost forgetting the use of her, from a long probation of water-gruel and cathartics— Such is the amiable state of our establishment, and such the horrors which I am sure you will have no objection to exchange for the warm rooms & rosy cheeks of our friends at Mayfield—[1] We have really been sad invalids, and Bessy was scarcely recovered herself before she had to undertake the nursing of *me*— Give our best regards to all at home, and tell your sister Isabella that John Cooper performed the commission for Bessy which she was kind enough to say she would undertake— Tell her too I am going to publish 'Oh yes—when the bloom' and, if she has no great objection to *suffer under* such an honour, I will dedicate it to her—[2]

Yours very truly
Thomas Moore.

We were rejoiced to hear that Caroline continued so well.

456. *To James Power*

Russell, ii. 89, no. 342

Sunday, Jan. 14. 1816.

My dear Sir,

I have been these two days past much better, have returned to my animal food and wine (which I think the cursed apothecary kept me from too long), and, except for a troublesome cough, which still hangs about me, am as well as ever. Many thanks for your kind solicitude about me. I shall certainly not encounter another winter in this coldest house of a most cold country, and I dare say it is somewhere near town that our next move will be to.

[1] Moore carelessly wrote 'Mayfield' instead of the name of another place to which Douglas had been invited.

[2] 'Oh, Yes! When the Bloom of Young Boyhood Is Over.' See *Melodies, Songs, Sacred Songs, and National Airs* (New York, 1825), p. 238. This poem was not included in the 1841 edition of Moore's works.

As to my spirits, they are, thank Heaven! pretty good. The only thing that sinks deep with me just now is the fear, almost to certainty, that I shall not be ready with my poem for the press till May,[1] which will put publication till after the summer quite out of the question. This annoys me, but I could not help it. I have not been idle; but my trip to Ireland threw me back most cruelly. I have received the proofs and copies of the words, and, in the course of this next week, shall put the whole job clean out of hand for you. I was doing a little song these few days past in spite of my headaches and weakness, but I shall throw it aside for the present, and think of nothing now but the dispatching the Sacred Songs for you. You must engrave 'Thou art, O God!'[2] as a single song.

Why have you not put in 'Ah! who shall see that glorious Day?'[3] It is in a style that we want very much, and I think you had much better include it. I hope you have sent duplicates of these last proofs to Stevenson, for of course he must see them.

I do not know how to thank you enough for your generosity about the pianoforte, neither am I quite sure that I can allow you to be so liberal to me; at least not till I am more settled than at present, for a gift of *yours* I should consider so sacred that I never could think of parting with it; and this might be inconvenient as long as we are in our vagabond state. So perhaps it is better to wait till I have some prospect of *fixing* somewhere; and, in the meantime, your interposition to delay my payment of Broadwood for this is quite as much as I can require of you; not that, after all, I think I am *by any means* likely to part with this sweet pianoforte; but one does not know what might happen to make it expedient. Ever yours, most truly,

Thomas Moore.

457. *To Mary Godfrey*

Russell, ii. 91, no. 343

Jan. 24. 1816.

You must not be angry with me for not writing to you: we have had nothing but illness in the house since you last heard from me. Scarcely had Bessy begun to show symptoms of recovery when *I* must needs imitate my betters, and be ill too. For about ten days I could hardly hold up my head; but I really think the apothecary

[1] *Lalla Rookh.*

[2] *Poetry*, p. 254.

[3] Probably 'Lord, Who Shall Bear that Day', *Poetry*, p. 260.

was, as usual, nine-tenths of my disease; for he starved and physicked me into such a state of debility, that, when the original complaint was gone, there was another, much worse, of his own manufacture, to proceed upon; but at last I took Molière's method of dealing with him, and am, accordingly, as well as ever: 'Il m'ordonne des remèdes; je ne les fais point, et je guéris.'[1] I wish I could say as much for poor Bessy, but her state of health gives me great uneasiness; indeed, she is not an instant free from pains, either in her back or head, and there appears a general weakness and derangement all over her: but her spirits and resolution keep her up wonderfully, and the regularity of our little *ménage* never suffers an instant from her indisposition. She went the other night to an Ashbourne assembly (the first time she has been in company since our return from Ireland), and the change in her looks struck every one. She feels, as I do, most sensibly your kindness in asking her to pass some time with you; and there is nothing she desires and raves of so incessantly as the seeing London, and the streets and the theatres once more; but no pleasure will tempt her to leave the children, and the impracticability of moving *with* them puts such a visit out of the question, till my present task is finished,[2] and I can shift my quarters nearer to you for good and all: indeed, *here* it is impossible to stay another winter; so I have said for these two winters past, and then, like the returning smiles of a mistress, the sweet summer looks of the little place made me fall in love with it again, and all the past was forgotten: but we have suffered too much, I think, *this* winter, from its damp, smokiness, and smallness, to let anything tempt us into a repetition of such horrors. How have *you* both stood the campaign? I fear, from what Rogers said in his letter, that my dear Lady Donegal has had some returns of her attacks,—is it so? Do tell me all particulars about yourselves; for your letters sometimes make me feel as if you thought I was a selfish fellow: I am so entirely the hero of them; but then, on second thoughts, I should *not* be *your* hero, if you thought me too much my *own;* so it is all right as it is, only *do* tell me a little more of your concerns—physical, moral, worldly, and spiritual.

We have had a melancholy event among us lately: a lovely young girl, of eighteen, left us a bride, and in six weeks afterwards was a corpse. It seemed as if her marriage bells had but just ceased, when we heard of her death. During her last delirium she sung

[1] See Moore's *Memoirs of Captain Rock* (Paris, 1835), chapter 9, p. 125, where the author quotes Molière's reply to Louis XIV, when the latter asked him what use Molière made of his physician.

[2] The writing of *Lalla Rookh.*

several of my Sacred Songs, of which the poor girl was a most enthusiastic admirer.[1] Good by. Ever faithfully yours,

Thomas Moore.

What account do you hear of Lord Byron and his wife? He never mentions her, but writes, I think, in lower spirits than usual.[2]

458. *To Lord Byron*

Moore, *Byron*, iii. 198

[January 1816]

And so you are a whole year married!—[3]

'It was last year I vow'd to thee
That fond impossibility.'[4]

Do you know, my dear B., there was a something in your last letter—a sort of unquiet mystery, as well as a want of your usual elasticity of spirits—which has hung upon my mind unpleasantly ever since.[5] I long to be near you, that I might know how you really look and feel; for these letters tell nothing, and one word, *a quattr'occhi*, is worth whole reams of correspondence. But only *do* tell me you are happier than that letter has led me to fear, and I shall be satisfied.

459. *To Lord Byron*

Sir John Murray

[January or February 1816]

My dear Byron—

I was very proud of the little you gave me at the beginning of your last letter, because I am sure you thought *twice* before you honoured me with it, and I hope I may long deserve it— As to my Poem, which you ask about, after many frights & miscarriages, it is at last in a fair way of being born and I think my Wife & I will lie in about the same time—June—but that is so late for a poetical parturition, and I am so very willing that the public *not* forget (for what will the public *not* forget?) the powerful impressions you have just made upon all their faculties, that I shall have no

[1] See letter No. 454, to his mother, 1 Jan. 1816.

[2] See letter No. 452, to Samuel Rogers, 26 Dec. 1815.

[3] Byron was married on 2 Jan. 1815.

[4] Lovelace, 'The Scrutiny', stanza 1.

[5] Moore is referring to the letter from Byron, 5 Jan. 1816 (*LJ*, iii. 252–4).

objection to let it sleep quietly over the summer, and try and fatten it up with hot-and-hot sunbeams in the dog-days—[1] I am sorry I must wait till 'we are veterans' before you will open to me

'The book, the story of your wandering life,
'Wherein you find more hours, *due* to *repentance*,
'Than time hath told you yet.—[2]'

Is it so with you? or are you, like me, reprobate enough to look back with complacency on what you have done?— I suppose repentance *must bring up the rear* with us all, but, at present, I should say with old Fontenelle 'Si je recommencais ma carrière, je ferois tout ce que j'ai fait'—[3]

There is *one* circumstance of your late life which I am *sure* I have guessed rightly—tho I sincerely hope it is not so bad as sometimes horrible imaginings would make it—you need not recur to it till we meet, nor even *then*, if you don't like it—but at all events with me you are safe & the same *malgré tout*—[4] I could love the Devil himself, if he were but such a bon diable as you are—and after all this is the true kind of affection— Your love that *picks* its *steps* was never worth a rush—

Good bye—if you have any *libels* that you wish to see in print, I am going to add two or three things, (since published) to the Fourteenth Edition of the bag,[5] and shall insert yours, as *from a friend*, with much delight—your lines about the bodies of Charles & Henry are, I find, circulated with wonderful avidity—even some Clods in this neighbourhood have had a copy sent by some 'Young ladies in town'—[6]

Ever yours
T. Moore

I hope I do not overload your privilege this time.

[1] Moore is alluding to the fact that Byron's *Giaour*, *Bride of Abydos*, and *Corsair* anticipated his own *Lalla Rookh*.

[2] Not identified.

[3] Not identified.

[4] Moore is probably referring to Byron's domestic difficulties. See letter No. 452, to Samuel Rogers, 26 Dec. 1815.

[5] *The Twopenny Post-Bag* was first published in 1813 and ran through at least eleven editions in the first year.

[6] Byron received a letter from Lady Melbourne, who passed on to him the story that an alteration in the tombhouse at Windsor had disclosed that Charles I and Henry VIII were buried in the same tomb. The Prince Regent was supposed to have superintended the opening of the tomb on 1 Apr. 1813. The funeral of his mother-in-law, the Duchess of Brunswick, having been held the day before, the Prince was in high spirits. He gave the centre sapphire of Charles's crown to Princess Charlotte and acted out the decapitation on one of his guests. Byron turned the story into a bit of satire against the Prince. See Byron, *Poetry*, vii. 35.

460. *To James Power*

New York Public

[Rec^{d} Feb^{r} 12th 1816]

When you are sending again, pray, let me have the First ms. of the German Melodies—you cannot think what a set was made at me to write for that work.[1]

Saturday Morning

My dear Sir— Just as I was finishing up these for the Caravan last night, I found the references under 'Fallen is thy throne'[2] were not given (as I rather think I gave them in *my* manuscript) fully & correctly—this delayed me till now—but if they go by the Traveller this morning, you will get them, I dare say, quite as soon as if they went last night— The receipt & letter for Lee, I will send thro Greville on Monday—

Ever yours
T. Moore

I must have Revise—how comes your Printer to be so sparing of his Presses?

461. *To Lord Byron*

Moore, *Byron*, iii. 200

[February 1816]

I am most anxious to hear from you, though I doubt whether I ought to mention the subject on which I am so anxious. If, however, what I heard last night, in a letter from town, be true, you will know immediately what I allude to, and just communicate as much or as little upon the subject as you think proper;—only *something* I should like to know, as soon as possible, from yourself, in order to set my mind at rest with respect to the truth or falsehood of the report.[3]

[1] The two German melodies included in the *National Airs* are 'There Comes a Time' and 'When the First Summer Bee', *Poetry*, pp. 239 and 247.

[2] *Poetry*, p. 255.

[3] Byron answered Moore's letter on 29 Feb. 1816 (*LJ*, iii. 266–8). 'In the meantime, I am at war "with all the world and his wife;" or rather "all the world and *my* wife" are at war with me, and have not yet crushed me,—whatever they *may* do.' He warned Moore against trying to defend him.

462. *To Leigh Hunt*

B.M. Add. MS. 37210, f. 172

Mayfield Cottage
March 7th 1816

My Dear Hunt— I *do* forgive you for your long silence tho you have much less right to be careless about our non-intercourse than *I* have—if I knew as little about you & your existence as you know of me, I should not feel quite so patient under the privation—but I have the advantage of communing with you, for a very delightful hour, every Tuesday evening:[1] of knowing your thoughts upon all that passes and exclaiming 'right!—bravo!—exactly!' to every sentiment you express—whereas, from the very few signs of life *I* give in the world, you can only take my existence for granted, as we do that of the

little woman under the hill,
Who, *if* she's not gone, must live there still—[2]

however I *do* forgive you—and only wish I could pay you back a millesimal part of the pleasure, which—in various ways—as poet, as politician, as partial friend, you have lately given me— Your Rimini[3] is beautiful—and its only faults such as I know you are aware of & prepared to justify—there is that maiden charm of originality about it—that 'integer, illibatusque succus' which Columella[4] tells us the bees extract—that freshness of the living fount, which we look in vain for in the bottled-up Heliconian of ordinary Bards—in short, it is Poetry—and notwithstanding the quaintnesses, the coinages and even affectations, with which, *here* and *there*

I had just got so far, my dear Hunt, when I was interrupted by a prosing neighbour, who has put every thing I meant to say out of my head—so, there I must leave you—impaled on the point of this broken sentence,—and wishing you as little torture there as the nature of the case will allow— I have only time to say again that your Poem is beautiful—and that, if I not exactly agree with [*sic*] *some* of your notions about versification & language the general spirit of the work has more than satisfied my utmost expectations of you— If you go on thus, you will soon make some of Apollo's guests sit 'below the salt'.— The additions to this latter Poem are excellent and the lines on Music at the end are full of beauty—[5]

[1] By reading the *Examiner*.

[2] One of the 'Mother Goose' rhymes.

[3] Hunt published *The Story of Rimini* in 1816.

[4] Lucius Junius Moderatus Columella, first century A.D., was a Roman writer on agriculture, author of *De Re Rustica*.

[5] Moore is probably referring here to Hunt's *Feast of the Poets*, which was

There are many of the lines of Rimini that 'haunt me like a passion'—[1] I don't know whether I ought to own that these are among the number—I quote from memory—

> The war was short, was fugitive, is past,
> The song that sweetens it may always last.[2]

I am afraid *you* will set this down among your regular, sing-song couplets—to me it is all music—

Is it true that our friend Lord B. has taken to the beautifully 'mammosa' Mrs. Mardyn, who after this will call him a 'searcher of dark bosoms'? Not a word to *him*, however, about this question of mine.[3]

Ever, my dear Hunt, most faithfully
Yours

Thomas Moore

I hope to deliver my mighty work into Longman's hands in May, but, of course, it will not go to press till after the summer.[4]

463. *To Lord Byron*

Moore, *Byron*, iii. 203

[March 1816]

I am much in the same state as yourself with respect to the subject of your letter, my mind being so full of things which I don't know how to write about, that *I* too must defer the greater part of them till we meet in May, when I shall put you fairly on your trial for all crimes and misdemeanors. In the mean time, you will not be at a loss for judges, nor executioners either, if they could have their will. The world, in their generous ardour to take what they call the weaker side, soon contrive to make it most formidably the strongest. Most sincerely do I grieve at what has happened. It has upset all my wishes and theories as to the influence of marriage on your life; for, instead of bringing you, as I expected, into something like a regular orbit, it has only cast you off again into infinite space, and left you, I fear, in a far worse state than it found you. As to

'amended and enlarged' in 1815. The last stanza but one lauds Moore as a singer.

[1] Wordsworth, 'Tintern Abbey', l. 77.

[2] Neither these lines nor others resembling them appear in *The Story of Rimini*.

[3] Marchand, *Byron*, 602 n., mentions the rumour that Byron had an intrigue with Mrs. Mardyn.

[4] *Lalla Rookh*.

defending you, the only person with whom I have yet attempted this task is myself; and, considering the little I know upon the subject, (or rather, perhaps, *owing* to this cause,) I have hitherto done it with very tolerable success. After all, your *choice* was the misfortune. I never liked,—but I'm here wandering into the *απορρητα*, and so must change the subject for a far pleasanter one, your last new poems, which, &c. &c.[1]

464. *To Lord Byron*

Moore, *Byron*, iii. 207

[March 1816]

I had certainly no right to say any thing about the unluckiness of your choice, though I rejoice now that I did, as it has drawn from you a tribute which, however unaccountable and mysterious it renders the whole affair, is highly honourable to both parties. What I meant in hinting a doubt with respect to the object of your selection did not imply the least impeachment of that perfect amiableness which the world, I find, by common consent, allows to her. I only feared that she might have been too perfect—too *precisely* excellent—too matter-of-fact a paragon for you to coalesce with comfortably; and that a person whose perfection hung in more easy folds about her, whose brightness was softened down by some of 'those fair defects which best conciliate love,' would, by appealing more dependently to your protection, have stood a much better chance with your good nature. All these suppositions, however, I have been led into by my intense anxiety to acquit you of any thing like a capricious abandonment of such a woman*; and, totally in the dark as I am with respect to all but the fact of your separation, you cannot conceive the solicitude, the fearful solicitude, with which I look forward to a history of the transaction from your own lips when we meet,—a history in which I am sure of, at least, *one* virtue—manly candour.

* It will be perceived from this that I was as yet unacquainted with the true circumstances of the transaction. [*Moore's note*]

[1] This was Moore's reply to Byron's letter of 29 Feb. 1816. See letter No. 461, to Lord Byron, February 1816.

465. *To Lady Donegal*

Russell, ii. 95, no. 345

Mayfield
April 4. 1816.

You know what it is to put off answering a letter; *right well* you know it; nobody better; and it is not to you I am going to apologise, but to my dear, trusty, and well-beloved correspondent at your side, who deserves all the punctuality, good letter-writing, wit, and fair penmanship I do *not* bestow upon her; and the fact is, when I got her last letter we were from home, actually smoked out of our house in those high winds, and blown into any of those of our neighbours that would give us shelter; and when we returned, I had so much to do for Power, besides my own never-ceasing job, that I could not muster up five minutes for letter-writing for the life of me. I cannot tell you how I am longing to be with you this sweet weather. I really believe spring has as much to do with friendship as with love, for I never think half so *genially* of all those I like as at this season. How soon do you leave town this year? I hope not till after June, as that will be about the period of my flourishing there. I have been thinking, as France is in such a ticklish state, to take a run over to Paris, just for about a fortnight, to take one peep into that great cauldron of revolutions, before the 'bubble, bubble' begins again, as it will before long, as sure as Louis is an old woman. By-the-bye, are you, or are you not, a little ashamed of your dear friends, the Ministers? I don't mean on the score of their wisdom, talents, &c., for in this respect they are, of course, as admirable as ever, but for the shabbiness with which they are daily surrendering so many wise, indispensable, and sine-qua-nonical measures to the bullies of Opposition. 'Time was, that when the brains were out, the man would die;'[1] or that when a Minister (as Dogberry says) 'was *proved* a fool, he would go near to be *thought* so too;'[2] but now we see that so he keeps his place, he need not be nice as to *whose* measures he keeps it by: if he hasn't the vigour or the sense to force what *he* thinks right upon his adversaries, he has the convenient passiveness to let them force what *they* please upon *him*. We shall soon have all measures originate with the Opposition: they will lay the eggs, and the kind Cuckoo Ministers will hatch them. Bessy, though a little better within these few days, continues in general as weak or even weaker than ever; but I look with much hope to the summer for her

[1] *Macbeth*, III. iv. 78.
[2] *Much Ado about Nothing*, IV. ii. 23.

amendment. The little ones are quite well, and Barbara, if she was but prettier, promises to be all we could wish her,—intelligent, sweet-tempered, and affectionate. How is *your* dear Barbara? You have not mentioned her to me this long time. I suppose I shall find her grown beyond redemption: what a pity they can't stay little young things for ever.

Be it known to you that on Saturday last I took the chair at the anniversary dinner of the Lancastrian Society[1] at Derby, and astonished not only the company but myself by sundry speeches, of which the Derby paper of to-day gives such a flourishing account, that I blush to the eyes; seriously, I never saw anything like the enthusiastic effect I produced, and of all exertions of talent, public speaking is certainly the most delightful: the effect is so immediately under one's own eyes, and the harvest of its fame so instantaneous. This was the first time I ever really prepared or exerted myself in speaking, and oh! what would I *not* give to have many and higher opportunities for it. Would *you* bring me in if you could? *that* you would, in spite of Dogberry and the Cuckoo Ministers; I know you would. Ever yours,

T. M.

In a letter I have had lately from Lord Byron he says, 'There is not existing a better, a brighter, or more amiable creature than Lady Byron.'[2] Is not this odd? What can be the reason of the separation?

466. *To his Mother*

Russell, ii. 98, no. 347

London
May [3] 1816.

My darling Mother,

Safe arrived—quite well, but more pulled about, fussed, and bustled than ever. To-night I go to the Queen's house to see the bride in all her nuptial glory.[3] Only think of Lady Donegal's courage to ask permission to take me.

I dine so early, for the purpose of being there in time, that I must bid good by, my own dearest mother. Love to father and Nell.

I must leave this letter with the Donegals in hope of a frank; but if she cannot get one, I have bid her send it off, and for once you must pay postage.

[1] See letter No. 373, to Samuel Rogers, 10 Apr. 1814.

[2] See *LJ*, iii. 272.

[3] See letter No. 467, to his mother, 4 May 1816.

467. *To his Mother*

Russell, ii. 99, no. 348

Saturday, May 4. 1816.

My dearest Mother,

What do you think of *me*, Tom Brown the Younger, having been at the Queen's house to see the royal bride in all her nuptial array? Lady Donegal had the courage to ask permission of the Princess Elizabeth for me to go. The Princess Charlotte stopped, as she passed, to shake hands with Lady Donegal, by whose side I stood, so that I had an admirable view of her. I am almost tired of the bustle of this place already, and even after a short week begin to sigh for my little cottage and Bessy again.

468. *To Francis Jeffrey*

Yale

London
May 23rd 1816 [postmark May 26, 1816]

My dear Jeffrey— Some friends of yours have just told me that I *ought* to write something for the Review, and one of them proposed 'Vathek' (the original French) to me— Now, tho all your kind praises have been ineffectual, in warming me into any degree of confidence in my own powers as a reviewer, yet, if you wish it & have employed no one better for the purpose, I *will* undertake Vathek, and shall set about it as soon as I receive your mandate, directed to me to Mayfield, for which place I shall be off the day after tomorrow heartily weary of the month's bustle I have had here—tho returning full of such strange knowledge, such monstrous recollections of men, women & things, as would astonish the innocent May-fieldians but to hint at—[1] How I should like to have a day's talk with you about Lord Byron, about *Glenarvon*, about all the extraordinary topics that are agitated 'usque ad nauseam' in this town!—but you & I, I fear, tho not paralells [*sic*] (would we were!) are destined never to meet— I had some idea of offering myself to you to quiz Christabel (out of which, by the bye, some one has applied a line to the Authoress of Glenarvon— 'What *can* ail the mastiff bitch?')—but I have been lately told

[1] Jeffrey replied to this letter on May 28 (Russell, ii. 100, no. 350). Although he accepted Moore's offer to review *Vathek*, the article was never printed. The chances are that Moore did not write it, choosing instead to write a comical piece about *Glenarvon*, which Jeffrey, following the advice of friends, did not publish. (See letter No. 474, to Mary Godfrey, 18 July 1816.)

that Coleridge is poor—so poor as to be obliged to apply to the Literary Fund—and as this is no laughing matter—why—I shall let him alone—[1]

I hope you mean to praise Rimini—I would do it *for spite*—Rogers is quite well, and has made me very happy by telling me how kindly you spoke of me at Paris.

Ever faithfully yours
Thomas Moore.

469. *To his Mother*

Russell, ii. 99, no. 349

Monday, May, 1816.

My dearest Mother,

I cannot get a frank, and have not time to write *round* through Joe, so I must dispatch this as it is; to tell you I am quite well, in *terrible* request, never half so much so before, and that, flattering as it is all, I am delighted at the idea of being off on Friday next (as I expect) to the cottage. This, I know, will give you more pleasure than any thing else, as it proves I am happy at home, which is the source of every comfort and virtue in this life. I only wish you were there to make it still happier to me. God bless my darling mother. Ever your own,

Tom.

[1] In spite of disclaimers by P. L. Carver, 'The Authorship of a Review of *Christabel* Attributed to Hazlitt', *JEGP*, xxix (1930), 562–78, and Catherine Macdonald Maclean, *Born under Saturn* (New York, 1944), pp. 362 and 600, the review of *Christabel* in the *Edinburgh Review*, xxvii, no. liii (September 1816), 58–67, has been persistently attributed to Hazlitt. In maintaining that it was Moore who wrote the article, Elisabeth Schneider, 'The Unknown Reviewer of *Christabel*: Jeffrey, Hazlitt, Tom Moore', *PMLA*, lxx (1955), 417–32, cites as external evidence a significant passage in T. F. Dibdin's *Reminiscences of a Literary Life* (London, 1836), i. 340. Dibdin claimed that he knew enough of the 'warm *Irish* heart of the reviewer' to affirm that the article would not be so harsh were it to be written again. Professor Schneider also calls attention to a letter from Coleridge to the Reverend Francis Wrangham in *Unpublished Letters*, ed. E. L. Griggs (New Haven, 1933), ii. 196–8, in which Coleridge maintained that 'Jeffrey wrote to Anacreon Moore, begging him, as a favour to supply a grand quiz of the poem'. She maintains further that the style, tone, and opinion expressed in the review are consistent with Moore's writings, but not with those of Hazlitt or Jeffrey.

Arguing solely from internal evidence (because of what he considers a lack of sufficient information from external sources), Hoover H. Jordan, 'Thomas Moore and the Review of *Christabel*', *MP*, liv (1956), 95–105, concludes that the review has 'something of Hazlitt and a good deal of Jeffrey' and suggests a kind of unofficial collaboration, in which the latter corrected and added to a manuscript submitted by the former. Professor Jordan maintains that internal evidence will not support the contention that Moore wrote the review.

For further evidence that Moore was not the author of the review see letter No. 484, to John Murray, 24 Dec. 1816.

470. *To Samuel Rogers*

Harvard, Widener Library

Mayfield
June 30th 1816

My dear Rogers— July will be here to-morrow, and yet not a word have we heard of the promised visit, which we are both, I assure you, looking very anxiously for, and beginning to think you as slow as the summer itself—do, let us know when we may expect you— yesterday evening (which was a very beautiful one) while Bessy on her donkey and I with a child in each hand were taking our after-dinner ramble, she said 'how I should like Mr Rogers to meet us all this way unexpectedly!'— We are going on Thursday next to pass four days with our worthy old friend, the Rector of Kegworth, whose garden you admired so much when you were there, and this is the only *gay* thing from home that we have before us during the summer—so that you are sure of us whenever you come, and the less hurry you are in to leave us again, the better— I see by the papers that poor Sheridan is nearly gone and that his numerous friends are so anxious in their enquiries that the knocker & bell are obliged to be taken off! This is excellent— 'Send for Burgess—I say—send for Burgess'—[1] There will be one subscriber less to the Monument, I think, for that night at Brookes's—our friend the speech-maker will never have the face to put down his name after your joke— How does the sale of the books go on? and will Lord H. be freer of his name in the title-page and preface than he was at the bottom of that awkward trier of friendship—a draft?—I dare I dare [*sic*] swear he will— I shall never forget the way in which you said, at Miss Pigon's dinner—talking of Brummel— 'I suppose his friends are too great to be of any use to him'— I knew what was in your mind—by the bye, How [*sic*] is *she?*

Let me entreat you to read 'Emma'—it is the very perfection of novel-writing—and I cannot praise it more highly than by saying it is often extremely like your own method of describing things—so much effect, with so little effort!—[2]

We do nothing but rain here—and so little sun has yet reached us that I doubt whether we shall muster up 'one green pea' (poor Brummel's favourite quantity) for your dinner while you stay with us—

Best remembrances to your sister from hers & yours ever

Thomas Moore

[1] Sheridan had a lawyer named Burgess.

[2] Jane Austen's *Emma* was published in 1816.

471. *To John E. Hall*

The Collector, ix (February 1896), 67[1]

Ashbourne, Derbyshire
June, 1816.

My Dear Sir: Your last letter reached me in Ireland and I lost no time in transmitting the inclosure for Mr. Adams to a friend of mine in London, who however was not able to find out any such person—so that I suppose Mr. Adams had already departed for America.

It gives me great pleasure to find that you remember me so kindly, and I would very willingly make my peace with those of your countrymen who think *otherwise* of me—this life however is just long enough to commit errors in, but too short to allow us time to repair them—and there are few of my errors I regret more sincerely than the rashness I was guilty of in publishing those crude and boyish tirades against the Americans.[2] My sentiments both with respect to their National and individual character are much changed since then, and I should blush as a lover of Liberty, if I allowed the hasty prejudices of my youth to blind me now to the bright promise which America affords of a better and happier order of things than the World has perhaps ever yet witnessed. If *you* but continue to be as good *republicans* as we of Europe seem to be determined to be good *royalists*, the new and the old World need soon have no other designation, than the Sphere of Freemen and the Hemisphere of Slaves.

My note about Washington to which you allude and which I had forgot with all the other nonsense of that work, has I find in recurring to the Editions of my Epistles, been ommitted in every one since the First, which was as speedy an admission as I could well make of the inconsiderateness and falsehood of the accusation.[3]

I have been living for these four or five years past in a country retirement, as happy as a most lovely and amiable wife, two or three little rosy children, a few books and a piano forte can make me. A Poetical work of mine for which Messrs. Longman & Co. have agreed to give me three thousand pounds will appear early next Spring.[4] As to my other occupations, I publish Irish Melodies from time to time and write occasionally in the Edinburgh Review,

[1] This letter was submitted to the *Collector* by Charles Henry Hart.

[2] See letter No. 87, to his mother, 13 June 1804.

[3] Moore must have meant Jefferson, since the attack in the *Epistles* was on him (see letter No. 87).

[4] *Lalla Rookh.*

and now your kind inquiries with respect to my pursuits are answered.

If any of the friends who were so hospitable to me in Philadelphia preserve but half the remembrance of *me* which I have of *them*, pray present my very warmest good wishes to them. To *Jacques*,[1] to Mr. and Mrs. Hopkins, and I fear I must not add poor Dennie; is he really gone? To yourself I wish every success which your talents and industry so well deserve and beg you will believe me.

Faithfully yours
Thomas Moore.

472. *To James Corry*

Russell, viii. 216

Mayfield
July 1. 1816.

My dear Corry,

It is not right that you and I, whatever may be our respective lazinesses, should continue so long without hearing from each other. I thought to provoke you into some signs of animation, by sending you, about a month or two since, a newspaper with some account of my oratorical proceedings at Derby.[2] But you were silent, and though I know of old that your epistolary fountain can run as readily as it runs pleasantly, yet, somehow, for *me* it has dried up of late, and you seem resolved to join the ranks of those unreasonable friends of mine, who will not write to me for that worst of all possible reasons, because *I* do not write to *them*. I was in hopes, as our friend Sam says, that you were above such 'vulgar prejudices.' Rogers and I, with *quantities* to say to each other, exchange letters about once a quarter. The Donegals (the most generous of you all) give me by regular agreement three letters for every one of mine; but Joe Atkinson is the most *favoured* of my correspondents, for he receives two letters from me every week—for my mother, and answers them punctually.

I heard from him, of your celebration of Richard Power's recovery, and I only wish, next to being there, that I had had your own account of it. When does he return?

Do you know, between ourselves, I think it not at all unlikely that I shall, after the publication of my poem, take to living for two or three years in or near Dublin? What do you say to this? Or will you still continue saying *nothing* to me? I have some

[1] Hart identifies 'Jacques' as Samuel Ewing.
[2] See letter No. 465, to Lady Donegal, 4 Apr. 1816.

thoughts of undertaking a very voluminous work about Ireland, (if properly encouraged by patres nostri—the Longmans,) and this will require my residence, for at least the time I have mentioned, in Dublin.[1] I think I shall be free, quite free, for the *Kilkenny* work,[2] by the time Richard Power returns; but really till I get this three-thousand pounder fired off,[3] it is in vain to think of doing any thing else *well*, and well should that be done which is done for you and him.

Sometimes Bessy and I have thought it possible we should receive a line from you to say that you were coming to England this summer, and would give us a sight of you and Mrs. Corry at the cottage,—now or never, 'tis our last summer here. I go to town in January; to *press* in February; and to the dogs (I mean the Critics) about the beginning of May.

Best love to Mrs. Corry. I'm afraid she does not like me so well since my marriage. Women never do. But if I wrong her, let her say so stoutly; and at all events, remembrances as warm as ever to her and you, from

Yours most faithfully,
Thomas Moore.

Bessy sends her kindest regards to you both.

473. *To his Mother*

Russell, ii. 102, no. 352

July 11. 1816.

My dearest Mother,

We got dear Nell's letter last night; and Bessy is afraid, by what she says, that she has not received a letter from her which I inclosed, I think, about a week ago. Perhaps, in my hurry, I may have omitted it, but I shall look among my papers. I sent one letter last week to you through Corry, which I fear you may not receive, from his being perhaps out of town.

Poor Sheridan! the Prince (I hear from town), after neglecting him, and leaving him in the hands of bailiffs all the time of his illness,

[1] Moore is probably referring to the *Memoirs of Captain Rock*, which Longman published in 1824. He evidently had not conceived the idea of writing the *History of Ireland*, the first volume of which did not appear until 1835.

[2] Moore was probably collaborating with Corry on a history of the Kilkenny Theatricals. See letters Nos. 277 and 311, to James Corry, 30 Dec. 1812 and June 1813.

[3] *Lalla Rookh*, for which he was to receive £3,000. See letter No. 407, to Longman & Company, 17 Dec. 1814.

sent him at last the princely donation of two hundred pounds, which Sheridan returned. I hope this is true.[1]

I have given notice to my landlord, and shall be off from this as soon as the winter shows his ugly face; that is, I suppose, about the latter end of October.

It grieves me to hear of the poor car's being such an invalid; and if my father could but get credit for a new one for a few months, I think I could manage to supply him by the time. Just now, and for two or three months to come, I shall be without one *extra* pound; if, indeed, I am lucky enough to have any *intra* ones; but *couldn't* you manage it somehow before the fine weather is all over, my dearest mother? the exercise is so necessary to you. Ever your own,

Tom.

474. *To Mary Godfrey*

Russell, ii. 103, no. 353

Mayfield
July 18. 1816.

I know you will say that I put off my letter to this 'last day of the world' in the hope of escaping, by *any* means, from the trouble of writing. But I am not quite so desperate, and I hope we shall have many 'more last' days (though of somewhat a sunnier kind than this is) to give me an opportunity of convincing you that, though appearances may be against me, I am really a very good correspondent. Do you know what the chemists call 'latent heat?' This I am full of. It is a property which some bodies have of keeping all their warmth to themselves; or, rather, *in* themselves; which makes them seem not half so warm as other bodies which have all their warmth on the surface. Now this is the case with me; and therefore, whenever you are long without hearing from me, set it down at once to 'latent heat,' and console yourself with the idea of its being all snug and warm in my heart, instead of lavishing its precious particles through the post-office. Seriously and really I ought to have written sooner; but, as I am very busy, and have no news for you,—nothing, in short, to send but a few bad jokes, which, like *over*-dead game, will hardly *keep* to town,—I thought I might as well let *you* begin with your 'How d'ye do?'

[1] Sheridan died on 7 July 1816. The rumour was circulated that he died in dire poverty and that offers of assistance were made by various people, including the Prince. Although certain offers were proffered and refused, Sheridan was not in need at the time of his death. See letter No. 697, to Charles Sheridan, 16 Apr. 1826.

and then, like Paddy Blake's echo, I could answer 'Very well, I thank ye.' I found Bessy, I thought, a little better on my return, which I attribute a good deal to her having passed the time away from home, and out of the reach of those domestic cares which, limited as they are, she feels much too anxiously and busily for that repose, both of mind and body, which is so necessary to her. If I could but afford the money and time, I am sure a few months of rambling and idleness would do her far more service than all the doctors in the world. She sometimes looks so wan and feeble as to make me quite miserable. I have given notice to our landlord, and, as soon as the winter months set in (at least those that don't call themselves summer ones, like the present), we shall hope to be off to you. My ulterior plans are so uncertain, that I think for the winter I shall only take a small furnished house somewhere near London.

Do you know that I was lately fool enough to waste a few days on a review of Glenarvon, and, thinking it rather comical, sent it to Jeffrey, who appears to have thought the same of it. But, in consequence of numerous applications he had from town, he pledged himself to more than one friend *not* to admit any mention of the book in his Review. Horner was one of the advisers, and I think, upon the whole, they were right.[1]

Those two little brothers, the Powers, are going to war ding-dong, and seem resolved to be 'belligerent Powers,' as well as their betters.[2] I am delighted that the work they come to issue upon is the Sacred Songs,[3] as from them not even Garrow[4] himself will be able to extract indecency.

Our little ones are quite well. Bessy was all delight at your presents, and is keeping the scarf for town display. Ever yours, with best love to Lady D. and sister Philly,

T. M.

475. *To his Mother*

Russell, ii. 105, no. 354

Sunday, July 21. 1816.

My dearest Mother,

For want of news I send you a letter we got last night from our Derby friend, Mr. Strutt, which will show you what kindness pursues me everywhere. There is nothing I should like better than

[1] See letter No. 468, to Francis Jeffrey, 23 May 1816.

[2] See letter No. 266, to James Power, 23 Nov. 1812.

[3] The *Sacred Songs* appeared in 1816.

[4] Probably Sir William Garrow. See the Glossary of Proper Names.

what he proposes, and it would do Bessy infinite service; but, besides the expense of joining them at Ramsgate (which I could not manage), it would unsettle all my plans of business for the rest of the summer; and Bessy, who is always self-denying and prudent, says, if *I* were wild enough to think of taking her, she would not let me. She was very ill all yesterday, but she is better to-day. Ever my darling mother's own,

Tom.

476. *To his Mother*

Russell, ii. 105, no. 355

Thursday [August 5] 1816.

My dearest Mother,

You will get either by to-day's or to-morrow's post a Morning Chronicle, with some lines on the death of Sheridan by *me*, which you must send back when you have done with them.[1] Let old Joe see them first; but you need not mention to any one else their being mine. Bessy has just been out walking to pay some bills, and call upon some of her poor sick women, to whom she is very kind and useful at very moderate expense. This delights her more than all the finery and company in the world. I never cease regretting, my dearest mother, that you have not an opportunity of seeing her in her own element—home and quiet. Mary Dalby (whose long and sincere attachment to me makes her a very quick-sighted judge) said to me at the end of a fortnight she passed with us, 'I do not think in the world you could have found another creature so suited to you as that.' And she was right. God bless you, my dearest mother. Ever your affectionate,

Tom.

477. *To his Mother*

Russell, ii. 106, no. 356

Sunday, August 18. 1816.

My dearest Mother,

I have only time to say that Rogers has just left us; he seemed to enjoy himself very much, and it was with some difficulty I got off going with him to the Lakes. Unluckily I cannot spare the time from my various jobs.

He made Bessy very happy by giving her, when he was going

[1] Moore's 'Lines on the Death of Sheridan', *Poetry*, p. 454, appeared in the *Morning Chronicle* on Monday, 5 Aug. 1816.

away, two pounds to lay out for the family of one of her poor women, whom he saw with her. He is an excellent fellow.

You will see by the Chronicle that my lines upon Sheridan were published in a pamphlet by some one, at 6*d.* price.[1] Rogers tells me they made a great sensation. Ever your own,

Tom.

478. *To Lady Donegal*

Russell, ii. 107, no. 358

Sept. 24. 1816.

I will not stop to make apologies for being so long without writing. My excuse is, that I had not time; but then, I have not time to make the excuse, as I merely seize the opportunity of a cover to Power to inclose a few hasty hieroglyphics to you. Part of my business lately has been gaiety; the business, of all others, I was born for. Bessy's doctor thought a trip to Matlock would do her good, and there accordingly we passed eight or nine days, dancing, walking, and keeping-never-minding any thing; for which Bessy, I think, was evidently better, and I, you may swear, not at all the worse. Rogers staid with us here from the Wednesday to Sunday, and left 'an image of himself' (I mean, intellectually speaking), *very favourable indeed*, on the minds both of Bessy and the little ones. He was indeed particularly amiable; and took no fright at the superfluity either of melted butter or of maids, and even saw with composure a little boy who comes to clean my shoes; not that I can quite answer for his subsequent reflections on these luxuries.

As the time approaches for leaving our cottage, I begin to feel a little reluctance, and shall, I dare say, linger on here till the period of my publishing is near.[2] Bessy is certainly a little better, and a break-up of our establishment just at this moment would be very deranging. She was delighted with the confidential frankness of your letter to her, and felt something far beyond the mere *honour* that it did her, though that was felt too, as it ought to be.

Tell our dear Mary that I look for it, under her own hand and seal, that she is quite as well and waggish as ever. Ever yours,

T. Moore.

[1] See letter No. 476, to his mother, 5 Aug. 1816.
[2] Until the publication of *Lalla Rookh*.

479. *To James Power*

Russell, ii. 108, no. 359

Tuesday, Sept. 24. 1816.

My dear Sir,

I send you a very short, but very beautiful Melody. It ought to have been a Sacred Song this time, but I took a fancy to this air, and was resolved to strike while the anvil was hot. I should be happy to think that my work now would prove as *durable* as it is *quick;* but though I post on in this way, I shall not be so unjust either to *you* or *myself* as to let either collection appear till I am perfectly satisfied with all their ingredients. There are two or three of the Irish ones equal to any I have done; and one in particular ('This Earth is the Planet'),[1] which will be very popular in my own singing of it; but our plan is to go on till we can select twelve *super-excellents.*

As the time approaches for our giving up the cottage, I begin to feel very reluctant, and shall probably linger on as long at least as there is any thing like tolerable weather; indeed, I feel a little afraid of a new place on account of the *finances;* for here, whenever I have not the supplies, I have at least, *credit*, which could not be expected in a new residence; we shall see, however. I have been expecting your answer about my Dedicatory Songs. Ever yours, very truly,

Thomas Moore.

Do you know that there is an edition of my Melodies published in Philadelphia. I wish we could get them.

480. *To his Mother*

Russell, ii. 106, no. 357

September, 1816.

My dearest Mother,

I was near letting this day go by, and it is the middle of the week, and then you would have reason to scold me for my neglect: but indeed you are very good and forgiving to all my little forgetfulnesses, which are not, after all, *very* heavy, for I never cease thinking of my own dears at home; and it is only business sometimes that make me seem (as Lord Moira expresses it) 'oblivious'[2]

[1] 'They May Rail at This Life', *Poetry*, p. 215. The last line of the first three stanzas is a refrain: 'This earth is a planet for you, love, and me.' The fourth stanza ends with a variation: 'And leave earth to such spirits as you, love, and me.'

[2] See letter No. 281, to Lady Donegal, December 1812.

of them. You will be amused at what Hunt says of my 'Magdalen' Hymns, in the Examiner I send you.[1] Bessy gives her best love. We have been paying visits to-day, and she is very tired. The little ones are quite well. I write in the midst of chatter, at Mrs. Belcher's. Ever your own,

Tom.

481. *To James Power*

Russell, ii. 109, no. 360

Wednesday, Oct. 1. 1816.

My dear Sir,

I send you a Sacred Melody, which is, I believe, rather of a 'Magdalen' cast[2] (as Hunt very prettily said of them the other day), but the remaining verses will retrieve this fault. I think Stevenson may harmonise the air for three voices very charmingly. I grieve much at your difference with him, and trust that it will never go so far as to separate our alliance; for, let them say what they will, no man in general could understand or please me half so well. He has done the little duet of 'If Thou'lt be Mine,'[3] beautifully; it is as pretty a thing, and will be as much sung, as any in the Melodies.

I have long been intending to ask you whether it is probable I shall be called upon by either you or your brother in the course of your law proceedings in Dublin this winter.[4] I wish to ascertain this point, as it might a good deal influence my movements on leaving Derbyshire.

I have had a letter from your brother, but have not time now to advert to its contents. Ever yours,

Thos. Moore.

[1] Moore is mentioned in a review of Byron's *Monody on the Death of Sheridan* (1816), the *Examiner*, Sunday, 22 Sept. 1816, no. 456, p. 603:

> [Byron's] character therefore as a poet is also his own;—a thing which can be said of perhaps but two other living poets,—Wordsworth and Moore, the former of whom is a metaphysical genius and the latter a refined Bacchanalanian one, living in a world of wit, garlands, and music.
>
> But as Mr. Wordsworth will never be a narrative poet nor Mr. Moore a very grave one (for his very hymns have a Magdalen air extremely reminiscent), so Lord Byron will never be skilful in addresses, nor in any other oratorical part of poetry.

[2] 'Were Not the Sinful Mary's Tears', *Poetry*, p. 258.

[3] *Poetry*, p. 214.

[4] See letter No. 266, to James Power, 23 Nov. 1812.

482. *To John Murray*

Sir John Murray

Mayfield Cottage, Ashbourne
Novr 21st 1816

My dear Sir— I shall thank you to send me down Lord Byron's two new Poems, as soon as the Prisoner of Chillon is published—[1] Where is *he* now? and could you forward a letter for me to him? *I* shall go to Press, I think, about the end of February, if Mr Hunt of Bristol will let any of us exist so long— What a time for Poetry!—

I shall have occasion, I think, in about two or three weeks hence, to draw upon the Longmans for a hundred pounds to meet my Christmas disbursements— Will it be trespassing too much upon your readiness both of money & good-nature, to ask you to discount the Bill for me?

When you write, pray tell me how it is that the Pirate of Cheapside pretends to have given Lord Byron five hundred guineas?[2]

Yours very truly
Thomas Moore.

483. *To his Mother*

Russell, ii. 110, no. 361

Nov. 22. 1816.

My dearest Mother,

We got my darling father's kind and heart-warming letter, and were both deeply gratified by it. I am glad, my own dear mother, that you *feel* how I love you. I can but *half* show it; but I would do more, if I could. Bessy is continually making projects for our all living together; and no later than this morning, at breakfast, imagined a very pretty scheme for our taking the house next to you, making a door in the wall, dining every day together, &c.

[1] In 1816 Byron published *The Siege of Corinth* and *Parisina* in one volume, as well as canto III of *Childe Harold* and *The Prisoner of Chillon*. Moore was probably referring to the last two poems.

[2] On Saturday, 16 Nov. a publisher named Johnson advertised that 'Lord Byron's "Pilgrimage to the Holy Land," "The Tempest," "Farewell to England," and "To My Daughter," with several other works, would go on sale the following Wednesday'. He also claimed 'that the copy-right of this work was consigned to him exclusively by the Noble Author himself, and for which he gave 500 guineas'. An injunction was sought in Court of Chancery by Sir Samuel Romilly, representing Byron, on 28 Nov. to restrain Johnson from publishing 'spurious and ungrammatical matter' as Byron's production. The injunction was granted. For further details see Byron's letter to Murray, 9 Dec. 1816 (*LJ*, iv. 19–22).

I am not without hopes that some of her visions may yet be realised.

God bless my sweet mother. Love from us both to father and our excellent Nell, and believe me, ever your own,

Tom.

484. *To John Murray*

Sir John Murray

Mayfield Cottage—
Decr 24th 1816

My dear Sir— I inclose you my Bill upon the Longmans, which you were so good as to say you would discount for me, and if you could conveniently send me a Bill of Exchange for the sum, it would save me some time, as I fear I should be obliged to send your draft back again to town to be cashed—however in this consult entirely your own convenience—you oblige me very much by accommodating me with the money, and I insist upon your deducting the discount from it—the Longmans always do, and I don't see why you are to be more generous to me than they—

The article upon Coleridge in the Ed. Rev. was altogether disgraceful both from its dulness and illiberality— You know I had some idea of laughing at Christabel myself—but when you told me that Coleridge was very poor and had been to the Literary Fund, I thought this no laughing matter, and gave up my intention—[1] I wonder much at Jeffrey letting that passage about Lord Byron appear—

The 3rd Canto of the Childe is magnificent—no man living can write up to it—

I have such a violent head-ache these two or three days, and such inflamed eyes that I can hardly see to write.

Every yours most truly
Thomas Moore

485. *To James Power*[2]

Quaker Collection, Haverford College

My head still troubles me—and I intend to have it bled copiously tomorrow—ten or twelve ounces. I must trouble you to pay the Postage of the inclosed for me—it is for Venice—

[1] See letter No. 468, to Francis Jeffrey, 23 May 1816.

[2] This letter is included in Russell's edition (ii. 111, no. 362).

Wednesday Jan^r^ 8 1817.

My dear Sir

I am glad you received the money safe, and rejoice that I could even, in such a trifling degree, be of service to you. I send three Irish Melodies, and shall make a parcel of the Proofs, as soon as I have the other two ready for you—

I suppose you have heard that my Father has lost his situation—[1] This is a heavy blow to me—as I shall have to support them all for the remainder of their lives— I am not yet in possession of the circumstances, but as there is no one to be appointed in his place, I suppose it is a part of the system of retrenchment—and if so, I cannot complain—but more of this another time.

Ever yours.
T. Moore

486. *To Lady Donegal*

Russell, ii. 111, no. 363

Jan. 12. 1817.

I have had various calamities lately. In the first place, my studies have been interrupted, in their very *capital*, by a violent pain, which was at first thought to proceed from too much blood, and I was accordingly cupped, scarified, leeched, and bleached by abstinence, physic, &c. &c. In the next and more serious place, my father has been turned out of his employment in Ireland;[2] and thus am I doomed to be a poor man for the remainder of my existence, as I must share my crust with him as long as he lives. They do not even give him half-pay;[3] and his dismission has been attended with some unfairness (as well as I can understand from his own account and Joe Atkinson's), which I have endeavoured to counteract by the inclosed letter to Lord Mulgrave.[4] You will smile at my having the impudence to write to him; but as I ask no favour, and merely entreat justice for my father, there could be no scruple on my part in addressing him; and, if *you* feel none in giving him the letter, I think it will be the means of drawing his attention more favourably to it. It was but this moment I thought of asking you to do me this kindness and I have not time for a

[1] Moore's father had been relieved of his post as Barrack-master of Island Bridge, Dublin. See letter No. 490, to his mother, 6 Mar. 1817.

[2] See letter No. 485, to James Power, 8 Jan. 1817.

[3] See letter No. 487, to James Power, 18 Jan. 1817.

[4] Lord Mulgrave, in his position as Master General of Ordnance, was responsible for notifying Moore's father that he was relieved of his post and later that he had been placed on half pay.

word more; except to say, that next month we move towards town, and that it will give me real happiness, amid all my perplexities, to find *you*, my very dear friend, as much better in health as my heart wishes you to be. Best love to Mary. Ever yours,

T. Moore.

My head is much better. You need not be afraid of the *tone* of the enclosed; nor think, with Davy, that 'it is, as I may say, a designing and malicious looking letter.'[1] I have written it with great respectfulness and humility, as I was in policy bound to do. You need not add any representations, I think, of your own, as I by no means wish to have the appearance of *making interest:* but the sooner you let him have it the better.

487. *To James Power*

Russell, ii. 113, no. 364

Saturday, Jan. 18. 1817.

My dear Sir,

You will be glad to hear that my father has got half-pay, which is a considerable relief compared with what we expected; and I write to you immediately, as I know you will be glad to hear it. *Between ourselves*, he never could have got it, had I not myself written to Lord Mulgrave on the subject:[2] but more of this when we meet. It is pleasant, as well in point of *character* as of *money;* for the liberal gentlemen at the other side wanted to make it appear that he had done something very wrong, which merited such a dismission; but Lord Mulgrave, in his letter to me, says, he 'can find nothing in Mr. Moore's conduct to prevent his receiving the retirement of half-pay; which he has accordingly directed.' Next Monday or Tuesday you shall have the proofs, &c.; but I have been all distraction and nervousness lately. Ever yours,

T. Moore.

Could you in the course of a week or ten days muster me up a few pounds (five or six), as I am almost without a shilling?

488. *To Lady Donegal*

Russell, ii. 113, no. 365

Thursday night, Jan. 23. 1817.

I am *upon* my *knees* before you. I find, from your statement, that I was quite wrong, and have not a word to say in my defence, except you can understand (what, perhaps, is unintelligible to any

[1] *The Rivals*, IV. i. 107.

[2] See letter No. 486, to Lady Donegal, 12 Jan. 1817.

but '*wrong-headed Irishmen*') the mortal dread I feel of being supposed to relax my principles in favour of my interest, or of being thought capable of attacking a man one day, and coming cap-in-hand to him on another, according as it suited my convenience so to do. Even now, so strongly do I labour under this wrong-headedness, that (simple as the transaction has been, and creditable, I think, to all of us) I should infinitely rather have worked to support my father myself *totally*, than have made one movement towards procuring this half-pay for him,[1] did I not know that the idea of depending wholly upon my exertions would have made my mother and him wretched. But this is only my own (perhaps morbid) feeling. It was that plaguy word about 'justice' in his note to you that set my fancy on horseback, and, as is the case with all beggars (which my fancy must be by this time, after an expenditure of six thousand lines), she rode to the devil with me. But *do* forgive me, my dearest friend, and, for Heaven's sake, write immediately to say you do; for among the calamities of this world I should rank as the *greatest*, my being in the slightest degree out of favour with you: indeed, I have not been happy ever since I wrote that hot-headed letter. Ever yours,

T. M.

I have inflicted double postage upon you, as I think the sooner he gets my acknowledgment the better, and I thought it would be satisfactory to you to see it. Do write soon, I entreat of you.

489. *To his Mother*

Russell, ii. 62, 317

Jan. 26. [1817]

My dearest Mother,

My father's last letter would have made us very unhappy indeed, if we had not the pleasing thought that by that time you had received the intelligence of Lord Mulgrave's letter,[2] and were lightened at least of *half* your sorrow; indeed, my darling mother, I am quite ashamed of the little resolution you seem to have shown upon this occurrence; it was an event *I* have been expecting for years, and which I know *you yourselves* were hourly apprehensive of; therefore, instead of looking upon it as such an overwhelming

[1] See letter No. 486, to Lady Donegal, 12 Jan., and No. 487, to James Power, 18 Jan. 1817.

[2] Lord Mulgrave notified Moore's father that he had been placed on half pay. See letters Nos. 486 and 488, to Lady Donegal, 12 and 23 Jan. 1817. Russell incorrectly dated this letter 1815. The date is obviously 1817, since it was at that time that Moore's father lost his position as Barrack-master.

thunderclap, you ought to thank Providence for having let you enjoy it so long, and for having deferred the loss till I was in a situation (which, thank God! I am now) to keep you comfortably without it. I venture to say 'comfortably,' because I *do* think (when the expenses of that house, and the et-ceteras which always attend an establishment are deducted), you will manage to live as well upon your 200£ a-year, as you did then upon your 350£., which I suppose was the utmost the place altogether was worth. Surely, my dear mother, the stroke was just as heavy to *us* as to *you*, for I trust we have no separate interests, but share clouds and sunshine equally together; yet you would have seen no gloom in *us*—nothing like it; we instantly made up our minds to the reduction and economy that would be necessary, and felt nothing but gratitude to Heaven for being able to do so well; and this, my sweet mother, is the temper of mind in which *you* should take it. If you knew the hundreds of poor clerks that have been laid low in the progress of this retrenchment that is going on, and who have no means in the world of supporting their families, you would bless our lot, instead of yielding to such sinful despondency about it. For my *father's* sake (who is by no means as stout himself as he ought to be) you ought to summon up your spirits, and make the best and the brightest of it.

Let him draw upon Power at two months for whatever he may want for the barrack money, and when the rent comes due in March, we shall take care of it. Ever, my dearest mother, your own affectionate,

Tom.

490. *To his Mother*

Russell, ii. 115, no. 366

Ashbourne
March 6. 1817.

My dearest Mother,

I arrived here yesterday morning, after having set the printers to work on my manuscript,[1] and fixed upon a cottage at Hornsey, within six miles of town. The way I have arranged my money matters with Longman is satisfactory and convenient to them, and, I should hope, safe for myself. I am to draw a thousand pounds for the discharge of my debts, and to leave the other two thousand in their hands (receiving a bond for it) till I find some mode of disposing of it to advantage. The annual interest upon this two

[1] The manuscript of *Lalla Rookh*.

thousand (which is a hundred pounds) my father is to draw upon them for quarterly, and this I hope, with his half-pay, will make you tolerably comfortable.[1] By this arrangement, you see, I do not touch a sixpence of the money for my own present use, and I consider myself very lucky indeed to be able to refrain from it. If my poem succeeds, I have every prospect of being very comfortable; and indeed, whether it succeeds or not, there is no fear of me.

I shall stay a few days here with our friends the Coopers, and, on Tuesday next, transport the whole colony (no easy or cheap matter, you may suppose) to London.

I was delighted to hear, by Ellen's letter through Lucy, that your spirits, my darling mother, were so much better. This is quite right; and I feel it the more joyfully, as I am sure your consideration for my wishes has been one great cause of your making the effort. God bless my sweet mother. Ever your own,

Tom.

Bessy is, I think, a little better, and the young ones are quite well.

491. *To his Mother*

Russell, ii. 116, no. 367

Ashbourne
Tuesday, March 11. 1817.

My dearest Mother,

We are off to-night for town.[2] I have taken the inside of one of the coaches to ourselves, and trust in Heaven that I shall carry all my little establishment safely to the end of their long journey. I have paid all my bills here, and believe that we carry with us the respect and good wishes of everyone. Indeed I have never experienced more real kindness than from some of our friends in this neighbourhood.

You will perceive that my poem is announced,[3] and I shall now have a most racketting time of it till I am published.

Bessy is a little better, and the young things are quite well. Ever your own,

Tom.

[1] See letter No. 487, to James Power, 18 Jan. 1817.
[2] See letter No. 490, to his mother, 6 Mar. 1817.
[3] See letter No. 494, to James Power, 26 Mar. 1817.

492. *To his Mother*

Russell, ii. 116, no. 368

Friday, March 13. 1817.

My dearest Mother,

We arrived quite safe, and the little ones bore the journey like heroines.[1] Bessy, too, went through it much more stoutly than I expected. We were at Drury Lane last night, and to-morrow we go to the Opera. This is merely to give Bessy a taste of London before we are off to our Hornsey cottage, where I shall be confined very closely to business for the next two months. We found a most comfortable and kind reception at the house of Bessy's friend (niece to Mrs. Ready), Mrs. Branigan, an excellent person, who appears to be very prosperously and comfortably married, and whose house will be a most valuable convenience to us whenever we visit London. We stay with them till Monday. Bessy is just gone out with Lady Donegal in her carriage to look for a new bonnet. God bless my dearest mother. Best love to Nell and my good father. Ever your own,

Tom.

I have taken Bessy this morning to see the new house: she likes it exceedingly. I am to pay ninety pounds for the year. It is well furnished; and this clears taxes and everything.

493. *To Joseph Strutt*

The Living Age, 7th Series, xxiii (1904), 438

Hornsey
Saturday, March 22, 1817.

My dear Sir,— I need not tell you how *scarce* time is with me just now—but by a friend like you I know that 'every little donation will be thankfully received.' The letter I got from you before I left Ashbourne, was so full of real kindness that I assure you I have looked over it often, very often, since—such things do one's heart good. I know too so well that expressions of kindness from you must have been felt strongly before you give them utterance—all this made your letter particularly gratifying to me.

This place is beautiful and I begin to feel at home in it,—though, at first, I was a good deal disgusted by finding that we were

[1] In March 1817 the Moores gave up Mayfield Cottage and moved to another house at the foot of Muswell Hill in Hornsey, only six miles from London, thus making easier the supervision of the publication of *Lalla Rookh*.

introduced to a disagreeable sort of *political* connection, viz., *Rats*, which the house appeared to abound with, when we came. I flatter myself, however, they felt ashamed of themselves in my presence, for they all seem to have disappeared and the place is now sweet and pure for the occupation of the 'Little dove' as soon as he will make his appearance—do let me have him as soon as possible, and if he cannot fly (though he looks as if he could) pray let him have the safest and speediest waftage this vulgar world of ours supplies—and tell his mother I send her a thousand loves of my own in exchange for him.

I find there must occur some delay in the getting out of 'Oft in the stilly night,'[1] on account of Powers' differences with his brother.[2] Isabella's song is not published, there were only those two copies taken, which I hope she secured safely.

Will you have the goodness to procure for me the Bill of Mr. Derby, the Tailor, who made some things for me? He at present enjoys the distinction of being the only person in Derbyshire to whom I owe any money.

Best regards to all.

Ever your very attached and obliged friend,

Thomas Moore.

Bessy sends her best remembrances.

494. *To James Power*

Huntington Library

Wednesday [March 26th 1817, *not in Moore's hand*]

My dear Sir— We must do with the Coals we get here, as those from town would be so expensive— I hope to see you on Friday, when we shall talk about the design— it *must* be from the Harp Song, as at present there is no other that would afford one—[3] Perhaps I might hit out something better in the two or three days I have still to write for the Number, but this would of course take too much time.

I feel quite sure you will not press me *now* (in the crisis of my fate) more than is absolutely necessary, nor oblige me to bring out the Number in a state I do not perfectly approve of— In addition to the feelings of kindness I know you have for me, it would evidently not be your own interest to do so—as if I fail in my Great Work, I shall still have my fame in the *lyrical* way to

[1] *Poetry*, p. 238.

[2] For an account of the legal difficulties between the Power brothers see letter No. 266, to James Power, 23 Nov. 1812.

[3] Probably 'My Gentle Harp, Once More I Waken', *Poetry*, p. 211.

retire upon—but, if I should so unluckily contrive it as at the same time to fail in *both*, I am *bedevilled*, and you with me, altogether— You may depend however upon my doing every thing to have the Number out as soon after the Poem as possible, but I am the more anxious to have it good, from looking upon it as a *corps du reserve* for my Fame, in case the *main attack* is unsuccessful—[1]

Ever truly yours,
Thomas Moore

495. *To his Mother*

Russell, ii. 117, no. 369

Hornsey, Middlesex
[March] 1817.

My dearest Mother,

We are at last settled, and I *begin* to feel at home. At first when we came, I was a good deal disgusted by finding that the place was full of rats, and that one of the rooms smoked,—indeed, you would have pitied me if you had seen the irritable state of fidget it put me into, everything now depending so much on my having these two next months free and quiet for the getting out my poem; but I think we have now got over all our grievances; and Bessy's exertions and good-humour throughout the whole, and the accommodating spirit with which she has encountered and removed every difficulty for me, has been quite delightful.

I hope my dear father has not suffered himself to want any supply: he may draw whenever he is in need of anything;[2] and as soon as the poem[3] is out I shall establish the *regular* channel through Longman for his annual hundred. Love to all. Ever your own,

Tom.

496. *To Mrs. Bentley*

Pforzheimer Misc. MS. 308

Hornsey
Wednesday [March 1817]

My dear Mrs Bentley— I am so confoundedly and confoundingly busy just now that I have hardly time to scribble you even this note— Write an epilogue!—you might as well (as old Wilson used

[1] The seventh number of the *Irish Melodies* was not published until October 1818. In the meantime *Lalla Rookh* appeared on 27 May 1817.

[2] See letter No. 490, to his mother, 6 Mar. 1817.

[3] *Lalla Rookh*.

to say) 'ask a man for a song while he had a tooth-drawing instrument in his mouth'— Let me but once get published and *damned* myself, and I will assist at the damnation of any one else you chuse.

Ever yours
T. Moore

497. *To his Mother*

Russell, ii. 118, no. 370

Tuesday, May 13. 1817.

My dearest Mother,

I am posting away, whip and spur, for the goal, which (you will have seen by the papers) I am to reach on the 22nd. Strange to say, the work is not finished yet, but I hope to give the last of it into the printer's hands before Saturday. I believe there is a good deal of anxiety for it, and the *first* sale will, I have no doubt, be rapid; but whether it will stick to that is the question, and I have my fears.[1]

I never was better, thank God! I have been (for the first time since I was your own little *boy*) a good Catholic all this week, not having tasted a bit of *meat* since Tuesday last. I found myself getting a little too full of blood, and this regimen has made me as cool and comfortable as possible. Love to all. Ever your own,

Tom.

498. *Addressee unknown*

Huntington Library

[May 15th 1817, *not in Moore's hand*]

My dear Sir— I should be particularly obliged by your calling upon Mr Sullivan for me—for I have been in great distress about him, the servants having mislaid his card—pray, tell him this & that I shall be in town for the next week, when I hope to see him.

Ever yours,
T. M.

499. *To his Mother*

Russell, ii. 119, no. 372

Hornsey
May 30. 1817.

My dearest Mother,

The book is going on famously; I believe I told you in my last that we were already going into a second edition, so that my

[1] For an account of the success of *Lalla Rookh* see letter No. 499, to his mother, 30 May 1817.

conscience as to the publishers' pockets is now quite at rest. I should suppose your copy was the first that arrived in Dublin. All the opinions that have reached me about it in London are very flattering; and I rather think I shall not be disappointed in the hope that it will set me higher in reputation than ever. Faults, of course, are found, but much less than I expected; and if I but get off well with the two Reviews, the Edinburgh and Quarterly,[1] I shall look upon my success as perfect. The latter, of course, is rather hostile to me from my politics, but I believe, on the present occasion, they will be pretty fair.

I have had most pressing solicitations from the Opposition to undertake the superintendence of a new paper they have set up, 'The Guardian,'[2] but it would not suit me; besides, living in London is what I do not now like at all. I dined and slept at Holland House on Wednesday last; we had Tierney, Lord Aberdeen, &c. &c. Bessy took a round with me, while we were in town, to return calls,—Lady Besborough, Asgill, Cork, Hastings, &c. &c.: we were let in at almost all, and she was very much amused. We go for a few days to Lady Donegal, on Wednesday next, children and all. Ever your own,

Tom.

I hope dear Kate and the little one are recovered: my love to her. I *think* she likes the book.

500. *To his Mother*

Russell, ii. 118, no. 371

Hornsey
Saturday, May, 1817.

My dearest Mother,

I received my father's letter yesterday, and am glad to find you did not omit the celebration of my birthday: I meant, indeed, to have stirred you up a little on the subject. We are delighted to find that dear Kate is recovered.

I received some Edinburgh papers the other day, full of praises of Lalla Rookh;[3] it seems, indeed, if I may judge from these

[1] *Lalla Rookh* was reviewed favourably in the *Edinburgh Review*, xxix (November 1817), 1–34. It was not reviewed in the *Quarterly*.

[2] *The Guardian, a New Daily Evening Paper*, was published from 12 Dec. 1819 to 25 Apr. 1824.

[3] *Lalla Rookh*, which appeared on 27 May 1817, was reviewed favourably in most of the leading newspapers and journals, although the Tory press, as might be expected, attacked it severely. For a summary of the reviews see Jones, *The Harp that Once*—, pp. 343–4.

journals, to have produced a great sensation in Scotland. One of these papers Bessy has forwarded to you, by the way of Derbyshire.

My father may draw upon the Longmans as soon as he pleases.[1] God bless my sweet mother. Ever your own,

Tom.

501. *To John Erskine Douglas*

Rice University

Hornsey
June 2nd 1817.

My dear Douglas— I wrote you a long letter last year, but I know you never received it— The bearer was a young Irishman, to whom I at the same time gave a letter of introduction to my poor friend Sir James Leith (and this, by the bye, shows it must have been more than a year since) but his destination, I heard, was soon after altered, and neither of the letters, I fear, ever were [*sic*] delivered— I have been often, very often, threatening to write to you lately, but the close attention I have been obliged to pay to the various literary tasks I had on hands, and particularly to the great & mighty Quarto Volume which has been so long expected from me, occupied every thought & moment so entirely, that till now I have not had an instant that I could call my own— At length however the *pregnant mountain* is delivered, and I only hope the world will not christen the child *Mouse* after all—[2] As yet indeed I have no cause to complain—the opinions that have reached me about it are all very favourable, and (what is the surest proof of its doing well) the Publishers are in high spirits, and the First Edition was gone in two or three days. I have ordered a Copy to be sent to you through Mr Branigan, who told me he knew of an opportunity the beginning of this week, and I hope it will arrive safe— Did you ever receive an introduction which I sent either to yourself or your sister for this gentleman on your first going out to Jamaica?— He is married to a particular friend of my wife's, and though I had never seen himself at that time, I knew I might venture to recommend him to your notice, and what makes me doubt your having received my letter on the subject, was your never (as he tells me) having mentioned the circumstance to him when he returned & saw you afterwards at Jamaica—

I have been delighted, my very dear friend, to hear of the success

[1] See letter No. 490, to his mother, 6 Mar. 1817.

[2] See letter No. 500, to his mother, May 1817.

that has attended you on your station—[1] It would have been one of those over-sights of Providence which sometimes seem to occur, if honour and industry and kind-heartedness such as *you* possess did not at last meet with the reward they deserve—and if there are many hearts to bless you as warmly as *mine* has always done, I do not wonder at their drawing down all kinds of prosperity upon you— The first who told me of your good-luck was Beresford; (Sir John)—he told it with a joy and cordiality that seemed to come from his very soul, and, I need not tell you, it went straight to mine—

You knew, I believe, that the Booksellers had agreed to give me three thousand pounds for my Poem, and they have very liberally fulfilled their agreement—[2] I thought it right (from the change that had taken place in the times since we made the bargain) to give them the full power of rescinding or modifying the terms if they chose it—they, however, with many compliments to me on what they called the liberality of this offer, professed themselves perfectly ready to adhere to the original agreement— I have drawn a thousand of the sum to pay my debts (two hundred of which lies waiting your draft at sight) and the remaining two thousand remaining in their hands, (till I can find some better way of disposing of it) as the *commencement* of a *fortune* for my two dear little girls —the interest of the two thousand I give to my poor father, who, in the course of the late retrenchments, has been reduced on half-pay, and it is a most providential thing that I have thus the means of helping him on in his old age—[3] You have now a full statement of *my* financial prosperity, and though it is but the keystone on which future industry must raise the arch, yet with the present quiet habits of my life, and the economical care of one of the most considerate young wives existing, I have no doubt I shall be able to ensure to myself a respectable independence; without being indebted to either place, pension or patron for it—

My friends Lady Donegall [*sic*] and Rogers (who, like yourself, are ever faithful and ever kind) often speak about you with the warmest interest— But there is *one* person particularly anxious to take you by the hand and present her two little babes to you, and I hope by the time you return to England, we shall have a house of our own (it being my great wish to purchase one) in which the Admiral shall always find a birth [*sic*] to turn into,

[1] Douglas was made Commander-in-Chief at Jamaica late in 1815. See letter No. 453, to his mother, December 1815.

[2] See letter No. 407, to Longman & Company, 17 Dec. 1814.

[3] See letter No. 490, to his mother, 6 Mar. 1817, and No. 486, to Lady Donegal, 12 Jan. 1817.

whenever he wants country air, warm welcome and little rosy playfellows—

You are to draw, recollect, upon Messrs Longman and Co. 39, Pater-noster Row, London—they are ready for you *at sight*, but, I dare say it would be a convenience to them to make your draft at a month or two—& it will make no difference to *you*. I took Mrs Moore to see your sisters, and they were very kind to her—We shall soon call upon them again—but she has not stirred to town from this during my labours—

I will not say any thing to you, my dear Douglas, about *interest* on the £200 till we meet—

God bless you— Ever your faithful friend

Thomas Moore.

502. *To his Mother*

Russell, ii. 121, no. 375

Keppel Street
June 25. 1817.

My dearest Mother,

Our College dinner on Saturday was a very curious one.[1] I dare say you will see the account of it copied into the Irish papers, and it will amuse you to find that Croker was the person that gave my health. I could not have a better proof of the station which I hold in the public eye than that Croker should claim friendship with me before such men as Peel, the Duke of Cumberland, &c. &c. I was received with very flattering enthusiasm by the meeting. Bessy and the children left Rogers's yesterday, and came here for a few days to the Branigans. About the tenth of the next month I shall set off for Paris; and, having passed a month there, it is my intention to run over to Dublin for a week or two, my darling mother, to see you and my own dears at home, as I have given up the thought of taking my whole establishment over, which would be imprudent unless I meant to live some time in Ireland, and *that*, I think, I had better *not* do. Bessy is pretty well in spite of all her racketting. She saw Kemble take leave on Monday night, Lady Besborough having sent to us to go to her box. Everybody is most kind to her. The little things are not quite well. God bless my own dear mother. Ever yours,

Tom.

[1] The dinner was given for the graduates of Trinity College, Dublin.

503. *To his Mother*

Russell, ii. 120, no. 373

Wednesday [June] 1817.

My dearest Mother,

What with you and my *other* love, Bessy, I am kept in continual pursuit of franks. I shall send this to Lord Byron, and take my chance for his sending it to-day. You cannot conceive how kind everybody is to me here, and my visit will do me all the good in the world by inspiring me with confidence, and showing me the high ground I stand upon. I am invited to *lecture* at the Royal Institution next year; a very flattering distinction, which, however, I am doubtful, from many reasons, whether I shall accept. Lord Lansdowne last night at Lady Besborough's said, he should feel delighted if I would fix my residence near his house in the country, and that my best way would be to take Bessy there on a visit to him and Lady Lansdowne this summer, and look about us for something.[1] Could anything be more pleasant or flattering than this?

I am very anxious to hear from you, my own dear mother; and with best love to father, Kate, and dear Nell, I am ever your own,

Tom.

504. *To Lady Holland*

The Earl of Ilchester[2]

11 Duke Street, St. James's
Sunday [July 1817].

Dear Lady Holland

I am most unluckily for myself obliged to return to Hornsey tomorrow evening, in consequence of the *Third Edition* of Lalla Rookh being about to go to Press,[3] and I am anxious to correct a few of its many many errors while it is printing. As I hear Lord Holland has done me the honour to read some of it, I should feel particularly flattered if he would point out any enormity that occured [*sic*] to him.—

[1] This mention of Lord Lansdowne's suggestion that Moore settle near him in Wiltshire is the first reference to the friendship which was established between the two men. The Moores settled in Sloperton Cottage, near Bowood, Lord Lansdowne's estate, in 1818. The spirit of friendliness and helpfulness which Moore had missed in Lord Moira was found in Lord Lansdowne, and their friendship lasted until the poet's death.

[2] Transcript provided by the Earl of Ilchester.

[3] The third edition of *Lalla Rookh* appeared in July 1817.

As soon as I have done my task I shall pay my respects at Holland House, and I beg of your Ladyship to believe me

Ever faithfully your obliged serv[t]
Thomas Moore.

505. *To his Mother*

Russell, ii. 122, no. 377

Hornsey
Saturday [5 July] 1817.

My dearest Mother,

I have come down here for a day or two, previous to my flight for France; and a bustling, crowded house I find it,—Branigan, his wife, two children, and two servants, in addition to our own establishment. Bessy has stowed us all away, though, very comfortably; and when *he* is gone to Scotland, and *I* to Paris, which will be the beginning of next week, she will get on very well with her group till our return. It is very delightful to her to have her friend with her while I am away.

I have seen the Daltons on their way to Paris. Poor fellow! his complaint seems to grow more near its fatal consummation every day. God bless my darling mother. Ever your own,

Tom.

My father has nothing to do with accounting for the difference of exchange: it is the same thing to the Longmans and me, and only puts a few pounds more in his own pocket.[1] How much does he receive for the twenty-five pounds British?

506. *To his Mother*

Russell, ii. 122, no. 376

Hornsey
Thursday [9 July] 1817.

My dearest Mother,

I am kept in the most perplexing state of bustle all this week by Rogers's delay of our departure: however, on Sunday he promises positively to be off. I will try and write again between this and then, and you shall hear from me as often while I am in France as possible. Bessy, too, shall write a line on the newspapers she sends you to tell you how I am. I expect much pleasure from the trip.

I take a letter of credit for three hundred pounds; pretty well, you'll say!—but this is mere form, and only for the dash of the

[1] See letter No. 490, to his mother, 6 Mar. 1817.

thing, as I dare say I shan't draw more than thirty. Ever my darling mother's own,

Tom.

507. *To his Mother*

Russell, ii. 123, no. 378

Amiens
July 16. 1817.

My dearest Mother,

I seize one moment, on my way, to write a line (if this cursed French ink *will* write) to tell you that I am quite well and merry, and enjoying myself in this grotesque country amazingly. Our passage from Dover to Calais was but three hours and a half, and I was as sick as need be; but the journey hither (we are within seventy or eighty miles of Paris) has quite set me up again: and I assure you, my own dears at home, that pleasant as this journey promises to be, I look forward to a still pleasanter one after it, in my trip to you all in Dublin.

God bless my own darling mother. Wherever I am, yours ever affectionately,

Tom.

508. *To James Power*

Russell, ii. 124, no. 379

Paris
August 7. 1817.

My dear Sir,

Though I have hardly one minute for writing, and Bessy always claims the little minute I have, yet, as I promised you should hear from me, here goes! Paris is the most delightful world of a place I ever could have imagined; and, really, if I can persuade Bessy to the measure, it is my intention to come and live here for two or three years. You *must* come and see it. Stevenson is *not* in very high force here; the ice is too cold for his stomach, and he cannot get whisky-punch for love or money—accordingly he droops. I cannot make out well his designs or wishes with respect to his business with you; but he says, that as to the two first years he has nothing to do with them; he has a receipt from you to prove their having been settled to your satisfaction.

I am called away. Best regards to Mrs. Power. Ever yours,

T. Moore.

509. *To his Mother*

Russell, ii. 124, no. 380

Wednesday, August 20. 1817.

My dearest Mother,

I have but this instant arrived safe and well, and am hastening, in great anxiety, to Hornsey; as I hear our poor dear Barbara is very ill indeed, from the fall she had a week ago. I suppose Bessy has told you of it. I have just seen Tegart; and I fear, from the way he speaks, that my dear child is in a very dangerous state. You shall know more by to-morrow's post.

God bless my darling mother. Ever your own,

Tom.

510. *To Joseph Strutt*

***The Living Age*, 7th Series, xxiii (1904), 439**

Hornsey
Sep. 1, 1817.

My dear Sir,— I should have answered your kind letter (which I found upon my return from Paris ten days ago) immediately but for the anxious state my mind has been in about our poor Barbara, who has been and still continues most seriously ill from a fall she had downstairs during my absence. Indeed, I have sometimes despaired of her, but I trust now the worst is over—and though her recovery must be slow I begin to hope she is out of danger. Bessy is wonderfully well considering that now for more than a month she has not had scarcely an hour of undisturbed sleep—being day and night at the call of the dear child, she will not let any one else touch her.

My visit to Paris was very delightful, but this was a sad blow for me on my return. Our delight at the accounts we hear of your dear Caroline's recovery is the warmer, I believe, from what we feel about our own poor child! May she be long spared to you! I am glad you are so pleased with 'Lalla Rookh,' and right glad that the world seems so pleased with her. The third Edition was three thousand, and you see a Fourth is out already—nay, they tell me a Fifth will be wanted this week.

Lord Byron has finished a fourth Canto of 'Childe Harold.'[1] I have just had a letter from him, and as I am not in a mood to amuse you myself, I shall transcribe for you some lines he has sent me, which I think you'll like. They are thus introduced in his letter:—

[1] The fourth canto of *Childe Harold* was published on 28 Apr. 1818.

'Do you remember . . . that damn'd supper of Rancliffe's which ought to have been a *dinner?* "Ah Master Shallow, we have heard the chimes at midnight." '[1]
But

My Boat is on the shore,
And my Bark is on the sea.
But before I go, Tom Moore,
Here's a double health to thee!

Here's a sigh to those who love me,
And a smile to those who hate,
And, whatever sky's above me,
Here's a heart for every fate.

Though the ocean roar around me,
Yet it still shall bear me on;
Though a desert should surround me,
It hath springs that may be won.

Wer't the last drop in the well,
As I gasp'd upon the brink,
Ere my fainting spirit fell,
'Tis to thee that I would drink.

With that water as this wine
The libation I would pour
Should be peace with thine and mine,
And a health to thee, Tom Moore.'[2]

I have never heard a word from Jeffrey about either my first manuscript or the other, and until I see what he does with 'Lalla Rookh,'[3] I do not like to write to him. The continuation of the article in the *Edinburgh Magazine* is most splendid and laudatory.—Love to all around you from

Yours and theirs ever
Thomas Moore.

511. *To his Mother*

Russell, ii. 125, no. 381

Sept. 10. 1817.

My dearest Mother,

Barbara is not at all better;[4] indeed, this morning we have been in very great alarm about her; but the medical man, who has just left us, says she is not worse. If she should get a little better,

[1] See Byron's letter to Moore, 10 July 1817 (*LJ*, iv. 147–50). For the quotation see *Henry IV*, *Part II*, III. ii. 229.
[2] Byron, *Poetry*, vii. 46.
[3] See letter No. 499, to his mother, 30 May 1817.
[4] See letter No. 509, to his mother, 20 Aug. 1817.

I mean to go for a day or two to Lord Lansdowne's, to look at a house which he has most friendlily written to me about, which he thinks would suit me exactly. He has been searching his neighbourhood for a habitation for me in a way very flattering indeed from such a man.

God bless my own dearest mother. Your

Tom.

512. *To his Mother*

Russell, ii. 125, no. 382

56. Davies Street, Berkeley Square
Saturday, Sept. 20. 1817.

It's all over, my dearest mother; our Barbara is gone.[1] She died the day before yesterday, and, though her death was easy, it was a dreadful scene to us both. I can bear such things myself pretty well; but to see and listen to poor Bessy makes me as bad as she is. Indeed, my dearest mother, you can only conceive what she feels by imagining *me* to have been snatched away from you at the age of Barbara. It will be some time before she can get over it; but she is very sensible and considerate; and her love for us that are left her will, I know, induce her to make every effort against the effect of this sorrow upon her mind. I succeeded yesterday in prevailing upon her to leave Hornsey, and come up to Lady Donegal's house, where we are now, as retired (for the family are at Tunbridge) and as comfortable as we could desire. It is a great consolation to us to reflect, from what Duggan told us in Dublin, and from what the medical men say here, that if Barbara had lived she must have been always a suffering invalid from the bad state of her inward parts; indeed, Tegart says that the fall was not of itself the cause of her death, but merely *hastened* what would otherwise have come on. God bless you. Ever your own affectionate,

Tom.

513. *To his Mother*

Russell, ii. 126, no. 383

Thursday [September] 1817.

My dearest Mother,

Poor Bessy, though she neither eats nor sleeps enough hardly to sustain life, is getting somewhat more composed in mind than she was, and will, I hope, soon recover from this sad shock.[2] I shall, as

[1] See letter No. 509, to his mother, 20 Aug. 1817.

[2] Moore's oldest child, Barbara, died on 18 Sept. 1817. See letter No. 512, to his mother, 20 Sept. 1817.

soon as possible, go down to Lord Lansdowne's, who (I think I told you) wrote most friendlily to me to say he had been looking for a house in his neighbourhood for me.[1] It would certainly be an object to be near such a man; his library, his society, all would be of use to me; not to mention the probability of his being some day or other able to do me more important services. Lady Donegal is very anxious that I should take the house he talks of.

We are anxious to hear from you. You had better direct to 56. Davies Street, Berkeley Square. We could not be more comfortable anywhere than we are here. Ever your own,

Tom.

514. *To his Mother*

Russell, ii. 127, no. 384

Bowood
Sunday, Oct. [5] 1817.

My dearest Mother,

I arrived here the day before yesterday, and found Rogers, Lord and Lady King, &c. Yesterday I looked at the three houses Lord Lansdowne had thought of for me; but there is only *one* of them at all within my reach, a little thatched cottage, with a pretty garden, for 25£. or 30£. a-year: it is, however, I fear, too small and humble even for our pretensions. I shall not decide till I return to Bessy, which I hope to do on Wednesday or Thursday.

It is a sad thing that my father cannot let his house; and I heartily wish it would suit us to live in Dublin, that I might take it from him.

My leg is not the worse for the use I have been obliged to make of it. Ever your own affectionate,

Tom.

515. *To his Mother*

Russell, ii. 127, no. 385

Saturday, Oct. 11. 1817.

My dearest Mother,

Bessy, who went off the night before last to look at the cottage near Lord Lansdowne's, is returned this morning, after travelling both nights. Power went with her. She is not only satisfied but delighted with it; which shows the humility of her taste, as it is a

[1] See letter No. 503, to his mother, June 1817.

small thatched cottage, and we get it *furnished* for 40£. a year! This is cheap, God knows. I am nursing my leg, which is free of the inflammation that my journey produced, and I hope, by giving it fair play, it will soon get well.

I have had so many letters to write to-day that my hand is quite weary. God bless my dearest mother. Ever your own,

Tom.

516. *To James Power*

Rice University

Friday* [October 1817][2]

My dear Sir—

I am at last able to breathe & think again, and was yesterday trying my fancy at a pretty little *Finland Air* for you—[3] You shall have it when I write next— Mind that these have nothing to do with my four original Songs—

I am obliged at last to draw for my usual sum, which, with the twenty five you have accepted for my Father makes a *whole quarter's allowance*—but I have many things to pay here, and I find my Father wants a little more of me, till after he has disposed of his House, which he hopes to do to advantage—[4]

We are very anxious about M^rs^ P.

Ever yours

T. Moore.

You will have the goodness to send the inclosed immediately

517. *To James Power*

Russell, ii. 128, no. 386

Sloperton, Devizes
Wednesday, Nov. 19. 1817.

My dear Sir,

We arrived safe, and are in possession: all looks as if we were likely to be very snug. Our maids (servants being always the hardest to please) look a little sulky at the loneliness of the place; but I dare say they will soon get reconciled.

[1] Sloperton Cottage, near Bowood, Lord Lansdowne's estate, in Wiltshire.

[2] Although the paper bears the watermark 1810, the contents of this letter indicate that it was written in 1817, probably in October.

[3] Evidently one of the *National Airs*, which first appeared in 1818.

[4] See letter No. 514, to his mother, 5 Oct. 1817.

I am just sallying out to my walk in the garden, with my head full of words for the Melodies. You shall have them as I do them. Ever yours,

T. Moore.

The pianoforte! the pianoforte!

518. *To Joseph Strutt*

The Living Age, 7th Series, xxiii (1904), 440

Sloperton Cottage, Devizes, Wilts.
[November 1817]

My dear Sir,—Your letter did not reach me so soon as a thing so very welcome ought, from Mr. Powers' having waited for the opportunity of a parcel he was sending me. If you had but put on it (what our friend Sir J. Stevenson writes on every letter he sends by the post) 'this with speed,' it would have been somewhat a more happy use of the injunction than his is. I have so often had occasion to thank you, my dear Sir, for kindnesses, that it puzzles even a poet's vocabulary to vary the phrases of gratitude—but, indeed, and in honest prose I do thank you for the cordiality with which you sympathize in our very severe loss[1] and the earnestness with which you offer us such an agreeable diversion to our thoughts as a visit to friends so very dear to us would be—but you see our fate is decided for the present. We have got a little thatched cottage within two miles of Lord Lansdowne (who has been very friendly in his exertions to bring us into his neighborhood) for which we pay 40 pounds a year furnished, and as yet, it promises to be the most comfortable dwelling we have had. I dare say we shall find it dreary enough through the winter, but then we must only console ourselves with thinking how pleasant it will be in summer and that 'cras melior erit' which cheats us on for ever, and luckily cheats us. It will be some time though before either of us enjoys any thing as we used to do. It is the first visit death has paid among those very dear to me, and it has left a desolate feeling behind it and a want of confidence in the blessings that still remain, which is very dreary indeed.

I have heard nothing from Jeffrey, but I understand 'Lalla Rookh' is to be the leading article in the next number—as the bolt therefore is shot, I feel myself free to write to him, and shall in the course of a few days—when I shall not forget to reclaim the precious MS. which he so unwarrantably withholds from me.[2]

[1] The death of his daughter Barbara. See letter No. 512, to his mother, 20 Sept. 1817.

[2] See letter No. 499, to his mother, 30 May, and No. 510, to Joseph Strutt, 1 Sept. 1817.

Though your dear Caroline is so well, I wish she would take it into her head that Bath or the neighborhood of it would make her still better, as I then might have some chance of receiving you for a day or two under my thatch. How I long to see her 'strong babe of Paradise'!

Love to all from Bessy and

Yours very faithfully,
Thomas Moore.

I must tell you a little triumph I have had. Wilkie & Murray are about to publish an Edition of Sheridan's Works complete, and they applied to me to write a poem on his Life and Graces to be prefixed, at the same time, sending me the first proof-sheet as a specimen of the typography. This proof-sheet was no less than a Dedication from the Publishers to the Prince Regent, in pursuance, as they expressed thereto, of Sheridan's own wish. I instantly said I could have nothing to do with the undertaking, as such a Life as I should write of Sheridan could not possibly be placed beside a Dedication to the P. R.—in consequence of which, after a little deliberation, they sacrificed his R. H. to me, and I am to write the Essay, for which they give me 500£. about 3£. a page. This (I mean about the dedication) is *entre nous.*

519. *To James Corry*

Russell, viii. 227

Sloperton Cottage, Devizes, Wilts
Dec. 8. 1817.

My dear Corry,

I owe you a letter, but I owe you much more for the kindness of that which you wrote, when you little knew to what extent we wanted such sympathy. Our loss has indeed been severe, and we feel it much more than those who mingle again with the world, and forget themselves in the distractions of society; for, in our quiet life, every little thing reminds us of the sad vacancy that has been left in it.[1] However, 'time and the hour' cures all.[2] We have got a very snug little thatched cottage here, which Lord Lansdowne most friendlily volunteered to find out for us. I pay for it furnished but forty pounds a year, and yet I think it promises to be by far the most comfortable dwelling we have had. Lord Lansdowne's Library is within a moderate walk of me, and as most of my

[1] The death of his daughter Barbara. See letter No. 512, to his mother, 20 Sept. 1817.

[2] *Macbeth*, I. iii. 146.

London friends come down to visit him in the course of the year, I shall have just those *glimpses* of society which throw a light over one's solitude, and enliven it.

I have not time now to tell you any particulars of myself, but I shall enclose you one or two of my twin weekly letters to my mother, in the course of this month, and shall accompany them with a word or two each time, to let you know some things you may like to hear.

Yours ever, with best regards to Mrs. Corry,

Thomas Moore.

520. *To Samuel Rogers*

Russell, viii. 228

Sloperton Cottage, Devizes, Wilts
Dec. 9. 1817.

My dear Rogers,

I wrote you a little note the other day to go in a packet to Power, but it was left out by mistake, and was not worth sending alone. We find our cottage as yet very comfortable; even during these last and stormy days it has neither smoked nor let in water—*et c'est beaucoup pour Slopperton.* The Lansdownes have not yet made their appearance, so that I suppose neither of them has returned to Bowood. Bowles was very early in his welcome of us, and has since brought Mrs. Bowles; but I was out, and Bessy did not venture to encounter them alone. How are *you* going on? I long to hear that you have achieved those remaining lines, and that Spring is likely to number you among her family as 'madre de' fiori, &c. Alas! the 'gioventù dell'anno' is not *our* youth, and I begin to think that Spring is but a tantalising recurrence. I am sorry to say these thoughts come rather too thick upon me of late, and, notwithstanding the society of the Fudges,[1] whom I endeavour to *make* as agreeable as I can, still I droop sometimes. I suppose it is natural that Death's first visit among those dear to us should leave this desolate feel behind it;[2] and a little time, perhaps, will make all right again. I have just finished a long letter from Mr. Fudge to Lord Castlereagh, and am beginning young Bob Fudge's account of a gourmand day in Paris—[3] excellent subjects, if I can but muster up gaiety of imagination enough to do them justice. You see the sixth edition of 'Lalla' is out, and (the Longmans tell me) a great many of it sold; so there I leave her—my paternal

[1] *The Fudge Family in Paris* appeared in 1818.
[2] See letter No. 512, to his mother, 20 Sept. 1817.
[3] *Poetry*, pp. 459–64.

anxieties are over, and she will now, I think, be able to shift for herself.

If you hear any comical anecdotes connected with French politics, or our own ministers, pray let me have them, or, if anything occurs to you in Miss Fudge's way, it will be but gallantry to communicate it for her, and, at all events, let me hear from you. Bessy has, for the first time, produced your beautiful book to stand in her book-case; and, indeed, it is the first time, poor girl, she has had a sitting-room fit for it. She sends her best remembrances to your sister and yourself, with those of, my dear Rogers, yours very truly,

Thomas Moore.

521. *To James Power*

New York Public, Stoddard Collection, photostat of letter in *Authors' Club MSS.*

Thursday Evening Dec[r] 11 1817

My dear Sir. There is nothing in the world more easy to be understood than the decision I proposed, and you have showed over & over in conversation with me that you *did* understand it—however, here it is again—that *Stevenson* should make up his number of twenty four each year from the commencement of your agreement to the end, and that you should pay him the full amount of the stipulated annuity— My arguments to induce you to sacrifice the contested points (viz his irregularity in the *time* of giving these things &c.) I shall not repeat; because, if they were good for any thing, you remember them & I thought, indeed, you were convinced by [them]. I perceive, however, the whole affair is as unsettled as e[ver and] I shall therefore, hopelessly, resign my office of arbitrator. What I meant by saying that 'I was sure *Stevenson* required no more than I proposed,' was that Stevenson *could* not require more as it was the utmost he could expect if he had been ever so punctual in his part of the transaction—and, indeed, no objection whatever to my decision *has* come from his side—

In addition to the above particulars of my decision between you, I also pledged myself to see that the compositions he gave you were such as would be creditable to him & you, & that he should arrange those songs of Handel which you required of him[1]

[1] The seventh number of the *Irish Melodies*, published in October 1818, was the last in which Moore was associated with Stevenson. Henry R. Bishop was engaged by Power to furnish music for the eighth, ninth, and tenth numbers.

I have now done with the business, my dear Sir, and am very sorry that my anxiety both for Stevenson & yourself induced me so officiously to interfere in it— You & I have got on so well together in our *own* transactions, that it is a pity our good-understanding should be risked by these entanglements with others—

I wrote you a letter this morning, but the one I have just received from you seems so *necessary* to be answered that I have lost not a minute in doing so.

Ever very truly yours
Thomas Moore

522. *To James Power*

Russell, ii. 128, no. 387

Dec. 20. 1817.

My dear Sir,

I hope all the corrections will be particularly attended to, as well as the notes I have added. If possible let 'Hark! the Vesper Hymn'[1] come *harmonised* before the single setting.

If you have any good place in the title-page, I should like to put this motto, 'Naturâ ad modos ducimur.'[2] Ever yours,

T. M.

I dare say the 'Tell me not'[3] is as bad as need be, but I'll try again for you; or is it that he *will* not sing any thing of mine?

523. *To John Murray*

Sir John Murray

Sloperton Cottage
Decr 23rd 1817

My dear Sir— I have just received a copy of the article that has been sent to you, and I lose not a moment in expressing my regret that I should have been the means of imposing so very indifferent a production upon you. I had much rather not be noticed at all— or even *well* abused than have my praises sounded through such a penny trumpet as this—therefore, pray, find some good excuse for rejecting it; and I think you could hardly have a better than the very unaccountable manner in which it mentions our friend Lord

[1] *Poetry*, p. 238.

[2] The 'motto', a quotation from Cicero, appears in the 'Advertisement' to the *National Airs*.

[3] Probably 'Tell Me Not of Joys above', one of the songs in *Lalla Rookh*, *Poetry*, p. 404.

Byron—though, of course, you will prefer alleging some other—and, whatever you do, I beseech you not to betray my own opinion of the article; for it was intended friendlily, and I would not for worlds hurt the feelings of the author about it—

The more I think & the more opinions I receive about the Life of Sheridan, the more I see reason to quake upon the subject— Truth will be deadly, and vague praise will be cowardly—so what am I to do?—[1] I am glad to see that Campbell's Work is coming out—[2] Let me have a copy of it immediately—

Yours very truly
Thomas Moore

I have been every day expecting to hear from you—

524. *To James Power*

Russell, ii. 129, no. 388

Dec. 23. 1817.

My dear Sir,

I am so anxious about a passage in one of the songs ('Dost thou remember'),[3] that I cannot help writing expressly to have it re-corrected, though I hope it may have happened that my former correction is not yet under the tool of the engraver. Instead of

'When, as the moonbeam fell tremblingly o'er thee
And lit thy blushes:'

let it be

'When, as the moonbeam, that trembled o'er thee,
Illum'd thy blushes.'

This passage has bothered me more than enough. You shall have the preface in a day or two. It will be very short. You need not mind about the motto. Yours very truly,

Thomas Moore.

[1] Murray published a two-volume edition of Sheridan's works in 1821, for which Moore wrote an introduction. *The Memoirs of the Right Honorable Richard Brinsley Sheridan* appeared on 13 Oct. 1825. Murray had offered 1,000 pounds for it after the publication of the two-volume *Works*, but it was finally taken over by the Longmans, since Moore's exile to France caused some delay in its preparation.

[2] Campbell published *Specimens of the British Poets*, 7 vols., in 1819.

[3] *Poetry*, p. 237. The correction was finally made as Moore requested. See letter No. 530, to James Power, 21 Jan. 1818.

525. *To John Murray*

Sir John Murray

Sloperton Cottage
Decr 29th 1817

My dear Sir— I perceive you are too *diplomatic* to write to me about the article; so I shall say no more on the subject—[1] You see the great gun from Edinburgh has fired—and considering how Jeffrey had committed himself by such a sweeping condemnation of my poetry altogether, I think I have got off pretty well—[2] I expect to be publishing again in March—*early* in March—and I then mean to come to close quarters with Sheridan—[3] By the Bye, would it be inconvenient to you & Mr Wilkie to let me have *half* my five hundred in advance? I would not ask it, but that I am just now particularly situated—as my agreement with Power is on the eve of terminating, and I do not like to *hurry* into a renewal of it—At all events, you will perhaps let me draw upon you for fifty or sixty pounds at two months for a present demand, & if it should not suit you & Mr Wilkie to let it go to the Sheridan account, I can pay it myself when it becomes due—This, of course, all between ourselves—

I heard a little of the new novel (Persuasion &c) read at Bowood the other night, which has given me a great desire for the rest—Will you send it to Power's for us?—or, indeed, send it off at once here—[4]

Ever yours truly
Thomas Moore—

526. *To John Murray*

Sir John Murray

Friday Jan^r^ 2, 1818

Many thanks, my dear Sir, for your letter, and the kind offer of the draft, which I shall avail myself of—you need not take any more trouble about the article—I have already managed the delicacies of the author—[5] Isn't it strange what things some men, who are

[1] See letter No. 523, to John Murray, 23 Dec. 1817.

[2] The *Edinburgh Review*, xxix (November 1817), 1–34. See letter No. 499, to his mother, 30 May 1817.

[3] See letter No. 523, to John Murray, 23 Dec. 1817.

[4] Jane Austen's *Persuasion* was published in December 1817, although it bore the date 1818 on the title-page (see R. W. Chapman's edition, Oxford, 1923, p. xiii).

[5] See letters Nos. 523 and 525, to John Murray, 23 and 29 Dec. 1817.

reputed clever, will do when they come to *write*—how the pen (as Curran used to say) remembers its allegiance to its old mother goose, when it is put into their hands— When I last wrote to you, I had only read the *censures* in Jeffrey's article;[1] for my eye had instinctively singled them out first—but I have since taken to the *praises*, and I really think he has been most kind & generous to me—I shall be happy if you can make me useful in your Monthly Journal, but I am but a bad littérateur—[2]

Pray don't mention any thing of my publishing in March—for, though I make up my mind to be found out, yet I had rather not be found out on my own authority—[3]

Mrs Moore is all gratitude for the novels, which fill up our intervals between dinner & ten most delightfully.

Ever yours
T. Moore

I have just written to Crabbe (who is a near neighbour) to say that as Jeffrey thinks 'Mr Moore & Mr Crabbe might approach a few degrees to each other with material advantage', the sooner we meet over a beefsteak & bottle of wine, the better.

527. *To Lady Donegal*

Russell, ii. 129, no. 389

Sloperton Cottage
Jan. 9. 1818.

A pang of conscience has just come over me for having been so long without writing; and, in addition to this pang, I have just received the long-strayed letter from Calne, which has been half over the country, but has reached me at last safe and inviolate. We are getting on here as quietly and comfortably as possible; and the only thing I regret is the want of some near and plain neighbours for Bessy to make intimacy with, and enjoy a little tea-drinking now and then, as she used to do in Derbyshire. She continues, however, to employ herself very well without them; and her favourite task of cutting out things for the poor people is here even in greater requisition than we bargained for, as there never was such wretchedness in any place where we have been; and the better class of people (with but one or two exceptions) seem to consider their contributions to the poor-rates as abundantly

[1] See letter No. 525, to John Murray, 29 Dec. 1817.

[2] Probably a reference to *The Representative*, which was published by Murray from 6 Jan. 1821 to 15 Apr. 1823.

[3] Moore is referring to his forthcoming *Fudge Family in Paris*.

sufficient, without making any further exertions towards the relief of the poor wretches. It is a pity Bessy has not more means, for she takes the true method of charity,—that of going herself into the cottages, and seeing what they are most in want of.

Lady Lansdowne has been very kind indeed, and has a good deal won me over (as, you know, kindness *will* do now and then). After many exertions to get Bessy to go and dine there, I have at last succeeded this week, in consequence of our being on a visit at Bowles's, and her having the shelter of the poet's old lady to protect her through the enterprise. She did not, however, at all like it; and I shall not often put her to the torture of it. In addition to her democratic pride,—which *I* cannot blame her for,—which makes her prefer the company of her equals to that of her superiors, she finds herself a perfect stranger in the midst of people who are all intimate; and this is a sort of dignified desolation which poor Bessy is not at all ambitious of. Vanity gets over all these difficulties; but pride is not so practicable. She is, however, very much pleased both with Lord and Lady Lansdowne; who have, indeed, been everything that is kind and amiable to her. Her health is, I think, somewhat better; and little Anastasia is perfectly well.

I trust, my dearest friend, that you have not had another attack since that which, I was grieved to find, you had suffered when the last letter was written: pray mention always particularly how you find yourself.

I am getting on wickedly with all the Fudges, and you cannot think how much your *list* embarrasses me; particularly with respect to that 'venerable and illustrious female,' whom I have now such an excellent precedent for attacking in the Memoirs of the patriotic and disappointed Bishop Watson.[1] She is, however, safe, though it has already cost me the strangling of two or three young epigrams in their cradle. *All*, in fact, shall be safe, except Lord Sidmouth; but that the author of the Circular, the patron of spies and informers, the father of the Green Bag, the eulogist of the Knights of Northampton (?), &c. &c., should not have a touch or two, is out of the nature of things. I only promise that he shall neither be called 'Doctor' nor 'Old Woman,' which is quite as much as his warmest friends could expect.[2]

[1] Moore is probably referring to the *Anecdotes of the Life of Richard Watson, Bishop of Landaff*, which was published in 1817.

[2] Lord Sidmouth was at this time Secretary of the Home Department. Although he was considered a kind, benevolent man in private life, his administration was noted for its severity. He prosecuted the Luddites; moved for a committee of secrecy for the suspension of the Habeas Corpus Act, and for the revival of laws against seditious meetings; and in 1817 issued a circular to the lord-lieutenants of the counties, instructing them in the proper methods of

Best love to sister Mary, and a thousand thanks for her copying out the French verses, which I have not yet read. Ever yours faithfully,

Thomas Moore.

A kiss to Barbara. Does she get stouter?

Jeffrey's article is pretty fair, though within an inch, now and then, of being otherwise: but the Longmans write me word it will do the book much service, and they are the best judges.[1]

528. *To James Corry*

Russell, viii. 231

Jan. 14. 1818.

My dear Corry,

If I did not feel a *craving* come over me now and then for a little intelligence from Lurgan Street I do not think you would ever receive a letter from me; so that it is pure and downright selfishness makes me write. Besides, extracting one of your long, delightful letters, by means of such hurried little scraps of notes as mine, is like the trick they play in foreign parts, of throwing pebbles at monkeys, in order to be pelted back with pine-apples in return; and therefore, with all my aversion to the *private* use of the pen (being doomed, for my sins, to the cursed *public* employ of it) I cannot resist, now and then, the temptations which such double compound interest on my notes offers. I very much agree with you about your character for the next Kilkenny, except as to Falstaff, of which I think you could give the *orations* most successfully. Power is a shabby fellow not to write to me; particularly as he has a house of mine on his hands, in *an unfinished condition*, which I expected long before now to have restored to me. Tell him this.

Lord Dandy *is* a good fellow; and I often remember with gratitude that he once condescended to call *me* a dandy. 'Laudari a Lord Dandies (laudandis) viris,' is something in this world.

dealing with those charged with the publication of pamphlets which law officers considered 'blasphemous and seditious'. The lines on Sidmouth in the *Fudge Family* are:

Reynolds and I—(you know Tom Reynolds—
  Drinks his claret, keeps his chaise—
Lucky the dog that first unkennels
  Traitors and Luddites now-a-days;
Or who can help to *bag* a few,
When S—d——th wants a death or two;)

Poetry, p. 470; Letter VI, ll. 22–27.

[1] See letter No. 525, to John Murray, 29 Dec. 1817.

Give my best love and remembrance to Mrs. Corry, and believe me,

Ever faithfully yours,
Thomas Moore.

In looking over this note, it strikes me that I have somewhere used the simile of the monkeys before: if to *you*, remember I am in your debt a new simile in place of it, which I shall take the first bright moment of discharging.

I am *not* writing Fudges in London. But, believe me, *personal* satire is the only one that will ever make fools and rascals *feel.* Any thing else is fudge indeed.

What is the story of Fanny Helsham?

529. *To Messrs. Locke, Hughes, and Company*

New York Public

Jan^{r} 15th 1818

In looking over the money you last sent me I find but thirty nine pounds—a £20 Bank of England, two £5 of Devizes and nine one pound notes—you can send your answer to Mrs Moore, as I am this instant off for Bath.

Yours &c.
Thomas Moore

530. *To James Power*

Pforzheimer Misc. MS. 302

Tuesday. Jan^{r} [21st, *not in Moore's hand*] 1818.

My dear Sir— I send back the Advertisement, of which I must see a Revise— The corrections I sent you (in a letter) of some of the words of 'Dost thou remember' is not at all as I desired it to be, and it is singular there could be any mistake, as I wrote it out quite plain—[1] I hope the work is not printed off, & that it can be set right again—as it totally destroys the sense of the words— I must never trust you with a correction in this way again—it was the same way with the Preface to my Songs— I have also detected a note wrong in the melody of 'Oh come to me',[2] which had escaped me before, & which is of much consequence—as it spoils the air—if it is too late to remedy these errors, I must only put an Errata [*sic*] under the Advertisement—

[1] See letter No. 524, to James Power, 23 Dec. 1817.

[2] *Poetry*, p. 238.

I was surprized on Sunday by a letter from your brother's attorney, giving me notice of my attendance being necessary in February at the trial of his action against you—[1] This is sad work every way—and will be devilish inconvenient to myself, besides the real & deep regret I feel at the explosion between you.

Lady Lansdowne is coming to call on Bessy this morning—when I mean to play the airs to her.

531. *To James Power*

Huntington Library

Sloperton Cottage, Devizes*
Tuesday, 27th Jan[r] 1818.

My dear Sir— I should not have written to you till tomorrow, (in expectation of a letter from you by to-day's post) but that I want to trouble you in the *fish* line—will you have the goodness to send me by tomorrow evening's coach a good Cod, not too large, and a lobster or two—*one* of the latter, if pretty sizeable, will be sufficient— We have some people to dine with us on Thursday, for whom I want this supply, and I know I can depend upon you—

Bessy is delighted at the prospect of having Jane, and would like if it be could be [*sic*] so managed that she should be here when I am away in town—but all this I shall talk more fully of, when I write again— We expect M[rs] Branigan down on a farewell visit some time soon—you know, I suppose, they are going to Jamaica for two years—

There is a great deal to be done to the 7th Number before it can make its appearance—but I shall lose no time about it—Stevenson's Songs I have nearly finished the inspection of & shall send them back to you with the National Melodies in a day or two—Lady Lansdowne was delighted with the latter—the Dedication is to be simply this

To the Marchioness of Lansdowne
this Volume is inscribed
by her Ladyship's obliged & faithful servant
Thomas Moore

[1] See letter No. 266, to James Power, 23 Nov. 1812.

532. *To Samuel Rogers*

Russell, viii. 233

Sloperton Cottage
Feb. 6. 1818.

My dear Rogers,

Though I think it not unlikely that I shall, in the course of next week, be shaking hands with you in St. James's Place (as those musical but inharmonious brothers, the Powers, who might well be called *brothers*-in-*law*, have given signal for combat on the 13th, and I fear I am to receive a subpœna on the occasion),[1] yet I cannot help writing you a short letter, just to ask how you do in this very cold weather. March was the month I looked to for being ready with the Fudges, and at the same time devoting three or four weeks to a rummage in London on the subject of Sheridan, who must be my *next* victim; but this cursed *law* trip will disconcert my plans a good deal; still, however, I shall contrive to be ready for the press in March, as I have now about 1400 lines written, and there will not be more in all than 17 or 1800. I have done it, I think, pretty well; but, as usual, not half so well as I had *pre*-imagined it. The Lansdownes have been particularly amiable to us. The day that Bessy dined there was indeed a sad operation to her, for there were a good many people, not one of whom she knew; and among whom she sat, poor girl, in a state of dignified desolation; but before they went to town Lord and Lady L., with Pamela*, walked over one morning and lunched with us, and listened to music; and then we all rambled together to the church at the other side of the valley, and Lady Lansdowne was all heartiness and good-nature; and Bessy, whose element is home, was seen, I flatter myself, to much advantage; so that we shall get on with them, I have no doubt, most comfortably; and, as they will only come like comets now and then into our system, we shall enjoy a little of their light and warmth without being either dazzled or scorched by them. I have, indeed, got to like Lady L. exceedingly; she is frank and sensible, unaffected, and certainly very pretty; and altogether she has so won me over that I am going to dedicate a set of national airs to her,— there's my anti-aristocracy for you![2] *He* is delightful; and, if I could but once forget he is a Lord, I could shake his hand as heartily as that of any

* Daughter of Lord Edward Fitzgerald; married Sir Guy Campbell. [*Russell's note.*]

[1] See letter No. 530, to James Power, 21 Jan. 1818.

[2] See letter No. 531, to James Power, 27 Jan. 1818.

good fellow I know. We passed three or four days at Bowles's since I last wrote to you. What an odd fellow it is! and how narrowly, by being a *genius*, he has escaped being set down for a *fool!* Even as it is, there seem to be some doubts among his brother magistrates; but he is an excellent creature notwithstanding; and if it is not of Helicon that his spirit has drunk, it is at least of very sweet waters, and to my taste very delightful. Bessy has had a long letter from Crabbe, with 'Fair Lady!' in every page: he, too, is an odd fellow. Then there's Crowe, whom I like much. He sent me a message that he wished to meet me, and we dined together at an ex-attorney's in Devizes; much to my gratification, for he certainly is one of the few, and there is something very racy even in his lees.

Tell the Donegals they are very lazy not to write to me; and, with best remembrances to your brother and sister, believe me,

My dear Rogers, faithfully yours,
Thomas Moore.

533. *To James Power*

B.M. Add. MS. 22488, f. 60

Saturday Night [March 30th 1818, *not in Moore's hand*]

My dear Sir— I forget to say, in sending off the parcel (which I hope you received yesterday) that, as there must, I suppose, be new plates for 'They may rail at this life'[1] it had *much* better be set a half note lower—that is E three sharps—it will make it many degrees more popular—and pray, let it be done correctly—as the transposition you had made of 'The girl I left behind me'[2] was rather carelessly done— I shall have an opportunity of looking over & correcting the new proofs, when I go to town, which I hope will be the week after next—

Another thing I want you to do is in the *first* verse of 'They may rail at this life' instead of the line

And until they can find me some *livelier* planet

make it

And until they can find me some *happier* planet.[3]

The only alteration is that of 'livelier' into 'happier.'—

I am still without a letter from you, *whereat* I marvel—

Ever yours sincerely
Thomas Moore

[1] *Poetry*, p. 215.

[2] 'As Slow Our Ship Her Foamy Track', *Poetry*, p. 212.

[3] The correction was made as Moore requested.

Bessy means to write soon to Jane about a young friend of ours who is going to her school.

534. *To his Mother*

Russell, ii. 131, no. 390

Saturday, March, 1818.

My dearest Mother,

We are still without a line from you, and I really begin to be apprehensive that something is the matter. We have had most dreadful weather here; the paling before the house was all blown in, and we were left bare to the road. How have you fared in Jervis Street?

Did I tell you that, when I was in town, I received an anonymous letter from some young girl, inclosing *three pounds*, as a token of her admiration of Lalla Rookh! It was wrong directed, and they made such work about it at the Post Office (as a *property* letter) that I really began to think there was something considerable in it; but I dare say it was as much to the poor girl as three hundred to another; and if every reader of Lalla Rookh would do the same, it would make us all pretty easy about money matters. I laid out the sum immediately in two sixteenths, and I hope they will be lucky to me.

They will soon go to press with a seventh edition of Lalla.

Poor Bessy is ailing with *her* new edition, and is often very low-spirited; but she keeps up for my sake, and does her utmost to make me happy and comfortable. God bless my darling father, and mother, and Nell. I often feel it dreary to be so long without seeing you all; but before the spring is over we shall meet, please Heaven. Ever your own,

Tom.

535. *To Lady Donegal*

Russell, ii. 132, no. 391

Sloperton, Devizes
April 2. 1818.

I was just going to write to you, when I received your letter, and why I have deferred it so long since is more than I can satisfactorily explain to you, except that we are very often apt to take *other* people's performance of their duty for our *own*. I grieve, most heartily grieve, for the annoyance and embarrassment these wretched people inflict upon you. I am afraid, after all, it is but a wicked world, and I am about too, myself, to be a victim of its wickedness. Within these twenty-four hours I have come to the knowledge of a circumstance which may very possibly throw me into a prison for life. You know I have had a deputy at Bermuda; he is nephew to very rich and respectable merchants (now my only hope), the Sheddons of Bedford Square.[1] I had every reason to suspect his playing me false with respect to my share of the profits during the American war, and I had written so often in vain to demand his accounts for the last year of the war, that I at last gave up the matter as hopeless. I had forgot both him and the office, when yesterday I was roused into most disagreeable remembrance of them by a monition from Doctors' Commons, calling upon me to appear there within fifteen days, in consequence of my deputy having refused to produce the proceeds of a sale of ship and cargo, which had been deposited in his hands during an appeal to the Court at home. I suppose the sum was considerable, and the fellow has absconded with it. I have no security for him, as the place was so mere a trifle at the time I appointed him, that no one would have thought it worth either asking or giving security; and, at present, I see no chance for my escape but in the forthcomingness of his uncle Sheddon, who, as having recommended him to me, is bound, I think (at least in honour), to be answerable for the defalcation. If he (which is highly probable) refuses, I suppose I have nothing for it but a prison; and all I shall ask of your friend Sir William Scott[2] is, that he will either make interest for the Rules for me, or at least let me have *two* rooms in whatever dungeon is to receive me. I dreamt, about a week ago, that I was walking home in full sunshine, and that suddenly a pitch-black cloud came all over the sky, like the forerunner of an earthquake, that made me cower down to the very earth, exclaiming, 'Oh, my dear Bessy and child!' Is this what they call one's dreams being *out?* Mind, I am only talking and anticipating now from what appears on the face of the monition, as I know nothing further of the particulars; but I wrote by last night's post to the Sheddons, and on their answer must depend a good deal of my comfort.[3]

[1] See letter No. 81, to his mother, 19 Jan. 1804.

[2] Sir William Scott was at this time Judge of the High Court of Admiralty.

[3] Because of his difficulties with the Admiralty, Moore was forced to live abroad from 1819 to 1821. In October 1821 he learned, while on a visit (in disguise) to England, that Lord Lansdowne had arranged a settlement and that his American creditors had agreed to accept £2,000 instead of the original £6,000 for which his deputy had made him liable.

For a summary account of his years of 'exile' see Jones, *The Harp that Once—*, pp. 206–16. For further details see the diary for 1819–21 (Russell, iii).

And now that I have given you grievance for grievance, I must say that our dear Mary's ill health gave us both very real concern; and I trust when I go up to town I shall find her much better, as well as yourself, in *every* way, as you both richly deserve to be.

Poor Bess, who—I don't know whether to be glad or sorry at it—is in the way of producing another little incumbrance for us (a little *prisoner* perhaps), is, as usual in that state, very weak and ailing.

Your friends, the Fudges, are nearly *out of hand*. It was well this shock did not come upon me sooner, as it might, perhaps, (though I doubt whether it would,) have damped my gaiety with them; but, I don't know how it is, as long as my conscience is sound, and that suffering is not attended by delinquency, I doubt whether even a prison will make much difference in my cheerfulness: 'Stone walls do not a prison make,' &c. &c.[1] I shall be in town next week. Ever yours,

T. Moore.

I need not remind you that this is not a case for interference with Sir W. Scott, or *any one*. The thing must take its course; and any interest you have must be reserved for my *prison comforts*.

536. *To Samuel Rogers*

Russell, viii. 238

April 6. 1818.

My dear Rogers,

I just dispatch a line to say that we shall meet, I hope, on Sunday or Monday next. I *may* be in town on Friday or Saturday, but shall be too busy with Proctors and *other* Fudges to call upon you. Proctors! only think; all my dreams of comfort and independence at once menaced, if not destroyed. I take for granted you have seen Lady Donegal, and heard my doleful story.[2] I was about answering a letter of hers, when I was served with the awful monition. I have heard no particulars; but the proceeds of a ship and cargo *must* be considerable, more, indeed, than I can ever *attempt* to pay. We are neither of us, however, thank Heaven! in the least cast down by it. As it is by no misdeed or extravagance of our own, conscience is, at least, left untouched, and *there* lies the spring of happiness after all. I have felt more, *at large*, from a small debt of my own than I shall feel, *in a prison*, from thousands thus incurred.

and letters written while he was living abroad, particularly No. 610, to Mrs. Belcher, 27 Oct. 1821.

[1] Lovelace, 'To Althea from Prison'.

[2] See letter No. 535, to Lady Donegal, 2 Apr. 1818.

I *ought* to have had security; but the place was so trifling, when I appointed him, that it was almost made a complaint his taking it. To show you, however, that it has not affected my spirits much, I have been able to write one of Biddy Fudge's gayest letters since I heard of it.

Good bye, my dearest Rogers. I *know* you will visit me in the Rules, when I can no longer be with those Pindaric poets who are '*lege solutis*.'

Ever yours faithfully,
Thomas Moore.

537. *To James Power*

Russell, ii. 135, no. 392

Monday, April 6. 1818.

My dear Sir,

I thought to have sent you back the proof of the duet by a parcel to the Longmans to-day; but it cannot go till to-morrow; and I can no longer delay congratulating you on the result of the arbitration,[1] which, I conclude from what you say, is as favourable as you could desire; I wish you joy upon it most sincerely. Your kind prayer for me on my wedding day has, I grieve to say, failed; and I have heard within these few days of a calamity which *may* have the effect of imprisoning me for life. My deputy at Bermuda, after keeping back from me my proper share of the receipts of the office, has now, it seems, made free with the proceeds of a sale of ship and cargo deposited in his hands, and *I* am called upon, by a monition from Doctors' Commons, to be accountable for it. I know not what may be the extent of his defalcation, but it *may* be more than I can even attempt to pay. What a life it is! I am not, however, thank Heaven! at all cast down by the prospect: as it is not by my own misdeeds I shall suffer, there will be nothing in it to embitter my conscience, and I shall smile at Fortune still. They cannot take away from me either my self-respect or my talents, and I can live upon them happily *anywhere*. Good by, my dear friend; I shall see you on Friday next. Best regards to Mrs. Power. From yours, very sincerely,

Thomas Moore.

[1] William Power had sued James for £5,000 in July 1817. Moore is referring to the successful arbitration of this suit. James Power was given exclusive publishing rights to the last four numbers of the *Irish Melodies*, but he was to send copy to William. He complied with copy for the seventh number (1818), but not for the eighth (1821). William hired Stevenson to write the music for the words, and James, who had engaged Henry Bishop, got out an injunction against his brother. (See Jones, *The Harp that Once*—, p. 159.)

538. *To his Mother*

Russell, ii. 136, no. 393

Sloperton Cottage
May 6. 1818.

My dearest Mother,

You cannot conceive how happy I am at finding myself quietly here again, out of the distracting bustle of London. I left my Bermuda affairs in as good train as I could, and, as my deputy has some landed property, I am in great hopes the burden will not fall so heavy on me as I first apprehended. In the mean time do not you, my darling mother, feel the least uneasiness about either our comforts or your own. The sum is so large that I could not think of attempting to pay it; and, as in the processes of the Admiralty Court they cannot touch *property*, let the worst come, my means of supporting myself, and continuing to contribute the little I do towards *your* comforts, will not be in the least diminished by it.

As soon as I rest a little, I hope to be off for about ten days (all I can spare now) to Dublin, and hope to find my own dears there well and comfortable. I want to persuade Bessy to go on as far as Derbyshire with me, where she might stay among our friends there till my return; but I am afraid she will not agree to it.

I left the Fudges prospering amazingly in town,—five editions in less than a fortnight,—and my share for that time (I go half and half with the Longmans) was 350 £.[1] Very convenient it was too, as I had overdrawn them; and it not only paid what was over, but gave me some *ready* in my pocket besides. God bless my darling mother. Ever your own,

Tom.

539. *To James Corry*

Russell, viii. 239

May 15. 1818.

My dear Corry,

The week after next I hope to present myself to you in Lurgan Street; and as I have but eight days to stay amongst you, you must make the most of me. I hope Richard Power continues in Dublin, but I heard some alarming rumours of his being expected in London soon after I left it. This will be indeed 'from love's shining circle, the *gem* dropped away;'[2] but I *will* hope I may be lucky

[1] *The Fudge Family in Paris* was published on 20 Apr. 1818.
[2] 'The Last Rose of Summer', *Poetry*, p. 202.

enough still to find him there; as for *you*, you *must* be there; it would be contrary to all laws, human and divine, that I should not have a glimpse, and many a glimpse, of you while I stay; and I am happy to find that my father's lodgings (where they have a bed for me) is close in your neighbourhood.

Happy as I am to see you all, it is with regret I leave my sweet, quiet cottage at this 'rosy time of the year,' where, in addition to the sunshine we have always, thank God, *within*, there is some prospect (if these ice-bergs would permit), of a warm gleam or two *without;* but you must make it up to me in your heartiest smiles; and be assured that, *there* or *here*, I am always, dear Corry,

Your very faithful friend,

Thomas Moore.

Love to Mrs. C.

Bessy bids me say she depends upon you for franking a letter of mine to her *every day*.

540. *To Lady Donegal*

Russell, ii. 137, no. 394

Sloperton

May 17. 1818.

I have been, not so much reproaching myself, as regretting that I did not get one shake of the hand from you before your flight; but I had taken it into my head that Wednesday was to be the day of your departure (I find since it was the day of taking possession), and, on Tuesday morning, I went very quietly to breakfast with you between eleven and twelve, but found nothing except Farrance, with a long list of memorandums in his hand, and myself and Childe Harold commemorated thereon. I was heartily mortified. How badly this world goes on with us all! It *used* to be much better, I think; or is it that the bitters *always* lie towards the bottom of the cup? Your disappointment about the house is too bad; but it is lucky you do not like Brighton much, as you will have a regret the less. I mean to set off this next week for Ireland. I shall be away but three weeks in all; and for nothing but to gratify my poor mother (who is ill and out of spirits) would I leave just now my sweet, quiet cottage, where, in spite of proctors, deputies, and all other grievances, I am as happy as, I believe, this world will allow any one to be; and, if I could but give the blessing of health to the dear cottager by my side, I would defy the devil and all his works, and Sir William Scott to boot. Poor Bessy is not at all well, and though she is very generous and considerate about these absences from her, yet, in her low state of health and spirits, they are not by any means pleasant. I am happy to hear *you* speak of the good effects of Brighton upon your health, and, disagreeable as it is otherwise, I shall be glad to hear you are enabled to stay there.

My Bermuda business remained, when I left town, *in statu quo*, 'nothing brighter or darker' than it was when I saw you. I have sent out a power of attorney to lay hold of whatever is forthcoming of my honest deputy's property, and I hope the person I have employed will do his duty.

Let me have a line from you in Dublin, directed 39. Upper Jervis Street. I shall be most anxious to hear whether you have got another tenant. Bessy sends her best love. Ever faithfully yours,

Thomas Moore.

541. *To the Reverend Thomas Lefanu*

William Lefanu

Jarvis Strand

Sunday Night [postmark June 8, 1818?]

My dear Sir— I deferred answering your first very kind letter in the hopes that I should have been able to pay you a visit at the Park—but every moment of my time has been so occupied & so distracted that I fear, after all, I shall be obliged to leave Ireland without accomplishing one of the chief objects I had in coming—that of procuring from you whatever materials you may possess relative to your uncle Mr Sheridan—*unless* you will have the goodness to come into town on Tuesday morning & meet me at Mr Power's, no. 4. Westmoreland at twelve o'clock— I am obliged to sail that night, and, if it be inconvenient for you to meet me, I must only trust to your goodness for leaving at my Father's whatever papers or memoranda you may feel inclined to communicate for this work.[1]

I hardly know what I write, I am so weary & sleepy after the day—but I hope you will be able to make out what I *mean* & I beg you to believe me, with many thanks for your kind attention to my request,

Yours very faithfully

Thomas Moore

[1] Moore was collecting material for his life of Sheridan and for this purpose had made a visit to Ireland in May and June 1818. See letter No. 540, to Lady Donegal, 17 May 1818, and No. 543, to James Power, 16 June 1818.

542. *To the Reverend Thomas Lefanu*

William Lefanu

Tuesday One o'clock* [postmark June 9, 1818 ?]

My dear Sir— I have deferred my sailing another day, and shall have the pleasure of calling upon you in the Park tomorrow morning about eleven o'clock, when, perhaps, you will be able to communicate at least a *part* of the information you possess about your uncle.[1]

Yours, my dear Sir, very truly
Thomas Moore

543. *To James Power*

Russell, ii. 139, no. 396

Tuesday, June 16. 1818.

My dear Sir,

I was kept in such a state of bustle while in Dublin, that I had not a minute to write to you. I suppose you heard all the enthusiasm my visit excited there—the grand dinner to me—the design of making it an anniversary—my reception at the theatre, &c. &c.[2] Nothing certainly was ever like it; and, if I had stayed there a week longer, it was very confidently said there would be a deputation to ask me to stand for the city of Dublin. I shall never say that Paddy is not national again.

I hope Mrs. P. is better. Ever yours, very sincerely,

Thomas Moore.

544. *To Samuel Rogers*

Russell, viii. 240

June 18. 1818.

My dear Rogers,

I am afraid you will think me a sad truant, but the truth is, I had persuaded myself, before I set off for Ireland, that I had really written to you soon after my leaving London, and that it was *you*

[1] See letter No. 541, to Thomas Lefanu, 8 June 1818.

[2] See letter No. 544, to Samuel Rogers, 18 June 1818. The public dinner was held on 7 June at Morrison's Great Rooms in Dawson Street. The chair was taken by Lord Charlemont, and guests included Lord Cloncurry, Lord Allen, Maturin, Charles Phillips, Samuel Lover, and Daniel O'Connell. Praise was heaped upon Moore from all sides, as the result of his success with *Lalla Rookh* and *The Fudge Family*. For a detailed account of the banquet see James Burke, *The Life of Thomas Moore* (Dublin, 1852).

who were in *my* debt a letter, but the startling truth of the case broke upon me one fine morning, in no less romantic a place than Manchester, as I was on my way to Ireland, and I sat down forthwith to write to you a long apology for my silence, when, *lo!* the arrival of the coach hurried me away; and from that moment to this I have been in such a giddifying labyrinth of bustle, acclamation, hurrahs, &c. that, though your name has often been upon my lips, I have never had a disposable minute to write a line to you. Never, certainly, was there anything more enthusiastic than my reception in Dublin. It was even better than Voltaire's at Paris, because there was more *heart* in it, and the call for me at the Theatre, and the bursts of applause when I appeared with my best bows at the front of the box (which I was obliged to repeat several times in the course of the night) were really all most overwhelmingly gratifying, and scarcely more delightful to me on my own account than as a proof of the strong spirit of nationality in my countrymen.[1]

There was a tolerably good report of the speeches at the dinner in the Irish papers; but I am not sorry that Perry has shortened the account so much, for we were none of us in very good taste, I think; and Phillips, who compiled the speeches, has left the marks of his own paint-brush upon us all; but the effect at the time was admirable, and never was there a day of more strong feeling witnessed.

I have heard, with some surprise, of your Poem lying at Murray's.[2] He kept the secret so well from me, that I was in hopes he would be equally secret with others. He has not, however, I believe, told more than that he had such a thing in his possession. What have you done with it? Do pray write to me soon, and do not visit my own transgressions upon me *in kind.*

I have had a *heavy* complaint from Wilkie about the unwillingness of Charles Sheridan, or his advisers, to come to anything decisive with respect to the sanctioning his publication of the works.

Good bye; best regards to your sister.

Ever yours,
T. Moore.

[1] See letter No. 543, to James Power, 16 June 1818. Voltaire arrived in Paris for the last time on 10 Feb. 1778 and was enthusiastically received by the Academy and society in general, although not directly by the Court. He lived to see the first performance of *Irène* (16 Mar.) but died during the night of 30 Mar.

[2] Probably *Human Life*, which was published in 1819.

545. *To Joseph Strutt*

The Living Age, 7th Series, xxiii (1904), 441

Sloperton, Devizes
June 18th, 1818.

My dear Sir,— Just returned. full [*sic*] of honors (of the best kind, because won by independence) from that land of kindness and patriotism, poor Ireland.[1] You cannot conceive anything much more enthusiastic than my reception there—and they were even planning, when I came away, a deputation to invite me to stand for the City of Dublin—but I have not time now to tell you more than that I was not forgetful of you and yours in the midst of all my intoxicating glories. I procured for you a most cordial letter to Denon from Lady Morgan and you shall have it as soon as the portmanteau that contains it reaches me—but (by one of those travelling accidents that happens oftener to me than any one else) my portmanteau has been carried off to town by one of my fellow-passengers in the medley instead of his own, which remains in my hands as my only pledge or hope for the recovery of the other. Luckily, both our names are, on brass plates, upon our respective portmanteaus, and I should hope, in a day or two, I may have some account of my leather vagabond. It contains, I am sorry to say, a MS. copy of Mrs. H. which her friends begged me to look over, in order to decide for them the propriety of publishing it.

Pray, let me hear from you immediately how soon you think of setting off, and, with warmest remembrances to the dear girls and Miss Lee, believe me

Ever faithfully yours,
Thomas Moore.

I have just heard that my portmanteau is safe.

546. *To Thomas Wilkie*

B.M. Add. MS. 29764, f. 19

I have the New Annual Register (beginning with 1780) up to 1796 inclusive, and should like to purchase the remaining volumes, if you can find them for me.

June 19th 1818

My dear Sir—

I found your letter on my return from Ireland, where I have been for the last three weeks— It has been a very serious disappointment

[1] See letter No. 543, to James Power, 16 June 1818.

to me not receiving the parcel of books, which I left with Mr Murray to be forwarded to me—and, with which I expected Dr Watkins's Life[1] and the other Works, necessary for my Sheridan business, would have come— But have had no intimation from Mr Murray whatever, either as to his reason for withholding *my* books or his not furnishing me with *others*— Will you have the goodness to call upon him, and see that the books at least which I left packed up in his care should be forwarded to me without any further delay— I regret exceedingly that Mr Charles Sheridan has not come to some explanation with you on the subject of his father's works, as it leaves me still in doubt how far I am authorized in making use of his papers for you.[2]

I am, Dear Sir, yours very truly
Thomas Moore

547. *To James Corry*

Russell, viii. 242

June 20. 1818.

My dear Corry,

You perceive how Perry has shorn us of our beams; between his stinginess of room and his zeal for *me*, he has made but an awkward monopolising concern of his report, and I most anxiously hope some of the other London papers may have done us more justice. You may guess how glad I was to see my quiet garden again, but I have hardly yet recovered from the giddiness of my Dublin fortnight. The hip, hip, hurrahs! seem still sounding in my ears, and I feel as if a good fit of sea-sickness (which, for the first time, I was not blessed with) would have been necessary to carry off the indigestion of glory I brought away with me. I arrived here at ten o'clock on Monday night, and found Bessy walking about the garden (as she had been for several nights before) watching for me. It seemed a long month to her. Your real and hearty kindness to me, my dear Corry, has not been forgotten in *my* report of the transactions to her, nor shall it ever be forgotten as long as I have a heart to feel and a hand to record my gratitude to you. I have often been regretting since that we had no conversation about the

[1] John Watkins, *Memoirs of the . . . Life of . . . R. B. Sheridan*, 2 vols. (1817).

[2] Charles Sheridan maintained that he had a right to share the profits of the biography since he had made his father's papers available to Murray and Moore. Murray was inclined to agree with him. For an account of Moore's difficulties with Charles Sheridan see Russell, iv. 155, and *passim*. See also letter No. 558, to Thomas Wilkie, 25 Aug. 1818.

Kilkenny Memoirs,[1] which, as I told Richard Power in Paris, I have not been unmindful of, but, whenever I have met with anything in my reading that bore upon it, have never failed to note it down, with a view to what, ere long, *you will see* I shall execute.

My 'Life of Sheridan' still remains in a very doubtful state, from the indecision of Charles Sheridan, with respect to any arrangement with the booksellers. Till the family are allowed some share in the publication, I feel delicate, of course, in availing myself of their papers for the advantage of the booksellers.[2]

How are *you* getting on, my dear fellow? I hope that plaguing pain is gone, and that you are as flourishing and happy every way as you deserve to be. I grieve that I did not see more of Mrs. Corry while I stayed, and most particularly grieve that I had not a better opportunity of singing her some of those new things, which I *know* she would have liked. My best regards to her, and believe me ever faithfully,

Hers and yours,
Thomas Moore.

548. *To Joseph Strutt*

The Living Age, 7th Series, xxiii (1904), 441

Sloperton, Devizes
Wednesday, June 24, 1818.

My dear Sir,— In reply to your very kind letter (whose cordiality was as welcome to me as any of my Irish glories) I have but just time to enclose Lady Morgan's letter—you will see whatever weight my name may have is thrown in too, and I wish most heartily it may be the means of procuring you some amusement.[3]

I have just received a newspaper from Ireland, with a Poem to me in it, which you ought to see, full of the warmest, saddest and deepest Irish feeling—but I have not time to copy it out.—

Yours ever faithfully,
Thomas Moore.

Bessy is not very well, but joins me vigorously in love and kind wishes to you all.

[1] An allusion to their collaboration on a book about the Kilkenny Theatricals. See letter No. 277, to James Corry, 30 Dec. 1812.

[2] See letter No. 546, to Thomas Wilkie, 19 June 1818.

[3] See letter No. 545, to Joseph Strutt, 18 June 1818.

549. *To James Power*

Trinity College, Dublin

Didn't I say that 'They may rail at this life'[1] was to be set half a note lower? It can't be helped now, I suppose.

June 26 1818

My Dear Sir—

Mrs Boyntun is the landlady for whom the 20 pounds was destined—my half-year's rent was due on the 18th & I am only surprized she has not been more prompt in sending for it—

You have not, I suppose, seen a full account of my Dinner as it appeared in the Irish papers—and I have not one to spare to send you—but I expect one from Dublin & then you shall see it.

I shall in the course of the summer make up my arrears to you in the way of detached Songs, besides finishing the Sacred ones.

The Longmans have behaved with uncommon generosity to me about the Fudges—they have added two hundred pounds to my share of the profits from their own, which is a thing, of course, I never could have dreamt of—[2]

Yours, my dear Sir, very truly
Thomas Moore.

If there be any fish you could send us on Saturday that would keep well till Monday (when we have the Bowles's to dine with us) I should be very glad of it— But do not venture unless the weather & the state of the fish is such as to promise certainty in its keeping— If you can get one salt salmon (done like Cod) it would be perhaps better.

550. *To John Murray*

Sir John Murray

June 26th 1818

My dear Sir—

I have set Wilkie on your back, in a letter I wrote him the other day—& I wish you joy of him.[3] Though I do not find that he has bored you into sending me the books I left with you near two months ago, to be forwarded *immediately*.— I have the pleasure to tell you that I have begun with Sheridan—taken to it *con amore*, and can promise it to you as a Christmas dish, without fail— You

[1] *Poetry*, p. 215.

[2] See letter No. 543, to James Power, 16 June, and No. 544, to Samuel Rogers, 18 June 1818.

[3] See letter No. 546, to Thomas Wilkie, 19 June 1818.

must however show more readiness to assist than you have done hitherto, and perhaps, after all, the shortest way for me to be supplied with the books I want (at least, some of them) is to subscribe to a Library—which I entreat you will do forthwith for me—Hookham's or Colbourn's, which-ever you think best—& send me down in the first batch (together with a Catalogue) Burke's Life, Pitt's Life, Fox's Life—in short make up the number of a Cat's, if you can muster them, not forgetting my great predecessor, Watkins,[1] which I have been three months asking Mr Wilkie for.

I really want some of these books of my own I left with you most grievously—particularly a manuscript Book there is among them, of the greatest value to me—so *do* send them as soon as possible.

Yours very truly
Thomas Moore

551. *Fragment to John Murray*

B.M. Add. MS. 29764, f. 43

[June 1818]

Will you have the goodness to tell Mr Wilkie that the boxes arrived safe—[2] I wish he had not done such a stupid thing as to take out the Music, which Mrs Moore had selected expressly for the purpose of bringing to me—tell him also that I shall write to him in a day or two.

Ever yours very truly
Thomas Moore

552. *To Thomas Wilkie*

B.M. Add. MS. 29764, f. 20

Sloperton Cottage, Devizes
July 9th 1818

Dear Sir.

I have received the books from Mr Murray & find his delay in forwarding them was entirely owing to his shopman's mistaking my directions—[3] He has also, by my desire, subscribed for me at Colbourn's, which will save him & you some trouble in procuring for me the books I may want— I must however beg of you to send me a copy of *Aristaenetus*,[4] which is not in Colbourn's catalogue,

[1] John Watkins, *Memoirs of the Life of Sheridan*, 2 vols. (1817).
[2] See letter No. 546, to Thomas Wilkie, 19 June 1818.
[3] See letter No. 546, to Thomas Wilkie, 19 June 1818.
[4] *The Love Epistles of Aristaenetus*, translated by Richard Brinsley Sheridan and N. B. Halhed (1771).

PLATE 2

HENRY PETTY-FITZMAURICE, third Marquess of Lansdowne by Henry Walton

but which, of course, I cannot do without, and the sooner I have it the better— As to the Annual Register, I should be glad to know what is the cheapest price you can get me a Dodsley's (from the beginning) for, and whether my seventeen volumes of Revington's[1] could be taken in exchange, so as to lighten the cost— They are bound and in good preservation.

I am getting on with the Life,[2] and think I can promise it to you with certainty before Christmas—indeed, if necessary, I could perhaps enable you to have it *out* at that time.

Will you have the goodness to make all possible search after a Pamphlet called 'Utrum Horum', written in 1790, upon the difference that took place between Burke & Sheridan, and let me have it—

Yours very truly
Thomas Moore

I must beg you also to send me the *Greek* Aristaenetus.

553. *To his Mother*

Russell, ii. 24, no. 282

[Sloperton]
Sunday, July 11 [1818]

My dearest Mother,

We feel it very long, indeed, since we heard anything from you, and though I grumble a little when a letter comes with an envelope on it that *ought* to be franked, there is no money I pay with more pleasure than that which brings me news from home. Bessy and I are particularly anxious about poor Kate, and hope another day will not pass over without bringing us some intelligence. Poor Joe Atkinson is at last gone! His death was easy, and no one ever lived a more prosperous or kind-hearted life.[3] Ever your own,

Tom.

[1] Moore is evidently referring to *The Annual Register*, which Robert Dodsley and Edmund Burke began in 1758. By 'Revington's' he evidently means *Rivington's New York Gazetteer: or the Connecticut, New Jersey, Hudson's River, and Quebec Weekly*, which was published by James Rivington in New York from 1773 until 1775.

[2] The *Life of Sheridan*.

[3] Russell dates this letter 'Mayfield, Sunday, July 11. 1814', but it is clear from Moore's diary that Joe Atkinson died in 1818. The index to Russell's edition of the *Memoirs and Correspondence* lists two entries under 'Atkinson, Joe, his death': vol. ii. 24, which is this letter, and vol. ii. 201, which falls in the October 1818 period of Moore's diary; but Atkinson's name does not appear on that page. On 25 Sept. 1818, however, Moore noted that he 'Wrote a few lines

554. *To John E. Hall*

The Collector, ix (February 1896), 67[1]

Devizes
July 12th, 1818.

My Dear Sir: I have just received your letter with an inclosed copy of the Lay Preacher[2] for Mrs. Moore, and have but time (as I find myself deeply in arrears of correspondence on my return from Ireland) to thank you most heartily for all your kind recollections of me. It is indeed very delightful to me to think that in spite of time and distance and other alienating circumstances, I am still remembered by you with such unchanging kindness, and I shall be most happy to have an opportunity of showing how sensibily I feel it. I have not seen the work on America you mentioned, though it is advertised in the London Papers; but I am very glad that you have given publicity to the paragraph of my letter alluded to by the author, and indeed I should not have had the least objections to your giving the *whole* of what I have said; as, though I do not precisely remember what it was, I seldom say or write anything political (at least since I have come to *years* of *discretion*) that I am not perfectly ready to abide by before the world. You are mistaken in thinking that my present views of politics are a change from those I formerly entertained—they are but a *return* to those of my school and college days—to principles, of which I may say what Propertius said of his mistress, 'Cynthia prima fuit, Cynthia finis erit.'

The only thing that has ever made them *vibrate* in their *orbit* was that foolish disgust I took at what I thought the consequences of democratic principles in America—but I judged by the *abuse*, not the *use* and the little information I took the trouble of seeking came to me through twisted and tainted channels—and in short I was a rash boy and made a fool of myself. But, thank Heaven, I soon *righted* again, and I trust it was the only deviation from the path of pure public feeling I ever shall have to reproach myself with. I mean to take some opportunity (most probably in the Life of Sheridan I am preparing) of telling the few to whom my opinion can be of any importance, how much I regret and how sincerely

of the epitaph for poor Joe Atkinson before breakfast', and on the following day, 'Finished my epitaph upon poor Joe' (Russell, ii. 173 and 174). Again on 1 Apr. 1819 he recorded, 'Finished the epitaph for poor Joe and hope I have now done with the subject' (Russell, ii. 285). The conclusion is that the letter was written from Sloperton Cottage rather than Mayfield, and that the date was 11 July 1818 rather than 1814.

[1] This letter was contributed to *The Collector* by Charles Henry Hart.

[2] A collection of essays by Joseph Dennie.

I retract every syllable injurious to the great cause of Liberty, which my hasty view of America and her society provoked me into uttering.[1]

Immediately on receiving your proposal with respect to Lalla Rookh, I mentioned it to the Longmans; but they told me they had already an established correspondent in America, which, of course, precluded my further interference on the subject.

Your Port Folios,[2] which you were so good as to offer me, I am sorry to say, I have not yet possessed myself of, from my having mislaid the order upon Mr. Souter, which you sent me—but when I next go to town I shall call upon him and perhaps he will take my word for my having your authority to receive the work.

Mrs. Moore begs her best thanks for the beautiful book (both *es*oterically and *ex*oterically)[3] which you have sent her and I entreat you to believe me my dear Sir

Always faithfully and cordially yours,
Thomas Moore.

555. *To James Corry*

Russell, viii. 246

July 13. 1818.

My dear Corry,

I have to thank you for two most welcome letters. I remember Cicero bids one of his correspondents write letters worthy of him,—'scribe literas te dignas:' he need never have given such a hint to *you;* but the worst of it is, *I* am always in too great a hurry to follow your example, and can only give you, what my friend William Spencer calls 'legs and wings of thoughts.' I don't even throw in the *merry-thoughts*, though I would if I could. In answer to Mrs. Corry's grave charge of 'not liking her as well as I did at Kilkenny'—how *can* she be so unjust? Only let her give me fair play,—I call for a ring and fair play: the bottle-holders shall be a few staunch hearts I could name; the ground either here or in Lurgan Street, the time of any duration she pleases, the longer the better; and if I don't beat her out and out in *liking*, why, I'll consent to wear the white feather of falsehood in my heart for ever after. *Like* her! 'like Ossian!'[4] says Werter [*sic*],—*love* is the word, and I hereby fling down the gauntlet upon it boldly.

[1] See letter No. 87, to his Mother, 13 June 1804, and No. 471, to John E. Hall, June 1816.

[2] A literary magazine, founded by Joseph Dennie.

[3] That is, both the contents and binding are beautiful.

[4] See letter No. 368, to Lord Byron, February 1814.

You delight me by your report of Peel's speech. He is one of the Dii Majores of our political Olympus, and I only wish he did not wield the Birmingham thunder of such Salmoneasses as his present masters. You know, at that college dinner it made me melancholy to think what a clever, manly-minded fellow they had got amongst them.

Poor Joe Atkinson is at last gone.[1] For this long time he has been but 'jocus, et preterea nihil;'[2] but his death was as gradual and easy, poor fellow, as his life had been prosperous and amiable. I shall miss him exceedingly.

I have written to Power to come to us. I hope he will.

Yours ever faithfully,
Thomas Moore.

I dine to-day at Poet Bowles's (whom I so shamefully omitted in my rigmarole of Bards) to meet Lord Lansdowne, Methuen, &c. &c.

556. *To his Mother*

Russell, ii. 139, no. 397

August 1. 1818.

My dearest Mother,

I have been just writing a long letter to the great Grecian, Doctor Parr, with whom I have entered into a correspondence about Sheridan;[3] so that I have but a few minutes left for you; but I know a few words to tell you we are well and happy are to *you*

'Sweeter than all the Heathen Greek
That Helen spoke when Paris woo'd.'[4]

Will you tell Miss Creagh, if you ever see her, how grateful I am for her kind recollections in sending me the pretty music she promised, so beautifully written out. Don't forget this! There was a concert in this neighbourhood the other night, where they had got nothing almost but *my* things to be performed, in expectation that I should be there, but I was not.

Love to all around you. Ever your own,

Tom.

[1] See letter No. 553, to his mother, 11 July 1818.

[2] A parody on 'Vox, et praeterea nihil.' Thought to have been said of Echo, or of the Nightingale. Plutarch, in his Apophthegm, *Lacon. Incert.* xiii, has a story of a man who, after plucking the nightingale and finding little flesh on it, remarked, 'Thou art voice, and nought else'. It is probable that the quotation is the Latin translation of Plutarch's anecdote.

[3] Moore printed a letter from Parr in his *Life of Sheridan*, i. 9.

[4] Not identified.

557. *To James Power*

Princeton

Friday 14th August [postmark 1818]

My dear Sir— The engraving will do very well & you may have it struck off as soon as you please—it is as neatly executed as I could wish—

I am full of grief & dismay, as usual, at the prospect of interminable war between you & your brother & I am seriously afraid it will have the effect of preventing any satisfactory arrangement between you & me—for I am sure to be hooked, some way or other, into the conflict, if I continue connected with either party—but we shall see.[1] The names of the five remaining songs are 'Poor broken flower'—'Tis all for thee'—'No—never think'—'Tis the soul within' and 'The Muse'.[2] I have sent two of them to Stevenson together with three Sacred Songs, to see if he will arrange them—I have not got his answer yet.

I wish when you are sending me the book-papers, you would let Wilkie in Paternoster Row (57, I think) know that you have a parcel for me & beg him to let you have Watkins's Sheridan[3] & any thing else he may have procured for me to send by the opportunity.

I think of going in a few days to Leamington Spa, for the purpose of having an interview with Mrs Lefanu, the only surviving sister of Sheridan— You may tell this to Wilkie, if you see him—

Ever yours very truly
Thomas Moore

558. *To Thomas Wilkie*

B.M. Add. MS. 29764, ff. 30, 31

Sloperton Cottage
August 25 1818

My dear Sir— I am but just returned from Leamington Spa, where I went for the purpose of seeing Mrs Lefanu, Sheridan's only surviving sister, who, I understood had made some remarks upon Watkins's Life, with the view of refuting his falsehoods, but had since given up the idea of publishing them.[4]

[1] See letter No. 266, to James Power, 23 Nov. 1812.

[2] 'Poor Broken Flower', and ''Tis All for Thee', *Poetry*, pp. 310 and 319. 'The Muse' is probably 'How Lightly Mounts the Muse's Wing', *Poetry*, p. 264. 'No—Never Think' and ''Tis the Soul within' were not included in the 1841 edition of Moore's works.

[3] John Watkins, *Memoirs of the Life of Sheridan*, 2 vols. (1817).

[4] See letter No. 557, to James Power, 14 Aug. 1818.

Those notes it was, of course, a great object for me to get possession of, and, after some letters had passed between us on the subject, I thought it better at once to go & manage the matter in person—particularly, as I could at the same time see Doctor Parr, with whom too I had some correspondence about Sheridan's school-days & the general extent of his literary acquirements— My journey has been as successful as I could desire— Mrs Lefanu has not only given me her remarks, but has told me much that I was anxious to know, & my conversations with Dr Parr have given me many new lights upon the subject— I wish you would make enquiries about Mr *Halhed* for me—the celebrated Halhed, Sheridan's early friend, but afterwards his antagonist on the Hastings business, who became a believer in the mission of Brothers, and is now, if living, in a state of wretched mental imbecillity— If you know anything about Major Scott Waring, he could inform you with respect to Halhed— I must also apply to Mr Thomas Grenville & Lord John Townshend, who, I suppose, have it in their power to give me any particulars— Indeed, independent of the *literary* difficulty of my task, it is, as a matter of mere *business*, a most anxious & troublesome undertaking, from the number of trifling circumstances upon which I have to make enquiries, and the various sources (some of them not very pleasantly accessible, such as Mr Grenville) to which I must apply in order to secure accuracy upon every particular.

I shall write immediately to Mr Linley as a few poems of his sister's would contribute most materially to embellish my Essay—[1] By the bye, I have thought of entitling it 'Some Account of the Life & Writings &c. &c.' as a less pretending title than 'An Essay on the Life & Genius &c.' but this we shall see.

I own I do not feel quite satisfied at the way in which we stand with respect to the Sheridan family— For there does not appear to have been any thing definitive arranged between you & Charles Sheridan,[2] and my friend Mr Rogers has not yet given me the papers that were in his possession—so that I am in fact, making use of materials for you upon which you have not yet established your

[1] On 16 Aug. 1818 William Linley wrote to Wilkie, saying that he had nothing at present in his possession but at one time had two very curious commonplace books in Sheridan's handwriting. One was a sketch of scenes and characters in *The Critic*. The other contained various character outlines intended to be introduced in an unfinished comedy, which was to be called *Affectation*. Sheridan, while on his death-bed, called for all his papers, and these were turned over to Charles Sheridan. Linley also noted that he had several beautiful poems by Sheridan's sister. (Original in the British Museum.)

[2] Sheridan wrote to Wilkie on 19 Nov. 1817 indicating that he would be glad for Moore to write a biography of his father and noting that the *School for Scandal*, in his father's handwriting, could be provided, but that the manuscript was then in Rogers's possession. (Original in the British Museum.)

claim—there being not only claims of the family yet to settle,[1] but a *lien* of Mr Rogers's on the property also—to say nothing of Ridgway's, which I know not how you have settled, but which has nothing whatever to do with *my* part of the business, though it would be a material & vital omission in the works—indeed it would be like the old story of the play of Hamlet with the character of Hamlet left out—so that I trust you will not *think* of publishing, *without* the School for Scandal. I am much obliged by your offer of allowing me to draw upon you, & if I should have occasion, will avail myself of your kindness.

Yours, my dear Sir, very truly
Thomas Moore

I want the Collection of Sheridan's speeches that is published—you will have the goodness to send it to Power for me.[2]

We shall be most happy to see you when you arrive in the country.

559. *To James Power*

New York Public

Friday, August 28, 1818

My dear Sir— On my return I found your letter with the account of poor Mr Cooper's death, and I have since had one from his son on the same subject— It appears to me to have been very like murder altogether— I inclose you a letter I have had from Stevenson, which, you see, leaves us in the lurch entirely as to our arrangements— I really do not know what is to be done— I detest the idea of giving my things into the hands of any one else, and yet, in justice to your claim upon them, they *must* be put into a finished state by *some* one— It would be very inconvenient for me to go to town just now or indeed for some time to come, and you can hardly fix upon any composer for the purpose till I am on the spot to consult with you— What state is your law-transaction with Stevenson in at present ?[3]

Ever yours, my dear Sir, very truly
Thomas Moore

[1] Sheridan wrote again to Wilkie on 20 July 1818, saying that he had furnished all the manuscript material, including the *School for Scandal* and a manuscript of a speech. He noted that Wilkie was to 'allow for the Benefit of Mr. T. Sheridan's widow & children one Guinea on each copy actually sold'. (Original in the British Museum.) See letter No. 546, to Thomas Wilkie, 19 June 1818.

[2] Sheridan's speeches were edited by 'a constitutional friend' in five volumes, 1798.

[3] In the difficulty between the Power brothers, Stevenson sided with William in Dublin, and James failed to engage him to make the arrangements for the eighth number of the *Irish Melodies*. Moore is probably referring to legal negotiations arising out of these circumstances.

Stevenson has not sent me back my MSS.
I am ashamed of having kept your portmanteau so long— Pray, pay Lord Byron's letter for me— Bessy's to Mrs Branigan must be in before Wednesday.

560. *To Mrs. Lefanu*

Russell, viii. 247

Sloperton Cottage
Sept. 16. 1818.

My dear Madam,

I have been prevented from acknowledging your very kind and useful communications by a visit of business which I was obliged to pay to London, and from which I am but just returned. I am sorry that Mrs. Canning[1] does not permit me to give her name, because her testimony to your brother's kindness of heart is very important, and would, of course, be much enhanced by the authority of the name. We must, however, be content to leave it anonymous, as she wishes it. You may depend upon my not committing you, in any way, with the important personage to whom you allude. Indeed, strong as is my feeling with respect to some parts of his conduct to your brother, I mean to let the facts speak for themselves, without any colouring or comment from me. I have not yet had time to look over the papers you have sent me; but I have no doubt that they are highly useful and interesting; and I shall take the liberty, whenever I find myself in any puzzle, to apply to you for a clue to help me out. Mr. W. Linley and I have had some correspondence lately, and he promises me not only several poems of his sister, but one or two of Mr. Sheridan's which have never been printed. I find too from my neighbour Lord Lansdowne that he expects Mr. Thomas Grenville at Bowood for a few days; so that I shall have an opportunity of uncorking (to use an old joke) all the remains of *Sherry* there are in *him*, which, you may suppose from the opinion I expressed of him, I do not expect to be of the most racy or sparkling quality. But, altogether, my materials (at least for the early part of the Life) are much more promising than I expected.

When I was in town, I took an opportunity of mentioning Miss Lefanu to the Longmans, and they beg that she will allow them to read her novel, when it is finished.[2] I added to my mention of her

[1] Evidently the wife of George Canning.

[2] Alicia Lefanu wrote some poetry and the *Memoirs of Mrs. Frances Sheridan, with Remarks upon a Late Life* [Watkins's] *of R. B. Sheridan* (1824), but she did not succeed in getting her novel published.

JAMES HENRY LEIGH HUNT by Samuel Laurence

name all that I was likely to feel after seeing and conversing with her; so that I trust she will find them disposed to do her every possible justice. But I need not tell you how little depends on *favour* in literature; even merit is not always sure of a good reception; *saleability* is the thing with the booksellers.

Pray tell Miss Lefanu how exceedingly obliged I am by the trouble she has taken in collecting and copying so much for me; and with my best regards to her and Mr. Lefanu, I beg you to believe me, my dear Madam, very faithfully,

Your obliged servant,
Thomas Moore.

561. *To John Murray*

Sir John Murray

Sept[r] 29 1818

My dear Sir—

I meant to have begged of you when I was in town to stop my subscription at Colbourn's, as I have picked their catalogue to the bone, and should like now to have my wicked will of Hookham for about a *quarter*— I perceive his catalogue is much more rich in Political Tracts than Colbourn's— Will you, therefore, have the goodness to arrange both these matters for me? Your *answering* for my payment to both will perhaps do as well as the actual bleeding—and if you will send Hookham's Catalogue to Power's for me quarterly, I shall be much obliged to you—

Have you got the books bound for me according to the Volumes I left for you? One, you know, was Lord Byron's Works, of which you were good enough to promise me the additional volume, & the other was Gifford's Jonson, which I wished to have bound like the volume of Ford's Works I left with you—[1]

Yours, my dear Sir, very truly
Thomas Moore

562. *To the Marquess of Lansdowne*

Bowood

Wednesday Evening [September 1818]

My dear Lord— I find M[rs] Moore had the courage to do what she knew I wished very much, but what I think I hardly should have ventured myself— She asked you to eat a Cottage dinner with us on Saturday, and, as you told me you have no company with you

[1] William Gifford edited the works of Massinger (1805), Jonson (1816), and Ford (1827).

on that day, I venture to hope you may still consent to do us this favour.— You shall have a mere poet's dinner— I don't mean an imaginary one, but something very near it.

Some think we, bards, have nothing real,
And that we live among the stars so
Our very dinners are ideal—
(Heav'n knows, they, but too often, are so!)
For instance—that we have instead
Of vulgar chops & stews & hashes,
First course—a Phoenix at the head,
Done on its own celestial ashes—
At foot, a cygnet, that kept singing
All the while its neck was wringing.
Side dishes—viz—Minerva's owl,
Or any such like learned fowl—
Doves, such as heaven's poulterer gets,
When Cupid shoots his mother's pets—
Larks, stewed in morning's roseate breath,
Or roasted by a sunbeam's splendour;
And nightingales, be-rhym'd to death,
Like young pigs whipp'd to make them tender.
Such fare may suit those bards, who're able
To banquet at Duke Humphrey's table,
But as for *me*, who've long been taught
To eat & drink like other people,
And can put up with mutton, bought
Where Bromham rears its antient steeple—
If Lansdowne will but deign to share
My humble feast, tho rude the fare,
Yet season'd by that salt he brings
From Attica's saliniest springs,
'Twill turn to dainties—and the bowl,
When brighten'd by his beams of soul,
Like Baucis' cup, when touch'd by Jove,
Will sparkle, fit for Gods above![1]

The longest extempore I ever wrote— If Saturday does not suit you, perhaps Sunday will—

Yours, my dear Lord, very faithfully
Thomas Moore

[1] *Poetry*, p. 533.

PRINTED IN GREAT BRITAIN
AT THE UNIVERSITY PRESS, OXFORD
BY VIVIAN RIDLER
PRINTER TO THE UNIVERSITY